Baking for All Occasions

Baking for All Occasions

A TREASURY OF RECIPES FOR EVERYDAY CELEBRATIONS

BY FLO BRAKER

PHOTOGRAPHS BY SCOTT PETERSON
FOREWORD BY CHUCK WILLIAMS

CHRONICLE BOOKS
SAN FRANCISCO

Library of Congress Cataloging-in-Publication Data
Braker, Flo.
    Baking for all occasions : a treasury of recipes for every celebration /
by Flo Braker.
        p. cm.
    Includes index.
    ISBN: 978-0-8118-4547-2
    1. Baking. I. Title.
TX763.B74 2008
641.8´15—DC22

Manufactured in China.

Designed by Frances Baca
Prop styling by Leigh Noe
Food styling by Kim Konecny

10 9 8 7 6 5 4 3 2 1

Chronicle Books LLC
680 Second Street
San Francisco, California 94107

www.chroniclebooks.com

Dedication and Acknowledgments

To my honey, our children, Jeff and Michal, Julie and Robert, and
our grandchildren, Joshua, Natalie and Daniel whose enduring support and love of desserts make life one sweet journey.

And, with great admiration to bakers everywhere who dream, create,
bake, share, and inspire me every day.

When you bake, the whole is greater than the sum of the parts.
Butter, sugar, eggs, and flour come together to make a dazzling
dessert. The same is true when you write a cookbook. A team of
talented individuals works in tandem to create the finished product.

I am profoundly grateful to a multitude of colleagues and friends
who have offered encouragement and support, sage advice and
feedback: Amy Albert, Nancy Baggett, Michael Bauer, Casey Ellis,
Louise Fiszer, Fran Gage, Marlene Sorosky Gray, Elinor Klivans,
David Lebovitz, Emily Luchetti, Nick Malgieri, Rosemary Mark,
Alice Medrich, Miriam Morgan, Patti Murray, Karen Nielsen, Greg
Patent, Amy Pressman, Susan Purdy, Mary Risley, Carole Walter,
Lisa Yockelson, and all the members of the amazing Bakers Dozen
organization in the San Francisco Bay Area. Both Ann Martin Rolke
and Cheryl Sternman Rule serendipitously came into my life in
the early stages of the project when their editing assistance made
it possible for me to move forward on the book.

I am deeply indebted to Jack Adler, Kevyn Allard, Anne Baker,
Allen Cohn, Melissa Eisenstat, Amanda Gold, David Grossblat,
Allison Komar, Shirley Rosenberg, Jeff Sherman, Susan Walter,
and Camille J. Zelinger who paid great attention to detail as they
diligently tested and tasted recipes.

Magnanimous assistance came from Laura Martin Bacon, Andrew
Baker, Janet Rikala Dalton, Nancy Kux, Evie Lieb, Christine Law,
and Nora Tong. These articulate and baking-savvy professionals were
always there to troubleshoot or share recipes, research sources, provide recipe math, clarify a lengthy paragraph, or come up with the
right words to express what I wanted to say. I will be eternally thankful.

My heartfelt thanks to all the great people at Chronicle Books for their
invaluable efforts. Very special appreciation is due to Bill LeBlond,
who first suggested that I write another book, and whose support
and insight guided me to the end. Editor Amy Treadwell, always
upbeat, offered great suggestions just when I needed them, and kept
me and the book on track through the editorial process.
A million thanks to Jane Dystel who is not only the hardest working
literary agent but also the best. Sharon Silva will forever hold the blue
ribbon for keen copy editing and a soft spot in my heart. And last,
but not least, bouquets to photographer Scott Peterson and food
stylist Kim Konecny for vividly bringing the recipes to life.

These loyal, talented people and my kind, loving family and close
friends helped me every step of the way. It was the sum of their
efforts that made this book a sweet reality.

CONTENTS

Foreword

WRITING THE FOREWORD to this cookbook, *Baking for all Occasions: A Treasury of Recipes for Everyday Celebrations*, was a very enjoyable project for me. First of all, it is not an ordinary cookbook, but one created with exceptional care for ingredients, mixing, baking, and timing. And, it is written by Flo Braker, whom I met soon after I opened the original Williams-Sonoma store on Sutter Street in San Francisco in 1958. Flo has devoted most of her life to developing her knowledge and perfection in baking.

I would like to take this opportunity to praise Flo on her expertise in home baking. In this book she has devoted many pages to teaching simple baking techniques. She answers the important questions: What can baking do for you? How can baking change the atmosphere of your kitchen? How should the sifting and folding of flour be done? How best to melt chocolate? What is the best way to fold ingredients? What is the correct procedure for whipping egg whites? For caramelizing sugar?

If you are really interested in learning the art of baking, I suggest you spend a little time in reviewing the first chapter of this book, A Baking Primer. It will give you the foundation you need to bake the recipes that follow. These recipes are not only clear and precise, but also inspiring and delicious. Every baker will be richly rewarded by this wonderful book.

—Chuck Williams

INTRODUCTION

oc·ca·sion (*noun*) 1. a particular time, especially a time when something happens;
2. a chance or opportunity to do something; 3. a cause of or reason for something;
4. the need for something or to do something; 5. an important or special event

—Anne Soukhanov, Ed., *Encarta World English Dictionary* [New York: St. Martin's Press, 1999], p. 1249

A glance through the dictionary reveals a smorgasbord of definitions for the word *occasion*. For me, the meanings come together like ingredients in a recipe, creating a delicious life that has nourished me on many levels—and given me the pleasure of nurturing others.

Baking is a way to commemorate all occasions and inspire everyday celebrations. In fact, the very process of baking can become an occasion in itself. As we peruse the pages of a favorite cookbook, we experience an exhilarating feeling of anticipation. Time seems to slow down as we measure and sift, mix and bake, and then decorate our creations. The kitchen fills with the sweet, buttery aromas of baking, perfuming the air with sugar and spice. Later, as we share our homemade delights with family and friends, the occasion is deposited in their memory banks—to be evoked, even years later, by a whiff of cinnamon or warm chocolate.

Whether your reason for baking is to indulge in the sweet pastime every now and then, to whip up treats for special events, or to make baking its own occasion, the simple joys it brings will last a lifetime. My personal story is testimony to that fact, defined by a series of unforgettable occasions that have allowed me to bake a life.

Baking is a harmonious blend of art and science, so it's not surprising that my career began with a chemistry set. As an insatiably curious nine-year-old, I spent endless hours happily ensconced at a card table in the basement of our family home. Spread out before me was an array of powders and liquids, along with a handbook of formulas and the equipment required for precise mixing. After I'd mastered the experiments in the book, I began

to mix the chemicals in my own original ways (thankfully, the makers of this child-friendly set had anticipated such self-motivated wizardry). I was fascinated to learn what would happen when I combined different things, observing wide-eyed as the mixtures bubbled and fizzed and transformed themselves with exciting new colors, smells, and textures. I duly recorded every reaction, scribbling my hypotheses, observations, and inspirations in a spiral-bound notebook—a habit that continues to this day.

My fascination with the alchemy of ingredients found its way to the kitchen when I was a young bride and stay-at-home mom in the early 1960s. Before then, my baking knowledge had been gleaned from a childhood and adolescence spent watching our family's beloved housekeeper and natural-born baker, Dorothy Temme, as she whipped up her signature pies, cakes, cookies, and breads. Now that I had my very own kitchen, my experimentation began in earnest. I read every cookbook I could get my hands on, and became notorious among friends for my obsession with scribbling down dessert recipes at dinner parties.

The more I observed and learned, the more passionate I became. Baking grew into a means of artistic and personal expression as I created special sweets for the people I loved. I went from baking occasionally to baking for every occasion I could think of, from family gatherings to school functions to fundraisers. It got to the point where the sheer volume of my baking exceeded my inner circle's consumption.

The occasion seemed perfect to begin baking professionally, so I opened a catering business, appropriately named Occasional Baking. I'd always loved to bake several things at once—stirring and tasting and transferring baking sheets with the multitasking zeal of a symphony conductor—and the business provided a bona fide reason for doing so. My repertoire expanded as clients requested desserts to sweeten the occasions in their lives. Weddings, birthdays, anniversaries, and family reunions filled my calendar—and long hours of trial and error filled my mind with the baking knowledge I craved.

I continued to build my culinary foundation in the solitude of my kitchen, teaching myself the skills and techniques I needed to master the European classics, from genoise to puff pastry. Just as a musician spends years practicing scales and learning the nuances of each note, I dedicated myself to perfecting the fundamentals of baking. I made a lot of mistakes along the way, analyzing and recording each one so that I wouldn't make it again.

To this day, I vividly recall the horror of finding ignominious white pills of flour in some cakes I had baked for a client. After staying up all night baking the cakes again, I finally figured out that I had been so diligent in creaming the butter and sugar that the mixture had liquefied too much to incorporate the flour. It was one of those things you wish your mother had warned you about.

Soon, it occurred to me that my mistakes might have a noble purpose: I could share my hard-earned knowledge with others by becoming a baking teacher. In those days, there weren't a lot of options for home bakers who wanted to expand their confidence and expertise. Although the San Francisco Bay Area was fertile ground for anyone who loved to cook, bake, and eat, it hadn't yet erupted into the spectacular scene it is today.

One day, after attending a cooking class led by Jack Lirio, a legendary local teacher, I worked up the nerve to ask if I could rent his school to teach baking classes on the days he wasn't using it. Jack told me to write a list of all the things I would like to teach. And I did. He liked my ideas, but instead of renting the school to me, he gave me a greater honor: Jack asked me to co-teach the baking classes with him. Over the years, many current Bay Area food luminaries—Alice Waters, Alice Medrich, Lindsey Shere, Narsai David—took a class or two. Best of all, I had the pleasure of working with other avid home bakers just like me.

I had found my life's vocation. The late James Beard, a wise teacher and good friend, once said, "When you cook, you never stop learning—that's the fascination of it." This is exactly what happens to me when I teach baking. Over the years, I've learned a tremendous amount from my students and from the readers of the baking column I began writing in the *San Francisco Chronicle* in 1989. Every question they pose inspires me to embark on an educational odyssey toward finding the answer, gaining a bounty of sometimes-unexpected knowledge in the process.

After I began teaching, I continued to regard every experience as an occasion for learning, and found creative inspiration in all sorts of places. My favorite shop was (and still is) Williams-Sonoma, where Chuck Williams taught me to see the myriad possibilities that lay within the store's gleaming array of baking pans, molds, and utensils.

Once my children were older, I was able to explore new echelons of the culinary world farther afield. The Great Chefs of France cooking classes at the Mondavi Winery in Napa, California, gave me the opportunity to learn from such legendary figures as Jean Troisgrois, Michel Guérard, and Gaston Lenôtre. On trips to Europe, tasting such delicacies as Sacher torte, apple strudel, *Kasesnitten*, *Sandkuchen*, and linzertorte in their native habitat was like finding the Holy Grail.

When I wrote my first book, *The Simple Art of Perfect Baking*, I found all of my knowledge coming together to create a compendium of what I had learned. I was also presented with a bit of advice from my mentor, the late Julia Child, that has served me well in writing, baking, and life. On hearing that I was nervous about undertaking a book project, Julia told me, "Just write what works for you." I did precisely that, both in that first book and in the one that followed, *Sweet Miniatures*. And now I tell my students and readers, "Just bake what works for you."

In *Baking for All Occasions*, you will find the perfect recipes for your landmark occasions, whether you are celebrating your fiftieth wedding anniversary or your baby's first tooth. I've searched every corner of my life to create this treasure trove of recipes that I hope will become favorites in your own family repertoire. Here, I've juxtaposed desserts from my childhood, baking business, and hard-at-work imagination with those generously shared by friends and colleagues. The result is a colorful culinary patchwork quilt guaranteed to bring many happy hours of warmth, comfort, and pleasure.

The chapter themes are organized with occasions in mind, making it easy to find just the recipe you need. In Blue-Ribbon Worthy, you will discover friendly, familiar fare with a new twist, all guaranteed to elicit rave reviews from your favorite people. Baking for a Rainy Day provides recipes you can prepare ahead of time, stash in the freezer or fridge, and then finish at a moment's notice.

When you need to bake a lot of delicious treats, turn to the Crowd-Pleasing Favorites for luscious cakes, tarts, and cookies that celebrate the occasion—and still leave you plenty of time to enjoy it. Ready to Share delivers a wealth of delectable (and easily transportable) options for those times when you've promised to bring a dessert to a party or other gathering.

To make the most of nature's bounty, consult Farmers' Market Fresh, where you will find recipes that celebrate the sweet pleasures of ripe, juicy seasonal fruits. Since I believe that every hour of the day is worth celebrating, I've included a chapter called Hearth and Home All Day Long. These rustic, homespun, deeply satisfying recipes showcase such old-fashioned traditions as rich, fragrant yeast coffee cakes.

Delight guests at dinner parties and buffets with the individual desserts in Singular Sensations. Beautiful and easy to serve, these petite masterpieces are favorites with dessert lovers because everyone gets his or her very own. Of course, sharing is a good thing, and so I've also included Say It with Cookies, an entire chapter devoted to conveying sweet sentiments.

For your grandest occasions and most memorable celebrations, you can rely on Red Letter Day Desserts to provide show-stealing recipes that won't also rob you of your sanity. Yielding desserts that are as impressive as the chapter title implies, each recipe is broken down into simple, manageable steps that allow you to calmly and confidently prepare your special creation over the course of a few days.

Whichever recipes you choose, I hope you will bake them with love and serve them with pride. The satisfaction of crafting a special dessert with your own hands is one of life's simplest and most profound pleasures. The knowledge, techniques, and recipes I offer here have brought great joy to me and to the people I love and admire. I wish the same for you.

Flo Braker

PART ONE

A Baking Primer

A journey of a thousand miles begins with a single step.

—Lao Tzu

WHAT YOU DO at the beginning of a recipe is vital to successful baking. From the very first step, each successive task is built on the one before it.

To make sure your home-baking journey is a gratifying and productive one, I have provided an occasional baker's primer of fundamental techniques along with the essential ingredients and equipment you will need to prepare the recipes. These baking techniques are organized according to the classic culinary practice of *mise en place*, that is, in the order they would be called for in a recipe.

FUNDAMENTAL BAKING TECHNIQUES

Preparing baking pans   Preparing pans properly guarantees successful removal of your homemade cake, whether from a layer cake pan or an intricately shaped pan. Warm cake structures are fragile, so preparing the pan aids in removing the cake in one piece, rather than having a portion stick to the sides or bottom. A perfectly shaped cake or one ready for decorating is a pleasure to glaze or frost, since the smoother the surface, the easier it is to cover. Keep in mind that your goal is to form just enough of a barrier between the metal pan and the batter to ease removal while still retaining the shape of the pan. Producing a perfectly formed cake or cake layer is an important first step in fashioning the dessert.

For round, square, loaf, layer, sheet cake, and spring-form pans, apply a film of softened butter or nonstick spray over the interior of the pan. I spread the butter over the sides and bottom with a paper towel or the paper wrapper from a stick of butter. If you prefer a nonstick spray, lightly coat the pan and then spray some on a paper towel and use the towel to spread the spray evenly over the pan. Dust the pan with flour (or use Wondra flour in a convenient shaker) and tap out the excess. Line the bottom with parchment paper.

For intricately shaped pans, first spread a thin film of room-temperature solid shortening over the pan with a paper towel, making sure you cover all of the ridges and crevices. Next, for insurance, lightly spray the pan with nonstick spray in case you missed a spot. Then dust the pan with flour and tap out the excess.

Pan preparation is determined by what you are baking. The butter and flour needed to prepare the cake, yeast bread, yeast coffee cake, and muffin pans for the recipes in this book are *in addition to the butter and flour amounts in the list of ingredients.* When a recipe requires a different form of pan preparation from the standard described here, the recipe explains the preparation.

Room-temperature ingredients   Many of my recipes remind you to have all of the ingredients at room temperature, and despite sounding like a Johnny-one-note, I feel compelled to say it one more time. Room-temperature ingredients are important to the success of many aspects of baking, but especially cake making. They make it possible to combine dry and liquid ingredients together easily to form a smooth batter. Depending on your kitchen's temperature and the time of year, allow ingredients such as butter, eggs, and milk to sit at room temperature for 45 to 60 minutes before using.

For example, cold eggs added to a fluffy, properly creamed mixture curdle it (breaks the emulsion) because air bubbles in the mixture break. This causes the loss of some of the lightness you want to achieve when making a butter cake. Also, you will not end up with a smooth, well-blended mixture if you add cold milk to melted butter or fold warm chocolate into whipped cream or a cold buttercream. Ingredients or mixtures that have similar consistencies and temperatures come together easily and unify the dry and liquid ingredients smoothly without overworking the mixture or losing its airy structure. That's why beginning with room-temperature ingredients is so important to creating a homogeneous cake or cookie batter.

ROOM-TEMPERATURE, SOFTENED, AND SOFT BUTTER   To achieve the desired texture and to blend well with other ingredients, butter must be at a certain consistency. How long it takes for butter to warm from its original cold, solid refrigerated state (35 to 40 degrees F) to the proper consistency depends on the time of year, where you live, and the temperature of your kitchen. For example, you want the maximum aeration when making most cake batters, so you need room-temperature butter, which you arrive at by letting it stand at room temperature until it is between 65 and 70 degrees F (see Instant-Read Thermometer, page 40).

But I find that the best way to judge the different temperature stages of butter is to rely on physical cues, rather than a thermometer. Press a finger into the butter, and if it still feels cool and your finger forms an indentation while the rest of the butter keeps its shape without cracking, it is at room temperature. For some cookie doughs, softened butter, and sometimes even soft butter, is necessary to bring the dough together with little manipulation (and without a lot of aeration, so the cookie holds its shape as it bakes). Press a finger into the butter, and if it is soft enough to yield to your finger but you can still pick it up without it being limp, it is softened butter. When the butter no longer can maintain its shape if you attempt to pick it up, it is soft butter, which is perfect for some cookie doughs, such as my Special Spritz Cookies (page 118) and Buttery Rosette Cookies (page 293).

Be careful if you use the microwave to soften butter. It works fast and you can easily end up with a portion of the butter soft and another portion almost melted. Use medium power (50 percent), very short bursts, rotate or turn over the butter with each burst, and monitor the progress vigilantly. If time is of the essence, soften butter quickly by cutting it into slices, and shortly the butter will be close to what you need it to be, 65 to 70 degrees F or even warmer.

Sifting   No sifting is necessary for the sake of accurate measurement in the book. (Of course, if you go by the weight measurements that I provide in every recipe, sifting is irrelevant.) All measurements for dry ingredients, such as flour, powdered sugar, and cocoa powder, begin with the ingredient unsifted. For measuring flour and powdered sugar, empty the bag or a portion of it into a bowl or a sturdy storage container. For cocoa powder, poke a fork in the cocoa powder in its container to break up any chunks, and then fluff up the contents slightly. My decision to omit sifting before measuring was influenced by my desire to simplify the preparation process where I could without affecting the outcome. So I modified the recipes just slightly to ensure the necessary balance of ingredients for successful results.

If a recipe does call for sifting, it is only to disperse all of the dry ingredients, such as flour, baking powder, baking soda, and salt, before making a cake. When I do sift, I put the dry ingredients in a fine-mesh sieve instead of a triple-sifter, and I carefully shake the sieve back and forth over a sheet of waxed paper until all of the particles fall through the sieve into a mound on the paper.

My switch from a triple-sifter to a fine-mesh sieve occurred when triple-sifters became hard to find in kitchenware shops and the kitchen-accessories departments of supermarkets. At the same time, I found that the amount of flour I typically needed to sift took an unusually long time to work its way through the triple screens (and coaxing it through by hitting the side of the sifter with the side of my hand made me fear that one day I'd chip a bone, if not throw my wristwatch out of whack), and that the sieve streamlined the process. And because using a sieve to add dry ingredients to my batters and doughs was easier and my results were just as successful as when I used the triple-sifter, I never looked back. However, if, for example, I don't think the cocoa blended thoroughly with the flour, I simply pass the mixture through the sieve a second time.

Folding   Proper folding is key to making a featherlight angel food cake, a chiffon pie filling, chocolate mousse, and many other cakes, fillings, and desserts. In order to combine two different ingredients or mixtures, such as melted chocolate into a cake batter, you must fold them together gently to achieve a smooth mixture. If folding in whipped ingredients, such as heavy cream or egg whites, your goal is to retain as much aerated volume as possible while still arriving at a smooth mixture.

Ingredients and mixtures of similar temperatures and consistencies are the easiest to fold together. A handy technique when the temperatures and/or consistencies are not the same is to fold a portion of the lighter mixture, such as whipped cream or whipped egg whites, into a thicker or heavier mixture, such as a pastry cream or lemon curd. This lightens the heavier mixture sufficiently, so that folding in the remaining whipped mixture is accomplished with more success.

To make folding dry ingredients into a cake batter more efficient, first sift the dry ingredients onto a sheet of waxed paper. Then, use a metal icing spatula to distribute them gently, one-third at a time, over the surface of the batter. If it is a sponge-cake batter, sprinkling, rather than dumping, the dry ingredients is especially important because it keeps them from clumping and deflating the batter.

To fold in any ingredient or mixture of ingredients, hold a rubber spatula over the center of the bowl with the broad side of the spatula, rounded edge down, facing you. Cut straight down into the mixture, pull the spatula along the bottom and then up the side of the bowl nearest you, and, with a flick of the wrist, lift the mixture up and over itself, letting it fall gently onto the mixture in the center of the bowl. Rotate the bowl a quarter turn and repeat the stroke. Continue in this manner, always rotating the bowl a quarter turn after each stroke. A few times during the process, bring the spatula up through the center of the mixture and check to make sure the added ingredient(s) are being evenly distributed. Fold no more than necessary to incorporate everything smoothly.

Water baths and bagged ice cubes   A warm- or hot-water bath (known as a bain-marie in France) provides a gentle heat environment and ensures that anything baked in it, from cheesecake to bread pudding, cooks evenly. An ice-water bath stops the cooking process of a hot filling, such as for a chiffon pie or other hot mixture, and helps to cool it down, with an occasional whisk or stir, in short order.

To create a warm- or hot-water bath, select a roasting pan or other ovenproof pan with 2- to $2^{1}/_{2}$-inch sides and large enough to accommodate the baking dish or pan with 1 to 2 inches of space between the dish and the pan sides. Or, select a rimmed baking sheet to accommodate the ramekins for Crème Fraîche Custard with Lacy Brûlée Wafers (page 263) or the muffin pan for Chocolate-Dipped Cheesecake-sicles (page 248). Set the baking dish in the roasting pan, or the ramekins or muffin pan in the baking sheet, and place the pan on the center rack of the oven. Using a pitcher, slowly and carefully pour hot water into the pan to reach about halfway up the sides of the vessel holding the baked item (or as directed in individual recipes), and then bake as directed. When finished baking, pull out the oven rack about one-third of the way, and use a turkey baster to transfer most of the water from the pan back into the pitcher. Using oven mitts, remove the pan from the oven and let cool as directed in individual recipes.

To create an ice-water bath, fill a large bowl one-third to one-half full with ice cubes and water. Be sure the bowl can accommodate the pan or bowl of hot filling or other mixture later. Set aside until needed.

If you are whipping a hot mixture, such as an Italian meringue or a sabayon, in a stand mixer, you can speed the cooling of the mixture by putting a few ice cubes in a resealable plastic bag, and holding the bag against the bottom of the bowl or as close to the bottom of the bowl as possible. Continue to apply the bag off and on as the recipe directs.

Toasting nuts   Toasting adds additional flavor and texture to nuts that impart extra richness to the recipes that use them. No special equipment or unusual tool is needed for this easy task. About 30 minutes before you want to use the oven, center a rack in it and preheat to 325 degrees F. Spread the nuts evenly on a shallow rimmed baking sheet (rimmed is best for containing the nuts as you move the sheet in and out of the oven). Soft nuts, such as walnuts, pecans, pine nuts, and macadamias, have a higher fat content than hazelnuts and almonds, which means they toast faster. Be sure to set a timer to avoid toasting them too long and wasting time and money. I always have several pounds of untoasted unblanched (sometimes referred to as raw or natural) nuts in the freezer. When I need some, I spread them straight from the freezer on the baking sheet and put them in the preheated oven. If you are toasting them straight from the freezer, you may need to add 1 to 3 minutes to the toasting times given below.

Toast walnuts, pecans, pine nuts, and macadamias until they are aromatic but have not begun to change color, 10 to 13 minutes.

Toast hazelnuts just until their dark, papery skin is beginning to crack and they are aromatic and are beginning to color, 10 to 17 minutes. If a recipe calls for skinned hazelnuts, wrap the hot nuts in a clean kitchen towel until they are cool enough to handle, roll them around in the towel briefly, and then rub them between your palms until you remove as much of the loose skin as possible. Transfer the nuts to a resealable plastic bag and put the bag in the freezer for at least 1 day or up to several days. Remove them from the freezer and rub them between your palms again. Freezing causes the nuts to contract from their skins, which makes it possible to remove more skin. Any skin that remains on the nuts after the second rubbing can stay.

Toast whole blanched or natural almonds just until they begin to color and are aromatic, 10 to 15 minutes. Natural or blanched sliced almonds are ready in 8 to 10 minutes.

Measuring and chopping nuts When you are measuring whole, chopped, or finely ground nuts for a recipe, pour or scoop them from the package with your hand, a serving spoon, or a metal spatula into a dry measuring cup. Don't pack them unless the recipe directs. When a recipe lists nuts as an ingredient, before chopping or finely grinding them, check their weight in the recipe, too, since you buy nuts in packages marked in ounces and grams (or bulk, where you weigh it yourself).

COARSELY CHOPPED NUTS Chop the nuts on a cutting board with a chef's knife, or put them in a food processor and process with brief (1-second) on-off pulses until the pieces are the desired size. Be careful not to overprocess or you will end up with uneven sizes.

FINELY CHOPPED NUTS When I want nuts chopped somewhere between fine and coarse, as in the Bundernuss Torte (page 134) and the Heavenly Brownie-on-Shortbread Bars (page 61), I use a nut mill (or nut grinder, the same item known by a different name). When chopped nuts are part of the bulk of the recipe, such as in the filling for the Pecan–Pine Nut Tassie Crostata (page 74), rather than present simply for their texture and flavor, I use a nut mill for chopping them. Since the mill allows for no variation in speed, intensity, or chopping time, the nut granules it produces will be the same proportion of slightly larger to slightly smaller pieces every time. This ensures that a given weight of nuts will consistently yield the same volume of chopped nuts. Chopping nuts with a chef's knife is not as speedy and is less accurate. With a nut mill, the nuts go in the top hopper, you turn the handle, and the chopped nuts fall into the glass container below. When you want to feature the nut, as in the Bundernuss Torte or the Pecan–Pine Nut Tassie Crostata, you have the option to put the nuts in a sieve, and shake out the nut "powder."

FINELY GROUND NUTS A small, handheld rotary cheese grater is fine for small amounts of nuts. For larger quantities (1/2 cup and up), I use a Zyliss grater (see Sources), which has a clamp that suctions onto a dry, smooth countertop. A sturdy plastic pusher keeps the nuts against the stainless steel drum while you turn the handle. Finely ground nuts not only flavor the baked good, but also often help give the cake, cookie, or meringue its structure, as in Frozen Lemon Glacier (page 140).

You can also use a food processor or an electric herb and spice mincer, but I recommend working with only a few ounces of nuts at a time to prevent their high fat content from making the ground nuts too oily.

Toasting coconut   Center a rack in the oven and preheat the oven to 350 degrees F. Spread unsweetened medium-shred dried coconut or sweetened flaked dried coconut over a shallow rimmed baking sheet and toast until the shreds or flakes are a mixture of pale, golden, and ivory, about 15 minutes for 2 cups coconut and up to 25 minutes for 5 cups coconut. The coconut around the outer edges of the baking sheet colors sooner, so every 5 to 7 minutes, use a metal spatula to toss the coconut toward the center of the sheet to blend all of the shreds or flakes.

Melting chocolate   Melted chocolate is added to many cake batters, frostings, fillings, and the like, so knowing how to melt chocolate properly is an important technique to master. Just a little heat is required to melt any brand of chocolate, no matter the amount. Excessive or direct heat can scorch it, sacrificing its flavor, and maybe even separating the cocoa butter from the chocolate solids. In other words, you want to melt chocolate to liquefy it, not to cook it.

THE WATER-BATH METHOD   I prefer the water-bath method (or makeshift double-boiler method), in which finely chopped chocolate is melted in a bowl that fits snugly over a container half filled with water at 95 to 120 degrees F (tap water hot to the hand). To ensure the water is the correct temperature, use an instant-read thermometer. The temperature range depends on the type of chocolate you are melting. If a recipe calls for melting finely chopped chocolate, chop it into matchstick-sized pieces (the small pieces speed the melting process) on a clean, dry cutting board with a large, sturdy serrated knife, a chef's knife, a *santoku* knife (page 42), or a cleaver. If it calls for melting coarsely chopped chocolate (usually when melting it with other ingredients, such as cream or butter), chop it into coarser chunks using the same tools.

Melt finely or coarsely chopped dark chocolate, including unsweetened, semisweet, and bittersweet, over water at 120 degrees F. As the water cools, replace it with more hot water as needed to melt the chocolate completely.

Melting milk and white chocolate, always finely chopped, requires more careful attention. If melted over water hotter than 95 to 110 degrees F, they tend to form small lumps, or seize. Allow the chocolate to sit over the water before stirring to give the chocolate closest to the heat source time to begin to melt, then stir gently. When almost all of the chocolate has melted, remove the bowl from over the water and stir gently. The residual heat in the bowl should melt the remaining chocolate. If not, return the bowl over the water, or replace the water if it has cooled too much to melt the chocolate. Remember that too much heat affects the milk proteins in the chocolate (a process known as denaturing), causing it to become lumpy. If the chocolate is overheated, nothing you do will restore it to its original flavor or gloss.

THE MICROWAVE METHOD   Following the same techniques described for the water-bath method, chop the chocolate finely for amounts up to 6 ounces (170 grams) and chop it coarsely for amounts from 6 ounces to 1 1/2 pounds (680 grams). Place in a microwave-safe bowl and microwave uncovered at 50 percent power (medium) until the chocolate appears shiny, 30 seconds to 2 minutes at a time with 30-second to 1-minute intervals. This will take a total of 1 to 5 minutes, depending on the microwave and the amount, brand, and type of chocolate. Remove the bowl from the microwave and stir the chocolate until melted. If any unmelted chocolate remains, microwave for additional 10-second bursts, stirring until smooth. Keep in mind that dark chocolates melted in a microwave can fool you because they retain their shape and appear solid even when they have liquefied. Press the chocolate with the blade of a dry rubber spatula to get a sense where the chocolate is soft and liquid. When you judge it to be almost all liquid, stir it until smooth.

Be vigilant when melting milk and white chocolate in a microwave. Watch them carefully and stir them often to prevent overheating.

MELTING CHOCOLATE WITH BUTTER   Some recipes, especially bar cookies like brownies, call for melting chocolate with butter. To streamline the process, cut the butter into a few pieces, place them in a microwave-safe bowl, put the coarsely chopped chocolate on top, and microwave the mixture uncovered at 50 percent power (medium) until the chocolate appears shiny and most of the butter is melted. Remove the bowl from the microwave and stir the ingredients together until smooth. If the mixture is not completely smooth, return the bowl to the microwave and heat for 10-second bursts, again stirring until smooth.

Grating citrus zest   Lightly pass the citrus fruit over the tiny sharp-edged holes on a Microplane grater, being careful not to remove any more of the white pith than necessary. Turning the fruit after each stroke makes this easier to accomplish. The Microplane is terrific because the shreds are quite fine and you can avoid removing any of the pith. I have discovered that 1 teaspoon zest removed with a Microplane grater does not provide the same flavor intensity as 1 teaspoon zest removed with a standard box grater. So I grate more zest and pack it firmly into the measuring spoon to ensure I get the flavor intensity I like in my recipes. The amount of citrus zest called for in the recipes is based on using a Microplane grater.

Caramelizing sugar   I regard the smooth, unctuous cream that results when you caramelize sugar to be one of the world's most delicious taste sensations. The sugar responsible for this magnificent, complicated flavor is sucrose, which is simply table sugar made from sugarcane or sugar beet. (I prefer sugarcane.) To turn sugar into caramel is not difficult, but to do it safely (sugar caramelizes between 320 and 350 degrees F) and correctly is vital to producing the amber-brown color that will eventually influence the color and flavor of a sauce.

As the sugar caramelizes, its flavor becomes more complex and pronounced, while its sweet characteristic is diminished. The longer the sugar cooks, the darker it becomes, changing from very light gold to dark amber. How dark you want it depends on the recipe.

Putting an apron on when you caramelize sugar is a given, but you should also be sure to wear a shirt with long sleeves to protect your arms. When you add liquid, such as water or cream, to caramelized sugar, it can produce steam and/or bubble wildly because of the extreme temperature difference between the caramel and the liquid. To lessen this result, gradually bring the liquid to room temperature. Adding liquid directly from the refrigerator will cause the caramelized sugar to bubble and sputter violently and probably to solidify slightly, making it difficult to form a smooth emulsion. Thin, runny sauces or smooth, semiliquid fillings made from caramelized sugar thicken as they cool.

Don't be seduced by the beautiful color of caramel or its rich aroma: from the beginning to the end of the caramelizing process, no matter how tiny a taste you want, never ever poke a finger into the hot caramel, or a burned finger will be your reward. Also, always wear oven mitts when holding the heavy saucepan in which you are preparing caramelized sugar or a caramel cream or sauce.

There are two methods for caramelizing sugar: wet and dry. The recipe on the right uses the wet method, which is especially helpful for people new to caramelizing sugar. It calls for dissolving the sugar in water over low heat, then raising the heat to medium-high and heating, without stirring, to evaporate the water. Once the sugar is concentrated, it will begin to show color. How dark you want the caramel depends on the recipe you are using.

The dry method calls for dissolving the sugar slowly over low heat in a heavy saucepan or skillet. When I am caramelizing sugar to make an ultrathin sheet for decorating the top of a tart or cake, I like to use a nonstick skillet. I melt the sugar until it is amber, pour it onto a silicone mat, and then set it aside to cool and firm up enough to lift off and break up into shards or pieces. I like using a skillet for the dry method because more of the surface of the sugar is exposed to the heat, which allows the sugar to melt more evenly. However, you can achieve the same results in a heavy saucepan, but you must stir the sugar with a wooden spoon to ensure it melts evenly.

The residual heat in a pan can cause an amber caramel to change color in a split second, so have a bowl of ice water on hand to stop the cooking. What you see in the pan is not what you get: to judge the color of caramel, once the sugar begins to color, occasionally dip a wooden chopstick or the tip of a wooden spoon into the molten sugar and drop a small sample onto a white plate.

BASIC CARAMEL CREAM

The best way to illustrate how to caramelize sugar correctly and safely, and the precautions you must take to avoid having to start over, is to provide a recipe that both tells you how and shows you how. For a more saucelike consistency—something to spoon over ice cream, to dip fruit in, or to pour over a poached pear—increase the ⅓ cup (2½ fl ounces/75 ml) heavy cream to ½ cup (4 fl ounces/120 ml). You may also double (or scale up further) this recipe. Just select a larger saucepan.

¼ CUP (2 FL OUNCES/60 ML) WATER
1 TABLESPOON LIGHT CORN SYRUP
¾ CUP (5¼ OUNCES/150 GRAMS) GRANULATED SUGAR
⅓ CUP (2½ FL OUNCES/75 ML) HEAVY CREAM,
    AT ROOM TEMPERATURE

Pour the water, corn syrup and sugar, in that order, into a 3- to 4-cup heavy saucepan. Swirl the pan to combine the ingredients and moisten the sugar. Place over low heat and stir occasionally until the sugar is dissolved. When the sugar has dissolved, stop stirring, raise the heat to medium-high, and boil the mixture. Keep a pastry brush in water to wash down any sugar crystals that form on the sides of the pan while the sugar solution cooks. The syrup may begin to color in one section of the pan first. Gently swirl the pan to distribute the heat evenly, and continue to cook until the caramel is amber. (To check for the desired color, dip a wooden chopstick or the tip of a wooden spoon into the molten sugar and drop a small sample on a white saucer.)

Remove from the heat and pour in the cream all at once. The mixture will bubble madly, climbing up the sides of the pan. It may appear that the mixture will overflow, but it won't. Stir the mixture with a small silicone spatula or wooden spoon to distribute the heat and blend the ingredients together. Set aside to cool for about 10 minutes, and then pour the caramel cream into a bowl.

Making brown butter Here is another delicious taste sensation that is right up there with caramelized sugar. Brown butter, or *beurre noisette*, is butter that is cooked to a hazelnut brown. To make it, you melt butter (I prefer unsalted) and then cook it until its milk solids toast slightly. It lends a unique, nutty depth of flavor to baked items, such as cookies, cakes, fillings, frostings, and waffles, and enhances the nuttiness of any type of nut in the recipe.

Be careful when browning the butter because while brown butter is fragrantly nutty and delicious, burned black butter is bitter and inedible. Generally, 8 ounces (2 sticks/225 grams) unsalted butter, melted, yields 1 cup (8 fl ounces/240 ml) butter. However, the browning process for the same amount of butter causes the moisture in the milk solids to evaporate, so the yield for brown butter starting with the same amount is about ¾ cup (6 fl ounces/180 ml).

To prepare brown butter, melt butter in a heavy saucepan over medium-low heat, and then continue cooking, watching closely, until the butter foams, just turns golden, and has a nutlike fragrance and the bottom of the pan is covered with golden specks. The timing will vary depending on the amount of butter and the heat level; 8 ounces butter will usually take 8 to 10 minutes. Remove from the heat, and strain the butter through a fine-mesh sieve, if desired. I let the golden specks remain in some recipes, like Brown Butter Bundtlettes (page 258) and Nancy's Brown Butter Buttons (page 290). Specific recipes in the book use brown butter slightly cooled, at body temperature yet still melted, cooled to room temperature, and when it is cold and solid from the refrigerator. Brown butter, tightly covered, will keep in the refrigerator for up to 1 week.

Whipping egg whites Here are a few important things to remember before you whip egg whites: Be sure the bowl and whisk are free of any trace of oil or egg yolk. Both will retard egg whites from reaching their optimum (not to be confused with maximum) volume because the fat emulsifies with the water in the whites, weighing them down and inhibiting volume. Crack eggs when cold because the yolk is firmer and less likely to break. The temperature of egg whites affects their foaming stability, with the ideal temperature about 60 degrees F, or slightly cooler than room temperature. A cooler white is thicker, more viscous, and the air bubbles that form hold better, with less tendency to overwhip. Room-temperature whites (about 70 degrees F) whip more quickly but with a greater risk of overwhipping. To reach that optimum temperature, separate the whites cold from the refrigerator and set them aside at room temperature for about 1 hour.

For many recipes, you are whipping whites until they form stiff peaks so they can be folded into another mixture. In general, the following technique is used: In the bowl of a stand mixer fitted with the whisk attachment (or with a handheld mixer), whip the egg whites on medium speed until foamy, 30 to 45 seconds. Add cream of tartar (if using), increase the speed to medium-high, and continue whipping until soft peaks form. Gradually add the sugar, about 1 tablespoon at a time, and continue to whip until shiny, stiff peaks form. To test if the whites are ready, lift some with the whisk. If they stand upright with a slight bend at the tip (yet are not so stiff that they cannot be folded into another mixture), they are ready. Keep in mind that the mixer speed at each stage can vary depending on how many whites you are beating, how much sugar you are using, and the specific recipe.

Whipping egg whites for an angel food cake calls for a slightly different technique, and doing it properly is particularly critical because the whites are the cake's only leavening. The best technique begins with mixing on medium-low speed to break up the egg whites until they are frothy. Then add the cream of tartar and whip on medium speed until soft peaks form. Continue whipping while gradually adding the granulated sugar, 2 tablespoons at a time, until the whites have thickened to form shiny, white, droopy peaks that appear dense yet elastic. It is better to err on the side of underwhipping than overwhipping. If you whip the whites too stiff, incorporating the other ingredients will require extra folding, and you will lose volume. The overextended air cells are also more likely to collapse in the oven, and the finished cake will be tough and chewy rather than melt-in-your-mouth tender. The result you want is egg whites that whip to an optimum, not maximum, capacity, so they can be incorporated easily with the other ingredients, leaving room to expand in the oven. The final batter should be fluffy yet fluid enough to be pourable, rather than spoonable.

Whipping cream   Begin with good-quality heavy cream, preferably 36 to 40 percent butterfat. For optimum results, have the bowl and whisk or beater(s) cold (from the refrigerator), especially for amounts larger than 2 cups, since the friction created with whipping can warm the cream and begin turning it into butter. The key is to whip it over a larger bowl half-filled with icy water to keep the cream cold during the process. Or, whip the cream until it just begins to thicken yet no peaks form, cover the bowl with plastic wrap, and refrigerate it. Prior to needing it, continue whipping until just before reaching the desired consistency, and then finish whipping by hand with a whisk, so you can judge the thickness by drawing the whisk through the middle to leave a track. The stability of the track will tell you how thick the cream is. The thickness can vary: thick enough to create swirls in the bowl (loosely whipped), soft peaks with enough body to be lifted onto a spatula without falling off (softly whipped), and soft peaks with more definition (moderately whipped).

When is it done?   My goal is to have the best-tasting, best-looking baked goods possible, so knowing when a batch of cookies or a loaf of bread is "done" is important. Gauging doneness can be tricky, though, since yeast breads, cookies, flaky pie crusts, even cream puffs or crisp meringues, all have different characteristics.

Never consider color the only cue. The best doneness tests use a combination of all of our senses (and don't forget common sense). Each recipe in this book tells you what to look for when it is properly baked and specifies an approximate baking time, or sometimes a range, after the visual cues. If something tests done before the time given in the recipe, remove it from the oven. If you miscalculate in measuring the ingredients or the baking time, taste the batter or pastry dough or the baked item. If the flavor is okay, it's okay. Perhaps your oversight created a new recipe.

Here are some additional tips to help you judge doneness:

- Baking time often depends on the pan you are using. A dull metal pan absorbs and holds the heat and may bake faster, while shiny pans do not absorb heat as evenly and usually bake slower. If you are using a pan with a dark finish, reduce the temperature 25 degrees F. If this is the first time you have baked in a specific pan, it's a good idea to check occasionally for signs of doneness before the time indicated.

- Yeast breads are typically done when they are golden to dark brown on the top and sides, pull away from the sides of the pan, and emit a resonant sound when tapped on the bottom. Some bakers use an instant-read thermometer to judge the doneness of their homemade breads. Insert the thermometer into one side of the loaf, aiming it toward the center, and when it registers between 190 and 200 degrees F, the bread is fully baked. (We have come a long way, technologically speaking. I remember a time when the test for doneness called for inserting a metal skewer into the bread as it emerged from the oven, and then immediately placing the skewer on one of your wrists. If after counting to five you said "Ouch," you declared the bread was done.)

- Cookies are ready when they are no longer shiny on top and are light brown on the bottom. For crisp cookies, whether drop, rolled, or molded, bake until firm to the touch and pale gold. I prefer to bake most drop cookies, like Bake-on-Demand Chocolate Chip Cookies (page 65), until pale gold yet still a bit soft in the center. As the cookies cool, their residual heat continues the baking process, so the end result is tender-crisp cookies rather than overbaked, tasteless ones. Cookies are the easiest of all the baked goods to overbake, so I heartily recommend baking just one cookie as a test. If it bakes successfully, neither overdone nor underdone, then proceed to bake the rest of the batch for the same length of time as your test-bake.

- Most cakes are done when they spring back slightly when lightly touched in the center, the sides contract from the pan (butter cakes), and a round wooden toothpick or skewer inserted in the center comes out clean. Sponge-type cakes are light golden brown, springy to the touch, and a wooden toothpick comes out clean.

- Brownies, chocolate butter cakes, and dense chocolate cakes must be monitored closely to avoid overbaking. Remove brownies and dense chocolate cakes from the oven while they are still slightly soft in the center. If they are overbaked, the chocolate will firm as it cools.

- Flaky pie crusts, puff pastries, and other laminated doughs (page 28) are finished baking when golden and a metal skewer gently stuck into the pastry resists and makes a crunchy sound, a sign that the pastry has baked completely through. If the pastry is underbaked inside, the skewer pierces easily without any sound. Then, as the baked pastry cools on the rack, the underbaked interior dries into a hard strip (similar to pasta) and is tough and unpleasant to eat.

- Pies are finished baking when the crust is golden brown. Baking pies in ovenproof clear-glass dishes makes it easy to see if the pastry is golden brown on the bottom as well. When baking fruit pies, a bubbly filling is a second cue indicating doneness.

Refrigerating and freezing   I think of the refrigerator as an extra pair of hands when I'm not certain if I'm going to use the cake I just baked or the dough I just made right away. I refrigerate cakes or pastry doughs for a short period of time, like a day or two. Place cakes in cake boxes or sturdy plastic containers, double wrap the boxes with plastic wrap, and refrigerate for up to 2 days. I store pastry doughs from the same recipe, individually wrapped in plastic wrap in resealable plastic bags in the refrigerator for up to 2 days. That gives me some time to decide whether to use the cake or dough or to freeze it for longer storage.

Every occasional baker should view the freezer as a personal assistant, sort of a frosty concierge. I have never believed in freezing whole desserts or their individual elements for long periods, but I have found that a couple of weeks is a good limit, unless I am freezing a frosting in an airtight container, in which case it will keep for 1 month. The freezer is a handy holding place to accommodate the occasional baker who wants to either make a dessert in stages or make the whole dessert ahead of time, such as cookies for a cookie exchange. It is a temporary storage spot, not a piece of equipment for housing food that will be consumed in a year or two.

After putting time and effort into making whatever you are going to freeze, you want it to emerge from its stint in the cold tasting and looking as great as when you stored it. Properly wrapping baked goods is key, as is putting them into in an odorless freezer. Store them in sturdy airtight containers or wrap in plastic wrap and overwrap with aluminum foil, and then label with the contents and date. Butter-based frostings and pie and tart pastries are especially prone to absorbing freezer (or refrigerator) odors. See individual recipes for additional freezing ideas and for how long an item can be frozen.

USING THE FREEZER FOR TEMPORARY STORAGE

- Chill pastry to firm the butter for flakiness and relax the gluten in the flour.

- Chill cakes before splitting or cutting into layers or different shapes.

- Store pie, puff pastry, and cream cheese pastry dough briefly—a holding pattern—until ready to use.

- Freeze freshly made cookie, pastry, or tart pastry dough that is too soft to roll just long enough for it to be manageable.

- Freeze berries in a single layer on a baking sheet, and then put them in a resealable bag.

- Flash-freeze a completely assembled and frosted cake until the frosting is firm enough to wrap for longer freezing without marring the cake.

WHAT CAN BE FROZEN

- Baked items, such as cookies, brownies and other bars, cupcakes, coffee cakes, snack cakes, phyllo turnovers, and scones, for from 3 days up to 2 weeks, depending on individual recipes.

- Parts of recipes when you pause between stages; times can range from 2 days up to 1 month, depending on individual recipes.

- Unfrosted cake layers.

- Frostings and buttercreams.

- Pastry-lined pie or tart pans.

- Tart pastry dough.

- Pie pastry dough.

- Cookie dough.

- Pastry dough scraps.

- Leftover fillings and glazes.

- Leftover frosted or unfrosted cakes, depending on individual recipes; always press pieces of plastic wrap or waxed paper against the cut surfaces to protect them from drying out.

Transporting cakes and other desserts   I'm often asked, "How do you transport your cakes and desserts from your house to your destination?" My response is "very carefully." And that's the truth. I have found that two tips work for me: a large cardboard box that fences the dessert in, and foam or a rubber mat to anchor the dessert in place in the car.

For a cake or dessert that is wrapped in plastic and not yet on a serving plate, I place it on a strip of foam or a rubber mat in the car so it won't slide once the car is moving. For an uncovered or unwrapped dessert or frosted cake on a plate, or a pie in its pie dish, I place it in a large cardboard box. If the box is larger than the plated dessert, I cut foam (it comes in a roll; see Sources) or a rubber mat to fit the bottom of the box, and then I place the plated dessert on the foam so the plate won't slide when the car is moving. If you are transporting a frosted, glazed, or decorated cake and you want to make sure you don't mar the finish, fashion a makeshift dome by placing several toothpicks around the top outer edge of the cake before covering it with a sheet of waxed paper or plastic wrap.

Key Techniques for Cake Making

At its simplest, creating a cake batter is a matter of blending dry and liquid ingredients into a silky smooth mixture. But how we achieve that depends on the type of cake we are baking. For most cake batters, such as butter and pound cakes, the ingredients must be at room temperature (65 to 70 degrees F) for them to blend smoothly and to incorporate air bubbles evenly for optimum baking results. The news here is that the consistency of the batter is a strong indication of the texture of the finished cake. For example, a smooth, thick, heavy batter (that you spoon into the baking pan) will transform into a dense, close-grained pound cake, while a smooth, fluffy, light batter (that you can pour into the pan) will emerge from the oven as a moist, airy sponge cake. The size of the sugar granule also dictates the cake's texture. Superfine granulated sugar (sometime known as bar sugar) will produce a smaller, closer grain, while granulated sugar will produce a slightly larger one.

The cake-making process   To create a perfect cake every time depends on the order in which you combine the ingredients and the manner in which you combine them. Different types of cakes require different mixing methods, each of which produces cakes with a distinctive texture.

The majority of the cakes in this book are butter or pound cakes that are created by beating (or "creaming") together room-temperature ingredients: first the butter and sugar thoroughly for 3 to 5 minutes (until the mixture appears fluffy and "creamy," thus the source of the expression "cream the butter and sugar") and then the eggs slowly to incorporate them. The sequence of the two beatings aerates the batter, which doubles or triples its volume (an imperative step in the process), and the millions of tiny trapped air bubbles that are produced naturally leaven the batter as it bakes, giving the cake its structure. Next, dry ingredients, which often include chemical leavenings such as baking powder (the leavening does not create additional bubbles; it only assists those already formed), are added alternately with more liquid, with each addition carefully blended in. This technique helps suspend the air bubbles that ensure a superior texture and maximum height.

Mixing the batter for springy, tender foam-style cakes, such as chiffon, sponge, and angel food, is dependent on properly whipping eggs, egg yolks, and/or egg whites, then carefully folding in the dry ingredients to create the cakes' distinctive lofty texture. The wonderfully adaptable classic American chiffon cake owes its fine-grained, tender texture to the gentle combining of two airy mixtures: an egg yolk batter containing a high percentage of liquid and oil to which you fold in whipped egg whites.

A successful angel food cake is dependent on an abundance of properly whipped egg whites, as in Chocolate Lover's Angel Food Cake (page 208). As the cake bakes, pressure builds in the air cells in the whipped egg whites, but most of the volume is created by the evaporation of the liquid in the egg whites, which creates steam that passes through the air cells to expand the cake.

Everything you need to produce the genoise, the most versatile of all the sponge cakes, happens in one bowl. A sugary egg mixture is whipped to a heavenly lofty, foamy state—a kind of whole-egg meringue—and then dry ingredients that define its texture are delicately folded into it. (It is also one of the easiest batters for practicing your folding skills.)

Measuring the capacity of cake pans   When I became seriously interested in baking, part of the fun was baking my favorite cakes in pans of different sizes and shapes. In those days, I estimated how much batter a pan could accommodate, I filled it with batter, placed it in the oven, set the timer, and then crossed my fingers and toes. (This was before self-cleaning ovens, too. Was I brave?) If you are interested in using a variety of pans, I can save you that same worry.

To check if a pan with a different shape and size from what the recipe calls for can be substituted successfully, you need to determine its capacity and compare it with the capacity of the original pan. Using a large measuring cup, and keeping track of how many times you fill it, pour water into the pan until it is close to the rim. Then, with a felt-tip permanent marker, record the cup capacity on the outside bottom of the pan. Compare this volume with the standard volume of the pan called for in the recipe (see Dimensions and

Capacity of Frequently Used Baking Pans, page 381). If the pan has a removable bottom, wrap aluminum foil tightly around the outer base before you fill the pan with water. (It still might leak a bit, but you will get a good sense of the pan's capacity.) See also Bakeware on page 35 for detailed measurements for all of the various pans used for cakes in this book.

Preparing cake pans   Generally speaking, you need to butter (preferably with soft butter) the bottom and sides of a pan, or coat them lightly and evenly with non-stick spray, and then flour them, tap out the excess flour, and finally line the bottom with parchment paper. To guarantee successful removal of a cake baked in a pan with an intricate shape, I take extra precaution, spreading it first with solid vegetable shortening, followed by a coating of nonstick spray, and then a dusting of flour.

Making parchment-paper cake liners   For easy removal of cakes from baking pans, it's helpful to line the bottom of the pan with parchment paper. I use precut parchment circles, 8, 9, or 10 inches in diameter. You can instead trace the bottom of the pan onto a sheet of parchment, and then cut it out. Then, when you invert the warm cake onto a wire rack, you lift off the pan, slowly peel off the parchment liner, turn the paper over so the sticky side faces up, and reposition it on top of the layer. Cover with another rack, invert the layer right side up, remove the original rack, and let the cake cool completely. Reusing the parchment liner in this way prevents the layer from sticking to the rack while it cools, and provides a temporary base for lifting the cake for storage or decorating without fear of it cracking.

Using a stand mixer   A stand mixer is a powerful machine, so try to match the speed for beating, whipping, or blending to the power of the action if you were doing it by hand. I seldom exceed medium speed in my recipes, such as when I am beating the butter and sugar for a butter cake. Then when I add the dry ingredients alternately with liquid ingredients, I often use the lowest speed. If I am whipping cream, I typically use medium speed as well, or when I whip egg whites, I start on medium-low speed

and then increase to medium speed as the whites thicken. Each recipe includes the correct mixer speed for each step.

Adding eggs   How you add eggs to a cake batter is a key element in successful cake making. First, lightly beat the eggs in a small bowl just to combine them. Then add them slowly to the mixture, from 2 tablespoons at a time up to about 1/4 cup at a time (the equivalent of 1/2 to 1 egg), always beating each addition until it is absorbed into the creamy mixture before adding more to keep the aerated mixture emulsified. Adding the eggs, which usually takes from 2 to 4 minutes, increases the volume of the batter.

Alternating dry and liquid ingredients   Usually you add the flour mixture in three or four stages alternately with the liquid in two or three stages, beginning and ending with the flour mixture. Making the dry ingredient the last addition binds the batter together to form the desirable consistency. Use the lowest speed on a stand or handheld mixer, and mix just until smooth after each addition, stopping to scrape down the sides of the bowl as needed. With a handheld mixer, you may have to mix longer and scrape down the bowl sides more often. If the ingredients are not added in stages and at low speed, air bubbles can burst and cause curdling, which will produce a cake with a reduced volume.

You can also add the dry and liquid ingredients by hand with a rubber spatula, which gives you greater control in producing a smooth batter. Mixing by hand reduces the risk of overmixing, which can encourage overdevelopment of the protein in the flour, yielding an undesirable texture, and overmanipulation of the baking powder, causing tunneling.

Filling baking pans   Using a large kitchen serving spoon, deposit equal amounts of batter into each pre-pared baking pan. If you want to make sure that each layer has the same amount, weigh each filled pan on a scale, a simple test that is particularly helpful if you want a perfectly symmetrical cake. For filling muffin (cupcake) pans with batter, I rely on ice cream scoops (which are also handy for chocolate truffles, cookie doughs, and even some cake fillings).

Spreading the batter to ensure even rising

Once the batter is in the pan, use a rubber spatula to spread it, working from the center outward, to create a slightly raised ridge around the outside rim. Since heat is conducted faster near the metal rim, mounding the batter around the edges ensures a more even baked layer. Batters containing one or more chemical leavenings also have a tendency to bake higher, or "dome," in the middle. The outer raised ridge compensates for this tendency.

Cooling cakes   Most cakes should be cooled on an elevated wire rack so that the air can freely circulate around them. Recipes provide details on how long to cool a cake before unmolding, and Making Parchment-Paper Cake Liners, above, includes specifics on removing paper liners. Angel food cakes and chiffon cakes are typically cooled by inverting the pan and resting it on legs on the pan or slipping the tube over a slim-necked bottle.

Splitting a cake into layers   Before you split a cake into layers, it must be completely cool. In fact, placing the cooled cake in the freezer for 20 to 40 minutes will make it easier to split and will produce fewer crumbs. (The timing depends on how cold your freezer is. The layer should feel well chilled but not be so firmly frozen that you can't easily cut through it.) To split a layer horizontally in half or into thirds is a simple two-step process. You need a small paring knife, a ruler, and a long, serrated knife, preferably with a blade at least 12 inches long, or 3 to 4 inches longer than the diameter of the cake. Place the cake on a piece of parchment or waxed paper on a work surface. If the cake is not level, make small shallow incisions horizontally in the top of the cake, or place several toothpicks around the cake to mark the thin layer that needs to be trimmed away. Then, using the markings around the cake, move the serrated knife across the cake, rotating the cake into the blade and sawing back and forth. If there are additional cake layers, trim them as well for the sake of symmetry.

To cut the cake into layers, measure the height of the cake with the ruler, and then use the paring knife to cut a shallow incision at the halfway point or at points for as many layers as you need. Then, with the paring knife,

cut an incision about 1 inch deep horizontally around the circumference of the cake. (Bending over the side of the cake slightly until your eyes are just above the level of the cake gives the best perspective for a straight, level cut.) Move the knife in a sawing motion, in and out, while simultaneously rotating the cake with your other hand, until you have circumnavigated the entire cake. Slip the serrated knife straight into the precut path at one edge of the cake. Rotate the cake as you cut through the entire layer, gently pushing the cake into the blade while simultaneously sawing back and forth.

To prevent cracking the layers when it is time to fill and frost them, transfer them, one at a time, by gently sliding a piece of corrugated cardboard, a small, rimless baking sheet, or the thin removable base from a tart pan under the layer and lifting it off the cake or work surface.

Compressing a cake roll   To ensure a rolled cake is uniform, such as Chocolate Roulade with Chocolate Diplomat Cream (page 307), Old-Fashioned Jelly Roll with a Twist (page 339), or Red Velvet Cake Roll (page 85), place the roll in its foil across the bottom third of a 24-inch-long piece of parchment paper. Bring the top edge of the paper toward you, and drape it over the cake roll, allowing a 2-inch overhang. Place the edge of a rimless baking sheet at a 45-degree angle to the roll and your work surface. Apply pressure against the roll, trapping the 2-inch overhang, and push while simultaneously pulling the bottom portion of paper toward you. This push-pull motion creates a resistance that results in compressing the log into a uniform shape. If any cracks appeared as you rolled the cake, they are consolidated in this compression and disappear from view. (Save any filling that might push out at the ends to use as an additional garnish when you serve the cake.) Carefully lift the cake roll in the aluminum foil and set it, seam side down, onto a second sheet of aluminum foil. Wrap the foil around the cake securely and refrigerate the cake for at least 2 hours or up to 1 day.

Making paper cones for decorating   These disposable cones are great for piping small amounts of chocolate, ganache, jelly, buttercream, and royal icing on your cakes. If you don't have precut paper triangles for paper cones, cut a 22-inch square from parchment paper. Fold it in half on the diagonal, and cut into 2 triangles. Hold a triangle in one hand with the longest side at the bottom and the thumb of your other hand in the center. Manipulate it into a cone shape so that the long side of the triangular-shaped paper becomes the tip and the point of the triangle (opposite the long side) becomes the opening of the cone. Fold the top of the point into the cone to hold it together. Fill the cone half full, fold the tops of the two sides toward the middle, and fold the top down to enclose the mixture. Cut the tip to the desired opening before piping.

HOW TO PIPE WITH A PAPER CONE Half fill a paper cone with the glaze, jelly, icing, or whatever ingredient a recipe directs. Snip a small opening at the end of the paper cone to allow a thin flow. Exerting light pressure on the cone, and never easing the pressure or halting the motion, pipe as the recipe directs.

Filling and using a pastry bag Pastry bags come in a variety of shapes and sizes (page 43). A 14- or 16-inch bag is the size I use most often. If it is a disposable bag, snip the opening with scissors to create a hole just large enough to accommodate the pastry tip you are using (the tip should extend halfway out of the opening). Slide the tip inside the bag down to the opening. Twist the bag a few times just behind the tip, and push the twisted portion into the tip itself. This seals the end so the bag can be filled. Fold the top of the bag about halfway down, to form a cuff that covers your hand. This makes filling the bag easier and keeps your hand clean.

Spoon the frosting, whipped cream, meringue, mousse, or other mixture into the bag, filling it no more than one-half to two-thirds full. If it is too full, you won't be able to exercise good control over the amount of pressure you apply as you pipe. Unfold the cuff and twist the top of the bag to force out any air and to pack the frosting down firmly into the tip. Once you begin piping, continue to twist the top as the mixture lessens, so the mixture is continuously forced into the tip.

Good control, the secret to good piping, involves three basic factors: the angle you hold the bag (from 45 degrees to 90 degrees), which is defined by the shape you are piping; the amount of pressure you apply, which depends on both the consistency of the mixture and the shape you pipe; and how smoothly you move. Don't be intimidated by the pastry bag. Practice makes perfect, and it won't be long before you will achieve a level of comfort. And although these piping instructions are included in the cake-making section, they apply to other baked goods, too, from cookies (Buttery Rosette Cookies, page 293) to cream puffs (Pumpkin Ice Cream Profiteroles with Caramel Sauce, page 152).

PIPING WITH EASE To maintain the steady movement needed for smooth piping, brace your arms against your body and move slowly in the direction you are piping. A gentle pressure creates a flow the same size as the tip; a heavier pressure increases the size of the flow, making it larger than the tip. Raising the tip slightly, along with increased pressure, will make the shape not only wider but also thicker.

For frosting a cupcake, hold the pastry bag at a 90-degree angle (perpendicular) to the baked cupcake and begin piping in the center, about 1 inch above the surface. Press out a string of the frosting, which should emerge from the bag the size of the tip. Work from the center outward, directing the initial curl of the mixture to curve and twist around as you enlarge the spiral shape, so that it ends with a wide rosette in the center. Many professional bakers like to cover the top almost completely, allowing only a small portion of the cake to show around the edges. This is especially true if there is a contrast between the cake and frosting.

For piping solid circular forms, hold the pastry bag at a 90-degree angle (perpendicular) to the surface with the tip about 1/2 inch above it. Pipe out the mixture, raising the tip as necessary, to create the height and width desired.

For piping a "dam" with whipped cream (Deluxe Boston Cream Pie, page 325), hold the pastry bag at a 90-degree angle (perpendicular) to the surface with the tip 1/2 inch above it and pipe a coil of whipped cream around the entire edge of the bottom layer. When you add the filling, this border will hold it in and make it easy to finish the exterior of the cake neatly.

To form a beaded border around the base of a cake, use a small plain open tip and pipe out small balls, or "pearls," of buttercream, creating a "string of pearls" in which each new pearl touches the one before it. Squeeze the pastry bag gently until a small ball begins to appear, then release pressure on the bag and guide the tip downward into the small ball of buttercream to tuck in the little point that forms when you lift the bag and to direct the pearl toward the cake. Repeat this action, piping another pearl directly next to the first one, and then continue in this way around the base of the cake to form the string of pearls. Before you start, you might find it helpful to practice piping by placing a large can, to represent a cake, on top of a cutting board and piping around the base of the can.

Key Techniques for Pie Making

Making the pie dough   A tender, flaky pie crust ideally has enough structure to hold fillings but not enough to remove the crust with its filling from the pan. To make the pastry, you basically mix flour (all-purpose), sugar (for browning), and salt (for flavor and to give support to the protein in the flour) in a large bowl (I prefer a metal bowl, but more on that later.) Then you cut in cold unsalted butter with a pastry blender (I prefer one that has stiff, rigid wires, rather than flexible ones) just until the mixture resembles a very coarse meal with many butter pieces ranging from the size of peas to the size of beans. Next, you cut in cold shortening until the mixture resembles a coarse meal with butter and shortening pieces varying in size from coarse crumbs to corn kernels to peas. How thoroughly you blend in the fats, their temperature, and the amount you use determine the final texture of your crust. I aim for the assorted pieces of chilled fat to provide the crust with both tenderness (smaller fat bits) and flakiness (medium and larger fat nuggets). Cutting in the fats is how you combine them with the flour, which in turn coats the flour (but not all of it; the proof is the loose flour in the bottom of the bowl, and that's fine, too).

Once the fat and flour are combined, sprinkle ice water over the mixture (to keep the fat chilled and solid and to keep gluten development at a minimum while you form the dough) 1 tablespoon at a time, tossing lightly with a fork (preferably a blending fork; see Sources) after every addition, just until the pastry is moist enough to hold together.

Transfer the dough to a lightly floured work surface, gently shape it into a ball, and flatten it into a disk (about 10½ ounces/300 grams) about ½ inch thick. Wrap it with plastic wrap and refrigerate for at least 2 hours or up to 2 days. For longer storage, overwrap in aluminum foil, date, label, and freeze for up to 1 month. To thaw, place in the refrigerator for about 4 hours or up to overnight. The dough should remain cold.

Rolling out pastry for a single-crust pie and lining a pie dish   Have on hand a glass pie dish. (A clear-glass dish allows you to view the baking process so you can judge when the bottom crust has finished baking.) To roll a circular shape for a round pie dish, begin with a circle, not a square or rectangle. Place the disk of dough on a lightly floured work surface. Center the rolling pin on the disk and push away from you in one stroke, using just enough pressure to extend the dough about 2 inches. Let up on the pressure as you near the edge. Gently lift the dough and rotate it a one-eighth turn in one direction. Dust the surface with additional flour as needed. Repeat the rolling, always working from the center out and always rotating the dough a one-eighth turn in the same direction after each stroke, until the circle of dough is 2 to 4 inches larger than the diameter of the pie dish (2½ to 3 inches larger for a single-crust pie and up to 4 inches larger for the bottom crust for a double-crust pie) and ⅛ to ³⁄₁₆ inch thick (or as individual recipes direct).

To maintain the shape of the circle and to avoid stretching the dough as you transfer it to the dish, fold the circle into quarters, lift it and place it in the pie dish with the point at the center, and then unfold it. Or, roll up the pastry loosely around the rolling pin and unroll it evenly over the pie dish. Gently ease the pastry into the contours of the dish, pressing down lightly with your fingertips, until it fits snugly against the sides and bottom. Trim the edges with scissors so there is a 1-inch overhang. Fold the overhang, tucking it under the edge of the pastry, and bring it up onto the dish rim, so it is flush with the lip of the dish. Pinch and flute the folded overhang decoratively to create a thick, high edge. Refrigerate the pastry-lined pie dish until it is time to blind bake it or fill it and bake it.

Blind baking a pie crust   Blind baking is baking pie pastry either partially or fully before adding the filling. It calls for weighting the dough (the source of the name of the technique, since you cannot see the pastry when it is weighted), which helps to hold it in place until it is sufficiently set to maintain its shape on its own. It also aids in sealing the dough, which protects against soggy pastry from a custard, juicy, or other liquidy filling.

Center a rack in the oven and preheat to 425 degrees F. Line a chilled unbaked pie crust with large, overlapping round coffee filters, preferably about 8 inches in diameter, or a sheet of parchment paper or aluminum foil, covering the bottom and sides completely. The pastry will bake more fully if using coffee filters or parchment because the heat will penetrate more easily. Fill the lined crust with 2 to 2½ cups dried beans. If possible, fold the edge of the liner over the outer rim of beans to expose the fluted edge to the heat.

Bake until the pastry appears set and dry near the edges and the edges no longer look raw or shiny, 10 to 15 minutes. Transfer the pan to a wire rack and carefully remove the lining with the beans. Prick the dough in a few places with a metal skewer or the tines of a fork to release some steam. Reduce the oven temperature to 375 degrees F, return the pie dish to the oven, and bake until the pastry is pale gold and appears set, about 15 minutes longer. This is a partially baked crust. Let cool completely on a wire rack before baking and filling as directed in individual recipes.

To fully bake the crust, proceed as directed for the partially baked crust, but after it bakes to a pale gold, reduce the oven temperature to 325 degrees F and continue to bake until light golden brown, 10 to 20 minutes longer. Let cool completely on a wire rack before filling.

Rolling out the pastry for a double-crust pie   Have on hand a glass pie dish. Using 1 dough disk, follow the directions for rolling out pastry for a single-crust pie and

lining a pie dish on page 27. Trim the edges as directed, leaving a 1-inch overhang. If not filling immediately, set the pastry-lined pie dish aside at room temperature.

Add the filling to the crust as directed in individual recipes. Then roll out the second dough disk the same way you rolled out the first one. Lightly moisten the overhang on the bottom pastry with water. Transfer the second dough disk to the pie dish the same way you transferred the first one, unfolding it or laying it over the filling. Gently press down along the edges to seal them firmly. With kitchen scissors, trim the excess pastry of the top and bottom crusts to within ¾ inch of the rim. Fold the overhang, tucking it under the edge of the bottom pastry, and bring it up onto the pie dish rim so it is flush with the lip of the pie dish. Pinch and flute the overhang decoratively to create a thick, high edge. Cut 1 or more vents in the center of the top crust (to allow steam to escape during baking) if directed in the recipe.

Key Techniques for Laminating Pastry Doughs

The recipes for PDQ (Pretty Darn Quick) Puff Pastry (page 367), Croissant Pastry ASAP (page 365), All-Butter Flaky Pastry (page 356), and Flaky Strudel Pastry (page 364) all read like a recipe for a pie dough because the same ingredients are used. But if you examine the proportions of the ingredients closely, you will notice that the ratio of fat to flour is higher than for a pie dough. How that fat is handled is the key to producing a multi-layered pastry. The technique is called lamination, and I have applied certain of its principles to some recipes, such as Apricot Flaky Scones (page 173) and the Sour Cream Flaky Pastry for Kouign Amman Express Pastries (page 69), that traditionally don't call for it because it takes them a cut above what they would have been without it. Lamination gives both the buttery sweet yeast pastry dough and even the simple scone dough a special flakiness and a puffy lift that changes their taste, texture, and appearance. All of this is possible with little effort. My method is a user-friendly one adapted to busy lives. It requires no time-consuming hand work, but does call for a few hands-off periods for resting the dough.

Laminating involves manipulating the dough so it forms horizontal layers of lean dough separated by thin films of fat that can expand, aerate, and leaven a pastry. However, rather than incorporating a block of butter into lean dough as you do for classic puff pastry and then rolling and folding the pastry in a specific pattern to distribute the fat as evenly as possible, my approach is less structured. Although the result is not as dramatic as its labor-intensive counterpart, the taste and texture are as good as gold, and my hope is that by simplifying these doughs, I can encourage other bakers to incorporate them into their baking repertoires and pass the pleasure forward.

Laminating pastry doughs   Most of my time-saving pastry recipes instruct you to make a dough similar to a pie crust dough. The primary difference is that you stop working in the butter when the butter nuggets are larger than you typically want for a pie crust. At that point, you add the liquid to bring everything together into a shaggy mass. Then, as directed in each recipe, you roll and fold the dough until its random pieces of butter are interspersed throughout the mixture, creating a structure of layers with different concentrations of butter.

As the pastry bakes, the moisture in the layers converts to steam, and as the steam attempts to escape, the pastry expands upward, creating air pockets. The gluten (protein) strands extend with pressure and at the same time tighten to contain the steam. The pressure and expansion continue until the gluten strands are set in place by the heat. Simultaneously, the butter melts and separates the layers from one another, creating a flaky texture with a lift that is puffier than pie pastry.

Preshrinking pastry doughs   The virtue of pre-shrinking pastry dough has been taught in my baking classes for years. It dates to a long-ago San Francisco class that included instructions for making puff pastry. My friend Sharon Lipson, who was attending the class, made an astute observation as I was rolling out the pastry. "Just like fabric, you're preshrinking the pastry," Sharon observed. What I do is roll out the dough, let it rest for just a few seconds, and then, with my fingertips, I gently lift the end of the pastry closest to me up and off the sur-

face, and then I set it back down on the same spot. This "release" from the surface shrinks the dough's dimensions a bit (relieves the tension created from rolling it), which in turn relaxes the dough, making it more docile, rather than elastic, as you continue rolling it. The result is pastry that shrinks less as it bakes. I never want to stop learning more about baking, and the learning is even more meaningful to me when I can share it with other bakers.

Key Techniques for Tart, Crostata, and Cookie Doughs

Tart doughs, my open-faced *crostata* dough (page 362), and many cookie doughs are related, though the cookie doughs are much sweeter. All three types of dough are low in moisture (with egg contributing some of the moisture) and have a high proportion of butter, which is thoroughly blended into the dry ingredients. These factors contribute to a short, crisp, and tender baked result. The egg and sugar contribute a slightly sticky quality to the dough that can make it tricky to roll, but if you follow my simple technique, you should have no trouble rolling and shaping the dough. Because the sugar and the amount of butter in these sweet doughs curtail gluten development, the risk of shrinkage and toughness is reduced.

Rolling out pastry for a tart pan and lining the pan   You can press tart dough into a pan with your fingertips, rather than roll it out. However, rolling is faster, results in a more even thickness, and requires less manipulation than pressing. Usually when you roll out dough, you dust the work surface with flour to ensure it rolls out smoothly and doesn't stick to the surface. But additional flour changes the flavor and texture of tart dough. Plus, you want to keep the dough scraps reusable and cleanup to a minimum. So, here's a technique for rolling out tart dough that doesn't involve extra flour so the ingredients remain in balance.

First, the dough must be pliable. Tart dough that you just made is often the perfect consistency for rolling. However, if it is too soft, refrigerate it for about 30 minutes to chill and firm it slightly. If it is too firm from the refrigerator, allow it to warm at room temperature until just malleable enough to roll and still cool to the touch, 15 to 30 minutes.

In the past, bakers rolled out tart pastry between 2 sheets of plastic wrap with considerable ease. But manufacturers have reformulated most plastic wraps for home use, so that the sheets stick together immediately, locking the dough in place as if it is shrink-wrapped, making expanding the dough as you roll out of the question. To circumvent the plastic-wrap problem, I roll the dough between a sheet of plastic wrap and a sheet of waxed paper or parchment paper.

Have ready a fluted round tart pan with a removable bottom. To roll a circular shape for a round container, begin with a circle, not a square or rectangle. Center the dough disk on a sheet of plastic wrap about 18 inches long, and center a sheet of waxed paper or parchment paper about 13 inches long on top of the dough. Center the rolling pin on the disk of dough, and push it away from you in one stroke, using just enough pressure to extend the dough about 2 inches and letting up on the pressure as you near the edge. Slip your hand between the plastic and the dough, gently lift the dough, and rotate it a one-eighth turn in one direction. Repeat the rolling, always working from the center out and always rotating the dough a one-eighth turn in the same direction after each stroke, until the circle of dough is 1/8 inch thick. The 1/8-inch thickness is critical. Any thicker and the tart will have more crust than filling.

Peel off and discard the waxed or parchment paper. To maintain the circular shape of the dough and avoid stretching it, use the overhang of the plastic wrap as handles, lifting the plastic wrap with the pastry on it and inverting it, pastry side down, over the tart pan. Gently peel away the plastic wrap, and discard it. With your fingertips, ease the pastry into the pan, fitting it carefully into the corners. If the pastry splits a bit, you can patch it easily by gently pressing the tear back together, or by firmly pressing a small amount of extra dough in place. Using kitchen scissors or a knife, trim any overhang to 1/2 inch, and then fold it inward to reinforce the sides. Use scraps to patch any gaps, if necessary. Place the pastry-lined pan in the freezer for about 20 minutes or in the refrigerator for at least 30 minutes or up to 1 day to chill and firm the dough. Any scraps can be frozen and used at another time.

Partially and fully baking a tart shell   Unlike a pie crust, which is flaky and thus needs weights to keep the dough in place until it bakes long enough to set (see Blind Baking a Pie Crust, page 28), most of my tart shells, including Three Tart Shells at One Time (page 360) and Chocolate Tart Pastry (page 363), stay in place without weights as they bake.

To partially bake a tart shell, center a rack in the oven and preheat the oven as directed in individual recipes (350 to 400 degrees F). Prick the bottom of the chilled unbaked tart shell with the tines of a fork or the tip of a knife, making small holes or tiny slashes about 1 1/2 inches apart, to allow the steam to escape as the tart shell bakes. Place in the oven and check the shell after 7 to 8 minutes to see if the pastry is bubbling. If it is, use a wooden skewer or the tip of a knife and gently prick the center of the bubble or blistered area to deflate, releasing the steam so the dough fits the pan snugly. After 10 to 15 minutes, check the color of the shell and rotate the pan 180 degrees if needed for even baking. Continue to bake until the surface of the dough looks dull and dry (no longer shiny), light gold, and feels firm to the touch, 5 to 10 minutes longer, for a total cooking time of 17 to 25 minutes. Remove from the oven and let cool on a wire rack as directed in individual recipes.

To fully bake the tart shell, proceed as directed for a partially baked shell, but bake until evenly golden, 5 to 10 minutes longer. Transfer to a wire rack and let cool completely before filling.

If you are not using the shell the same day you bake it, wrap it securely in plastic wrap, overwrap with aluminum foil, and set aside at room temperature for up to 2 days. For longer storage, label with the contents and date and freeze for up to 10 days. Thaw at room temperature for about 2 hours before filling.

Mixing large batches of tart or cookie dough
I am partial to making some sweet doughs in a food processor. I have found that it incorporates less air than a

stand mixer, making it especially suitable for cookies and tarts where I specifically do not want a lot of puffing or lifting as they bake. However, there are circumstances, such as when doubling or scaling up a cookie or tart dough recipe, or when all of the ingredients in a recipe won't fit in my standard food processor, that I make the dough in a stand mixer on the lowest speed to emulate the food processor in slower motion. Three Tart Shells at One Time (page 360) is a good example.

In these instances, and especially when a recipe calls for a small amount of liquid in relation to its amount of dry ingredients (the case with most cookie and tart doughs), I use a method that reverses the usual order of mixing. I add softened butter to the flour and sugar, rather than first beating the butter and sugar until fluffy and then adding the flour. This method, known as reverse mixing, blends ingredients together simply and easily without overworking the dough.

Fraisage: Forming a smooth, cohesive sweet dough   Place room-temperature or still-cool-to-the-touch dough on a work surface, lightly dusting the surface with flour first if the recipe calls for it. Beginning at the far end, and using the heel of your hand, push a small amount of the dough (about the size of an extra-large egg) away from you, smearing it on the work surface. Repeat with the remaining dough in small amounts. When you have worked all of the dough in this manner, give it a couple more strokes to bring it together. French bakers call this kneading process *fraisage*, and it is used in this book in a variety of recipes, including Tangy Lemon Custard Tart with Pomegranate Gelée (page 71) and Three Tart Shells at One Time (page 360). It helps create a smoother, more cohesive dough that is less likely to tear or crack while it is being rolled or while it is being rolled around the pin for fitting into a pan.

Rolling out and partially baking pastry for an open-faced crostata   Preheat the oven as directed in individual recipes. Line a large rimmed baking sheet with parchment paper, and dust the paper with flour. If the dough is cold and firm, set it aside at room temperature until it is slightly pliable yet still cool to the touch,

about 30 minutes. On a lightly floured surface, roll out the dough into a circle 10 inches in diameter. As you roll, lift the pastry occasionally to make sure it isn't sticking and rotate it one-eighth turn to maintain a well-shaped circle. Carefully transfer the pastry circle to the prepared baking sheet, lightly flour the top of the pastry, and continue to roll it into a circle 12 inches in diameter and about 3/16 inch thick.

Using your fingertips, gently roll up about 1 inch of the outer edge of the pastry circle to form a raised border that stands about 1/2 inch high. The circle will now be about 11 inches in diameter. Don't worry if the circle is slightly irregular, rather than a perfect round. A *crostata* is meant to be a homey, rustic tart. Check that there are no gaps in the border, so the filling won't leak out during baking. With the tines of a fork, prick the bottom of the pastry about every 1 1/2 inches.

Bake the pastry until it is dry, no longer shiny on top, feels slightly firm to the touch in the center, and is beginning to color, 20 to 22 minutes. Check after baking for about 8 minutes. If the pastry is puffed up, prick the center of the blistered area with a wooden skewer or the tip of a knife, and it should deflate. If it doesn't, gently press it down with your fingertips and then continue baking. When the pastry is ready, remove the pan to a wire rack and let cool for about 10 minutes before filling.

Rolling out dough for cutout cookies   Have the dough at room temperature, so it is pliable enough to roll out between 2 sheets of waxed paper. (Parchment paper can be used for rolling out cookie dough too, but waxed paper is less expensive and works fine.) Place the dough between the 2 sheets of paper and roll out into the shape and thickness specified in individual recipes.

If rolling out more than 1 dough portion, leave the rolled-out dough between the sheets of paper, put the packages on a baking sheet, and refrigerate until firm, or for as long as the recipe directs. Line 1 or more baking sheets with parchment paper. If using 1 baking sheet, center a rack in the oven, and if using 2 baking sheets, position one rack in the lower third of the oven and another in the upper third of the oven, then preheat the oven to the temperature specified in individual recipes.

Remove 1 dough package at a time from the refrigerator, peel off the top sheet of waxed paper, replace it loosely on top, and flip the entire package over. Peel off and discard the second sheet of waxed paper. Using a cutter, cut out shapes in the dough and transfer to the prepared baking sheets. Bake as directed in specific recipes.

Compressing a cookie-dough log   To ensure a cookie-dough log is uniform, such as for Chocolate-Vanilla Swirl Cookies (page 276), place the log across the bottom third of a 24-inch-long piece of parchment paper. Bring the top edge of the paper toward you, and drape it over the log, allowing a 2-inch overhang. Place the edge of a rimless baking sheet at a 45-degree angle to the roll and your work surface. Apply pressure against the roll, trapping the 2-inch overhang, and push while simultaneously pulling the bottom portion of paper toward you. This push-pull motion creates a resistance that results in compressing the log into a uniform shape. Wrap the log securely in plastic wrap or foil and refrigerate as directed.

Maintaining the round shape of cookie-dough logs   For almost thirty-five years, I've had a hollow steel rod in my kitchen that looks like it was cut from plumbing pipe. Years ago, when French-style rolling pins were not yet available in cookware shops, I used this rod for a rolling pin. In fact, I packed it with my clothes and other odd pieces of equipment when I first began to travel and teach. One afternoon, after I finished forming several logs of cookie dough, I got the idea to slip two of the logs inside my makeshift rolling pin to maintain their round form while they chilled in the refrigerator.

Now I save the cardboard cylinders at the center of plastic wrap, waxed paper, and even wrapping-paper rolls. I slip the just-formed cookie logs (wrapped in plastic) into the cardboard cylinders, and put the cylinders in the refrigerator. As the dough firms up, the cylinders prevent a flat spot from forming on the bottom of the rolls. Then when you are ready to cut a slice from the roll, the slice will be round every time. I've read this tip in cooking magazines and other cookbooks, so all I can say is that this technique falls under the category of nothing is new under the sun.

Key Techniques for Sweet Yeast Baking

It's no longer necessary to take a day out of your life to bake with yeast. I used to spend the entire day, so rather than be a slave to baking with yeast, I often bought all sorts of coffee cakes and sweet rolls. But since it's more gratifying to bake my own, I've discovered how to make time even with my busy schedule. True, yeast baking requires a few brief periods of hands-on work. However, you don't have to be home from the beginning to the end. You don't even need to do the steps of the recipe in succession. I've found several places in the operation where it's okay to pause.

Sweet yeast doughs are malleable and can be pulled, twisted, patted, sculpted, woven, and even pushed down only to have them pop up again. While cakes rely on a pan to give them their characteristic silhouette, yeast doughs will take any shape your imagination can give them. It's how you cut and shape them that makes it possible to create a variety of shapes and sizes.

Although a rich yeast dough requires time to develop and rise, there are ways to simplify its preparation and improve your efficiency without compromising the finished result. Most of my recipes employ fast-acting yeast, which quickly blends with the other ingredients, and the food processor or stand mixer, which speeds up the mixing and some of the kneading steps.

Yeast basics   Nowadays, so many types of yeast are available that it's difficult to know which type is best to use for various kinds of baking. After extensive testing with various kinds of yeasts, I can cut to the chase and say that many of my sweet yeast recipes call for instant yeast (also labeled rapid or quick rise and bread machine). Active dry yeast and occasionally fresh yeast is what I used in my early days of yeast baking, and though I always still have a packet or two of active dry yeast on hand just in case I'm baking a family or friend's recipe that calls for it, instant yeast is what I regularly use. (I no longer use fresh yeast because few markets carry it and it has a short shelf life.)

Instant yeast streamlines yeast baking because you don't need to proof it (dissolve it in water, and then wait for tiny bubbles to appear on the surface to give "proof" that it was alive or active) and rising times are shorter. When I purchase yeast, I note the expiration date for freshness, and then, for a little extra insurance, I refrigerate it when I am back in the kitchen to maintain its viability. In each recipe that calls for yeast, I have listed the type of yeast that tested best in the recipe, and in the case of yeast recipes that people shared with me, I have used the yeast that was in the original recipe.

Probably the most common mistake home bakers make is to kill the yeast (a plantlike living organism) in an environment that is too hot. This is less likely to happen when you use instant yeast in a recipe. Try this method: First, follow the proportions in your recipe using instant yeast in place of active dry yeast, which is easy, since you add it directly to the flour, rather than proofing it first. In a large bowl, stir together the instant yeast with some or all of the flour and other dry ingredients, such as sugar, spices, and salt. Next, heat the liquid over low heat with the butter in the recipe just until the butter melts. Off the heat, check the temperature of the mixture with an instant-read thermometer. Don't let it get too hot. If the liquid is over 140 degrees F, it will kill the yeast. Let it cool to 120 degrees F before you add it to the flour mixture. In my kitchen, the yeast seems to come to life sooner at this temperature than any other. And based on my experience, instant yeast is quite hardy and tolerates the sugar and butter in sweet doughs beautifully.

To purchase instant yeast, look for SAF, Fleischmann's, or Fermipan brand—all of which are sold in 1-pound vacuum "bricks" and can be stored unopened at room temperature—and for bread machine yeast in jars. For smaller amounts of instant yeast sold in strips of three packets, use Fleischmann's RapidRise or Red Star Quick-Rise. All of these brands can be used interchangeably in recipes calling for instant yeast. A good rule of thumb is to refrigerate all yeasts, whether in a jar, brick, or packet, sealed or open. Also, don't allow instant yeast to come in contact with ice or cold water, which will slow down its action.

Flour basics   Bleached and unbleached all-purpose flour are called for in my yeast baking recipes. Bleached has been treated with a chemical to hasten its aging process, while unbleached is aged naturally. When I began yeast baking many years ago, I used bleached flour because unbleached flour was not as widely available (except at health-food stores). In those early days of teaching baking—and even today—I don't use hard-to-find ingredients in my recipes. And since the baked goods were to everyone's satisfaction (including the students), I got into the habit of baking with bleached flour. I know people who insist they can taste the difference, and since taste is what baking is all about, they should bake with unbleached flour. And I do use unbleached when the structure of the dough that I am making will benefit from a higher percentage of protein, such as PDQ (Pretty Darn Quick) Puff Pastry (page 367) and Croissant Pastry ASAP (page 365). Some bakers insist on using organic flours, which are becoming more readily available and produce fine baked goods. But their accessibility remains limited, and because I only test with flour that is widely available, I did not develop my recipes with organic flour.

The stages of yeast baking   Here's where you will discover that pauses in the process are possible. For example, when mixing the dough, you can delay its development by using cold, rather than room-temperature, ingredients. Or, after kneading the dough, you can set it in a cool place, rather than a warm one, or you can even put it in the refrigerator overnight.

MEASURING   For best results, weigh the flour rather than use the volume measures. Weighing is the best way to respect the correct proportions in the recipe.

MIXING   To create most of my sweet yeast doughs, I mix the yeast in with a portion of the flour, sugar, salt, and any other dry ingredients, such as spices, and then I add the liquid. Have an instant-read thermometer on hand to make sure the temperature of the liquid is between 120 and 130 degrees F before you add it to the flour mixture.

KNEADING   If you are used to working with bread doughs, keep in mind that sweet yeast doughs are softer and stickier because they are enriched with eggs and sugar and sometimes milk. This means they require a different kneading technique. First, kneading by hand is recommended over kneading in a stand mixer, which can easily result in overkneaded dough. Hand kneading lets you strengthen the dough just enough without overworking it or adding too much additional flour. You can feel its consistency—how wet, dry, soft, or sticky it is—and you can better judge when you have kneaded it just enough. As you work, you will be tempted to add more flour to alleviate the stickiness. But in most cases the dough simply needs more time to absorb the flour you have just kneaded into it. Too much flour can compromise the dough's soft, smooth texture, which will change the flavor, texture, and crumb of the finished baked item. It's always best to err on the side of adding less flour, which will yield more tender results. The dough is sufficiently kneaded when it comes together in a smooth, homogeneous mass, is slightly tacky, and has tiny beadlike blisters on the surface. It should not be too elastic, which can mean that it has developed the protein in the flour for strength or structure, desirable for breads but not for sweet yeast baking.

Rather than add more flour to reduce the stickiness, I sometimes pick up the dough in one hand and slam it onto the work surface. Then I slip a dough scraper under the dough, pick it up again, and slam it down. After three or four times of repeating this action, you will notice the dough has a different texture. It is not as shiny or sticky and has tiny blisters on the surface. This technique, known as slap-kneading, efficiently shortens the kneading process. The sweet yeast doughs in this book that are treated to a combination of gentle hand kneading and slap-kneading are usually kneaded for only 5 to 7 minutes.

REFRIGERATING THE DOUGH   I'm a firm believer in refrigerating sweet yeast dough after kneading it to make it easier to handle. Chilling retards the rising process by inhibiting the yeast's growth, so the dough can be refrigerated for as briefly as 1 hour or as long as 24 hours. More important, a well-chilled sweet yeast dough can adjust to your schedule for its next steps. It gives you time to pause—go to the dentist or take the kids to the movies—and then proceed to the next step when it is convenient.

RISING AND PUNCHING DOWN   I can't tell you how many times I have put a yeast dough aside to rise and then waited and waited for it to show some life. The rising times in the recipes are based on room-temperature ingredients, so if your ingredients are colder, the dough will take longer to rise. The temperature of your kitchen (my kitchen's average temperature is between 68 and 70 degrees F) is another factor, as are the other ingredients and their amounts. For example, the type of yeast or water (high in minerals or heavily chlorinated) and the amount of sugar and butter can contribute to or hinder the speed of the rise. Just remember that no matter what the temperature is, the dough will eventually rise. It is just a question of when. While I wait, I find that the time goes faster if I go on with my life in as productive a way as possible. For example, I run an errand or take a walk. Of course, it's often just when I stop checking that suddenly the dough is puffy and fully risen.

Yeast doughs do not necessarily need a warm place to rise. Each recipe indicates whether warmth is preferable to room temperature or refrigeration. A 2-quart Pyrex glass bowl allows you to monitor the dough's rise. It's important to cover the bowl or container tightly with a sheet of plastic wrap or a lid. Covering it tightly keeps the dough moist, which eliminates the need to butter or oil the bowl and then turn the dough in the bowl to coat it with the fat. Alternatively, you can put the dough in a resealable plastic bag, squeeze out the air, and seal the bag, leaving room for the dough to expand. Or, you can create a temporary proof box by placing the dough on its baking sheet or in its pan in a large sturdy rectangular plastic container and then cover the container with a lid.

To check if the dough has risen sufficiently, gently press a finger into it. If the indentation remains, the dough is ready for the next step. If it is the rise directly after kneading, the dough is ready to be shaped. If it is the rise after shaping, the dough is ready to go into the oven.

For me, *punching down* is simply too strong a phrase for the sweet yeast doughs in this book. Instead, gently deflate the dough by pressing it with the palm of your hand.

SHAPING   Chilled dough is easier to roll out or shape than room-temperature dough. It is more relaxed, which makes it more apt to stay where you roll it, without it shrinking up and acting like a rubber band as it expands. Chilling reduces the chance of overworking it, too, which can result in a dough that does not bake up as tender as you would like. Shape sweet yeast doughs as directed in individual recipes.

BAKING, COOLING, SERVING, AND STORING   Almost all of the rich sweet yeast doughs in this book bake most evenly at 350 or 375 degrees F. Baking them at higher temperatures is tricky because the butter, sugar, eggs, and/or milk that they contain cause them to brown quickly, which means they can be done on the outside before they finish baking on the inside.

We home bakers don't use preservatives in our baking, so as soon as the coffee cakes, buns, and swirls cool, they become firm. For that reason, I am careful to bake them just to the point—or, should I say, catch them just at the point—at which they are either a bit underdone or test done (according to the timing and visuals given in individual recipes). In other words, I take them out of the oven before they are very firm or overly brown on the top, sides, or bottom. This is especially true of individual buns, which are exposed to heat on all sides.

Individual rolls clustered together in a baking pan to form a single coffee cake take longer to finish baking for obvious reasons. However, these clusters also benefit from underbaking slightly; otherwise, they dry out when you reheat them. Transfer them still in the pan to a wire rack to cool completely. Wrap them securely (still in the pan is fine if it is completely cool) in aluminum foil and freeze for another time. When ready to use, rewarm them in their foil wrapping in a preheated 325 degree F oven, or thaw at room temperature for 30 to 45 minutes and then place in a 350 degree F oven and finish baking until golden. Serve without delay as though freshly made. This bake-on-demand technique of rewarming sweet yeast pastries is especially appreciated at breakfast or brunch.

For optimum taste and texture, serve sweet yeast items soon (up to 6 hours) after baking, warm or at room temperature. However, I taste-tested all of my sweet yeast recipes, and the flavor and crumb of many of them still tasted freshly baked even after 10 hours.

ESSENTIAL EQUIPMENT

Whether you are creating a sumptuous dessert for a holiday celebration or baking cookies to sweeten a rainy afternoon, a well-equipped kitchen will make your experience even more enjoyable. Using the right tool for a particular task ensures preparation is faster, easier, and more efficient.

Part of the joy of occasional baking is that you don't need a lot of esoteric or expensive equipment. The recipes in this book can be prepared with a few fundamental tools, all designed to streamline your time in the kitchen. Although the equipment I recommend is basic, I advise purchasing the best-quality tools you can find. Quality costs a bit more, but well-made equipment performs better, yields more reliable results, and often lasts a lifetime.

On the following pages, you'll find a handpicked selection of equipment that will help you make the most of your time as an occasional baker.

Bakeware

As you can imagine, I'm a big fan of bakeware and take great pleasure in using pans of all shapes, sizes, and fabrications. A good baking pan contributes to the personality of a dessert, and using the right pan for any recipe helps ensure its success. Because the taste and texture of baked goods are affected by the surface on which they are cooked, it is important to choose pieces that conduct heat efficiently and uniformly. Also, when measuring baking pans, I measure from the inner rims, and my recipes reflect those sizes. To calculate the volume of a baking pan, fill it with water, and then measure the liquid (see Measuring the Capacity of Cake Pans, page 23). See Dimensions and Capacity of Frequently Used Baking Pans (page 381) and below for measurements for some of the most frequently used pans.

METAL BAKEWARE

I prefer dull, heavy-gauge pans made of aluminum, tinned steel, or aluminum-coated steel, all of which retain heat well and encourage even baking. Many baking pans are available with nonstick surfaces to promote easy release and facilitate cleanup. If I have a choice of finishes, I'll opt for a traditional surface, rather than a nonstick coating. However, there are some intriguingly shaped pans that are only available with nonstick finishes, and I sometimes use them because I can't resist certain shapes perfectly suited for specific occasions that I enjoy. Even when using nonstick pans, I advise greasing and flouring the interiors to ensure that baked goods rise to their optimum heights. It's also important to note that dark-colored pans—nonstick or not—tend to absorb more of the oven's heat than their lighter counterparts, which can result in overbaking and overbrowning. To compensate, reduce the baking temperature specified in a recipe by 25 degrees F.

Baking sheets   Sturdy baking sheets, both rimless and rimmed, are used in many of my recipes. I rely on them for baking a variety of cookies, pastries, and cakes. They are invaluable for holding baked cakes or a stack of cookie-dough circles sandwiched between waxed paper in the refrigerator or freezer. The two pan sizes that I use the most are 15½ by 12 inches and 17 by 14 inches, both with a 45-degree-angle, ½-inch rim on all four sides, *open* at the corners. I recommend owning at least 2 pans in each of these or comparable sizes. A 13 by 9 by 1-inch quarter sheet pan is ideal for baking bar cookies, while a slightly deeper 13 by 9 by 2-inch quarter sheet pan is perfect for baking a full cake recipe that also produces a three-layer 8-inch or a two-layer 9-inch cake. An 18 by 13 by 1-inch pan, known as a half sheet pan, is used for the sheet cakes for Coffee Cup Tiramisu (page 250) and Raspberry Sheet Cake (page 110).

When I want to remove warm, flexible cookies quickly without fear of them sticking, I use nonstick baking sheets. (You'll find nonstick baking sheets are especially useful for Bonnie's Best-Selling Almond Tuiles on page 273.) For cake rolls, I use a 15½ by 10½ by 1-inch pan, also known as a jelly-roll pan. Rimmed perforated baking sheets are useful for placing underneath flexible silicone pans to give them support in and out of the oven during baking (see Silicone Bakeware on page 38). Sometimes I put a tart pan or pie dish on a large rimmed pizza pan or baking sheet to ensure that any overflow from the tart or pie is contained in the pan and not on the floor of the oven.

Bundt pan   In the past, Bundt pans were confined to a single design and shape, but nowadays they are fashioned in a variety of ways, making it easy for bakers to create a wide range of intricately sculpted and shaped cakes. They're typically made of cast aluminum with a non-stick coating, usually with a 10- to 12-cup capacity. In my recipe for Spicy Yogurt Pound Cake (page 189), I call for a pan 10 inches in diameter with a 10- to 12-cup capacity and 3-inch sides. All of the recipes in this book calling for a Bundt pan will fit comfortably in this same-size pan because the 10-cup mark is ½ to ¾ inch below the rim, and the 12-cup mark is almost level with the rim. In other words, you don't need to worry about the cake batter overflowing the sides of the pan.

Cake pans   When selecting cake pans, I prefer straight sides, which produce an attractive dessert that's easy to frost and convenient to serve. My most frequently used sizes are 8- and 9-inch round and square pans (you need 2 pans of each size). I occasionally use 4 by 2-inch round pans with a 2-cup capacity, 6 by 3-inch round pans with a 6-cup capacity, a 7 by 3-inch round pan with an 8-cup capacity, and a 10 by 2¾-inch round pan with a 14-cup capacity.

Loaf pan   This is the ideal pan for baking quick breads and for many of my yeast-leavened loaves. The most commonly used size is 9 by 5 by 3 inches, and I recom-mend you have on hand 2 pans of this size.

Mud pan   One of my favorite pans is actually a main-stay in the building trades. The tapered rectangular pan is known among contractors as a mud pan, and I use it for Frozen Fruit Rainbow Terrine (page 143). Reusable and inexpensive, this sturdy plastic pan measures 14 by 3 by 3¼ inches and has an 11-cup capacity. You can find mud pans at most hardware stores. If you don't have time to shop, use two 9 by 5 by 3-inch loaf pans and divide the recipe equally between the two pans.

Muffin (cupcake) pans   Traditional muffin pans are also perfect for baking cupcakes. They are widely available in standard, jumbo, and miniature muffin sizes. For example, for Three Cheers for Tiny Pumpkin Pies (page 261), you will need a 12-cup miniature muffin pan (each cup should measure 1⁷⁄₈ inches across the top and ¾ inch deep), and for Cinnamon Bubble Buns (page 77), you'll need a 12-cup standard muffin pan (each cup should measure 2¾ inches across the top, and 1½ inches deep).

Popover plaque   This pan's deep, widely spaced cups cause popover batter to expand and "pop over" the sides. For the Popovers with Bourbon-Buttermilk Sauce (page 160), you'll need a 6-cup popover plaque, each cup measuring 2 inches wide at the top and base and 2½ inches high.

Pullman loaf pan   Also known as a *pain de mie* pan, this 13 by 4 by 4-inch covered baking pan yields a compact, brick-shaped loaf with a thin, golden crust when used for baking the traditional *pain de mie* loaf. However, I use the pan to make Mocha-Almond O'Marble Cake (page 88), a marbleized showstopper.

Ring molds   These metal molds, some of which are highly decorative, come in handy for baking all kinds of cakes. I use plain ring molds for my Bishop's Cake (page 58), which calls for a 10-inch mold (6 cups) and can be baked in a 10-inch ring mold.

Springform pans   Perfect for my Almond-Rhubarb Snack Cake (page 79), Banana-Split Cream Pie (page 98), and Ultimate Cappuccino Cheesecake (page 210), this pan has sides that spring free from the base when the clamp is released, so you can remove baked goods without breakage. The pie calls for a 10-inch round springform pan, and the snack cake and cheesecake use a 9-inch round springform pan. The depth of these pans varies, with some 2¾ inches deep and some 3 inches deep. Either depth will work for these desserts.

Tart pans   Classic tart pans have removable bottoms that make getting the finished tart out of the pan intact easy and foolproof. I call for a 9½ by 1-inch fluted round (Double-Crust White Peach–Polenta Tart with Sweetened Crème Fraîche, page 222), an 11 by 1-inch fluted round (Brown Butter Pear Tart, page 226), a 9 by 1-inch fluted square (Sour Cream Custard Tart, page 230), and 2 fluted rectangular pans, 8 by 11¼ by 1 inch (Lily's Extraordinary Linzer Tart, page 146) and 13¾ by 4¼ by 1 inch (Rhubarb and Pistachio Tart, page 319). I also use 4 by ¾-inch tartlet pans for my Milk Chocolate S'More Tartlets with Homemade Marshmallow Topping (page 270).

Timbale mold   I use round high-sided, aluminum timbale molds to make my Cheesecake Timbales (page 247). Each mold measures 2⅛ inches wide by 2 inches deep and has a ½-cup capacity.

Tube pan   A 10 by 4¼-inch tube pan, also called an angel food cake pan, is a round pan with a tube in the center. Some tube pans have removable centers, which I prefer. Many also have small metal feet for holding the inverted pan above the work surface when you are cooling a cake. However, I prefer to cool the cake by "hanging" it upside down on a bottle with a long neck or an inverted heatproof funnel. I use a tube pan to bake my Tender Butter Cake with Nut-Crunch Topping (page 83) and Chocolate Lover's Angel Food Cake (page 208).

Ceramic and Glass Bakeware

I rely on ovenproof glass and ceramic baking dishes for a variety of recipes, particularly pies, cobblers, and other fruit desserts. These materials are efficient heat conductors, so foods bake and brown beautifully. Glass and ceramic baking dishes also tend to be aesthetically pleasing, making it possible to bake and serve in the same vessel.

Baking dishes   The most often-used baking dish in this book is a 13 by 9 by 2-inch ovenproof glass or ceramic baking pan. I also use a 10 by 1-inch round gratin dish and a 14 by 9 by 2-inch oval gratin dish for fruit cobblers and other fruit desserts, like Almost-Last-Minute Summer Fruit Crumble (page 234).

Pie dish   For pie baking, I use a 9-inch round Pyrex glass dish, which makes it easy to monitor browning on the bottom of the crust.

Ramekins   Made of ovenproof glass or porcelain, these circular, straight-sided dishes are typically 4 inches in diameter and have a ½-, ¾-, or 1-cup capacity. They are perfect for baking crème brûlées or individual soufflés and are also ideal for mousses and other chilled desserts. Flag-Raising Mixed-Berry Potpies (page 229) is one of my favorite desserts calling for ramekins.

SILICONE BAKEWARE

Many of the pieces listed above in both the metal and the glass and ceramic bakeware sections are fashioned in silicone as well, and silicone mats for lining baking sheets are also available. They offer a nonstick surface and a flexibility that ensures foolproof release, plus they can be used in the oven, refrigerator, and freezer.

Silicone baking molds   These versatile molds can be used for everything from baking cakes and muffins to molding frozen desserts, mousses, and puddings. Whether you are baking or chilling, always place the flexible molds on top of baking sheets for stability. My only caveat about baking in silicone molds is that your baked goods can emerge from the oven looking a bit pale on the bottoms and sides.

To improve heat circulation and ease transfer, place the baking mold on a perforated or traditional baking sheet and then bake according to the recipe instructions, keeping in mind that times may be slightly shorter than with metal baking pans because silicone bakes a bit hotter. To remove baked items from the molds, let cool for 10 minutes if miniature cakes or completely if a regular-size cake, then invert the molds. Miniature cakes should fall out. To release larger cakes, apply pressure to the bottom of the mold while carefully peeling back or twisting the sides. Use the same technique for chilled or frozen recipes, and the perfectly shaped creations will pop right out.

Silicone mats   Reusable silicone baking mats, such as the popular Silpat brand, provide a nonstick surface for sheet pans. Originally designed to replace parchment paper during baking, they can be used any time you need to keep food from sticking. They can go directly from freezer to oven, and wipe clean in no time. I bake cream puffs (page 152) on silicone mats, rather than on buttered and floured baking sheets. Silicone mats can be purchased in sizes to line quarter and half sheet pans.

Cookware

Double boiler   A double boiler will help ensure success for heat-sensitive tasks, such as melting chocolate, whipping up a 7-minute frosting, or making Milk 'n' Honey Sabayon (page 121). In this double-vessel arrangement, you place a bowl over a saucepan of simmering water to moderate the heat, which allows the contents of the bowl to reach the desired temperature without scorching or burning. You can purchase a conventional double boiler (a set of two pans, one nested in the other) at a cookware store, or you can do as I do and improvise with a saucepan and a stainless-steel or heatproof glass mixing bowl. To find pans and bowls that fit together, just shop around your kitchen for combinations that work well. If you will be whipping ingredients in the bowl, make sure the capacity is adequate to accommodate the increased volume.

Saucepans   Saucepans are indispensable for melting butter, caramelizing sugar, and preparing dessert sauces. Choose heavy-gauge pans to guarantee uniform heating, and make sure they are made of a nonreactive material (such as stainless steel or anodized aluminum). Saucepans lined with stainless steel or enamel are also fine. Reactive metals (such as nonanodized aluminum or unlined copper) can leave a metallic aftertaste when you cook with citrus or other acidic ingredients. The most often-used sizes in my recipes are small (3 to 4 cups), medium (1½ to 2½ quarts), and large (4½ quarts).

Roasting pan   I usually use a metal roasting pan (about 13 by 7 by 2½ inches) to create a water bath for baking my Mile-High Cheesecake (page 154).

Small Appliances and Kitchen Electrics

Food processor   The food processor is a great multi-purpose tool. I use one when I want to make a dough quickly and easily without adding a lot of air to it, such as

Chocolate Tart Pastry (page 363). This efficient machine also offers a fast, easy way to crush the praline into tiny golden crumbs for the filling in my Black-Bottom Praline Chiffon Pie (page 320). Fitted with its truncated dough blade, a food processor helps you make divine challah (page 184). When you're using a food processor to chop or blend ingredients, always err on the side of less rather than more: once something is overprocessed, it is too late. You can help ensure precision processing by using the pulse feature (my pulses are 1 second long each).

Stand mixer   A worthwhile investment for bakers, a powerful, heavy-duty stand mixer is a kitchen workhorse. I use mine for making everything from cake batters, meringues, and buttercreams to yeast doughs and pastry doughs—even doughs for flaky puff pastry and croissants. One great convenience of a stand mixer is that it leaves your hands free to add ingredients or scrape down the sides of the bowl. To guarantee the most efficient mixing, kneading, and aerating, many stand mixers feature planetary action: the attachments not only spin but also rotate around the work bowl. Most models come with a handful of attachments, including a paddle beater, a balloon whisk, and a dough hook. I use the paddle attachment the most: to mix cake batters and yeast doughs, to beat cream cheese until smooth, to beat butter until smooth and creamy as the first step of making a butter cake, to break up almond paste before adding other ingredients.

Handheld mixer   Although I rely on my stand mixer for most tasks, I do use a handheld electric mixer for certain jobs. For example, a handheld mixer is convenient for blending or whipping ingredients on the stove top, such as when making a sabayon. It's also handy for such small jobs as whipping a few egg whites or some heavy cream (for times when you don't want to whip them by hand) or for making a frosting.

If you don't own a stand mixer, a handheld model can be used in its place. It has less power than a stand mixer, however, so you will need to adjust the speed specified in the recipes, which were written for stand mixers. For instance, if a recipe says to use a stand mixer set at medium-low speed, compensate by raising the speed setting on your hand mixer to medium.

Know your oven   Because ovens vary, the amount of time we preheat them can produce subtle variations in the appearance, texture, and even flavor of your baked goods.

Use a small, portable oven thermometer to check the accuracy of your thermostat, centering it in the oven. Surprisingly, even though your oven may indicate it is "ready," it is still 50 to 100 degrees below the set temperature. That's due in part to the fact that many portable oven thermometers have a lag time, and they need longer to register the accurate, most stable reading. If after preheating, it does not register the temperature you want, adjust the oven temperature control up or down until the thermometer displays the correct temperature, disregarding the setting on the oven panel.

Preheat, preheat, preheat. A thoroughly preheated oven gives you better control of the baking process. Most of us think an oven is fully preheated when the red light goes out or the ding sounds, and we immediately put the cake in the oven. Think again. We really need an additional 10 to 15 minutes for the oven to heat and cycle and reheat, so plan on about 30 minutes total for a thorough preheat.

Microwave oven   I never bake with a microwave oven, but I do find this appliance handy for simple tasks like melting chocolate (page 17) or butter, melting butter and chocolate together, or for quickly heating up liquids, such as coffee or milk.

Measuring Equipment

Measuring cups and spoons   Since successful baking depends on accurate measuring, scientifically calibrated measuring cups and spoons are essential equipment. You'll use them every time you measure ingredients by volume, so be sure to buy sturdy, high-quality tools. I recommend purchasing multiple sets. That way, you won't have to stop to wash a cup or spoon in the middle of a recipe. To measure dry ingredients, I use nesting stainless-steel cups with long, sturdy handles that make it easy to scoop out ingredients. These are most commonly found in ¼-, ⅓-, ½-, 1-, and 2-cup sizes. For liquids, I use 1- and 2-cup Pyrex glass measuring cups marked with ounce, cup, and pint (on the larger cup) gradations on one side and milliliters on the other. I use stainless-steel measuring spoons to measure small amounts of dry or liquid ingredients, such as spices, leavening agents, or flavoring extracts. The most common sizes include ⅛ teaspoon, ¼ teaspoon, ½ teaspoon, 1 teaspoon, and 1 tablespoon.

Scale A scale is my all-time favorite equipment for gauging accurate measurements of both liquid and dry ingredients. Weighing ingredients is not only faster, more precise, and more reliable than measuring them by volume, but it is also more convenient because you can weigh multiple ingredients in the same bowl. I own an electronic scale with a digital readout displayed in both ⅛-ounce and gram increments. A tare feature allows you to weigh an ingredient, set the reading back to zero, then add the next ingredient. I like to use a scale that can accommodate any size bowl or pan and has a total capacity of 11 pounds (5 kilograms). Refer back to page 379 for more on weighing ingredients.

Thermometers Thermometers are used for a variety of baking tasks, from double-checking the temperature of your oven to caramelizing sugar. To test a thermometer for accuracy, place it in a saucepan of boiling water, making sure the tip of the probe sensor does not touch the bottom of the pan. The gauge should read 212 degrees F. It's best to select a thermometer with a clip that allows you to slide the tool up and down along the side of your saucepan, adjusting the thermometer's height for whatever you are cooking. Don't try to clean a battery-operated thermometer by immersing it in water. Instead, hold the probe end under warm running water, then gently wipe it dry. I use several Taylor brand thermometers and a Thermapen digital thermometer.

OVEN THERMOMETER The only way to be sure your oven has reached the desired temperature is to use an oventhermometer. Available at hardware stores and kitchen-supply shops, this small, portable tool is a reasonably priced necessity.

CANDY THERMOMETER A candy thermometer tracks the stages of cooking sugar syrups, such as for the Divinity Frosting for the All-American Chocolate Cake (page 331), and the Italian Meringue topping (page 329) for the Dee-luscious Lemon Meringue Pie. For recipes like these, I prefer an analog thermometer attached to a 12 by 1¾-inch stainless-steel strip with a clip, so it can be easily slipped onto the rim of the saucepan. It makes it easy to track both rising temperatures and stages of cooking (for example, soft ball, hard ball, and the like), giving you a sense of how much time is left before you'll need to switch to the next phase of the recipe, like whipping egg whites for the buttercream.

INSTANT-READ THERMOMETER When I'm baking, an instant-read analog or digital thermometer is always within easy reach. Analog models usually register temperatures up to 220 or 240 degrees F, while the range of digital versions vary, with some measuring up to about 450 degrees F. If the day's recipe is Chocolate Lover's Angel Food Cake (page 208), my instant-read thermometer lets me know when the egg whites have reached 60 to 70 degrees F, the optimum temperature for whipping. When melting chocolate, I use the thermometer frequently to check the temperature of the chocolate and of the water in the pan under the bowl of chocolate. If you are making crème anglaise, the thermometer will let you know when it reaches 160 degrees F, the point at which the custard has thickened enough. To test whether your challah has finished baking (190 degrees F), you can insert the thermometer through one side of the loaf to the center. Or, if you want to know if your butter is at room temperature (65 to 70 degrees F), you can slide the thermometer lengthwise into the center of the cube. In these cases, I prefer a digital thermometer that gives me an instant readout so I don't overbake or overwarm. If you bake often, you may want to invest in the professional Super-Fast Thermapen instant-read thermometer, which gauges temperatures (from −58 to 572 degrees F) in just 4 seconds.

Timer   Time, like ingredients, needs to be measured accurately. I use a portable digital timer with an easily audible alert signal.

Measure and weigh for consistent results Weighing with a kitchen scale is the only accurate method of measuring dry ingredients. For example, if you use the weight specified for 1 cup all-purpose flour in a recipe it will always weigh 4 1/2 ounces (130 grams) no matter whether you packed it down in the bowl, fluffed it with a fork, scooped it out of the bottom of a bag, or spooned it out of a canister.

If you must use volume measurement, use dry-ingredient measuring cups for items like flour, granulated and powdered sugars, and nuts; use liquid measuring cups for ingredients such as milk and egg whites.

To measure flour, empty the entire bag into a container with a lid to insulate it from any moisture. Lightly fluff the flour with a scoop, spoon, or large fork to loosen and aerate it, ensuring a lighter pack in the cup. Now, scoop enough flour into your dry-measuring cup until it mounds slightly over the top, and then use a flat metal icing spatula to sweep off the excess. This is known as the spoon-and-sweep method. Do not tap or pack the flour in the cup, or you will alter the measurement. I also use the spoon-and-sweep method to measure other dry ingredients like granulated and powdered sugars.

For measuring liquids, such as water and egg whites, the glass Pyrex cup is my gold standard. To check that the liquid is at the exact mark, bend down and view the marking on the cup at eye level.

Volume and weight measures for most liquids are the same or nearly the same. Since 2 *fluid* ounces of water or milk also weighs 2 *dry* ounces, using volume measures for these ingredients is fine. A greater variation exists between volume and weight measures of heavy liquids, such as molasses and corn syrup. Because of this, my recipes calling for these dense liquids include measures by volume and by dry ounce (rather than by fluid ounce).

Baking and Decorating Tools

Blending fork   A cast-aluminum blending fork whose tine area measures 2 1/2 inches long by 1 1/2 inches wide is useful for blending pie crust ingredients. The generously sized tines provide superb control and promote efficient mixing.

Cooling racks   An elevated wire rack helps baked goods cool faster and more evenly because it allows air to circulate freely underneath. Because it keeps condensation from forming underneath, it also prevents the baked goods from getting soggy. Use a 12 1/2-inch round cooling rack for circular cakes and tarts; an 18 by 13-inch rack works well for square or rectangular desserts. An extra-large rack is best for cookies because it accommodates a batch without overlapping or crowding. You'll find a sturdy rack is also handy for icing glazed desserts, such as my Eggnog Pound Cake with Crystal Rum Glaze (page 180). For glazing cookies, like my Scalloped Butter Cookies (page 299), I prefer a cooling rack with a grid of closely spaced wires that keep the cookies steady and prevent them from slipping through the rack. A rack is useful for inverting cakes, cupcakes, quick breads, and yeast coffee cakes. After transferring a galette or *crostata* to a cooling rack, I can peek at the pastry's underside for signs of gold or light brown to determine if the pastry has baked long enough.

Cookie and pastry cutters   You can never own too many cookie and pastry cutters. We all like to have the appropriate cutter on hand for any occasion that pops up on the calendar. Nested sets of round cutters in graduated sizes, with plain and fluted edges, are among the most useful. It's also nice to collect an assortment of different shapes. Among my favorites are hearts, used in this book for Heart-to-Heart-to-Heart Cookies (page 285). Look for nested sets of sturdy plastic cutters that snap together when not being used. Heavy tinned-steel cutters are also recommended. They don't bend easily and usually have sharp edges that cut cleanly through even the stickiest doughs.

Cookie press   The secret asset of busy bakers, this tool is great for making a lot of beautiful cookies in surprisingly little time. Just fill the barrel with soft dough, squeeze the handle, and cookie dough is piped through a decorative disc onto your baking sheet. Some presses have a window in the stainless-steel barrel that allows you to gauge dough level at a glance. The tool of choice for making my Special Spritz Cookies (page 118), a cookie press typically includes a dozen or more discs in a wide variety of seasonal shapes.

Decorator's turntable   A turntable makes applying frostings and putting the finishing touches on cakes and desserts easier. You place the dessert on the rotating top, then turn it with one hand as you frost or decorate with the other. As the wheel pivots, you can easily apply icing, scatter on toppings, or use a pastry bag to pipe on decorative designs. An inexpensive, sturdy plastic lazy Susan sold for holding bottles or condiments is a good alternative.

Dough scraper   This versatile tool, also known as a pastry scraper, typically features a wide plastic or stainless-steel blade. Primarily used for scraping your work surface clean, it's also ideal for lifting and turning soft bread or pastry doughs. I often rely on mine to help knead yeast doughs, using the blade to lift a ball of dough and slap it back down onto the work surface. Many pastry chefs also use a scraper as an impromptu ruler to measure and mark sections of dough. A giant spatula or lightweight dough scraper is optional though extremely useful. It is an oversized version of the standard scraper and is great to have for lifting large sections of pastry dough, or for transferring a freshly baked galette, tart, or *crostata* to a serving plate without cracking it.

Ice cream scoops   Bakers can use these hardworking tools to scoop neat, uniform portions of everything from cookie dough and cake batter to meringue and ganache. I prefer models with a thumb press that operates a blade mechanism on the interior of the scoop, efficiently sweeping the contents into a baking pan or onto a baking sheet.

Scoops are available with round or oval bowls, and come in a variety of sizes. The sizing of scoops has not been standardized, but most are marked with a number indicating the number of scoops per quart of ice cream. That means the larger the scoop number, the smaller the scoop will be. These numbers vary among manufacturers, however, so I always provide the diameter of the scoop, too. One of my favorite scoops is so tiny it doesn't even merit a number. With a capacity of about 1 teaspoon, it's ideal for depositing small dollops of cookie dough or forming truffles for chocolate Trufflewiches (page 279) and "Be My Valentine" Heartwiches (page 281). You can also use it to portion soft butter for greasing a pan before filling it with batter. Other frequently used sizes include #100 (about 1 1/8 inches), #70 and #60 (about 1 1/4 inches), #50 and #40 (about 1 1/2 inches), #24 (scant 2 inches), and #16 (about 2 1/4 inches). In general, the smaller sizes are excellent for cookie doughs and fillings, while the larger ones work well for scooping cake or muffin batter into baking pans.

Knives   Most cooks and bakers count knives among their most prized culinary tools—and I'm no exception. For the occasional baker, I recommend several sizes and blade styles. *Santoku* knives (an Asian-style chef's knife with grooves on the blade that prevent food from sticking as you slice) are mainstays in my kitchen. Exceptionally well-balanced and easy to handle, they're perfect for most everyday cutting jobs, including chopping, mincing, and slicing. I value my serrated knives and especially recommend them for chopping chocolate, either finely or coarsely. A chef's knife with a 7- to 8-inch blade is handy for chopping nuts and slicing fruit. A small paring knife is ideal for peeling and trimming fresh produce. For splitting or trimming the sides of cake layers, I rely on a 12-inch-long serrated blade.

Mixing bowls   I'm famous for telling my students that you can never own too many mixing bowls. Always one to practice what I teach, I have a collection that includes every shape and size imaginable. I recommend every baker own a variety of sturdy, lightweight stainless-steel bowls. Use shallow bowls for mixing and folding and for holding prepped ingredients. The most useful sizes include 1, 1 1/2, 2, and 3 quarts. Also have on hand a deep, U-shaped

$1\frac{1}{2}$-quart bowl, perfect for whipping cream and egg whites (the smaller surface area promotes fast, efficient aeration), and some microwave-safe bowls (heat-resistant glass, glass ceramic, and some plastics) for melting or heating ingredients in the microwave.

Nut mill   My preferred tool for grinding or chopping nuts finely is a rotary mill or grinder, which produces a uniform dry grind (the nuts look somewhat diced). It's inexpensive and very easy to use: just place the nuts in the hopper and turn the crank. Since nuts contain a high amount of fat that can turn rancid quickly, I only grind as much as I'll need for the recipe I'm preparing. For more information on measuring, chopping, grinding, and toasting nuts, see pages 15–16.

Pastry bag and tips   Bakers can use a pastry bag to pipe frostings and fillings with professional results. I always have two types on hand: 12-, 14-, and 16-inch pastry bags made of lightweight, flexible nylon, and 12- and 18-inch disposable clear plastic decorating bags. The nylon bags are reusable and easy to manipulate, while the disposable ones save time by eliminating cleanup. Whichever you use, fill the bag no more than two-thirds full, and twist the upper third tightly closed to prevent the mixture from escaping out the top as you pipe.

Buttercream and whipped cream look especially attractive when piped through a pastry tip. You will also find that piping a dough, batter, or filling is often the fastest and easiest way to accomplish the task at hand. Even though I have a drawer full of different sizes and shapes, I usually use just a few plain open tips ($\frac{1}{8}$, $\frac{1}{4}$, and $\frac{1}{2}$ inch) and a few star tips. I indicate the diameter of the tip to be used in each recipe since the number marked on each tip varies among manufacturers.

Pastry blender   For light, flaky pastry, I use a pastry blender to mix the cold butter or solid vegetable shortening into the flour—a classic technique often described as "cutting in the fat"—quickly and efficiently. I prefer a pastry blender with four rigid stainless-steel wires, which provides excellent control over blending and keeps the mixture cool as you work.

Pastry brush   A pastry brush is the tool of choice for applying glazes, egg washes, or melted butter. It is also ideal for brushing excess flour off puff pastry dough during the layering process. I feel more comfortable with the precision of traditional bristle-headed brushes, but some bakers swear by silicone versions. Try both to see which works best for you.

Pastry roller   I consider this little tool (sometimes called a pizza roller) a must. Guaranteed to make pastry rolling easier and more efficient, it has a $2\frac{1}{2}$- to 4-inch-long roller, which is just the right size for neatly smoothing shortbread, cookie dough, or tart dough into a pan. I place a piece of plastic wrap over the dough and roll it out right in the pan. Then I peel off the plastic wrap and proceed as the recipe directs. Or, I sometimes partially roll out the dough on a work surface and then use the roller to extend it once it is in the pan.

Peeler   Equipped with a sharp, double-edged blade, a peeler (sometimes called a vegetable peeler) is indispensable for removing the skins or rinds from fresh fruits. I recommend a serrated peeler for soft, juicy fruits, such as peaches, nectarines, and mangoes. I also use the tool to cut these fruits into ultrathin slices that can be twisted into attractive shapes, like ruffles for decorating cakes or tarts. To peel firm fruits such as apples or pears, I advise using a peeler with a straight-edged blade.

Pie weights   When recipes call for blind baking a pastry crust, pie weights make the process easier and more reliable. Weights prevent the crust from shrinking or blistering during baking, ensuring an attractive pastry shell that will hold its shape when filled. Some people use commercial metal or ceramic pie weights, but I find their weight makes them unwieldy. My first choice is dried beans, which I store in a canister and reuse many times.

Rolling pin   A well-designed rolling pin eases rolling out a thin disk of pastry without stretching, tearing, or overworking the dough. A French-style rolling pin, measuring 16 inches long and 2 inches in diameter, works best for me. Resembling a smooth, straight dowel, this handle-free tool provides exceptional control, allowing me to direct its course easily and apply just the amount of pressure I want. It also provides an easy way to lift and transfer rolled-out dough without the dough losing its shape. I simply flip the dough over the pin, and then slide the dough onto my tart pan, pie dish, or parchment-lined baking sheet. Of course, as with so many baking tools, choosing a rolling pin is a matter of personal preference. If you're more comfortable with a wooden or silicone pin with ball bearings and handles, by all means use it.

Ruler   I swear by my 18-inch ruler for measuring all sorts of things, from pan sizes to pastry dough. Other handy tools include a tape measure and yardstick.

Sieves and strainers   The primary distinction between sieves and strainers is that a sieve is meant to refine texture, while a strainer is used for separating liquids from solids. For some uses, such as sifting, the two are interchangeable. I rely on fine sieves and strainers for sifting together dry ingredients—flour, baking powder, baking soda, salt, spices—for cake making. They are also ideal for sifting powdered sugar or cocoa over a cake or cookies. For refining sauces, I recommend using a sieve made from a nonreactive metal, such as stainless steel. Medium mesh is ideal for fruit sauces, while fine mesh works well for crème anglaise or similar mixtures. I also keep a fine-mesh sieve close at hand for "recipe rescues," using it to save me when I've inadvertently put together a less-than-silken batter, filling, frosting, or glaze.

Scissors   I use kitchen scissors, or shears, for all sorts of tasks, including trimming pastry dough, snipping dried fruit into uniform bits, and cutting thin strips of delicate sponge cake. Shears are also handy for cutting parchment paper to line baking pans.

Spatulas   A well-equipped kitchen includes several different types of spatulas. A rubber spatula performs flawlessly for a variety of kitchen tasks, from scraping out saucepans and bowls to blending, stirring, and folding ingredients. The best ones have flexible silicone heads that withstand extremely high temperatures and won't absorb flavors or odors. Spatulas with flat or offset metal blades are indispensable for spreading batters, frostings, and fillings. I use four sizes: 8, 10, 13, and 15 inches long. As with any frequently used tools, I recommend buying extra spatulas so you don't have to pause in the middle of a recipe to wash them.

Tart tamper   This handy little tamper, also known by the brand name Breezy Tart Maker, simplifies making miniature tartlet shells, such as the ones used for my Three Cheers for Tiny Pumpkin Pies (page 261). It is easy to use: You put a ball of dough in the cup of a miniature muffin pan. Then you dip the tamper into a little flour, dusting it lightly, and press down on the dough to create a perfectly even pastry shell in the cup. Finally, you gently lift out the tamper and proceed to the next ball of dough.

Torch   A kitchen torch (home models are powered with butane, professional kitchen models are powdered with propane) allows you to quickly and easily brown meringues (page 329) or a marshmallow topping (page 270).

Whisks   When a recipe doesn't call for sifting, I use a standard whisk to mix the dry ingredients thoroughly. For whipping heavy cream or egg whites by hand, I use a balloon whisk about 11 1/2 inches long. For whisking sauces, I use a sauce whisk about 10 inches long. When I cook Crème Anglaise (page 369) or the filling for my lemon meringue pie (page 329), I use a narrow sauce whisk about 10 inches long.

Wooden toothpicks and skewers   To determine whether a cake is perfectly baked, I use round wooden toothpicks or slim wooden skewers as testers. A cake is done if a wooden toothpick or skewer inserted into the center emerges crumb free. A metal skewer is ideal for checking the doneness of pie crusts and puff pastries: if the pastry emits a crisp, crunchy sound when stuck with the skewer, it is done.

Zester   I use grated citrus zest to add fresh, lively flavor to many recipes in this book, from Spicy Citrus Swirly Buns (page 174) to my Almond Tea Cake with Tangerine Glaze (page 182). You can use any one of a variety of tools to separate the colorful, fragrant citrus zest from the bitter white pith, but the one I like best is the Microplane rasp grater. Based on a carpenter's rasp, it was created by a woodworker's wife seeking the perfect tool for removing orange zest. If you don't have a rasp grater, you can use the fine holes on a box grater, or you can remove the zest with a citrus zester (fine strips) or a straight-bladed peeler (wider strips) and then mince it finely. Both of these tools are handy when recipes call for zest in strips, rather than grated. Keep in mind that you'll need to pack your measuring spoon tightly to guarantee the proper quantity of zest.

Lining and Wrapping Products

Aluminum foil   Aluminum foil is a kitchen superhero, thanks to its exceptional flexibility and strength. It molds easily over the exterior of an upside-down baking pan, such as a 13 by 9 by 2-inch baking pan (quarter sheet pan), to make a custom-fit liner for easy removal of Congo Brownies (page 102). Because foil won't absorb the butter from the cookies, it's ideal for lining cardboard boxes or layering between cookies in airtight metal tins. Bakers can also roll small pieces of foil to make springlike shapes that fit between spaces to protect cookies against breakage. I line a baking sheet with foil when I want a thin cake, such as the Chocolate Roulade with Chocolate Diplomat Cream (page 307) or Red Velvet Cake Roll (page 85), to release easily and in perfect form after it has cooled.

Coffee filters   When blind baking a pastry crust, I use 3 or 4 overlapping 8-inch paper coffee filters to cover the dough, then top them with a layer of dried beans.

Fluted paper or foil liners   For an attractive presentation in a gift box or on a serving tray, use fluted paper or foil bonbon cups. Pack the cups with cookies (set on their sides, like files in a filing cabinet), or fill each cup with an individual bar, a small cupcake, or a miniature cake. Cupcake liners measuring 1 3/8 inches across the bottom and 3/4 inch deep are ideal for baking Classic Butter Cake Cupcakes with White Chocolate–Sour Cream Frosting (page 92) and 24-Karat Cupcakes with Orange Cream Cheese Icing (page 239).

Parchment paper   This is my number-one choice for lining baking sheets and cake pans. I rely on reusable parchment paper to promote uniform baking of many types of baked goods, from a batch of cookies to a strudel to a *crostata*. It's also wonderful for rolling out dough. For example, I roll out *crostata* dough on a lightly floured sheet of parchment paper, then transfer the whole thing to a baking sheet. Parchment paper is a real time-saver when I'm baking drop cookies. I cut sheets of parchment paper the same size as my baking sheets and line them up on my countertop. Then, I drop the cookie dough directly onto the parchment rectangles, ready to transfer to baking sheets. This forms a sort of assembly line for baking: I can have one batch of cookies in the oven and the others waiting on the paper.

Plastic wrap   Wrapping cylinders of cookie dough in plastic wrap keeps them from drying out when refrigerated. Or, for storing several dough circles (pie or cookie dough, separated by waxed paper), stack them on a baking sheet and then wrap the entire stack and the pan with sturdy plastic wrap and put in the refrigerator or freezer. To help keep a cake fresh, wrap the outside of the cake box in plastic wrap before refrigerating. This will keep out excess moisture and protect your cake from being spoiled by unwanted flavors and odors.

Waxed paper   Waxed paper is one of my primary kitchen assistants, aiding me every time I bake. I recommend using a sieve to sift flour and other dry ingredients over a sheet of waxed paper. You can then lift the sheet and twist it to form a spout, perfect for slowly funneling the ingredients into a mixing bowl. Rolling out cookie dough between two sheets of waxed paper before refrigerating to firm it is another technique I strongly endorse, especially for my Heart-to-Heart-to-Heart Cookies (page 285) and chocolate Trufflewiches (page 279).

Storage Containers

Whenever I store baked goods, my goal is to fit them into the container as snugly as possible to avoid breakage. Also, I want as little room as possible between the food and the lid of the container to prevent stale air from penetrating the freshly baked sweets.

Metal containers   Airtight metal containers are best for cookies, meringues, and *dacquoise* that must remain crisp. I also use a special trick for cookies that are highly sensitive to humidity, such as Bonnie's Best-Selling Almond Tuiles (page 273). To prevent the cookies from absorbing moisture at room temperature, I store them in an airtight metal container with a desiccant (nontoxic blue crystals that absorb moisture; see Sources). When the crystals turn pale lilac, put them in a hot oven to reactivate them.

Plastic containers   Sturdy, airtight plastic containers are useful when I want to ensure that moist or chewy cookies remain that way, such as Fruit-Nut Florentine Cookie Triangles (page 283). These containers are also perfect for freezing pastries, such as Year-Round Little Peach Pies (page 268), Cheesecake Timbales (page 247), Double-Cranberry Mini Cakes (page 255), Apple Cider Baby Chiffon Cakes (page 242), and Cookie-Dough Hamantaschen (page 294). When I store Croissant Pastry ASAP (page 365) or any yeast dough for proofing in the refrigerator, I typically use an 11 by 7 by 3-inch container. If the dough is shaped and refrigerated overnight, I usually use a larger, deeper rectangular container.

INGREDIENTS

The best baked goods begin with the best-quality ingredients. In *Baking for All Occasions*, almost all of the ingredients called for in the recipes are straightforward and easy to acquire. If you begin with quality ingredients, even if you make a mistake along the way, you will usually end up with a decent dessert. In other words, you will be able to eat your mistake. Wherever I call for a relatively esoteric item, such as unsweetened large-flake dried coconut in Chocolate Lover's Angel Food Cake (page 208), I let you know that Sources includes information on where to find it.

When you shop for baking ingredients, the most important criteria are that the items are fresh and taste good. Once you get the foods home, label them with their date of purchase and store them with care. Taking a bit of extra time for careful storage will help keep your carefully chosen ingredients looking and tasting their best.

What follows are the ingredients you will need to make the recipes in this book and brief guidelines on selecting and storing them, based on what works for me in my kitchen.

Flour

Today's bakers have a tremendous variety of flours from which to choose. In this book, I use wheat flours that differ primarily in protein content. The varying levels of protein in flour are what make the difference between a light, tender cake and a dense, chewy bread, so the type of flour I use in a recipe depends on what I'm baking. Most of my recipes call for all-purpose flour, which has a moderate level of protein. Below are the four types of flour I use in this book.

All-purpose flour   This general-use flour is milled from a mixture of soft and hard wheat, with the bran and germ removed. It has an average protein content of 10 to 11.5 percent, the optimal amount for providing good structure for many cakes, cookies, quick breads, scones, and pastries. All-purpose flour is available in two basic forms: bleached and unbleached. In most of my recipes, I use bleached flour, which has been chemically treated to whiten it (unbleached flour is cream colored) and which seems to yield a more tender result. I call for unbleached flour in my puff pastry recipe (page 367), which requires slightly more structure. Generally speaking, I use Gold Medal bleached all-purpose flour, King Arthur unbleached all-purpose flour, and Gold Medal organic unbleached flour.

Cake flour   The low protein (8 to 9 percent) and high starch content of cake flour mean that it blends easily into a batter and absorbs and retains moisture during baking. The result is an impressively tender, delicate cake with a fine crumb, such as my Favorite Buttermilk Cake (page 344). Milled from soft wheat, cake flour is widely available in grocery stores. I used two brands for testing the recipes in this book, Softasilk and Queen Guinevere from King

Arthur. If you can't find cake flour at your local market, you can make your own by sifting together three parts all-purpose flour to one part cornstarch. I customize a blend of all-purpose flour in combination with cake flour for the Strawberry-Mango Shortcakes with Basil Syrup (page 81).

Bread flour   With an average protein content of 12 to 16 percent, this hard-wheat flour creates an elastic dough that gives breads such as Evie Lieb's Processor Challah (page 184) their structural strength and high rise. I use Bob's Red Mill, Stone Buhr, and King Arthur brands.

Wondra flour   Available in convenient shaker canisters at most grocery stores, this brand-name all-purpose flour is more granular than conventional all-purpose flour. I often use Wondra for prepping baking pans, sprinkling the fine granules evenly over all the buttered surfaces.

Butter and Other Fats

Butter   Flavor is paramount to bakers—and butter delivers flavor better than any other fat. Butter enriches your home-baked items, contributing exceptional tenderness and moistness. It's also responsible for the flaky texture of biscuits, scones, pie crusts, strudels, croissants, and puff pastry.

Because of its sweet, creamy flavor and aroma, I prefer U.S. Grade AA unsalted butter, which is made from the highest-quality fresh cream. It is used almost exclusively in my recipes, all tested using the widely available Land O'Lakes brand. I'm also a fan of the European-style butters that have become increasingly available in American supermarkets and specialty-foods stores. Containing a higher percentage of butterfat (up to 86 percent) and less water than most commercial butters, they increase the flakiness of puff pastry and other laminated doughs and enhance the flavor and texture of pound cakes.

I keep 2 to 3 pounds of butter in the refrigerator, always drawing from my ample supply in the freezer. Butter easily picks up flavors from other stored foods, so always securely wrap any opened portions with plastic wrap.

Depending on temperature, the texture of butter can vary dramatically from very cold and brittle to very soft and oily. Since the temperature of butter is often vital to the success of a recipe, each of my recipes lets you know what temperature will produce the best results.

Soft butter is the ideal consistency for buttering cake pans. I reserve a stick of butter for this use, keeping it wrapped in its paper in a designated place in my refrigerator. When time permits, I cut off ¼-inch-thick slices (the number of slices depends on the size of the pan) and set them aside at room temperature on a small plate to soften. Or, I use a box grater to grate the butter into shavings that thaw almost the moment they touch the pan.

Brown butter   For information on brown butter, see page 19.

Nonstick spray   Over the decades, I have tried every pan spray available, and I prefer only two: Bak-klene and Everbake (see Sources). Bak-klene, a blend of wheat starch and pure vegetable oil, works well for most baked goods, from breads and rolls to berry muffins. Everbake is pure vegetable oil, with a fine mist that coats evenly. For best results, spray using a side-to-side motion, and shake well and often during use. If you can't find either of these brands, I recommend using a pure vegetable oil spray (hold it at least 10 inches away from the pan when spraying) since many grocery-store brands contain starch that often leaves a powdery white coating on baked goods.

Solid vegetable shortening   For my Single-Crust Flaky Pie Pastry (page 354), Double-Crust Flaky Pie Pastry (page 355), and Four Pie Crusts at One Time (page 357), I combine a small amount of vegetable shortening with unsalted butter. Solid shortening contributes tenderness to the pastry, while butter enhances the flavor. I also use solid shortening to prepare intricately detailed baking pans for cakes (page 24). To keep the shortening fresh, always store it in the refrigerator. If using it to prepare a pan, let it come to room temperature so it is easier to spread evenly.

Vegetable oil   To give chiffon cakes their characteristic light, tender crumb, I use a flavorless vegetable oil, such as canola or safflower.

Sugars and Other Sweeteners

Brown sugar   Distinguished by its rich flavor and soft, moist texture, brown sugar is simply granulated sugar that has been colored with molasses. It is widely available in two varieties: mild-flavored golden (light brown) and more intensely flavored dark brown. Muscovado sugar is a fine-grained, dark brown specialty sugar appreciated for its deep molasses flavor. Since brown sugar dries out easily, I keep mine in a jar that has a rubber or plastic gasket topped with an airtight wire-bale lid. If you are measuring brown sugar by volume rather than weight, use recently purchased sugar so that it is softer and thus easier to pack firmly in the measuring cup.

Granulated white sugar   The most commonly used sugar is granulated white sugar, which can be extracted from either sugarcane or sugar beets. I recommend using only sugar labeled "pure cane sugar." In some recipes, I specify superfine (bar or caster) sugar. This is a more finely ground granulated sugar, typically called for because it dissolves almost instantly. Pearl sugar, sometimes called coarse sugar, is granulated white sugar that has been processed into larger, snowy white irregular grains. It is a decorative sugar, used for sprinkling on the top crust of a pie or on a sweet bread before it goes in the oven or on other baked goods.

Powdered sugar   Also called confectioners' sugar and icing sugar, this popular sweetener combines crushed granulated sugar with a bit of cornstarch to prevent clumping. It is typically used to make frostings and icings, or sprinkled over baked goods as a simple finishing touch. When I measure powdered sugar by volume, I use a method that is similar to the way I measure flour. I pour about a pound of powdered sugar into a large canister or sturdy container, fluff it slightly with a fork, and then use the spoon-and-sweep method (page 41) to measure the amount I need.

Raw sugar   Among the most popular raw sugars is turbinado, commonly sold under the brand name Sugar in the Raw. (It is not literally raw. Instead, it is an early stage in the processing of sugarcane for granulated white sugar.) This coarse, pale blond sugar adds appealing color and crunch to streusels or as a topping for a cake, pie, or scones.

Sanding sugar   So-called because each crystal is the size of a grain of sand, this sparkling sugar is available in every color imaginable. I'm fond of the vibrant hues, but my favorite is clear white sanding sugar because it reflects the light in a truly amazing way. Sometimes called decorating sugar, sanding sugar gives baked goods a special finishing touch. You will find it at gourmet markets, specialty-foods stores, and cake-decorating supply shops.

Liquid Sweeteners

Corn syrup   Made from cornstarch, corn syrup contributes moisture and chewiness to baked goods and aids in preventing crystallization of granulated sugar when cooked to make syrups. It's available in two types: milder-tasting light syrup and a stronger-flavored dark version.

Golden syrup   Popular in England, golden syrup is a sugar-derived syrup with a buttery caramel flavor. I use it interchangeably with light corn syrup in ganache and cookie recipes, such as Lacy Brûlée Wafers (page 263) and World-Traveling Crispy ANZAC Cookies (page 204). The most readily available brand is Lyle's Golden Syrup, which can be found at most specialty-foods stores and well-stocked supermarkets.

Honey   A natural sweetener made from flower nectar by the proverbial busy bees, honey derives its color from the nectar's source and adds delicate sweetness to baked goods. As a general rule, darker honeys have a more intense flavor. I tested the recipes with two relatively light honeys, orange and clover.

Maple syrup   This indigenous American sweetener is made by boiling maple sap until it forms a thick syrup. For recipes such as Maple-Pecan Medjool Date Rugelach (page 165) and Maple-Pecan Custard Pie (page 205), I prefer Grade B maple syrup, notable for its rich flavor and deep amber hue. But you can use any grade you like, as long as it is pure maple syrup.

Molasses   A by-product of sugar refining, molasses varieties typically include mild (light), dark, and blackstrap. The term *sulfured* or *unsulfured* on the label indicates whether or not sulfur dioxide played a role in the processing. I prefer unsulfured molasses (no sulfites have been added) for baking since sulfured molasses can leave a slight taste of sulfur in your baked goods. Generally, the lighter the color, the sweeter and milder the molasses. I use mild or dark molasses depending on how strong a flavor I want. For example, in my Triple-Ginger Gingerbread (page 90), I use dark molasses. In recipes calling for small amounts, such as Golden Gingersnap Stars (page 287), I leave the choice to you. I like two brands, Brer Rabbit (mild and full flavor) and Grandma's.

Eggs   Since eggs are one of the most important ingredients in many baked goods, it pays to select and treat them with care. I purchase only Grade AA large eggs from refrigerated cases. At home, always refrigerate eggs in their original cartons, which should be marked with a date to indicate freshness. Transferring eggs to the egg compartment in your refrigerator door exposes them to odors and increases the risk of breakage. Be sure to keep eggs refrigerated at all times, and never use an egg that has a cracked shell. For information on measuring eggs and the roles they play in baking, see page 24.

Milk and Other Dairy Products

Milk   In baking, I use whole milk, which adds moistness and encourages the browning reactions that are characteristic of baked goods like pastry crusts, cookies, and biscuits. Whole milk also adds fat, which in turn creates a richer taste and softer crumb in butter cakes. When used in yeast breads, milk helps prolong storage life. Although I use whole milk in baking, I use nonfat milk in Milk 'n' Honey Sabayon (page 121). Today nonfat milk no longer appears "blue" and watery because additional nonfat milk solids have been added. And it's the protein in these milk solids that enhances the foaming ability as well as supports the foam structure of the sabayon.

Buttermilk   In days gone by, buttermilk referred to the liquid that remained after butter had been made from cream. Today, buttermilk is made from pasteurized skim milk that has been cultured with bacteria to produce lactic acid. The lactic-acid culture develops flavor and gives the original skim milk a thicker, creamier consistency. Some producers add tiny flecks of butter for flavor and to suggest the attractive appearance of old-fashioned buttermilk. Bakers add buttermilk to baked goods for moistness and tenderness and to give them a mildly tangy flavor. Always shake the carton before measuring the buttermilk for a recipe.

Cream cheese   Cream cheese is best known among American bakers for its starring role in cheesecakes. For baking, I use cream cheese made from milk, cheese cultures, salt, and gum arabic as a stabilizer, sold in 8-ounce and 3-ounce packages. It is consistently less watery than other cream cheeses and yields excellent results in baked goods, such as my Mile-High Cheesecake (page 154), Ultimate Cappuccino Cheesecake (page 210), and Cheesecake Timbales (page 247). For best results in baking, use cream cheese at room temperature (unless stated otherwise in the recipe) and mix until smooth with no lumps before adding any other ingredients. Use cream cheese without a stabilizer for no-bake recipes or for spreading on English muffins or bagels.

Crème fraîche   Crème fraîche combines the richness of heavy cream with a pleasant tang. Ranging in texture from that of sour cream to almost as solid as softened butter, it has a slightly nutty flavor and a velvety nap that enriches without being heavy. I rely on this tart-sweet dairy product to add luxurious texture and flavor to many desserts, including Crème Fraîche Custard (page 263). To make a homemade version of crème fraîche, add 1 tablespoon buttermilk to 1 cup heavy cream (preferably at least 40 percent milk fat) and heat to 100 degrees F. Pour the mixture into a jar, cover with a lid, and shake well. Set the mixture aside at room temperature until it thickens slightly, 8 to 12 hours, depending on the temperature of the room. Store in the refrigerator for up to 10 days (the mixture will thicken further).

Evaporated milk and sweetened condensed milk   My students have often questioned me about the difference between evaporated milk and sweetened condensed milk. They are two different products, each with its own distinct characteristics. While both have a percentage of their water removed under vacuum, evaporated milk is the more versatile of the two because it can be used in almost any recipe calling for milk. Sweetened condensed milk has added sugar to provide extra sweetness and a thicker consistency. When caramelized, sweetened condensed milk becomes *dulce de leche*, prized for its rich caramel flavor. For ultimate safety, sweetened condensed milk can be caramelized in one of three approved methods: oven, stove top, or microwave. In Dulce de Tres Leches Fiesta Cake with Red Fruit Sauce (page 309), I use the oven method. Always heed the warning that appears on cans of sweetened condensed milk: never heat an unopened can in simmering or boiling water. The process is *very* unstable and can be dangerous.

Heavy cream   As the saying goes, cream rises to the top—and this is certainly true in baking. In dessert sauces and ice creams, heavy cream acts not only as a liquid but also as a fat that adds richness and, not surprisingly, "creaminess." In baking, it produces tender cakes and pastries with a luscious flavor. Whipped heavy cream is indispensable for topping and filling cakes and pastries. Or, folded into lemon curd or pastry cream, it lightens the mixture and creates a flawlessly smooth texture. Look for heavy cream (sometimes labeled "heavy whipping cream" or "whipping cream") with at least 36 percent butterfat content.

Mascarpone cheese   Used in Coffee Cup Tiramisu (page 250), mascarpone is an unripened Italian dessert cheese made from fresh cream. When you're baking with mascarpone, follow the guidelines for cream cheese and select a good-quality unsalted brand. I most often use BelGioioso brand.

Sour cream   Sour cream is cream that has been cultured with lactic-acid bacteria to create fermentation and impart the characteristic tangy flavor. Rich and acidic in nature, this semiliquid acts as a fat to produce moist, tender textures in cakes and pastries. Most commercial sour cream is made from light cream, so it is 18 to 20 percent fat. It is interesting to note that sour cream tastes more sour and has less fat than crème fraîche. In baking, low-fat sour cream is a fine substitute for the full-fat variety, but nonfat sour cream will yield unsatisfactory results.

Yogurt   Yogurt is made by adding friendly bacteria, such as acidophilus, to milk (whole, low fat, or nonfat), resulting in a creamy cultured dairy product with a bright, tangy flavor. In baking, plain yogurt helps create tenderness, as in Spicy Yogurt Pound Cake (page 189).

Leavenings and Stabilizers

Baking powder   Baking powder is a mixture of baking soda and an acidic powder that, when moistened and heated, react with each other to form carbon-dioxide bubbles that leaven a baked good. Double-acting baking powder, the most common type of baking powder and the one I recommend, means that only a small amount of the bubbles are released when mixed with other ingredients, and the strongest reaction—the rest of the bubbles— begins at about 180 degrees F. Store baking powder in an airtight container to help it stay effective longer.

Baking soda   Technically sodium bicarbonate or bicarbonate of soda, baking soda is an alkaline that reacts with an acidic ingredient in a batter or dough, giving off carbon dioxide that aerates the baked good. Baking soda starts forming carbon dioxide as soon as it is mixed with liquid, so it's important to bake a batter containing baking soda as soon as it is assembled, although its strongest reaction begins at about 140 degrees F. Among the acidic foods that combine with baking soda to form carbon dioxide are sour cream, buttermilk, molasses (which contains a small amount of organic acids), brown sugars (which have small amounts of molasses clinging to the crystals), honey, bananas, fruit juices, maple syrup, and natural cocoa powder (but not Dutch processed). Baking soda generally has a yellowing effect on batters and doughs, with the exception of devil's food cake, which develops a reddish hue. Unlike baking powder, it doesn't deteriorate with age.

Cream of tartar   Officially known as potassium acid tartrate, cream of tartar is a fine white powder derived from white wine. It is used to stabilize egg whites and to inhibit crystallization when caramelizing sugar. For me, the real value of cream of tartar is in the oven, particularly in recipes where whipped egg whites are a main contributor to the volume and structure of a batter. Cream of tartar stabilizes the air bubbles in the heat, preventing them from collapsing before they set.

Yeast   I use primarily two types of yeast, active dry and instant, in my sweet yeast baking. Unlike active dry yeast, which requires activation with liquid before adding other ingredients, instant yeast is combined with the flour and then the liquid is added to activate it. Since instant yeast contains more living cells than active dry yeast, the dough rises faster. Many bakers prefer active dry yeast because it generates a slower rise that translates to more time for the dough to develop flavor (especially in bread baking). However, sweet yeast doughs are made with ingredients like sugar, honey, spices, eggs, butter, sour cream, and milk that amplify their flavor, so the long rise is not as important. Doughs rich in these ingredients that once took a long time to rise are enhanced today by the additional living cells in instant yeast. For more information on yeast, see Key Techniques for Sweet Yeast Baking (page 32).

Flavorings

Vanilla beans and extract   Vanilla is the most commonly used flavoring in this book. As a rule, I call for pure vanilla extract, which is made by soaking macerated vanilla beans in an alcohol-water solution. I prefer Madagascar Bourbon vanilla because its sweet, creamy flavor marries well with a wide variety of ingredients. Vanilla beans— actually the seedpods of a tropical orchid—are also used to great advantage. For example, I rely on vanilla beans to add distinctive flavor and aesthetic appeal to the glaze on

Brown Butter Bundtlettes (page 258). One of my favorite tricks for making the most of vanilla beans is to store one right in my bottle of vanilla extract. In addition to keeping the bean moist and ready for use, this technique gives the extract an added boost of flavor.

Miscellaneous flavoring extracts   I recommend you use only pure flavoring extracts (as opposed to those with artificial ingredients). To impart a delicate floral note, I use rose water (also known as rose flower water), a centuries-old flavoring made by distilling rose petals. It is a particularly wonderful companion to such fruits as raspberries and strawberries. Orange flower water, a distillation of orange blossoms, adds subtle flavor to yeast doughs, such as Lemon-Scented Pull-Apart Coffee Cake (page 163). A little goes a long way, so be judicious if you don't want to end up serving a baked good that tastes like perfume. When it comes to pistachio flavorings, pure extracts can be difficult to find. I advise substituting pistachio paste (see Sources) or pure almond extract.

Salt

Salt is used in baking to balance the flavors of other ingredients in the recipe, especially those calling for unsalted butter (as mine do). To make it easy for you to prepare the recipes in this book, I've specified table salt (iodized salt) as a basic ingredient. However, if you can find fine-grained sea salt at your local market, feel free to use it. As a finishing touch for the Swiss Engadiner Squares (page 104), *fleur de sel* is a welcome surprise. This prized French sea salt—its name translates "flower of salt"—is harvested from the coastal waters of Brittany. It has a subtle flavor and delicate crunch that make the flaky, grayish ivory salt a harmonious complement to sweet ingredients, with a special affinity for caramel and chocolate.

Spices

You will find an interesting range of spices sprinkled throughout the recipes. Among the most frequently used are cinnamon, ginger, allspice, and nutmeg (with the latter freshly grated if you like). When you buy spices, mark the containers with the date of purchase. I recommend buying only small amounts because spices lose their flavor and aroma over time. Once they are on your pantry shelf, check them for freshness occasionally and discard any that have lost their vibrancy.

Chocolate

When it comes to chocolate, there is no substitute for the real thing. Authentic chocolate comes from the bean of the cacao tree, which grows only in equatorial climates. To make chocolate, the beans are fermented, roasted, and shelled, leaving only the prized nibs. The heart of the cacao bean, nibs are ground into a rich paste known as chocolate liquor. Various types of chocolate are defined according to how much chocolate liquor each contains.

If you buy chocolate in bulk, cover the wrapped chocolate with heavy-duty aluminum foil to prevent it from absorbing other flavors. Store all types of chocolate in a dark, cool, dry place to protect them from moisture. Semisweet and bittersweet chocolate have a longer shelf life than white or milk chocolate, which contain milk products.

Bittersweet and semisweet chocolate   Whether to use bittersweet or semisweet is a matter of taste preference. In fact, the two terms are often used interchangeably. Bittersweet chocolate is usually less sweet and contains a higher percentage of chocolate liquor (usually listed as cacao percentage on the label) than semisweet chocolate. The semisweet and bittersweet chocolates used in the recipes in this book are made up of between 50 and 82 percent chocolate liquor.

Cacao nibs   Also known as cocoa nibs, these precious morsels are the basic raw material for chocolate production. They're also delicious ingredients on their own, used by bakers and pastry chefs to add intense chocolate flavor to desserts, ice cream, and cookies such as Cacao Nib Meringue Kisses (page 274).

Cocoa powder   This unsweetened powder is the solid portion of chocolate liquor that remains after nearly all of the cocoa butter has been removed. Cocoa powder

is available in two forms: natural and Dutch processed. Both types play a role in baking, and neither is considered superior to the other. Natural cocoa is distinguished by its rich, fruity flavor and reddish brown hue. Dutch-processed (also called Dutched) cocoa has been treated with an alkalizing agent to reduce bitterness, darken its color, and make it more soluble. Even though it's darker than natural cocoa, Dutch-processed cocoa has a milder, more mellow flavor. Because the two types of cocoa powder have different reactions to leavenings, be sure to use the one called for in a recipe. If no particular type is specified, feel free to use either one. In all cases, however, be careful not to confuse cocoa powder with sweetened cocoa beverage mixes. I use a variety of cocoa powder brands, including Hershey's, Scharffen Berger, Bensdorp, Droste, Dagoba, Valrhona, and Cacao Barry.

Milk chocolate   This familiar chocolate has a mellower flavor than its semisweet and bittersweet cousins. In addition to cocoa butter and sugar, it contains anywhere from 10 percent to about 40 percent chocolate liquor and about 12 percent milk solids. As a general rule, it shouldn't be substituted for other chocolates in baking.

Unsweetened chocolate   Often referred to as baking chocolate, unsweetened chocolate is pure chocolate liquor, consisting of roughly half cocoa butter and half cocoa solids. This product, reserved for baking and cooking, is too bitter to eat out of hand. It is an essential ingredient in all the other types of chocolate, with the exception of white chocolate.

White chocolate   White chocolate is the only chocolate that doesn't contain any chocolate liquor. To be considered authentic white chocolate, it should contain no fats other than a minimum of 20 percent cocoa butter and slightly less than 4 percent butterfat, along with milk solids. What I like about white chocolate are its pristine ivory hue and rich, creamy flavor. It provides a dramatic contrast to the darker chocolates, and adds its unique aesthetic appeal to such desserts as Frozen Lemon Glacier (page 140) and Night and Day Torte (page 322). Be especially careful when melting white chocolate, as the added milk solids make it more sensitive to heat. To prevent the delicate chocolate from forming tiny lumps, chop it finely and melt it over water no hotter than 95 to 110 degrees F (page 17).

Nuts and Nut Products

Nuts   Nuts play a key role in many of my recipes, where I use them to add flavor, texture, and decorative appeal. The types used most frequently in this book are walnuts, almonds, pecans, macadamia nuts, hazelnuts, and pine nuts. Because the natural oils in nuts can quickly turn rancid, I store unopened packages in the freezer. Once the packages are opened, you should use the nuts as soon as possible. Nuts may be labeled with a variety of terms, including natural or raw (skins intact) and blanched (skins removed). Because toasting gives nuts a deeper, richer flavor, I think all types of nuts benefit from being toasted before you use them in a recipe.

Almond paste   A mixture of finely ground almonds and sugar, authentic almond paste can be made only by machine. It's a primary ingredient in marzipan, as well as in fillings such as frangipane, a classic pastry cream. Since I use almond paste often, I keep a large can of it in the refrigerator, where it will stay fresh almost indefinitely. My preferred brands are Blue Diamond and American Almond.

Marzipan   A favorite among pastry chefs and confectioners, marzipan is a sweet, pliable mixture made from almond paste and additional sugar. It is often tinted and molded into whimsical shapes, including fruits, animals, and holiday-themed decorations. It can also be rolled into thin sheets and cut into strips to create ribbons, bows, and other festive finishing touches. I use store-bought marzipan when I don't have time to make my own. It is stocked in most supermarkets, in cans or in plastic-wrapped logs. Store commercial marzipan, well wrapped, at cool room temperature, and keep homemade marzipan in an airtight container in the refrigerator.

Nutella   Reminiscent of classic Italian *gianduia* (sometimes *gianduja*), Nutella is a rich chocolate-hazelnut spread. Once difficult to find outside of Europe, it is now widely available in American grocery stores, usually stocked alongside peanut butter and other nut butters.

Dried Fruits

The deep colors and concentrated sweetness of dried fruits make them stellar ingredients. Many markets carry an impressive variety of dried fruits, commonly offering cherries, cranberries, peaches, apricots, prunes, raisins, and tropical fruits. I feature combinations of dried fruits in several of my recipes, including Autumn Dried Fruit–Nut Tart (page 198) and Minced-Fruit Strudel (page 214). When choosing dried fruits, always make sure your selections are soft, moist, and plump. Storing dried fruits in airtight bags or containers will help preserve their moist texture. Two of my favorite dried fruits require some explanation, which is provided below.

Coconut   Dried coconut enhances baked goods with its signature nutty flavor and chewy texture. Most grocery stores sell dried coconut in sweetened forms, including shredded, flaked, and grated. When I use one of them in a recipe, I reduce the salt in the recipe by half because sweetened coconut contains salt. Unsweetened dried coconut can be found in well-stocked grocery stores and in natural-foods stores and specialty-foods markets. I use both types in my recipes, calling for the unsweetened coconut when I want the flavor and texture of coconut without intensifying a dessert's sweetness as in Ultimate Coconut Macaroons (page 301). For garnishing, I often call for toasted coconut, which has a deep, nutty taste and golden brown hue.

Prunes   These succulent dried fruits have been going through something of an identity crisis, answering to the names of prune, dried plum, and dried prune plums. The California Sunsweet growers refer to them as dried prune plums. Whatever you choose to call them, the plump fruits add rich flavor and texture to a wide range of baked goods. Assuming the form of a luscious puree, they play a key role in the filling for my Crème Fraîche Custard (page 263), Prune Plum–Apricot Oversized Frangipane Tart (page 96), and Bohemian Kolaches (page 171).

PART TWO

Blue-Ribbon Worthy

I'VE ONLY ENTERED ONE RECIPE contest in my life. Years ago, I thought of a novel idea: an ice cream sandwich made with cookies, similar to the It's-It frozen treat that originated in San Francisco. I tested and tinkered to make the recipe perfect before mailing it off. Weeks later, I found out that the judges chose a more humdrum recipe. But it really didn't matter to me. I was hooked on the thrill of creating.

Since then, I have never stopped baking for new occasions. I am drawn to what attracts others, so when I discover that my friends or family favor an ingredient, I am inspired to incorporate it into my recipe repertoire.

Looking through this chapter, you will see desserts that look familiar. Indeed, many of them come from my childhood. But I have given the recipes innovative touches that move them from tried-and-true to terrific.

Who doesn't love brownies? And the zing of a lively herb makes Fresh Mint Brownies all the better. Two breakfast classics—both moist and cakey—find a happy harmony in Blueberry Muffins with Doughnut Topping. And letting one ingredient star to its full potential is why the unadorned flavor of Walnut Breton Cake is so appealing.

Prizewinning is different from showstopping. The presentation of these desserts is casual, and the techniques are straightforward. They will, however, win the hearts, minds, and taste buds of those who enjoy them. For instance, Strawberry-Mango Shortcakes with Basil Syrup is assembled in a few easy steps, but the result is a wow-factor dessert that belies its simplicity. Likewise, Any Day All-Occasion Snack Cake goes together with little effort, but the accolades it brings are sensational.

I probably won't enter a recipe contest again anytime soon, but when I want to offer guests my A-list, these are the desserts I prepare time and again. In my mind, the best prize is the praise of my loved ones.

Banana-Bottom Pineapple-Swirl Cupcakes

Your first bite into one of these cupcakes reveals a luscious pineapple–cream cheese filling—a perfect match for the flavorful banana cake that hides the surprise. The creamy swirl on top is like an invitation to discover the secret pineapple center.

For me, bananas are at their optimum for incorporating into most cakes when their skins are yellow with a moderate sprinkling of brown flecks. And please note: for this recipe, I think the banana flavor is more intense if you mash the bananas in a bowl with a pastry blender or oversized fork, rather than puree them in a small electric chopper or food processor. Any small nugget of fruit that remains from the hand-processed mashing delivers the very essence of banana flavor. Then I spoon the mashed banana pulp into a measuring cup to calculate the amount needed. **YIELD: 15 CUPCAKES**

PINEAPPLE SWIRL FILLING

ONE 8-OUNCE (225-GRAM) CAN CRUSHED PINEAPPLE

6 OUNCES (170 GRAMS) CREAM CHEESE, AT ROOM
    TEMPERATURE

¼ CUP (1 ¾ OUNCES/50 GRAMS) GRANULATED SUGAR

1 LARGE EGG

⅛ TEASPOON SALT

BANANA CUPCAKES

1 ¾ CUPS (7 OUNCES/200 GRAMS) CAKE FLOUR

1 TEASPOON BAKING POWDER

½ TEASPOON BAKING SODA

½ TEASPOON SALT

1 CUP (9 OUNCES/255 GRAMS) MASHED RIPE BANANAS
    (2 MEDIUM OR 3 SMALL)

3 TABLESPOONS WHOLE MILK

1 TEASPOON PURE VANILLA EXTRACT

4 OUNCES (1 STICK/115 GRAMS) UNSALTED BUTTER,
    AT ROOM TEMPERATURE

1 CUP (7 OUNCES/200 GRAMS) GRANULATED SUGAR

1 LARGE EGG

Before baking: Center a rack in the oven and preheat the oven to 350 degrees F. Lightly coat a 12-cup standard muffin pan with nonstick spray, then flour the cups, tapping out the excess flour. Or, butter and flour the cups. Or, line the cups with fluted paper or foil liners. Repeat with a second muffin pan, preparing only 3 cups and spacing them evenly around the pan. Spacing the cups promotes even baking when not all of the cups are filled. Have all of the ingredients at room temperature.

To make the Pineapple Swirl Filling: Drain the pineapple in a sieve over a small bowl. Press the pineapple against the sieve with the back of a spoon to release as much of the juice as possible. Drain the pineapple further on a few sheets of paper toweling. Discard the liquid.

In the bowl of a stand mixer fitted with the paddle attachment (or use a handheld mixer), beat the cream cheese on very low speed until smooth. Add the sugar and beat until the mixture is smooth. Add the egg and salt, mixing just until the ingredients are blended and creamy. Gently twist the paper towels around the crushed pineapple to absorb any additional juice, and then stir in ⅓ cup of the pineapple; save the remainder for another use.

To make the Banana Cupcakes: Sift together the flour, baking powder, baking soda, and salt onto a sheet of waxed paper. Put the bananas into a medium bowl, add the milk and vanilla, and mix together with a rubber spatula. In the bowl of the stand mixer fitted with the paddle attachment (or use a handheld mixer), beat the butter and sugar on medium speed until well blended, about 3 minutes. Beat in the egg just until incorporated. Add the banana mixture (it will look curdled but that's okay; it won't after you add the flour mixture) and beat on medium-low speed until it is incorporated. On the lowest speed, add the flour mixture in two or three additions, mixing just until smooth after each addition.

Spoon 1 tablespoon of the cupcake batter into each prepared muffin cup, spoon 1 tablespoon of the pineapple filling over the batter, and then top each with 2 more tablespoons of the batter.

If your oven is wide enough, bake 2 muffin pans side by side, spacing them about 1 inch apart. If not, put the second pan on a rack in the upper third of the oven. Bake the cupcakes until they are golden and spring back without leaving an impression when gently pressed, 22 to 24 minutes. Transfer to a wire rack and let cool in the pan for 10 minutes. Gently tap the pan on a counter to see if the cupcakes release from the sides. If not, trace around each form with a small knife to free the cupcakes. Invert a rack on top of the cupcakes, invert the cupcakes onto it, and carefully lift off the pan. Place the cupcakes right side up on the rack and let cool completely.

These cupcakes freeze beautifully. Place them in a sturdy covered container, label with the contents and date, and freeze for up to 10 days. Thaw at room temperature for about 1 hour.

Bishop's Cake

This ring-shaped cake is studded with golden raisins, glacéed red cherries, chocolate chips, and sliced almonds in perfect balance. The almonds melt into the cake, lending both flavor and crunch. Icing drizzled in a lattice pattern on top provides numerous spots to secure additional fruits, nuts, and chocolate chips—a reflection of the delectable ingredients inside.

There's plenty of fascinating folklore regarding the origin of the bishop's cake, but not a lot of fact, according to my friend and culinary historian Laura Martin Bacon. She has found that when it comes to this quick bread, legends abound, both European and American. My favorite story is rooted in frontier folklore. In the American West of the nineteenth century, it was common for circuit-riding preachers to travel from village to far-flung village on horseback, stopping for refreshment and conversation at the residences of their parishioners. According to one story, a Kentucky bishop unexpectedly dropped in for breakfast at the family home of a woman who was an accomplished and resourceful baker. With no time to dash out to the general store (or a neighboring farm) for groceries, the creative hostess concocted a sumptuous quick bread using the luxurious ingredients in her own pantry and larder. The bishop was delighted—and American home bakers have been serving the fruit-studded cake on special occasions ever since.

YIELD: ONE 10-INCH RING CAKE, ABOUT 12 SERVINGS

CAKE

⅓ CUP (ABOUT 2 OUNCES/55 GRAMS) GOLDEN RAISINS

⅓ CUP (ABOUT 2½ OUNCES/70 GRAMS) GLACÉED RED CHERRIES, QUARTERED

⅓ CUP (2¼ OUNCES/65 GRAMS) SEMISWEET CHOCOLATE CHIPS

⅓ CUP (1 OUNCE/30 GRAMS) NATURAL OR BLANCHED SLICED ALMONDS

1 TABLESPOON MEDIUM-DRY SHERRY OR FRESH ORANGE JUICE

1¼ CUPS PLUS 2 TABLESPOONS (6½ OUNCES/185 GRAMS) ALL-PURPOSE FLOUR

¼ TEASPOON BAKING POWDER

¼ TEASPOON SALT

8 OUNCES (2 STICKS/225 GRAMS) UNSALTED BUTTER, AT ROOM TEMPERATURE

1 CUP PLUS 2 TABLESPOONS (8 OUNCES/225 GRAMS) GRANULATED SUGAR

3 LARGE EGGS, LIGHTLY BEATEN

2 LARGE EGG YOLKS

1½ TEASPOONS PURE VANILLA EXTRACT

2 TABLESPOONS WHOLE MILK

TOPPING

⅔ CUP (2½ OUNCES/70 GRAMS) POWDERED SUGAR

1 TABLESPOON MEDIUM-DRY SHERRY OR FRESH ORANGE JUICE

MIXTURE OF GOLDEN RAISINS, QUARTERED GLACÉED RED CHERRIES, CHOCOLATE CHIPS, AND SLICED ALMONDS

Before baking: Center a rack in the oven and preheat the oven to 350 degrees F. Lightly coat a 10-inch metal ring mold (6-cup capacity) or a 9 by 2-inch square cake pan with nonstick spray, then flour it, tapping out the excess flour. Or, butter and flour the pan. Have all of the ingredients at room temperature.

To make the cake: Using your fingertips, blend together the raisins, cherries, chocolate chips, almonds, and sherry in a small bowl; set aside. Sift together the flour, baking powder, and salt onto a sheet of waxed paper; set aside.

In the bowl of a stand mixer fitted with the paddle attachment, beat the butter on medium speed until creamy and smooth, 30 to 45 seconds. Add the sugar and continue to beat until light and fluffy, about 6 minutes. Stop the mixer occasionally to scrape down the sides of the bowl. Add the eggs, about 3 tablespoons at a time, beating after each addition only until incorporated, and stopping to scrape down the sides of the bowl as needed. Add the egg yolks and beat just until incorporated. Then beat in the vanilla and the milk until combined. On the lowest speed, add the flour mixture in two additions, mixing after each addition until combined and stopping the mixer occasionally to scrape down the sides of the bowl. Detach the paddle and bowl from the mixer, and tap the paddle against the side of the bowl to free the excess batter. Using a rubber spatula, gently fold in the raisin mixture. Spoon the batter into the prepared pan, spreading evenly with the spatula.

Bake the cake until it springs back when lightly touched in the center and is beginning to come away from the sides of the pan, 43 to 45 minutes. Transfer to a wire rack and let cool in the pan for about 10 minutes. Invert a wire rack on top of the cake, invert the cake onto the rack, and carefully lift off the pan. Slide a sheet of waxed paper under the rack (it will catch any drips when the topping is applied). Let cool completely before topping.

To make the topping: In a small bowl, stir together the powdered sugar and the sherry until smoothly blended. Drizzle crisscrossing lines over the cake (or create a web of sorts) from the tip of a spoon or from fork tines. Press raisins, cherries, chocolate chips, and almonds randomly on the glaze. Set aside to allow the glaze to set, 35 to 45 minutes, before serving.

Blueberry Muffins
with Doughnut Topping

Chock-full of blueberries, these moist muffins grace the top-ten list of nearly everyone who has tried them. They can be put together quickly, baked in short order, and enjoyed on the go. The best part, though, is the topping. Dipping the warm muffins in butter and cinnamon sugar leads you to wonder, are these muffins or doughnuts? No matter: anyone with a soft spot for blueberry muffins is sure to find them irresistible. You can use other fruits, such as fresh cranberries or dried cherries, cranberries, or coarsely chopped apricots, in place of the blueberries.   **YIELD: 1 DOZEN MUFFINS**

MUFFINS

2 CUPS (9 OUNCES/255 GRAMS) ALL-PURPOSE FLOUR

½ CUP (3½ OUNCES/100 GRAMS) GRANULATED SUGAR

2 TEASPOONS BAKING POWDER

½ TEASPOON BAKING SODA

½ TEASPOON SALT

¾ CUP (6 FL OUNCES/180 ML) COLD WELL-SHAKEN BUTTERMILK

3 OUNCES (¾ STICK/85 GRAMS) UNSALTED BUTTER, MELTED AND TEPID

2 LARGE EGGS

2 TEASPOONS FINELY GRATED LEMON ZEST

1 TEASPOON PURE VANILLA EXTRACT

1½ CUPS (ABOUT 8 OUNCES/225 GRAMS) BLUEBERRIES, PICKED OVER FOR STEMS

DOUGHNUT TOPPING

½ CUP (3½ OUNCES/100 GRAMS) GRANULATED SUGAR

1½ TEASPOONS GROUND CINNAMON, OR 1 TEASPOON GROUND CINNAMON AND ½ TEASPOON GROUND CARDAMOM

3 OUNCES (¾ STICK/85 GRAMS) UNSALTED BUTTER, MELTED

Before baking: Center a rack in the oven and preheat the oven to 375 degrees F. Lightly coat a 12-cup standard muffin pan with nonstick spray, then flour the cups, tapping out the excess flour. Or, butter and flour the cups. Or, line the cups with fluted paper or foil liners. Have all of the ingredients at room temperature except the buttermilk.

To make the muffins: In a large bowl, whisk together to blend the flour, sugar, baking powder, baking soda, and salt.

In a medium bowl, stir together the buttermilk, butter, eggs, lemon zest, and vanilla until combined. Add the buttermilk mixture to the flour mixture and stir gently with a rubber spatula just until moistened. Don't beat until smooth, or the muffins will have a coarse texture. Using the spatula, fold in the blueberries just enough to incorporate them into the batter.

Using an ice-cream scoop about 2¼ inches in diameter (#16) or a spoon, fill the muffin cups three-fourths full. Bake the muffins until they are golden, spring back when gently pressed in the center, and are starting to pull away from the muffin cups, 18 to 23 minutes. Cool in the pan just until they can be handled, 10 to 15 minutes.

To make the Doughnut Topping: In a small bowl, stir together the sugar and cinnamon.

While the muffins are still warm, gently remove them from the pan one at a time, dip the tops in the melted butter, roll in the cinnamon sugar to coat, and then place on a wire rack.

Serve warm or at room temperature. Store at room temperature under a cake dome for up to 2 days, or freeze for up to 10 days in a sturdy covered container. Thaw at room temperature 1 to 1½ hours.

Heavenly Brownie-on-Shortbread Bars

Baking the silky, intense chocolate topping on crunchy (firm) shortbread makes for neatly cut brownies that will lend panache to any dessert time. I prefer to chop the nuts for this recipe in a nut mill (page 42) for consistently evenly chopped nuts. For a more attractive finish, after you chop the nuts, sieve them to remove nut "dust" before topping the brownie.

YIELD: 3 DOZEN BROWNIES

SHORTBREAD

1 ⅓ CUPS (6 ¼ OUNCES/175 GRAMS) ALL-PURPOSE FLOUR

⅓ CUP (2 ¼ OUNCES/65 GRAMS) GRANULATED SUGAR

¼ TEASPOON SALT

4 OUNCES (1 STICK/115 GRAMS) COLD UNSALTED BUTTER, CUT INTO ½-INCH SLICES

1 TEASPOON PURE VANILLA EXTRACT

HEAVENLY BROWNIE

⅔ CUP (3 OUNCES/85 GRAMS) ALL-PURPOSE FLOUR

⅛ TEASPOON SALT

4 OUNCES (1 STICK/115 GRAMS) UNSALTED BUTTER, CUT INTO ½-INCH SLICES

5 OUNCES (140 GRAMS) BITTERSWEET CHOCOLATE, COARSELY CHOPPED

1 CUP FIRMLY PACKED (7 OUNCES/200 GRAMS) LIGHT BROWN SUGAR

3 LARGE EGGS

1 TEASPOON PURE VANILLA EXTRACT

1 CUP PACKED (4 ½ OUNCES/130 GRAMS) HAZELNUTS, FINELY CHOPPED TO YIELD 1 CUP

Before baking: Center a rack in the oven and preheat the oven to 350 degrees F. Press a sheet of aluminum foil to cover the outside bottom and sides of a 9 by 2-inch square pan. Lift off the foil, invert the pan, and gently press the foil into the pan to fit the contours.

To make the shortbread: In a food processor, combine the flour, sugar, and salt and process briefly to blend. Scatter the butter pieces over the top and process with 1-second bursts. Add the vanilla and continue with 1-second bursts until the ingredients form small clumps. Stop before the mixture forms a ball. Scatter the clumps over the bottom of the prepared pan, and press with fingertips to line the bottom evenly.

Bake the shortbread until it is pale gold and firm to the touch, 27 to 32 minutes. Let cool in the pan, about 20 minutes.

To make the Heavenly Brownie: Briefly whisk together the flour and salt in a medium bowl to blend; set aside. In a small, heavy saucepan, melt the butter and chocolate over very low heat, stirring with a silicone spatula until smooth. Remove from the heat and stir the sugar into the chocolate mixture, combining thoroughly. Set aside for 5 to 7 minutes.

In a medium bowl, whisk the eggs until lightly beaten. Add the slightly cooled chocolate mixture to the eggs, stirring to blend. Stir in the vanilla, then the flour mixture. Pour the batter over the shortbread, and spread evenly with a rubber spatula. Sprinkle the nuts evenly over the batter. Gently pat them in place.

Bake the brownie until the top looks slightly cracked about 1 inch from the edge around the pan and feels soft to the touch, 27 to 30 minutes. Don't overbake; the brownie will firm as it cools. Transfer to a wire rack and let cool completely in the pan, at least 3 hours or up to overnight.

To serve, using the edges of the foil as handles, lift the brownie slab onto a cutting board. Using a sharp knife, cut the brownies straight down through the shortbread into 1 ½-inch squares. To store, return the bars to the pan, cover with aluminum foil, sealing the foil around the edges of the pan, and keep at room temperature for up to 3 days.

Double-Crust Butter-Pecan Apple Pie

Incorporating candied pecans into an all-American favorite raises the bar on a beloved dessert. Candying the nuts adds a crisp, sweet coating and ensures that they will maintain some of their crunch during baking. If you are weighing your ingredients, you will notice that when you divide the candied nuts for the filling and the garnish, the weights don't seem correct when viewed alongside the volume measures. That's because when you candy the nuts, they are not all evenly coated, and those are the weights that my scale showed when I tested the recipe.

For pies, I peel the whole apples, cut them in half, core them, put them cut side down on the cutting board, and slice them horizontally, rather than slicing them from the stem end to the blossom end. This way, you create slices that lie flat, making it easier to pile a lot of them in the pie dish. **YIELD: ONE 9-INCH PIE, 8 SERVINGS**

CANDIED BUTTER PECANS

⅓ CUP (2¼ OUNCES/65 GRAMS) GRANULATED SUGAR

3 TABLESPOONS LIGHT CORN SYRUP

3 TABLESPOONS UNSALTED BUTTER

⅛ TEASPOON SALT

1 CUP (4 OUNCES/115 GRAMS) PECAN HALVES

1 RECIPE DOUBLE-CRUST FLAKY PIE PASTRY (PAGE 355)

FILLING

7 MEDIUM (3 POUNDS/1.4 KG) PIPPIN, BRAEBURN, GRANNY SMITH, OR ASSORTED COOKING APPLES, PEELED, CUT IN HALF VERTICALLY, CORED, AND CUT CROSSWISE INTO ¼-INCH-THICK SLICES (ABOUT 9 CUPS/ 2½ POUNDS/1.1 KG)

½ CUP (3½ OUNCES/100 GRAMS) GRANULATED SUGAR

2 TABLESPOONS FIRMLY PACKED LIGHT BROWN SUGAR

⅓ CUP (1½ OUNCES/45 GRAMS) ALL-PURPOSE FLOUR

⅛ TEASPOON SALT

⅔ CUP (3 OUNCES/85 GRAMS) CANDIED BUTTER PECANS

2 OUNCES (½ STICK/55 GRAMS) UNSALTED BUTTER, MELTED

1 TABLESPOON FRESH LEMON JUICE

1 TABLESPOON HONEY

1 TO 2 TABLESPOONS WHOLE MILK

2 TABLESPOONS SANDING SUGAR, RAW SUGAR, OR GRANULATED SUGAR

OPTIONAL GARNISHES

PREMIUM VANILLA ICE CREAM, OR 1 CUP (8 FL OUNCES/ 240 ML) HEAVY CREAM, WHIPPED TO SOFT PEAKS

⅓ CUP (2 OUNCES/55 GRAMS) CANDIED BUTTER PECANS

To make the Candied Butter Pecans: Line a baking sheet with a silicone mat or aluminum foil. In a 10-inch heavy skillet, combine the sugar, corn syrup, butter, and salt and stir over low heat until the sugar dissolves and the butter melts. Increase the heat to medium-low. When the mixture reaches a simmer, add the pecans and cook just until the syrup turns deep amber and large, thick bubbles form. Stir the pecans occasionally to prevent burning and to coat them. Pour the nuts out onto the prepared baking sheet and, without delay, separate them, using metal or wooden skewers or fork tines. Set aside to cool. The nuts will keep in an airtight container at room temperature for up to 10 days. You should have about 1 cup (5 ounces/140 grams).

Before baking: Center a rack in the oven and preheat the oven to 425 degrees F. Have ready a 9-inch glass pie dish.

To line the pie dish: Following the directions on page 27 for rolling out pie pastry and lining a pie dish, roll out 1 pastry disk into a 13-inch circle about ³⁄₁₆ inch thick, transfer the pastry to the pie dish, and trim the edge with scissors to leave a 1-inch overhang. Set aside at room temperature.

To fill the pie crust: Put the apple slices in a large bowl. In a small bowl, mix together the sugars, flour, and salt. Sprinkle the sugar mixture, candied pecans, butter, lemon juice, and honey over the apples and toss the apples to coat evenly. Pile the apples into the pie crust, mounding them in the center, and scrape any juices and sugar in the bowl over the filling.

To finish the pie: Roll out the second dough disk into a 13-inch circle, then, following the directions on page 28, top the pie and finish the edges. Using the tip of a small, sharp paring knife, cut out a 3-inch circle in the center of the top crust for decoration and to allow steam to escape during baking. Brush the crust lightly with the milk and then sprinkle it with the sanding sugar.

Place the pie on a rimmed baking sheet (to catch drips) and bake for 15 minutes. Reduce the temperature to 375 degrees F and bake the pie until the apples are tender when pierced with the tip of a knife, the filling starts to bubble, and the crust is golden and bubbly, about 40 minutes longer. Transfer to a wire rack and let cool for about 1 hour to serve warm, or to room temperature to serve later. (During this rest, most of the juices return to the apples and the filling thickens.)

Cut the pie into wedges and accompany with vanilla ice cream. Garnish each serving with a few candied pecans, if desired.

Chocolate-Chip Cookie Cake

Here's a recipe you will use again and again. It's a standard in our family. I selected a dough from my repertoire of chocolate-chip cookie recipes, placed it in a rectangular pan (which most people have on hand), and baked it as though it were a cake. The result is a super-easy informal indulgence that can be whipped up at the last minute. It makes an ideal birthday cake for someone who lives for chocolate chip cookies: simply pop a candle in the center and serve it straight from the pan. If you can resist eating it immediately, wrap it securely and freeze for later enjoyment.

A speedy way to soften butter is to set the unwrapped butter on a plate, and cut it into ¼-inch slices. The butter softens in 30 to 60 minutes (depending on the temperature of the room). The key to this recipe is not to incorporate a lot of air, or the dough will expand too much during baking. You want to create a texture similar to a cookie, rather than a cake.

For a more complex flavor, substitute ½ teaspoon ground cardamom for half of the ground cinnamon in the recipe. If you wish, omit the nuts and mix in an additional 1 cup (6 ounces/170 grams) chocolate chips.   **YIELD: ONE 13 BY 9-INCH CAKE, 1½ TO 3½ DOZEN PIECES, DEPENDING ON SIZE**

2⅓ CUPS (10½ OUNCES/300 GRAMS) ALL-PURPOSE FLOUR

⅔ CUP (4½ OUNCES/130 GRAMS) GRANULATED SUGAR

⅔ CUP FIRMLY PACKED (4½ OUNCES/130 GRAMS) LIGHT BROWN SUGAR

1 TEASPOON SALT

1 TEASPOON GROUND CINNAMON (OPTIONAL)

½ TEASPOON BAKING SODA

8 OUNCES (2 STICKS/225 GRAMS) UNSALTED BUTTER, SOFTENED

1 LARGE EGG

1 TEASPOON PURE VANILLA EXTRACT

2 CUPS (12 OUNCES/340 GRAMS) SEMISWEET CHOCOLATE CHIPS

1 CUP (4 OUNCES/115 GRAMS) CHOPPED WALNUTS, PECANS, OR HAZELNUTS, OR A COMBINATION

Before baking: Center a rack in the oven and preheat the oven to 350 degrees F. Have ready a 13 by 9 by 2-inch pan (quarter sheet pan).

In a stand mixer fitted with the paddle attachment, combine the flour, sugars, salt, cinnamon (if using), and baking soda and mix on the lowest speed just until blended. Add the butter and continue to mix on low speed just until small, moist crumbs form (they are larger than crumbs that don't clump together) that look similar to streusel, about 1 minute. Add the egg and vanilla and beat on low speed until the mixture begins to form a cohesive dough. Increase the speed to medium just as you add the chocolate chips and nuts and beat just until they are incorporated into the dough, 20 to 30 seconds.

Spoon dollops of the thick dough evenly over the bottom of the baking pan, and then spread the dough over the pan with a rubber spatula. To distribute the dough evenly, lay a sheet of plastic wrap over the dough and pat it evenly with your fingertips.

Bake the cake until it is golden brown and feels more solid than soft when pressed in the center, 37 to 40 minutes. Be careful not to overbake; it will firm as it cools. Transfer to a wire rack and let cool in the pan for 30 to 35 minutes.

Slip a thin metal spatula between the still-warm cake and the pan and run the spatula carefully along the entire perimeter of the pan. Lift the pan, tilt it slightly, and tap it on a counter to help release the cake. Invert a large wire rack on top of the cake, invert the cake onto it, and carefully lift off the pan. Invert another large wire rack on top, invert the cake so it is right side up, and remove the original rack. Let cool completely.

If serving within 2 days, wrap the cake tightly in aluminum foil and store at room temperature. For longer storage, label with the contents and date and freeze for up to 1 month. Thaw in the wrapping at room temperature for about 3 hours.

To serve, cut the cake into squares, rectangles, or sticks with a sharp knife.

Chocolate Chip Biscotti Variation

YIELD: ABOUT 4 ½ DOZEN BISCOTTI

1 RECIPE CHOCOLATE-CHIP COOKIE CAKE DOUGH
   (OPPOSITE PAGE)

Bake the Chocolate-Chip Cookie Cake as directed and place on a wire rack to cool for 30 minutes. Leave the oven on (350 degrees F), and line 2 large baking sheets with parchment paper.

Unmold the still-warm cookie cake as directed in the recipe. Cut the cake into thirds, to yield three 9 by 4-inch pieces. Using a long-bladed sharp knife, cut each piece into sticks ½ inch thick and 4 inches long. Cut carefully and slowly to prevent the sticks from breaking. (Each cookie strip will yield about fourteen 4 by ½-inch sticks.) It's always best to cut the sticks while the cake is warm; as it cools, the cake crisps, making it difficult to cut without shattering. Carefully transfer the sticks, cut side down, to the prepared baking sheets, spacing them about ½ inch apart.

Bake the sticks until they are crisp, 10 to 13 minutes. Transfer to wire racks and let cool on the pans for about 10 minutes. Transfer the sticks to a wire rack and let cool completely. To store, wrap securely in aluminum foil or stack in a sturdy airtight container and store at room temperature for up to 2 days. For longer storage, freeze for up to 1 month as directed for the cake.

Bake-on-Demand Chocolate Chip Cookies Variation

YIELD: ABOUT 4 DOZEN COOKIES

1 RECIPE CHOCOLATE-CHIP COOKIE CAKE DOUGH
   (OPPOSITE PAGE)

Before baking: Center a rack in the oven and preheat the oven to 350 degrees F. Line a baking sheet with parchment paper.

Make the dough as directed. Using an ice cream scoop about 1 ½ inches in diameter (#40 or #50), scoop up the dough and place the balls (each weighing ¾ to 1 ounce) on the prepared baking sheet, spacing them about 1 inch apart. (Alternatively, scoop up a level tablespoon of dough for each ball.) To ensure the cookies bake evenly, dip the tines of a fork into some flour and flatten each cookie slightly.

Bake the cookies just until the undersides are golden, 11 to 13 minutes. Transfer the baking sheet to a wire rack and let cool on the pan for 2 to 3 minutes. Then transfer the cookies to the rack and let cool completely (they will firm as they cool). To store, wrap securely in aluminum foil or stack in a sturdy airtight container and store for up to 2 days at room temperature. For longer storage, freeze for up to 1 month as directed for the cake.

To make bake-on-demand cookies: Scoop out the dough and arrange on baking sheets as directed. Freeze just until the cookies are firm, about 30 minutes. Then, transfer the cookies to resealable plastic bags and freeze until needed or for up to 2 weeks.

If you can plan ahead, remove just the number of cookies needed from the freezer to the refrigerator the day before baking, and then arrange them on a parchment paper–lined baking sheet. If you can't plan ahead, place the cookies straight from the freezer on the parchment-lined baking sheet and allow them to thaw at room temperature until only partially frozen, 20 to 30 minutes. Bake the cookies as directed. If they went into the oven partially frozen, check them after 13 minutes. They may need to bake for 2 to 3 minutes longer.

Any Day All-Occasion Snack Cake

This versatile cake, welcome on the table at any time of day, has brought eating pleasure to many people in my life. It's a simple cake with an infinite number of variations possible according to the season. Fresh blueberries, raspberries, and cranberries; shredded carrots; diced apples; and even shredded raw pumpkin—about 1 cup (about 5 ounces/140 grams) total—can be added to the batter after the buttermilk. Ideal for picnics or tailgate parties, this traditional Braker family cake is a great keeper. Add your own special touches to make it part of your family's traditions. **YIELD: ONE 13 BY 9-INCH CAKE, 12 TO 16 SERVINGS**

2⅓ CUPS (10½ OUNCES/300 GRAMS) ALL-PURPOSE FLOUR

¾ CUP (5¼ OUNCES/150 GRAMS) GRANULATED SUGAR

½ TEASPOON SALT

1½ TEASPOONS GROUND CINNAMON

1 CUP FIRMLY PACKED (7 OUNCES/200 GRAMS) LIGHT BROWN SUGAR

¾ CUP (6 FL OUNCES/180 ML) FLAVORLESS VEGETABLE OIL SUCH AS CANOLA OR SAFFLOWER

1 CUP (4 OUNCES/115 GRAMS) CHOPPED WALNUTS, PECANS, OR HAZELNUTS

1 TEASPOON BAKING POWDER

1 TEASPOON BAKING SODA

1 CUP (8 FL OUNCES/240 ML) WELL-SHAKEN BUTTERMILK

1 LARGE EGG

Before baking: Center a rack in the oven and preheat the oven to 350 degrees F. Lightly coat a 13 by 9 by 2-inch pan (quarter sheet pan) with nonstick spray, then flour it, tapping out the excess flour. Or, butter and flour the pan. If desired, line the bottom with parchment paper to facilitate unmolding the baked cake.

To make the cake batter: Sift together the flour, granulated sugar, salt, and ½ teaspoon of the cinnamon into a large bowl. Using a rubber spatula or whisk, briefly mix in the brown sugar just until the ingredients are blended. Stir in the oil, mixing well.

To make the crumb topping: Remove enough of the flour mixture to measure ¾ cup loosely packed. Add the nuts and the remaining 1 teaspoon cinnamon and blend well with your fingertips; set aside.

To finish the cake batter, stir in the baking powder and baking soda. Add the buttermilk and egg and stir until the mixture is smooth. Pour the batter into the prepared pan and spread evenly with the rubber spatula. Sprinkle the reserved topping evenly over the batter, and then gently pat the topping to ensure it bakes evenly.

Bake the cake until a round wooden toothpick inserted in the center comes out free of cake, about 35 minutes. Transfer to a wire rack and let cool in the pan for 10 to 15 minutes.

Tilt and rotate the pan while gently tapping it on a counter to release the cake sides. Invert a large wire rack on top of the cake, invert the cake onto it, and carefully lift off the pan. If you have used parchment, slowly peel it off, turn it over so that the sticky side faces up, and reposition it on top of the cake. Invert another rack on top, invert the cake so it is right side up, and remove the original rack. Let cool completely.

If serving the cake within 24 hours, wrap in plastic wrap and store at room temperature. For longer storage, over-wrap with aluminum foil, label with the contents and date, and freeze for up to 2 weeks. Thaw at room temperature in its wrapping for about 3 hours. If desired, unwrap the package after an hour at room temperature, and using the aid of a rimless baking baking sheet or a giant spatula, carefully transfer the cake to a serving platter. Cover it lightly with plastic wrap and let the cake continue to thaw.

To serve, cut the cake into squares or rectangles with a sharp knife.

Fresh Mint Brownies

This is truly an old favorite with a completely new dimension. Infusing the batter with fragrant fresh mint leaves is a simple technique that complements the chocolate with a depth and intensity of flavor that can't be achieved with an oil or extract. Frosted mint leaves garnish the top of each brownie to provide a natural finish with a taste that is indisputably the real thing.

YIELD: SIXTEEN 2-INCH SQUARE BROWNIES

BROWNIES

1½ CUPS (6¼ OUNCES/175 GRAMS) ALL-PURPOSE FLOUR

½ TEASPOON SALT

¼ TEASPOON BAKING SODA

6 OUNCES (1½ STICKS/170 GRAMS) UNSALTED BUTTER

4 OUNCES (115 GRAMS) UNSWEETENED CHOCOLATE, COARSELY CHOPPED

2 TABLESPOONS WATER

½ CUP FINELY CHOPPED FRESH MINT

2 CUPS (14 OUNCES/400 GRAMS) GRANULATED SUGAR

4 LARGE EGGS, LIGHTLY BEATEN

CANDIED MINT LEAVES

ORGANIC FRESH MINT LEAVES, AT LEAST 1 LEAF PER BROWNIE

1 EGG WHITE, LIGHTLY BEATEN UNTIL FOAMY

¾ CUP (5¼ OUNCES/150 GRAMS) GRANULATED SUGAR

Before baking: Center a rack in the oven and preheat the oven to 325 degrees F. Press a sheet of aluminum foil to cover the outside bottom and sides of a 9 by 2-inch square pan. Lift off the foil, invert the pan, and gently press the foil into the pan to fit the contours.

To make the brownies: Sift together the flour, salt, and baking soda onto a piece of waxed paper; set aside. In a small, heavy saucepan, melt the butter and chocolate over very low heat, stirring with a silicone spatula until smooth. Or, combine in a medium microwave-safe bowl and melt in a microwave oven at 50 percent power (medium) for 30-second bursts, stirring after each burst, until melted, 1 to 1½ minutes. Remove from the heat, stir in the water, and then stir in the mint. Set aside to cool for 5 minutes.

Press the chocolate mixture through a medium-mesh sieve into a large bowl; discard the mint. Stir in the sugar and then the eggs just until thoroughly blended. Add the flour mixture, stirring until well blended.

Pour the batter into the prepared pan, spreading evenly with the spatula. Bake the brownie until the top is no longer shiny and a thin crust appears, 42 to 45 minutes. Don't overbake; the brownie will firm as it cools. Transfer to a wire rack and let cool completely in the pan, at least 3 hours or up to overnight.

To make the Candied Mint Leaves: Gently rinse the leaves and pat thoroughly dry with paper toweling. Select a baking sheet that will fit in your refrigerator and line it with aluminum foil; set aside. Have the egg white and sugar ready in separate small bowls. Using a small, clean paint brush or pastry brush, and working with 1 leaf at a time, lightly coat the leaf with the egg white. Immediately sprinkle the leaf lightly on both sides with the sugar, or dip both sides into the bowl of sugar to coat lightly. As the leaves are coated, place them in a single layer on the prepared baking sheet. Let dry in the refrigerator for at least 1 hour or up to 3 days.

To serve, using the edges of the foil as handles, lift the brownie slab onto a cutting board. Using a *santoku* (page 42) or other sharp knife, cut the slab into 2-inch squares. Top each brownie with a candied leaf. To store after cutting, return the brownies to the pan, cover with aluminum foil, sealing the foil around the edges of the pan, and keep at room temperature for up to 3 days.

Walnut Breton Cake

This is my answer-to-everything cake: I make it for meetings, I take it as a hostess gift for a weekend visit, it goes to a friend who is convalescing at home after surgery. Here's delicious proof yet again that blending just a few simple ingredients can produce something quite extraordinary. The cake is a specialty of bakers in Brittany and the Basque region of France. Your first bite will divulge a buttery, not-too-sweet dense cake with a texture similar to tender shortbread. The amount of salt in the recipe is key because salt amplifies other flavors.   **YIELD: ONE 8-INCH ROUND CAKE, 12 TO 14 SERVINGS**

1 ½ CUPS PLUS 3 TABLESPOONS (7 OUNCES/200 GRAMS) CAKE FLOUR

½ TEASPOON SALT

8 OUNCES (2 STICKS/225 GRAMS) UNSALTED BUTTER, AT ROOM TEMPERATURE

1 CUP (7 OUNCES/200 GRAMS) GRANULATED SUGAR

4 LARGE (⅓ CUP/2 ½ FL OUNCES/75 ML) EGG YOLKS

1 TABLESPOON ARMAGNAC OR OTHER BRANDY

½ CUP (2 OUNCES/55 GRAMS) FINELY CHOPPED WALNUTS (OPTIONAL)

Before baking: Center a rack in the oven and preheat the oven to 350 degrees F. Lightly butter an 8 by 2-inch round cake pan, then flour it, tapping out the excess flour. Or, lightly coat the pan with nonstick spray and flour it. Line the bottom with parchment paper. Have all of the ingredients at room temperature.

Sift together the flour and salt onto a sheet of waxed paper; set aside. In the bowl of a stand mixer fitted with the paddle attachment, beat the butter on medium speed until it is lighter in color, clings to the sides of the bowl, and has a satiny appearance, about 45 seconds. Maintaining the same speed, add the sugar in a steady stream. When all of the sugar has been added, stop the mixer and scrape down the sides of the bowl. Then continue to beat at medium speed until the mixture is very light in color and fluffy, about 3 minutes.

With the mixer still on medium speed, pour in the yolks, slowly at first. As each addition is absorbed, add the next one. Continue to beat, stopping to scrape down the sides

of the bowl at least once. Add the Armagnac during the final moments of mixing. When the mixture appears fluffy and velvety and has increased in volume, detach the paddle and bowl from the mixer. Tap the paddle against the side of the bowl to free the excess batter.

Using a rubber spatula, stir in about one-third of the flour mixture at a time. Scrape down the sides of the bowl often, and stir until smooth after each addition. Stir in the walnuts, if using. Spoon the thick batter into the prepared pan, spreading it evenly with the spatula. Use fork tines to create a lattice design on the surface.

Bake the cake until it is golden brown on top, feels firm to the touch, and is beginning to contract from the sides of the pan, 45 to 50 minutes. Transfer to a wire rack and let cool in the pan for 5 to 10 minutes.

Tilt and rotate the pan while gently tapping it on a counter to release the cake sides. Invert a wire rack on top of the cake, invert the cake onto it, and carefully lift off the pan. Slowly peel off the parchment liner, turn it over so that the sticky side faces up, and reposition it on top of the cake. Invert another rack on top, invert the cake so it is right side up, and remove the original rack. Let cool completely.

If serving the cake within 24 hours, wrap in plastic wrap and store at room temperature. For longer storage, overwrap with aluminum foil, label with the contents and date, and freeze for up to 3 weeks. To thaw, remove the foil and leave at room temperature for about 3 hours.

To serve, cut the cake into small wedges with a sharp knife.

Kouign Amman Express Pastries

This sugary yeast cake's slightly unprepossessing appearance belies its ineffably delicious butter and caramel flavor. *Kouign amman* is Celtic (an ancient language today confined to Brittany, Scotland, Ireland, Wales, and the Scottish highlands) for "cake" and "butter," respectively, and the authentic pastry originated in nineteenth-century Brittany. This serendipitous takeoff—and speedier version—evolved after I rolled out a flaky sour cream pastry (without yeast) in powdered sugar. To my delight, the sugar mixed with the moisture in the pastry and caramelized during baking. On cooling, the pastry became crunchy, much like the traditional *kouign amman*. I fill each pastry with small amounts of coconut and preserves, yielding a chewy, macaroon-like texture.   **YIELD: ABOUT 2½ DOZEN PASTRIES**

SOUR CREAM FLAKY PASTRY

2 CUPS (9 OUNCES/255 GRAMS) ALL-PURPOSE FLOUR

¼ TEASPOON SALT

8 OUNCES (2 STICKS/225 GRAMS) COLD UNSALTED BUTTER, CUT INTO ¼-INCH SLICES

½ CUP (4 OUNCES/115 GRAMS) COLD SOUR CREAM

¼ CUP (2 FL OUNCES/60 ML) WATER

COCONUT FILLING

2 CUPS (6 OUNCES/170 GRAMS) SWEETENED FLAKED DRIED COCONUT

6 TABLESPOONS (3 OUNCES/85 GRAMS) GRANULATED SUGAR

2 TABLESPOONS ALL-PURPOSE FLOUR

2 LARGE EGG WHITES

1 TEASPOON PURE VANILLA EXTRACT

½ CUP (1¾ OUNCES/50 GRAMS) POWDERED SUGAR

To make the Sour Cream Flaky Pastry: In a large bowl, stir together the flour and salt. Scatter the butter pieces over the flour mixture. With a pastry blender, cut in the butter until the mixture has many pieces of butter ranging in size from fava or lima beans to pinto beans and rolled oats.

In a small bowl, stir together the sour cream and water. Drizzle the sour cream mixture over the flour mixture and stir with a fork until the mixture begins to come together. Form into a rough mass on your work surface, working any loose flour into the dough. Shape the dough into a flattened rectangle about 8 by 5 inches, and transfer it to a lightly floured work surface.

Roll out the dough to a 16 by 8-inch rectangle. Fold the dough into thirds like a business letter: working from a short end, lift the bottom one-third of the rectangle up over the center and then fold the top third down to cover, forming a 5½ by 8-inch rectangle. Rotate the dough 90 degrees, lightly flour the work surface, and again roll the dough out into a 16 by 8-inch rectangle. Fold the dough again into thirds, wrap in plastic wrap, and refrigerate for at least 30 to 40 minutes to firm the butter and relax the pastry before using.

Return the dough to a lightly floured work surface, roll it out again into a 16 by 8-inch rectangle, and fold it again into thirds. Wrap the dough in plastic wrap and refrigerate until cold and firm, at least 4 hours or up to 3 days. For longer storage, overwrap with aluminum foil, label with the contents and date, and freeze for up to 1 month. Thaw the dough in its package in the refrigerator overnight.

Before baking: Center a rack in the oven, and preheat the oven to 375 degrees F. Lightly coat three 12-cup miniature muffin pans with nonstick spray. Line a baking sheet with parchment paper.   CONTINUED ▶

To make the Coconut Filling: In a small bowl, stir together the coconut, sugar, and flour with a rubber spatula until blended. Add the egg whites and vanilla and stir just until well blended; set aside.

To assemble the pastries: Divide the cold pastry in half (about 12 ounces/340 grams each). Wrap 1 portion in plastic wrap and refrigerate it while rolling the other portion. Lightly sprinkle some powdered sugar over a work surface, place the pastry on the surface, and then lightly sprinkle some powdered sugar over the top of the pastry. Roll out the pastry into a 12½- to 13-inch square about ⅛ inch thick. (The sugar draws out the moisture in the pastry much like salt does to zucchini slices, so the dough can soften. However, it is this thin film of sugar and moisture that bakes to create the crunchy, sweet shell of the pastries.) As you roll, apply additional powdered sugar on the work surface and the top of the pastry as needed to prevent sticking. (If the pastry softens a bit and gets slightly sticky to handle, just "stick" with it. The end product is worth it. If it is close to the dimensions suggested, the pastry is easy to expand just a bit more by lifting an edge or two and gently stretching it with your fingertips.) With a ruler and a pastry wheel, trim the ragged edges. Then measure and cut the pastry into 3-inch squares.

Lay the pastry squares across the top of the prepared cups of the miniature muffin pans, and spoon about 1½ teaspoons of the filling on each square. Bring the opposite corners of each square to the center, and press lightly to seal them. This procedure eases the pastry into each cup. (During baking, the pastries open slightly to reveal the filling.) Refrigerate the pastries in the muffin pans for 10 to 15 minutes before baking. Roll, cut, fill, and shape the remaining pastry half in the same fashion. When filling the third pan, shape the pastries in every other cup to ensure more even baking.

Place the muffin pans in the oven, spacing them about 1 inch apart. Bake the pastries until lightly golden, 20 to 25 minutes. Remove the pans from the oven. Using a thin-bladed knife to ease the pastries out of the cups, transfer the pastries to the prepared baking sheet. Return the pastries to the oven. Bake until the pastries are golden and sugary crisp, 5 to 10 minutes longer. Transfer the pastries to a wire rack to cool completely. Serve at room temperature.

If not serving the pastries the same day they are baked, stack them in sturdy airtight containers and freeze for up to 2 weeks. To serve, reheat the pastries (either frozen or thawed at room temperature) in a preheated 325 degree F oven until warm, 7 to 12 minutes. Let cool slightly before serving.

Tangy Lemon Custard Tart with Pomegranate Gelée

Jewels of pomegranate gelée decorate this colorful citrus tart, which is accented with both lemon and lime. The crunch of cornmeal in the crust provides a slightly sweet textural contrast to the creamy custard filling. Apply the gelée over the tart and then pepper it randomly with the pomegranate arils, or seeds. This tart is best served the day it is baked; refrigerate any leftovers.

To remove the seeds from a pomegranate, cut the crown end off the pomegranate, removing some of the white pith with it. Try not to pierce the seeds inside. Lightly score the rind (skin) in quarters, from the stem to the crown end. Firmly yet gently break the sections apart, following the score lines. Bend back the skin and gently scoop the seed clusters into a bowl, and then remove the pith. **YIELD: ONE 9½-INCH TART, 8 SERVINGS**

POMEGRANATE GELÉE

1 CUP (8 FL OUNCES/240 ML) BOTTLED POMEGRANATE JUICE, PREFERABLY POM BRAND

1½ TEASPOONS UNFLAVORED POWDERED GELATIN

1 TABLESPOON GRANULATED SUGAR

PASTRY

1¼ CUPS (5½ OUNCES/160 GRAMS) ALL-PURPOSE FLOUR

¼ CUP (1¾ OUNCES/50 GRAMS) GRANULATED SUGAR

2 TABLESPOONS YELLOW CORNMEAL

½ TEASPOON FINELY GRATED LEMON ZEST

½ TEASPOON FINELY GRATED LIME ZEST

⅛ TEASPOON SALT

1 LARGE EGG YOLK

1 TEASPOON PURE VANILLA EXTRACT

4 OUNCES (1 STICK/115 GRAMS) COLD UNSALTED BUTTER, CUT INTO ¼-INCH SLICES

LEMON CUSTARD FILLING

3 LARGE EGGS, AT ROOM TEMPERATURE

¾ CUP (5¼ OUNCES/150 GRAMS) GRANULATED SUGAR

⅓ CUP (3 FL OUNCES/75 ML) STRAINED FRESH LEMON JUICE

1 TABLESPOON STRAINED FRESH LIME JUICE

⅓ CUP PLUS 1 TABLESPOON (3 FL OUNCES/90 ML) HEAVY CREAM

½ CUP (2¾ OUNCES/75 GRAMS) POMEGRANATE SEEDS

To make the Pomegranate Gelée: Pour the pomegranate juice into a measuring cup. Sprinkle the gelatin over the surface, and set aside for about 5 minutes to soften. Then pour into a small saucepan, add the sugar, and heat over low heat just to dissolve the gelatin and sugar. Do not allow to boil. Remove from the heat and pour into an 8-inch round cake pan. The mixture should be ⅛ inch deep. Cover and refrigerate until set, about 1 hour.

To make the pastry: In a food processor, combine the flour, sugar, cornmeal, lemon zest, lime zest, and salt and pulse 3 or 4 times to blend. In a small bowl, mix together the egg yolk and vanilla just to combine. Scatter the butter pieces over the flour mixture. Pulse using 1-second bursts until the mixture resembles a combination of bread crumbs and coarse meal, 15 to 20 seconds. Add the egg yolk mixture and continue to pulse just until the ingredients come together.

Transfer the dough to a work surface. Beginning at the far end, and using the heel of your hand, push a small amount of the dough (about the size of an extra-large egg) away from you, smearing it on the work surface. Repeat with the remaining dough in small amounts. When you've worked all the dough in this manner, give it a couple more strokes to bring it together CONTINUED ▸

into a smooth, homogeneous unit. (This kneading technique, described on page 31, is known as *fraisage*.) Flatten the dough into a disk. Wrap in plastic wrap and refrigerate until chilled and slightly firm, at least 1 hour or up to 3 days.

Before baking: Center a rack in the oven and preheat the oven to 375 degrees F. Have ready a 9½ by 1-inch round fluted tart pan with a removable bottom.

Remove the dough from the refrigerator. If it is too firm to roll, let sit at room temperature until it is malleable enough to roll yet still cool to the touch, 15 to 30 minutes. Press the dough evenly into the bottom and up the sides of the tart pan. Or, roll out the dough on a lightly floured work surface into a 12-inch circle ⅛ to 3/16 inch thick. (Although this is a tart, the pastry is more like a pie pastry; see the directions for rolling out pie pastry on page 27.) Roll up the pastry around the rolling pin, and suspend the pin about 1 inch above the pan. Aligning the edge of the dough with the rim of the pan farthest from you, unroll it toward you. Then gently fit the dough into the pan, easing it into the crevices and up the sides. Trim away the excess dough by rolling the pin over the top of the pan. (Save any scraps for another use, if desired.)

Bake the tart shell until it is pale gold and the surface no longer looks wet, raw, or shiny, 15 to 20 minutes. Check after baking for about 5 minutes. If the pastry is puffed up, prick the center of the blistered area with a metal or wooden skewer or fork tines to release the steam. Don't prick more than is needed. Transfer to a wire rack and let cool while you prepare the filling. Leave the oven on.

To make the Lemon Custard Filling: In a medium bowl, beat the eggs with a fork just to combine. Add the sugar, lemon juice, and lime juice and mix just until blended. To remove any unincorporated egg to create a smooth filling, pour the mixture through a fine-mesh sieve set over another bowl. Stir in the cream slowly just until blended.

Place the tart pan on a rimmed baking sheet (to catch drips), and carefully pour the filling into the pastry shell. Place the tart on the baking sheet in the oven and bake until the filling appears set yet shiny on top, the center quivers a bit when the pan is gently shaken, and the edges of the crust are golden, 18 to 20 minutes. Transfer to a wire rack and let cool on the pan for about 20 minutes. Set the tart pan on a narrower elevated surface, such as a tin can, so the bottom of the pan is released as the metal rim slips down. Return the tart to the wire rack and let cool to room temperature.

To serve: At least 30 minutes before serving, remove the gelée from the refrigerator. With the tip of a paring knife, cut lines about ⅛ inch apart in both directions (the pattern will look like graph paper) to form the pomegranate jewels.

With a wide metal spatula (similar to what you would use to turn pancakes), lift the gelée from the pan to break the cut pieces apart. Lift some of the pomegranate gelée onto the same spatula, and scatter the gelée over the lemon filling. Then, scatter the pomegranate seeds over the top. Refrigerate the tart just long enough to chill the gelée pieces, about 30 minutes.

Cut the tart into wedges with a sharp knife.

Peanut Butter Pound Cake with Coconut-Date Topping

This five-ingredient pound cake is so easy to prepare, you can whip it up on a moment's notice with ingredients you probably have in your kitchen. The sweet, chewy topping of coconut and dates adds a special homey touch. **YIELD: ONE 9 BY 5-INCH CAKE, 12 SERVINGS**

PEANUT BUTTER POUND CAKE

8 OUNCES (2 STICKS/225 GRAMS) UNSALTED BUTTER, AT ROOM TEMPERATURE

1½ CUPS (10½ OUNCES/300 GRAMS) GRANULATED SUGAR

½ CUP (5 OUNCES/140 GRAMS) CREAMY PEANUT BUTTER

5 LARGE EGGS, LIGHTLY BEATEN

2 CUPS (9 OUNCES/255 GRAMS) ALL-PURPOSE FLOUR

COCONUT-DATE TOPPING

2 TABLESPOONS UNSALTED BUTTER

⅓ CUP FIRMLY PACKED (2¼ OUNCES/65 GRAMS) LIGHT BROWN SUGAR

3 TABLESPOONS HEAVY CREAM

½ CUP (1¼ OUNCES/35 GRAMS) SWEETENED SHREDDED DRIED COCONUT

5 PITTED DATES (1¼ OUNCES/35 GRAMS), COARSELY CHOPPED

Before baking: Center a rack in the oven and preheat the oven to 350 degrees F.

Butter a 9 by 5 by 3-inch loaf pan, then flour it, tapping out the excess flour. Or, lightly coat the pan with nonstick spray and flour it. Have all of the ingredients at room temperature.

To make the Peanut Butter Pound Cake: In the bowl of a stand mixer fitted with the paddle attachment, beat the butter on medium-low speed until smooth, about 45 seconds. Scrape down the sides of the bowl. On medium speed, add the sugar in a steady stream, and beat until the mixture is light, stopping the mixer occasionally to scrape down the sides of the bowl. Add the peanut butter and beat until fluffy and well incorporated, 2 to 3 minutes. Maintaining the same speed, add the eggs, about 3 tablespoons at a time, beating after each addition until

incorporated. With the mixer on the lowest speed, add the flour in two additions, mixing after each addition until combined. Pour the batter into the loaf pan, and spread evenly with a rubber spatula.

Bake the cake until golden brown and a round wooden toothpick or skewer inserted in the center comes out clean, about 65 minutes. Transfer to a wire rack and let cool in the pan for about 10 minutes. Tilt and rotate the pan while gently tapping it on a counter to release the cake sides. If they don't release, slip a thin metal spatula between the still-warm cake and the pan and run the spatula carefully along the entire perimeter of the pan. Invert a wire rack on top of the cake, invert the cake onto it, and carefully lift off the pan. Invert another rack on top, invert the cake so it is right side up, and remove the original rack. Let cool completely before making the topping.

To make the Coconut-Date Topping: Transfer the cooled cake to an unlined rimmed baking sheet; set aside. Have on hand a kitchen torch, or place an oven rack about 6 inches from the oven broiler and preheat the broiler to medium-high while preparing the topping. In a small, heavy saucepan, melt the butter with the sugar over low heat. Add the cream, coconut, and dates and stir until blended. Remove from the heat and spread the mixture over the top of the cake (you may not need all of it). Toast the topping with the kitchen torch, or broil the topping for 45 to 90 seconds. It is ready when it is bubbly and golden. Let cool completely before serving.

To serve, slice the cake with a serrated knife.

Pecan–Pine Nut Tassie Crostata

Pecan tassie tartlets are one of the South's signature sweets and are my inspiration for this dessert. Similar to an Italian *crostata* (an open-faced tart) in form and in spirit, the tender cookie-like dough of the tassie is rolled thinly and shaped to reveal a slightly chewy pecan–pine nut filling. Cutting one large *crostata* into narrow wedges serves many, eliminating the need to form individual tartlets. **YIELD: ONE 11-INCH *CROSTATA*, ABOUT 14 SERVINGS**

1 RECIPE SINGLE-CRUST CROSTATA PASTRY (PAGE 362), MADE WITHOUT VANILLA EXTRACT

FILLING

1 LARGE EGG

⅔ CUP FIRMLY PACKED (4½ OUNCES/130 GRAMS) LIGHT BROWN SUGAR

1 TABLESPOON UNSALTED BUTTER, MELTED AND LUKEWARM

1 TEASPOON PURE VANILLA EXTRACT

⅛ TEASPOON SALT

⅓ CUP (1¾ OUNCES/50 GRAMS) PINE NUTS

⅓ CUP (1¼ OUNCES/35 GRAMS) FINELY CHOPPED PECANS

Before baking: Center a rack in the oven and preheat the oven to 350 degrees F. Line a large baking sheet with parchment paper, and dust the paper with flour.

Following the directions on page 31, roll out the pastry into a 12-inch circle about ³⁄₁₆ inch thick and shape into a *crostata* crust on the baking sheet. Bake partially for 20 to 22 minutes. Remove the baking sheet to a wire rack and let the *crostata* crust cool for about 10 minutes while you prepare the filling.

To make the filling: In a medium bowl, mix together the egg, sugar, butter, vanilla, salt, pine nuts, and pecans in that order, until blended.

Pour the filling into the center of the pastry and spread it evenly over the dough with an offset spatula. Bake the *crostata* until the filling is set (it will form a thin, smooth semitranslucent layer over the nuts with a slight sheen) and the pastry border is golden, 20 to 23 minutes. Transfer the pan to a wire rack and let cool completely.

To serve, cross 2 long, sturdy spatulas and slip under the *crostata*, or slip 1 large, wide metal spatula or a rimless baking sheet under the *crostata*, and transfer it to a serving plate. Cut into wedges with a sharp knife. Wrap any leftovers in aluminum foil and store at room temperature for up to 2 days.

Fresh Pineapple Crumble Cake

The pairing of tangy pineapple and rich hazelnuts in this moist, streusel-topped cake creates an unexpected combination sure to bring kudos to the baker. This is an ideal cake to make year-round, since fresh pineapple is always available.

A rotary nut (cheese) grinder is the best tool for grinding the hazelnuts, but you can use a food processor. Process the nuts with 2 tablespoons of the sugar until finely ground and powdery. The texture of the cake will be slightly coarser than if the nuts were ground in a rotary grinder, but the flavor remains delicious. **YIELD: ONE 9-INCH ROUND CAKE, 12 SERVINGS**

STREUSEL

6 TABLESPOONS (1¾ OUNCES/50 GRAMS) ALL-PURPOSE FLOUR

6 TABLESPOONS FIRMLY PACKED (2¾ OUNCES/75 GRAMS) LIGHT BROWN SUGAR

3 TABLESPOONS UNSALTED BUTTER, SOFTENED

¼ TEASPOON GROUND CINNAMON

FRESH PINEAPPLE CAKE

1½ CUPS (9½ OUNCES/270 GRAMS) MEDIUM-SIZED FRESH PINEAPPLE CHUNKS (ABOUT 38 CHUNKS)

1½ CUPS (6¾ OUNCES/195 GRAMS) ALL-PURPOSE FLOUR

1 TEASPOON BAKING POWDER

¼ TEASPOON SALT

½ CUP PLUS 2 TABLESPOONS (3 OUNCES/85 GRAMS) HAZELNUTS, FINELY GROUND TO YIELD 1 CUP

8 OUNCES (2 STICKS/225 GRAMS) UNSALTED BUTTER, AT ROOM TEMPERATURE

1 CUP (7 OUNCES/200 GRAMS) GRANULATED SUGAR

3 LARGE EGGS, LIGHTLY BEATEN

1 TEASPOON PURE VANILLA EXTRACT

2 TABLESPOONS POWDERED SUGAR FOR GARNISH

Before baking: Center a rack in the oven and preheat the oven to 350 degrees F. Butter a 9 by 2-inch round cake pan, then flour it, tapping out the excess. Line the bottom with parchment paper. Have all of the ingredients at room temperature.

To make the streusel: In a medium bowl, mix together the flour, sugar, butter, and cinnamon with your fingertips until the mixture is lumpy; set aside.

To make the Fresh Pineapple Cake: Set the pineapple chunks on a couple of strips of paper toweling to absorb some of their juice; set aside while preparing the batter.

Sift together the flour, baking powder, and salt onto a sheet of waxed paper. Pour the hazelnuts on top of the flour mixture and set aside.

In the bowl of a stand mixer fitted with the paddle attachment, beat the butter on medium speed until creamy and smooth, 30 to 45 seconds. Add the sugar in a steady stream and continue to beat until light and fluffy, 2 to 3 minutes, stopping the mixer occasionally to scrape down the sides of the bowl. Add the eggs, about 3 tablespoons at a time, beating after each addition until incorporated. Add the vanilla toward the end of mixing in the eggs. On the lowest speed, gradually add the flour mixture and beat just until incorporated. Stop the mixer occasionally to scrape down the sides of the bowl.

Spoon half of the batter into the prepared pan and smooth the surface evenly with a rubber spatula. Scatter half of the pineapple chunks (about 19) over the top and press them gently into the batter. Spoon the remaining batter over the pineapple, and smooth it with the spatula. Scatter the remaining pineapple chunks over the top and press them gently into the batter. Sprinkle the streusel evenly over the top.

Bake the cake until it is golden on top, springs back when gently pressed in the center, and a round wooden toothpick inserted into the center comes CONTINUED ►

out free of cake, 43 to 45 minutes. Transfer to a wire rack and let cool in the pan for 10 minutes. Tilt and rotate the pan while gently tapping it on a counter to release the cake sides. If they don't release, slip a thin metal spatula between the still-warm cake and the pan and run the spatula carefully along the entire perimeter of the pan. Invert a wire rack on top of the cake, invert the cake onto it, and carefully lift off the pan. Slowly peel off the parchment liner, turn it over so that the sticky side faces up, and reposition it on top of the cake. Invert another rack on top, invert the cake so it is streusel side up, and remove the original rack. Let cool completely before dusting with the powdered sugar.

This cake freezes beautifully. Wrap it securely in plastic wrap, then overwrap with aluminum foil, label with the contents and date, and freeze for up to 1 week. Thaw at room temperature, 3 to 4 hours. Dust with the powdered sugar before serving.

To serve, cut the cake into wedges with a sharp knife.

Cinnamon Bubble Buns

These whimsical buns remind me of my college days at the University of Michigan, when Dorothy Temme, our family's loving housekeeper and an awesome baker, sent them to me in care packages. Although I've adapted the recipe a bit and added more sour cream for extra richness, the unique look of the buns remains the same. Unlike many yeast doughs, this one contains baking soda, which enables the buns to brown despite the presence of sour cream. (Because sour cream is an acid, it can inhibit browning.) Each bun resembles a cluster of bubbles like the clusters children blow on carefree summer days.

You can mix the dough, knead it, place it in a large bowl, cover the top of the bowl securely, and refrigerate it for 8 hours and up to overnight before shaping. When you are ready to shape the buns, remove the dough from the refrigerator, gently punch it down, let it stand at room temperature for 30 minutes, shape the buns, set aside to rise for an hour, and then bake as directed.

YIELD: 1 DOZEN BUNS

SOUR CREAM YEAST DOUGH

2¼ TEASPOONS (1 ENVELOPE) ACTIVE DRY YEAST

¼ CUP (2 FL OUNCES/60 ML) WARM WATER (100 TO 110 DEGREES F)

3 TABLESPOONS UNSALTED BUTTER, MELTED AND COOLED

⅔ CUP (5½ OUNCES/155 GRAMS) SOUR CREAM

3 TABLESPOONS GRANULATED SUGAR

1 LARGE EGG

1 TEASPOON PURE VANILLA EXTRACT

2½ CUPS (11¼ OUNCES/320 GRAMS) ALL-PURPOSE FLOUR, PLUS 1 TO 2 TABLESPOONS FOR KNEADING, IF NECESSARY

½ TEASPOON SALT

¼ TEASPOON BAKING SODA

CINNAMON-SUGAR COATING

⅓ CUP FIRMLY PACKED (2¼ OUNCES/65 GRAMS) LIGHT BROWN SUGAR

1 TEASPOON GROUND CINNAMON

2 TABLESPOONS UNSALTED BUTTER, MELTED

TRANSLUCENT VANILLA GLAZE

1¼ CUPS (4¾ OUNCES/135 GRAMS) POWDERED SUGAR

1 TABLESPOON UNSALTED BUTTER, MELTED

1 TABLESPOON WHOLE MILK

1 TEASPOON PURE VANILLA EXTRACT

To make the Sour Cream Yeast Dough: Sprinkle the yeast over the water in the bowl of a stand mixer; set aside for 5 to 10 minutes until bubbly. Add the butter, sour cream, sugar, egg, and vanilla to the yeast mixture and stir to combine with a rubber spatula. Attach the bowl to the mixer, and fit the mixer with the paddle attachment. Beat in 2 cups (9 ounces/255 grams) of the flour, the salt, and baking soda on medium-low speed until incorporated, 30 to 45 seconds. Add the remaining ½ cup (2¼ ounces/65 grams) flour and beat until a smooth, moderately soft dough forms.

Turn the dough out onto a lightly floured work surface and knead until smooth and satiny, about 3 minutes. At first the dough will be sticky. Add no more than 1 to 2 tablespoons additional flour during the kneading to combat the stickiness. Place the dough back in the bowl, cover tightly with plastic wrap, and let rise in a warm place (about 70 degrees F) until doubled in size, about 1 hour. The dough is ready when a finger gently pressed into it leaves an indentation. Meanwhile, prepare the pan and make the Cinnamon-Sugar Coating. CONTINUED ➤

Before baking: Center a rack in the oven and preheat the oven to 350 degrees F. Lightly coat a 12-cup standard muffin pan with nonstick spray, then flour the cups, tapping out the excess flour. Or, butter and flour the cups.

To make the Cinnamon-Sugar Coating: In a small bowl, stir together the sugar and cinnamon; set nearby. Place the melted butter in a small, shallow dish.

To shape the buns: Gently punch the dough down to deflate it. Form it into a long cylinder, and divide it into 12 equal portions (each portion is about 1¾ ounces/ 50 grams). Using kitchen scissors, a small metal spatula, or a dough scraper, divide 1 portion into 6 equal pieces, and then shape each piece into a ball. One at a time, roll the balls first in the butter and then in the cinnamon sugar. Arrange 5 balls next to one another in a circle in each prepared muffin cup, and then, using a fingertip, poke the sixth ball down slightly in the center. Repeat with the remaining 11 dough portions. Loosely cover the buns with plastic wrap and set them aside in a warm place (about 70 degrees F) until puffy and doubled in volume, about 40 minutes. The dough is ready to bake when a finger gently pressed into it leaves an indentation.

Bake the buns until golden, 20 to 22 minutes. Transfer the pan to a wire rack and let cool for 5 to 8 minutes. Then tilt the pan and gently tap it on a counter to release the buns. If necessary, slip a knife blade between the pan and the bun to release. Transfer the buns to a wire rack.

To make the Translucent Vanilla Glaze: In a small bowl, stir together the sugar, butter, milk, and vanilla until smooth and just the right consistency to apply a thin glaze over each bun. If it is too thick, add water, 1 teaspoon at a time.

The buns can be warm or at room temperature when you glaze them. Slip a sheet of waxed paper under the rack holding the buns to catch any drips. Using a pastry brush, coat each bun with the glaze. Serve the buns warm or at room temperature.

For the best taste and texture, serve the buns the same day they are baked. For longer storage, bake as directed and let cool completely after baking but do not glaze. Place the unglazed buns in a sturdy airtight container, label with the contents and date, and freeze for up to 2 weeks. To reheat, wrap the frozen buns in aluminum foil and place them in a preheated 300 degree F oven until heated through, about 10 minutes. Make the glaze and glaze the buns while they are warm.

Almond-Rhubarb Snack Cake

With its elegant, celery-like stalks and rosy complexion, rhubarb serves as my pivot point from winter to spring. It's essential to pair rhubarb with a generous amount of sugar and to cook it long enough to mellow its astringency. You will be rewarded with a unique and toothsome flavor perfectly suited to this simple, buttery cake. Cutting the stalks into thin slices ensures that they'll cook through quickly and prevents them from sinking to the bottom during baking.   YIELD: ONE 9-INCH ROUND CAKE, 10 SERVINGS

CAKE

1¾ CUPS (7 OUNCES/200 GRAMS) CAKE FLOUR

½ TEASPOON BAKING SODA

¼ TEASPOON SALT

⅛ TEASPOON BAKING POWDER

4 OUNCES (1 STICK/115 GRAMS) UNSALTED BUTTER, AT ROOM TEMPERATURE

1 CUP (7 OUNCES/200 GRAMS) GRANULATED SUGAR

½ TEASPOON PURE ALMOND EXTRACT

½ TEASPOON PURE VANILLA EXTRACT

2 LARGE EGGS, LIGHTLY BEATEN

¾ CUP (6 FL OUNCES/180 ML) WELL-SHAKEN BUTTERMILK

4½ OUNCES (130 GRAMS) NARROW RHUBARB STALKS (ABOUT 3), TRIMMED AND CUT INTO ⅛-INCH-THICK SLICES TO YIELD 1 CUP PACKED

½ CUP (1¾ OUNCES/50 GRAMS) NATURAL OR BLANCHED SLICED ALMONDS

ALMOND TOPPING

2 TABLESPOONS UNSALTED BUTTER, MELTED

1 TABLESPOON ALL-PURPOSE FLOUR

1 TABLESPOON HEAVY CREAM

⅓ CUP (2¼ OUNCES/65 GRAMS) GRANULATED SUGAR

⅓ CUP (1 OUNCE/30 GRAMS) NATURAL OR BLANCHED SLICED ALMONDS

Before baking: Center a rack in the oven and preheat the oven to 350 degrees F.

Butter a 9-inch round springform pan with 2¾- or 3-inch sides. Line the bottom with parchment paper.

To make the cake: Have all of the ingredients at room temperature. Sift together the flour, baking soda, salt, and baking powder onto a sheet of waxed paper; set aside. In the bowl of a stand mixer fitted with the paddle attachment, beat the butter on medium speed until smooth and creamy, 30 to 45 seconds. Add the sugar in a steady stream, stopping the mixer occasionally to scrape down the sides of the bowl. Continue to beat on medium speed until the mixture is very light in color and texture, about 3 minutes. Add the extracts during the final moments of mixing.

With the mixer on medium speed, add the eggs, about 3 tablespoons at a time, beating after each addition until incorporated. When the mixture is fluffy, reduce the speed to low and add the flour mixture in three additions alternately with the buttermilk in two additions, beginning and ending with the flour mixture and mixing after each addition only until incorporated. Stop the mixer and scrape down the sides of the bowl after each addition. Fold in the rhubarb slices with a rubber spatula. Spoon the batter into the pan, and spread evenly with the spatula.

Bake the cake until a round wooden toothpick inserted in the center comes out free of cake, 40 to 45 minutes.

About 15 minutes before the cake is ready, begin making the Almond Topping: In a small saucepan, mix together the butter, flour, cream, and sugar and stir over low heat just until blended.   CONTINUED ▶

About 10 minutes before the cake is ready, remove the cake from the oven, pour the topping mixture over it, and sprinkle the almonds over the top. Return the cake to the oven and bake until the topping spreads over the cake and just begins to bubble, about 10 minutes. Transfer to a wire rack and let cool in the pan for 20 minutes.

Slowly release the springform clasp and carefully remove the pan sides. Let the cake cool on its base on the rack for 10 minutes longer. Then invert a wire rack on top of the cake, invert the cake onto it, and carefully lift off the base. Slowly peel off the parchment liner, turn it over so that the sticky side faces up, and reposition it on top of the cake. Invert another rack on top, invert the cake so it is right side up, and remove the original rack. Let cool completely.

Serve at room temperature, cut into wedges with a sharp knife. Cover any leftover cake with aluminum foil and store at cool room temperature for up to 2 days.

Strawberry-Mango Shortcakes with Basil Syrup

This not-too-sweet yet rich shortcake gets a pleasant boost of flavor from a drizzle of basil syrup, which complements the fruits perfectly. I look for strawberries that have an exceptionally sweet flavor and deep red color throughout. Often the berries are organic, but don't overlook local-grown varieties. The taste test just can't be beat when it comes to selecting the best. Plan in advance when you need mangoes, as it is rare to find ripe ones in the supermarket (they can take up to a week to ripen). Years ago, I was privileged to be in the same place at the same time as noted actress and cookbook author Madhur Jaffrey, and heard her say, "Put the mangoes under your bed. When you can smell their fragrance, they're ripe."

A deluxe filling of crème fraîche and heavy cream lets you know you are indeed eating a shortcake, but this version elevates the traditional concept from ordinary to extraordinary. The shortcake recipe doubles easily. If you increase the recipe, divide the dough in half, wrap one piece loosely in plastic wrap, and refrigerate while you are forming shortcakes from the other half. Place all of the shortcakes on a large baking sheet, if possible, and bake them at the same time.

YIELD: 6 TO 8 SHORTCAKES, 6 TO 8 SERVINGS

FRUIT FILLING

2 PINTS (8 TO 10 OUNCES/225 TO 280 GRAMS) STRAWBERRIES, HULLED AND SLICED HORIZONTALLY TO YIELD ABOUT 4 CUPS

¼ TO ½ CUP (1¾ TO 3½ OUNCES/50 TO 100 GRAMS) GRANULATED SUGAR, DEPENDING ON SWEETNESS OF FRUIT

¼ CUP FRESH BASIL LEAVES, CUT INTO CHIFFONADE (FINE STRIPS)

3 MEDIUM (ABOUT 7 OUNCES/200 GRAMS EACH) OR 2 LARGE (ABOUT 1 POUND/455 GRAMS EACH) RIPE MANGOES

SHORTCAKE BISCUITS

1 CUP (4½ OUNCES/130 GRAMS) ALL-PURPOSE FLOUR

1 CUP (4 OUNCES/115 GRAMS) CAKE FLOUR

2 TABLESPOONS GRANULATED SUGAR

1 TABLESPOON BAKING POWDER

½ TEASPOON SALT

4 OUNCES (1 STICK/115 GRAMS) COLD UNSALTED BUTTER, CUT INTO 10 SLICES

⅔ TO ¾ CUP (5½ TO 6 FL OUNCES/165 TO 180 ML) COLD WHOLE MILK

2 TABLESPOONS SANDING OR GRANULATED SUGAR

CREAM FILLING

2 CUPS (16 FL OUNCES/480 ML) HEAVY CREAM

1 CUP (8 OUNCES/225 GRAMS) CRÈME FRAÎCHE

1 TABLESPOON GRANULATED SUGAR

1 TEASPOON PURE VANILLA EXTRACT

POWDERED SUGAR FOR DECORATION

To prepare the fruit: Put the strawberries in a large bowl, pour the sugar over the berries, sprinkle with the basil, and toss gently. Cover and set aside at room temperature for at least 2 hours.

Using a fork, mash one-third of the berries in the bowl, toss the mixture again, and let stand for another hour. (You can make this 1 day ahead. Refrigerate CONTINUED ▸

the mixture after mashing some of the berries, and bring the berries to room temperature before serving.)

Peel the mangoes and cut lengthwise into ½-inch-thick slices, cutting from one side and then the other side of the large central pit. Cut the slices lengthwise into ¾-inch-wide sticks. Cut the sticks crosswise into ¾-inch cubes, place in a medium bowl, cover, and set aside at room temperature.

Before baking: Center a rack in the oven and preheat the oven to 400 degrees F. Line a baking sheet with parchment paper. Have ready a sturdy 2½-inch round metal cutter.

To make the Shortcake Biscuits: In a large bowl, whisk together the flours, sugar, baking powder, and salt. Scatter the butter pieces over the flour mixture. With a pastry blender, cut in the butter just until the mixture resembles a very coarse meal. Add the milk, about one-third at a time, and toss gently with a fork (preferably a blending fork) after each addition until the mixture develops moist clumps and leaves the sides of the bowl to form a dough.

Turn the dough out onto a floured work surface and knead gently only 2 or 3 times to bring it together into a cohesive ball. Pat or roll out the dough about ½ inch thick.

Using the cutter, cut out 6 circles. Be sure to press the cutter straight down to cut each circle. Twisting the cutter seals the edges of the biscuits and limits their rise. (Using a glass as a cutter does not cut as cleanly as a metal cutter. As you press the glass into the dough, it tends to seal the edges, which affects how high the biscuits will rise as

they bake. When you cut with a metal cutter, both the top and bottom of the biscuit remain open, so that air can escape as you press down.)

Set the dough circles about 2 inches apart on the prepared baking sheet. Sprinkle the tops evenly with the sanding sugar. If desired, gather the scraps, gently pat the dough ½ inch thick, and cut out another circle or two (the biscuits made from scraps won't be as tender as the first ones, but they will be tender).

Bake for 10 minutes, then reduce the heat to 375 degrees F and bake until the shortcakes are golden, about 10 minutes longer. Transfer the biscuits to a wire rack and let cool completely. For the best texture and flavor, serve them at room temperature as soon as possible after they have cooled and no more than a few hours.

To make the Cream Filling: In a large bowl, combine the cream, crème fraîche, sugar, and vanilla and whip with a handheld electric mixer on medium-low speed or by hand with a whisk just until soft peaks form.

To assemble the shortcakes: Split the biscuits in half horizontally either by gently pulling them apart with your fingertips or cutting them with a serrated knife. Place a biscuit bottom, cut side up, on each plate. Spoon ⅓ to ½ cup of the strawberries on the biscuit bottom, top with about ¼ cup of the mango pieces, and then ¼ to ⅓ cup of the whipped cream. Cover with the top half of the biscuit, cut side down. Lightly dust each shortcake and its plate with powdered sugar.

Tender Butter Cake with Nut-Crunch Topping

No frosting required on this easy-to-assemble rich butter cake. To make the dessert, pour the syrupy topping into the pan, and then spread the batter on top. Together they bake into one large, handsome cake that, when inverted, has its candy-like topping already in place. The unusual topping was inspired by the late, great Richard Sax (author of *Classic Home Desserts*), a kind and generous man who was one of our nation's most talented, popular, and prolific food writers, and someone whom I was privileged to call a friend. **YIELD: ONE 10-INCH TUBE CAKE, 12 TO 14 SERVINGS**

GLAZE

2½ OUNCES (5½ TABLESPOONS/70 GRAMS) UNSALTED BUTTER, AT ROOM TEMPERATURE

½ CUP (1¾ OUNCES/50 GRAMS) NATURAL OR BLANCHED SLICED ALMONDS

½ CUP (2½ OUNCES/70 GRAMS) COARSELY CHOPPED HAZELNUTS

¼ CUP (1¾ OUNCES/50 GRAMS) GRANULATED SUGAR

¼ CUP FIRMLY PACKED (1¾ OUNCES/50 GRAMS) LIGHT BROWN SUGAR

2 TABLESPOONS HONEY

2 TABLESPOONS STORE-BOUGHT PLAIN FINE BREAD CRUMBS

CAKE

2½ CUPS (10½ OUNCES/300 GRAMS) CAKE FLOUR

1 TEASPOON BAKING POWDER

⅛ TEASPOON SALT

9 OUNCES (2¼ STICKS/255 GRAMS) UNSALTED BUTTER, AT ROOM TEMPERATURE

1¾ CUPS (11½ OUNCES/325 GRAMS) GRANULATED SUGAR

5 LARGE EGGS, LIGHTLY BEATEN

1 TEASPOON PURE VANILLA EXTRACT

⅛ TEASPOON PURE ALMOND EXTRACT

¼ CUP (2 FL OUNCES/60 ML) WHOLE MILK

Before baking: Center a rack in the oven and preheat the oven to 350 degrees F. Generously butter a 10 by 4¼-inch tube pan. (If the pan has a removable bottom, that's fine.) Have all of the ingredients for making the cake at room temperature.

To make the glaze: In a small, heavy saucepan, melt the butter over medium heat. Add the almonds and hazelnuts and cook for 1 minute, stirring occasionally. Add the sugars and the honey and stir just until the sugars dissolve and the glaze bubbles, about 2 minutes. Remove from the heat and let cool for 5 minutes. Pour the glaze into the prepared pan. Let cool for another 5 minutes, then use a rubber spatula to distribute it evenly over the bottom and about 1 inch up the sides of the pan. Add the bread crumbs to the pan and tilt and tap the pan as necessary to coat it evenly.

To make the cake: Sift together the flour, baking powder, and salt onto a sheet of waxed paper; set aside. In the bowl of a stand mixer fitted with the paddle attachment, beat the butter on medium-low speed until creamy, about 45 seconds. Increase the speed to medium and add the granulated sugar in a steady stream. Continue to beat until the mixture is very light in color and texture, 3 to 4 minutes. Stop the mixer occasionally to scrape down the sides of the bowl.

With the mixer on medium speed, add the eggs slowly at first, about 1 tablespoon at a time, beating after each addition until incorporated. If the mixture appears curdled, stop adding the eggs, increase the speed slightly and beat until the mixture looks smooth again. Resume beating at medium speed and add the remaining eggs. Continue beating until the mixture is fluffy and pale ivory in color. The entire process of CONTINUED ▶

adding and beating in the eggs should take about 3 minutes. Toward the end of mixing, add the extracts. On the lowest speed, add the flour mixture in three additions, mixing after each addition until incorporated. Stop the mixer occasionally to scrape down the sides of the bowl. Pour in the milk and mix just until blended and smooth. Spoon the batter into the prepared pan and spread it evenly with a rubber spatula.

Bake the cake until it is golden, the top springs back when pressed lightly, and a round wooden toothpick or skewer inserted in the center comes out free of batter, 55 to 65 minutes. Transfer the pan to a wire rack and let cool for about 15 minutes. Invert a wire rack on top of the cake, invert the cake onto it, and carefully lift off the pan (the glaze that was in the bottom of the pan is now on top of the cake). Let cool completely before serving.

To store, place under a cake dome or cover lightly with aluminum foil and keep at room temperature for up to 2 days. (The glaze does not freeze well.)

Red Velvet Cake Roll

My twist on the classic red velvet cake takes the form of a roulade rolled around a silky white chocolate cream. To disguise the red color from unsuspecting guests, I dust the cake with powdered sugar. Only when you slice the roulade do you see the filling and the cake's shocking color. Here, raspberries accompany each serving, but you can instead pair the cake with Red-Hot Poached Pears (page 372), which will mirror its red and white design.

YIELD: ONE 15-INCH ROLLED CAKE, 12 TO 14 SERVINGS

CAKE

1 CUP (4½ OUNCES/130 GRAMS) ALL-PURPOSE FLOUR

2 TABLESPOONS UNSWEETENED NATURAL COCOA POWDER

½ TEASPOON BAKING SODA

⅛ TEASPOON SALT

½ CUP (4 FL OUNCES/120 ML) MILK

1 TEASPOON PURE VANILLA EXTRACT

1 TEASPOON APPLE CIDER OR WHITE VINEGAR, 5% ACIDITY

4 OUNCES (1 STICK/115 GRAMS) UNSALTED BUTTER,
    AT ROOM TEMPERATURE

¾ CUP (5¼ OUNCES/150 GRAMS) GRANULATED SUGAR

1 LARGE EGG, LIGHTLY BEATEN

1 TABLESPOON LIQUID RED FOOD COLORING
    (½ FL OUNCE/15 ML)

WHITE CHOCOLATE–CREAM CHEESE FILLING

ONE 8-OUNCE (225-GRAM) PACKAGE CREAM CHEESE,
    AT ROOM TEMPERATURE

5 OUNCES (140 GRAMS) WHITE CHOCOLATE, MELTED (PAGE 17)

2 OUNCES (½ STICK/55 GRAMS) UNSALTED BUTTER, SOFTENED

⅓ CUP (1¼ OUNCES/35 GRAMS) POWDERED SUGAR, SIFTED

½ TEASPOON PURE ALMOND EXTRACT

1 CUP (4 TO 5 OUNCES/115 TO 140 GRAMS) RED RASPBERRIES,
    PICKED OVER FOR STEMS (OPTIONAL)

POWDERED SUGAR FOR DECORATION

RED RASPBERRIES, PICKED OVER FOR STEMS, FOR SERVING

Before baking: Center a rack in the oven and preheat the oven to 375 degrees F. Coat a small area in the center of a 15½ by 10½ by 1-inch pan (jelly-roll pan) with nonstick spray. Line the pan with aluminum foil, pressing the foil into the contours of the pan and leaving a 2-inch overhang at each short end (the spray anchors the foil in place to make buttering easier). Butter the foil, then flour it, tapping out the excess flour. Have all of the ingredients at room temperature.

To make the cake: Sift together the flour, cocoa, baking soda, and salt onto a sheet of waxed paper; set aside. In a small bowl, stir together the milk, vanilla, and apple cider. In the bowl of a stand mixer fitted with the paddle attachment, beat the butter on medium-low speed until creamy and smooth, about 1 minute. Increase the speed to medium and add the granulated sugar in a steady stream. Continue to beat until light in color and fluffy in texture, about 2 minutes, stopping the mixer occasionally to scrape down the sides of the bowl.

With the mixer on medium speed, add the egg slowly, about 1 tablespoon at a time, beating after each addition until incorporated and stopping the mixer occasionally to scrape down the sides of the bowl. On the lowest speed, add the flour mixture in two or three additions alternately with the milk mixture in one or two additions, beginning and ending with the flour mixture and mixing after each addition only until incorporated smoothly. Stop the mixer after each addition and scrape down the sides of the bowl. Maintaining the same speed, add the food coloring and mix well to color the batter evenly. Without delay, spoon the batter into the prepared pan, spreading evenly with a rubber spatula.

Bake the cake until it is set on top and springs back when lightly pressed in the center, about CONTINUED ➤

10 minutes. Transfer the pan to a wire rack. If necessary, run a thin knife blade around the perimeter of the pan to loosen the cake sides. Then pull up on the foil overhang and carefully transfer the cake to a wire rack. Without delay, place a sheet of foil over the cake and manipulate the foil to make a shallow tent (a tent holds in the moisture as the cake cools, but prevents the foil from sticking to the cake). Let cool for about 45 minutes, then proceed to assemble the dessert.

While the cake is cooling, make the White Chocolate–Cream Cheese Filling: In a bowl of the stand mixer fitted with the paddle attachment, beat the cream cheese on medium-low speed until smooth. Pour in half of the chocolate and beat until smooth, stopping the mixer occasionally and scraping the mixture clinging to the sides into the center of the bowl. Pour in the remaining chocolate and beat just until combined. Add the butter and then the sugar and almond extract and beat until smooth and creamy. Use right away, or store in a covered container in the refrigerator. When ready to use, remove from the refrigerator, bring to room temperature, and beat with a rubber spatula, small whisk, or fork until smooth and creamy. You should have about 1⅓ cups.

To assemble the cake: Remove the foil from the top of the cake. Transfer the cake on its bottom sheet of foil to a work surface, placing it so that one of its long sides is parallel to the edge of the surface closest to you. Place another long sheet of aluminum foil on the work surface nearby. Using an offset spatula, spread 1 cup plus about 2 tablespoons of the filling evenly over the cake, leaving a ½-inch border uncovered on the long side farthest from

you. (The leftover filling, along with a few berries, makes a good kitchen snack for the baker.) Place the raspberries, if using, randomly on the filling along the length of the cake.

Begin rolling the cake by flipping the edge nearest you over onto itself. Then, with the aid of the foil that extends beyond the short sides, roll up the cake lengthwise until you reach the far long side. As you work, wrap the foil around the roll to assist in rounding the shape (otherwise the cake will stick to your hands). Place the roll in its foil across the bottom third of a 24-inch-long piece of parchment paper, and follow the directions on page 25 for compressing the cake into a uniform roll. Carefully lift the roll in the aluminum foil and set it, seam side down, on the fresh sheet of foil. Wrap the cake securely in the foil. Transfer the foil-wrapped roll to a baking sheet or shallow tray and refrigerate for about 30 minutes to help set the filling.

To serve: Remove the cake from the refrigerator and peel off and discard the foil. Carefully lift the roll onto a serving plate with the aid of a long, wide spatula or a rimless baking sheet. (If not serving right away, cover loosely with plastic wrap to keep the cake's surface from drying out and return to the refrigerator to serve the same day.) Dust the cake with powdered sugar. Using a serrated knife and a sawing motion, cut the roll into ½-inch-thick slices. Center each portion on a dessert plate. Accompany with the raspberries.

Crowd-Pleasing Favorites

WHEN I BAKE FOR LARGE GROUPS—whether family, friends, or colleagues—I set aside my penchant for thinking too far outside of the box. For such occasions, I search my recipe files for desserts that have two qualities: they provide enough generous servings to accommodate the guest list, and they contain ingredients that are all-time favorites. A few careful calculations help me figure out if I'll need more than one recipe's worth, or a few different kinds of desserts to satisfy the multitude.

I always find that the cakes, cookies, and pies that please crowds the most evoke memories of delights people have eaten in the past. And yet, to keep the spark of excitement alive in a large gathering, the recipes need to be innovative enough to make everyone stop and take notice.

Butterscotch Spiral Coffee Cake is a wonderful example. It may trigger a memory of Grandma making her best homemade pudding. The same cherished flavor is there, for sure, but the form is novel and will invite tasters to take a second piece, both to relive the recollection and to experience a present-day pleasure.

Some gatherings necessitate finger-friendly fare. I suggest Congo Brownies, two layers of widely loved flavors: nutty Congo bars and chocolaty brownies. And Classic Butter Cake Cupcakes topped with a swirl of White Chocolate–Sour Cream Frosting are just as fun to eat as when you were a kid. Millionaire's Shortbread is a clever way to congratulate someone's recent promotion. No matter how big the dollar sign attached to the advancement is, everyone who samples the decadent bars will be happy to be part of the celebration.

Other get-togethers allow you to serve fork-and-plate desserts, like Banana-Split Cream Pie, which will have everyone thinking back to the traditional ice-cream parlor version and marveling at how the flavors have been reimagined in a new presentation. Or, one slice of Mocha-Almond O'Marble Cake will have your guests mesmerized by the marbling of the almond batter and chocolate-mocha batter.

With a few of these recipes, it may become so easy to please a crowd that you will have a hard time sending them away.

Mocha-Almond O'Marble Cake

This cake is the baker's answer to a magic trick. No matter how many times I bake it, it never ceases to amaze me. The recipe is similar to one I saw in a magazine in the late 1960s, and I've derived a lot of pleasure from baking it in different ways. Whether you bake it in a Bundt pan, a loaf pan, or an angel-food cake pan, the design varies with stunning results. Spread the chocolate batter over the vanilla, bake it, and then when you remove it from the pan, you will witness a part of the enchantment: in the oven, the heavier batter (chocolate) flipped positions with its lighter counterpart. But to see the rest of the wizardry you need to cut a slice from the cake, causing dessert lovers to exclaim, "Ohhh . . . marble!" YIELD: ONE 13 BY 4-INCH CAKE, ABOUT 20 SERVINGS (2 OR 3 THIN SLICES PER SERVING)

1 TEASPOON INSTANT ESPRESSO POWDER

1 TABLESPOON HOT WATER

¾ CUP (6 FL OUNCES/180 ML) CHOCOLATE SYRUP SUCH AS HERSHEY'S

3 CUPS (13¾ OUNCES/390 GRAMS) ALL-PURPOSE FLOUR

2 TEASPOONS BAKING POWDER

½ TEASPOON SALT

8 OUNCES (2 STICKS/225 GRAMS) UNSALTED BUTTER, AT ROOM TEMPERATURE

2 CUPS (14 OUNCES/400 GRAMS) GRANULATED SUGAR

3 LARGE EGGS, LIGHTLY BEATEN

1 CUP (8 FL OUNCES/240 ML) WHOLE MILK

1½ TEASPOONS PURE VANILLA EXTRACT

1 TEASPOON PURE ALMOND EXTRACT

¼ TEASPOON BAKING SODA

Before baking: Center a rack in the oven and preheat the oven to 350 degrees F. Lightly coat a 13 by 4 by 4-inch straight-sided Pullman pan (also called a *pain de mie* pan, page 37) with nonstick spray, then flour it, tapping out the excess flour. Or, butter and flour the pan. Have all of the ingredients at room temperature.

In a small bowl, stir the espresso powder with the hot water until dissolved. Stir the mixture into the chocolate syrup; set aside. Sift together the flour, baking powder, and salt onto a sheet of waxed paper. Set aside.

In the bowl of a stand mixer fitted with the paddle attachment, beat the butter on medium-low speed until creamy and smooth, about 45 seconds. Increase the speed to medium and add the sugar in a steady stream, stopping the mixer occasionally to scrape down the sides of the bowl. Continue to beat until the mixture is very light in color and texture, 4 to 5 minutes, again stopping the mixer occasionally to scrape down the sides of the bowl.

With the mixer on medium speed, add the eggs very slowly, about 1 tablespoon at a time, at the beginning. If the mixture appears curdled, stop adding the eggs, increase the speed to high, and beat until the mixture looks smooth again. Resume on medium speed and add the remaining eggs 1 to 2 tablespoons at a time. Continue beating until the mixture is fluffy and pale ivory in color. The entire process of adding and beating the eggs should take 3 to 4 minutes.

On the lowest speed, add the flour mixture in three additions alternately with the milk in two additions, beginning and ending with the flour mixture and mixing after each addition only until incorporated. Stop the mixer occasionally to scrape down the sides of the bowl. Add the extracts during the final moments of mixing.

Spoon two-thirds of the batter into the prepared pan, and spread evenly with a rubber spatula. Stir the baking soda into the chocolate syrup–espresso mixture, then add the mixture to the remaining batter in the bowl, mixing well. Without delay, pour the chocolate batter on top of the batter in the pan and spread evenly.

Bake the cake until the top springs back when pressed lightly and a round wooden toothpick or skewer inserted in the center of the cake comes out free of batter, 65 to 70 minutes. Transfer to a wire rack and let cool for 10 to 15 minutes.

Tilt and rotate the pan while gently tapping it on a counter to release the cake sides. If they don't release, slip a thin metal spatula between the still-warm cake and the pan and run the spatula carefully along the entire perimeter

of the pan. Invert a wire rack on top of the cake, invert the cake onto it, and carefully lift off the pan. Invert another rack on top, invert the cake so it is right side up, and remove the original rack. Let cool completely.

For the best flavor and texture, wrap the cake securely in plastic wrap, store at room temperature, and serve the day after baking. It will keep for up to 3 days. For longer storage, overwrap with aluminum foil, label with the contents and date, and freeze for up to 1 month. Thaw at room temperature, 3 to 4 hours.

To serve, cut into thin slices with a serrated knife.

Triple-Ginger Gingerbread

The fragrant aroma of this moist, chestnut brown, spicy cake fresh from the oven is bound to conjure memories of a lazy winter afternoon spent sitting in front of a fire reading a book, sipping hot chocolate, and nibbling on a slice of gingerbread. If you like, you can skip the whipped cream and the pomegranate sauce and seeds and frost the top of the cooled cake with the Bittersweet Chocolate Frosting on page 116, using one-half of the recipe.   **YIELD: ONE 13 BY 9-INCH CAKE, 16 SERVINGS**

POMEGRANATE SAUCE

2 CUPS (16 FL OUNCES/480 ML) POMEGRANATE JUICE, PREFERABLY POM BRAND

⅓ CUP (2¼ OUNCES/65 GRAMS) GRANULATED SUGAR

CAKE

2⅔ CUPS (1¾ OUNCES/330 GRAMS) ALL-PURPOSE FLOUR

2 TEASPOONS GROUND CINNAMON

2 TEASPOONS GROUND GINGER

1½ TEASPOONS BAKING SODA

½ TEASPOON BAKING POWDER

½ TEASPOON SALT

½ TEASPOON GROUND CLOVES

½ TEASPOON GROUND ALLSPICE

¼ TEASPOON GROUND BLACK PEPPER

1 CUP (12 OUNCES BY WEIGHT/340 GRAMS) DARK UNSULFURED MOLASSES

1 CUP (8 FL OUNCES/240 ML) WATER

¼ CUP (2 FL OUNCES/60 ML) FLAVORLESS VEGETABLE OIL SUCH AS CANOLA OR SAFFLOWER

2 TABLESPOONS FINELY GRATED OR CHOPPED, PEELED FRESH GINGER

4 OUNCES (1 STICK/115 GRAMS) UNSALTED BUTTER, AT ROOM TEMPERATURE

1 CUP (7 OUNCES/200 GRAMS) GRANULATED SUGAR

2 LARGE EGGS, LIGHTLY BEATEN

2 OUNCES CRYSTALLIZED GINGER (ABOUT 6 SMALL DISKS), FINELY MINCED TO YIELD ¼ CUP

1 TEASPOON FINELY GRATED ORANGE ZEST

1 CUP (8 FL OUNCES/240 ML) HEAVY CREAM, WHIPPED

½ CUP (2¾ OUNCES/75 GRAMS) POMEGRANATE SEEDS (SEE PAGE 71 FOR DIRECTIONS ON REMOVING THE SEEDS)

To make the Pomegranate Sauce: In a medium-sized, heavy saucepan, heat the pomegranate juice and sugar over low heat until the sugar dissolves. Increase the heat to medium and cook until the mixture is reduced by half and is the consistency of syrup, about 25 minutes. Set aside to cool for about 20 minutes. Pour into a jar or other sturdy container with a tight-fitting lid and store at room temperature for up to 5 days. For longer storage, refrigerate for up to 2 weeks. If cold, bring to room temperature or heat briefly in a microwave to pouring consistency before serving.

Before baking: Center a rack in the oven and preheat the oven to 350 degrees F. Lightly coat a 13 by 9 by 2-inch pan (quarter sheet pan) with nonstick spray, then flour it, tapping out the excess flour. Or, butter and flour the pan.

To make the cake: Sift together the flour, the cinnamon, ground ginger, baking soda, baking powder, salt, cloves, allspice, and pepper onto a piece of waxed paper; set aside.

In a small bowl, stir together the molasses, water, and oil until well blended. Stir in the fresh ginger; set aside. In the bowl of a stand mixer fitted with the paddle attachment, beat the butter on medium-low speed until creamy and smooth, 30 to 45 seconds. Increase the speed to medium and add the sugar in a steady stream, stopping the mixer occasionally to scrape down the sides of the bowl. Continue to beat until the mixture is very light in color and texture, about 3 minutes, again stopping the mixer occasionally to scrape down the sides of the bowl.

With the mixer on medium speed, add the eggs, 2 to 3 tablespoons at a time, beating after each addition until incorporated. On the lowest speed, add the flour mixture in three additions alternately with the molasses mixture in two additions, beginning and ending with the flour mixture and mixing after each addition only until incorporated. Stop the mixer to scrape down the sides of the bowl as needed. Detach the paddle and bowl from the mixer, and tap the paddle against the side of the bowl to free the excess batter. Using a rubber spatula, fold in the crystallized ginger and orange zest. Pour into the prepared pan, spreading evenly with the spatula.

Bake the cake until it springs back when lightly touched in the center, about 45 minutes. Transfer the pan to a wire rack. To serve warm, allow the cake to cool for 45 to 60 minutes, or let cool to room temperature. Cut the cake into squares or rectangles with a serrated knife. Transfer the pieces to individual plates and, using a spoon, drizzle some Pomegranate Sauce over each piece. Spoon a dollop of whipped cream alongside and sprinkle pomegranate seeds randomly over the cake, cream, and plate.

Classic Butter Cake Cupcakes with White Chocolate–Sour Cream Frosting

Light in hand, and with a delicate crumb, these cupcakes bake just as you want a cupcake to look, with a healthy topknot. You can place the unfrosted cupcakes in a sturdy covered container and freeze them for up to 2 weeks. Frosted cupcakes must first be refrigerated or flash-frozen just long enough to firm up the frosting to prevent marring it. Then, wrap each cupcake in plastic wrap or in a small, resealable plastic bag before placing all of them in a sturdy container for freezing. Each cupcake can thaw in its own package without affecting the other cupcakes with its moisture. It's an easy way to give my grandkids and their friends something sweet to eat that they don't have to share.

The frosting, which can be made a day or two ahead and stored in the refrigerator, can be piped or spread on the cupcakes.   **YIELD: 28 CUPCAKES**

CUPCAKES

3 CUPS (12¼ OUNCES/350 GRAMS) CAKE FLOUR

2½ TEASPOONS BAKING POWDER

½ TEASPOON SALT

1 CUP (8 FL OUNCES/240 ML) WHOLE MILK

1½ TEASPOONS PURE VANILLA EXTRACT

¾ TEASPOON PURE ALMOND EXTRACT

8 OUNCES (2 STICKS/225 GRAMS) UNSALTED BUTTER, AT ROOM TEMPERATURE

2 CUPS (14 OUNCES/400 GRAMS) GRANULATED SUGAR

4 LARGE EGGS, LIGHTLY BEATEN

WHITE CHOCOLATE–SOUR CREAM FROSTING

12 OUNCES (340 GRAMS) WHITE CHOCOLATE, FINELY CHOPPED

1½ CUPS (12 OUNCES/340 GRAMS) SOUR CREAM, AT ROOM TEMPERATURE

Before baking: Center a rack in the oven, place another rack in the upper third of the oven, and preheat the oven to 350 degrees F. Very lightly coat *only* the top surface of three 12-cup standard muffin pans with nonstick spray. Or, very lightly butter them. The cupcakes rise above the muffin cups during baking, so this ensures that the top portion of each cupcake will not stick to the surface of the pan and each cupcake will easily release from its cup.

Place fluted paper or foil liners in 28 of the muffin cups, filling the cups in 2 of the pans and spacing the 4 liners in the third pan evenly around the pan. Spacing the cups promotes even baking when not all of the cups are filled. Have all of the ingredients at room temperature.

To make the cupcakes: Sift together the flour, baking powder, and salt onto a piece of waxed paper; set aside. In a liquid measuring cup, stir together the milk and both extracts.

In the bowl of a stand mixer fitted with the paddle attachment, beat the butter on medium speed until creamy and smooth, about 45 seconds. Add the sugar in a steady stream, stopping the mixer occasionally to scrape down the sides of the bowl. Continue to beat on medium speed until the mixture is very light in color and texture, 3 to 4 minutes, again stopping the mixer occasionally to scrape down the sides of the bowl.

With the mixer still on medium speed, add the eggs slowly, about 1 tablespoon at a time, beating after each addition until incorporated and stopping the mixer occasionally to scrape down the sides of the bowl. If the mixture appears curdled, stop adding the eggs, increase the speed slightly, and beat until the mixture looks smooth again. Resume beating on medium speed and add the remaining eggs. Continue beating until the mixture is fluffy and pale ivory in color. The entire process of adding and beating the eggs should take 4 to 5 minutes. On the lowest speed, add the flour mixture in four additions alternately with the milk mixture in three additions, beginning and ending with the flour mixture and mixing only until incorporated after each addition. Stop the mixer occasionally to scrape down the sides of the bowl.

Without delay, using an ice cream scoop a scant 2 inches in diameter (#24) or a spoon, deposit mounded portions of the batter into the prepared cups, filling them no more than two-thirds full.

If your oven is wide enough, bake 2 muffin pans side by side, spacing them about 1 inch apart on the center rack, and the third pan on a rack in the upper third of the oven. If your oven can't accommodate all of the pans at one time, put a full pan on each of the racks and set the third muffin pan with the batter for 4 cupcakes aside at room temperature (or in the refrigerator if it's a very warm day), and bake these cupcakes after the others have finished baking. Bake the cupcakes until lightly golden, the tops spring back when lightly pressed, and a round wooden toothpick inserted in the center of a few of the cupcakes comes out free of batter, 21 to 23 minutes. Be careful not to overbake. If the cupcakes are browning unevenly, gently rotate the pans when a little more than half of the baking time has elapsed. The cupcakes will rise above the paper liners. Transfer the pans to wire racks and let cool for 10 to 15 minutes.

Tilt a pan and tap it gently on a counter to help free the cupcakes. (Don't invert the cupcakes onto a rack or you will mar their shape.) Carefully remove the warm cupcakes from the pan and place them, right side up, on the racks. Repeat with the second and third pan. Let the cupcakes cool completely before frosting them. If you are not frosting them right away, cover them with a kitchen towel to prevent them from drying out.

To make the White Chocolate–Sour Cream Frosting: Half fill a bowl with hot water (95 to 110 degrees F). Put the chocolate in a bowl and place it over (but not touching) the hot water. When you can see that a portion of the chocolate has melted in the bottom of the bowl, stir slowly to blend. Let the chocolate melt until creamy and smooth, stirring slowly occasionally. Remove from the water bath and set aside to cool to a temperature similar to the room-temperature sour cream.

Gradually stir the sour cream into the cooled chocolate and set the mixture aside at room temperature until it thickens to a spreading consistency, about 2 hours, depending on the temperature of the room. If you are not using it before it thickens, store it in an airtight container in the refrigerator for up to 2 days. Before using, bring to room temperature and beat until creamy and smooth with a rubber spatula. You should have about 2 cups.

To frost the cupcakes: Spoon the frosting into a large pastry bag fitted with a ¹⁄₂-inch star tip, filling the bag half full. Following the directions on page 26, pipe the frosting onto the cupcakes. Alternatively, using a flexible metal spatula, spread 2 to 3 tablespoons of the frosting on top of each cupcake, mounding the frosting in the center.

Serve the cupcakes the same day they are baked. Or, place in a sturdy covered container or cake box, securely wrapped with plastic wrap, and store at room temperature for up to 1 day.

Note: You can leave the batter plain, or you can create colorful ribbonlike layers or swirls in the cupcakes by splitting the batter and tinting it 3 different colors. Split one-fourth of the batter into 3 equal portions, and place each portion in a small bowl. Tint each portion with a few drops of the food coloring of your choice, gently stirring each portion until the mixture reaches the desired depth of color. Fill each muffin cup about two-thirds full with the plain batter as directed. Using the same spoon you used to blend the color into each portion of the reserved batter, drop the equivalent of about 1½ teaspoons of each color next to one another on the surface of each cupcake. Using a wooden skewer or toothpick, swirl the colors on top, dragging the skewer slightly below the surface of the batter with just a few strokes. Bake as directed.

Spicy Applesauce Cake

Homemade applesauce cakes have been popular for generations. The cake's flavor is especially heightened by the addition of other fruity flavors, such as golden raisins and dried currants, and a combination of spices to produce a moist, spicy cake that appeals to everyone. A coffee frosting is the perfect finishing touch. Cut the cake into squares, or mark the frosting to suggest squares, and then center a toasted walnut half on each square for decoration. You may want to begin making the frosting when the cake is about halfway through baking to give the brown butter time to cool until just warm. However, it's fine if you make the brown butter a day or two ahead and store it in a covered container in the refrigerator. When needed, melt it over low heat and proceed with the frosting recipe as directed. **YIELD: ONE 13 BY 9-INCH CAKE, 15 TO 20 SERVINGS**

CAKE

⅓ CUP (2 OUNCES/55 GRAMS) GOLDEN RAISINS

⅓ CUP (1½ OUNCES/40 GRAMS) DRIED CURRANTS

2¾ CUPS PLUS 2 TABLESPOONS (13 OUNCES/370 GRAMS) ALL-PURPOSE FLOUR

1½ TEASPOONS BAKING POWDER

1 TEASPOON GROUND CINNAMON

¾ TEASPOON GROUND ALLSPICE

½ TEASPOON SALT

¼ TEASPOON BAKING SODA

¼ TEASPOON NUTMEG, PREFERABLY FRESHLY GRATED

¼ TEASPOON GROUND CLOVES

8 OUNCES (2 STICKS/225 GRAMS) UNSALTED BUTTER, AT ROOM TEMPERATURE

1¼ CUPS (8¾ OUNCES/250 GRAMS) GRANULATED SUGAR

½ CUP FIRMLY PACKED (3½ OUNCES/100 GRAMS) LIGHT BROWN SUGAR

3 LARGE EGGS, LIGHTLY BEATEN

1 TEASPOON PURE VANILLA EXTRACT

1½ CUPS (11½ OUNCES/325 GRAMS) UNSWEETENED APPLESAUCE, PREFERABLY SMOOTH TEXTURED

⅓ CUP (1½ OUNCES/40 GRAMS) CHOPPED WALNUTS, TOASTED (PAGES 15–16)

BROWN BUTTER FROSTING

4 OUNCES (1 STICK/115 GRAMS) UNSALTED BUTTER

1 TEASPOON HOT WATER OR STRONG BREWED COFFEE

¼ TEASPOON INSTANT ESPRESSO POWDER

2 CUPS (7 OUNCES/200 GRAMS) POWDERED SUGAR, SIFTED, PLUS MORE FOR THICKENING, IF NECESSARY

1 TABLESPOON WHOLE MILK, PLUS MORE FOR THINNING, IF NECESSARY

2 TEASPOONS FINELY GRATED LEMON ZEST

15 TO 20 WALNUT HALVES, TOASTED (PAGES 15–16)

Before baking: Center a rack in the oven and preheat the oven to 350 degrees F. Lightly coat a 13 by 9 by 2-inch pan (quarter sheet pan) with nonstick spray, then flour it, tapping out the excess flour. Or, butter and flour the pan. Line the bottom with parchment paper. Have all of the ingredients at room temperature.

To make the cake: Place the golden raisins and currants in a small sieve. Briefly hold the fruits under hot tap water just to rinse them, rather than to soak them. Deposit the dried fruits onto paper toweling; wrap the toweling around the fruits and gently press on them with the toweling to absorb the excess water. Unwrap the towel and fluff the fruits with your fingertips to separate them and to break up any clumps. Set aside.

Sift together the flour, baking powder, cinnamon, allspice, salt, baking soda, nutmeg, and cloves onto a sheet of waxed paper; set aside. In the bowl of a stand mixer fitted with the paddle attachment, beat the butter on medium speed until creamy and smooth, 30 to 45 seconds. Add both sugars in a steady stream, stopping the mixer occasionally to scrape down the sides of the bowl. Continue to beat on medium speed until the mixture is very light in color and texture, 2 to 3 minutes, again stopping the mixer occasionally to scrape down the sides of the bowl.

With the mixer on medium speed, add the eggs slowly at first, 1 to 2 tablespoons at a time, beating after each addition until incorporated. Continue adding the eggs, now a little faster, until they are completely incorporated and the mixture is light and fluffy, stopping the mixer and scraping down the sides of the bowl at least once. Add the vanilla during the final moments of mixing. This entire process of adding and beating the eggs should take 2 to 3 minutes.

On the lowest speed, add the flour mixture in three additions alternately with the applesauce in two additions, beginning and ending with the flour mixture and mixing only until incorporated after each addition. Stop the mixer occasionally to scrape down the sides of the bowl. Detach the paddle and bowl from the mixer, and tap the paddle against the side of the bowl to free the excess batter. Using a rubber spatula, gently fold in the raisins, currants, and nuts. Spoon the batter into the prepared pan, and spread it evenly with the spatula.

Bake the cake until it is light brown on top, springs back when lightly touched in the center, and is beginning to come away from the sides of the pan, 40 to 45 minutes. Transfer to a wire rack and let cool for 10 minutes. Tilt and rotate the pan while gently tapping it on a counter to release the cake sides. If they don't release, slip a thin metal spatula between the still-warm cake and the pan and run the spatula carefully along the entire perimeter of the pan. Invert a large wire rack on top of the cake, invert the cake onto it, and carefully lift off the pan. Slowly peel off the parchment liner, turn it over so that the sticky side faces up, and reposition it on the top of the cake. Invert another rack on top, invert the cake so it is right side up, and remove the original rack.

You can frost the cake while it is still warm, or you can let the cake cool completely and frost it the next day. For the best flavor, serve the cake the day after baking to give the spicy flavors time to mellow. Wrap it in plastic wrap and store at room temperature. For longer storage, overwrap with aluminum foil, label with the contents and date, and freeze for up 2 weeks. Remove the aluminum foil and thaw at room temperature, 3 to 4 hours.

To make the Brown Butter Frosting: Following the directions for making brown butter on page 19, melt the butter in a small, heavy saucepan over medium-low heat and heat just until it begins to turn a delicate brown, 5 to 7 minutes. Remove from the heat, pour into a small bowl, and let cool just until warm. The browning process reduces the moisture in the butter, so though you began with 4 ounces (8 tablespoons/115 grams), you will have less than that now. For this recipe, measure 6 tablespoons (3 fl ounces/90 ml) of the brown butter into a medium bowl. (Any remaining brown butter, which will be less than 2 tablespoons, can be stored in the refrigerator in a small, covered container and used as a sauce for pancakes, waffles, or even freshly cooked vegetables.)

In a very small bowl, stir together the hot water and espresso powder until the powder dissolves. Stir 1 cup of the sugar into the brown butter with a rubber spatula. Add the coffee liquid, milk, and lemon zest and stir until smooth. Then stir in the remaining 1 cup sugar until you have a smooth spreading consistency. If the mixture is too thin, add 1 tablespoon sugar at a time until you achieve the desired consistency. If it is too thick, add 1 teaspoon milk at a time until you achieve the desired consistency.

Spread the frosting over the top and sides of the warm cake, and decorate with the walnut halves (see headnote). As the cake cools, the frosting develops a sheen. If you don't plan to serve the cake within 12 hours, set aside at room temperature, covered with a cake dome, for up to 1 day. (Do not cover it with aluminum or plastic wrap, as they will mar the frosting.)

To serve, cut the cake into squares or rectangles with a sharp knife.

Prune Plum–Apricot Oversized Frangipane Tart

A handsome, oversized tart with a duet of poached fruit: one half is dimpled with dried apricots and the other with prune plums. The presentation creates a divided effect that gives the impression of two desserts in one. A layer of creamy almond filling brings everything together. Cut into bars and arrange on a platter to add a splash of color to any occasion. You will be glad the recipe serves a crowd, since anyone who sees it will want to taste both halves. For the summer months, put fresh raspberries or blackberries on one side and fig slices or plum wedges on the other. Lightly coat kitchen scissors with nonstick spray and use them to cut the dried fruit.

YIELD: ONE 10 BY 15-INCH TART, 2½ DOZEN BARS

DRIED FRUIT

½ CUP (4 FL OUNCES/120 ML) FRESH ORANGE JUICE

2 TABLESPOONS GRANULATED SUGAR

8 (3 OUNCES/85 GRAMS) PITTED, MOIST DRIED PRUNE
    PLUMS, QUARTERED

8 (2½ OUNCES/70 GRAMS) LARGE, MOIST DRIED
    APRICOTS, QUARTERED

PASTRY

2 CUPS (9 OUNCES/255 GRAMS) ALL-PURPOSE FLOUR

½ CUP (3½ OUNCES/100 GRAMS) GRANULATED SUGAR

⅛ TEASPOON SALT

6 OUNCES (1½ STICKS/170 GRAMS) COLD UNSALTED BUTTER,
    CUT INTO ¼-INCH SLICES

1 LARGE EGG, LIGHTLY BEATEN

FRANGIPANE FILLING

2¼ CUPS (8 OUNCES/225 GRAMS) SLICED NATURAL ALMONDS

1 CUP (7 OUNCES/200 GRAMS) GRANULATED SUGAR

4 LARGE EGGS

8 OUNCES (2 STICKS/225 GRAMS) UNSALTED BUTTER, SOFTENED

1 TABLESPOON DARK RUM

½ TEASPOON PURE VANILLA EXTRACT

½ TEASPOON PURE ALMOND EXTRACT

To prepare the dried fruit: In a small saucepan, combine the orange juice and sugar. Bring to a boil and cook until the liquid is reduced by almost one-third, about 3 minutes. Reduce the heat to low and add the prunes and apricots, keeping each to one side of the pan (they'll be easier to fish out this way). Simmer for about 3 minutes, stirring occasionally. Remove from the heat and set aside to cool. (If desired, prepare up to 2 days in advance.)

Before baking: Center a rack in the oven and preheat the oven to 350 degrees F. Have ready a 15½ by 10½ by 1-inch pan (jelly-roll pan).

To make the pastry: In a food processor, combine the flour, sugar, and salt and pulse 3 or 4 times to blend. Scatter the butter pieces over the flour mixture and pulse until the mixture resembles cornmeal. Add the egg and process just until the dough comes together into a ball.

Transfer the dough to a lightly floured work surface and pat it into a 6 by 4-inch rectangle. Roll out the dough into a 12 by 9-inch rectangle. Roll the rectangle loosely around the rolling pin, center the pin over the baking sheet, and unroll the pastry over the pan. Press the dough with your fingertips to extend it to cover the bottom of the pan. (If you own a pastry roller with a 2½- to 4-inch-long roller, it's helpful for extending the dough over the bottom of the pan.)

Partially bake the crust until it is pale gold and the surface no longer looks wet, raw, or shiny, 10 to 13 minutes. Transfer the pan to a wire rack and let cool while you prepare the filling.

To make the Frangipane Filling: In the food processor, combine the almonds and sugar and process until the mixture has the consistency of cornmeal. Add the eggs, butter, rum, and extracts and process just until creamy.

Pour the filling onto the cooled crust, spreading evenly with a rubber spatula. Score a shallow line to divide the tart in half vertically. Remove the fruit from the juice (you don't need to pat it dry; the juices will evaporate during baking). On one-half of the tart, arrange the apricot quarters in 5 rows of 6 pieces each. On the other half of the tart, arrange the prune plums in the same manner. Gently press the pieces into the filling (the filling should not cover the fruit pieces completely).

Bake the tart until the top is pale golden and springs back when lightly pressed, 25 to 30 minutes. Transfer the pan to a wire rack and let cool completely. Using a sharp knife, cut into 1¾ by 3-inch bars.

Banana-Split Cream Pie

I've taken the classic components of the banana split and transformed them into a pie with a chocolate crumb crust, a banana cream filling, and a strawberry-raspberry topping. To make the dessert big enough to serve a crowd of banana-split lovers, I had to assemble the pie in something larger than a standard pie dish. The answer is a 10-inch round springform pan. A small amount of gelatin in the filling provides just enough support to make a dessert of this size easy to cut and serve. Layering the banana slices between the crust and the filling creates a barrier that prevents the crust from becoming soggy. **YIELD: ONE 10-INCH PIE, 12 TO 14 SERVINGS**

CHOCOLATE CRUMB CRUST

33 (6½ OUNCES/185 GRAMS) STORE-BOUGHT CHOCOLATE WAFER COOKIES SUCH AS NABISCO FAMOUS

⅓ CUP PLUS 1 TABLESPOON (1½ OUNCES/40 GRAMS) CHOPPED PECANS

3 TABLESPOONS GRANULATED SUGAR

4½ OUNCES (1 STICK PLUS 1 TABLESPOON/130 GRAMS) UNSALTED BUTTER, MELTED

BANANA CREAM FILLING

3 TABLESPOONS WATER

1½ TEASPOONS UNFLAVORED POWDERED GELATIN

5 LARGE (SCANT ½ CUP/3 FL OUNCES/90 ML) EGG YOLKS

⅔ CUP (4½ OUNCES/130 GRAMS) GRANULATED SUGAR

⅓ CUP PLUS 1 TABLESPOON (1¾ OUNCES/50 GRAMS) CORNSTARCH

⅛ TEASPOON SALT

2¾ CUPS (22 FL OUNCES/660 ML) WHOLE MILK

2 TABLESPOONS UNSALTED BUTTER

1 TEASPOON PURE VANILLA EXTRACT

1 TEASPOON DARK RUM

4 MEDIUM, FIRM BUT RIPE BANANAS

STRAWBERRY-RASPBERRY WHIPPED CREAM

½ CUP (2½ OUNCES/70 GRAMS) STRAWBERRIES, HULLED AND QUARTERED

⅓ CUP (2½ OUNCES/70 GRAMS) RED RASPBERRIES, PICKED OVER FOR STEMS

¼ CUP (1¾ OUNCES/50 GRAMS) GRANULATED SUGAR

1 CUP (8 FL OUNCES/240 ML) COLD HEAVY CREAM

Before baking: Center a rack in the oven and preheat the oven to 350 degrees F. Lightly coat a 10-inch round springform pan with at least 2-inch sides with nonstick spray or with flavorless vegetable oil such as canola or safflower.

To make the Chocolate Crumb Crust: Break the chocolate wafers into pieces and place in a food processor. Add the pecans and sugar and process until fine crumbs form to yield about 2½ cups. Transfer to a medium bowl. Pour the butter over the mixture and toss with a fork until thoroughly coated and crumbly. Pour into the prepared pan, and use your fingertips to press the crust firmly and evenly over the bottom and about 1½ inches up the sides of the pan.

Bake the crust for 10 minutes only. It will be soft when lightly touched with a fingertip, but it will firm as it cools. Transfer to a wire rack and let cool completely.

To make the Banana Cream Filling: Pour the water into a measuring cup. Sprinkle the gelatin over the water and set aside for at least 5 minutes to soften.

Rest a sieve over a large bowl; set nearby. In a medium bowl, whisk the egg yolks until blended. In a medium saucepan, whisk together the sugar, cornstarch, and salt. Gradually pour in the milk while whisking constantly. Place over medium heat and cook, stirring slowly and often with a silicone spatula, until the mixture just begins to bubble and thicken, 6 to 8 minutes. Continue to cook, slowly stirring constantly, for about 1 minute longer. Remove from the heat.

Pour about one-third of the hot mixture into the yolks, while stirring to combine. Pour the mixture back into the saucepan, and return it to medium-low heat. Cook, stirring constantly, until the mixture is thick, somewhat bubbly, and an instant-read thermometer registers 170 degrees F, 2 to 3 minutes longer.

Remove from the heat, and pour the custard through the sieve. Stir in the butter, softened gelatin, vanilla, and rum until all of the ingredients are thoroughly blended and the butter is melted. Without delay, pour the mixture into a large bowl and cover with plastic wrap, pressing it directly on the surface to prevent a skin from forming. Poke vents in the plastic wrap with the tip of a paring knife. Set aside at room temperature until lukewarm, about 10 minutes.

Peel 3 of the bananas and cut into about 1/4-inch-thick slices, allowing the slices to fall into the crumb crust. The slices should cover the bottom of the crust completely. Pour the warm custard over the banana slices, spreading it with the spatula to cover them evenly. Press a piece of plastic wrap directly on the surface of the filling, and refrigerate up to 1 hour before serving.

To make the Strawberry-Raspberry Whipped Cream: Combine the strawberries, raspberries, and the sugar in the bowl of a stand mixer fitted with the whisk attachment. Mash the berries lightly with a fork. Pour 1/2 cup (4 fl ounces/120 ml) of the cream on top. Whip the ingredients on medium speed until the berries are partially crushed and dispersed throughout the cream, about 45 seconds. Add the remaining 1/2 cup cream and continue to whip on medium speed until soft peaks form.

Peel the remaining banana and cut into about 1/8-inch-thick slices, scattering the slices over the pie filling. Spread the berry whipped cream evenly over the sliced bananas. Refrigerate until serving. This pie tastes best the same day it is prepared.

To avoid disturbing the crumb-coated sides, slowly release the springform clasp and carefully remove the sides. With a narrow metal spatula, smooth the whipped cream evenly around the sides of the pie. If desired, slip a wide metal spatula under the metal base and transfer the dessert to a serving plate.

Cut the pie into wedges with a sharp knife, and carefully lift off the base of the pan with a pie spatula. To store any leftovers, reattach the ring to the pan base, cover securely with aluminum foil, and store in the refrigerator for up to 1 day.

Butterscotch Spiral Coffee Cake

Imagine a cinnamon bun large enough to feed a crowd. Here's a giant one in coffee-cake form that's simple to make. The cinnamon-butter filling and butterscotch glaze pair beautifully, and an array of spices—cardamom, nutmeg, and cinnamon—give the yeast dough an old-time flavor. Not one sweet tooth will be disappointed. You can also spread a thin layer of apple butter, homemade or store-bought, over the cinnamon butter and then bake as directed.

YIELD: ONE 9-INCH ROUND CAKE, 14 TO 16 SERVINGS

DOUGH

2½ TO 2¾ CUPS (11½ TO 12¼ OUNCES/325 TO
    350 GRAMS) ALL-PURPOSE FLOUR

¼ CUP (1¾ OUNCES/50 GRAMS) GRANULATED SUGAR

2¼ TEASPOONS (1 ENVELOPE) INSTANT YEAST

½ TEASPOON SALT

½ TEASPOON GROUND CARDAMOM

⅛ TEASPOON NUTMEG, PREFERABLY FRESHLY GRATED

⅛ TEASPOON GROUND CINNAMON

⅓ CUP (2½ FL OUNCES/75 ML) WHOLE MILK

2 OUNCES (½ STICK/55 GRAMS) UNSALTED BUTTER

¼ CUP (2 FL OUNCES/60 ML) WATER

2 LARGE EGGS, AT ROOM TEMPERATURE

1 TEASPOON PURE VANILLA EXTRACT

BUTTERSCOTCH GLAZE

½ CUP FIRMLY PACKED (3½ OUNCES/100 GRAMS) LIGHT
    BROWN SUGAR

2 OUNCES (½ STICK/55 GRAMS) UNSALTED BUTTER

2 TABLESPOONS DARK CORN SYRUP

CINNAMON-BUTTER FILLING

½ TEASPOON GROUND CINNAMON

2 TABLESPOONS UNSALTED BUTTER, MELTED

To make the dough: Stir together 2 cups (9 ounces/ 255 grams) of the flour, the sugar, yeast, salt, cardamom, nutmeg, and cinnamon in the bowl of a stand mixer; set aside. In a small, heavy saucepan, combine the milk and butter and heat over low heat just until the butter melts. Add the water and set aside until warm (120 to 130 degrees F), about 1 minute.

Pour the milk mixture over the flour-yeast mixture and mix well with a rubber spatula until all of the dry ingredients are moistened. Attach the bowl to the mixer, and fit the mixer with the paddle attachment. With the mixer on low speed, add the eggs, one at a time, beating after each addition until incorporated. Add the vanilla in the final moments of mixing. Stop the mixer, add ½ cup (2¼ ounces/65 grams) more flour, and resume mixing on low speed until smooth, 30 to 45 seconds. Add 2 tablespoons additional flour and resume mixing on medium speed until the dough is smooth, still soft, and slightly sticky, about 45 seconds.

Sprinkle the work surface with 1 tablespoon of the flour, and center the dough on the flour. Knead the dough gently until it is smooth and no longer sticky, adding an additional 1 to 2 tablespoons flour only if necessary to prevent stickiness. Place the dough in a large bowl, cover the bowl securely with plastic wrap, and let the dough rise in a warm place (70 degrees F) until doubled in bulk, 45 to 60 minutes. The dough is ready when a finger gently pressed into it leaves an indentation. Meanwhile, prepare the baking pan, the glaze, and the filling.

To make the Butterscotch Glaze: Lightly coat a 9 by 2-inch round cake pan with nonstick spray, or butter the pan. Combine the sugar, butter, and corn syrup in a small, heavy saucepan and set over low heat until the butter is completely melted. Pour the mixture into the prepared pan and tilt the pan to cover the bottom evenly; set aside. (The glaze might thicken slightly before it's time to place the dough in the pan, but it will liquefy again as the coffee cake bakes.)

To make the Cinnamon-Butter Filling: In a small bowl or cup, stir the cinnamon into the butter; set aside.

Before baking: Center a rack in the oven and preheat the oven to 350 degrees F.

To assemble the coffeecake: Gently deflate the dough. On a lightly floured work surface, roll out the dough into a 16 by 12-inch rectangle. Using a pastry brush, spread the butter-cinnamon mixture evenly over the dough. Cut the dough lengthwise into six 2-inch-wide strips. (A pizza cutter is helpful here.) Loosely (so the dough has some give as it expands in the oven) roll up 1 strip and place it, cut edge up, in the center of the prepared pan on top of the glaze. One at a time, coil the remaining dough strips around the center strip, starting each strip at the end of the previous one, to make a single large spiral. As you roll the dough strips around the coffee cake, the butter-cinnamon side of the dough strips should be facing inside. (When you finish forming the spiral there will be plenty of space left in the pan. The spaces around the dough will fill in as the dough bakes.) Loosely cover the pan with plastic wrap and let the cake rise in a warm place until it is almost doubled in size, about 30 minutes. The dough is ready when a finger gently pressed into it leaves an indentation.

Bake the coffee cake until the top is deep golden brown, about 35 minutes. Check after 20 minutes to make sure the cake is not browning too fast. If it is, cover the top loosely with aluminum foil for the last 10 to 15 minutes of baking to prevent overbrowning. Transfer to a wire rack (if you have used foil, remove it) and let cool for 10 minutes.

Gently tilt the pan and tap the sides on a counter to release the cake sides, then invert a serving plate on top of the cake, and invert the pan and the plate. Leave the pan on the cake for 1 minute, so the glaze transfers to the cake, then gently lift off the pan. Using a rubber spatula, scrape out any butterscotch syrup remaining in the pan and spread it over the warm surface of the cake.

Serve the cake warm or at room temperature, cut into wedges gently with a serrated knife. This coffee cake is best eaten the day it is baked.

Congo Brownies

You will never have to choose between a brownie and a blondie again, since these nut-studded bars have layers of both to double your pleasure. These easy-to-eat-out-of-hand bars will leave sweet impressions when you take them to a group picnic or a bake sale, or tuck them into lunch boxes. To keep the bars fresh for several days, wrap them individually in plastic wrap or clear cellophane.   YIELD: 2 TO 4 DOZEN BARS, DEPENDING ON THE SIZE

CONGO LAYER

1⅓ CUPS (6¼ OUNCES/175 GRAMS) ALL-PURPOSE FLOUR

1¼ TEASPOONS BAKING POWDER

¼ TEASPOON SALT

3 OUNCES (¾ STICK/85 GRAMS) UNSALTED BUTTER, MELTED AND COOLED

1¼ CUPS FIRMLY PACKED (8 OUNCES/225 GRAMS) LIGHT BROWN SUGAR

1 LARGE EGG

1 LARGE EGG WHITE

1 TEASPOON PURE VANILLA EXTRACT

1 CUP (4 OUNCES/115 GRAMS) CHOPPED WALNUTS

BROWNIE LAYER

1 CUP PLUS 2 TABLESPOONS (5 OUNCES/140 GRAMS) ALL-PURPOSE FLOUR

¼ CUP (¾ OUNCE/25 GRAMS) UNSWEETENED DUTCH-PROCESSED COCOA POWDER

⅛ TEASPOON BAKING POWDER

¼ TEASPOON SALT

4 OUNCES (1 STICK/115 GRAMS) UNSALTED BUTTER

4 OUNCES (115 GRAMS) UNSWEETENED CHOCOLATE, COARSELY CHOPPED

1½ CUPS (9¼ OUNCES/260 GRAMS) GRANULATED SUGAR

2 LARGE EGGS, LIGHTLY BEATEN

1 LARGE EGG YOLK

2 TEASPOONS PURE VANILLA EXTRACT

CHOCOLATE GLAZE

3 OUNCES (85 GRAMS) SEMISWEET OR BITTERSWEET CHOCOLATE, FINELY CHOPPED

3 TABLESPOONS HEAVY CREAM

Before baking: Center a rack in the oven and preheat the oven to 350 degrees F. Lightly butter a 13 by 9 by 2-inch pan (quarter sheet pan), then flour it, tapping out the excess flour.

To make the Congo Layer: Sift together the flour, baking powder, and salt onto a sheet of waxed paper; set aside. In a large bowl, stir together the butter, brown sugar, egg, egg white, and vanilla just until blended. Stir in the flour mixture just until the batter is smooth.

Scoop the thick, sticky batter onto 8 or 9 different areas on the bottom of the prepared pan. With an offset spatula, spread the batter to cover the pan as evenly as possible. Sprinkle the walnuts evenly on top and gently press them into the batter.

Partially bake the layer until it is no longer shiny on top and is beginning to come away from the sides of the pan, about 20 minutes. Transfer the pan to a wire rack to cool while you prepare the Brownie Layer.

To make the Brownie Layer: Sift together the flour, cocoa powder, baking powder, and salt onto a sheet of waxed paper; set aside. In a small, heavy saucepan, melt the butter and chocolate over very low heat, stirring with a silicone spatula until smooth. Or, combine in a medium microwave-safe bowl and melt in a microwave oven at 50 percent power (medium) for 30-second bursts, stirring after each burst, until melted, 1 to 1½ minutes. Transfer to a medium bowl and let cool for 5 minutes.

Stir the sugar into the chocolate mixture until incorporated. Add the eggs, egg yolk, and vanilla and stir until well blended. Stir in the flour mixture just until the batter is smooth. Scoop the thick, sticky batter onto 8 or 9 different areas of the still-warm Congo Layer. With the offset spatula, spread the batter as evenly as possible.

Bake the brownie until the top is no longer shiny; appears set; feels firm, rather than soft; and a round wooden toothpick inserted in the center comes out with moist chocolate crumbs attached, about 25 minutes. Transfer the pan to a wire rack and let cool completely. The top layer will set up as it cools.

To make the Chocolate Glaze: Place the chocolate in a medium bowl. In a small saucepan, bring the cream just to a boil over medium-low heat. Pour the cream over the chocolate and let it stand for 30 seconds. Whisk together until smooth and creamy. Set the mixture aside at room temperature just until it cools a bit and begins to thicken slightly.

Fashion a small cone out of parchment paper (page 26) and half fill it with the liquid glaze. Snip a small opening at the end of the paper cone to allow a thin flow of glaze. Exerting light pressure on the cone, and never easing the pressure or halting the motion, pipe thin lines of chocolate in a zigzag pattern over the cooled surface of the brownie. Set aside at room temperature until the glaze is set, 1 to 1 1/2 hours.

To serve, cut the brownie lengthwise into seven 1 3/4-inch-wide strips, and then cut crosswise into seven 1 1/4-inch-wide strips, to yield forty-nine 1 3/4 by 1 1/4-inch bars. Or, cut lengthwise into 6 strips and crosswise into 4 strips to yield twenty-four 2-inch squares.

To store, cover the pan tightly with aluminum foil and keep at room temperature for up to 3 days. For longer storage, bake and cool as directed but do not glaze. Cover tightly with aluminum foil and freeze for up to 2 weeks. Thaw at room temperature, 2 to 3 hours, then glaze as directed.

Swiss Engadiner Squares

I'll never forget the first time I laid eyes on this gorgeous creamy dessert, named after the Engadine Valley in Switzerland. It was during one of my trips to Europe in the 1960s, and its flavor transformed me into a caramel-aholic. My version is inspired by that trip and a recipe from my baking mentor, Jack Lirio, with whom I taught classes in the 1970s. A filling of cream, honey, walnuts, and caramelized sugar is poured over a cookielike base. Extra dough forms a lattice on top; when you cut down the center of each lattice strip, it frames the filling, much like a picture frame. Sometimes I use an assortment of pine, pistachio, and pecan nuts to create an interesting variation.   **YIELD: 4 DOZEN BARS**

DOUGH

3½ CUPS (1 POUND/455 GRAMS) ALL-PURPOSE FLOUR

¾ CUP (5¼ OUNCES/150 GRAMS) GRANULATED SUGAR

1 TEASPOON FINELY GRATED LEMON OR ORANGE ZEST

¼ TEASPOON SALT

8 OUNCES (2 STICKS/225 GRAMS) UNSALTED BUTTER,
    AT ROOM TEMPERATURE, CUT INTO ½-INCH SLICES

2 LARGE EGGS

2 TEASPOONS PURE VANILLA EXTRACT

FILLING

¼ CUP (2 FL OUNCES/60 ML) WATER

1⅓ CUPS (9¼ OUNCES/260 GRAMS) GRANULATED SUGAR

1 CUP (8 FL OUNCES/240 ML) HEAVY CREAM, AT ROOM
    TEMPERATURE

3 TABLESPOONS HONEY

3 CUPS (12 OUNCES/340 GRAMS) COARSELY CHOPPED
    TOASTED WALNUTS (PAGES 15–16)

1 LARGE EGG, LIGHTLY BEATEN, FOR EGG WASH (OPTIONAL)

FLEUR DE SEL FOR SPRINKLING (OPTIONAL)

To make the dough: In a food processor, combine the flour, sugar, zest, and salt and pulse 3 or 4 times to blend. Scatter the butter pieces over the flour mixture and pulse until the mixture has the consistency of cornmeal. In a small bowl, whisk the eggs and the vanilla until blended. With the motor running, pour the egg mixture down the feed tube and process until the mixture forms a ball.

Divide the dough in half, and flatten each half into a disk. One at a time, place each disk between 2 sheets of waxed paper and roll out a rectangle 13 by 12 inches and about ³⁄₁₆ inch thick. Put 1 rectangle (still between the sheets of waxed paper) on a baking sheet, and place in the refrigerator for about 45 minutes or in the freezer for about 25 minutes to firm. Remove the top sheet of waxed paper from the other rectangle, lift the waxed paper with the dough on it, and position the pastry, top side down, on the bottom of a 13 by 9 by 2-inch pan (quarter sheet pan). Gently peel away the other piece of waxed paper, and press the dough onto the bottom and about halfway up the sides of the pan. Using a dough scraper, trim the edges of the dough so they are even.

To make the filling: In a medium-sized, heavy saucepan, combine the water and sugar over low heat and heat, stirring occasionally with a silicone spatula, until the sugar dissolves. Raise the heat to medium-high and cook until the sugar turns amber, about 7 minutes. Remove from the heat, add the cream, and stir with the spatula until the caramelized sugar blends with the cream (be careful, as the mixture will bubble up when you add the cream). Stir in the honey, and then the nuts. Set aside to cool slightly, 30 to 45 minutes. The mixture will thicken a bit as it cools.

Before baking: Center a rack in the oven and preheat the oven to 350 degrees F for at least 30 minutes.

Spread the cooled filling evenly over the dough in the pan. Remove the pan with the second dough rectangle from the refrigerator. Peel off the top sheet of waxed paper, loosely replace it, and then turn the package over and peel off the second sheet of paper. Cut 5 strips each 12 inches long and ¹/₂ inch wide from the dough, and place them lengthwise over the filling. Then cut 7 strips each 8 to 9 inches long and ¹/₂ inch wide from the dough and place them crosswise over the filling. This creates 8 squares in one direction and 6 squares in the other direction. Finally, cut enough ¹/₄-inch-wide strips from the remaining dough to encircle the pan completely. Lay them on top of the edge of the dough and press down

gently to adhere, creating an attractive border. Brush all of the pastry strips with the egg wash, if using. (You will have some pastry scraps; you can use them to make some cutout cookies.) Top evenly with a very light sprinkling of *fleur de sel*, if desired.

Bake until the pastry strips are pale gold and the filling bubbles thickly in a few places, about 45 minutes. Transfer the pan to a wire rack and let cool completely.

To serve, using a sharp knife, cut into squares by cutting down the center of each pastry strip. Cover leftovers securely with aluminum foil and store at room temperature for up to 3 days.

Luscious Lime Bars
with Milk Chocolate Glaze

A new look at an old favorite lemon recipe: fresh lime juice and toasted coconut—a touch of the tropics—with a shiny milk-chocolate topping. The sweet piquancy of the filling blends superbly with the milk chocolate and its hint of rich caramel.   **YIELD: 2 DOZEN 1½ BY 3-INCH BARS**

SHORTBREAD

2 CUPS (9 OUNCES/255 GRAMS) ALL-PURPOSE FLOUR

½ CUP (3½ OUNCES/100 GRAMS) GRANULATED SUGAR

¼ TEASPOON SALT

8 OUNCES (2 STICKS/225 GRAMS) UNSALTED BUTTER,
    AT ROOM TEMPERATURE, CUT INTO ¼-INCH SLICES

ZESTY LIME FILLING

½ CUP PLUS 2 TABLESPOONS (2 OUNCES/55 GRAMS)
    UNSWEETENED MEDIUM-SHRED DRIED COCONUT

2 CUPS (14 OUNCES/400 GRAMS) GRANULATED SUGAR

2 TABLESPOONS ALL-PURPOSE FLOUR

½ TEASPOON BAKING POWDER

4 LARGE EGGS

⅓ CUP PLUS 1 TABLESPOON (3 FL OUNCES/90 ML) FRESH LIME
    JUICE (FROM 3 TO 4 LIMES)

2 TABLESPOONS FINELY GRATED LIME ZEST

MILK CHOCOLATE GLAZE

12 OUNCES (340 GRAMS) MILK CHOCOLATE, FINELY CHOPPED

½ CUP PLUS 1 TABLESPOON (4½ FL OUNCES/135 ML)
    HEAVY CREAM

3 TABLESPOONS FRESH LIME JUICE

Before baking: Center a rack in the oven and preheat the oven to 350 degrees F.

Press a sheet of aluminum foil to cover the outside bottom and sides of a 13 by 9 by 2-inch pan (quarter sheet pan). Lift off the foil, invert the pan and gently press the foil into the pan to fit contours. Lightly coat the foil-lined sides of the pan with soft butter or nonstick spray.

To make the crust: In a food processor, combine the flour, sugar, and salt and pulse 3 or 4 times to blend. Scatter the butter pieces over the flour mixture and pulse until the mixture resembles rolled oats with some small chunks of dough. Stop before the mixture forms a ball. Scatter the clumps over the bottom of the prepared pan, and press with fingertips to line the bottom of the pan evenly.

Bake the shortbread until it is no longer shiny on top and is light gold, 25 to 30 minutes. Transfer the pan to a wire rack to cool while you prepare the filling. Leave the oven on.

To make the Zesty Lime Filling: Spread the coconut on a baking sheet, place in the oven, and toast, tossing the coconut with a metal spatula as needed to ensure even baking, until lightly golden, 5 to 6 minutes. Distribute the toasted coconut evenly over the partially baked crust and set aside to cool.

In a medium bowl, combine the sugar, flour, and baking powder and stir with a rubber spatula or whisk until blended. In another medium bowl, combine the eggs and lime juice and zest and mix with a rubber spatula until blended. Add the flour mixture to the egg mixture and mix until thoroughly combined.

Pour the filling over the coconut-topped crust, return the pan to the oven, and bake until the filling no longer looks wet or shiny, is slightly crusty on top, and feels softly set yet doesn't quiver when gently touched or the pan is moved, 20 to 25 minutes. Transfer to a wire rack and let cool completely before glazing. The filling firms slightly as it cools.

To make the Milk Chocolate Glaze: Place the chocolate in a medium bowl. In a small, heavy saucepan, bring the cream just to a boil over medium-low heat. Pour the cream over the chocolate and let stand for about 30 seconds. Pour the lime juice on top and whisk together until smooth and creamy. Using an offset spatula, spread the glaze evenly over the cooled filling. Set aside in a cool room for a few hours until the glaze is set. To retain the vibrant appearance of the glaze, do not refrigerate.

To serve, using the edges of the foil as handles, lift the slab onto a cutting board. Using a *santoku* (page 42) or other sharp knife, cut the slab lengthwise into six 1½-inch-wide strips, wiping the blade clean with a damp towel after each cut. Then cut the slab crosswise into four 3-inch-wide strips, again wiping the blade after each cut. To store after cutting, return the bars to the pan, cover with aluminum foil, sealing the foil around the edges of the pan, and keep at room temperature for up to 2 days.

Millionaire's Shortbread

Here is a traditional British bar cookie that I first tasted in London. Later, when I visited a tea shop adjacent to a magnificent castle in Scotland, I met a generous baker, Tusanee Scott, who was selling millionaire's shortbread: thick caramelized milk filling (similar to *dulce de leche*) on a shortbread base, topped with rich chocolate icing. When I raved, she responded by writing the recipe for me on the spot.   YIELD: 2 TO 4 DOZEN SQUARES OR BARS, DEPENDING ON SIZE

SHORTBREAD

1¾ CUPS (8 OUNCES/225 GRAMS) ALL-PURPOSE FLOUR

¼ CUP (1¾ OUNCES/50 GRAMS) GRANULATED SUGAR

6 OUNCES (1½ STICKS/170 GRAMS) COLD UNSALTED BUTTER, CUT INTO ½-INCH SLICES

DULCE DE LECHE FILLING

1 CAN (14 OUNCES/SCANT 400 GRAMS) SWEETENED CONDENSED MILK

4 OUNCES (1 STICK/115 GRAMS) UNSALTED BUTTER

½ CUP (3½ OUNCES/100 GRAMS) GRANULATED SUGAR

CHOCOLATE GLAZE

6 OUNCES (170 GRAMS) SEMISWEET CHOCOLATE, FINELY CHOPPED

2 OUNCES (½ STICK/55 GRAMS) UNSALTED BUTTER

Before baking: Center a rack in the oven and preheat the oven to 350 degrees F.

To make the shortbread: In a food processor combine the flour and sugar, and process 3 or 4 seconds to blend. Scatter the butter pieces over the flour mixture and pulse until the mixture resembles small crumbs. Scatter the crumbs over the bottom of a 13 by 9 by 2-inch pan (quarter sheet pan), and press with fingertips to line the bottom of the pan evenly. If needed, place a sheet of plastic wrap on the surface of the dough, and use a 2½- to 4-inch pastry roller (or even a soda can) to help spread it evenly. Prick the surface with the tines of a fork.

Bake the shortbread until pale gold and firm to the touch, 20 to 25 minutes. Transfer the pan to a wire rack to cool while you prepare the filling.

To make the Dulce de Leche Filling: In a heavy 1½-quart saucepan, combine the milk, butter, and sugar and heat over low heat, swirling the pan occasionally to blend the ingredients, until the sugar dissolves. Bring to a boil, stirring occasionally with a silicone spatula, then reduce the heat and simmer gently, stirring frequently, until the mixture begins to come away from the sides of the pan, has thickened slightly, and is straw colored, 8 to 10 minutes. (Be careful not to undercook the filling, and watch closely to make sure it doesn't scorch.) Pour the filling over the shortbread base and spread it evenly with an offset spatula. Set aside at room temperature to cool for at least 2 hours or up to overnight.

To make the Chocolate Glaze: Half fill a bowl with hot water (120 degrees F). Put the chocolate and butter in a bowl and place it over (but not touching) the hot water. Let melt until creamy and smooth, stirring slowly occasionally. (Replace the water with more hot water, if needed, to melt the chocolate smoothly.)

Pour the glaze over the filling, and use the offset spatula to cover the filling in a thin, even layer. Place in the refrigerator for only 5 minutes to begin setting the chocolate. Remove from the refrigerator and let stand in a cool room until the surface is dry, shiny, and firm, 30 to 60 minutes.

To serve, use a thin-bladed, sharp paring knife to cut the slab into 1½-inch squares or 2 by 1-inch or 3 by 1-inch bars. To create neat, trim bars, dip the knife blade into very hot water and wipe it dry before each cut.

Flourless Banana Chiffon Cake

No one will ever guess that this cake is made without flour. This very moist chiffon cake is well suited to people who celebrate Passover or who can't tolerate flour, and to everyone else, too. One of the best cakes, period, the recipe came from a fabulous baker and friend, the late Ruth Kolm, and it tastes as good plain as it does frosted with sweetened whipped cream and garnished with fresh berries or assorted pieces of fruits spooned around the base of the cake.

YIELD: ONE 10-INCH TUBE CAKE, 12 TO 14 SERVINGS

1 CUP PLUS 2 TABLESPOONS (5½ OUNCES/155 GRAMS) MATZOH CAKE MEAL

¼ CUP PLUS 2 TABLESPOONS (2 OUNCES/55 GRAMS) POTATO STARCH

1½ CUPS (10½ OUNCES/300 GRAMS) GRANULATED SUGAR

½ TEASPOON SALT

¾ CUP (6 OUNCES/170 GRAMS) MASHED RIPE BANANAS (2 SMALL OR 1 LARGE)

6 LARGE EGGS, SEPARATED

1 LARGE EGG

¼ CUP PLUS 2 TABLESPOONS (3 FL OUNCES/90 ML) FLAVORLESS VEGETABLE OIL SUCH AS CANOLA OR SAFFLOWER

2 TEASPOONS FINELY GRATED LEMON ZEST

1 TEASPOON PURE VANILLA EXTRACT

Before baking: Center a rack in the oven and preheat the oven to 325 degrees F. Have ready a 10 by 4¼-inch tube pan, preferably with a removable bottom, and a long-necked bottle or large heat-resistant funnel for cooling the cake.

Sift together the cake meal, potato starch, ¾ cup (5¼ ounces/150 grams) of the sugar, and the salt into a large bowl. Make a well in the center and add the bananas, egg yolks, egg, oil, lemon zest, and vanilla to the well. Using a rubber spatula, stir together the banana mixture with the dry ingredients until smooth, thick, and well blended.

In the bowl of a stand mixer fitted with the whisk attachment, whip the whites on medium-low speed until soft peaks form, about 1½ minutes. Increase the speed to medium and gradually add the remaining ¾ cup sugar. Continue whipping until glossy white, stiff but not dry peaks form, about 2 minutes. Using a clean rubber spatula, fold ¾ to 1 cup of the whipped whites into the egg yolk mixture to lighten it. Then fold in the remaining whites just until combined. Spoon the batter into the tube pan, spreading the batter evenly with the spatula.

Bake the cake until lightly golden, the top springs back when touched lightly, and a round wooden toothpick inserted near the center comes out free of cake, 55 to 60 minutes. Remove the pan from the oven and immediately invert it over the long-necked bottle. Let cool completely, about 2 hours.

To remove the cake from the pan, tilt the cake pan on its side, and gently tap the bottom against a counter to loosen the cake. Rotate the cake pan, tapping it a few more times as you turn it, until the cake appears free from the sides of the pan. Invert a wire rack on top of the cake, or top with a cardboard round, and as you invert the cake, tap it firmly on the surface. Lift the pan from the cake. Or, if the pan has a removable bottom, when the cake sides are free, push up the bottom to release the cake from the pan completely. The cake should come out cleanly and beautifully, like a pillow taken out of a slipcover.

If serving the cake within 24 hours, wrap in plastic wrap and store at room temperature. For longer storage, over-wrap with aluminum foil, label with the contents and date, and freeze for up to 10 days. To thaw, remove the foil and leave at room temperature for about 3 hours.

To serve, cut the cake with a sharp knife. Store any leftovers, under a cake dome or wrapped in plastic wrap, at room temperature.

Raspberry Sheet Cake

This light pound cake is enriched with a small amount of almond paste, which adds flavor without making the batter heavy. I use a ruler to mark neat 3-inch squares that create perfectly sized individual portions when cut. I prefer squares to other shapes, since there are no scraps when you cut them. My recipe is adapted from a recipe that appears in *The Taste of Summer* (1988), one of the first of several fabulous books written by the very talented Diane Worthington, and it is the exact dessert that I brought to her book party all those years ago. Raspberries suspended in the cake create a whimsical, polka-dot effect. Here's a wonderful way to feed a crowd with something that looks like it takes much more effort to make than it actually does.

You will enjoy the simple, tailored decoration. Place strips of paper on top of the cake, on the diagonal and spaced ½ inch apart; sprinkle the cake with powdered sugar; and carefully remove the strips. Or, for a different decorative touch, apply lengths of string in any design you like to the cake's surface, sprinkle the cake with powdered sugar, and then carefully lift the strings to reveal the design. **YIELD: TWENTY 3 BY 3 ¼-INCH PIECES OR 3-INCH CIRCLES**

3 ½ CUPS (1 POUND/455 GRAMS) ALL-PURPOSE FLOUR

1 ½ TEASPOONS BAKING POWDER

½ TEASPOON SALT

¼ CUP (2 OUNCES/55 GRAMS) ALMOND PASTE

2 ½ CUPS (1 POUND, 2 OUNCES/500 GRAMS) GRANULATED SUGAR

15 OUNCES (3 ¾ STICKS/430 GRAMS) UNSALTED BUTTER, AT ROOM TEMPERATURE, CUT INTO 1 ½-INCH PIECES

2 TEASPOONS PURE VANILLA EXTRACT

½ TEASPOON PURE ALMOND EXTRACT

8 LARGE EGGS, LIGHTLY BEATEN

3 CUPS (12 TO 15 OUNCES/340 TO 420 GRAMS) FIRM BUT RIPE RED RASPBERRIES, OR A MIXTURE OF BERRIES OF CHOICE, PICKED OVER FOR STEMS

⅓ CUP (1 ¼ OUNCES/35 GRAMS) POWDERED SUGAR

Before baking: Center a rack in the oven and preheat the oven to 350 degrees F. Butter an 18 by 13 by 1-inch pan (half sheet pan), then flour it, tapping out the excess flour. Line the bottom with parchment paper. Have all of the ingredients at room temperature.

To make the cake: Sift together the flour, baking powder, and salt onto a sheet of waxed paper; set aside. In the bowl of a stand mixer fitted with the paddle attachment, beat the almond paste on low speed for 30 seconds just until it is a crumbly mixture. Maintaining the same speed, add ½ cup (3 ½ ounces/100 grams) of the sugar in a steady stream and continue to beat until the almond paste has broken up and is well combined with the sugar, about 1 minute. Then beat in the remaining 2 cups (14 ounces/400 grams) sugar in a steady stream until combined, scraping down the sides of the bowl as needed.

Continue beating on low speed while adding the butter, 1 piece at a time. Stop the mixer occasionally to scrape the mixture clinging to the sides down into the center of the bowl. Increase the speed to medium-low and beat until the mixture is smooth, lighter in color, and fluffy in texture, 3 to 4 minutes. Add the extracts during the last few moments of mixing.

With the mixer on medium speed, add the eggs, 3 to 4 tablespoons at a time, beating after each addition until incorporated. Continue to beat, stopping the mixer to scrape down the sides of the bowl at least once, until the mixture appears light in color and texture, about 2 minutes.

On the lowest speed, add the flour mixture in four additions, stopping the mixer occasionally to scrape down the sides of the bowl and beating until the batter is smooth. Detach the paddle and bowl from the mixer, and tap the paddle against the side of the bowl to free the excess batter. Sprinkle the berries on top of the batter and gently fold them into the batter with a rubber spatula. Spoon the batter into the prepared pan, spreading as evenly as possible with the rubber spatula.

Bake the cake for 30 minutes, then rotate the pan 180 degrees and continue to bake until the cake is pale gold on top, springs back when touched lightly, and a round wooden toothpick inserted in the center comes out free of cake, 20 to 25 minutes longer. Transfer the pan to a wire rack and let cool completely.

To cut the cake into neat pieces, you need a sharp knife and an 18-inch ruler to measure and cut 3 by 3$\frac{1}{4}$-inch pieces. Place the ruler next to one of the long sides (18 inches) of the pan. With the tip of the knife, mark $\frac{1}{2}$-inch notches in the cake every 3$\frac{1}{4}$ inches along the entire length. Repeat on the opposite side, so that the notches line up directly across from each other. Repeat this procedure on the short sides of the pan, too, marking the notches in the cake every 3 inches. With the knife, cut through the cake in straight lines, using the notches and the ruler as guides. When you are finished, the pattern for the squares has been formed. Alternatively, cut out circles using a 3-inch round cutter.

The cake is so moist that it may remain in the baking pan, uncovered, for several hours or even overnight before serving. For longer storage, cover the cake in the pan with aluminum foil, securing it around the edges of the pan, and freeze for up to 1 week. Thaw at room temperature for 1 to 2 hours.

Before serving, cut $\frac{1}{4}$- or $\frac{1}{2}$-inch-wide strips of parchment or waxed paper about 15 inches long (some of the strips are longer than needed; just clip them close to size, if you wish), and place them diagonally on top of the cake. Sprinkle the powdered sugar evenly over the cake. Carefully remove the strips, revealing the design. Using a small metal spatula, transfer each square to a paper case. If desired set the cakes on their paper cases on a platter or tray for ease in serving. Any leftover cake squares can be placed in a sturdy airtight container and frozen for up to 1 week.

Chocolate–Sour Cream Pound Cake with Cheesecake Swirl

A chocolate lover's delight, this rich, dark pound cake features a velvety cream cheese swirl enhanced with ground hazelnuts, dried cherries, and a dash of kirsch. Whenever I bake it, I can't wait to cut it to see how the filling has swirled itself through the cake, creating an artistic decoration for every slice. I make this cake in the traditional Bundt, which has simple lines. If you select a Bundt pan that has an intricate design or detail, you need to prepare the pan differently to ensure that the baked cake will release from it in one piece (page 24). If you bake the cake in a pan with a dark surface, reduce the oven temperature indicated in the recipe by 25 degrees F. Pans that have a dark finish tend to bake hotter than those that don't, so lowering the oven temperature will ensure the cake is done in the same amount of time.

YIELD: ONE 10-INCH TUBE CAKE, 20 SERVINGS (3 THIN SLICES PER SERVING)

CHEESECAKE SWIRL

ONE 8-OUNCE (225-GRAM) PACKAGE CREAM CHEESE, AT ROOM TEMPERATURE

¼ CUP (1¾ OUNCES/50 GRAMS) GRANULATED SUGAR

1 LARGE EGG

1 TEASPOON PURE VANILLA EXTRACT

2 TABLESPOONS HAZELNUTS, TOASTED AND SKINNED (PAGES 15–16), THEN FINELY GROUND TO YIELD ¼ CUP (½ OUNCE/15 GRAMS)

2 TABLESPOONS COARSELY CHOPPED DRIED SOUR CHERRIES

1 TABLESPOON KIRSCH (OPTIONAL)

CHOCOLATE–SOUR CREAM POUND CAKE

¾ CUP (2¼ OUNCES/65 GRAMS) UNSWEETENED NATURAL COCOA POWDER

¾ CUP (6 FL OUNCES/180 ML) WARM WATER (100 TO 120 DEGREES F)

2¼ CUPS (9¼ OUNCES/260 GRAMS) CAKE FLOUR

1½ TEASPOONS BAKING SODA

½ TEASPOON BAKING POWDER

½ TEASPOON SALT

6 OUNCES (1½ STICKS/170 GRAMS) UNSALTED BUTTER, AT ROOM TEMPERATURE

1¾ CUPS PLUS 2 TABLESPOONS (13¼ OUNCES/375 GRAMS) GRANULATED SUGAR

3 LARGE EGGS, LIGHTLY BEATEN

2 TEASPOONS PURE VANILLA EXTRACT

¾ CUP (6 OUNCES/170 GRAMS) SOUR CREAM

Before baking: Center a rack in the oven and preheat the oven to 350 degrees F (or 325 degrees F if the pan has a dark finish). Butter a 10 by 3-inch Bundt pan, lightly coat it with nonstick spray, then flour it, tapping out the excess flour. Or, butter and flour a 10 by 4¼-inch tube pan with or without a removable bottom. For the cake batter, in a medium bowl, whisk together the cocoa powder and warm water until blended; set aside to cool. Have all of the remaining ingredients at room temperature.

To make the Cheesecake Swirl: In a medium bowl, beat the cheese with a rubber spatula just until the cheese is smooth and creamy. Or, use a handheld electric mixer on low, being careful not to whip in too much air. Beat in the sugar until well blended. Add the egg and vanilla and mix until combined and creamy. By hand, stir in the nuts, cherries, and kirsch, if using, until evenly distributed. Set aside.

To make the Chocolate–Sour Cream Pound Cake: Sift together the flour, baking soda, baking powder, and salt onto a sheet of waxed paper; set aside. In the bowl of a stand mixer fitted with the paddle attachment, beat the butter on medium speed until creamy and smooth, 30 to 45 seconds. Add the sugar in a steady stream. Continue to beat until light in color and texture, 3 to 4 minutes, stopping the mixer occasionally to scrape down the sides of the bowl.

With the mixer on medium speed, add the eggs, 2 to 3 tablespoons at a time, beating after each addition until incorporated and stopping the mixer occasionally to scrape down the sides of the bowl. Add the vanilla and sour cream to the cooled cocoa mixture and stir to combine. With the mixer on the lowest speed, add the flour mixture in three additions alternately with the cocoa mixture in two additions, beginning and ending with the flour mixture and mixing after each addition until incorporated. Again, stop the mixer occasionally to scrape down the sides of the bowl.

Spoon half of the batter into the prepared pan and spread it with the rubber spatula, working from the center outward to create a slightly raised ridge around the rim. Carefully spoon the cream cheese filling over the batter, trying to contain it within the rim. If you are able to keep the filling from touching the pan, it will remain concealed when the cake is finished baking. Spoon the remaining batter over the filling and smooth the top.

Bake the cake until the center springs back when lightly touched and a round wooden toothpick inserted in the center comes out free of cake, 60 to 70 minutes. Transfer the pan to a wire rack and let cool for 10 to 15 minutes.

Tilt and rotate the pan while gently tapping it on a work surface to release the cake sides. Invert a wire rack on top of the cake, invert the cake onto it, and carefully lift off the pan. Let cool completely.

To serve, cut the cake into thin slices with a serrated knife. Store any leftovers under a cake dome at room temperature.

Brown Sugar–Almond Slices

Eating this cookie reminds me of a favorite childhood snack that I enjoyed with a tall glass of cold milk. It is a crispy-thin, not-too-sweet icebox cookie with lots of nuts to make it extraordinary. It is adapted from a recipe given to me by ace baker Shirley Rosenberg, who has diligently and lovingly tested my recipes for years, and it is great with fruit sorbets and chocolate and caramel ice creams.

This recipe makes oodles of cookies. Keep the dough in your freezer, and when you want some cookies, transfer a portion of the dough to the refrigerator to thaw, so that later you can slice just what you need and bake it. With little effort, cookies are ready to be mounded in a napkin-lined basket for sharing with family and friends.   **YIELD: 9 TO 12 DOZEN COOKIES**

5 CUPS (1 POUND, 7 ½ OUNCES/670 GRAMS)
   ALL-PURPOSE FLOUR

1 TABLESPOON GROUND CINNAMON

1 TEASPOON BAKING SODA

¼ TEASPOON SALT

1 POUND (4 STICKS/455 GRAMS) UNSALTED
   BUTTER, SOFTENED

2⅓ CUPS FIRMLY PACKED (1 POUND/455 GRAMS) LIGHT
   BROWN SUGAR

3 LARGE EGGS

2 TEASPOONS PURE VANILLA EXTRACT

1¾ CUPS (5 ½ OUNCES/155 GRAMS) SLICED ALMONDS,
   PREFERABLY BLANCHED

Line a 9 by 2-inch square pan with heavy-duty aluminum foil, pressing it into the contours of the pan and allowing 2 to 3 inches to overhang each side. Alternatively, line the pan with a double layer of regular foil the same way (a single layer of regular foil may tear when you lift the firm, heavy cookie dough out of the pan later).

Sift together the flour, cinnamon, baking soda, and salt onto a sheet of waxed paper; set aside. In the bowl of a stand mixer fitted with the paddle attachment, beat together the butter and sugar on medium speed until thoroughly blended and the mixture clings to the sides of the bowl and is smooth and creamy, about 45 seconds. Maintaining the same speed, add the eggs, one at a time, beating after each addition until incorporated. Then beat in the vanilla. Stop the mixer to scrape down the sides of the bowl as needed.

On the lowest speed, add the flour mixture, about ¾ cup at a time (6 or 7 additions), beating after each addition until incorporated. Detach the paddle and bowl from the mixer, and return any dough on the paddle to the bowl. Using a rubber spatula, reach down to the bottom of the bowl to make sure all of the flour has been incorporated into the dough. Stir in the almonds, evenly distributing them throughout the dough. Spoon the soft dough into the prepared pan, place a sheet of plastic wrap on the surface of the dough, and pat the dough to spread it evenly. A 2½- to 4-inch pastry roller (or even a soda can) is helpful for spreading the dough evenly in the pan. Refrigerate the dough until firm, at least 6 hours or up to overnight.

Center a rack in the oven and preheat the oven to 350 degrees F. Line a large baking sheet with parchment paper. If you plan to bake more than one-fourth of the dough, line at least 2 baking sheets with parchment paper. This way you can work in tandem: slice and arrange unbaked cookies on the cool baking sheet while the other cookies are baking. If you prefer to bake 2 sheets at the same time, position one rack in the lower third of the oven and a second rack in the upper third of the oven and switch the pans between the racks and rotate them 180 degrees halfway through baking.

Using the foil flaps to help, lift the chilled dough from the pan. Peel off and discard the foil. Alternatively, turn the pan upside down and let the dough, which is stuck to the foil, release onto the work surface. Slice the dough into three 3-inch-wide or four 2¼-inch-wide strips. Wrap any strips you are not cutting and baking now in plastic wrap and refrigerate for up to 5 days. For longer storage, overwrap with aluminum foil, label with the contents and date, and freeze for up to 3 months. Using a sharp knife (serrated is fine), cut each strip crosswise into slices a scant ¼ inch thick, and space them 1 inch apart on the prepared baking sheets.

Bake the cookies, 1 or 2 sheets at a time, until golden yet not dark brown, 8 to 10 minutes. Transfer the cookies with a metal spatula to a wire rack to cool. They will become crispy as they cool. To store, stack in airtight containers and store at room temperature for up to 1 week.

Inside-Out Chocolate Layer Cake

One of the sweet mysteries in American baking history is that desserts like this one are always called chocolate layer cakes, even though the only chocolate element is the rich frosting between the layers of moist, tender yellow cake. Here, I've opted to defy tradition and call my version of this classic exactly what it is: an inside-out chocolate layer cake. Made with my Signature Yellow Cake and a decadent chocolate frosting, the old-fashioned recipe is reminiscent of one my Aunt Julia used to bake. Her luscious layer cake went on to become a legend in our family, as I hope this one will be in yours. Great for birthdays and other special occasions, the cake's personality can be varied by using different fillings, including alternating the decadent Bittersweet Chocolate Frosting featured here with colorful fruit preserves. **YIELD: ONE 9-INCH, 4-LAYER ROUND CAKE; 14 OR MORE SERVINGS**

1 RECIPE (TWO 9-INCH OR THREE 8-INCH ROUND LAYERS) SIGNATURE YELLOW CAKE (PAGE 348)

BITTERSWEET CHOCOLATE FROSTING

8 OUNCES UNSWEETENED CHOCOLATE, COARSELY CHOPPED

2 CUPS (7 OUNCES/200 GRAMS) POWDERED SUGAR

¼ CUP (2 FL OUNCES/60 ML) HOT WATER

4 TO 5 TABLESPOONS (2 TO 2½ FL OUNCES/60 TO 75 ML) HEAVY CREAM

1½ TEASPOONS PURE VANILLA EXTRACT

6 OUNCES (1½ STICKS/170 GRAMS) UNSALTED BUTTER, SOFTENED

Bake the cake layers as directed, and let cool completely on wire racks.

To make the Bittersweet Chocolate Frosting: Half fill a bowl with hot water (120 degrees F). Put the chocolate in a bowl and place it over (but not touching) the hot water. Let the chocolate melt until creamy and smooth, stirring slowly occasionally. (Replace the water with more hot water, if needed, to melt the chocolate smoothly.) Remove from the water bath. Or, put the chocolate in a medium microwave-safe bowl and melt in a microwave oven at 50 percent power (medium) for 45-second bursts, stirring after each burst, until melted, about 3½ minutes.

Pour the sugar into a sieve or sifter and sift it on top of the melted chocolate, without stirring. Add the hot water, 4 tablespoons of the cream, and the vanilla and stir together with a rubber spatula briefly and briskly. Stir in the butter just until it is smooth and homogeneous. Stir in an additional tablespoon of cream if the mixture is too thick. (Stirring in quickly to incorporate the additions is fine, but whisking is not recommended. It introduces too much air, which lightens the rich dark color of the frosting.) The frosting is usually easiest to spread as soon as you finish making it. However, the temperature of your kitchen and of the ingredients can affect the consistency of the frosting. If it is too runny, more like a glaze than a frosting, set it aside for 15 to 20 minutes until it just thickens to a spreadable consistency before using. After frosting the cake, the chocolate will set up as it cools, which makes the frosting thicker. You should have 2¾ cups (about 1½ pounds/680 grams).

To assemble the cake: Using a 12-inch serrated knife, split each layer in half horizontally (page 25). Place 1 of the bottom cake layers, cut side up, on a sturdy cardboard round, or place it on a cake plate and slip about 3 strips of waxed paper under the cake to protect the plate. (A decorator's turntable is helpful when frosting the cake. If using the turntable, place the cake on its cardboard on the platform and frost as directed. After frosting the cake, lift it off of the turntable on its cardboard base and transfer to a cake plate.) If you baked 2 cake layers and split them to create 4 layers, using a metal icing spatula, spread a scant ⅔ cup frosting evenly over the layer all the way to the edges. Place the matching layer on top of the frosting, lining up the edges. Spread about ²/₃ cup frosting on the layer all the way to the edges. Repeat with the remaining layers, spreading each with frosting. If you baked 3 cake layers and split them to create 6 layers, spread ¹/₃ cup plus 1 tablespoon frosting over each layer. Center the last layer, golden side up, on top of the frosting, and spread the sides and top of the cake evenly with the remaining frosting.

To serve, cut the cake with a sharp knife, wiping the blade clean with a damp towel after each cut. Store any leftovers under a cake dome at room temperature, or place a piece of plastic wrap directly on the exposed portion of cake to keep it from drying out.

Special Spritz Cookies

Count on this recipe and your trusty cookie press to turn you into a veritable cookie factory, producing lots of beautiful treats in a gratifyingly short time. I often make these delectable cookies for large gatherings, from Champagne tastings to family reunions to school functions. I especially enjoy baking them for young children, since the size is easily tailored for a toddler's hands. For a friend blessed with twin grandchildren (a boy and a girl), I decorated the cookies with translucent sugar glazes in pale pink and blue.   **YIELD: ABOUT 6 DOZEN 1½-INCH CORAL COOKIES OR TWENTY-ONE 2¾- TO 3-INCH-LONG RIBBON SANDWICH COOKIES**

COOKIE DOUGH

2¼ CUPS (10¼ OUNCES/290 GRAMS) ALL-PURPOSE FLOUR

¼ TEASPOON SALT

8 OUNCES (2 STICKS/225 GRAMS) UNSALTED BUTTER, AT ROOM TEMPERATURE

⅔ CUP (4½ OUNCES/130 GRAMS) GRANULATED SUGAR

2 LARGE EGG YOLKS

1 TEASPOON PURE VANILLA EXTRACT

¼ TEASPOON PURE LEMON EXTRACT

¼ TEASPOON PURE ALMOND EXTRACT

½ CUP (4 OUNCES/115 GRAMS) SANDING SUGAR (OPTIONAL)

5-PETAL FLOWER COOKIE SUGAR GLAZE

½ CUP (1¾ OUNCES/50 GRAMS) POWDERED SUGAR

4 TEASPOONS WATER

FOOD COLORING (OPTIONAL)

RIBBON SANDWICH COOKIES

½ CUP (5 OUNCES/140 GRAMS) FAVORITE RED JAM OR JELLY

6 OUNCES (170 GRAMS) WHITE OR DARK SEMISWEET CHOCOLATE, FINELY CHOPPED

1 TEASPOON SAFFLOWER OR CANOLA OIL

2 CUPS ASSORTED SPRINKLES OR FINELY CHOPPED NUTS SUCH AS PISTACHIOS, BLACK WALNUTS, OR NATURAL ALMONDS

Before baking: Center a rack in the oven and preheat the oven to 350 degrees F. If you prefer to bake 2 sheets of cookies at the same time, position one rack in the lower third of the oven and a second rack in the upper third of the oven. Line 1 or 2 large baking sheets with a silicone mat, rough side up. (If you bake these cookies

on an ungreased baking sheet, the dough forms perfectly from the press, but it sticks as it bakes and the cookies break when you try to remove them with a spatula. Parchment avoids the sticking problem, but the dough does not release cleanly from the press on the paper.) Insert a cookie-design plate into the ring on a cookie press, and then tightly screw the ring back onto the cookie-press barrel. For this recipe, I use 2 different design plates: a 5-petal flower and a ribbon (sometimes called a washboard). But feel free to select any design plate you like.

To make the cookie dough: In a medium bowl, whisk together the flour and salt just to blend; set aside. In a stand mixer fitted with the paddle attachment, beat together the butter and sugar on medium-low speed until very creamy and well blended, about 1 minute. Beat in the egg yolks and the extracts. On the lowest speed, add the flour mixture, about ½ cup at a time, mixing well after each addition. A soft dough will form.

To use the dough right away, divide it into thirds; each third will weigh about 8 ounces (225 grams). Pack 1 portion of the dough into the plate-outfitted cookie-press barrel. When filling the barrel with dough, pack it firmly. (If not using all of the dough at this time, wrap the remaining portions separately in plastic wrap and refrigerate for up to 3 days. For longer storage, overwrap with aluminum foil, label with the contents and date, and freeze for up to 2 weeks. Before using, bring the dough to room temperature until it is pliable enough to force through the press.)

For a 5-petal flower design, hold the press perpendicular to the prepared baking sheet and press out the cookies, spacing them about ½ inch apart. (Most cookie presses have a lever for adjusting the amount of dough that is extruded each time you depress the lever.) As you press the dough, it will stick to the silicone mat, making it easy to form each cookie. After forming each cookie, simply lift up the press and the cookie dough will release from the press and adhere to the mat.

Ribbon (or washboard) cookies are formed slightly differently, depending on your press. Tilt the press slightly so that you are holding it similar to how you hold a pencil when you are writing. (For most shapes, such as snowflakes, stars, Christmas trees, and wreaths, the press is held perpendicular, as it is for the 5-petal flower.) Then, press out a strip of dough onto the baking sheet in the length you want. (I prefer strips 2¾ to 3 inches long.) To stop the flow of dough at the length you want, you may need to cut it with a small metal spatula to release it from the design plate. Then press or squeeze again to form the next strip. Sprinkle sanding sugar over the cookies, if desired.

Bake the cookies just until they are firm to the touch and their edges are barely golden, 12 to 14 minutes. If you are baking 2 sheets of cookies at the same time, switch the pans between the racks and rotate them 180 degrees halfway through baking. Transfer the pan(s) to a wire rack, let cool for 5 minutes, and then transfer the cookies to a wire rack and let cool completely. Repeat with the remaining dough portions.

To glaze the 5-petal flower cookies: To make the glaze, in a small bowl, stir together the sugar, water, and a drop or two of food coloring, if using, until smooth and evenly colored. Or, mix together the sugar and water, divide into 2 or more batches, and color each batch a different color. With a pastry brush, splatter the top of each cookie with the glaze. Or, dab a small amount of glaze on the surface of each cookie, perhaps one color (like pink) on one-half of the cookie and another color (like blue) next to the pink. Set the cookies aside at room temperature to allow the glaze to set and dry before storing.

To make ribbon sandwich cookies: In a small, heavy saucepan, bring the jam to a boil and boil for 1 minute to evaporate some of its liquid. Remove from the heat and let cool until warm. Turn over half of the cookies, and spoon about ½ teaspoon jam or jelly onto each cookie. Top with the remaining plain cookies, bottom side down, and press gently so the jam spreads just to the edge of the sandwiched cookies.

To glaze the ribbon sandwich cookies: Half fill a bowl with hot water (95 to 110 degrees F for white chocolate and 120 degrees F for dark chocolate). Put the chocolate and oil in a bowl and place it over (but not touching) the hot water. Let the chocolate melt until creamy and smooth, stirring slowly occasionally. (Replace the water with more hot water, if needed, to melt the chocolate smoothly.) Remove from the water bath. Put the sprinkles in a bowl. Dip one or both short edges of each cookie in the chocolate, and then dip the edge(s) into the sprinkles, pressing them with your fingertips to make sure they adhere. As each cookie is coated, set it aside on a clean baking sheet. Set the baking sheet aside in a cool room just to firm the chocolate (or place it briefly in the refrigerator just until the chocolate is set).

To store undecorated, unfilled cookies, stack them in an airtight container and store at room temperature for up to 10 days. Store decorated cookies in a single layer in an aluminum foil–lined, covered cardboard container, such as a cake box, at room temperature for up to 3 days.

Orange Chiffon Tweed Cake with Milk 'n' Honey Sabayon

Tweed is a timeless fabric that exemplifies good taste—as does this divine dessert. This tender, fine-textured cake is inspired by an orange chiffon cake that I first tasted years ago at Gayle's Bakery in Capitola, California, home to some of the most sumptuous cakes, breads, pies, pastries, cookies, and coffee cakes I've ever eaten. Capitola is located between San Francisco and the Carmel-Monterey area, so if you should find yourself in either place, a detour to Gayle's is definitely worth the drive. I've enriched the tangy orange batter with finely grated semisweet and milk chocolate, creating handsome tweedy flecks in the finished cake. For a simple, yet festive finishing touch, accompany the dessert with San Francisco pastry chef and consultant Janet Rikala Dalton's ethereal milk-and-honey sabayon.

The key to creating a fine-textured chiffon cake is to gently fold well-beaten egg whites into a fluffy egg-yolk mixture. The orange peel in the batter guarantees an orange flavor that won't disappear during baking. The pith on a citrus peel is the soft, spongy white tissue that separates the peel from the flesh. It is usually quite bitter, so you want as little of it as possible to remain on the peel. It is worth owning a serrated peeler, which slices so finely that almost no pith remains on the peel. **YIELD: ONE 10-INCH TUBE CAKE, 14 TO 18 SERVINGS**

ORANGE CHIFFON TWEED CAKE

5 STRIPS ORANGE PEEL, EACH ABOUT 1½ INCHES LONG BY ½ INCH WIDE

1½ CUPS (10½ OUNCES/300 GRAMS) GRANULATED SUGAR

2¼ CUPS (9¼ OUNCES/260 GRAMS) CAKE FLOUR

1 TABLESPOON BAKING POWDER

1 TEASPOON SALT

6 LARGE EGGS, SEPARATED

2 LARGE EGG WHITES

½ CUP (4 FL OUNCES/120 ML) CANOLA OIL

¾ CUP (6 FL OUNCES/180 ML) FRESH ORANGE JUICE

2 OUNCES (55 GRAMS) SEMISWEET CHOCOLATE, FINELY GRATED

1 OUNCE (30 GRAMS) MILK CHOCOLATE, FINELY GRATED

MILK 'N' HONEY SABAYON

½ CUP (4 FL OUNCES/120 ML) HEAVY CREAM

6 LARGE (½ CUP/4 FL OUNCES/120 ML) EGG YOLKS

⅓ CUP (4 OUNCES BY WEIGHT/115 GRAMS) ORANGE CLOVER HONEY

⅓ CUP (2½ FL OUNCES/75 ML) NONFAT OR 1-PERCENT MILK

⅓ CUP (2½ FL OUNCES/75 ML) ORANGE LIQUEUR, SUCH AS COINTREAU, OR ORANGE JUICE

Before baking: Center a rack in the oven and preheat the oven to 350 degrees F. Have ready a 10 by 4¼-inch tube pan, preferably with a removable bottom, and a long-necked bottle or large heat-resistant funnel for cooling the cake.

To make the Orange Chiffon Tweed Cake: Place the orange peel and 2 tablespoons of the sugar in a small food processor or chopper and process until the peel is finely chopped, about 1 minute; set aside. (Alternatively, in a small bowl, mix 2 tablespoons of the sugar with ¼ cup finely grated orange zest from 2 oranges.)

Sift together the flour, ¾ cup (5¼ ounces/150 grams) of the sugar, the baking powder, and the salt into a large bowl. With a rubber spatula, make a well in the center and set aside. In a medium bowl, combine the 6 egg yolks, oil, 2 tablespoons of the orange-flavored sugar, and the orange juice. Using a handheld mixer, beat the egg yolk mixture on medium speed just to aerate it, 40 to 50 seconds. Pour the egg yolk mixture into the well of the flour mixture and then beat on medium-low speed just until the batter is completely smooth and homogeneous, about 30 seconds. Stop the mixer occasionally to scrape down the sides of the bowl.

In the large bowl of a stand mixer fitted with the whisk attachment, whip the 8 egg whites on medium-low speed until small bubbles appear and the surface is frothy, about 30 seconds. Increase the speed to medium and whip until soft white peaks form, about 45 seconds. Maintaining the same speed, add the remaining sugar (scant ⅔ cup/4½ ounces/130 grams) in a slow, steady stream and whip until glossy white, stiff but not dry peaks form, 1 to 1½ minutes.

Detach the whisk and bowl from the mixer, and tap the whisk against the side of the bowl to free the excess whites. Using the rubber spatula, gently stir about one-third of the egg whites into the batter to lighten it. Then fold in the remaining egg whites and the grated chocolates just until no white streaks remain. Carefully pour the batter into the prepared pan, spreading evenly with the rubber spatula.

Bake the cake until it is light brown on top, springs back when lightly pressed, and a round wooden toothpick inserted near the center comes out free of batter and is not sticky when touched, about 45 minutes. Remove the pan from the oven and immediately invert it over the long-necked bottle. Let cool completely, about 3 hours.

To remove the cake from the pan, slip just the tip of a small metal spatula or paring knife between the cake sides and the pan, and slowly trace the perimeter to release any cake sticking to the pan. Tilt the cake pan on its side, and gently tap the bottom against a counter to loosen the cake further. Rotate the cake pan, tapping it a few more times as you turn it, until it appears free. Invert a rack on top of the cake, or top with a cardboard round, and as you invert the cake, tap it firmly on a counter. Lift the pan from the cake. Or, if the pan has a removable bottom, when the cake sides are free, push up the bottom to release the cake from the pan completely. It should come out cleanly and beautifully, like a pillow taken out of a slipcover.

If serving the cake within 24 hours, wrap in plastic wrap and store it at room temperature. For longer storage, overwrap with aluminum foil, label with the contents and date, and freeze for up to 2 weeks. To thaw, remove the foil and leave at room temperature for about 3 hours.

To make the Milk 'n' Honey Sabayon: Using a whisk or a handheld mixer, whip the cream in a deep, medium bowl until soft peaks form. Cover and refrigerate. Prepare an ice-water bath by filling a large bowl one-third to one-half full with ice and water; set aside. Select a large stainless-steel bowl that will fit snugly in the top of a saucepan, and combine the egg yolks and honey in the bowl. Fill the saucepan about one-third full with water and bring to a gentle simmer. Meanwhile, using a handheld electric mixer, whip the egg yolk mixture on medium speed until thick and pale in color, 2 to 3 minutes. Set the bowl over (not touching) the simmering water and continue to whip while gradually adding the milk and liqueur. Continue to whip on medium to medium-low speed until the mixture is fluffy and light, has almost tripled in volume, and forms a soft peak when the beater is lifted, 3 to 4 minutes. Transfer the bowl to the ice-water bath to cool the mixture rapidly, gently stirring once or twice.

When the mixture is cool, fold in the whipped cream with a rubber spatula. Use right away, or cover and refrigerate for up to 1 day. Whisk to blend the ingredients before serving.

To serve, slice the cake with a serrated knife, using a sawing motion. Spoon a dollop (or if you own an oval-shaped ice-cream scoop, an oval dollop) of the sabayon on top of or alongside each slice of cake.

Double-Crust Sweet Ricotta Galette

Fashioned after an unforgettable breakfast pastry I enjoyed one morning in a Chicago hotel, this heavenly galette combines an exceptionally flaky, buttery crust with a thin layer of sweet ricotta filling. The simple filling, enhanced with a hint of orange zest and a dash of vanilla, allows the pure, wholesome flavor of ricotta cheese to shine through. Distinguished by its endearingly rustic, handcrafted appearance, the freshly baked galette is a wonderful addition to brunch, lunch, or supper.

YIELD: ONE 11½- TO 12-INCH DOUBLE-CRUST GALETTE, 12 SERVINGS

SWEET RICOTTA FILLING

1 CUP (8 OUNCES/225 GRAMS) WHOLE-MILK RICOTTA CHEESE

½ CUP (1¾ OUNCES/50 GRAMS) POWDERED SUGAR

1 LARGE EGG YOLK

FINELY GRATED ZEST OF 1 SMALL ORANGE

1 TEASPOON PURE VANILLA EXTRACT

¼ TEASPOON PURE ALMOND EXTRACT

PINCH OF SALT

1 RECIPE ALL-BUTTER FLAKY PASTRY (PAGE 356)

GLAZE

WHOLE MILK FOR BRUSHING

1 TABLESPOON SANDING OR GRANULATED SUGAR

To make the Sweet Ricotta Filling: Spoon the ricotta into a sieve placed over a bowl and cover with plastic wrap, pressing it directly on the surface of the cheese. Let drain for at least 1 hour or preferably overnight in the refrigerator. Don't fret if nothing drips from the ricotta; different brands have different amounts of moisture.

When ready to bake, transfer the ricotta to a bowl and discard any collected liquids. Add the sugar, egg yolk, orange zest, both extracts, and salt and mix well; set aside.

Before baking: Center a rack in the oven and preheat the oven to 400 degrees F. Line a large baking sheet with parchment paper.

To form the galette: Remove the pastry from the refrigerator and cut it in half (just cut across the plastic-wrapped package with a sharp knife). Return 1 portion to the refrigerator to keep it cold. Remove and discard the plastic wrap from the other portion and place the dough on a lightly floured work surface. Roll out the dough into an 11- to 12-inch square. As you roll, lightly flour the dough and the work surface as needed; lift and move the dough to make sure it is gliding and expanding on the surface, not sticking to it; and never roll off the edges. If you own a 2½- to 4-inch pastry roller, you might find it helpful in expanding the dough into a 12½- or 13½-inch square. If not, continue to roll with the rolling pin to reach this size. Roll the square loosely around the rolling pin, center the pin over the prepared baking sheet, and unroll the pastry, top side down, onto the baking sheet.

Spread the filling over the dough, leaving a 1-inch border uncovered around the ragged edges. (You don't need to refrigerate this portion while rolling the other half of dough.) Remove the second portion of dough from the refrigerator, and roll it out into a square the same size as the first square. Again, loosely roll up the pastry onto the rolling pin, and then suspend it about 1 inch over the filling. Carefully unroll it, top side down and centered, over the filling. With kitchen scissors or a sharp paring knife, trim the ragged edge of the top layer of dough ½ to 1 inch smaller than the edge of the bottom layer of pastry. Then gently press together the top and bottom layers at the point where they meet.

Using a paring knife, cut a 1-inch triangle of dough from each corner of the galette, so that the pastry is not so thick when you crimp the edges. Beginning on the section closest to you, form a border: Lift the extended bottom layer and roll it up about 1 inch toward the center, over the top layer of dough, to seal the two layers together. Rotating the pan as needed, repeat until you have sealed the edge of the galette completely and have created an attractive border.

To glaze the pastry, lightly brush the pastry with the milk. Using the tip of the paring knife, make 5 shallow, horizontal lines, parallel to one another and about 1 inch apart, across the top of the galette. Sprinkle the sugar evenly over the top.

Bake the galette until the pastry is golden, flaky, and puffed on top, 38 to 42 minutes. Transfer the pan to a wire rack to cool.

To serve, cross 2 long, sturdy spatulas and slip under the galette, or slip 1 large, wide metal spatula or a rimless baking sheet under the galette, and transfer it to a serving plate. Serve warm or at room temperature, cut into 12 squares with a sharp knife. This is best eaten the same day it is baked.

Five-Layer Checkerboard Cake with Dark Chocolate Ultra-Satin Frosting

Invite the neighbors to your house when you serve this American classic. It's guaranteed to surprise everyone when it's sliced and reveals a five-layer checkerboard cake. You will need to purchase a Chicago Metallic checkerboard cake kit (see Sources) to make this cake. It includes three 9 by 1½-inch nonstick aluminum cake pans and 1 plastic batter ring, and is modestly priced. The batter ring is made up of 2 metal concentric rings linked by a narrow metal strip, with the center ring about 2¾ inches in diameter and the second ring about 5½ inches in diameter. The edge of the pan, 9 inches in diameter, forms the third ring. To create the checkerboard effect, you must be careful to stack the cake layers so the outside colors alternate, and the frosting between the layers must be thin enough to complete the checkerboard pattern.

The intensely flavored, glossy chocolate frosting has the consistency of a glaze when freshly made. As it cools at room temperature, it thickens to a marvelous spreadable state. You will not be disappointed in either form. The original recipe for this stunning frosting dates back to an adult education cake-decorating class I took in the 1960s. **YIELD: ONE 9-INCH, 5-LAYER ROUND CAKE, 14 SERVINGS**

CHECKERBOARD CAKE

4 CUPS (15½ OUNCES/450 GRAMS) CAKE FLOUR

1 TABLESPOON BAKING POWDER

½ TEASPOON SALT

9 OUNCES (2 STICKS PLUS 2 TABLESPOONS/255 GRAMS) UNSALTED BUTTER, AT ROOM TEMPERATURE

2½ CUPS (1 POUND, 1½ OUNCES/500 GRAMS) GRANULATED SUGAR

6 LARGE EGGS, LIGHTLY BEATEN

1½ CUPS (12 FL OUNCES/360 ML) WHOLE MILK

2 TEASPOONS PURE VANILLA EXTRACT

4 OUNCES (115 GRAMS) UNSWEETENED CHOCOLATE, MELTED (PAGE 17) AND TEPID

DARK CHOCOLATE ULTRA-SATIN FROSTING

7½ OUNCES (215 GRAMS) UNSWEETENED CHOCOLATE, VERY COARSELY CHOPPED

ONE 12-FL OUNCE (360-ML) CAN EVAPORATED MILK (1½ CUPS)

1½ CUPS (10½ OUNCES/300 GRAMS) GRANULATED SUGAR

6 OUNCES (1½ STICKS/ 170 GRAMS) UNSALTED BUTTER, SOFTENED

2 TEASPOONS PURE VANILLA EXTRACT

Before baking: Center a rack in the oven and preheat the oven to 350 degrees F. Lightly coat three 9 by 1½-inch round cake pans with nonstick spray, then flour them, tapping out the excess flour. Line the bottoms with parchment, and place the batter divider that comes with the checkerboard cake kit (see headnote) in one of the prepared pans. If your oven is wide enough, bake the cake pans side by side, spacing them 1 inch apart. Otherwise, when preheating the oven, position a rack in the upper third of the oven to hold the third pan. Have all of the ingredients at room temperature.

To make the Checkerboard Cake: Sift together the flour, baking powder, and salt onto a large sheet of waxed paper. In the bowl of a stand mixer fitted with the paddle attachment, beat the butter on medium speed until smooth and creamy, about 45 seconds. Add the sugar in a steady stream, stopping the mixer occasionally to scrape down the sides of the bowl. Continue to beat on medium speed until the mixture is light in color and texture, 3 to 5 minutes.

With the mixer on medium speed, add the eggs, 1 to 2 tablespoons at a time, beating after each addition until incorporated and stopping the mixer occasionally to scrape down the sides of the bowl. Continue to beat on medium speed until the mixture is white, fluffy, and has increased in volume. This entire process of adding and beating the eggs should take 2 to 4 minutes.

On the lowest speed, add the flour mixture in four additions alternately with the milk in three additions, beginning and ending with the flour mixture and mixing only until incorporated after each addition. Stop the mixer occasionally to scrape down the sides of the bowl. Add the vanilla during the final moments of mixing.

Transfer about one-third of the batter (4½ cups) to a medium bowl. Stir the melted chocolate into this batter just until the batter is a uniform color. Have the pan with the batter divider at hand. Spoon the vanilla batter into the outer and center rings of the divider, filling half to two-thirds up the rings. Spoon about 1 cup of the chocolate batter into the middle ring (the ring between the outer and center rings). Gently lift the divider from the pan, place it in the second pan, and fill this pan with the vanilla and chocolate batters in the same pattern as you did for the first pan. Again, gently lift the divider from the pan and scrape any vanilla batter still clinging to the divider into the bowl of vanilla batter and any chocolate batter still clinging to the divider into the bowl of chocolate batter.

For the third cake pan, reverse the procedure: Place the divider into the pan and spoon the chocolate batter into the outer ring and the center ring. Spoon the remaining vanilla batter (about 1 cup) into the middle ring. It is important that each layer have approximately the same amount of batter, so that the layers will be the same thickness when baked. Lift the divider gently, and scrape off any remaining vanilla batter, distributing it in the appropriate circles of batter. Repeat this with any clinging chocolate batter.

Bake the cakes until the chocolate portions of the cakes spring back without leaving an impression when gently pressed, 25 to 30 minutes. The chocolate batter will bake slightly faster than the vanilla, so don't overbake the cakes or the chocolate cake will become dry as it cools. If the cakes are browning unevenly, gently rotate the pans when a little more than half of the baking time has elapsed. Transfer the pans to wire racks and let cool for 10 minutes.

Tilt and rotate a pan while gently tapping it on a counter to release the cake sides. If they don't release, slip a thin metal spatula between the still-warm cake and the pan and run the spatula carefully along the entire perimeter of the pan. Invert a wire rack on top of the cake, invert the cake onto it, and carefully lift off the pan. Slowly peel off the parchment liner, turn it over so that the sticky side faces up, and reposition it on top of the cake. Invert another rack on top, invert the cake so it is right side up, and remove the original rack. Repeat with the remaining 2 pans. Let cool completely before frosting.

If serving the cake within 24 hours, wrap each layer with plastic wrap and store at room temperature. For longer storage, overwrap with aluminum foil, label with the contents and date, and freeze for up to 10 days. To thaw, remove the foil and leave at room temperature until still cold and firm (to ease splitting the layers).

To make the Dark Chocolate Ultra-Satin Frosting:
Place the chocolate in a large bowl; set aside. In a tall, heavy 2-quart saucepan, preferably 6 inches wide, combine the evaporated milk and sugar and stir with a silicone spatula. Place over medium-low heat and heat, stirring occasionally with the spatula, just until the sugar dissolves. Raise the heat to medium and bring the mixture just to a boil. Reduce the heat to low and cook just until the mixture registers 220 degrees F on an instant-read thermometer, about 12 minutes. Pour the milk mixture over the chocolate and let stand for 15 to 20 minutes to cool to 125 degrees F. Then stir with the silicone spatula to melt the chocolate and emulsify the mixture. Set aside at room temperature until lukewarm, 95 to 100 degrees F, 15 to 20 minutes. Stir the CONTINUED ▶

butter into the chocolate mixture to incorporate and emulsify it (not to melt it). The mixture thickens as the butter is incorporated. Finally, stir in the vanilla. You should have about 4 cups.

This frosting can be used right away as a glaze for this cake or for other cakes or cupcakes. To use as a filling or frosting for spreading or piping onto cakes, cupcakes, cookies, or pastries, set aside to thicken at room temperature for 2 to 6 hours, depending on the desired consistency. To store, pour into a sturdy airtight plastic container and refrigerate for up to 2 weeks. To use, leave the container at room temperature just until the frosting is malleable, about 2 hours. Or, to speed up the process, portion out the amount you need into a heatproof bowl and slowly stir it over a hot-water bath (120 degrees F) until it is close to the consistency you wish. Off the water bath, stir it just to bring the entire mixture together to a smooth, spreadable consistency.

To assemble the cake: Place the cake layers in the freezer for about 20 minutes to firm them just enough to make splitting the layers easier. Using a 12-inch serrated knife, split each layer in half horizontally (page 25) to create 6 layers. (If the layers have been frozen, thaw until still cold and firm.) You need only 5 layers to form the appropriate checkerboard pattern. (The remaining layer makes a delicious snack for the baker and a few of the baker's friends.) As you proceed to stack and frost each layer, be sure to alternate the layers in the proper order to create the checkerboard pattern.

Place one of the bottom cake layers, cut side up, on a sturdy cardboard round, or place it on a cake plate and slip about 3 strips of waxed paper under the cake to protect the cake. (A decorator's turntable is helpful when frosting the cake. If using the turntable, place the cake layer on its cardboard round on the platform and frost as directed. After frosting the cake, lift it off of the turntable on its cardboard base and transfer to a cake plate.) Using a long metal icing spatula, spread a scant ½ cup frosting on the layer, spreading it all the way to the edges of the cake. Place the contrasting layer on top of the frosting, lining up the edges. Spread a scant ½ cup frosting on the layer, again spreading it all the way to the edges of the cake. Repeat with the next 3 layers, alternating the layers as before and spreading the frosting over each layer in the same way. Center the last layer on top of the frosting, top side up, and spread the sides and top of the cake evenly with the remaining frosting. Remove the waxed-paper strips, if used. Set aside until serving the same day. If serving the next day, store under a cake dome or in a covered cake box at room temperature.

To serve, cut the cake into wedges with a sharp knife, wiping the blade clean with a damp towel after each cut.

Baking for a Rainy Day

I LIKE TO HAVE DESSERTS on hand to serve to impromptu guests, or to bring out when I don't have the time to bake something from step one to completion.

Here is a collection of recipes that goes far beyond what you might expect. The fridge and freezer play a crucial role in keeping your delectable arsenal at the ready, and some of the finished products wait at room temperature, like Bundernuss Torte and Naomi's Date-Nut Slices. A kaleidoscope of textures and presentations is possible—and in the case of the Frozen Fruit Rainbow Terrine with its colorful layers of cake, sorbet, and ice cream, it *is* a kaleidoscope.

These are the desserts you pull out when, for example, the neighbors and their kids come over for a pool party or backyard barbecue. Then—mark my words—the Over-the-Top Super-Duper Ice Cream Sandwiches will bring oohs and ahs, and more than a few guesses about the other delights you have stored away. Once your secret is out, don't be surprised if people start peeking into your freezer to see what else it holds.

When you are invited to a last-minute gathering, it's a good thing you have Lily's Extraordinary Linzer Tart or the slice-and-serve frozen Sunshine Orange Semifreddo at the ready. Or, you may need to rush something special over to a family that needs emotional encouragement. I suggest the spirits-lifting Great Peanut Butter Grated-Dough Bars.

Rainy-day baking also comes in handy when I face a busy week. I serve Quintessential Cheese Blintzes at brunch or for a light supper. The recipe is prepared days or weeks ahead (and refrigerated or frozen until needed), but when everyone sits down to eat, the results are no less spectacular.

I have also tucked a pair of first-rate rainy-day pastry recipes—Four Pie Crusts at One Time (page 357) and Three Tart Shells at One Time (page 360)—in The Baker's Handbook: Basic Recipe Components (see page 343). Each one of them guarantees you will be ready to use the abundance garnered from a neighbor's fruit trees or a foray to the farmers' market.

If you are busy—and who isn't?—this is the chapter for you.

Peanut Butter Crunch Cake, Squared

A luxurious peanut butter ganache sandwiched between tender buttermilk cake layers topped with an easy-to-make candylike peanut-sesame crunch is a dessert you will serve with pride again and again. You can get most of the work done ahead because the cake layers freeze well for 3 weeks, and the nutty-seed crunch stores perfectly in an airtight container at room temperature for up to 10 days. The popular ingredients make it an ideal birthday cake for a teenager or a special-event cake for the people in your office. After filling the cake layers and topping them with the peanut-sesame crunch, the cake's square form makes it a cinch to trim the edges, creating a simple, tailored finish that reveals the inviting layers and leaves the impression you worked hours on making dessert.   **YIELD: ONE 8-INCH, 3-LAYER SQUARE CAKE, 9 TO 12 SERVINGS**

1 RECIPE (8-INCH SQUARE) FAVORITE BUTTERMILK CAKE
  (PAGE 344)

PEANUT-SESAME CRUNCH

1 CUP (5 OUNCES/140 GRAMS) SALTED PEANUTS

1 LARGE EGG WHITE

¼ CUP (1 OUNCE/30 GRAMS) WHITE SESAME SEEDS

⅓ CUP (2¼ OUNCES/65 GRAMS) GRANULATED SUGAR

PEANUT BUTTER–WHITE CHOCOLATE GANACHE

⅓ CUP PLUS 1 TABLESPOON (3 FL OUNCES/90 ML) HEAVY CREAM

6 TABLESPOONS (3¼ OUNCES/90 GRAMS) CREAMY
  PEANUT BUTTER

5 OUNCES (140 GRAMS) WHITE CHOCOLATE,
  COARSELY CHOPPED

Bake the cake as directed, and let cool completely on a wire rack.

Before baking the Peanut-Sesame Crunch: Center a rack in the oven and preheat the oven to 350 degrees F. Have ready a large baking sheet, preferably lined with a silicone mat.

To make the Peanut-Sesame Crunch: Coarsely chop the peanuts on a cutting board to yield 1 cup. Place the egg white in a medium bowl and add the peanuts. Sprinkle the sesame seeds and sugar over the nuts and toss with a rubber spatula to coat the nuts. Spread the coated nuts in a thin layer on the prepared baking sheet.

Bake the nuts for about 35 minutes, tossing with a rubber spatula every 5 to 7 minutes to redistribute them so they dry and toast evenly. At first the mixture will resemble a syrup with nuts, but as it bakes, the sugar will dissolve and the mixture will caramelize and become crisp and golden. Transfer the pan to a wire rack and let cool completely, then store in a sturdy airtight container at room temperature for up to 10 days. If desired, crush with a rolling pin before sprinkling over the cake (or over cookies or pies). You should have 1¾ cups.

To make the Peanut Butter–White Chocolate Ganache: In a small, heavy saucepan, heat the cream and peanut butter over medium heat and whisk to combine the ingredients. Half fill a saucepan with warm water (95 to 110 degrees F). Put the white chocolate in a bowl and place it over (but not touching) the warm water. Allow to sit just until some of the white chocolate on the bottom of the bowl is liquid. Remove the bowl of chocolate and stir with a rubber spatula just until most of the chocolate is melted (a few tiny pieces of chocolate might remain). Stir the slightly warm peanut butter mixture into the white chocolate until smooth. Take care not to overmix or the ganache might separate. Set aside at room temperature until needed. The mixture will thicken as it cools. You should have about 1¼ cups.

To assemble the cake: Cut an 8-inch cardboard square, and cover one side of the square with aluminum foil. Place the cake, right side up, on a cutting board. Using a 12-inch serrated knife, split the cake horizontally into 3 layers, each ⅝ inch thick (page 25).

Place the bottom cake layer on the foil-covered square. Spread about half of the ganache evenly over the layer and center the second cake layer on top. Spread all but 2 tablespoons of the remaining ganache on top. Top with the last cake layer and spread the remaining 2 tablespoons ganache on top in a thin layer just to cover the surface. Refrigerate just to firm the frosting, 15 to 30 minutes.

Remove from the refrigerator and, using the serrated knife and a sawing motion, trim about ¼ inch off of all 4 sides of the cake, exposing the peanut butter filling. Scatter the Peanut-Sesame Crunch over the top of the cake.

Transfer the dessert to a cake stand or large cake plate. Serve at room temperature, cutting square portions with a serrated knife.

Quintessential Cheese Blintzes

Good make-ahead recipes inspire great eating, and these cheese blintzes are no exception. I use the same batter that I use for crepes, but I cook the crepes on only one side before filling with farmer cheese (sometimes called pot cheese). The crepes can be made ahead (and stacked between sheets of waxed paper), and the blintzes can be assembled and frozen and then heated in a skillet or in the oven when needed. For a delicious blueberry-cheese version, fold 1 cup (4 ounces/115 grams) blueberries into the cheese filling and proceed as directed in the recipe (blueberry-cheese blintzes freeze well, too).

Blintzes are delectable any time of the day. They can be a quick, comforting meal, or a great breakfast or brunch dish when you have overnight guests. Busy people can make them in stages over 3 days, but not necessarily 3 consecutive days.

Day 1: Make the crepes as directed in the recipe. When the first 10 have cooled, stack them. Then, place a sheet of waxed paper on top as a marker. Make, cool, and stack 10 more crepes. This will help you keep track of how many crepes you have. Wrap the stack and refrigerate overnight or freeze for up to 2 weeks. Bring the crepes to room temperature before filling.

Day 2: Make the filling, assemble the blintzes, and sauté them in butter until lightly browned as directed in the recipe. Let the blintzes cool, and then arrange them in a single layer in a lightly buttered baking dish, cover with aluminum foil, and refrigerate overnight. Or, for longer storage, line a baking sheet with plastic wrap, arrange the sautéed blintzes in a single layer on the prepared sheet, and freeze just until firm. Transfer the blintzes to a resealable plastic freezer bag or an airtight container and freeze for up to 2 weeks.

Day 3: To serve the blintzes, center a rack in the oven and preheat the oven to 400 degrees F. Set the baking dish with the sautéed blintzes in the oven and immediately reduce the heat to 350 degrees F. Bake just until hot, 15 to 20 minutes. Serve directly from the dish. Or, if you have frozen the sautéed blintzes, remove them from the bag or container, arrange them in a single layer in a buttered baking dish, and bake in a preheated 350 degree F oven until hot, 20 to 27 minutes. Serve directly from the oven.   YIELD: ABOUT 20 BLINTZES, 2 OR 3 PER SERVING

CREPES

1¼ CUPS (10 FL OUNCES/300 ML) MILK, PLUS MORE IF NEEDED
    TO THIN THE BATTER

4 LARGE EGGS

¼ CUP (2 FL OUNCES/60 ML) WATER

1 TABLESPOON UNSALTED BUTTER, MELTED, PLUS 3 OUNCES
    (¾ STICK/85 GRAMS) FOR COOKING CREPES

½ TEASPOON SALT

1 CUP (4½ OUNCES/130 GRAMS) ALL-PURPOSE FLOUR

CHEESE FILLING

2 CUPS (1 POUND/455 GRAMS) FARMER CHEESE

½ CUP (3½ OUNCES/100 GRAMS) GRANULATED SUGAR

1 LARGE EGG
2 TEASPOONS PURE VANILLA EXTRACT
1 TEASPOON FINELY GRATED TANGERINE OR LEMON ZEST
¼ TEASPOON SALT

UNSALTED BUTTER FOR BROWNING BLINTZES
SOUR CREAM OR CRÈME FRAÎCHE FOR SERVING
FAVORITE FRUIT JELLY, JAM, OR PRESERVES FOR SERVING

To make the crepes: In a food processor or blender, combine 1¼ cups milk, the eggs, water, 1 tablespoon melted butter, and the salt and process just to combine the ingredients. Add the flour and process just until the mixture is smooth. Transfer the mixture to a bowl, cover, and refrigerate for 1 to 2 hours before cooking.

Before cooking the crepes, whisk the batter to emulsify the ingredients. If necessary, add more milk, tablespoon by tablespoon, to the batter to thin it to the consistency of heavy cream. Line a plate with a sheet of waxed paper. Heat a nonstick skillet or crepe pan 6 or 7 inches in diameter (measuring the flat bottom surface) over medium-high heat. When a drop of water flicked onto the bottom of the pan sizzles, add 1 to 2 teaspoons butter and swirl the pan to coat it thinly. Pour 2½ to 3 table-spoons batter (I use a ¼-cup/2–fl ounce/60-ml ladle and fill it half to two-thirds full) into the center of the pan all at once, and immediately tilt and swirl the pan to distribute the batter thinly and evenly to the edges. Cook until the top surface of the crepe appears set and dry and its underside is speckled golden brown, about 45 seconds. Loosen the edges of the crepe with a silicone spatula (be careful, as the crepe can tear easily when it's hot) and slide it out onto the waxed paper–lined plate, speckled (cooked) side up. (You don't cook the other side.) Repeat with the remaining batter, melting 2 teaspoons butter in the pan each time, stirring the batter occasionally, adjusting the heat as necessary, and stacking the crepes, separated by small pieces of waxed paper, on the plate. You should have about 20 crepes.

If you will be filling the crepes within 3 hours, leave them at room temperature. Otherwise, let the stacked crepes cool completely, cover securely with plastic wrap, and refrigerate for up to 2 days, or overwrap the package with aluminum foil, label with the contents and date, and freeze up to 2 weeks. If frozen, thaw for several hours or overnight in the refrigerator. Bring the refrigerated crepes to room temperature before attempting to separate them to avoid tearing them.

To make the filling: In a medium bowl, combine the cheese, sugar, egg, zest, vanilla, and salt and stir together.

To assemble the blintzes: Working with 1 crepe at a time, place it, cooked side up, on a work surface. Spoon about 1½ tablespoons of the filling slightly off the center onto the crepe and spread it over the surface just a bit. Fold the bottom end over the filling, fold in the sides, pat lightly to flatten, and then roll the filled crepe to completely enclose the filling in a neat rectangular package. Place seam side down on a large platter if cooking right away, and repeat with the remaining blintzes and filling. If not cooking right away, place the blintzes in a sturdy covered storage container and refrigerate for up to 1 day.

Butter a shallow baking dish large enough to hold the blintzes in a single layer. Center a rack in the oven and preheat the oven to 225 degrees F. To brown the blintzes, melt about 1 tablespoon butter in a skillet over medium-low heat. Working in batches, add the blintzes, seam side down and not too close together, and sauté, flipping them gently once, until pale gold to golden, about 2 minutes total, adding more butter as needed. Transfer the blintzes to the prepared baking dish, cover loosely with aluminum foil, and place in the oven until serving.

Alternatively, generously butter a shallow baking dish large enough to hold the blintzes in a single layer. Center a rack in the oven and preheat the oven to 350 degrees F. Place the blintzes, seam side down, in the prepared baking dish and bake, turning once after 6 to 8 minutes, until pale gold and heated through, 12 to 15 minutes.

Divide the blintzes among dessert plates. Serve warm with sour cream and fruit preserves.

Over-the-Top Super-Duper Ice Cream Sandwiches

Take a brownie, omit the chocolate, and add brown sugar and a healthy dose of chopped macadamia nuts and you have a butterscotch-flavored, chewy bar cookie called a blondie. Ice cream—butter pecan, pistachio, coffee, *dulce de leche*, mint chip, or whatever you like—is layered inside, creating a kid- and adult-friendly finale. Individual sandwiches are cut from this large sandwich cookie sheet, their sides are dipped into the crunchy sweet crumble, and then the sandwiches are wrapped and returned to the freezer until needed. Pack these on dry ice and cart them to the beach or serve them alfresco in your backyard.

The sweet crumble stays crumbly and crisp in an airtight container at room temperature for about 2 weeks. It also makes a great topping for cakes, cupcakes, ice cream, peaches, and other fresh or poached fruits and is great layered in parfaits. **YIELD: 20 SMALL (2 BY 1¾ INCHES) SANDWICHES**

SWEET CRUNCHY CRUMBLE

1¾ CUPS PLUS 2 TABLESPOONS (8½ OUNCES/240 GRAMS) ALL-PURPOSE FLOUR

6 TABLESPOONS (2¾ OUNCES/75 GRAMS) GRANULATED SUGAR

6 TABLESPOONS FIRMLY PACKED (2¾ OUNCES/75 GRAMS) LIGHT BROWN SUGAR

¼ TEASPOON SALT

6 OUNCES (1½ STICKS/170 GRAMS) UNSALTED BUTTER, MELTED AND COOLED

BLONDIE BARS

1 CUP (4½ OUNCES/130 GRAMS) ALL-PURPOSE FLOUR

½ TEASPOON BAKING POWDER

¼ TEASPOON SALT

6 TABLESPOONS (3 OUNCES/85 GRAMS) UNSALTED BUTTER, AT ROOM TEMPERATURE

¾ CUP FIRMLY PACKED (5¼ OUNCES/150 GRAMS) LIGHT BROWN SUGAR

1 LARGE EGG

1 TABLESPOON WATER

1 TEASPOON PURE VANILLA EXTRACT

½ CUP (2 OUNCES/55 GRAMS) FINELY CHOPPED MACADAMIA NUTS

2 PINTS PREMIUM ICE CREAM IN YOUR FLAVOR OF CHOICE

Before baking: Center a rack in the oven and preheat the oven to 350 degrees F. Line a baking sheet with parchment paper.

To make the Sweet Crunchy Crumble: In a medium bowl, stir together the flour, sugars, and salt. Pour the butter over the flour mixture and toss with a rubber spatula until it is well combined and large crumbs have formed. Alternatively, in the bowl of a stand mixer fitted with the paddle attachment, combine all of the ingredients and mix on low speed just until large crumbs have formed. With fingertips, sprinkle the crumbs onto the prepared baking sheet. Break up the larger crumbs a bit as you sprinkle to cover the entire surface.

Bake the crumbs until golden, 35 to 45 minutes. Transfer to a wire rack and let cool completely. Spoon the crumble into a sturdy airtight container and store at room temperature for 2 weeks. For longer storage, label with the contents and date and freeze for up to 1 month.

To make the Blondie Bars: Center a rack in the oven and preheat the oven to 350 degrees F. Line a 15½ by 10½ by 1-inch baking sheet (jelly-roll pan) with aluminum foil, then lightly butter the foil.

Sift together the flour, baking powder, and salt onto a sheet of waxed paper; set aside.

In the bowl of a stand mixer fitted with the paddle attachment, beat together the butter, sugar, egg, water, and vanilla on low speed just until the mixture is smooth. Maintaining the same speed, add the flour mixture and nuts and beat just until the ingredients are well combined. Using an offset spatula, spread the thick batter evenly over the prepared baking sheet.

Bake the blondie until it is no longer shiny on top, is pale gold, and is supple rather than crisp, 13 to 15 minutes. Transfer to a wire rack and let cool in the pan for about 5 minutes. Invert a large rack or another baking sheet on top, invert the blondie onto it, lift off the pan, and carefully peel off the foil. Let cool completely.

Meanwhile, transfer the pints of ice cream from the freezer to the refrigerator to give them time to soften a bit, about 15 minutes. Line the original (jelly-roll) pan with plastic wrap. Scoop the ice cream into a large bowl and mix it with a rubber spatula just enough to combine the soft and firm portions (or transfer it to the bowl of the stand mixer fitted with the paddle attachment and blend briefly on the lowest speed). Spread the ice cream evenly over half of the lined pan to form a rectangle about 10 by 7$\frac{1}{2}$ inches. Place the baking sheet in the freezer to firm the ice cream, 1 hour or longer.

Up to 1 hour before serving, cut the blondie bar in half to create 2 rectangles, each about 10 by 7$\frac{1}{2}$ inches. Remove the ice cream from the freezer, and set 1 blondie rectangle on top of the ice cream, pressing lightly so the blondie sticks to the ice cream. Wrap the whole thing in plastic wrap and place in the freezer until the blondie feels cold, 15 to 30 minutes.

Line the same pan with a fresh piece of plastic wrap. Remove the blondie-covered ice cream from the freezer, unwrap, and invert it, blondie side down, onto the prepared baking sheet. Set the other blondie rectangle on top of the ice cream, again pressing lightly. Wrap the whole thing in the plastic wrap and return it to the freezer for 15 to 30 minutes. Do not leave it in the freezer too long or the blondie will be too firm to cut.

Remove the package from the freezer and unwrap on a cutting board. Using a sharp knife, cut it into individual sandwiches in any size you like. Spread the crumble over a shallow pan, such as a 13 by 9 by 2-inch pan (quarter sheet pan). One at a time, dip all of the edges of each sandwich into the crumble, and then wrap the sandwiches individually in aluminum foil. Label with the contents and date, and then decorate with permanent markers in assorted colors, if desired. Return the sandwiches to the freezer for up to 1 week.

Bundernuss Torte

The combination of buttery tart pastry, moist macaroon filling, and hazelnut caramel topping is like a candy bar in a crust. Make the torte up to 3 days in advance and it will taste as if you made it the same day. The stunning solid blanket of chopped hazelnuts applied to the caramel topping is created by chopping the nuts in a nut grinder or mill, an inexpensive device sold in kitchen-supply shops and in the housewares sections of supermarkets and department stores. I prefer the nut mill when I want the chopped nuts to be as uniform as possible. Using a food processor is tricky because it works too quickly to ensure uniform pieces.   **YIELD: ONE 9-INCH TORTE, 12 TO 14 SERVINGS**

⅓ RECIPE (ONE 10-OUNCE/280-GRAM DISK) THREE TART
    SHELLS AT ONE TIME (PAGE 360)

MACAROON FILLING

¼ CUP (2 OUNCES/55 GRAMS) ALMOND PASTE

2 TABLESPOONS UNSALTED BUTTER, AT ROOM TEMPERATURE

1 TABLESPOON GRANULATED SUGAR

1 TEASPOON DARK RUM

1 LARGE EGG WHITE

2 TEASPOONS ALL-PURPOSE FLOUR

HAZELNUT CARAMEL TOPPING

¾ CUP PLUS 1 TABLESPOON (6½ OUNCES/185 GRAMS)
    HAZELNUTS, TOASTED AND SKINNED (PAGES 15–16),
    AND THEN FINELY CHOPPED TO YIELD 1¾ CUPS

3 TABLESPOONS WATER

1 TABLESPOON LIGHT CORN SYRUP

⅔ CUP (4½ OUNCES/130 GRAMS) GRANULATED SUGAR

2 OUNCES (½ STICK/55 GRAMS) UNSALTED BUTTER,
    CUT INTO 3 PIECES

⅛ TEASPOON SALT

¼ CUP (2 FL OUNCES/60 ML) HEAVY CREAM, AT ROOM
    TEMPERATURE

Before baking: Center a rack in the oven and preheat the oven to 375 degrees F. Have ready a 9 by 2-inch round cake pan.

To line the pan with the pastry dough: Following the directions on page 29 for rolling out tart pastry, roll out the dough into an 11-inch circle about ⅛ inch thick, line the cake pan, and neatly trim the top edge of the pastry with a plastic dough scraper. Chill the pastry-lined pan in the freezer for about 20 minutes or in the refrigerator for at least 30 minutes or up to 1 day.

Prick the bottom of the pastry with the tines of a fork and partially bake for 17 to 25 minutes as directed for tarts on page 30. It's natural for the pastry to settle down the sides during baking to about 1½ inches in height. Transfer to a wire rack and let the pastry cool for about 10 minutes before filling. Leave the oven on.

To make the Macaroon Filling: In a food processor, combine the almond paste, butter, sugar, rum, egg white, and flour and process just until the mixture is smooth. (This is a small amount, so lift the lid occasionally and scrape the mixture close to the metal blade before processing again.) Spoon the filling into the tart shell, spreading evenly with a rubber spatula.

Bake the torte until the top is just set (appears dry, not wet), about 15 minutes. (It will bake more after the topping is made.) Transfer to a wire rack and let cool in the pan while you make the caramel topping. Leave the oven on.

To make the Hazelnut Caramel Topping: Place the nuts in a medium heatproof bowl; set aside. In a heavy 1½-quart saucepan, combine the water, corn syrup, and sugar, in that order, and heat over low heat, stirring occasionally with a wooden spoon, until the sugar dissolves. Raise the heat to medium-high and boil the mixture without stirring until the mixture turns amber, about 5 minutes. (Although you can't stir, you can gently tilt and swirl the pan occasionally to distribute the sugar syrup, which results in the caramel cooking more evenly.) Remove from the heat and add the butter, salt, and cream all at once. Be careful, as the mixture will bubble vigorously and rise in the pan. Carefully stir the mixture with the wooden spoon to distribute the heat and blend the ingredients. If lumps form in the caramel, return the pan to very low heat and stir slowly until the caramel is smooth.

Pour the caramel over the nuts in the bowl and toss them with a silicone spatula to coat evenly with the caramel. Pour the nut topping over the macaroon filling, spreading evenly with the spatula. Bake until the nuts are lightly golden and the mixture is bubbling lightly, 15 to 20 minutes. Transfer to a wire rack and let cool almost completely in the pan.

Tilt the pan slightly and gently tap it on a counter to release the torte sides. Invert a wire rack on top of the torte, invert the torte onto it, and carefully lift off the pan. Invert a serving platter on top, invert the torte so it is right side up, and remove the rack.

For the best flavor, allow the tart to cool at room temperature for several hours or up to overnight. For longer storage, wrap securely in plastic wrap, overwrap with aluminum foil, and store at room temperature for up to 1 week.

To serve, cut the torte into thin wedges with a sharp knife.

Dark Chocolate Baby Cakes

I enjoy making 6-inch round cakes to have on hand in the freezer for gifting to friends for birthdays, anniversaries, engagements, get well wishes, one less baby tooth, happy first day of school, because it's rainy outside, because there's a blue moon, and other special occasions. Their charm isn't lost on children either, who feel quite important with a diminutive cake to call their own. The chocolate frosting recipe, which yields enough to fill and frost both cakes, couldn't be easier to make or to spread over the cakes.   **YIELD: TWO 6-INCH, 3-LAYER ROUND CAKES, 6 TO 8 SERVINGS EACH**

1 RECIPE (TWO 6-INCH ROUND LAYERS) DARK CHOCOLATE CAKE
    (PAGE 350), MADE WITH WATER INSTEAD OF COFFEE

COFFEE–WHITE CHOCOLATE GANACHE (OPTIONAL)

6 OUNCES WHITE CHOCOLATE, FINELY CHOPPED

½ CUP (4 FL OUNCES/120 ML) HEAVY CREAM

2 TEASPOONS INSTANT ESPRESSO POWDER

1 TEASPOON PURE VANILLA EXTRACT

FUDGY CHOCOLATE FILLING AND FROSTING

4 OUNCES (115 GRAMS) UNSWEETENED CHOCOLATE,
    FINELY CHOPPED

3¾ CUPS (1 POUND/455 GRAMS) POWDERED SUGAR

⅛ TEASPOON SALT

4 OUNCES (1 STICK/115 GRAMS) UNSALTED BUTTER, SOFTENED

½ CUP (4 FL OUNCES/120 ML) WHOLE MILK

2 TEASPOONS PURE VANILLA EXTRACT

Bake the 2 cake layers as directed, and let cool completely on wire racks.

To make the Coffee–White Chocolate Ganache:
Place the chocolate in a medium heatproof bowl. In a small saucepan, heat the cream just until it comes to a boil. Pour the cream over the chocolate, add the espresso powder and vanilla, and let stand for about 30 seconds. Whisk together until smooth and creamy and set aside to cool and thicken, about 15 minutes. You should have about 1 cup (8 fl ounces/240 ml). Divide the ganache in half, and use half for each cake.

If not assembling the cakes right away, spoon the ganache into a small, sturdy container, and set aside for a few hours. Or, refrigerate for up to 5 days. To use, remove

from the refrigerator and let stand at room temperature until it has a spreading consistency, about 1 hour.

To make the Fudgy Chocolate Filling and Frosting:
Half fill a bowl with hot water (120 degrees F). Put the chocolate in a bowl and place it over (but not touching) the hot water. Let the chocolate melt until creamy and smooth, stirring slowly occasionally. (Replace the water with more hot water, if needed, to melt the chocolate smoothly.) Remove from the water bath. Set aside until cool yet still creamy smooth.

In a food processor, combine the sugar, salt, and butter and pulse just until mixed. Pour in the milk and vanilla and process until smooth. Add the melted chocolate and process until well blended, smooth, and creamy. Divide the frosting in half, and use half for filling and frosting each cake.

If not assembling the cakes right away, pour the frosting into a small, sturdy container and set aside at room temperature for a few hours (it will thicken). Or, refrigerate for up to 5 days. To use, remove from the refrigerator and let stand at room temperature until it has a spreading consistency, 1 to 1¼ hours. You should have 2½ cups, enough to fill and frost the two 6-inch layer cakes here, two 8- or 9-inch layer cakes, or one 9- or 10-inch tube pan.

To assemble the cakes: Using a 12-inch serrated knife, split 1 cake into thirds horizontally (page 25) to create 3 equal layers each slightly thicker than ¾ inch. Place the bottom layer, cut side up, on a sturdy cardboard round the same diameter as the cake. If the cardboard is too large, cut it ⅛ to ¼ inch larger than the diameter of the cake to allow room for the frosting. (A decorator's turntable is helpful when frosting the cake. If using the turntable, place the cake on its cardboard on the platform and frost as directed.)

Have the ganache and frosting nearby. Using a flexible metal icing spatula, spread about ½ cup of the frosting evenly over the cake layer. Center the second layer on top and spread the ganache evenly over the cake layer to the edge. If not using the ganache, spread another ½ cup of the frosting over the cake layer to the edge. Top with the third layer. Spread the remaining frosting over the top and sides of the cake, making swirls with the icing spatula or the back of a spoon. If frosting the second baby cake now, repeat the entire procedure, beginning with splitting the cake into 3 layers.

To flash-freeze the frosted cakes, set them, uncovered, on a baking sheet and place in the freezer until the frosting is firm to the touch, 45 to 60 minutes. Transfer the frosted cakes to airtight containers, or wrap the cakes in plastic wrap and overwrap in aluminum foil; label with the contents and date and return them to the freezer. To thaw, transfer the cakes to the refrigerator for 6 to 24 hours before serving. To speed thawing, transfer to a cool room after the cake has been refrigerated for a few hours.

For optimum flavor, serve the cakes at room temperature. Cut into slices with a sharp knife, wiping the blade clean with a damp towel after each cut.

Sunshine Orange Semifreddo

You will notice that the initials of this sunny *semifreddo* are SOS—and it truly lives up to that billing. A godsend for hosts with hectic schedules, this cool, creamy dessert actually benefits from being made ahead, achieving its ultimate texture only after a good, long chill in the freezer. Perfect for everything from summer celebrations to holiday get-togethers to dinner-with-just-friends parties, the *semifreddo* (Italian for "semifrozen") combines a crisp, chocolate-speckled crust with a light, Grand Marnier–orange zabaglione.   **YIELD: 14 SERVINGS**

CRUMB CRUST

18 (5 ¼ OUNCES/150 GRAMS) ZWIEBACK TOASTS
    (1½ PACKAGES FROM THE BOX)

2 TABLESPOONS POWDERED SUGAR

2 OUNCES (55 GRAMS) 50 TO 60% SEMISWEET CHOCOLATE

3 OUNCES (¾ STICK/85 GRAMS) UNSALTED BUTTER, MELTED
    AND COOLED

FILLING

2 CUPS (16 FL OUNCES/480 ML) STRAINED FRESH ORANGE JUICE

1 CUP (8 FL OUNCES/240 ML) HEAVY CREAM

½ CUP (3 ½ OUNCES/100 GRAMS) GRANULATED SUGAR

4 LARGE (⅓ CUP/2 ½ FL OUNCES/75 ML) EGG YOLKS

2 TABLESPOONS LIGHT CORN SYRUP

2 TABLESPOONS ORANGE-FLAVORED LIQUEUR SUCH AS
    BRAND GARNIER OR COINTREAU

Before baking: Center a rack in the oven and preheat the oven to 350 degrees F. Lightly coat the sides of a 9-inch round springform pan with at least 2¾-inch sides with nonstick spray and then lightly rub the sides to remove excess spray.

To make the crumb crust: Break the zwieback toasts into pieces and place in a food processor. Add the sugar and chocolate and pulse until finely ground. Add the butter and pulse briefly to blend. Pour into the prepared pan and use your fingertips to press the mixture evenly and firmly over the bottom of the pan.

Bake the crust just until firm to the touch (the chocolate melts during baking and binds the mixture together perfectly), about 10 minutes. Transfer to a wire rack and let cool completely, and then place the pan in the freezer.

To make the filling: Have ready for easy access in the freezer about 15 ice cubes for cooling the filling quickly. In a 2½-quart saucepan, bring the orange juice to a boil and cook until reduced to 1 cup, 20 to 30 minutes. Set aside to cool to room temperature.

Using a whisk or a handheld mixer, whip the cream in a deep, medium bowl until soft peaks form. Cover and refrigerate. Place a fine-mesh sieve over the bowl of a stand mixer; set aside.

In a heavy 1½-quart saucepan, combine the cooled orange juice, sugar, egg yolks, and corn syrup and whisk to blend. Place over medium-low heat and heat, whisking constantly, until the mixture registers 170 degrees F on an instant-read thermometer, about 6 minutes. Remove from the heat and pour through the sieve into the bowl. Attach the bowl to the mixer, fit the mixer with the whisk attachment, and start whipping on medium speed. As you begin to whip, put a few of the reserved ice cubes into a resealable plastic bag and hold the bag against the bottom of the bowl, or as close to the bottom of the bowl as possible, to speed the cooling. Continue to do this off and on for about 2 minutes, changing the ice cubes as they begin to melt. Then continue beating at medium speed until the mixture is cold, thicker, and fluffy, about 20 minutes. The texture, which should be homogeneous and foamy, will be close to that of a zabaglione, though not as thick. Add the liqueur toward the end of whipping.

Detach the whisk and bowl from the mixer, and tap the whisk against the side of the bowl to free the excess orange mixture. Using a rubber spatula, fold the whipped cream into the orange mixture just until combined. Remove the springform pan from the freezer and pour the filling into it, spreading evenly with the spatula. Cover with aluminum foil and freeze until firm, at least overnight or up to 1 week.

To unmold, remove the *semifreddo* from the freezer, and apply a warm wet cloth to the outside of the pan for 1 to 2 minutes. Resoak the cloth in warm water, squeeze out most of the water, and reapply it to the pan at least twice during this time. Gently tilt the pan to see if the mixture is coming away from the sides. When it appears to be free from the sides, slowly release the springform clasp and carefully lift off the sides. You can place the dessert (still on the base) on a platter and serve it immediately, or you can return it on the base to the freezer until ready to serve.

To serve, cut the *semifreddo* into small wedges with a sharp knife and transfer to individual plates with a thin spatula.

Frozen Lemon Glacier

Here, three layers of hazelnut *dacquoise* are each thinly coated with white chocolate and then filled and frosted with a luscious blend of whipped cream and lemon curd to produce a knockout pale yellow dessert that's a great keeper, literally. It can be fully assembled and frozen without losing its crisp texture or sweet-tangy flavor.

Finely grate the hazelnuts to a powdery consistency with a rotary grater, preferably a Zyliss model with a suction device that makes it easy to operate (page 16). The fine hazelnut powder acts like a flour in the *dacquoise*.   YIELD: ONE 8-INCH, 3-LAYER ROUND CAKE, 14 SERVINGS

HAZELNUT DACQUOISE

½ CUP PLUS 1 TABLESPOON (3 OUNCES/85 GRAMS) HAZELNUTS, FINELY GROUND TO YIELD 1⅓ CUPS

1 CUP PLUS 2 TABLESPOONS (4 OUNCES/115 GRAMS) POWDERED SUGAR, SIFTED

¾ CUP (6 FL OUNCES/180 ML) EGG WHITES (5 TO 6 LARGE)

¾ CUP (5¼ OUNCES/150 GRAMS) GRANULATED SUGAR

WHITE CHOCOLATE FLAKES

1-POUND (455-GRAM) BAR WHITE CHOCOLATE

LEMON CURD FILLING AND FROSTING

1½ CUPS (12 FL OUNCES/360 ML) HEAVY CREAM

1 RECIPE LEMON CURD (PAGE 370)

WHITE CHOCOLATE FILLING

6 OUNCES (170 GRAMS) WHITE CHOCOLATE, FINELY CHOPPED

Before baking: Place a rack in the upper third and another rack in the lower third of the oven and preheat the oven to 250 degrees F. Line 2 baking sheets with parchment paper. Using a pencil and a template such as a saucepan lid or cake pan, trace two 7-inch circles on the paper in 1 pan and one 7-inch circle on the paper in the other pan. Turn the parchment paper over (the circles show through the paper). Fit a large (16-inch) pastry bag with a ½-inch plain open tip.

To make the Hazelnut Dacquoise: Place the ground hazelnuts in a medium bowl, add the powdered sugar, and stir to blend. Pour the egg whites into the bowl of a stand mixer fitted with the whisk attachment. Whip the whites on low speed until small bubbles appear and the

surface is frothy, 30 to 45 seconds. Increase the speed to medium-low and pour in 2 tablespoons of the granulated sugar in a steady stream. Continue whipping until soft, white peaks form, about 45 seconds. Raise the speed to medium and gradually add the remaining granulated sugar in a steady stream. Continue whipping until a small amount rubbed between your thumb and forefinger feels smooth, not granular, about 2 minutes.

Detach the whisk and bowl from the mixer, and tap the whisk against the side of the bowl to free the excess whites. Sprinkle the nut-sugar mixture over the whites and fold the two together with a rubber spatula.

Apply a tiny dollop of the meringue under each corner of the parchment sheets to secure them to the baking sheets. Without delay, scoop the meringue mixture into the pastry bag. Starting in the center of each marked circle, pipe the mixture in a continuous spiral, filling the circles completely. When the spiral reaches the pencil line, lift the tip slightly to cut off the flow. As the mixture bakes, the *dacquoise* will expand slightly outside the lines.

Using the extra meringue in the pastry bag, pipe a few disks each about 1½ inches in diameter on each baking sheet. These are samples to test to see if the large disks are ready to be removed from the oven.

Bake the disks until dry and ivory colored, 65 to 70 minutes. About halfway through the baking, rotate the baking sheets 180 degrees to ensure even baking. Test for doneness by examining a sample. If a small disk is firm and dry to the touch and releases easily and if it snaps in half and is uniformly crisp after cooling for 5 to 10 minutes, the large disks are done. Don't worry about leaving the large disks in the oven while you cool a smaller one; the additional time will not harm them.

Transfer the baking sheets to wire racks to cool. As soon as you can lift the sheets of parchment paper, lift them with the disks on them to a large rack and let cool completely. When cool, slip a spatula under each disk to release it from the paper. Or, if you want to store the disks for a while before using, don't release them from the paper. Instead, cut around the paper with kitchen scissors to remove the excess paper, and place the disks in a large, airtight metal container. The paper provides support and keeps the disks from breaking. Store for up to 1 week at room temperature. You should have three 7-inch disks.

To make the White Chocolate Flakes: For convenience, make the flakes ahead and store them in a sturdy covered container in the freezer, lifting the shavings into the container with a dough scraper. The heat of your fingers can melt the flakes when you apply them to the cake. Keeping the shavings as cold as possible before you use them helps to prevent this from happening so quickly.

To make the flakes, hold a shallow, 3 by 1-inch tartlet tin (not fluted) upside down in one hand and draw its edge down the surface of the chocolate bar, allowing the shavings to fall onto a clean work surface. (I have called for a 1-pound bar here, but the larger the bar, the easier it will be to hold steady, plus a larger chocolate surface makes creating the shavings easier. Just shave the larger bar until you have used about 1 pound.) The temperature of the room and the texture of the chocolate (white chocolate is not as firm or brittle as dark chocolate) will determine the size of your flakes.

To make the Lemon Curd Filling and Frosting: In a bowl, using a stand mixer fitted with the whisk attachment or a handheld mixer, whip the cream on medium speed until stiff peaks form. The peaks should be soft but defined, and a track made in the cream should stay in place for a while, then move only slightly. Using a rubber spatula, fold the cream into the curd. Cover and refrigerate until needed.

To make the White Chocolate Filling: Half fill a bowl with hot water (95 to 110 degrees F). Put the chocolate in a bowl and place it over (but not touching) the warm water. Let the chocolate melt until creamy and smooth, stirring slowly occasionally. (Replace the water with more hot water if needed to melt the chocolate smoothly.) Remove from the water bath. Set aside to cool to lukewarm.

To assemble the cake: Have ready an 8-inch cardboard round (or thin metal round) to support the layers. (You can use the cardboard as a guide to make the disks more uniform, cutting with scissors or a small paring knife. However, keep in mind that the dessert will be completely covered with frosting and any little imperfections won't be visible.) Place the *dacquoise* disks, flat side up, on a work surface. Pour 3 tablespoons of the melted white chocolate over each disk and, using a flexible metal icing spatula, spread it evenly over the surface. Set aside. The white chocolate will firm and set up.

Place 1 *dacquoise* layer, spiral side down, on the cardboard round. (A decorator's turntable is helpful here. If using the turntable, place the cake on its cardboard on the platform and fill and frost as directed.) Using the flexible metal spatula, spread about 1 cup of the lemon cream evenly over the disk. Top with a second *dacquoise* layer, spiral side down, and spread with about 1 cup of the lemon cream. Top with the third layer, spiral side down, and frost the top and sides completely with the remaining lemon cream. Transfer to a baking sheet or a 12-inch round pizza pan and place in the freezer, uncovered, just until the lemon cream is firm, about 2 hours. Then, transfer the cake on its cardboard to a covered cake box and cover the box with plastic wrap, or put the cake into a sturdy airtight container and freeze for up to 1 week.

The cake should be served firm, almost frozen. Remove from the freezer to the refrigerator 1 hour before serving. Sprinkle a generous amount of the chocolate flakes on the sides and top of the cake. Refrigerate the cake if not serving immediately.

To serve, cut the cake into small wedges with a sharp knife and transfer to individual plates with a sturdy metal spatula.

Great Peanut Butter Grated-Dough Bars

Years ago, while reading a European cookbook, I discovered a clever technique for thawing frozen butter quickly: grate it on a box grater onto a cutting board. Here, I apply that same technique to logs of frozen peanut butter dough, which I shred into a mound of shaggy shards about the size of a medium apple. I carefully lift the mound with a dough scraper and transfer it into the baking pan, distributing it evenly. I then repeat the process until the shards cover the pan evenly. Don't be tempted to pat the dough into the pan. Leave it shaggy. A delicious sandy shortbread is your reward.   **YIELD: 2 TO 4 DOZEN BARS**

3 CUPS (13¾ OUNCES/390 GRAMS) ALL-PURPOSE FLOUR

¼ TEASPOON SALT

8 OUNCES (2 STICKS/225 GRAMS) UNSALTED BUTTER, SOFTENED

⅓ CUP (3 OUNCES/85 GRAMS) CREAMY PEANUT BUTTER

1⅓ CUPS (9¼ OUNCES/260 GRAMS) GRANULATED SUGAR

1 LARGE EGG WHITE

1 TEASPOON PURE VANILLA EXTRACT

½ CUP (2½ OUNCES/70 GRAMS) UNSALTED OR SALTED MACADAMIA NUTS, CHOPPED TO YIELD ½ CUP PLUS 2 TABLESPOONS

1 CUP (ABOUT 10 OUNCES/280 GRAMS) RED JAM OR PRESERVES SUCH AS STRAWBERRY, CHERRY, OR RASPBERRY

In a medium bowl, combine the flour and salt and stir to blend; set aside. In the bowl of a stand mixer fitted with the paddle attachment, beat together the butter, peanut butter, and sugar on low speed until very creamy and well blended. Beat in the egg white and vanilla. Gradually add the flour mixture on low speed and beat just until the mixture starts to appear crumbly.

To form the bars: Remove half of the dough from the bowl to a clean work surface, and form it into a cohesive ball. Using your palms, roll the ball back and forth on the work surface until it forms a thick log about 6 inches long. Wrap the log in plastic wrap and freeze until firm, 2 to 3 hours.

Sprinkle the nuts over the remaining dough in the bowl and, using a rubber spatula, toss gently to disperse the nuts evenly throughout the dough. Turn the dough into

a 13 by 9 by 2-inch pan (quarter sheet pan) and use your fingertips to press it gently and evenly over the bottom. Cover the surface with a sheet of plastic wrap and set aside at room temperature until you are ready to bake.

Before baking: Center a rack in the oven and preheat the oven to 350 degrees F.

Remove and discard the plastic wrap from the baking pan. Bake the cookie base until the dough is set, about 10 minutes. Transfer to a wire rack and let cool until almost completely cool, about 20 minutes. Then spread the jam evenly over the cookie base and set aside until needed.

To form the grated cookie layer: Place a box grater on a cutting board and, using the coarsest holes on the grater, grate the dough log until you have a mound equivalent to about ½ cup. If the dough is frozen, wrap a paper towel around one end to make it easier to hold steady while grating. Slip a dough scraper under the mound, lift carefully, and sprinkle over the jam layer. Repeat, always grating about ½ cup, until you have covered the jam layer evenly with all of the dough.

Bake until the dough on top is firm to the touch and tinged a light gold, 40 to 45 minutes. Transfer to a rack and let cool completely. Using a sharp paring knife, cut into 1½- to 2-inch squares or 2 by 1½-inch rectangles. Cover the pan with aluminum foil and store at room temperature for up to 4 days.

Frozen Fruit Rainbow Terrine

Here's my template for a frozen dessert that I make every summer. It is a festive, frosty striped sorbet, ice cream, and cake terrine with five layers in all: a layer of homemade Blackberry–Red Raspberry Sorbet, a layer of homemade Orange Sorbet, a layer of store-bought vanilla ice cream, a layer of homemade Strawberry Sorbet, and ending with a layer of cake. It's an ideal time to take out that extra Silver Cake with Poppy Seeds from your freezer (you need only half of the cake). When you invert the frozen dessert onto a platter, the cake layer becomes the base and stabilizes the terrine to make it easy to cut into slices. It was on a quick stop at a hardware store one sunny summer day that I spied a long, slender pan that served as inspiration for this terrine. It's known in the construction business as a mud pan, and Sheetrock installers use it for holding the "mud" they apply to Sheetrock to smooth the surface. For me, I see it as an ideal container for this frozen dessert: it's inexpensive, reusable, and available at most hardware stores. Here's the imprint information on the bottom of the pan that will lead you to the correct purchase: 14-inch plastic Mud Pan; cat. #PP 14 by Walboard Tools. The measurement across the top, rim to rim, is 15¾ by 4¾ inches.

Choose fruit that is ripe, fragrant, and full of flavor for the sorbets. Two sugar syrup recipes follow, one for soft fruit puree sorbets and one for fruit juice sorbets. Both have been fine-tuned to balance the sweetness and to yield an ideal texture (not too coarse or icy and not too sweet or dense). Do what I do in the warm summer months: keep a couple of large jars of sugar syrup in the refrigerator ready for impromptu sorbet making.

Try the version that follows or create a terrine with your own favorite flavor combinations. You can vary the fruits used for the sorbets, depending on what is available. Feel free to skip the cake layer, substituting another ice cream or sorbet layer in its place.   YIELD: ONE 5-LAYERED FROZEN DESSERT, ABOUT 20 SERVINGS

SUGAR SYRUP FOR SOFT FRUIT PUREE SORBETS SUCH AS BLACKBERRY, RASPBERRY, AND STRAWBERRY

1½ CUPS PLUS 1 TABLESPOON (12½ FL OUNCES/375 ML) WATER, PREFERABLY FILTERED

1½ CUPS PLUS 2 TABLESPOONS (12 OUNCES/340 GRAMS) GRANULATED SUGAR

SUGAR SYRUP FOR FRUIT JUICE SORBETS SUCH AS ORANGE, BLOOD ORANGE, TANGERINE, AND LEMON

SCANT ½ CUP (3¾ FL OUNCES/110 ML) WATER, PREFERABLY FILTERED

¾ CUP PLUS 2 TABLESPOONS (6 OUNCES/170 GRAMS) GRANULATED SUGAR

BLACKBERRY-RASPBERRY SORBET

2 CUPS (ABOUT 10 OUNCES/280 GRAMS) BLACKBERRIES, PICKED OVER FOR STEMS, TO YIELD ¾ CUP PUREE (6 FL OUNCES/180 ML)

1 CUP (5 OUNCES/140 GRAMS) RED RASPBERRIES, PICKED OVER FOR STEMS, TO YIELD ½ CUP PUREE 4 FL OUNCES/120 ML)

1¼ CUPS (10 FL OUNCES/300 ML) SUGAR SYRUP FOR SOFT FRUIT PUREE SORBETS   CONTINUED ▸

¼ CUP (2 OUNCES/55 GRAMS) COLD CRÈME FRAÎCHE OR
    SOUR CREAM

ORANGE SORBET

¾ CUP (6 FL OUNCES/180 ML) SUGAR SYRUP FOR FRUIT
    JUICE SORBETS

2 CUPS (16 FL OUNCES/480 ML) PLUS 1 TABLESPOON
    STRAINED FRESH ORANGE JUICE

VANILLA ICE CREAM

1 PINT PREMIUM VANILLA ICE CREAM

STRAWBERRY SORBET

2 CUPS (ABOUT 8 OUNCES/225 GRAMS) STRAWBERRIES,
    HULLED, TO YIELD 1 CUP PUREE (8 FL OUNCES/ 240 ML)

1 CUP (8 FL OUNCES/240 ML) SUGAR SYRUP FOR FRUIT
    PUREE SORBETS

1 TABLESPOON FRESH LIME JUICE

CAKE LAYER

½ (9 BY 6½ INCHES) SILVER CAKE WITH POPPY SEEDS
    (PAGE 346), OR 3 SLICES ORANGE CHIFFON TWEED CAKE
    (PAGE 120), EACH ¾ INCH THICK

To prepare the pan: Line a 14 by 3 by 3¼-inch sturdy
plastic mud pan with tapered sides (11-cup capacity) with
two layers of plastic wrap, one overlapping the other
in order to cover the bottom and sides of the pan completely. Press it into the contours of the pan and leave a
5-inch overhang at the top of each end for easy removal
of the frozen dessert from the pan; set aside. If you don't
have a mud pan, use two 9 by 5 by 3-inch loaf pans or
one 13 by 4 by 4-inch straight-sided Pullman loaf pan
(also called a *pain de mie* pan, page 37).

To make the Sugar Syrup for Soft Fruit Puree Sorbets:
In a medium, heavy saucepan, combine the water and
sugar over medium heat and bring to a boil, stirring
occasionally to dissolve the sugar. Remove from the heat
and set aside to cool, then cover and refrigerate until well
chilled before using (it will keep indefinitely). You should
have 2¼ to 2½ cups (18 to 20 fl ounces/540 to 600 ml)
syrup, enough to make both berry sorbets for the terrine.

To make the Sugar Syrup for Fruit Juice Sorbets: In a
small, heavy saucepan, combine the water and sugar over
medium-low heat and heat, stirring occasionally, until
the sugar dissolves. Raise the heat to medium and boil

for 2 minutes only. Remove from the heat and set aside to
cool, then cover and refrigerate until well chilled before
using (it will keep indefinitely). You should have ¾ cup
(6 fl ounces/180 ml) syrup, enough to make the Orange
Sorbet for the terrine.

**To make and freeze the Blackberry-Raspberry
Sorbet layer:** Place a fine-mesh sieve over a large bowl;
set aside. In a food processor, combine the blackberries
and raspberries and process until a puree forms. Pour the
puree into the sieve and, using a rubber spatula, stir the
puree to force the pulp through the sieve, catching the
tiny seeds in the mesh. As the puree drips into the bowl,
press on the contents of the sieve to help release as much
of the juice and pulp from the seeds as possible. Pour the
puree into a 2-cup (16 fl ounce/480 ml) liquid measure,
and discard the contents of the sieve. You need 1¼ cups
(10 fl ounces/300 ml) puree. If the yield is less, puree
additional fruit to make up the difference. If the yield is
more than 1¼ cups, stir the extra into a glass of carbonated water for a refreshing drink. The puree can be used
immediately or covered and refrigerated for up to 2 days
before continuing.

Add the cold sugar syrup and crème fraîche to the
puree, and blend thoroughly with a whisk or rubber
spatula. Freeze in an ice cream maker according to the
manufacturer's instructions. You should have 3 cups sorbet. Without delay, transfer the 3 cups soft sorbet to the
prepared pan, tapping the bottom of the pan to level the
sorbet. Cover the surface with plastic wrap, and place
the pan in the freezer for several hours to firm the sorbet
(before preparing the next recipe to create the next layer).
This can remain in the freezer for several days before
adding another layer. (Spoon any extra sorbet into a
sturdy container and place in the freezer for several hours
to firm; serve as an accompaniment to fruit, cake, or pie.)

To make and freeze the Orange Sorbet layer: In a
medium bowl, combine the sugar syrup and orange juice
and stir until thoroughly blended. Cover and refrigerate.
When the mixture is cold, freeze it in the ice cream maker
according to the manufacturer's instructions. You should
have 3 cups sorbet. Remove the pan from the freezer

and uncover the berry sorbet. Without delay, spread the 3 cups soft orange sorbet evenly over the top. Cover the surface with plastic wrap, and return the pan to the freezer for several hours to firm the sorbet (before preparing the ice cream for the next layer). This can remain in the freezer for several days before adding another layer. (Spoon any extra sorbet into a sturdy container and place in the freezer for several hours to firm; serve as an accompaniment to fruit, cake, or pie.)

To make the Vanilla Ice Cream layer: Soften the ice cream in the refrigerator for about 10 minutes. Remove the pan from the freezer, uncover the orange sorbet, and set the pan nearby. Transfer the ice cream to a large bowl and mix it with a rubber spatula to combine the soft and firm portions. Spread the ice cream evenly over the orange sorbet, cover the surface with plastic wrap, and return the pan to the freezer for several hours to firm (before adding the next layer). This can remain in the freezer for several days before adding another layer.

To make the Strawberry Sorbet layer: In a food processor, process the berries until a puree forms. Pour into a liquid measure. You need 1 cup puree (8 fl ounces/ 240 ml). If the yield is less, puree additional fruit to make up the difference. If the yield is more than 1 cup, stir the extra into a glass of carbonated water for a refreshing drink. The puree can be used immediately or covered and refrigerated for up to 2 days before continuing.

Add the cold sugar syrup and the lime juice to the puree and blend thoroughly with a rubber spatula.

Freeze in an ice cream maker according to the manufacturer's instructions.

While the sorbet is freezing, using a 12-inch serrated knife, split the cake in half horizontally (page 25) to create two ¾-inch-thick layers. Then cut the layers to fit the top of the pan. (Snack on the remaining cake or use it for the trifle recipe on page 267.)

You should have 2 cups sorbet. Remove the pan from the freezer and uncover the vanilla ice cream. Without delay, spread the 2 cups soft strawberry sorbet evenly over the top. Top the sorbet with the cake pieces, gently pressing to ensure that the cake adheres to the sorbet. Cover the pan securely with aluminum foil, and return the pan to the freezer for several hours to firm before serving. The terrine can remain in the freezer for several days before serving.

To serve the frozen terrine: Remove the pan from the freezer, remove the wrapping, and lift the plastic-wrap flaps to loosen the terrine. Invert a serving platter on top of the pan and then invert the pan and platter together and carefully lift off the pan. (The cake layer will now be on the bottom.) Peel off the plastic wrap. Using a sharp knife, cut the terrine into ¾-inch-thick slices, dipping the knife blade in hot water and wiping it dry with a towel before each cut.

Lily's Extraordinary Linzer Tart

Having visited Linz, Austria, and savored more than my share of the city's eponymous tarts, I can decisively state that this one is the best of the best. Its authentic Austrian recipe is one I requested from the gentle, loving Lily Gerson, an incredible baker and a fellow member of our popular Bakers Dozen group in Northern California. Everything about it is perfect, from the tender, nutty pastry crust to the luscious raspberry filling. If you are using preserves with seeds, Lily recommends straining half of the amount specified in the recipe to reduce the total amount of seeds in the finished tart. A small amount of seeds is traditional in this tart.

The rainy day feature of this tart is that the pastry freezes well. So shape the pastry into a disk and freeze it for up to a month to use another time. However, I often divide the dough in half and roll out one portion between sheets of waxed paper and plastic wrap, fit it to the contours of the baking pan, and then wrap the pan securely in plastic wrap and freeze it. I roll out the second pastry portion the same way into a rectangle the same size and transfer the rectangle, still sandwiched between the waxed paper and plastic wrap, to a baking sheet. I wrap plastic wrap securely around the baking sheet, overwrap the sheet with aluminum foil, and freeze it, too. Now, I have a superb dessert almost ready for baking whenever the opportunity comes.

If time permits, thaw the dough-lined pan and the rolled-out dough sheet in the refrigerator overnight. Otherwise, let the dough-lined pan sit at room temperature for 30 to 60 minutes before filling. The sheet of dough thaws at room temperature quickly, so don't leave it out for more than about 5 minutes. It's better to let the jam-filled dough in the pan wait for the dough sheet to soften enough to cut out the strips for the latticework, rather than the other way around.

YIELD: ONE 11½ BY 8-INCH TART, 8 TO 12 SERVINGS

PASTRY

2 CUPS (9 OUNCES/255 GRAMS) ALL-PURPOSE FLOUR

½ CUP (2⅛ OUNCES/60 GRAMS) STORE-BOUGHT PLAIN FINE
    BREAD CRUMBS

1½ CUPS (6 OUNCES/170 GRAMS) GROUND
    NATURAL ALMONDS

1 TEASPOON GROUND CINNAMON

⅛ TEASPOON NUTMEG, PREFERABLY FRESHLY GRATED

⅛ TEASPOON GROUND ALLSPICE

8 OUNCES (2 STICKS/225 GRAMS) UNSALTED BUTTER,
    AT ROOM TEMPERATURE

⅔ CUP (4½ OUNCES/130 GRAMS) GRANULATED SUGAR

1 LARGE EGG

FINELY GRATED ZEST OF 1 LEMON

FILLING

1 TABLESPOON FRESH LEMON JUICE

1 CUP (10 OUNCES/280 GRAMS) RASPBERRY PRESERVES

DECORATION

1 LARGE EGG, LIGHTLY BEATEN

½ CUP (1¾ OUNCES/50 GRAMS) SLICED NATURAL ALMONDS

To make the pastry: In a large bowl, combine the flour, bread crumbs, ground almonds, cinnamon, nutmeg, and allspice and whisk or stir to mix. Set aside.

In the bowl of a stand mixer fitted with the paddle attachment, beat together the butter and sugar at the lowest speed until smooth. Add the egg and lemon zest and beat until incorporated. Maintaining the same speed, gradually add the flour mixture until it comes together to form a dough. Divide the dough in half and shape each half into a rectangle. Wrap separately in plastic wrap and refrigerate until firm enough to roll, about 1 hour.

For longer storage, overwrap each package with aluminum foil, label with the contents and date, and freeze for up to 1 month. Thaw the dough in its packaging in the refrigerator overnight, and remove to room temperature about 1 hour before rolling it out.

To assemble the tart: Have ready an 11¼ by 8 by 1-inch fluted tart pan with a removable bottom. Place 1 piece of the dough on a sheet of plastic wrap and cover it with a sheet of waxed paper. Roll out the dough into an 11½ by 8-inch rectangle. Peel off and discard the waxed paper. Lift the plastic wrap with the pastry on it, and center it, pastry side down, over the tart pan. Gently peel away the sheet of plastic wrap and discard it. With your fingertips, ease the pastry into the pan, fitting it carefully into the corners. If the pastry splits a bit, gently press the tear back together to patch it. Roll the rolling pin over the rim of the tart pan to cut off any excess dough. Chill the pastry-lined pan in the refrigerator for at least 30 minutes or up to 1 day. Roll out the remaining half of the dough the same way and to the same dimensions as the first half. Slide the package onto a baking sheet and refrigerate until firm, at least 30 minutes.

Before baking: Center a rack in the oven and preheat the oven to 350 degrees F.

To make the filling: In a bowl, stir the lemon juice into the raspberry preserves.

Spoon the filling into the pastry-lined pan. Remove the dough package from the refrigerator. Peel off the waxed paper from the dough, replace it loosely on top, and flip the entire package over. (This frees the pastry from the waxed paper so the strips won't stick to it.) Peel off and discard the plastic wrap. Using a pastry wheel or a knife, cut the dough sheet on the diagonal into fourteen ½-inch-wide strips. (You need 7 strips for each diagonal direction to form a lattice pattern, and cutting on the diagonal yields the longest strips.) Arrange the strips on top of the jam filling, forming a lattice. If at any time the pastry strips become too soft to lift, slip a rimless baking sheet under the dough and place it in the freezer for about 10 minutes. If desired, lightly brush the tart edges and strips with the beaten egg wash. Sprinkle the sliced almonds along the edges of the tart.

Bake the tart until it is nicely browned on top and the preserves are bubbling slightly, 30 to 35 minutes. Transfer to a wire rack and let cool completely. Set the tart pan on a narrower elevated surface, such as a tin can, so the bottom of the pan is released as the metal rim slips down. Carefully slide the tart still on its thin metal base onto a serving platter.

To serve, cut the tart into 1½-inch squares, or any size desired.

Chocolate Marquise
with Graham Crackers

Anyone who has eaten the chocolate *marquise* at the restaurant Taillevent in Paris will never forget it. When the copy of the recipe disappeared in the blizzard of papers in my study, I emailed the restaurant requesting the recipe. To my happy surprise, a kind reply appeared on my computer screen in no time, with the recipe attached. The *marquise*, like a rich, dense chocolate mousse, is perfect to make now and reserve in the refrigerator for serving later in the week. I took the liberty of folding in small shards of graham crackers, so when you slice into it you see an artistic pattern and can enjoy the unexpected interplay of textures. If you are seeking a terrific, sophisticated make-ahead chocolate dessert, look no further. Serve a thin slice atop a pool of luxurious vanilla-bean crème anglaise. *Note:* This simple, intensely chocolate, no-bake dessert may be made with pasteurized eggs if you have any reservations about eating uncooked eggs. (And yes, I am sneaking this *marquise* into a baking book even though it doesn't go near the oven. That's because it is wonderfully dramatic with only moderate effort, the graham crackers make it unique in both design and flavor, and it is wildly popular with anyone who has ever tasted it.)

YIELD: ONE 10 BY 4-INCH *MARQUISE*, ABOUT 24 SERVINGS

4 (2 OUNCES/55 GRAMS) STORE-BOUGHT WHOLE HONEY GRAHAM CRACKERS SUCH AS NABISCO

12 OUNCES (340 GRAMS) BITTERSWEET CHOCOLATE, FINELY CHOPPED

8 OUNCES (2 STICKS/225 GRAMS) UNSALTED BUTTER, CUT INTO ½-INCH SLICES

8 LARGE (⅔ CUP/5½ FL OUNCES/165 ML) EGG YOLKS

¾ CUP (5¼ OUNCES/150 GRAMS) GRANULATED SUGAR

½ CUP (1¾ OUNCES/50 GRAMS) UNSWEETENED DUTCH-PROCESSED COCOA POWDER, SIFTED

1 TEASPOON PURE VANILLA EXTRACT

4 LARGE (½ CUP/4 FL OUNCES/120 ML) EGG WHITES

1 RECIPE CRÈME ANGLAISE (PAGE 369)

Moisten a paper or cloth towel with water and rub the towel lightly over the bottom and sides of a 10 by 4¼ by 3-inch loaf pan (6-cup capacity) with slanted sides. Line the pan with plastic wrap (you may have to use 2 sheets of plastic wrap, one overlapping the other slightly, to cover the bottom and sides completely), pressing it into the contours of the pan and leaving about a 3-inch overhang at each end (the water anchors the plastic liner in place); set aside.

Carefully break each graham cracker (following the markings on the crackers) into 4 sections and place on a cutting board. One at a time, and using a sharp knife, cut each 2½ by 1-inch cracker horizontally into thirds, so each piece is about ¾ inch wide. Transfer the cracker pieces to a small bowl; set aside.

In a heavy 1½-quart saucepan, combine the chocolate and butter and heat over low heat, stirring occasionally with a rubber spatula, until the mixture is smooth. Off the heat, add the egg yolks, two at a time, stirring after each addition until well incorporated. Stir in the sugar, reserving 2 teaspoons to use with the egg whites later. Stir the cocoa powder into the chocolate mixture, and then add the vanilla.

In the bowl of a stand mixer fitted with the whisk attachment, whip the egg whites on medium-low speed until foamy. Increase the speed to medium, add the reserved 2 teaspoons sugar, and whip until soft, glossy peaks form. Using the spatula, fold the egg whites into the chocolate mixture just until combined. Then fold in the graham cracker pieces.

Pour the mixture into the prepared pan and tap the pan on a counter to eliminate any air pockets and to compact the mixture. Cover securely with the overhanging plastic wrap, then wrap tightly with aluminum foil and refrigerate for at least 8 hours before serving. The *marquise* keeps well, refrigerated, for up to 3 days. For longer storage, label with the contents and date and freeze for up to 2 weeks. To store any leftover *marquise*, rewrap securely and return to the refrigerator freezer for serving on another occasion. Thaw in the refrigerator for at least 8 hours or up to overnight before serving.

To serve, lift the plastic wrap at both ends of the pan to loosen the *marquise*. Cover the top of the pan with a cutting board (or invert a serving platter over it). Invert the pan and cutting board together, lift off the pan, and peel away and discard the plastic wrap.

Using a sharp knife, cut the *marquise* into $^3/_8$- to $^1/_2$-inch-thick slices, dipping the blade in hot water and wiping it dry with a towel before each cut. Spoon a pool of Crème Anglaise onto each plate and top with a *marquise* slice.

Naomi's Date-Nut Slices

Naomi Klughaupt gave me this recipe and I consider it a special gift. It's easy to prepare, delicious to eat, nutritious, and aesthetically handsome—no two slices look the same. A few thin slices make a perfect serving, resembling an artist's mosaic on the plate. You may slather them with softened cream cheese, though I prefer mine plain. Coffee, hot chocolate, or tea will never taste better than when sipped while munching on a few date-nut slices. This dessert benefits from being made ahead: its flavor deepens and it is easier to cut. Look for whole pitted dates and pecan halves at well-stocked supermarkets, greengrocers, and specialty-food stores. The dates should be moist, not dry or hard, and the pecans should be sweet and tender. I don't recommend using the delicious Medjool dates. They're full of sugar, which makes them too soft for the lengthy baking time. **YIELD: ONE 9 BY 5-INCH LOAF, 20 TO 30 SERVINGS, DEPENDING ON THE THICKNESS OF THE SLICES**

1 POUND (1¾ PACKED CUPS/455 GRAMS) PITTED WHOLE DATES SUCH AS DEGLET NOOR

4 CUPS (1 POUND/455 GRAMS) PECAN HALVES

3 LARGE EGGS, AT ROOM TEMPERATURE

1 CUP (7 OUNCES/200 GRAMS) GRANULATED SUGAR

1 CUP (4½ OUNCES/130 GRAMS) ALL-PURPOSE FLOUR

Before baking: Center a rack in the oven and preheat the oven to 350 degrees F. Generously grease a 9 by 5 by 3-inch loaf pan with solid vegetable shortening, then flour it, tapping out the excess flour.

Place the dates and pecans in a large bowl and toss with fingertips to mix them; set aside.

In the bowl of a stand mixer fitted with the paddle attachment, beat the eggs on low speed to break them up. Increase the speed to medium and gradually add the sugar in a steady stream. Continue to beat the mixture until it is pale yellow and fluffy, about 1 minute. On the lowest speed, gradually add the flour, beating just until incorporated. Detach the paddle and bowl from the mixer, and tap the paddle against the side of the bowl to

free the excess batter. Using a rubber spatula, fold in the dates and nuts until thoroughly incorporated. Spoon the batter into the pan.

Bake for 70 to 80 minutes. Toward the end of baking, the outside of the loaf will darken, as will some of the dates and nuts on the surface. But the interior remains light in color, so your best guide for doneness is when the top is dark brown and feels firm when pressed with a fingertip. Apply the round wooden toothpick or skewer to the center of the loaf before removing it from the oven. The toothpick should be free of any batter. Transfer the pan to a wire rack and let cool completely. Then invert the pan onto the rack and carefully lift off the pan.

For the best flavor and texture, wait a day or two before serving. To store, wrap in plastic wrap, overwrap with aluminum foil, and keep at room temperature for up to 1 week. Or, label with the contents and date and freeze for up to 3 weeks. To thaw, leave at room temperature in its packaging for 3 to 4 hours.

To serve, cut into ¼-inch-thick slices (or any thickness you like) with a serrated knife.

Peppermint Candy Ice Cream Cake Roll

Capturing the sweet magic of the holidays, this festive dessert combines two of the season's signature flavors: deep, dark chocolate and cool, refreshing peppermint. Decadent chocolate sponge cake is rolled with vanilla ice cream and crushed peppermint candies, creating a beautiful dessert that needs only a peppermint stick or candy cane for the perfect garnish.

The most efficient way to crush the peppermint candy is to break up a few candy canes and place the pieces in a sturdy resealable plastic bag, releasing as much air from the bag as possible. Set the bag on a cloth towel on a cutting board, fold the towel over the bag, and pound gently with the end of a rolling pin or with a meat pounder until the candy is in small pieces. Pour the contents of the bag into a sieve and shake it over a sink to sift out candy crumbs. Store the crushed candy in an airtight tin or glass jar until needed. **YIELD: ONE 18-INCH ROLLED CAKE, 12 TO 16 SERVINGS**

1 RECIPE CHOCOLATE GENOISE SHEET CAKE (PAGE 352)

FILLING

2 PINTS PREMIUM VANILLA ICE CREAM

1 OR 2 DROPS RED FOOD COLORING

⅔ CUP (3 OUNCES/85 GRAMS) CRUSHED PEPPERMINT CANDY

¼ CUP (¾ OUNCE/20 GRAMS) POWDERED SUGAR

Make the genoise sheet cake and let cool, tented with aluminum foil, as directed.

To make the filling: Transfer the ice cream from the freezer to the refrigerator so it will soften a bit, about 10 minutes. Meanwhile, remove the foil from the top of the cake. Using a thin metal spatula, gently release any portion of cake sticking to the long sides of the pan. One at a time, pull up on the foil overhangs to release the foil from the pan, and then transfer the cake on its foil liner to a work surface, placing it so that one of its long sides is parallel to the edge of the surface closest to you. Place another long sheet of aluminum foil on the work surface nearby.

Scoop the ice cream into a large bowl and mix it with a rubber spatula to combine the soft and firm portions (or transfer to the bowl of the stand mixer fitted with the paddle attachment and blend briefly on the lowest speed). Add the red coloring and stir it through the ice cream with the spatula to create a streaked effect reminiscent of peppermint candy. Then fold in the peppermint candy.

Using an offset spatula, spread the ice cream evenly over the cake, leaving a 1-inch border uncovered on the long side farthest from you. (Some of the filling will move to that end as you roll up the cake.) Begin rolling by flipping the edge nearest you over onto itself. Then, with the aid of the foil that extends beyond the short sides, roll up the cake lengthwise until you reach the far long side. As you work, wrap the foil around the roll to assist in rounding the shape (otherwise the cake will stick to your hands). Carefully lift the roll and set it, seam side down, on the fresh sheet of foil. Wrap the cake securely in the foil. Freeze for at least 2 hours or up to 2 days.

To serve: Remove the cake from the freezer and peel off and discard the foil. Using a serrated knife and a sawing motion, cut off both ends of the roll on the diagonal for eye appeal, and dust the roll evenly with the powdered sugar. Lift the roll onto a serving plate with the aid of a long, wide spatula or a rimless baking sheet. Using the serrated knife, cut the roll into 1-inch-thick slices.

Pumpkin Ice Cream Profiteroles with Caramel Sauce

A thin cookie-dough circle placed on each unbaked cream puff creates a festive lacy topping after baking. These two-bite ice cream bonbons should be placed on a platter directly from the freezer and popped in your mouth as quickly as possible. They're great for offering to standing guests at large parties. To serve diners around your Thanksgiving table, spoon some warm caramel sauce into bowls, set 2 to 3 profiteroles on top, and spoon additional sauce over the profiteroles. If desired, serve with fresh pear slices or a sprinkling of toasted nuts.

YIELD: ABOUT 4 DOZEN 1½-INCH CREAM PUFFS

COOKIE TOPPING

2 OUNCES (½ STICK/55 GRAMS) UNSALTED BUTTER, AT ROOM TEMPERATURE

½ CUP PLUS 1 TABLESPOON (4 OUNCES/115 GRAMS) GRANULATED SUGAR

1 LARGE EGG

1¼ CUPS PLUS 2 TABLESPOONS (6½ OUNCES/ 185 GRAMS) ALL-PURPOSE FLOUR

CREAM PUFF PASTRY (PÂTE À CHOUX)

¾ CUP PLUS 2 TABLESPOONS (3¾ OUNCES/105 GRAMS) ALL-PURPOSE FLOUR

¼ CUP (2 FL OUNCES/60 ML) WHOLE MILK

½ CUP (4 FL OUNCES/120 ML) WATER

1½ TEASPOONS GRANULATED SUGAR

¼ TEASPOON SALT

3 OUNCES (¾ STICK/85 GRAMS) UNSALTED BUTTER, CUT INTO ½-INCH PIECES

¾ CUP (6 FL OUNCES/180 ML) EGGS, AT ROOM TEMPERATURE (ABOUT 4 LARGE)

⅔ CUP (5½ FL OUNCES/165 ML) BOURBON-BUTTERMILK SAUCE (PAGE 160) OR A FAVORITE STORE-BOUGHT CARAMEL SAUCE

1 QUART PREMIUM PUMPKIN ICE CREAM

To make the Cookie Topping: In the bowl of a stand mixer fitted with the paddle attachment, beat the butter and sugar together on low speed until smooth. Add the egg and then the flour and continue to beat until a smooth, well-blended dough forms. Divide the dough in half. Place each dough portion between 2 sheets of waxed paper and roll out into a 9-inch circle a scant ⅛ inch thick. Stack the circles, still between their sheets of waxed paper, on a baking sheet and refrigerate until firm, at least 2 hours. Or, wrap plastic wrap around the dough circles and the baking sheet and refrigerate for up to 3 days.

Before baking: Center a rack in the oven and preheat the oven to 400 degrees F. Have ready an ice cream scoop about 1⅛ inches in diameter (#100) for forming the cream puffs, or fit a large pastry bag with a ½-inch plain open tip. Line 2 large baking sheets with silicone mats. Or, lightly butter 2 baking sheets, then lightly flour them, tapping out the excess flour.

To make the Cream Puff Pastry: Sift the flour onto a sheet of waxed paper; set nearby. In a heavy 1½-quart saucepan, bring the milk, water, sugar, salt, and butter to a rolling boil over medium heat. Immediately remove from the heat and stir to combine the ingredients. Add the flour all at once, stirring vigorously with a wooden spoon and scraping the sides of the pan, until a stiff paste forms and comes together in a ball. Return to low heat and beat for about 30 seconds to eliminate extra moisture. The paste should be smooth, thick, and glossy. Remove from the heat and transfer to a large bowl to cool, about 10 minutes.

Using a handheld mixer on low speed, add the eggs, one at a time, to the dough, mixing well after each addition. After incorporating the eggs, the dough should be smooth, glossy, and stiff yet hold a soft peak that droops slightly when lifted with a spoon.

Using the ice cream scoop, drop mounds of the paste about 1 inch in diameter on the prepared baking sheets. Or, fill the pastry bag half full with the paste and pipe bite-sized mounds about 1 inch in diameter. Space the cream puffs ½ inch apart to allow for expansion. (If the paste is piped, dip a pastry brush in cool water and lightly "glaze" each cream puff. The brush helps shape each puff smoothly.)

Remove a cookie-dough circle from the refrigerator. Peel off the top sheet of waxed paper, replace it loosely on top, and flip the entire package over. Peel and discard the second sheet of waxed paper from the dough. Using a 1¼-inch round cutter, cut out circles in the dough. Set 1 circle of cookie dough on top of each unbaked mound of cream puff paste. Repeat with the second dough circle, cutting out only as many circles as you need to top the remaining mounds of cream puff paste. (Scraps and leftover dough make great cookies. Reroll, cut out, and bake in a preheated 350 degree F oven until lightly golden and crisp, 8 to 11 minutes.)

Bake the cream puffs, 1 sheet at a time, until the cookie topping is crackly, the puffs are pale gold, and the sides of the puffs are rigid enough that they won't collapse when removed from the oven, 24 to 30 minutes. Transfer the cream puffs from the baking sheets to wire racks and let cool completely. Space them well apart on a wire rack. If they are too close together, steam will soften the puffs and make them soggy. If not using right away, freeze in a sturdy container in the freezer for up to 1 week.

Using a small serrated knife, cut off the top one-third of each puff, including the cookie crown, and set the tops nearby. Remove any soft, uncooked paste from inside the puffs. Spoon ½ to 1 teaspoon caramel sauce inside each puff. Then, using an ice cream scoop about 1¼ inches in diameter (#60), fill the puffs with about 1 tablespoon of the pumpkin ice cream. Set a cream puff top on each filled base.

Place the filled puffs on a baking sheet and place it in the freezer until the puffs are firm, about 1 hour. Then, cover the baking sheet loosely with aluminum foil and freeze for up to 3 days. Serve directly from the freezer.

Mile-High Cheesecake

Manhattan is world-renowned for many things, including its famous cheesecake. With a perfect balance of sweetness and tang, this dense, creamy, melt-in-your-mouth version is reminiscent of the legendary Lindy's cheesecake. As lofty as the city's iconic skyscrapers, this towering cake freezes beautifully, so you can enjoy it whenever you find yourself in a New York state of mind. For perfect results, be sure to give the cream cheese time to soften at room temperature, so it will blend smoothly into the batter. To test when it is ready, press it gently with your finger. If it easily leaves an indentation, the cheese is soft enough to make the batter. To speed the process, unwrap the cream cheese and cut it into small pieces. (Softening cream cheese in a microwave is not recommended for this recipe. Things happen quickly in a microwave, and there is a fine line between softening the cheese and melting it.) Also, be careful not to overbeat the batter, which will incorporate too much air. Because the air has nowhere to go, it will cause cracks to form on the surface of the finished cake.   **YIELD: ONE 7-INCH ROUND CAKE, 10 TO 12 SERVINGS**

1 TABLESPOON UNSALTED BUTTER, SOFTENED

2 TABLESPOONS BLANCHED ALMONDS, FINELY GROUND TO YIELD ¼ CUP (¾ OUNCE/20 GRAMS)

2½ POUNDS (FIVE 8-OUNCE/225-GRAM PACKAGES) CREAM CHEESE

1½ CUPS (10½ OUNCES/300 GRAMS) GRANULATED SUGAR

5 LARGE EGGS, LIGHTLY BEATEN

1 TABLESPOON PURE VANILLA EXTRACT

2 TABLESPOONS HEAVY CREAM

2 TABLESPOONS ALL-PURPOSE FLOUR

FINELY GRATED ZEST OF 1 ORANGE

FINELY GRATED ZEST OF 1 LEMON

Before baking: Center a rack in the oven and preheat the oven to 350 degrees F. Generously rub the butter on the sides of a 7 by 3-inch round cake pan. Coat the sides with the almonds, tapping out the excess. Line the bottom with parchment paper. Select a medium roasting pan with sides 2 to 2½ inches deep and large enough to accommodate the cake pan with at least 1 to 2 inches of space between the sides of the cake pan and the roasting pan. Have all of the ingredients at room temperature.

In the bowl of a stand mixer fitted with the paddle attachment, beat the cream cheese on low speed until smooth, about 45 seconds, stopping to scrape down the sides and the bottom of the bowl once or twice. Maintaining the same speed, add the sugar in a steady stream. When all of the sugar has been added, increase the speed to medium-low and beat until completely smooth. Stop the mixer occasionally to scrape the mixture clinging to the sides into the center of the bowl.

Beat in the eggs, 3 to 4 tablespoons at a time, mixing after each addition until incorporated. Reduce the mixer speed to low and add the vanilla and heavy cream, and then add the flour, mixing until incorporated. Detach the paddle and bowl from the mixer, and tap the paddle against the side of the bowl to free the excess batter. Using a rubber spatula, stir in the orange and lemon zest. Pour the mixture into the prepared pan. Place the pan in the roasting pan, set the roasting pan on the oven rack, and pour in hot tap water to come slightly more than halfway up the sides of the cake pan.

Bake the cake until it is a rich brown on top with no cracks on its surface (it will still be soft inside) and an instant-read thermometer inserted about $1\frac{1}{2}$ inches from the center registers 140 to 150 degrees F, $1\frac{1}{2}$ to $1\frac{3}{4}$ hours. Using a turkey baster, remove at least half of the water from the water bath and discard. With oven mitts, carefully lift the cake pan out of the water bath and place it on a wire rack. Let cool to room temperature, 2 to 3 hours. (As the cheesecake cools, it becomes firm yet remains creamy inside, and it becomes even firmer after refrigeration.)

To unmold, tilt and rotate the pan while gently tapping it on a counter to release the cake sides. Invert a serving plate on top of the pan; invert the cake onto it, working carefully so as not to mar the cake; and gently lift off the pan. Refrigerate the cake until firm and cold, about 2 hours, and then cover securely with plastic wrap until serving.

For longer storage, cover an 8- or 9-inch cardboard round with aluminum foil, and overwrap the cardboard round with plastic wrap. Unmold the cake onto the cardboard round as described for the serving plate. Refrigerate the cake on the round until firm and cold, about 2 hours, and then wrap securely with plastic wrap, overwrap with foil, label with the contents and date, and freeze for up to 2 weeks. To thaw, remove the foil, plastic wrap, and cardboard round, place the frozen cheesecake on a serving plate, and cover securely with plastic wrap. Set the package in the refrigerator overnight before serving.

To serve, cut the chilled cake into small wedges with a sharp knife, wiping the blade clean with a damp towel after each cut.

Hearth and Home All Day Long

ASK DIFFERENT PEOPLE about what home means to them, and you are bound to get different answers. But if you ask different bakers what home signifies, they will probably talk about aromas. There is something comforting—and inviting—about freshly baked breads, cakes, pastries, and desserts. Taste is certainly part of the equation. But even before the first crumb of a batch of apricot scones or oatmeal cookies hits your tongue, you smell their scent in the air. The best advertising any baker can do is to open the windows when the oven is on.

Don't take the title of this chapter literally. You will not be at home all day waiting for these recipes to be ready. Many of the doughs can sit unattended overnight in the refrigerator, since they don't suffer from a long, slow rise. In fact, chilled doughs are easier to form into loaves, buns, or twists.

The idea here is that baking with a variety of doughs and batters complements different times of the day. Olfactory temptations can start in the morning, with the air filled with a heady mix of cinnamon, nutmeg, and warm blackberries from Focaccia for Breakfast, or with orange and lemon zest from Spicy Citrus Swirly Buns. At midday, perhaps the delightful scent of Banana Streusel Snack Cake or Popovers with Bourbon-Buttermilk Sauce will attract hungry souls to the hearth. And at any time, the fragrance of Croissant Cinnamon Sticks or Pain d'Épices—both perfect for snacking—will entice everyone within sniffing distance of your kitchen.

Throughout the day, these recipes rise to the occasion.

Banana Streusel Snack Cake

This cake evolved from a favorite banana bread recipe from my childhood. Now it is gussied up for any occasion, be it a housewarming gift, a bake sale, or an impromptu tea party. It is also a great addition to a lunch box. The bananas should be mashed, but not pureed, for this recipe. Any small nugget of banana that remains from the hand-smashing delivers the very essence of the fruit's flavor. You can also bake this cake in an 8 by 2-inch square pan for about 35 minutes.

YIELD: ONE 9 BY 5-INCH CAKE, 12 SERVINGS

STREUSEL

6 TABLESPOONS (1¾ OUNCES/50 GRAMS) ALL-PURPOSE FLOUR

6 TABLESPOONS FIRMLY PACKED (2¾ OUNCES/75 GRAMS) LIGHT BROWN SUGAR

3 TABLESPOONS UNSALTED BUTTER, SOFTENED

¼ TEASPOON GROUND CINNAMON

CAKE

2 CUPS (8 OUNCES/225 GRAMS) CAKE FLOUR

1 TEASPOON BAKING POWDER

½ TEASPOON BAKING SODA

½ TEASPOON SALT

1 CUP (9 OUNCES/255 GRAMS) MASHED RIPE BANANAS (2 MEDIUM OR 3 SMALL)

3 TABLESPOONS WHOLE MILK

1 TEASPOON PURE VANILLA EXTRACT

4 OUNCES (1 STICK/115 GRAMS) UNSALTED BUTTER

1 CUP (7 OUNCES/200 GRAMS) GRANULATED SUGAR

1 LARGE EGG, LIGHTLY BEATEN

To make the streusel: In a medium bowl, mix together the flour, sugar, butter, and cinnamon with your fingertips until the mixture is lumpy; set aside.

Before baking: Center a rack in the oven and preheat the oven to 350 degrees F. Lightly coat a 9 by 5 by 3-inch loaf pan with nonstick spray, then flour it, tapping out the excess flour. Or, butter and flour the pan. Have all of the ingredients at room temperature.

To make the cake: Sift together the flour, baking powder, baking soda, and salt onto a sheet of waxed paper; set aside. Put the mashed bananas in a medium bowl and stir in the milk and vanilla; set aside.

In the bowl of a stand mixer fitted with the paddle attachment (or a handheld mixer), beat together the butter and sugar on medium-low speed until fluffy, 2 to 3 minutes. Add the egg and beat until completely incorporated. Add the banana mixture (it will look curdled, but that's okay) and beat until combined. Reduce the mixer to its lowest speed and gradually add the flour mixture, beating just until incorporated. Spoon the batter into the prepared pan and smooth the surface with a rubber spatula. Sprinkle the streusel evenly over the batter.

Bake the cake until it springs back when gently pressed in the center and a round wooden toothpick inserted in the center comes out free of batter, 40 to 50 minutes. Transfer to a wire rack and let cool in the pan for 10 minutes.

Tilt and rotate the pan while gently tapping it on a counter to release the cake sides. If they don't release, slip a small metal spatula between the still-warm cake and the pan and run the spatula carefully along the entire perimeter of the pan. Invert a rack on top of the cake, invert the cake onto it, and carefully lift off the pan. Invert another rack on top, invert the cake so it is streusel side up, and remove the original rack. Let cool completely before cutting.

This cake freezes beautifully. Wrap securely in plastic wrap, overwrap with aluminum foil, label with the contents and date, and freeze for up to 2 weeks. To thaw, remove the foil and leave at room temperature for about 3 hours.

To serve, cut into slices with a sharp knife.

Focaccia for Breakfast

The serendipitous story of this recipe begins at the popular Cetrella Bistro and Café in Half Moon Bay, California. I always look forward to the restaurant's chewy, full-flavored focaccia, and was hoping I could include the recipe in this book. My request was graciously granted by the very talented Lewis Rossman, who at the time was executive chef. A conversation with my friend Christine Law, former pastry chef of Postrio restaurant in San Francisco and Spago in Palo Alto (and ice cream guru par excellence) gave me the secret (and her recipe) to transforming the world-class savory bread into a sweet sensation: plump fresh blackberries and a gorgeous brown sugar–olive oil streusel. Note to night owls: Bake the focaccia in the late afternoon or evening, and it will still have that fresh-from-the-oven taste for breakfast, brunch, or even a tailgate the next day.

For the best results, it is important to respect the proportion of flour to other ingredients in the recipe. Weigh the flour for accuracy, since the volume measure of 1 pound (455 grams) bread flour varies with the brand used.   YIELD: ONE 15½ BY 10½-INCH COFFEE CAKE, ABOUT 15 SERVINGS

DOUGH

1 TEASPOON ACTIVE DRY YEAST

1 TEASPOON GRANULATED SUGAR

1⅓ CUPS (10½ FL OUNCES/315 ML) WARM WATER (98 TO 100 DEGREES F)

5 TABLESPOONS (2½ FL OUNCES/75 ML) OLIVE OIL, PREFERABLY A FRUITY ONE

1 POUND (455 GRAMS) UNBLEACHED BREAD FLOUR (3 CUPS PLUS 3 TO 8 TABLESPOONS, DEPENDING ON FLOUR BRAND)

2 TEASPOONS SALT

OLIVE OIL STREUSEL

½ CUP (3 OUNCES/85 GRAMS) WHOLE NATURAL ALMONDS

¼ CUP (2 FL OUNCES/60 ML) FRUITY OLIVE OIL

⅛ TEASPOON SALT

½ CUP PLUS 2 TABLESPOONS (3 OUNCES/85 GRAMS) ALL-PURPOSE FLOUR

¼ CUP (1¾ OUNCES/50 GRAMS) GRANULATED SUGAR

¼ CUP FIRMLY PACKED (1¾ OUNCES/50 GRAMS) DARK BROWN SUGAR

½ TEASPOON GROUND CINNAMON

½ TEASPOON NUTMEG, PREFERABLY FRESHLY GRATED

2½ OUNCES (5 TABLESPOONS/70 GRAMS) COLD UNSALTED BUTTER, CUT INTO ½-INCH PIECES

2 CUPS (10 OUNCES/280 GRAMS) BLACKBERRIES (ABOUT 48), PICKED OVER FOR STEMS

To make the dough: In the bowl of a stand mixer, sprinkle the yeast and a pinch of the sugar over the warm water and set aside to proof for about 10 minutes. Add the olive oil, flour, the remaining sugar, and the salt, in that order. Attach the dough hook to the mixer and beat on low speed for about 12 minutes, stopping to scrape down the sides of the bowl once or twice. When the dough is smooth yet slightly sticky, elastic, and comes away from the sides of the bowl in a cohesive ball, stop the mixer, detach the hook and bowl, and loosely cover the bowl with a kitchen towel or plastic wrap. Set the dough aside at room temperature to rise until almost doubled in bulk, 30 to 35 minutes. Press the dough gently with a fingertip. If the indentation remains, the dough is ready for the next step.

Before baking: Center a rack in the oven and preheat the oven to 350 degrees F.

To make the Olive Oil Streusel: While the dough is rising, spread the almonds on a baking sheet and toast them in the oven until hot and fragrant but not yet starting to color, about 8 minutes. Carefully transfer the hot almonds to a small cup and pour the olive oil over them. (The cup should be small and tall enough so the nuts are fully submerged.) Set aside to cool completely. Leave the oven on.

Drain the nuts, reserving the olive oil, and place them in a food processor. Sprinkle the salt over them and pulse briefly to chop the nuts to about half of their original size. Add the flour, sugars, cinnamon, nutmeg, and butter, in that order, and pulse briefly until the mixture appears mealy with clumps the size of small peas. Drizzle in $1\frac{1}{2}$ tablespoons of the almond-infused olive oil and pulse briefly. Transfer the streusel to a small bowl and refrigerate, uncovered, until ready to use.

To form the focaccia: Increase the oven temperature to 375 degrees F. Lightly coat a $15\frac{1}{2}$ by $10\frac{1}{2}$ by 1-inch pan (jelly-roll pan) with nonstick spray. Line the bottom with parchment paper, and brush the paper with 1 tablespoon of the reserved almond-infused olive oil.

Gently deflate the dough and press it over the bottom of the prepared pan. It will be slightly elastic, even a bit slippery, due to the oil on the parchment paper. When the dough resists too much, just let it rest for 1 minute at a time, then resume coaxing it to cover the bottom of the pan. It won't take long to achieve this. Cover the pan with plastic wrap or a kitchen towel and set the dough aside in a warm place (about 70 degrees F) to rise until doubled in size, 60 to 70 minutes.

When a floured finger gently pressed into the dough leaves an indentation, the dough is ready for topping. Brush 1 to $1\frac{1}{2}$ more tablespoons of the almond-infused oil on top. Gently poke the blackberries in the dough, forming 6 rows and spacing the berries about 1 inch apart. Break up any large pieces of the streusel into pea-sized pieces and then sprinkle the streusel evenly over the dough.

Loosely cover the pan with plastic wrap or a cloth towel and set aside to rise until the dough has almost doubled in bulk and a floured finger gently pressed into the dough leaves an indentation, 30 to 35 minutes more.

Bake the focaccia, rotating the pan 180 degrees midway through baking, until the dough is lightly golden (especially around the edges of the pan), the streusel is golden brown, and the blackberries are bubbly, 40 to 45 minutes. Transfer the pan to a wire rack and let cool for at least 30 minutes.

Serve the focaccia warm or at room temperature. Cut into 3-inch squares (or any size desired) with a serrated knife. Slip a sturdy metal spatula under the pieces to remove them from the pan.

Popovers with Bourbon-Buttermilk Sauce

Baking popovers is a magical experience, as the oven's heat transforms a simple batter into lofty, golden brown muffins with the shape of a chef's toque. They call for ingredients that most of us have on hand—and with a blender or food processor, you can make the thin, pancakelike batter in seconds. Serve the popovers for dessert, topped with San Francisco pastry chef Susan Brinkley's incredible Bourbon-Buttermilk Sauce. A luxurious complement to the airy popovers, the rich, creamy sauce is one of the biggest crowd-pleasers on her menus.   **YIELD: 6 POPOVERS**

POPOVERS

2 LARGE EGGS

1 CUP (8 FL OUNCES/240 ML) WHOLE MILK, AT ROOM TEMPERATURE

1 TABLESPOON UNSALTED BUTTER, MELTED

1 CUP (4½ OUNCES/130 GRAMS) ALL-PURPOSE FLOUR

½ TEASPOON SALT

BOURBON-BUTTERMILK SAUCE

1 CUP (7 OUNCES/200 GRAMS) GRANULATED SUGAR

½ CUP (4 FL OUNCES/120 ML) WELL-SHAKEN BUTTERMILK

½ TEASPOON BAKING SODA

⅛ TEASPOON SALT

4 OUNCES (1 STICK/115 GRAMS) UNSALTED BUTTER

¼ CUP (2 FL OUNCES/60 ML) BOURBON

Before baking: Center a rack in the oven and preheat the oven to 400 degrees F. Thoroughly and generously coat the cups in a 6-cup popover plaque (each cup measures 2 inches in diameter and 2½ inches deep) with softened butter.

To make the popovers: In a blender or food processor, combine the eggs, milk, butter, flour, and salt and process until completely smooth, about 40 seconds, stopping to scrape down the sides of the bowl twice. Alternatively, in a large bowl, whisk together the eggs, milk, and butter. Add the flour and salt and beat until very smooth and about the consistency of heavy cream. Pour the batter into the prepared cups, dividing it evenly and filling each cup one-half to two-thirds full.

Bake until golden brown, 35 to 40 minutes. Resist opening the oven door until the end of the baking time, or the popovers will collapse. While the popovers are baking, make the sauce.

To make the Bourbon-Buttermilk Sauce: In a high-sided 2- to 2½-quart saucepan, combine the sugar, buttermilk, baking soda, salt, and butter and stir to blend. (Adding the stick of butter whole, rather than cut up, means that it will melt slowly, which helps regulate the cooking of the sauce so that it doesn't "break.") Place over medium heat and cook, stirring constantly, until the mixture registers 225 degrees F on a candy thermometer, about 10 minutes. (The baking soda causes the mixture to foam up the sides of the pan as it cooks.) Remove from the heat, let cool for 5 minutes, and whisk in the bourbon. You should have 1¼ cups (10 fl ounces/300 ml) sauce.

When the popovers are ready, transfer the plaque to a wire rack. Pour some of the warm sauce onto each dessert plate and center a warm popover on each pool of sauce. Serve warm. Pour the remaining sauce in a pitcher and pass the pitcher at the table. Using a fork and knife, eat the popover as if it were a waffle.

Rhubarb, Apple, and Raspberry Jalousie

This traditional pastry derives its evocative name from the French word for Venetian blinds, describing the enticing way the fruit filling peeks out from beneath the slatted crust. I've briefly roasted the rhubarb and apple to evaporate some of their moisture and intensify their rich fruit flavors. If you've been too intimidated to make your own puff pastry dough, the PDQ recipe used here is a surefire cure. Its speedier, more streamlined process makes it a cinch to create an irresistibly light, flaky pastry. **YIELD: ONE 12½ BY 7½-INCH PASTRY, 8 SERVINGS**

FRUIT

11 OUNCES (310 GRAMS) NARROW RHUBARB STALKS (5 OR 6 STALKS), TRIMMED AND CUT INTO 1½-INCH PIECES TO YIELD ABOUT 2½ CUPS (ABOUT 10½ OUNCES/300 GRAMS)

2 MEDIUM (ABOUT 6 OUNCES/170 GRAMS EACH) GOLDEN DELICIOUS APPLES, PEELED, HALVED, CORED, EACH HALF CUT LENGTHWISE INTO 4 STRIPS, AND EACH STRIP CUT CROSSWISE INTO THIRDS TO YIELD ABOUT 3½ CUPS (ABOUT 5½ OUNCES/155 GRAMS)

1 MEDIUM (ABOUT 6 OUNCES/170 GRAMS) BRAEBURN OR SIMILAR TART APPLE VARIETY, PEELED, HALVED, CORED, EACH HALF CUT LENGTHWISE INTO 4 STRIPS, AND EACH STRIP CUT CROSSWISE INTO THIRDS TO YIELD ABOUT 1¾ CUPS (ABOUT 5¾ OUNCES/165 GRAMS)

5 TABLESPOONS (2¼ OUNCES/60 GRAMS) GRANULATED SUGAR, DIVIDED

2 TABLESPOONS UNSALTED BUTTER, CUT INTO SMALL CUBES

½ RECIPE (ABOUT 1¼ POUNDS/570 GRAMS) WELL-CHILLED PDQ (PRETTY DARN QUICK) PUFF PASTRY (PAGE 367)

1 CUP (ABOUT 5 OUNCES/140 GRAMS) RED RASPBERRIES, PICKED OVER FOR STEMS

1 TABLESPOON CORNSTARCH

ABOUT 1 TEASPOON WATER

1 TABLESPOON GRANULATED SUGAR

Before baking: Center a rack in the oven and preheat the oven to 400 degrees F.

Spread the rhubarb and apple pieces on a rimmed baking sheet, sprinkle with 3 tablespoons of the sugar, and scatter the butter over the fruits. Roast the fruits, tossing occasionally to ensure that they bake evenly and some of their juices evaporate, until they are lightly glazed with their juices and partially cooked, 14 to 17 minutes. Remove from the oven, transfer to a bowl, and let cool completely. Although you began with about 7½ cups fruit (about 1 pound, 6 ounces/625 grams), you will have only about half that amount after partially roasting. Leave the oven on. While the fruits cool, begin readying the pastry.

To prepare the pastry: Line 2 rimmed baking sheets with parchment paper; set aside. Take the puff pastry package from the refrigerator, and place it on a lightly floured work surface. Cut the pastry in half. Return 1 portion, unwrapped, to the refrigerator briefly. On a lightly floured work surface, roll out the remaining portion into a 14 by 8-inch rectangle about ⅛ inch thick. Transfer it to 1 of the prepared baking sheets, trim any ragged edges with a sharp knife, cover the pastry loosely with plastic wrap, and refrigerate for just as long as it takes to roll out the other piece of pastry. Remove the second pastry portion from the refrigerator and roll it out into a 14 by 8-inch rectangle about ⅛ inch thick. Transfer it to the other prepared baking sheet, trim it, cover it loosely with plastic wrap, and refrigerate.

Remove the first baking sheet from the refrigerator. Add the raspberries to the cooled fruits, sprinkle the cornstarch over the top, and toss to blend the fruits with the cornstarch and with any of the buttery juices that have flowed to the bottom of the bowl. Spoon the filling lengthwise onto the pastry, mounding it CONTINUED ▶

evenly over the center and leaving a 1- to 1½-inch border uncovered on all sides. Sprinkle the additional 2 tablespoons sugar over the filling.

Remove the baking sheet with the other pastry rectangle from the refrigerator. Fold the rectangle in half lengthwise, and cut across the fold at about ¼-inch intervals, stopping 1¼ inches from the long end (to keep the strips attached). Once the pastry is cut, you can slip it, still folded, into the freezer for 5 to 10 minutes so it gets very cold, which will make it easier to move it to the top of the tart.

With a pastry brush, apply a very light coat of water to the border of the fruit-topped pastry rectangle. Gently lift the chilled folded pastry and line up a long edge of it with a long edge of the fruit-laden pastry. Unfold the pastry over the fruit filling. (If the strips are not straight after the transfer, you will have a chance to adjust them soon.) Seal the edges of the top to the bottom pastry by pressing them together gently with your fingertips. With a sharp, large knife, trim the edges of the pastry to

even them (after trimming, the jalousie is about 12½ by 7½ inches). Carefully adjust any of the ¼-inch strips that are stuck together or need to be realigned. Then, holding the dough in place with 1 fingertip, scallop the edges of the pastry at close intervals with the back of a small paring knife (the dull edge). This action both decorates the edges and seals the layers together. (Scalloping the edges is a classic technique for ensuring an even rise as the pastry bakes.) Chill the jalousie, uncovered, in the refrigerator for about 30 minutes.

Brush the jalousie very lightly with the water and sprinkle evenly with the sugar. Bake until golden, 40 to 45 minutes. Transfer to a wire rack and let cool on the pan.

For optimum flavor and texture, serve the jalousie the same day it is baked, either warm or at room temperature. To serve, cut crosswise into 1½-inch-wide pieces with a serrated knife.

Lemon-Scented Pull-Apart Coffee Cake

Lemon and cream cheese have long been classic companions in American baking, and this fun-to-assemble, sweet-tart filled coffee cake makes it easy to see why. Showcasing the lively flavors of fresh citrus, the sweet, buttery filling is made with fluffy, fragrant lemon and orange zest. The warm loaf is brushed with a zippy cream cheese icing, whose tangy flavor marries marvelously with the sunny taste of citrus. Enjoy a slice of this pull-apart coffee cake whenever you need an instant pick-me-up. **YIELD: ONE 9 BY 5-INCH COFFEE CAKE, ABOUT 14 SERVINGS**

SWEET YEAST DOUGH

ABOUT 2¾ CUPS (12¼ OUNCES/350 GRAMS) ALL-PURPOSE FLOUR

¼ CUP (1¾ OUNCES/50 GRAMS) GRANULATED SUGAR

2¼ TEASPOONS (1 ENVELOPE) INSTANT YEAST

½ TEASPOON SALT

⅓ CUP (2½ FL OUNCES/75 ML) WHOLE MILK

2 OUNCES (½ STICK/55 GRAMS) UNSALTED BUTTER

¼ CUP (2 FL OUNCES/60 ML) WATER

1½ TEASPOONS PURE VANILLA EXTRACT

2 LARGE EGGS, AT ROOM TEMPERATURE

LEMON PASTE FILLING

½ CUP (3½ OUNCES/100 GRAMS) GRANULATED SUGAR

3 TABLESPOONS FINELY GRATED LEMON ZEST (3 LEMONS)

1 TABLESPOON FINELY GRATED ORANGE ZEST

2 OUNCES (½ STICK/55 GRAMS) UNSALTED BUTTER, MELTED

TANGY CREAM CHEESE ICING

3 OUNCES (85 GRAMS) CREAM CHEESE, SOFTENED

⅓ CUP (1¼ OUNCES/35 GRAMS) POWDERED SUGAR

1 TABLESPOON WHOLE MILK

1 TABLESPOON FRESH LEMON JUICE

To make the Sweet Yeast Dough: Stir together 2 cups (9 ounces/255 grams) of the flour, the sugar, the yeast, and the salt in the bowl of a stand mixer; set aside. In a small saucepan, heat the milk and butter over low heat just until the butter is melted. Remove from the heat, add the water, and set aside until warm (120 to 130 degrees F), about 1 minute. Add the vanilla extract.

Pour the milk mixture over the flour-yeast mixture and, using a rubber spatula, mix until the dry ingredients are evenly moistened. Attach the bowl to the mixer, and fit the mixer with the paddle attachment. With the mixer on low speed, add the eggs, one at a time, mixing after each addition just until incorporated. Stop the mixer, add ½ cup (2¼ ounces/65 grams) of the remaining flour, and resume mixing on low speed until the dough is smooth, 30 to 45 seconds. Add 2 more tablespoons flour and mix on medium speed until the dough is smooth, soft, and slightly sticky, about 45 seconds.

Sprinkle a work surface with 1 tablespoon flour and center the dough on the flour. Knead gently until smooth and no longer sticky, about 1 minute, adding an additional 1 to 2 tablespoons flour only if necessary to lessen the stickiness. Place the dough in a large bowl, cover the bowl securely with plastic wrap, and let the dough rise in a warm place (about 70 degrees F) until doubled in size, 45 to 60 minutes. Press the dough gently with a fingertip. If the indentation remains, the dough is ready for the next step. While the dough is rising, make the filling.

To make the Lemon Paste Filling: In a small bowl, mix together the sugar and the lemon and orange zests. Set the sandy-wet mixture nearby (the sugar draws out moisture from the zests to create the consistency).

Before baking: Center a rack in the oven and preheat the oven to 350 degrees F. Lightly butter a 9 by 5 by 3-inch loaf pan. Or, lightly coat the pan with nonstick spray.

CONTINUED ▶

To shape the coffee cake: Gently deflate the dough. On a lightly floured work surface, roll out the dough into a 20-by-12-inch rectangle. Using a pastry brush, spread the melted butter generously over the dough. Cut the dough crosswise into 5 strips, each about 12 by 4 inches. (A pizza cutter is helpful here.) Sprinkle 1½ tablespoons of the zest-sugar mixture over one of the buttered rectangles. Top with a second rectangle and sprinkle it with 1½ tablespoons of the zest-sugar mixture. Repeat with the remaining dough rectangles and zest-sugar mixture, ending with a stack of 5 rectangles. Work carefully when adding the crumbly zest filling, or it will fall off when you have to lift the stacked pastry later.

Slice the stack crosswise through the 5 layers to create 6 equal strips, each about 4 by 2 inches. Fit these layered strips into the prepared loaf pan, cut edges up and side by side. (While there is plenty of space on either side of the 6 strips widthwise in the pan, fitting the strips lengthwise is tight. But that's fine because the spaces between the dough and the sides of the pan fill in during baking.) Loosely cover the pan with plastic wrap and let the dough rise in a warm place (70 degrees F) until puffy and almost doubled in size, 30 to 50 minutes. Press the dough gently with a fingertip. If the indentation remains, the dough is ready for baking.

Bake the coffee cake until the top is golden brown, 30 to 35 minutes. Transfer to a wire rack and let cool in the pan for 10 to 15 minutes.

While the coffee cake bakes, make the Tangy Cream Cheese Icing: In a medium bowl, using a rubber spatula, vigorously mix the cream cheese and sugar until smooth. Beat in the milk and lemon juice until the mixture is creamy and smooth.

To remove the coffee cake from the pan, tilt and rotate the pan while gently tapping it on a counter to release the cake sides. Invert a wire rack on top of the coffee cake, invert the cake onto the rack, and carefully lift off the pan. Invert another rack on top, invert the cake so it is right side up, and remove the original rack. Slip a sheet of waxed paper under the rack to catch any drips from the icing. Using a pastry brush, coat the top of the warm cake with the icing to glaze it. (Cover and refrigerate the leftover icing for another use. It will keep for up to 2 days.)

Serve the coffee cake warm or at room temperature. To serve, you can pull apart the layers, or you can cut the cake into 1-inch-thick slices on a slight diagonal with a long, serrated knife. If you decide to cut the cake, don't attempt to cut it until it is almost completely cool.

Maple-Pecan Medjool Date Rugelach

No one with a sweet tooth will be able to resist these festive bite-sized pastries. Their indulgent goodness comes from the use of Medjool dates, which are as delectably sweet and rich as candy. Toasted pecans add a bit of crunch, while maple lends its own unique flavor. The cream cheese dough is a baker's dream: rich, tender, and a joy to handle. Shaping the rugelach is fun and easy: just spread the filling over a thin circle of dough, cut it into triangular wedges, and then roll each one into a handsome little crescent. **YIELD: 8 DOZEN PASTRIES**

1 RECIPE CREAM CHEESE PASTRY (PAGE 359)

FILLING

⅔ CUP FIRMLY PACKED (4½ OUNCES/130 GRAMS) LIGHT
 BROWN SUGAR

½ TEASPOON GROUND CINNAMON

⅓ CUP (3 OUNCES BY WEIGHT/85 GRAMS) PURE MAPLE SYRUP,
 PREFERABLY GRADE B

2 CUPS (7½ OUNCES/215 GRAMS) FINELY CHOPPED PECANS

24 MEDJOOL DATES, PITTED AND QUARTERED

GLAZE

6 TABLESPOONS (1½ OUNCES/40 GRAMS) POWDERED SUGAR

4 TEASPOONS PURE MAPLE SYRUP

2 TEASPOONS HOT WATER

⅓ CUP (1¼ OUNCES/35 GRAMS) FINELY CHOPPED PECANS

Make the pastry as directed, divide it into 8 equal pieces, flatten each piece into a disk, wrap separately in plastic wrap, and refrigerate until firm, about 4 hours.

Before baking: Center a rack in the oven and preheat the oven to 350 degrees F. Line 2 large baking sheets with parchment paper.

To form the rugelach: In a small bowl, stir together the sugar and cinnamon for the filling. Remove 1 dough package from the refrigerator about 5 minutes before rolling it; keep the other dough pieces chilled. On a lightly floured surface, roll out the dough into an 8-inch circle about ⅛ inch thick. Using a small pastry brush, apply a light film of maple syrup over the circle. Sprinkle with a scant 2 tablespoons cinnamon sugar, and then

with ¼ cup of the nuts. With the rolling pin, lightly roll to press the filling ingredients into the dough.

Using a sharp knife, cut the circle into 12 pie-shaped wedges. Place a date quarter ¼ inch in from the wide edge of each wedge. Beginning at the wide edge, roll up each wedge. Place the rolls, point down, on the prepared baking sheet, spacing them about 1 inch apart. Repeat to shape and fill the additional dough portions until the baking sheet is full.

Bake the pastries until they are pale gold and not shiny or soft to the touch on top and golden on the bottom, 15 to 18 minutes.

While the pastries are baking, prepare the glaze: In a small bowl, stir together the powdered sugar and maple syrup (it will be slightly thick). Add the hot water and stir until the mixture is thoroughly blended and smooth. Put the pecans in a small, shallow bowl.

When the pastries have finished baking, transfer the pan to a wire rack. While the pastries are still warm, dip the top of each pastry into the glaze and then dip the glazed portion into the pecans. As each pastry is coated, set it on a wire rack to cool completely. Repeat the shaping, baking (on the second baking sheet) and glazing with the remaining dough portions, filling, and glaze.

Store the pastries in an airtight container at room temperature. They will keep for up to 1 week.

Old-World Braided Coffee Cake

This lavish nut-filled coffee cake is reminiscent of heirloom recipes from eastern Europe. A pleasure to enjoy at any time of day, it is one of those intricate, yeast-leavened cakes that looks as though it takes a master baker's expertise and many long hours to prepare—even though it doesn't. Both the dough and the rich walnut filling are gratifyingly straightforward, as is forming the handsome design. The secret? You simply braid the filling into the dough, which obligingly bakes into an impressive chevron pattern. Serve the sliced braid with a favorite honey or soft unsalted butter.   **YIELD: 1 RECTANGULAR COFFEE CAKE, ABOUT 14 SERVINGS**

SWEET YEAST DOUGH

3 CUPS PLUS 1 TABLESPOON (14 OUNCES/400 GRAMS) ALL-PURPOSE FLOUR

¼ CUP (1¾ OUNCES/50 GRAMS) GRANULATED SUGAR

2¾ TEASPOONS (1 ENVELOPE PLUS ½ TEASPOON) ACTIVE DRY YEAST

½ TEASPOON SALT

½ CUP (4 FL OUNCES/120 ML) WHOLE MILK

2 OUNCES (½ STICK/55 GRAMS) UNSALTED BUTTER

1½ TEASPOONS PURE VANILLA EXTRACT

2 LARGE EGGS, LIGHTLY BEATEN

WALNUT FILLING

2 CUPS (8 OUNCES/225 GRAMS) WALNUTS, FINELY GROUND TO YIELD 2½ CUPS

¼ CUP (1¾ OUNCES/50 GRAMS) GRANULATED SUGAR

2 TABLESPOONS FIRMLY PACKED BROWN SUGAR

1¼ TEASPOONS GROUND CINNAMON

⅛ TEASPOON SALT

⅓ CUP (2½ FL OUNCES/75 ML) HEAVY CREAM

1 TABLESPOON PURE MAPLE SYRUP

1 TEASPOON PURE VANILLA EXTRACT

2 LARGE EGG WHITES

GLAZE

1 TABLESPOON GRANULATED SUGAR

1 TABLESPOON WATER

To make the Sweet Yeast Dough: Stir together 2 cups (9 ounces/255 grams) of the flour, the sugar, the yeast, and the salt in the bowl of a stand mixer; set aside. In a small, heavy saucepan, heat the milk and butter over low heat until the butter melts; set aside until warm (120 to 130 degrees F), 1 to 3 minutes. Add the vanilla.

Pour the milk mixture over the flour-yeast mixture and, using a rubber spatula, mix until the dry ingredients are evenly moistened. Attach the bowl to the mixer, and fit the mixer with the paddle attachment. With the mixer on low speed, add the eggs, one at a time, mixing after each addition just until incorporated. Stop the mixer and scrape down the sides of the bowl. Add 1 cup (4½ ounces/130 grams) of the flour and resume mixing on medium-low speed until the dough is smooth, soft, and slightly sticky, about 45 seconds.

Sprinkle a work surface with the remaining 1 tablespoon flour and center the dough on the flour. Knead gently until smooth and just slightly tacky, about 5 minutes. (No additional flour is necessary while kneading.) Place the dough in a large bowl, cover the bowl securely with plastic wrap, and let the dough rise in a warm place (70 degrees F) until doubled in size, 45 to 60 minutes. Press the dough gently with a fingertip. If the indentation remains, the dough is ready for shaping. While the dough is rising, make the filling.

To make the Walnut Filling: In a medium bowl, combine the nuts, sugars, cinnamon, and salt and whisk just until mixed. In a small saucepan, bring the cream and maple syrup to a simmer over medium-low heat, and then pour the mixture over the nuts.

In a deep, medium bowl, using a handheld mixer, whip the egg whites on medium speed until stiff (not dry) peaks form. Using a rubber spatula, fold the egg whites into the nut mixture just until incorporated. Set aside.

Before baking: Center a rack in the oven and preheat the oven to 375 degrees F. Line a large rimmed baking sheet with parchment paper; set aside.

To form the coffee cake: Gently deflate the dough. On a lightly floured surface, roll out the dough into a 16 by 12-inch rectangle. Roll the rectangle loosely around the rolling pin, center the pin over the baking sheet, and unroll the pastry. Reshape the rectangle as needed.

Although one of the last steps of finishing the coffee cake is to form a braid (which serves not only as a way of enveloping the filling but also as a handsome decoration), some advance preparation will make it easier to do when it is time. With a 16-inch side facing you, and using a ruler, measure the dough into 3 equal vertical strips. Mark these 3 rectangular strips by lightly poking the dough with the tines of a fork from one long side to the other, forming a continuous line of "dots" (each strip is 5⅓ inches wide and 12 inches long). You don't want to cut the dough, just make faint markings in it. Spread the filling down the center rectangular strip to within 1 inch of the faintly scored marks and of the top and bottom.

To encase the filling, you need to create a short flap at each end in the middle strip of dough. Using the tip of a paring knife, make a ¾-inch cut at each dotted line on both sides (4 cuts total). Fold the top and bottom flaps over the filling.

Now, along the 2 outside strips and starting at the top of the pastry, cut 1-inch-wide strips on the diagonal with a sharp knife, slanting downward toward the center. Starting at one end, and alternating from side to side with each fold, fold the strips at an angle across the filling. Overlapping the dough strips over the filling creates a crisscross braid reminiscent of a chevron pattern. Tuck under any excess dough from the top and bottom to seal the package.

Loosely cover the braid with a kitchen towel or plastic wrap and let it rise in a warm place (about 70 degrees F) until puffy and almost doubled in size, 35 to 45 minutes. Press the dough gently with a fingertip. If the indentation remains, the dough is ready for baking.

Bake the braided cake until golden brown, about 25 minutes. Transfer the pan to a wire rack to cool.

To glaze the cake: In a small bowl, stir together the sugar and water until well mixed. Brush the glaze over the braid while it is warm. Then lift the parchment with the braided cake onto a second wire rack. Serve warm, or let cool completely and serve at room temperature. The coffee cake is best served the same day it is baked. Cut into thin slices with a serrated knife. Offer a favorite honey or soft unsalted butter to accompany the slices.

To make ahead to serve later: Wrap the cooled braided cake securely in plastic wrap, overwrap with aluminum foil, label with the contents and date, and freeze for up to 1 week. Unwrap and thaw at room temperature for about 2 hours, then rewrap the loaf in foil and reheat in a preheated 325 degree F oven until warm, 15 to 20 minutes.

Overnight Cinnamon Buns

Thanks to my neighbor Megan McCaslin for gifting me one grand spring day with these fragrant, light-as-a-feather home-baked buns, and the fine recipe from the *More-With-Less Cookbook* by Doris Janzen Longacre. My adaptation is enhanced with sweet spices and buttery macadamia nuts.

YIELD: 2 DOZEN BUNS

POTATO

1 MEDIUM (ABOUT 8 OUNCES/225 GRAMS) RUSSET POTATO, PEELED AND QUARTERED

SWEET YEAST POTATO DOUGH

2¼ TEASPOONS (1 ENVELOPE) ACTIVE DRY YEAST

⅓ CUP (2½ FL OUNCES/75 ML) RESERVED POTATO WATER, WARMED TO 105 TO 110 DEGREES F

1⅓ CUPS (10½ FL OUNCES/315 ML) WHOLE MILK, WARMED TO 100 DEGREES F

⅔ CUP (ABOUT 5 OUNCES/140 GRAMS) RESERVED MASHED POTATO

5½ TABLESPOONS (2¾ OUNCES/75 GRAMS) UNSALTED BUTTER, AT ROOM TEMPERATURE

⅓ CUP (2¼ OUNCES/65 GRAMS) GRANULATED SUGAR

ABOUT 4½ CUPS (1 POUND, 6 OUNCES/630 GRAMS) UNBLEACHED BREAD OR UNBLEACHED ALL-PURPOSE FLOUR, DIVIDED

1 LARGE EGG, LIGHTLY BEATEN

1 TEASPOON SALT

2 TEASPOONS FINELY GRATED ORANGE ZEST

FILLING

½ CUP (2½ OUNCES/70 GRAMS) MACADAMIA NUTS

⅔ CUP FIRMLY PACKED (4½ OUNCES/130 GRAMS) LIGHT BROWN SUGAR

1¼ TEASPOONS GROUND CINNAMON

¼ TEASPOON GROUND CLOVES

¼ TEASPOON NUTMEG, PREFERABLY FRESHLY GRATED

2 OUNCES (½ STICK/55 GRAMS) UNSALTED BUTTER, MELTED

ICING

1 CUP (3½ OUNCES/100 GRAMS) POWDERED SUGAR

2 TABLESPOONS WHOLE MILK

1 TABLESPOON UNSALTED BUTTER, MELTED

½ TEASPOON PURE VANILLA EXTRACT

¼ TEASPOON NUTMEG, PREFERABLY FRESHLY GRATED

PINCH OF SALT

To prepare the potato: In a small, heavy saucepan, combine the potato pieces with cold water to cover and bring to a boil over medium-high heat. Cook until tender when pierced with a fork, 10 to 15 minutes. (Resist adding salt to the cooking water.) Drain, reserving ⅓ cup (2½ fl ounces/75 ml) of the water, and place the potato pieces in a small bowl. Using a potato masher, mash the potato until smooth. Measure out ⅔ cup (about 5 ounces/140 grams) of the mashed potato and set aside to cool with the reserved potato water. Save the remaining potato and potato water for another use or discard.

To make the Sweet Yeast Potato Dough: In a small bowl, sprinkle the yeast over the potato water and set aside until bubbly, about 5 minutes. Meanwhile, place the warm milk, mashed potato, butter, and sugar in a large bowl, and stir to blend. (Some of the butter will melt, while the remaining butter will be soft.) Let cool to lukewarm. Add the yeast mixture and 2 cups (9 ounces/255 grams) of the flour and stir with a rubber spatula until the mixture is smooth. Cover the bowl securely with plastic wrap. Let stand until bubbles appear on the surface (slightly foamy), about 20 minutes.

Stir only 2 tablespoons of the beaten egg into the yeast mixture. Gradually add 2 cups of the flour and the salt and stir with a rubber spatula or a large wooden spoon until incorporated. Add another ⅓ cup (1½ ounces/40 grams) of the flour. A soft dough should form.

Lightly dust a work surface and center the dough on the flour. Knead the dough gently until it is smooth with tiny blisters on the surface, feels moist, and is just slightly sticky though still soft, about 2 minutes, adding an additional 2 to 3 tablespoons flour only if necessary to lessen the stickiness. The secret to a tender bun is to work just enough flour (not too much) into the dough until the dough handles easily. The dough will remain slightly sticky, so rather than adding more flour and risk changing the balance of the recipe, slip a dough scraper under the dough to release it from the surface and slap it down onto the work surface. Repeat this slap-kneading action about 5 times to strengthen the dough.

Return the dough to the bowl, place a piece of plastic wrap directly on the surface of the dough, and cover the bowl tightly with aluminum foil or plastic wrap. Refrigerate the dough from 8 hours up to 24 hours. Although the action of the yeast will slow in the refrigerator, the dough will rise slightly until it is chilled completely throughout. To preserve the action of the yeast for after you form the buns, gently deflate the dough when it is almost cold to hasten the chilling, then re-cover its surface again with the plastic wrap, and re-cover the bowl securely with foil.

To make the filling: Before forming the buns, place the nuts in a food processor and pulse just until they are tiny pieces to yield about 1/2 cup. (That's correct. Your eyes are not deceiving you. You began with 1/2 cup nuts, and after pulsing, you still have 1/2 cup but in another form. Macadamias are soft nuts, so be careful not to grind them finely.) Transfer the nuts to a small bowl, add the sugar, cinnamon, cloves, and nutmeg, and mix well; set aside. Reserve the butter for brushing on the dough.

To form the buns: Gently deflate the dough, divide it in half, loosely cover it with a kitchen towel or plastic wrap, and set it aside to rest for 10 minutes. Wrap one-half in plastic wrap and refrigerate it while you shape the other half. Lightly coat two 13 by 9 by 2-inch pans (quarter sheet pans) with nonstick spray. Line the bottoms with parchment paper.

On a lightly floured work surface, roll out half of the dough into a 17 by 9-inch rectangle. Brush the entire surface with the butter, and then sprinkle evenly with half of the filling mixture. Starting from a long side closest to you, roll up the rectangle jelly-roll fashion, and pinch the bottom edge with your fingertips to seal the log. Using

your palms, gently roll the log back and forth on the work surface until it is uniform. In the process, it will expand to about 18 inches long. Repeat with the remaining dough half, butter, and filling.

Using a ruler, make shallow cuts with a serrated knife at 1 1/2-inch intervals. Then, using the knife and a slow sawing motion, cut the log crosswise into 12 slices. (Or, if you prefer, place an 18-inch-long piece of thread or dental floss under the rolled dough log at each notch. Pull the thread up and around the sides, then crisscross the thread at the top and pull quickly. This method is often better for cutting because the pressure of a knife can sometimes result in squashed slices.) Place the spirals, cut side down, in 1 of the prepared pans, spacing them about 1 inch apart. Loosely cover the buns with a kitchen towel or plastic wrap and set aside to rise in a warm place (about 70 degrees F) until puffy and doubled in size, about 1 hour. Press the dough gently with a fingertip. If the indentation remains, the dough is ready for baking.

Before baking: Center a rack in the oven and preheat the oven to 400 degrees F.

One pan at a time, bake the buns until pale golden brown, 22 to 28 minutes. About halfway through the baking, rotate the pan 180 degrees to ensure even baking. While the buns are baking, make the icing.

To make the icing: In a small bowl, stir together the sugar, milk, butter, vanilla, nutmeg, and salt until smooth and creamy. If it is too thick, add more milk, 1 teaspoon at a time, until you achieve a smooth spreading consistency.

When the buns are done, transfer the pan to a wire rack. Without delay, use a small pastry brush to coat each roll with the icing. Let the buns cool for 10 to 15 minutes, then invert a rack on top of the buns, invert the buns onto it, lift off the pan, and carefully peel off the parchment paper. Invert a platter on top of the buns, invert the buns so they are right side up, and remove the rack. Bake the second sheet of buns, ice them, and unmold them the same way. For the best flavor and texture, serve the buns warm or at room temperature the same day they are baked.

Pain d'Épices

My recipe for this simple spice-honey bread was inspired by a recipe from the late French chef Joseph Donon. The French version of an American quick bread, only chewier and not as moist, it is delicious thinly sliced and served plain or sandwiched with unsalted butter, lightly whipped cream cheese, or perhaps a creamy mild cheese. For the best flavor, wrap it well after it cools completely and leave it overnight before serving to give the richly spiced flavors a chance to mellow and age. This aromatic loaf is delicious served with coffee, tea, or wine. The variety of spices, sweeteners, and flours makes this unusual bread oh so interesting when sandwiched with a favorite ice cream flavor, such as coffee, butter pecan, *dulce de leche*, or vanilla.   **YIELD: ONE 9 BY 5-INCH LOAF, 16 SERVINGS**

3½ CUPS (1 POUND/455 GRAMS) ALL-PURPOSE FLOUR

½ CUP (2 OUNCES/60 GRAMS) DARK RYE FLOUR

2½ TEASPOONS BAKING SODA

1½ TEASPOONS GROUND CINNAMON

1½ TEASPOONS GROUND GINGER

½ TEASPOON SALT

¼ TEASPOON NUTMEG, PREFERABLY FRESHLY GRATED

⅛ TEASPOON GROUND CLOVES

½ TEASPOON ANISEEDS

2 OUNCES (½ STICK/55 GRAMS) UNSALTED BUTTER, SOFTENED

1 LARGE EGG, AT ROOM TEMPERATURE

1 CUP (12 OUNCES BY WEIGHT/340 GRAMS) HONEY, PREFERABLY LAVENDER

1 CUP (8 FL OUNCES/240 ML) WATER

1 TABLESPOON FINELY GRATED ORANGE ZEST

Before baking: Center a rack in the oven and preheat the oven to 350 degrees F.

Lightly coat a 9 by 5 by 3-inch loaf pan with nonstick spray, then flour it, tapping out the excess flour. Or, butter and flour the pan.

Sift together the flours, baking soda, cinnamon, ginger, salt, nutmeg, and cloves onto sheet of waxed paper. Sprinkle the aniseeds over the flour mixture; set aside.

In the bowl of a stand mixer fitted with the paddle attachment, combine the butter, egg, and honey, in that order, and mix on low speed until well blended. On the lowest speed, add the water and orange zest. Maintaining the same speed, add the flour mixture in three additions, stopping the mixer to scrape down the sides of the bowl after each addition and continuing to mix just until the batter is smooth and thoroughly blended. Pour the batter into the prepared pan and spread it evenly with a rubber spatula.

Bake the bread until it feels firm when lightly pressed in the center with a fingertip and a round wooden toothpick inserted in the center comes out free of batter, 60 to 70 minutes. (It bakes dark on top.) Transfer to a wire rack and let cool in the pan for 10 minutes before removing from the pan. Then turn out onto the rack, turn the bread right side up, and let cool completely before serving.

To serve, cut the bread into ¼-inch-thick slices with a serrated knife.

Bohemian Kolaches

One of the joys of baking at home is the freedom to make whatever matches your mood. When I'm feeling nostalgic, the aroma of a sweet yeast dough takes me back in time. As a child I savored *kolaches*, old-fashioned sweet buns. Years later, after moving to California, my craving was so strong that I experimented and finally came up with this recipe. Originally from Czechoslovakia and Poland, *kolaches* are subject to innumerable variations: the name can be spelled *kolachy*, *kolachke*, or *kolacky*; the filling might be jam or sweet cheese; and the yeast dough recipe can vary from family to family.

As much as I relish the first comforting bite of a warm *kolache*, nowadays I'm patient enough to let the dough develop more flavor and become easier to handle by refrigerating it for several hours (it will keep for up to a day). After the dough has risen, I gently deflate it, divide it in half, and shape each half into a smooth, round form on a work surface. I then slip each half into a gallon-sized resealable plastic bag and refrigerate them for up to a day. When I am ready to use the dough, I remove a portion at a time from the refrigerator, shape the *kolaches*, let them rise in a warm place for 45 to 60 minutes (they take slightly longer to rise than room-temperature dough), and they are ready to bake.   **YIELD: 2 DOZEN BUNS**

SWEET YEAST DOUGH

3¼ CUPS (14½ OUNCES/415 GRAMS) PLUS 1 TABLESPOON
  ALL-PURPOSE FLOUR

5 TABLESPOONS (2¼ OUNCES/65 GRAMS) GRANULATED SUGAR

2¼ TEASPOONS (1 ENVELOPE) INSTANT YEAST

¾ TEASPOON SALT

¾ CUP (6 FL OUNCES/180 ML) WHOLE MILK

6 OUNCES (1½ STICKS/170 GRAMS) UNSALTED BUTTER,
  AT ROOM TEMPERATURE

¼ CUP (2 FL OUNCES/60 ML) WATER

1 TEASPOON PURE VANILLA EXTRACT

3 LARGE (¼ CUP/2 FL OUNCES/60 ML) EGG YOLKS,
  LIGHTLY BEATEN

PRUNE PLUM OR APRICOT FILLING

6 OUNCES (170 GRAMS) PITTED DRIED PRUNE PLUMS OR
  DRIED APRICOTS (ABOUT 1 CUP)

⅓ CUP (2½ FL OUNCES/75 ML) WATER

3 TABLESPOONS GRANULATED SUGAR

1 TABLESPOON LIGHT CORN SYRUP

2 TEASPOONS FINELY GRATED ORANGE ZEST

¼ TEASPOON GROUND CINNAMON

TOPPING

2 OUNCES (½ STICK/55 GRAMS) UNSALTED BUTTER, MELTED

¼ CUP (1¾ OUNCES/50 GRAMS) GRANULATED SUGAR

To make the Sweet Yeast Dough: Stir together 2½ cups (11¼ ounces/320 grams) of the flour, the sugar, the yeast, and the salt in the bowl of a stand mixer; set aside. In a small, heavy saucepan, heat the milk and butter over low heat just until the butter is melted. Remove from the heat, add the water, and set aside until warm (120 to 130 degrees F), about 3 minutes. Add the vanilla.

Pour the milk mixture over the flour-yeast mixture and, using a rubber spatula, mix until the dry ingredients are evenly moistened. Attach the bowl to the stand mixer, and fit the mixer with the paddle attachment. With the mixer on low speed, add the egg yolks and mix until incorporated. Stop the mixer and scrape down the sides of the bowl. Add ½ cup (2¼ ounces/65 grams) of the flour, and resume mixing on low speed until the dough is smooth, about 30 seconds. Add ¼ cup (1 ounce/ 30 grams) of the flour, increase the speed to   CONTINUED ▶

medium, and mix until the dough is smooth, soft, and slightly sticky, 45 to 60 seconds.

Sprinkle a work surface with 1 tablespoon of the flour, and center the dough on the flour. Knead gently until satiny smooth and no longer sticky, about 5 minutes, adding an additional 1 to 2 tablespoons flour only if necessary to lessen the stickiness. Place the dough in a large bowl, preferably clear glass (which will allow you to monitor the rise), and place a piece of plastic wrap directly on the surface. Cover the bowl securely with another piece of plastic wrap and let the dough rise in a warm place (about 70 degrees F) until doubled in size, 1 to 1 1/2 hours. Press the dough gently with a fingertip. If the indentation remains, the dough is ready for shaping. While the dough is rising, make the filling.

To make the Prune Plum or Apricot Filling: In a small, heavy saucepan, combine the dried fruit and water, place over medium-low heat, bring to a simmer, and simmer until almost all of the water has evaporated, 3 to 5 minutes. Remove from the heat, let cool for about 5 minutes, and transfer to a food processor. Add the sugar, corn syrup, orange zest, and cinnamon and process until a smooth, sticky paste forms; set aside. You should have 1/2 cup plus 2 tablespoons filling.

Before baking: Center a rack in the oven and preheat the oven to 350 degrees F. Line 2 large baking sheets with parchment paper.

To form the buns: Gently deflate the dough, and divide it in half. On a very lightly floured work surface, roll each half into a log 11 to 12 inches long. Divide each log into 12 equal pieces, each weighing about 1 1/4 ounces (35 grams). Shape each piece into a ball: Set a piece on the work surface, pull up the sides, and pinch them together on top to form a small knot in the center. Continue this pulling and pinching until you have shaped a tight, round ball. Turn the unfinished portion (the surface that isn't smooth) of the ball over, cup your hand over it, and roll the dough ball on an *unfloured* surface until you have a smooth ball. Place the balls on the prepared baking sheets, spacing them about 2 inches apart. Cover loosely with

plastic wrap or a kitchen towel and set aside to rise in a warm place until puffy, about 30 minutes. Press a ball gently with a fingertip. If the indentation remains, the buns are ready to be filled and baked.

To fill the buns: Make an indentation in the center of each ball with a sturdy tart tamper (page 43), leaving the edges a bit higher. (If the tamper sticks to the dough, lightly dip it into flour before making each indentation.) Fill each indentation with about 1 1/4 teaspoons of the filling. Using a metal or wooden skewer, poke about 8 holes straight down, positioning them all around the edge of the filling and its indentation. (This helps maintain the indentation and the shape of the bun as it bakes.) Or, instead of making the indentations with a tart tamper, use kitchen scissors to gently snip an X, 1/4 to 1/2 inch deep, in the top of each bun. Snip carefully so you don't deflate the buns too much. Deposit the filling in the center of each opening. This is an easy, speedy way to create the same effect as you do with a tart tamper, and the indentation is slightly deeper and stays in place better. Place a couple of sheets of plastic wrap loosely over the buns, and set aside at room temperature to rest for about 5 minutes before baking.

One pan at a time, bake the *kolaches* until they are golden on top and golden brown on the bottom, 17 to 20 minutes. About halfway through the baking, rotate the baking sheet 180 degrees to ensure even baking. Transfer the pan to a wire rack and proceed to bake the second baking sheet the same way.

To top the buns: Without delay, using a pastry brush, brush the hot rolls with the melted butter and then sprinkle lightly with the sugar. For the best flavor and texture, serve the buns warm or at room temperature the same day they are baked.

Place any leftover buns in an airtight container, label with the contents and date, and freeze for up to 1 week. To serve, place the frozen rolls, spaced 1 inch apart, on a parchment paper–lined baking sheet and let thaw partially at room temperature for about 30 minutes. Reheat in a preheated 300 degree F oven until hot to the touch, 12 to 15 minutes.

Apricot Flaky Scones

The sweet, tangy flavor of dried apricots perks up these not-too-sweet scones. Or, you can use dried pears, figs, cherries, and cranberries, alone or in combination, in place of the apricots. The pistachios are optional, but they add wonderful color and texture and their own distinctive flavor. The scones are even delicious made without any dried fruit or nuts. Serve them with butter and homemade preserves. **YIELD: 14 SCONES**

SCONES

3 CUPS (13¾ OUNCES/390 GRAMS) ALL-PURPOSE FLOUR

⅓ CUP PLUS 2 TABLESPOONS (3¼ OUNCES/90 GRAMS) GRANULATED SUGAR

2½ TEASPOONS BAKING POWDER

¾ TEASPOON SALT

½ TEASPOON BAKING SODA

6 OUNCES (1½ STICKS/170 GRAMS) COLD UNSALTED BUTTER, CUT INTO ¼-INCH SLICES

½ CUP PLUS 2 TABLESPOONS (4 OUNCES/115 GRAMS) MOIST DRIED APRICOTS (11 TO 12 LARGE), FINELY DICED TO YIELD ¾ CUP

½ CUP (2½ OUNCES/70 GRAMS) UNSALTED, SHELLED PISTACHIO NUTS, COARSELY CHOPPED (OPTIONAL)

2 TEASPOONS FINELY GRATED ORANGE ZEST

1 CUP (8 FL OUNCES/240 ML) COLD WELL-SHAKEN BUTTERMILK

GLAZE

2 TABLESPOONS WELL-SHAKEN BUTTERMILK

3 TABLESPOONS TURBINADO OR OTHER RAW SUGAR

Before baking: Center a rack in the oven and preheat the oven to 400 degrees F. Line a large baking sheet with parchment paper; set aside.

To make the scones: In a large bowl, combine the flour, sugar, baking powder, salt, and baking soda and whisk to blend. Scatter the butter pieces over the flour mixture. With a pastry blender, cut in the butter just until the majority of the butter chunks range in size from peas to coarse crumbs. Stir in the apricots and nuts, if using.

Stir the orange zest into the buttermilk, and drizzle half of the buttermilk evenly over the surface of the flour mixture. Toss lightly with a fork. Then add the remaining buttermilk and toss until the mixture comes together in a shaggy mass. If any areas remain dry, gradually add more buttermilk, 1 to 2 teaspoons at a time, tossing lightly to distribute the buttermilk. With lightly floured hands, transfer the dough to a lightly floured work surface, shape it into a rough, semicohesive mass, and knead gently about three times.

On the lightly floured surface, roll out the dough into a 12 by 5-inch rectangle. Fold the dough into thirds like a business letter: working from a short end, lift the bottom one-third of the rectangle up over the center and then fold the top third down to cover. This folding creates layers of dough and fat, so the scones will puff up slightly as they bake and will have a flaky texture. Roll out the dough again into a 14 by 5½ by ¾-inch rectangle. Transfer it to a baking sheet, place a piece of plastic wrap on top, and refrigerate for 20 to 30 minutes, to rest and to partially chill the dough.

Carefully transfer the chilled dough to a cutting board. Cut 13 small wedges with a sharp knife. Place the wedges, about 1½ inches apart, on the prepared baking sheet. Gently press the 2 end pieces from the rectangle together to form a wedge, and add it to the others on the baking sheet.

To glaze the scones: Brush the tops of the scones with the buttermilk and sprinkle with the sugar.

Bake the scones until golden brown, 20 to 25 minutes. Transfer the scones to a wire rack to cool. Serve warm or at room temperature the same day they are baked.

Spicy Citrus Swirly Buns

I've borrowed the technique for forming these incredible buns from baker par excellence Kathleen Stewart of the family-owned Downtown Creamery in Healdsburg, California. Whatever Kathleen creates is guaranteed to be the best of the best. **YIELD: 1½ DOZEN BUNS**

SWEET CITRUS PASTE FILLING

5 TABLESPOONS FINELY GRATED LEMON ZEST
 (4 TO 5 LEMONS)

1 TABLESPOON FINELY GRATED TANGERINE ZEST
 (2 TANGERINES)

2 TABLESPOONS FINELY GRATED ORANGE ZEST
 (1 LARGE ORANGE)

¼ TEASPOON PURE ALMOND EXTRACT

½ TEASPOON PURE VANILLA EXTRACT

1⅓ CUPS (9¼ OUNCES/260 GRAMS) GRANULATED SUGAR

1 TEASPOON GROUND CINNAMON

1 RECIPE CROISSANT PASTRY ASAP (PAGE 365)

To make the Sweet Citrus Paste Filling: Place all of the zests in a small bowl, add the extracts, and mix with a fork to evenly distribute the ingredients. Add the sugar and cinnamon and stir with the fork until all of the sugar is coated. Set the sandy-wet mixture nearby.

Before baking: Center a rack in the oven and preheat the oven to 375 degrees F. Lightly coat two 12-cup standard muffin pans with nonstick spray.

To form the buns: Remove the croissant pastry dough from the refrigerator. Unwrap it, saving the plastic wrap and discarding the foil. Divide the dough in half and place one-half on a lightly floured work surface. Wrap the remaining dough with the plastic wrap and return it to the refrigerator. Roll out the dough into a rectangle about 13 by 10 inches. Scatter half of the filling evenly over the entire surface of the dough. Lightly roll the rolling pin over the dough to ensure that the filling adheres to the dough. Starting from a long side closest to you, roll up the rectangle jelly-roll fashion, and pinch the bottom edge with your fingertips to seal the log. Using your palms, gently roll the log back and forth on the work surface until it is uniform. In the process, it will expand to about 14 inches long.

Using a ruler, make shallow cuts with a serrated knife at 1½-inch intervals. Then, using the knife and a slow sawing motion, cut the log crosswise into 9 slices. (Or, if you prefer, place an 18-inch-long piece of thread or dental floss under the rolled dough log at each notch. Pull the thread up and around the sides, then crisscross the thread at the top and pull quickly. This method is often better for cutting because the pressure of a knife can sometimes result in squashed slices.) Tuck the tail end of each bun underneath and place the buns, with the tucked portion on the bottom, in the prepared muffin cups. Repeat with the remaining dough and filling. When putting the buns in the second pan, place them in every other cup. Alternating full and empty cups promotes even baking when not all of the cups are filled. As each batch is ready, loosely cover the buns with plastic wrap or a kitchen towel and let rise in a warm place (about 70 degrees F) until they rise above the rim of the muffin cups, 1 to 2 hours. Press the dough gently with a fingertip. If the indentation remains, the buns are ready to bake.

Bake the buns until golden brown, 20 to 25 minutes. About halfway through the baking, rotate the pans 180 degrees to ensure even baking. Transfer the pans to wire racks and let cool for about 5 minutes. Using a small metal spatula, carefully remove the buns (they are very hot and might unravel), and place them on the rack to cool. Removing them from the pan while they are warm allows them to cool more evenly and ensures they won't stick to the cups. For the best flavor and texture, serve the buns warm or at room temperature the same day they are baked.

Place any leftover buns in an airtight container, label with the contents and date, and freeze for up to 1 week. To serve, remove from the freezer and leave at room temperature for about 1 hour. Wrap the buns, 3 or 4 to a package, in aluminum foil and reheat in a preheated 325 degree F oven until heated through, 12 to 15 minutes.

Croissant Cinnamon Sticks

As much fun to bake as they are to eat, these spicy pastry twists are perfect for nibbling throughout the day. They are made with my ASAP croissant dough, sprinkled liberally with cinnamon sugar, and then speedily cut into strips and twisted into shape. I like to put the freshly baked sticks in a handsome pitcher, tall glass, or vase, making it easy—and especially tempting—for people to help themselves. Offer them at breakfast or lunch or along with a latte, cappuccino, or tea during the day, or leave them on the kitchen counter for family snacks. Any way you present them, I promise they'll disappear fast. If you want to create twice as many sticks, simply double the recipe. **YIELD: 20 TO 24 TWISTS**

½ CUP (3½ OUNCES/100 GRAMS) GRANULATED SUGAR

¾ TEASPOON GROUND CINNAMON

¾ TEASPOON GROUND ALLSPICE

⅛ TEASPOON NUTMEG, PREFERABLY FRESHLY GRATED

½ RECIPE (1¼ POUNDS/570 GRAMS) CROISSANT PASTRY ASAP (PAGE 365)

⅓ CUP (2½ FL OUNCES/75 ML) OLIVE OIL, PREFERABLY FRUITY

Line the center of 2 large baking sheets with parchment paper, leaving a 3-inch border uncovered on each long side. In a small bowl, stir together the sugar, cinnamon, allspice, and nutmeg. Scatter the mixture over the bottom of a 13 by 9 by 2-inch pan (quarter sheet pan); set aside.

To shape the pastries: Remove the dough from the refrigerator. Unwrap it, saving the plastic wrap and discarding the foil. Divide the dough in half and place one-half on a lightly floured work surface. Wrap the remaining dough with the plastic wrap and return it to the refrigerator.

Lightly moisten the uncovered sides on 1 of the baking sheets. Roll out the dough into a 12 by 10-inch rectangle. With a sharp knife, cut the rectangle into about 10 to 12 strips, each ¾ to 1 inch wide and 12 inches long. Brush both sides of each strip with half of the olive oil. Working with 1 strip at a time, gently dip both sides of the strip in the spiced sugar, coating evenly. With fingertips holding each end, twist the strip 4 or 5 times. Place the twists on the baking sheet, pressing each end onto the

moist unlined portion of the pan to anchor it firmly. (This prevents the strip from unwinding as it bakes.) Repeat with the remaining dough and sugar mixture, spacing the strips 1½ to 2 inches apart on the baking sheets. Loosely cover the strips with a sheet of plastic wrap and let them rise in a warm place (about 70 degrees F) until they are puffy and have expanded just slightly, 45 to 60 minutes. Press the dough gently with a fingertip. If the indentation remains, the sticks are ready to bake.

Before baking: Center a rack in the oven and preheat the oven to 375 degrees F (be sure to do this once just after you set the strips aside to rise, so the oven will be fully preheated by the time they are ready to bake).

One pan at a time, bake the pastries until golden brown, 18 to 22 minutes. About halfway through the baking, rotate the pan 180 degrees to ensure even baking. Transfer the pan to a wire rack and let cool for 5 minutes. Using a metal spatula, transfer the twists to the wire rack to cool completely. For the best flavor and texture, serve the twists the same day they are baked.

Place any leftover twists in an airtight container and store at room temperature for 1 day, or label with the contents and date and freeze for up to 1 week. To serve, place the frozen twists on a parchment paper–lined baking sheet and let thaw at room temperature for 30 minutes. Reheat in a preheated 325 degree F oven just until crisp, 5 to 7 minutes.

Coconut Twist Coffee Cake

This coffee cake looks complicated. But looks are deceiving. It is fun-to-make, easy-to-eat, not-too-sweet finger food with no fancy decoration. There's no trick to mixing the dough, and it has a forgiving, easy-to-stretch consistency, so you don't have to be a pro with a rolling pin. If desired, prepare the dough one day, refrigerate it overnight, and set it out at room temperature for 30 minutes before shaping it.

The coffee cake's intriguing design, which I originally saw in a national magazine, looks like a wheel, complete with spokes. You cut wedges from a stack of dough circles and, without detaching them from the center, twist each wedge to form a spiral. Glaze the warm coffee cake to seal in its moisture and create an attractive sheen. **YIELD: ONE 12-INCH ROUND COFFEE CAKE, 16 SERVINGS**

SWEET YEAST DOUGH

3½ CUPS (15 OUNCES/430 GRAMS) UNBLEACHED ALL-PURPOSE FLOUR, DIVIDED

⅓ CUP (2¼ OUNCES/65 GRAMS) GRANULATED SUGAR

2 TEASPOONS INSTANT YEAST

¾ TEASPOON SALT

1 CUP (8 OUNCES/240 ML) WHOLE MILK

2½ OUNCES (5 TABLESPOONS/70 GRAMS) UNSALTED BUTTER

1 TEASPOON HONEY

1 LARGE EGG

2 LARGE EGG YOLKS

1 TEASPOON PURE VANILLA EXTRACT

COCONUT FILLING

1¼ CUPS (2½ OUNCES/70 GRAMS) UNSWEETENED FINE-SHRED DRIED COCONUT

2 TABLESPOONS GRANULATED SUGAR

3 TABLESPOONS UNBLEACHED ALL-PURPOSE FLOUR

⅛ TEASPOON SALT

2 OUNCES (½ STICK/55 GRAMS) UNSALTED BUTTER

1 LARGE EGG WHITE

½ TEASPOON FINELY GRATED LEMON ZEST

½ TEASPOON PURE VANILLA EXTRACT

GLAZE

½ CUP (4 FL OUNCES/115 ML) STRAINED APRICOT JAM, WARMED

½ CUP (1¾ OUNCES/50 GRAMS) POWDERED SUGAR

4 TEASPOONS WHOLE MILK

½ TEASPOON PURE VANILLA EXTRACT

To make the Sweet Yeast Dough: Stir together 2 cups (9 ounces/255 grams) of the flour, the sugar, the yeast, and the salt in the bowl of a stand mixer; set aside. In a small, heavy saucepan, heat ⅔ cup (5½ fl ounces/165 ml) of the milk with the butter over low heat just until almost all of the butter is melted. Remove from the heat, add the honey and the remaining ⅓ cup (2½ fl ounces/75 ml) milk, and set aside until warm (120 to 130 degrees F), 1 to 2 minutes.

Pour the milk mixture over the flour-yeast mixture and, using a rubber spatula, mix until the dry ingredients are evenly moistened. Attach the bowl to the mixer, and fit the mixer with the paddle attachment. With the mixer on low speed, add the egg and egg yolks, one at a time, mixing after each addition just until incorporated. Add the vanilla in the final moments of mixing. Stop the mixer occasionally to scrape down the sides of the bowl. Add 1 cup (4½ ounces/130 grams) of the flour and mix on medium-low speed until a smooth, soft dough forms. Add ¼ cup (1 ounce/30 grams) of the flour, increase the speed to medium, and mix until the dough is smooth, soft, and slightly sticky, about 30 seconds. Stop the mixer to scrape down the sides of the bowl. Add 2 tablespoons of the flour, reduce the speed to medium-low, and mix until the dough is more cohesive but not yet coming away from the sides of the bowl into a ball.

Sprinkle a work surface with 1 tablespoon of the flour, and center the dough on the flour. Sprinkle the remaining 1 tablespoon flour on top of the dough and knead gently until smooth, soft, and elastic, about 3 minutes, adding an additional 1 to 2 tablespoons flour only if necessary to lessen the stickiness. To strengthen the dough without adding additional flour (too much flour diminishes the chance of producing a tender dough), slip a pastry scraper under the dough to release it from the surface and slap it down onto the work surface. Repeat this slap-kneading action about 5 times to strengthen the dough.

Place the dough in a large bowl, place a piece of plastic wrap directly on the surface, and then cover the bowl securely with plastic wrap. Let the dough rise in a warm place (about 70 degrees F) until doubled in size, 1 to 1½ hours. Press the dough gently with a fingertip. If the indentation remains, the dough is ready to shape. While the dough is rising, make the filling.

To make the Coconut Filling: In a food processor, combine the coconut, sugar, flour, and salt and pulse to blend. Add the butter, egg white, lemon zest, and vanilla and process just until smooth. Transfer the filling to a small bowl; set aside.

Before baking: Center a rack in the oven and preheat the oven to 350 degrees F. Lightly coat a 12-inch rimmed pizza pan with softened butter, then flour it, tapping out the excess flour.

To shape the coffee cake: Gently deflate the dough and divide it into thirds (10½ ounces/300 grams each). On a lightly floured work surface, roll out 1 portion into a 12-inch circle and transfer it to the prepared pan. If necessary, adjust the dough to cover the bottom of the pan by stretching it gently with your fingertips. Because the pan has been lightly buttered, the dough circle will adhere to it easily without shifting too much. Using half of the filling, pinch off small pieces and scatter them evenly over the dough. Place a sheet of waxed paper on top. Using a 2½- to 4-inch pastry roller (or even a soda can), roll over the waxed paper to spread the filling thinly and evenly over the pastry. Carefully lift the waxed paper and save it for the next layer of filling.

Lightly flour the work surface again and center the second portion of dough on it. With your fingers, press the dough into a flat disk about ½ inch thick. Lift the dough and lay it over the back of the fist of one of your hands. Place the fist of your other hand under the dough. Gently and slowly move your hands in opposite directions to stretch and rotate the dough at the same time until it is close to a thin 12-inch circle. (You will notice that the weight of the soft dough helps stretch it. This method, similar to forming a pizza crust, is quicker and works the dough less than rolling it.) Carefully center the dough on top of the filling-topped pastry circle. Repeat pinching off small pieces of the remaining filling and scatter them evenly over the dough. Place the sheet of waxed paper on top and again roll over the waxed paper to spread the filling thinly and evenly over the pastry. Carefully lift the waxed paper and discard it. Repeat the rolling and stretching to form another 12-inch circle and center it on top of the 2 stacked pastry circles.

Invert a small drinking glass about 2 inches in diameter and set it in the center of the dough circle. (Don't allow it to cut through the dough.) With the handle of a wooden spoon, and working from the edge of the glass outward, lightly score the large dough circle into 16 wedges. Using kitchen scissors or a sharp chef's or *santoku* knife (page 42), cut through the layers of dough, using the indentations as a guide, to form 16 wedges: begin at the edge of the dough circle and cut just up to the glass. Gently twist each wedge (in the same direction) about 3 times, spiraling each piece of dough and pressing the end onto the pan to anchor it. Remove the glass. Loosely cover the dough with a kitchen towel or plastic wrap and let rise in a warm place (about 70 degrees F) until almost doubled in size, 25 to 30 minutes. Press the dough gently with a fingertip. If the indentation remains, the coffee cake is ready for baking. CONTINUED ▶

Bake the coffee cake until golden, 30 to 35 minutes.

While the cake is baking, make the glaze: Have the warmed jam ready. In a small bowl, stir together the sugar, milk, and vanilla to form a thin liquid.

When the coffee cake is ready, transfer to a wire rack and let cool on the pan for no more than 10 minutes. Brush the surface of the warm cake with the warm apricot jam. Using a clean pastry brush, spread the sugar mixture thinly over the jam. Let the cake cool slightly, then detach the wedges or cut them apart with a knife.

Serve the wedges warm or at room temperature. For optimum flavor and texture, serve the coffee cake the same day it is baked. Wrap leftovers in aluminum foil and store at room temperature for 1 day.

Ready to Share

A BAKER SHOULD NEVER let distance stand in the way of sharing—at least I never have. For my mother's eightieth birthday, I created the Deluxe Lemon-Lavender Mail-a-Cake, incorporating her favorite flavors. The sturdy, fruity-floral cake slides into a box and, with some careful packaging, can be sent to someone special.

Of course, sharing the bounty of your kitchen can be simpler and more immediate. The recipes in this chapter make gifts from the heart that are delicious and travel well, with their texture not suffering in the process. Tuck a box of World-Traveling Crispy ANZAC Cookies into a care package and let the sweet combination of coconut and oats brighten the day of a friend or relative across the miles.

I love desserts that are portable and do not need any added attention once you arrive at a friend's home, a potluck, or a neighbor's housewarming. For those occasions, I carry along a Chocolate Lover's Angel Food Cake or a Spicy Yogurt Pound Cake. Their flavors complement a wide variety of dishes that may already be on the menu. And on the off chance that your hostess or host winds up with too many good things to serve, both cakes can be set aside to enjoy a day or two later.

Enjoying food together—especially baked goods—puts everyone at ease. Keep that in mind the next time you must attend an early-morning meeting or make it through a particularly difficult work project. A rich Cyrano Chocolate Cake or a fluffy Blackberry-Blueberry Chiffon Cream Pie may be the most deliciously disarming thing to share.

Eggnog Pound Cake with Crystal Rum Glaze

This inviting holiday cake is the next best thing to eggnog in a cup. The dense yet tender cake showcases the incomparable flavor of eggnog, while rum, nutmeg, and currants add a complementary dimension. Bake it in your favorite patterned Bundt pan, and brush the warm cake with the rum glaze. As the cake cools, the crystallized topping clings attractively to the crevices, creating a special effect. **YIELD: ONE 10-INCH TUBE CAKE, 20 SERVINGS (3 THIN SLICES PER SERVING)**

SCANT ½ CUP (2¼ OUNCES/65 GRAMS) DRIED CURRANTS

2 TABLESPOONS DARK RUM OR WATER

3 CUPS (13¾ OUNCES/390 GRAMS) ALL-PURPOSE FLOUR

2 TEASPOONS BAKING POWDER

¼ TEASPOON SALT

¼ TEASPOON NUTMEG, PREFERABLY FRESHLY GRATED

8 OUNCES (2 STICKS/225 GRAMS) UNSALTED BUTTER, AT ROOM TEMPERATURE

2 CUPS (14 OUNCES/400 GRAMS) GRANULATED SUGAR

3 LARGE EGGS, LIGHTLY BEATEN

1 CUP (8 FL OUNCES/240 ML) STORE-BOUGHT REFRIGERATED (RATHER THAN CANNED) EGGNOG

1 TEASPOON PURE VANILLA EXTRACT

CRYSTAL RUM GLAZE

¾ CUP (5¼ OUNCES/150 GRAMS) GRANULATED SUGAR

2 TABLESPOONS DARK RUM

2 TABLESPOONS WATER

Before baking: In a small bowl, combine the currants and rum and set aside to macerate for 15 minutes. Center a rack in the oven and preheat the oven to 350 degrees F (or 325 degrees F if the pan has a dark finish). Butter a 10 by 3-inch Bundt pan, lightly coat it with nonstick spray, then flour it, tapping out the excess flour. Or, butter and flour a 10 by 4¼-inch tube pan with or without a removable bottom. If the pan has an intricate design or detail, prepare it as directed on page 24 to ensure the finished cake releases in one piece. Have all of the ingredients at room temperature.

To make the cake: Sift together the flour, baking powder, salt, and nutmeg onto a sheet of waxed paper; set aside. Using a stand mixer fitted with the paddle attachment, beat the butter on medium-low speed until creamy and smooth, 30 to 45 seconds. Stop the mixer and scrape down the sides of the bowl. Add the sugar in a steady stream and continue to beat on medium speed until light in color and fluffy, about 5 minutes, stopping the mixer occasionally to scrape down the sides of the bowl.

With the mixer still on medium speed, add the eggs, 1 to 2 tablespoons at a time, beating after each addition until incorporated and stopping the mixer occasionally to scrape down the sides of the bowl. On the lowest speed, add the flour mixture in four additions alternately with the eggnog in three additions, beginning and ending with the flour mixture and mixing after each addition until incorporated. Stop the mixer as needed to scrape down the sides of the bowl. Add the vanilla during the final moments of mixing. Detach the paddle and bowl from the mixer, and tap the paddle against the side of the bowl to free the excess batter. Using a rubber spatula, gently fold in the currants and any remaining rum. Spoon the batter into the prepared pan and spread evenly with the spatula.

Bake the cake just until the top springs back when lightly touched in the center and the sides are beginning to come away from the pan, 55 to 65 minutes. Transfer to a wire rack and let cool in the pan for about 10 minutes while you prepare the glaze.

To make the Crystal Rum Glaze: In a small bowl, combine the sugar, rum, and water and stir with a rubber spatula just until blended.

Without delay, tilt and rotate the cake pan while gently tapping it on a counter to release the cake sides. Invert a wire rack on top of the cake, invert the cake onto it, and carefully lift off the pan. Slide a sheet of waxed paper under the rack to catch any drips from the glaze. Using a pastry brush, coat the top and sides of the warm cake with all of the glaze. Let the cake cool completely before serving.

To serve, slide the base of a tart pan, a small rimless baking sheet, or a large offset spatula under the cake and carefully transfer it to a serving platter. Cut the cake into thin slices with a sharp or serrated knife.

Almond Tea Cake with Tangerine Glaze

Enlivened with a tangy tangerine glaze, this rich, moist almond cake is perfect to bring to almost any occasion, from a board meeting or an impromptu brunch to a bridge game at your neighbor's house. It is easy to transport from home to your destination, where it will arrive just as glamorous as it was before you left. The secret to the sparkling citrus character of the glaze is a combination of fresh juice and fragrant zest, which captures the very heart of the tangerine's delicate flavor and aroma. Use a Microplane zester or a serrated peeler, rather than a vegetable peeler, and you will have no trouble removing just the colorful zest without the bitter white pith.

YIELD: ONE 10-INCH TUBE CAKE, 20 SERVINGS (3 THIN SLICES PER SERVING)

CAKE

2⅓ CUPS PLUS 2 TABLESPOONS (10 OUNCES/280 GRAMS) CAKE FLOUR

1½ TEASPOONS BAKING POWDER

¼ TEASPOON SALT

⅔ CUP (5 OUNCES/140 GRAMS) ALMOND PASTE

1 CUP (7 OUNCES/200 GRAMS) GRANULATED SUGAR

8 OUNCES (2 STICKS/225 GRAMS) UNSALTED BUTTER, AT ROOM TEMPERATURE

4 LARGE EGGS, LIGHTLY BEATEN

½ CUP (4 FL OUNCES/120 ML) WHOLE MILK

½ TEASPOON PURE ORANGE EXTRACT

TANGERINE GLAZE

¾ CUP (3 OUNCES/85 GRAMS) POWDERED SUGAR, SIFTED

1 TABLESPOON UNSALTED BUTTER, SOFTENED

1 TABLESPOON FRESH TANGERINE JUICE

1½ TEASPOONS FINELY GRATED TANGERINE ZEST

Before baking: Center a rack in the oven and preheat the oven to 350 degrees F (or 325 degrees F if the pan has a dark finish). Butter a 10 by 3-inch Bundt pan, lightly coat it with nonstick spray, then flour it, tapping out the excess flour. Or, butter and flour a 10 by 4¼-inch tube pan with or without a removable bottom. If the pan has an intricate design or detail, prepare it as directed on page 24 to ensure the finished cake releases in one piece. Have all of the ingredients at room temperature.

To make the cake: Sift together the flour, baking powder, and salt onto a sheet of waxed paper; set aside. In the bowl of a stand mixer fitted with the paddle attachment, beat the almond paste on low speed just to break it up, about 30 seconds. Slowly add the sugar and beat until incorporated. Maintaining the mixer's speed, add the butter, tablespoon by tablespoon, taking about 45 seconds total. Stop the mixer and scrape down the sides of the bowl.

With the mixer on medium-low speed, add the eggs, 2 to 4 tablespoons at a time, beating after each addition until incorporated. Continue beating until the mixture is light in color and fluffy, about 3 minutes. Stop the mixer as needed to scrape down the sides of the bowl. On the lowest speed, add the flour mixture in three additions alternately with the milk in two additions, beginning and ending with the flour mixture and mixing after each addition until incorporated. Stop the mixer as needed to scrape down the sides of the bowl. Add the orange extract during the final moments of mixing. Detach the paddle and bowl from the mixer, and tap the paddle against the side of the bowl to free the excess batter. Spoon the batter into the prepared pan and spread evenly with the spatula.

Bake the cake until the top springs back when lightly touched and a round wooden toothpick inserted near the center comes out free of cake, about 55 minutes. Transfer to a wire rack and let cool in the pan for about 10 minutes while you prepare the glaze.

To make the Tangerine Glaze: In a medium bowl, combine the sugar, butter, and tangerine juice and zest and mix together until smooth.

Without delay, tilt and rotate the cake pan while gently tapping it on a counter to release the cake sides. Invert a wire rack on top of the cake, invert the cake onto it, and carefully lift off the pan. Slide a sheet of waxed paper under the rack to catch any drips from the glaze. Using a pastry brush, coat the top and sides of the warm cake with all of the glaze. Let the cake cool completely before serving.

To serve, slide the base of a tart pan, a small rimless baking sheet, or a large offset spatula under the cake and carefully transfer it to a serving platter. Cut the cake into thin slices with a sharp or serrated knife.

Evie Lieb's Processor Challah

Evie Lieb, one of the best bakers I know and a loving, generous friend, has been teaching baking and cooking classes since 1976. Her challah is just one of her many signature baked goods. Through the years, we have had great times exchanging recipes and information on all things baking, and Evie has shared many of her invaluable baking tips, especially on baking with yeast. She regularly makes two smaller breads from this recipe, one for her family and one to freeze or give as a gift. Although challah is traditionally baked for the Jewish Shabbat and holidays, it is a superb bread for every baker, Jewish and not.

The joy about making this bread from scratch is that you can do the work in stages, fitting the steps to your daily routine. For example, you can make the dough and let it rise in the refrigerator for 2 to 24 hours, and then form a braided loaf as the recipe directs. After braiding the dough, a second rise is necessary. This second rise can also be in the refrigerator for 2 to 24 hours. If you are baking the loaf the next day be sure to leave plenty of time to preheat your oven.

Here's a tip for braiding a perfectly symmetrical three-strand challah that longtime family friend Jacques Adler, another fine challah baker, taught me years ago: Start braiding the strands from the center of the loaf out to each end, being sure to pinch the ends of the strands together tightly. (You may find it easier to turn the other side of the braid around so that the unbraided portion is facing you.)

Before you begin, consult the instruction book of your food processor to make sure that your model can accommodate this amount of dough. **YIELD: 1 LOAF, 12 TO 16 SERVINGS**

4 CUPS (ABOUT 1¼ POUNDS/570 GRAMS) UNBLEACHED
    BREAD FLOUR

1 TABLESPOON PLUS 1½ TEASPOONS GRANULATED SUGAR

2¼ TEASPOONS (1 ENVELOPE) ACTIVE DRY YEAST

1½ TEASPOONS SALT

1 CUP (8 FL OUNCES/240 ML) VERY WARM WATER
    (120 TO 130 DEGREES F)

6 TABLESPOONS (3 FL OUNCES/90 ML) FLAVORLESS
    VEGETABLE OIL SUCH AS CANOLA OR SAFFLOWER

2 EXTRA-LARGE EGGS

1 TO 1½ TABLESPOONS SESAME SEEDS OR POPPY SEEDS

Place the flour, sugar, yeast, and salt in the bowl of a food processor fitted with the *dough blade*; pulse several times to combine the ingredients. Combine the warm water and oil in a glass measure with a pouring lip.

(Make sure the temperature of the combined liquids does not exceed 130 degrees F.)

With the motor running, add the warm liquid to the flour mixture through the feed tube, pouring only as fast as the liquid can be absorbed. Using the same glass measure, lightly beat the eggs until blended. Remove 2 tablespoons of the beaten egg and set aside to use for glazing the loaf. In the same manner as above, add the remaining beaten egg to the flour mixture. After all the egg has been added, continue to process until the dough cleans the sides of the bowl and forms a rough ball, then process for 40 to 60 seconds to knead the dough. If the dough seems sticky, pulse in flour, 1 tablespoon at a time, until you have a soft, elastic dough that may be slightly tacky but does not stick to your hand.

Remove the dough to a work surface and knead by hand for 1 minute. You will feel the dough firm up a little. (A little tackiness, if there is any, will disappear when it is kneaded for this final minute.) Place the dough in a resealable plastic bag, press out the air, and seal, leaving room for the dough to expand to double its bulk. Or, place the dough in a bowl and cover securely with plastic wrap. Let the dough rise at room temperature until doubled in bulk, 30 to 45 minutes or longer if the room is chilly. Press the dough gently with a fingertip. If the indentation remains, the dough is ready to shape.

Before baking: Center a rack in the oven and preheat the oven to 350 degrees F. Line a baking sheet with parchment paper or a silicone mat; set aside.

Gently deflate the dough and shape it into 1 large challah. The traditional shape is a braid, which can have a variable number of strands (ropes) and be simple or elaborate.

To shape the strands for braiding: Directions for making a two-tier challah and a three-tier challah follow. The directions here for shaping the strands are used for both forms. First, using a knife or a dough scraper, divide the dough into the number of pieces you need for the challah you have decided to make. For a precision-made loaf, weigh the portions. If you estimate the size, the resulting loaves may be a little more rustic, but they will be fine.

Line up the pieces of dough and work with each one in turn. Place 1 piece in front of you and use the heel of your hand to press it into a rough rectangle about ½ inch thick with a long side parallel to the edge of the work surface. Starting with the side nearest you, roll the dough into a tight log. Place your hands on top of the log and move them outward from the center as you roll the dough back and forth to elongate the dough into a smooth strand. Don't flour your work surface for this step. It is easier to manipulate and form the strands when they stick slightly. Make each strand a little longer than the desired length of the finished braid. Check to make sure that the seam has smoothed out, and pinch it firmly closed if necessary. Leave the center of each strand a

little thicker, and taper the ends so the loaf will be thicker in the middle and the ends can be tucked under neatly.

Working the dough will cause it to become quite elastic, so as the strands are formed and set aside they will creep back to a shorter length. This is not a problem; the dough will relax as it sits and you will be able to reroll the strands to restore their length when you are ready to form the braid.

To form a two-tier challah: Divide the dough into 4 equal pieces. To form the bottom tier, shape 3 of the pieces into strands about 12 inches long as described above. Lay them on the work surface parallel to one another and braid them. Divide the remaining piece into thirds, shape each piece into a strand, and make a small braid. In judging the length of the strands for the upper tier, keep in mind that the finished second braid should be longer (although thinner) than the first one. This will allow you to tuck the ends under and pinch them firmly to the bottom of the challah. To stack the braids, with the side of your hand make a trench down the length of the larger braid. Place the little braid on top, pressing it into the trench; seal the ends underneath.

To form a three-tier challah of any size: Use the same method for stacking the braids as for a two-tier challah, but follow these proportions. First, divide the dough in half. Then, form one-half into 3 strands and make a braid; this is the bottom of the challah. Divide the remaining half into 4 equal pieces. Use 3 pieces to make a 3-strand braid, and place it on top of the first braid. Divide the remaining piece of dough into 3 equal pieces and roll them into thin ropes that are longer than the two-tier challah you have shaped. Place this little braid on top of the other 2 braids, and seal the ends underneath.

Place the challah on the prepared baking sheet. Brush the loaf with some of the reserved 2 tablespoons beaten egg, and sprinkle with 1 tablespoon sesame seeds. To prevent the three-tier loaf from falling over while baking, generously grease wooden skewers with solid vegetable shortening, and push them through top to bottom at about 5 places along the loaf. Leave these CONTINUED ▸

in place while the loaf is rising; push them down to the baking sheet if they have lifted up with the rising dough. Remove the skewers when the challah has firmed up in the oven, about halfway through the baking time.

Loosely cover the loaf with plastic wrap and let it rise at room temperature until doubled in size, about 30 minutes or longer if the room is chilly. Press the dough gently with a fingertip. If the indentation remains, the loaf is ready to bake.

Brush the challah again with some of the beaten egg and add more seeds if the rising of the dough has created gaps without seeds. Bake for 15 minutes, then apply the egg glaze one last time and more seeds if needed. Return the bread to the oven until the interior temperature reaches 200 degrees F on an instant-read thermometer and there is a resonant sound when it is tapped on the bottom, about 15 minutes longer. The loaf should be nice and brown. Remove the pan from the oven and transfer the loaf to a wire rack. Let cool completely before storing or serving.

The challah tastes best if it is eaten the same day it is baked (or freshly thawed if frozen), but it will keep, wrapped in aluminum foil, at room temperature for up to 3 days. For longer storage, wrap in heavy-duty aluminum foil and freeze for up to 1 month. Thaw at room temperature in its wrapping for 4 to 5 hours.

Banana–Poppy Seed Cake

Here's one of my all-time favorite cakes for picnics, tailgate parties, and casual gatherings with family and friends. Guaranteed to disappear as quickly as you can cut it, this cake can be served right out of the pan. For on-the-go occasions, I use a pan that is easy to transport in a wicker basket, or sometimes I line a basket with a couple of colorful kitchen towels and set the cooled cake in its baking pan on top. For a great addition to a brunch buffet, I rely on a tried-and-true ceramic baking dish. If desired, scatter about 1 cup (5 ounces/140 grams) blueberries over the top of the batter before baking. The plump, juicy berries partially disappear into the cake and are a delicious counterpoint to the sweetness of banana and delicate crunch of poppy seeds. **YIELD: ONE 10-INCH ROUND CAKE, 8 TO 10 SERVINGS**

CAKE

1¾ CUPS (7 OUNCES/200 GRAMS) CAKE FLOUR

1½ TEASPOONS BAKING POWDER

½ TEASPOON BAKING SODA

½ TEASPOON GROUND CINNAMON

¼ TEASPOON SALT

3½ TEASPOONS POPPY SEEDS

¾ CUP (6 OUNCES/170 GRAMS) MASHED RIPE BANANAS (2 SMALL OR 1 LARGE)

⅓ CUP PLUS 1 TABLESPOON (3 FL OUNCES/90 ML) WELL-SHAKEN BUTTERMILK

4 OUNCES (1 STICK/115 GRAMS) UNSALTED BUTTER, AT ROOM TEMPERATURE

¾ CUP (5¼ OUNCES/150 GRAMS) GRANULATED SUGAR

2 LARGE EGGS, LIGHTLY BEATEN

LEMON DRIZZLE

½ CUP (1¾ OUNCES/50 GRAMS) POWDERED SUGAR

1 TABLESPOON FRESH LEMON JUICE

1 TEASPOON FINELY GRATED LEMON ZEST

½ TEASPOON PURE VANILLA EXTRACT

1 TABLESPOON POPPY SEEDS

Before baking: Center a rack in the oven and preheat the oven to 350 degrees F. Butter a 10 by 2-inch round ceramic gratin dish (6-cup capacity), a scant 10 by 2-inch round, fluted metal pan with sloping sides and a removable bottom (scant 8-cup capacity), or a 10 by 2-inch round cake pan (10-cup capacity), then flour it, tapping out the excess flour. Or, coat the pan lightly with nonstick spray and flour it. If you plan on removing the cake from its pan after baking, line the bottom with parchment paper (except for the pan with the removable bottom). Have all of the ingredients at room temperature.

To make the cake: Sift together the flour, baking powder, baking soda, cinnamon, and salt onto a sheet of waxed paper; add the poppy seeds on top and set aside. In a small bowl, stir together the bananas and buttermilk; set aside.

In the bowl of a stand mixer fitted with the paddle attachment, beat the butter on medium-low speed until creamy and smooth, 30 to 45 seconds. Stop the mixer and scrape down the sides of the bowl. On medium speed, add the sugar in a steady stream and continue beating until the mixture is lighter in color and texture, 2 to 3 minutes. Stop the mixer occasionally to scrape down the sides of the bowl.

With the mixer on medium speed, add the eggs, about 2 tablespoons at a time, mixing after each addition until incorporated. Continue beating until the mixture is fluffy and pale ivory. The entire process of adding and beating the eggs should take about 2 minutes. On the lowest speed, add the banana-buttermilk mixture until blended. Detach the paddle and bowl from the mixer, and tap the paddle against the side of the bowl to free CONTINUED ▶

the excess batter. Using a rubber spatula, stir in the flour mixture in three additions. With each addition, scrape down the sides of the bowl and continue mixing until the batter is smooth. Spoon the batter into the prepared pan. With the spatula, spread the batter from the center outward, creating a slightly raised ridge around the outside rim. (Since heat is conducted faster near the metal rim, mounding the batter around the edges ensures the cake will bake more evenly and will be more level.)

Bake the cake until it is golden, springs back when gently touched in the center, and the sides are beginning to pull away from the pan, 35 to 40 minutes. (The baking time may be shorter depending on which pan you used, so to avoid overbaking, start checking for doneness after 30 minutes.) Transfer the pan to a wire rack and let cool completely.

Or, to remove the cake from the pan, let it cool in the pan for 5 to 10 minutes. Then, tilt and rotate the pan while gently tapping it on a counter to release the cake sides. If they don't release, slip a small metal spatula between the still-warm cake and the pan and run the spatula carefully along the entire perimeter of the pan. Invert a wire rack on top of the cake, invert the cake onto it, and carefully lift off the pan. Slowly peel off the parchment liner, turn it over so that the sticky side faces up, and reposition it on the top of the cake. Invert another rack on top, invert the cake so it is right side up, and remove the original rack. (If you have used a pan with a removable bottom, set the pan on a narrower elevated surface, such as a tin can, so the bottom of the pan is released as the metal rim slips down. Return the cake to the wire rack.) Let the cake cool completely. Slip a sheet of waxed paper under the rack and proceed to glaze the cake.

To make the Lemon Drizzle and decorate the cake:
In a small bowl, stir together the sugar, lemon juice and zest, and vanilla until smooth. Drizzle the glaze over the cooled cake from the tines of a fork, then sprinkle the poppy seeds over the cake.

To store, place the cake in a sturdy covered container and store at room temperature for up to 1 day. For longer storage, label with the contents and date, and freeze for up to 2 weeks. The glaze does not freeze well, however, so wait to glaze the cake until the day of serving. Thaw at room temperature, about 2 hours, then glaze the cake.

To serve, cut the cake into wedges with a sharp knife.

Spicy Yogurt Pound Cake

This moist cake is a magical example where a sweet and spicy alchemy creates a whole that far exceeds the sum of its parts. From aromatic spices and finely ground walnuts to cocoa powder and orange zest, every ingredient adds its own dimension to the cake's unique flavor and texture. For a memorable, easy-to-create fruit garnish, use a serrated peeler to thinly slice a mango, nectarine, and/or plum, creating a kind of fruit carpaccio, and then gather the slices into ruffles and arrange them on or around the cake—the choice is yours. **YIELD: ONE 10-INCH TUBE CAKE, 20 SERVINGS (3 THIN SLICES PER SERVING)**

CAKE

2 ½ CUPS (11 ¼ OUNCES/320 GRAMS) ALL-PURPOSE FLOUR

1 TEASPOON GROUND CINNAMON

1 TEASPOON BAKING POWDER

1 TEASPOON UNSWEETENED NATURAL OR DUTCH-PROCESSED COCOA POWDER

½ TEASPOON GROUND ALLSPICE

½ TEASPOON BAKING SODA

½ TEASPOON SALT

⅛ TEASPOON GROUND CLOVES

⅛ TEASPOON NUTMEG, PREFERABLY FRESHLY GRATED

⅛ TEASPOON FRESH GROUND BLACK PEPPER

1 TEASPOON PURE VANILLA EXTRACT

1 CUP (8 OUNCES/225 GRAMS) PLAIN LOW-FAT YOGURT

8 OUNCES (2 STICKS/225 GRAMS) UNSALTED BUTTER, AT ROOM TEMPERATURE

½ CUP (3 ½ OUNCES/100 GRAMS) GRANULATED SUGAR

1 CUP FIRMLY PACKED (7 OUNCES/200 GRAMS) LIGHT BROWN SUGAR

4 LARGE EGGS, LIGHTLY BEATEN

1 CUP (3 OUNCES/85 GRAMS) FINELY GROUND WALNUTS

1 TABLESPOON FINELY GRATED ORANGE ZEST

GARNISH

1 LARGE, RIPE MANGO; FIRM YET RIPE RED-SKINNED, RED- OR YELLOW-FLESHED PLUM; AND/OR FIRM YET RIPE NECTARINE

Before baking: Center a rack in the oven and preheat the oven to 350 degrees F (or 325 degrees F if the pan has a dark finish). Butter a 10 by 3-inch Bundt pan, lightly coat it with nonstick spray, then flour it, tapping out the excess flour. Or, butter and flour a 10 by 4 ¼-inch tube pan with or without a removable bottom. If the pan has an intricate design or detail, prepare it as directed on page 24 to ensure the finished cake releases in one piece. Have all of the ingredients at room temperature.

To make the cake: Sift together the flour, cinnamon, baking powder, cocoa powder, allspice, baking soda, salt, cloves, nutmeg, and pepper onto a sheet of waxed paper; set aside. Stir the vanilla into the yogurt; set aside.

In the bowl of a stand mixer fitted with the paddle attachment, beat the butter on medium speed until creamy and smooth, 30 to 45 seconds. Stop the mixer and scrape down the sides of the bowl. Add the sugars all at once and continue to beat on medium speed until light tan and fluffy, 3 to 5 minutes. Stop the mixer occasionally to scrape down the sides of the bowl.

With the mixer on medium speed, add the eggs, 2 to 4 tablespoons at a time, mixing after each addition until incorporated and stopping occasionally to scrape down the sides of the bowl. On the lowest speed, add the ground nuts. Then add the flour mixture in four additions alternately with the yogurt mixture in three additions, beginning and ending with CONTINUED ▶

the flour mixture and mixing only until incorporated after each addition. Stop the mixer occasionally to scrape down the sides of the bowl. Detach the paddle and bowl from the mixer, and tap the paddle against the side of the bowl to free the excess batter. Using a rubber spatula, gently stir in the grated orange zest. Pour the batter into the prepared pan. With the spatula, spread the batter from the center outward, creating a slightly raised ridge around the outside rim. (Since heat is conducted faster near the metal rim, mounding the batter around the edges ensures the layer will bake more evenly and will be more level.)

Bake the cake until the center springs back when lightly touched, 40 to 45 minutes. Transfer the pan to a wire rack and let cool for about 10 minutes. Tilt and rotate the pan while gently tapping it on a counter to release the cake sides. Invert a wire rack on top of the cake, invert the cake onto it, and lift off the pan. Let the cake cool completely before serving.

To make the garnish: If using the mango, peel it; leave the nectarine and/or plum unpeeled. Using a serrated peeler, cut paper-thin slices from 1 or more of the fruits. Loosely roll up the slices to resemble ruffles on a blouse, and place them on top of the cake or around the base.

To serve, cut the cake into thin slices with a serrated knife. Garnish each serving with some of the fruit.

Cheery Cherry Chocolate Tart

The seductive pairing of sweet, juicy cherries and deep, dark chocolate along with almonds and cocoa nibs encased in a chocolate pastry makes this tart the ultimate finale for a dinner, romantic or otherwise. (That said, if you own a shallow heart-shaped tart pan, this recipe is begging to be baked in it.) Eminently portable, it is easily carried to friends' or a sweetheart's favorite dining spot. If fresh cherries aren't in season, substitute a mixture of dried sweet and tart cherries (about ½ cup/2¼ ounces/65 grams of each), along with ⅓ cup (3 ounces/ 85 grams) red seedless grapes that have been rinsed, drained on paper towels, and cut in half.

YIELD: ONE 9½-INCH TART, 8 TO 12 SERVINGS

1 RECIPE CHOCOLATE TART PASTRY (PAGE 363)

CHERRY FILLING

2 OUNCES (½ STICK/55 GRAMS) UNSALTED BUTTER

1 CUP (3½ OUNCES/100 GRAMS) POWDERED SUGAR

2 TABLESPOONS WHOLE NATURAL ALMONDS, FINELY GROUND TO YIELD 6 TABLESPOONS (1 OUNCE/30 GRAMS)

⅓ CUP (1½ OUNCES/40 GRAMS) ALL-PURPOSE FLOUR

⅓ CUP (2½ FL OUNCES/75 ML) EGG WHITES (3 LARGE)

½ TEASPOON PURE VANILLA EXTRACT

¼ TEASPOON PURE ALMOND EXTRACT

2 TABLESPOONS FINELY CHOPPED COCOA NIBS (OPTIONAL)

10 OUNCES (280 GRAMS) BING OR OTHER FULL-FLAVORED SWEET CHERRIES (ABOUT 25), STEMMED, PITTED, AND LEFT WHOLE

CHOCOLATE DRIZZLE

2½ OUNCES (70 GRAMS) SEMISWEET OR BITTERSWEET CHOCOLATE, FINELY CHOPPED

3 TABLESPOONS HEAVY CREAM

Before baking: Center a rack in the oven and preheat the oven to 350 degrees F. Have ready a 9½ by 1-inch round fluted tart pan with a removable bottom.

To line the pan with the pastry dough: Following the directions on page 29, roll out the pastry into an 11-inch circle about ⅛ inch thick and line the tart pan. Chill the pastry-lined pan in the freezer for about 20 minutes or in the refrigerator for at least 30 minutes or up to 1 day.

Bake the tart shell for 10 minutes. Remove from the oven, prick the dough in a few places with the tines of a fork, and return to the oven until the surface appears set (dry and no longer shiny), about 5 minutes longer. Transfer the pan to a wire rack and let cool completely before filling. (The tart shell can also be baked ahead; see instructions for storage on page 30.) Leave the oven on.

To make the Cherry Filling: Following the directions for making brown butter on page 19, melt the butter in a small, heavy saucepan over medium-low heat and heat just until it begins to turn a delicate brown, 3 to 5 minutes. Pour the butter into a small bowl and set aside to cool, about 5 minutes.

In a medium bowl, stir together the sugar, ground nuts, and flour. In another medium bowl, whisk the egg whites just until foamy. Add the flour mixture and stir until combined. Gradually stir in the brown butter to blend thoroughly. Stir in the vanilla extract, almond extract, and cocoa nibs. Let the mixture rest at room temperature until slightly thickened, about 30 minutes.

Spoon the filling into the tart shell. Press all but 3 of the cherries into the filling around the perimeter of the tart. Press the 3 reserved cherries in the center of the filling. The filling should reach about halfway up the cherries, dimpling the filling in a handsome manner. CONTINUED ▶

Bake the tart until the surface is dull, no longer appears wet or shiny, and springs back when lightly pressed, 22 to 25 minutes. Transfer the pan to a wire rack and let cool completely. When completely cool, set the tart pan on a narrower elevated surface, such as a tin can, so the bottom of the pan is released as the metal rim slips down. Set the tart aside.

To make the Chocolate Drizzle: Place the chocolate in a small bowl. In a small, heavy saucepan, bring the cream just to a boil over medium-low heat. Pour the cream over the chocolate and let stand for about 15 seconds. Whisk together until smooth and creamy. Set aside at room temperature just until the mixture cools a bit and begins to thicken.

Set the tart on a baking sheet or a long strip of waxed paper for easy cleanup. Fashion a small cone out of parchment paper (page 26) and half fill it with the chocolate. Snip a small opening at the end of the paper cone to allow a thin flow. Exerting light pressure on the cone, and never easing the pressure or halting the motion, pipe thin lines of chocolate in a zigzag pattern over the surface of the tart. Set the tart aside at room temperature to set up the chocolate.

To serve, cut the tart into wedges with a sharp knife.

Pumpkin Strudel

A creative idea for Thanksgiving dinner and other autumn celebrations, this crowd-pleasing dessert is essentially a pumpkin pie in the classic shape of a strudel. My recipe calls for a user-friendly cream cheese dough that yields an exceptionally tender, flaky pastry. Ideal for time-pressed bakers, both the pastry dough and the rich, spicy pumpkin filling can be prepared in advance, so you can easily assemble and bake the strudel at the last minute. Serve with lightly sweetened whipped cream flavored with brandy or hard or regular apple cider.

YIELD: ONE 13-INCH-LONG STRUDEL, 8 SERVINGS

½ RECIPE (11 OUNCES/310 GRAMS) FLAKY STRUDEL PASTRY (PAGE 364)

PUMPKIN FILLING

1⅔ CUPS CANNED PUMPKIN PUREE (ONE 15-OUNCE/ 430-GRAM CAN)

⅔ CUP (4½ OUNCES/130 GRAMS) GRANULATED SUGAR

1 TABLESPOON FINELY GRATED ORANGE ZEST

1 TEASPOON GROUND CINNAMON

½ TEASPOON SALT

½ TEASPOON GROUND GINGER

¼ TEASPOON GROUND CLOVES

¼ TEASPOON GROUND ALLSPICE

¼ CUP (2 FL OUNCES/60 ML) FRESH ORANGE JUICE

2 LARGE EGGS, LIGHTLY BEATEN

2 TABLESPOONS COLD UNSALTED BUTTER, CUT INTO PIECES

To prepare the pastry: On a lightly floured work surface, roll out the pastry into a 13 by 8-inch rectangle. Fold the dough into thirds like a business letter: working from a short end, lift one-third up over the center and then fold the top third down to cover. Rotate the dough 90 degrees, and repeat the rolling, this time into a 12 by 7-inch rectangle, and folding into thirds. Wrap in plastic and refrigerate until cold and firm, about 3 hours. (If the pastry recipe is freshly made, it will keep in the refrigerator for up to 3 days before continuing.)

To make the Pumpkin Filling: In a heavy 1½-quart saucepan, combine the pumpkin puree, sugar, orange zest, cinnamon, salt, ginger, cloves, and allspice and stir with a silicone spatula until well blended. Stir in the orange juice and eggs. Put the butter pieces on top of the mixture, place the pan over medium heat, and stir constantly until the butter melts into the mixture. Reduce the heat to medium-low and cook, stirring frequently, until an instant-read thermometer registers 170 degrees F, about 8 minutes. The filling will bubble occasionally and thicken slightly toward the end of cooking. Pour it into a bowl and set aside to cool completely. Cover securely with plastic wrap and refrigerate until cold or for up to 2 days. For longer storage, pour the cooled filling into a sturdy covered container, label with the contents and date, and freeze for up to 2 weeks.

Before baking: Center a rack in the oven and preheat the oven to 375 degrees F. Line a rimmed baking sheet with parchment paper.

To assemble the strudel: On a lightly floured work surface, roll out the pastry into a 13-by-8-inch rectangle. Spoon the filling lengthwise down the center of the pastry in a strip about 3 inches wide, leaving a 1-inch border uncovered on each short end. Fold each short end of the pastry over the filling, creating a 1-inch flap. Fold 1 uncovered long side over the filling, creating a flap about 2½ inches wide. Then fold the other uncovered side over the filling, overlapping the first flap by about 3 inches. Press to seal. With both hands, gently lift the strudel and transfer it, seam side down, onto the prepared baking sheet. Using the tip of a paring knife, score the top of the strudel in a simple pattern of intersecting CONTINUED ▸

lines to form Xs. Cut 2 small holes in the top with the tip of the knife to allow steam to escape during baking.

Bake the strudel, rotating the baking sheet 180 degrees at the midpoint to ensure even baking, until golden, 35 to 40 minutes. (Some of the butter might melt from the pastry toward the end of baking, but it will remain within the rimmed pan. A small amount of butter leaking from the pastry doesn't affect the pastry.) Transfer the pan to a wire rack and let cool for about 15 minutes. Using a large

metal spatula, carefully transfer the strudel to the rack and let cool almost completely before serving.

To serve, using a serrated knife, cut across the strudel into 2- to 2^1/$_2$-inch-wide slices. Serve warm or at room temperature. Lightly cover any leftover strudel with waxed paper and store at room temperature. Although the pastry is not as crisp the second day, it is still quite delicious.

Cream Cheese Pound Cake with Spearmint-Lime Glaze

One of my best-loved flavor pairings is citrus and mint, which I've featured here in a simple glaze. The cool, fresh character of spearmint harmonizes beautifully with the bright flavor and delicate floral aroma of fresh lime juice. Cream cheese, a favorite baking ingredient, gives the pound cake its velvety smooth texture, luxurious moistness, and subtle tang. Enjoy this at any backyard party or on a leisurely picnic beneath a shady tree. Fresh spearmint, more subtle in flavor than cool, spicy fresh peppermint, is the variety most often available in supermarkets.

YIELD: ONE 10-INCH TUBE CAKE, 20 SERVINGS (3 THIN SLICES PER SERVING)

CAKE

3¼ CUPS (13 OUNCES/370 GRAMS) CAKE FLOUR

¼ TEASPOON BAKING SODA

¼ TEASPOON SALT

9 OUNCES (2¼ STICKS/255 GRAMS) UNSALTED BUTTER, AT ROOM TEMPERATURE

ONE 8-OUNCE (225-GRAM) PACKAGE CREAM CHEESE, AT ROOM TEMPERATURE

3 CUPS (1 POUND, 5¼ OUNCES/600 GRAMS) GRANULATED SUGAR

6 LARGE EGGS, LIGHTLY BEATEN

1 TEASPOON PURE VANILLA EXTRACT

3 TABLESPOONS FRESH LIME JUICE

2 TEASPOONS FINELY GRATED LIME ZEST

SPEARMINT-LIME GLAZE

6 TABLESPOONS (3 FL OUNCES/90 ML) WATER

2 TABLESPOONS FRESH LIME JUICE

2 TABLESPOONS UNSALTED BUTTER

¼ CUP LIGHTLY PACKED SPEARMINT LEAVES

1¼ CUPS PLUS 2 TABLESPOONS (5 OUNCES/140 GRAMS) POWDERED SUGAR

2 TEASPOONS FINELY GRATED LIME ZEST

Before baking: Center a rack in the oven and preheat the oven to 350 degrees (or 325 degrees F if the pan has a dark finish). Butter a 10 by 3-inch Bundt pan, lightly coat it with nonstick spray, then flour it, tapping out the excess flour. Or, butter and flour a 10 by 4¼-inch tube pan with or without a removable bottom. If the pan has an intricate design or detail, prepare it as directed on page 24 to ensure the finished cake releases in one piece. Have all of the ingredients at room temperature.

To make the cake: Sift together the flour, baking soda, and salt onto a sheet of waxed paper; set aside. In the bowl of a stand mixer fitted with the attachment, beat together the butter and cream cheese on medium speed until creamy and smooth, 30 to 45 seconds. Stop the mixer and scrape down the sides of the bowl. On medium speed, add the sugar in a steady stream and continue to beat until light in color and fluffy, about 5 minutes. Stop the mixer occasionally to scrape down the sides of the bowl.

With the mixer still on medium speed, add the eggs, 2 to 4 tablespoons at a time, beating after each addition until incorporated. The entire process of adding and beating the eggs should take 2 to 3 minutes. Add the vanilla and lime juice during the final moments of mixing. On the lowest speed, gradually add the flour mixture, mixing after each addition only until incorporated and stopping the mixer occasionally to scrape down the sides of the bowl. The entire process of adding the flour mixture should take about 2 minutes. Detach the paddle and bowl from the mixer, and tap the paddle against the side of the bowl to free the excess batter. Using a rubber spatula, fold in the lime zest. Spoon the batter into the prepared pan and spread evenly with the spatula. CONTINUED ▸

Bake the cake until golden and a round wooden tooth-pick inserted near the center comes out clean, about 1¼ hours. Transfer the pan to a wire rack and let cool for about 10 minutes while you prepare the glaze.

To make the Spearmint-Lime Glaze: In a small sauce-pan, combine the water, lime juice, butter, and mint leaves over low heat just until the mixture bubbles around the edges. Remove from the heat and let steep for 1 minute.

Without delay, tilt and rotate the cake pan while gently tapping it on a counter to release the cake sides. Invert a wire rack on top of the cake, invert the cake onto it, and lift off the pan. Slide a sheet of waxed paper under the rack to catch any drips from the glaze.

Press the mint leaves against the side of the saucepan to release most of the moisture, and then discard the mint leaves. Stir the sugar and lime zest into the liquid until smooth. Using a pastry brush, coat the top and sides of the warm cake with all of the glaze. Let the cake cool completely before serving. As the cake cools, the glaze sets up to form a shiny coating.

To serve, slide the bottom of a tart pan, a small rimless baking sheet, or a large offset spatula under the cake and carefully transfer it to a serving platter. Cut into thin slices with a serrated knife.

Cyrano Chocolate Cake

Like France's legendary Cyrano de Bergerac, this captivating chocolate dessert is remarkable not for its appearance but for its unforgettable flavor. Guaranteed to seduce any chocolate lover (including Julia Child, in whose kitchen I baked this cake back in the 1980s), the not-too-sweet dessert woos the palate with its intense chocolaty goodness. The water bath (bain-marie) baking method ensures gentle, uniform heating, making the cake irresistibly rich and creamy.

YIELD: ONE 9-INCH ROUND CAKE, 8 TO 10 SERVINGS

5 OUNCES (1 ¼ STICKS/140 GRAMS) UNSALTED BUTTER

12 OUNCES (340 GRAMS) SEMISWEET CHOCOLATE, FINELY CHOPPED

3 TABLESPOONS UNSWEETENED NATURAL OR DUTCH-PROCESSED COCOA POWDER

3 LARGE EGGS

1 LARGE EGG YOLK

½ CUP (3 ½ OUNCES/100 GRAMS) GRANULATED SUGAR

1 TABLESPOON PURE VANILLA EXTRACT

POWDERED SUGAR, OR ¾ CUP (6 FL OUNCES/180 ML) HEAVY CREAM LIGHTLY WHIPPED WITH 2 TEASPOONS GRANULATED SUGAR

Before baking: Center a rack in the oven and preheat the oven to 375 degrees F. Have ready a 9 by 2-inch round cake pan. Select a shallow roasting pan that will accommodate the cake pan with 1 to 2 inches of space between the cake pan and the sides of the roasting pan. Set the cake pan in the roasting pan and pour warm water into the roasting pan to reach slightly over halfway up the sides of the cake pan. Remove the cake pan from the water and place the roasting pan with the water in the oven while it is preheating. Butter the cake pan, then flour it, tapping out the excess flour. Line the bottom with parchment paper. Have all of the ingredients at room temperature.

To make the cake: In a heavy 1-quart saucepan, melt the butter and chocolate over very low heat, stirring with a rubber spatula until smooth. Or, combine in a medium microwave-safe bowl and melt in a microwave oven at 50 percent power (medium) for 30-second bursts, stirring after each burst, until melted, 2 to 3 minutes. Transfer to a medium bowl and let cool for 5 minutes. Stir in the cocoa powder.

In the bowl of a stand mixer, stir together the eggs, egg yolk, and granulated sugar. Attach the bowl to the mixer, fit the mixer with the whisk attachment, and whip the mixture on medium speed until fluffy, pale yellow, and double in volume, about 3 minutes. When the whisk is lifted, the mixture should fall back into the bowl in a ribbon that rests softly on the surface and remains there for about 3 seconds before dissolving back into the mixture. Add the vanilla during the final moments of whipping. Fold one-third of the egg mixture into the chocolate to lighten it. Fold in the remaining egg mixture. Pour the batter into the prepared pan and carefully place the pan in the water bath.

Bake the cake until an instant-read thermometer inserted into the center registers about 160 degrees F, about 30 minutes. The chocolate firms as the cake cools, so be careful not to overbake. Transfer the cake pan to a wire rack and let cool for about 10 minutes. Then invert a serving plate on the cake and invert the cake onto it. Slowly peel off the parchment paper and let the cake cool completely.

To serve, using a fine-mesh strainer, dust the top of the cake with powdered sugar. Or, using an offset spatula, frost the top with the whipped cream. Cut into wedges with a sharp knife, dipping the knife blade in hot water and wiping it dry with a towel before each cut.

Autumn Dried Fruit–Nut Tart

When it comes to desserts, I love surprises—like the jewel-toned apricot filling that is revealed when I cut into this double-layered tart. The intense, fruity flavor of dried apricots is perfectly balanced by the richness of natural almonds. You can vary this wonderfully portable dessert by substituting dried peaches or nectarines for the apricots. To cut dried fruit into strips with ease, lightly coat the blades of your kitchen scissors with a flavorless oil or nonstick spray. For this tart, you need to bake the crust partially before filling it to ensure that the filling and the pastry are done at the same time. **YIELD: ONE 10¼-INCH ROUND TART, 12 TO 14 SERVINGS**

1 RECIPE TENDER TART PASTRY (PAGE 361)

DRIED APRICOT AND NUT FILLING

1 CUP (4 OUNCES/115 GRAMS) DRIED APRICOTS, CUT INTO
    ¼-INCH-WIDE STRIPS

½ CUP (4 FL OUNCES/120 ML) BOILING WATER

2 TABLESPOONS ORANGE LIQUEUR, SUCH AS COINTREAU,
    OR FRESH ORANGE JUICE

⅓ CUP (2½ FL OUNCES/75 ML) FRESH ORANGE JUICE

3 TABLESPOONS GRANULATED SUGAR

1 TEASPOON FINELY GRATED ORANGE ZEST

½ CUP (1¾ OUNCES/50 GRAMS) NATURAL OR BLANCHED
    SLICED ALMONDS, TOASTED (PAGES 15–16)

2¾ OUNCES (½ STICK PLUS 1½ TABLESPOONS) UNSALTED
    BUTTER, SOFTENED

½ CUP PLUS 2½ TABLESPOONS (2¾ OUNCES/75 GRAMS)
    POWDERED SUGAR

¾ CUP (2¾ OUNCES/75 GRAMS) GROUND NATURAL ALMONDS

1 LARGE EGG, LIGHTLY BEATEN

Before baking: Center a rack in the oven and preheat the oven to 400 degrees F. Have ready a 10¼ by 1-inch round fluted tart pan with a removable bottom.

To line the pan with the pastry dough: Following the directions on page 29, roll out the pastry into a 12-inch circle about ⅛ inch thick and line the tart pan. Chill the pastry-lined pan in the freezer for about 20 minutes or in the refrigerator for at least 30 minutes or up to 1 day.

Partially bake the tart shell for 17 to 25 minutes as directed on page 30. Transfer to a wire rack and let cool completely. The tart shell is fragile while warm but becomes crisp as it cools. Reduce the oven heat to 350 degrees F. While the tart shell is baking, proceed to make the filling.

To make the Dried Apricot and Nut Filling: In a 1-quart saucepan, combine the apricots and boiling water and set aside to soak for 30 minutes. Add the liqueur and orange juice, place over medium heat, and bring the mixture to a boil. Reduce the heat to medium-low and simmer until almost all of the liquid has evaporated, about 15 minutes. Toward the last moments of cooking, stir in the granulated sugar. Remove from the heat, stir in the orange zest, and then stir the mixture briskly to bring it together into a smooth, thick paste. Add the sliced almonds, and spread the apricot mixture over the bottom of the tart. Set aside while preparing the nut filling.

In a medium bowl, using a rubber spatula, beat together the butter, powdered sugar, and ground nuts until the mixture is smooth. Add the egg and mix just until the ingredients are well blended. Spread the nut mixture evenly over the apricot filling.

Bake the tart until the top is set (feels firm, not dry or hard, rather than soft), 35 to 40 minutes. Transfer the pan to a wire rack and let cool completely.

Serve the tart at room temperature. Cut into wedges with a sharp knife.

Fruit-Studded Cornmeal Cake

Like an accomplished pianist who has a well-polished repertoire, a home baker needs to have a few favorite recipes that are perfect at any time of the year and for any occasion that calls for bringing something you baked for everyone to share. A golden butter cake with the addition of cornmeal harmonizes perfectly with a variety of dessert flavors. Fresh cherries, prune plums, or grapes, depending on the season, pressed into the batter before baking, peek through and dimple this simple snack cake.   **YIELD: ONE 8-INCH SQUARE CAKE, 16 SERVINGS**

½ CUP (2¾ OUNCES/75 GRAMS) YELLOW CORNMEAL, PLUS ADDITIONAL CORNMEAL FOR COATING THE PAN

1 CUP PLUS 2 TABLESPOONS (5 OUNCES/140 GRAMS) ALL-PURPOSE FLOUR

¾ TEASPOON BAKING POWDER

¼ TEASPOON SALT

6 OUNCES (1½ STICKS/170 GRAMS) UNSALTED BUTTER, AT ROOM TEMPERATURE

¾ CUP (5¼ OUNCES/150 GRAMS) GRANULATED SUGAR

3 LARGE EGGS, LIGHTLY BEATEN

1 TEASPOON PURE VANILLA EXTRACT

16 BING CHERRIES (ABOUT 6 OUNCES/170 GRAMS), STEMMED, PITTED, AND LEFT WHOLE; 8 (ABOUT 5 OUNCES/140 GRAMS) SMALL ITALIAN OR FRENCH PRUNE PLUMS, HALVED AND PITTED; OR ½ CUP (3½ OUNCES/100 GRAMS) GRAPES, PREFERABLY SEEDLESS RED, HALVED

1 CUP (5 OUNCES /140 GRAMS) PINE NUTS

Before baking: Center a rack in the oven and preheat the oven to 350 degrees F. Lightly coat an 8 by 2-inch square pan with nonstick spray, then dust with cornmeal, tapping out the excess cornmeal. Have all of the ingredients at room temperature.

Sift together the flour, cornmeal, baking powder, and salt onto a sheet of waxed paper; set aside.

In the bowl of a stand mixer fitted with the paddle attachment, beat the butter on medium speed until creamy and smooth, 30 to 45 seconds. Stop the mixer to scrape down the sides of the bowl. On medium speed, add the sugar in a steady stream and continue to beat until light in color and fluffy, 2 to 3 minutes.

With the mixer on medium speed, add the eggs, 2 to 4 tablespoons at a time, beating after each addition until incorporated and stopping the mixer occasionally to scrape down the sides of the bowl. Add the vanilla during the final moments of mixing. Detach the paddle and bowl from the mixer, and tap the paddle against the side of the bowl to free the excess butter mixture. Using a rubber spatula, stir in the flour mixture until well blended. Spoon the batter into the prepared pan, spreading evenly with the spatula. Press the cherries just halfway (so they are still visible) into the batter: 4 rows of 4 cherries each, evenly spaced over the surface. If using the prune plums, press them cut side up into the batter; if using the grapes, press them cut side down. Sprinkle the pine nuts evenly over the surface.

Bake the cake until a round wooden toothpick inserted in the center comes out free of cake, 40 to 45 minutes. Transfer to a wire rack and let cool in the pan for about 10 minutes.

Tilt and rotate the pan while gently tapping it on a counter to release the cake sides. Invert a wire rack on top of the cake, invert the cake onto it, and lift off the pan. Invert another rack on top, invert the cake so it is right side up, and remove the original rack. Let cool completely.

To serve, cut the cake into squares with a sharp knife.

Gingerbread-Pecan Tart

Like almost everyone I know, I tend to cook the same dishes at Thanksgiving year after year. The only exception—you guessed it—is dessert. Our holiday tradition is for me to surprise the family with a new dessert. Throughout the year I consider many candidates, and selecting the recipe is an enjoyable challenge. A favorite is one that haunted me from the day I first ate it at Sara Beth's Kitchen in New York. After that taste, I promised myself that someday I would take the time to try to duplicate its unique combination of flavors: a rich tart with a gingerbread-cookie-like crust and a pecan filling.

Since Thanksgiving is a holiday for family and friends, the day is often spent cooking for a crowd. This tart is ideal for just that kind of occasion: it's rich enough to cut into many servings, with their size geared to individual appetites. Don't hesitate to serve each portion with a dollop of sweetened whipped cream spiked with rum or bourbon to balance the spiciness of the tart dough and the sweetness of the filling. **YIELD: ONE 13 BY 9-INCH TART, 12 TO 24 SERVINGS, DEPENDING ON SIZE**

PASTRY

2 CUPS (9 OUNCES/255 GRAMS) ALL-PURPOSE FLOUR

½ CUP (3½ OUNCES/100 GRAMS) GRANULATED SUGAR

¾ TEASPOON GROUND GINGER

½ TEASPOON GROUND CINNAMON

⅛ TEASPOON GROUND CLOVES

⅛ TEASPOON GROUND BLACK PEPPER

⅛ TEASPOON GROUND ALLSPICE

⅛ TEASPOON SALT

6 OUNCES (1½ STICKS/170 GRAMS) COLD UNSALTED BUTTER, CUT INTO ¼-INCH SLICES

1 LARGE EGG

1 TABLESPOON UNSULFURED MOLASSES

1 TEASPOON PURE VANILLA EXTRACT

PECAN FILLING

6 LARGE EGGS, LIGHTLY BEATEN

1⅓ CUPS (1 POUND BY WEIGHT/455 GRAMS) DARK CORN SYRUP

1 CUP FIRMLY PACKED (7 OUNCES/200 GRAMS) DARK BROWN SUGAR

2 OUNCES (½ STICK/55 GRAMS) UNSALTED BUTTER, MELTED

1 TABLESPOON PURE VANILLA EXTRACT

2 CUPS (8 OUNCES/225 GRAMS) PECAN PIECES

1 CUP (4 OUNCES/115 GRAMS) PECAN HALVES

WHIPPED CREAM TOPPING

1 CUP (8 FL OUNCES/240 ML) COLD HEAVY CREAM

1 TABLESPOON GRANULATED SUGAR

1 TO 2 TABLESPOONS DARK RUM OR BOURBON

Before baking: Center a rack in the oven and preheat the oven to 350 degrees F. Lightly coat a 13 by 9 by 2-inch pan (quarter sheet pan) with nonstick spray.

To make the pastry and line the pan: In a food processor, combine the flour, sugar, spices, and salt and pulse 3 or 4 times to blend. Scatter the butter pieces over the flour mixture, and pulse until the mixture is the consistency of cornmeal.

In a small bowl, whisk together the egg, molasses, and vanilla until blended. With the motor running, pour the egg mixture down the feed tube and process until a soft dough forms.

Transfer the dough to a work surface. Beginning at the far end, and using the heel of your hand, push a small amount of the dough (about the size of an extra-large egg) away from you, smearing it on the work surface. Repeat with the remaining dough in small amounts.

When you've worked all the dough in this manner, give it a couple more strokes to bring it together into a smooth, homogeneous unit. (This kneading technique, described on page 31, is known as *fraisage*.)

On a lightly floured work surface, roll or pat the dough into a rectangle 8 or 9 inches by 5 inches. Gently lift the rectangle and center it in the prepared pan. With floured fingertips, press the dough evenly over the bottom and 1 inch up the sides of the pan. (Or, place a sheet of plastic wrap on top of the dough and use a 2 1/2- to 4-inch pastry roller to expand the dough over the bottom and up the sides of the pan, then remove the plastic.) Set aside while preparing the filling.

To make the Pecan Filling: In a large bowl, combine the eggs, corn syrup, sugar, butter, and vanilla and stir to mix. Stir in the pecan pieces and halves. Pour the filling into the tart shell. The filling should come right to the top edge of the dough.

Bake the tart until set (when you lightly press the center, it doesn't quiver or feel soft), 46 to 50 minutes. Transfer to a wire rack and let cool. Serve lukewarm or, preferably, cooled to room temperature.

To make the Whipped Cream Topping: Using a whisk or a handheld mixer, whip together the cream, sugar, and rum to taste in a deep, medium bowl until soft peaks form. Cover and refrigerate. Just before serving, use a whisk just to bring the whipped cream together.

To serve, cut the tart into squares with a sharp knife. Spoon a dollop of the whipped cream on top of each serving or alongside it. The tart is still delicious the day after baking, so you can make it the day before you plan to serve it. Cover it with aluminum foil and store at room temperature.

Deluxe Lemon-Lavender Mail-a-Cake

When circumstances forced me to celebrate one of my mother's birthdays from a distance, I was determined to give something more creative than the easy-to-send flowers, cards, and gifts. "What can I give that would be thoughtful?" I asked myself. "Of course," I thought, "what is more fitting than the family baker commemorating the day with a homemade cake?" I found out, however, that mailing the cake is the challenge, not making it.

The first consideration is the type of cake. Those frosted with whipped cream, filled with ice cream and fresh fruit, and studded with lit candles are out of the question for obvious reasons. The best cake is one that is sturdy enough to endure the rigors of shipping, like this lemon-lavender pound cake. Light, airy sponge cakes lose their shape, and traditional butter-cake layers are prone to cracking. But a dense, fine-grained pound cake remains intact.

Here's the two-step schedule for mailing the cake:

1. Bake the cake, let it cool completely on a wire rack, and then wrap it securely in plastic wrap. Overwrap with another layer of plastic wrap, and freeze for at least 24 hours or up to 1 week before shipping.

2. On shipping day, use the double-box technique. Put packing insulation, such as bubble wrap or Styrofoam "peanuts," in the bottom of a sturdy cardboard box measuring about 12 inches square and 10 inches deep. I use crumpled paper bags for insulation because they are environmentally friendly and more economical. Place the wrapped frozen cake in a sturdy cardboard box (or cake box) and set it on the insulation layer in the larger box. Fill the remaining spaces with more insulation so there is cushioning on all sides.

Eureka lemons are the variety most often sold in supermarkets. Their sharp, zesty flavor is ideal for this cake. **YIELD: ONE 10-INCH TUBE CAKE, 20 SERVINGS (3 THIN SLICES PER SERVING)**

CAKE

3 CUPS (12¼ OUNCES/350 GRAMS) CAKE FLOUR

½ TEASPOON BAKING POWDER

½ TEASPOON BAKING SODA

⅛ TEASPOON SALT

8 OUNCES (2 STICKS/225 GRAMS) UNSALTED BUTTER, AT ROOM TEMPERATURE

2 CUPS (14 OUNCES/400 GRAMS) GRANULATED SUGAR

1 TABLESPOON PESTICIDE-FREE DRIED LAVENDER FLOWERS (SEE SOURCES)

3 LARGE EGGS, LIGHTLY BEATEN

1 CUP (8 FL OUNCES/240 ML) WELL-SHAKEN BUTTERMILK

2 TABLESPOONS FINELY GRATED LEMON ZEST (2 LEMONS)

2 TABLESPOONS FRESH LEMON JUICE

Before baking: Center a rack in the oven and preheat the oven to 350 degrees F (or 325 degrees F if the pan has a dark finish). Butter a 10 by 3-inch Bundt pan, lightly coat it with nonstick spray, then flour it, tapping out the excess flour. Or, butter and flour a 10 by 4¼-inch tube pan with or without a removable bottom. If the pan has an intricate design or detail, prepare it as directed on page 24 to ensure the finished cake releases in one piece. Have all of the ingredients at room temperature.

To make the cake: Sift together the flour, baking powder, baking soda, and salt onto a sheet of waxed paper; set aside.

In the bowl of a stand mixer fitted with the paddle attachment, beat the butter on medium speed until it is lighter in color, clings to the sides of the bowl, and has a satiny appearance, 30 to 45 seconds. Add the sugar and the lavender in a steady stream, then stop the mixer and scrape the gritty, sandy mixture clinging to the sides of the bowl into the center. Resume beating at medium speed until the mixture is light in color and fluffy, 4 to 5 minutes. Stop the mixer as needed to scrape down the sides of the bowl.

With the mixer on medium speed, add the eggs, 2 to 4 tablespoons at a time, beating after each addition until incorporated. If at any time the batter appears watery or shiny (signs of curdling), stop adding the eggs, increase the speed to medium-high, and beat until the mixture looks smooth and silky again. Resume beating on medium speed and add the remaining eggs. On the lowest speed, add the flour mixture in three additions alternately with the buttermilk in two additions, beginning and ending with the flour mixture and mixing after each addition until incorporated. Stop the mixer and scrape down the sides of the bowl after each addition. Detach the paddle and bowl from the mixer, and tap the paddle against the side of the bowl to free the excess batter. Using a rubber spatula, stir in the lemon zest and juice. Spoon the batter into the prepared pan and spread evenly with the spatula.

Bake the cake until a round wooden toothpick inserted in the center comes out free of cake, 60 to 65 minutes. Transfer to a wire rack and let cool in the pan for 20 minutes.

Tilt and rotate the pan while gently tapping it on a counter to release the cake sides. Invert a wire rack on top of the cake, invert the cake onto it, and lift off the pan. Let the cake cool completely.

If serving the cake within 24 hours, place under a cake dome or wrap in plastic wrap and store at room temperature. For longer storage, overwrap with aluminum foil, label with the contents and date, and freeze for up to 1 month. To thaw, remove the foil and leave at room temperature for about 3 hours.

To serve, cut the cake into thin slices with a serrated knife.

World-Traveling Crispy ANZAC Cookies

Here's a crisp, crunchy cookie that has traveled around the world via Australia and New Zealand only to win the hearts of all who eat it. It first appeared during World War I, with the theories on its origin varied. But the story I've heard the most often is that the cookies, which can survive a long journey, were created for sending to loved ones who were fighting at the front (ANZAC is an acronym for the Australian and New Zealand Army Corps). The distinctively flavored Lyle's golden syrup can be found in well-stocked supermarkets, usually shelved with the pancake syrups. If you use an ice cream scoop to portion out the dough, the cookies will bake evenly and will all be the same size. To vary the flavor, add 3 tablespoons chopped dried cherries, dried dates, candied orange peel, crystallized ginger, or dried apricots to the dry ingredients before adding the liquids. **YIELD: ABOUT 4 DOZEN COOKIES**

1 ½ CUPS (6 ¾ OUNCES/195 GRAMS) ALL-PURPOSE FLOUR

1 ½ CUPS (10 ½ OUNCES/300 GRAMS) GRANULATED SUGAR

1 ½ CUPS (4 ½ OUNCES/130 GRAMS) UNSWEETENED MEDIUM-SHRED DRIED COCONUT

1 ½ CUPS (4 ½ OUNCES/130 GRAMS) OLD-FASHIONED ROLLED OATS

1 TEASPOON BAKING SODA

6 ¾ OUNCES (1 ½ STICKS PLUS 1 ½ TABLESPOONS/ 190 GRAMS) UNSALTED BUTTER

5 TABLESPOONS (3 ¼ OUNCES BY WEIGHT/90 GRAMS) LYLE'S GOLDEN SYRUP OR HONEY

3 TABLESPOONS HOT WATER

1 TEASPOON FINELY GRATED LEMON ZEST

Before baking: Center a rack in the oven and preheat the oven to 350 degrees F. Line 2 large baking sheets with parchment paper.

In a large bowl, stir together the flour, sugar, coconut, oats, and baking soda. In a small saucepan, melt the butter over medium-low heat. Turn off the heat and stir the syrup and hot water into the butter, and then stir in the lemon zest. Stir the butter mixture into the flour mixture.

Using an ice cream scoop about 1 ½ inches in diameter (#40 or #50) or a tablespoon, scoop out the dough (it is a bit crumbly) into the palm of your hand and squeeze it into a ball. Set it on a prepared baking sheet and carefully, with the palm of your hand, flatten the ball slightly to a disk about 2 inches in diameter. Continue in this fashion, spacing the cookies 2 inches apart.

One pan at a time, bake the cookies until golden brown, 12 to 13 minutes. The cookies might be soft and puffy in the center but will deflate as they cool. (Or, you can position 1 rack in the center of the oven and a second rack in the upper third of the oven and bake as directed, switching the pans between the racks about halfway through baking to ensure even baking.) Transfer to a wire rack and let the cookies cool on the pan for 2 minutes (they are fragile when they are warm). Then, using a metal spatula, transfer the cookies to the rack and let cool completely. The cookies will crisp as they cool.

To store, stack the cookies in an airtight container and store at room temperature for up to 10 days.

Baking for All Occasions

COLOR PLATES

ABOVE **Lemon-Scented Pull-Apart Coffee Cake** P163
LEFT **Red Velvet Cake Roll** P85

ABOVE **Strawberry-Mango Shortcakes with Basil Syrup** P81

RIGHT **Evie Lieb's Processor Challah Bread** P184

ABOVE **Fruit-Nut Florentine Cookie Triangles** P283
LEFT **Milk Chocolate S'more Tartlets with Homemade Marshmallow Topping** P270

ABOVE **Peanut Butter Crunch Cake, Squared** P128

RIGHT **All-American Chocolate Cake with Divinity Frosting and Milk Chocolate Paint** P331

ABOVE **Fruit Cocktail Trifles with Crème Anglaise** P267
LEFT **Mocha-Almond O'Marble Cake** P88

ABOVE **Tangy Lemon Custard Tart with Pomegranate Gelée** P71
RIGHT **Frozen Lemon Glacier** P140

ABOVE **Butterscotch Spiral Coffee Cake** P100
LEFT **Flag-Raising Mixed-Berry Potpies** P229

ABOVE **Heart-to-Heart-to-Heart Cookies** P285
RIGHT **Chocolate-Dipped Cheesecake-sicles** P248

ABOVE **Cinnamon Bubble Buns** P77

LEFT **Cupid's Strawberry Cake with Cream Cheese Buttercream** P314

ABOVE **Congo Brownies** P102
RIGHT **Sour Cream Custard Tart** P230

ABOVE **Focaccia for Breakfast** P158

LEFT **Chocolate-Vanilla Swirl Cookies** P276

Eggnog Pound Cake with Crystal Rum Glaze P180

Maple-Pecan Custard Pie

Iconic autumn flavors make this rich custard pie the perfect dessert to share at seasonal gatherings. Evoking sweet memories of good friends, this pie is my tribute to Billy Cross and the late Michael James, two longtime food professionals who had a fabulous Beverly Hills pie business in the 1980s. One of their pies was a showstopping dessert that inspired this recipe, enriched with sweet maple syrup and the mellow, buttery crunch of toasted pecans. Since pecans play a starring role, be sure to taste before you buy to make sure they are at their peak of freshness. For the best flavor, use Grade B maple syrup, which is darker and more flavorful than Grade A syrup. It's sold at some supermarkets and specialty-foods stores. If you've planned ahead and have a frozen 9-inch pie crust on hand, here's a great opportunity to use it.   **YIELD: ONE 9-INCH PIE, 8 TO 10 SERVINGS**

ONE 9-INCH PIE CRUST FROM FOUR PIE CRUSTS AT ONE TIME (PAGE 357)

MAPLE-PECAN CUSTARD FILLING

1 ½ CUPS (12 FL OUNCES/340 ML) HEAVY CREAM

¾ CUP (5 ¼ OUNCES/150 GRAMS) GRANULATED SUGAR

¾ CUP (8 ¼ OUNCES BY WEIGHT/230 GRAMS) PURE MAPLE SYRUP, PREFERABLY GRADE B

2 CUPS (8 OUNCES/225 GRAMS) PECAN HALVES

2 LARGE EGGS, LIGHTLY BEATEN

1 ½ TEASPOONS PURE VANILLA EXTRACT

WHIPPED CREAM TOPPING (OPTIONAL)

⅔ CUP (5 ½ FL OUNCES/165 ML) HEAVY CREAM

1 TABLESPOON FIRMLY PACKED LIGHT BROWN SUGAR

1 ½ TEASPOONS FINELY GRATED LEMON ZEST

Before baking: Center a rack in the oven and preheat the oven to 425 degrees F for 30 minutes. Have the pie crust ready to bake.

Following the directions for blind baking a pie crust on page 28, partially bake the pie crust for 25 to 30 minutes. Transfer to a wire rack and let cool completely before filling. Leave the oven on at 425 degrees F.

To make the Maple-Pecan Custard Filling: In a deep, 2- to 2 ½-quart saucepan, combine the cream and sugar and bring to a gentle boil over low heat (be careful; it boils up). Cook until reduced to 1 ¼ cups

(10 fl ounces/300 ml), 12 to 15 minutes. Stir in the maple syrup and set aside to cool for about 10 minutes.

Meanwhile, scatter the pecan halves over the bottom of the partially baked crust. Gently whisk the eggs and vanilla into the maple cream until well blended. Pour the custard filling into the pie crust (the pecans will rise to the surface).

Bake the pie until the filling puffs slightly, is set around the edges, and jiggles a bit in the center when the pan is moved slightly, 30 to 40 minutes. If the edges of the pastry are browning too quickly toward the end of baking, cover them with aluminum foil. Transfer the pan to a wire rack and let cool for at least 1 ½ hours before serving. As the pie cools, the filling will firm.

While the pie cools, make the Whipped Cream Topping, if desired: Using a whisk or a handheld mixer, whip together the cream, sugar, and lemon zest in a deep, medium bowl until soft peaks form. Cover and refrigerate. Just before serving, use a whisk to bring the whipped cream together.

For the best flavor and texture, let the pie cool for 1 ½ hours as directed above and then serve at room temperature within 4 hours. Cut into wedges with a sharp knife, and spoon a dollop of the whipped cream on each serving.

Old-Time Pound Cake with Candied Cranberry-Pineapple-Ginger Topping

It's the baking teacher in me that wants to introduce you to an heirloom baking technique—and to show you there's more than one way to make a perfect pound cake. My inspiration for this recipe came to me years ago when I happened on the concept in Paula Peck's immortal cookbook, *The Art of Fine Baking*. My curiosity took over right away and I applied her method to one of my favorite recipes. Although it may sound like heresy, this recipe calls for beating butter with flour, whipping eggs with sugar, and then blending the two mixtures. The result is a simple yet stunning buttery cake with an exceptionally fine texture. I first made this cake decades ago using a faithful old Sunbeam stand mixer I'd fondly dubbed Bessie. Although Bessie has long been out to pasture, this cake remains a staple in my baking repertoire.

In fall and winter, I serve it with the Candied Cranberry-Pineapple-Ginger Topping, roasted pears, or apples and dried apricots, or I toast it and drizzle it with honey. In spring and summer, there's nothing like a dollop of brown sugar–sweetened whipped cream and sliced peaches and strawberries to accompany it, or you might lightly grill the cake and accompany it with a scoop of your favorite ice cream.   **YIELD: ONE 9 BY 5-INCH CAKE, 12 SERVINGS**

POUND CAKE

1¾ CUPS (7 OUNCES/200 GRAMS) CAKE FLOUR

¼ TEASPOON SALT

8 OUNCES (2 STICKS/225 GRAMS) UNSALTED BUTTER, AT ROOM TEMPERATURE

1 TABLESPOON BRANDY SUCH AS CALVADOS OR COGNAC

1 TEASPOON PURE VANILLA EXTRACT

5 LARGE EGGS

1½ CUPS (10½ OUNCES/300 GRAMS) GRANULATED SUGAR

CANDIED CRANBERRY-PINEAPPLE-GINGER TOPPING

⅓ CUP (3½ OUNCES/100 GRAMS) RED CURRANT JELLY

⅓ CUP (2½ FL OUNCES/75 ML) APPLE CIDER

½ CUP (3½ OUNCES/100 GRAMS) GRANULATED SUGAR

1½ CUPS (6 OUNCES/170 GRAMS) FRESH OR THAWED FROZEN CRANBERRIES, PICKED OVER FOR STEMS

⅓ CUP (1¾ OUNCES/50 GRAMS) COARSELY CHOPPED DRIED PINEAPPLE

2 TABLESPOONS FINELY DICED CRYSTALLIZED GINGER

Before baking: To ensure success in making this cake, a stand mixer and 2 bowls are best. If you own only one mixer bowl, transfer the contents to a large bowl after beating the first mixture, wash and dry the bowl, and proceed to whipping the next mixture. Center a rack in the oven and preheat the oven to 350 degrees F. Butter a 9 by 5 by 3-inch loaf pan, then flour it, tapping out the excess flour. Have all of the ingredients at room temperature.

To make the Pound Cake: Sift together the flour and salt onto a sheet of waxed paper; set aside. In the bowl of a stand mixer fitted with the paddle attachment, beat the butter on medium-low speed until creamy, 30 to 45 seconds. Stop the mixer and scrape down the sides of the bowl.

With the mixer on low speed, gradually add the flour-salt mixture. (You might want to wrap a kitchen towel around the back and sides of the mixer bowl, or use a bowl shield to contain the mixture in the bowl, since even the lowest speed might cause the flour to fly out of the bowl.) When all of the flour is added, stop the mixer and scrape down the sides into the center of the bowl. Then, with the mixer on medium speed, beat until the mixture is light, fluffy, and white, 5 to 7 minutes. (As the mixture becomes fluffier, you will hear a slapping sound in the bowl.) Gradually beat in the brandy and vanilla toward the end of beating. Detach the paddle and bowl from the mixer. Scrape the batter from the beater and the sides into the center of the bowl and set the bowl nearby.

Place the eggs and the sugar in another mixer bowl and fit the mixer with the whisk attachment. Whip on medium-high speed until thick and almost tripled in volume, 5 to 8 minutes. Detach the whisk and bowl from the mixer. Add 1 cup (8 fl ounces/240 ml) of the egg foam to the butter-flour mixture, gently whisking it in by hand. Add another cup of the egg foam and again whisk in gently. Then add the remaining sugar-egg mixture and fold it in with a rubber spatula, being careful not to over-mix. If the mixture appears slightly curdled, whisk the entire mixture fairly briskly for about 30 seconds in an attempt to emulsify the batter. Spoon the batter into the prepared pan and spread evenly with the rubber spatula.

Bake the cake until it springs back slightly when lightly touched in the center, a round wooden toothpick inserted in the center comes out free of cake, and the sides begin to pull away from the pan, 55 to 65 minutes. Transfer the pan to a wire rack and let cool for 10 to 15 minutes.

Tilt and rotate the pan while gently tapping it on a counter to release the cake sides. If they don't release, slip a thin metal spatula between the still-warm cake and the pan and run the spatula carefully along the entire perimeter of the pan. Invert a wire rack on top of the cake, invert the cake onto it, and lift off the pan. Invert another rack on top, invert the cake so it is right side up, and remove the original rack. Let the cake cool completely.

If serving the cake within 24 hours, wrap in plastic wrap and store at room temperature. For longer storage, over-wrap with aluminum foil, label with the contents and

date, and freeze for up to 1 month. To thaw, remove the foil and leave at room temperature for about 3 hours. Prepare the topping and serve the cake the same day the topping is made.

To make the Candied Cranberry-Pineapple-Ginger Topping: In a heavy 1 1/2-quart saucepan, melt the jelly over medium-low heat. Stir in the apple cider and cook for about 1 1/2 minutes to reduce some of the moisture. Add the sugar and stir to blend. Cook over medium-low heat until a digital instant-read thermometer registers 240 degrees, about 3 minutes. Remove from the heat, add the cranberries, and stir to coat with the syrup. Return the pan to very low heat and cook gently, stirring occasionally, until the berries are heated through, 1 1/2 to 2 minutes. Don't allow a majority of the cranberries to pop or you will end up with a sauce. Remove from the heat and let cool, stirring occasionally to coat the cran-berries with the syrup, until the mixture is close to room temperature, about 30 minutes. (The cranberries actually poach in the syrup as the mixture cools, which avoids additional cooking that would break down the cranberries into a sauce.)

Pour the cranberry mixture through a sieve set over a medium bowl. Save the syrup, which thickens as it cools, for topping ice cream, waffles, or pancakes or for blend-ing into an orange juice drink. Transfer the cranberries to a large bowl and let cool to room temperature.

Put the pineapple and ginger on top of the cooled cran-berries and, using a rubber spatula, toss the mixture only three times. You want to avoid overmixing, or you will submerge the pineapple and ginger in any syrup that has accumulated in the bottom of the bowl and they will turn red, making them indistinguishable from the cranberries.

Transfer the cake to a serving plate. Spoon the topping onto the top of the cake, attractively mounding it slightly. Using a serrated knife, cut the cake into slices about 3/4 inch thick (1 slice per serving) or about 1/4 inch thick (3 slices per serving). Alternatively, cut the cake as directed and spoon the topping onto each serving.

Chocolate Lover's Angel Food Cake

This is an exceptional angel food cake not only because of its rich chocolate flavor and moist texture, but also for its versatility. It's great for Passover, though you don't have to be Jewish to enjoy this cake, and it is also great for anyone who is looking for a gluten-free cake. This recipe is similar to one in my first book, *The Simple Art of Perfect Baking*. It makes a tall, majestic cake that can easily serve a crowd, and from the raves it has received over the years, I include it for you to enjoy—in the best of health.

To convert the cake to serve at Passover, substitute ¼ cup (1 ounce/30 grams) matzoh cake meal and ¼ cup (1½ ounces/40 grams) potato starch for the cake flour, and replace the cream of tartar with lemon juice. This cake is also delicious served unfrosted, and if well wrapped, it freezes beautifully for up to a month. Thaw at room temperature for at least 3 hours or up to overnight before serving. **YIELD: ONE 10-INCH TUBE CAKE, 20 SERVINGS (3 THIN SLICES PER SERVINGS**

CHOCOLATE ANGEL FOOD CAKE

2 CUPS (16 FL OUNCES/480 ML) EGG WHITES (14 TO 16 LARGE)

1 CUP (3½ OUNCES/100 GRAMS) UNSWEETENED NATURAL OR DUTCH-PROCESSED COCOA POWDER

½ CUP (2¼ OUNCES/65 GRAMS) CAKE FLOUR

2¼ CUPS (SCANT 1 POUND/450 GRAMS) GRANULATED SUGAR, DIVIDED

¼ TEASPOON SALT

1½ TEASPOONS CREAM OF TARTAR

1½ TEASPOONS PURE VANILLA EXTRACT

FROSTING

1¾ CUPS (14 FL OUNCES/420 ML) HEAVY CREAM

2 TABLESPOONS SOUR CREAM OR CRÈME FRAÎCHE

2 TABLESPOONS GRANULATED SUGAR

1½ TEASPOONS PURE VANILLA EXTRACT

ONE 12-OUNCE (340-GRAM) PACKAGE UNSWEETENED LARGE-FLAKE DRIED COCONUT (SEE SOURCES)

Before baking: About 1 hour before making the batter, place the cold egg whites in the bowl of a stand mixer (so that by the time you begin making the cake, the whites will be close to 60 degrees F, slightly below room temperature). Center a rack in the oven and preheat the oven to 325 degrees F. Be organized, as this cake comes together quickly. Have ready a 10 by 4¼-inch tube pan, preferably with a removable bottom, and a long-necked bottle or large heat-resistant funnel for cooling the cake.

To Make the Chocolate Angel Food Cake: Sift together the cocoa powder, flour, 1 cup (7 ounces/200 grams) of the sugar, and the salt onto a sheet of waxed paper; set aside.

Before you begin whipping the egg whites, review the directions on whipping egg whites for angel food cakes on page 000. Fit the stand mixer with the whisk attachment, and whip the egg whites on medium-low speed until foamy. Add the cream of tartar, increase the speed to medium, and whip just until soft peaks form, about 2 minutes. Gradually add the remaining 1¼ cups (8¾ ounces/250 grams) sugar, about 2 tablespoons at a time, and continue whipping until the whites have thickened and formed soft, droopy white peaks, 1 to 1½ minutes. Add the vanilla during the final moments of whipping. The mixture should be fluffy but fluid enough to be pourable.

Detach the whisk and the bowl from the mixer, and tap the whisk against the side of the bowl to free the excess whites. Using a metal icing spatula, sprinkle one-third of the flour mixture over the whites and fold in with a rubber spatula. Repeat with the remaining flour mixture in two additions, using a minimum of strokes to preserve the foam structure and stopping as soon as the mixtures are blended. Gently pour the batter into the tube pan.

Bake the cake until the top is no longer shiny but dull brown and springs back when touched and the sides are beginning to come away from the pan, 55 to 65 minutes. Do not overbake or the cake will be dry. Remove the pan from the oven and immediately invert it over the bottle or funnel. Let cool completely, about 2 hours.

To remove the cake from the pan, slip just the tip of a small metal spatula or paring knife between the cake sides and the pan, and slowly trace the perimeter to release any cake sticking to the pan. Tilt the cake pan on its side, and gently tap the bottom against a counter to loosen the cake further. Rotate the cake pan, tapping it a few more times as you turn it, until it appears free. Invert a rack on top of the cake or top with a cardboard round, and as you invert the cake, tap it firmly on the surface. Lift the pan from the cake. It should come out cleanly and beautifully, like a pillow taken out of a slipcover. Or, if the pan has a removable bottom, when the cake sides are free, push up the bottom to release the cake from the pan.

To store for another time, place unfrosted cake in a sturdy, deep covered plastic container, label the contents and date, and freeze for up to 1 month. To thaw, remove from the container and leave at room temperature for about 3 hours.

To make the frosting: In the bowl of the stand mixer fitted with the whisk attachment, combine the cream, sour cream, sugar, and vanilla and whip on medium-low speed until soft peaks form.

Place the cake on a sturdy cardboard round, or place it on a cake plate and slip about 3 strips of waxed paper under the cake to protect the plate. (A decorator's turntable is helpful when frosting the cake. If using the turntable, place the cake on its cardboard round on the platform and frost as directed.) Using a flexible metal icing spatula, frost the top and sides of the cake. Remove the waxed-paper strips, if used. If using the cardboard round, place the coconut on a rimmed baking sheet. Hold the cake on its cardboard base directly over the coconut. Tilt the cake slightly, and sprinkle the large coconut flakes all over the entire cake to cover. With the cake still slightly tilted, gently press the coconut into the cream with your free hand, and then put the cake on another baking sheet. If the cake is on a plate, sprinkle the coconut over the cake, covering it as completely as possible with the coconut, and then gently press the coconut into the cream. Cover the cake very loosely with plastic wrap, and refrigerate for a few hours (the coconut flakes will soften) before serving. Remove the cake from the refrigerator 1 hour before serving. To serve, cut into thin slices with a serrated knife using a sawing motion.

Ultimate Cappuccino Cheesecake

This espresso-infused sour cream cheesecake, topped with a whisper of cocoa powder and cinnamon, is the perfect choice when you've volunteered to bring dessert to a dinner party. Echoing the sophisticated flavors and festive layers of a cappuccino, the cake calls for a crust made from zwieback crumbs, whose subtle, not-too-sweet taste blends particularly well with other flavors. Zwieback toasts are typically found in the baby-food section of the supermarket.

YIELD: ONE 9-INCH ROUND CHEESECAKE, 14 SERVINGS

CRUMB CRUST

12 (3 ½ OUNCES/100 GRAMS) ZWIEBACK TOASTS (1 PACKAGE FROM THE BOX)

2 TABLESPOONS GRANULATED SUGAR

2 ½ OUNCES (5 TABLESPOONS/70 GRAMS) UNSALTED BUTTER, MELTED

CAPPUCCINO CHEESECAKE

4 TEASPOONS INSTANT ESPRESSO POWDER

2 TEASPOONS PURE VANILLA EXTRACT

2 CUPS (1 POUND/455 GRAMS) SOUR CREAM

1 ½ POUNDS (THREE 8-OUNCE/225-GRAM PACKAGES) CREAM CHEESE, AT ROOM TEMPERATURE

1 ½ CUPS (10 ½ OUNCES/300 GRAMS) GRANULATED SUGAR

6 LARGE EGGS, LIGHTLY BEATEN

2 OUNCES (85 GRAMS) SEMISWEET CHOCOLATE, FINELY GRATED TO YIELD ½ CUP

1 TABLESPOON UNSWEETENED NATURAL OR DUTCH-PROCESSED COCOA POWDER

½ TEASPOON GROUND CINNAMON

Before baking: Center a rack in the oven and preheat the oven to 300 degrees F. Have ready a 9-inch round springform pan with 2 ¾- or 3-inch sides. Have all of the cheesecake ingredients at room temperature.

To make the Crumb Crust: Break the zwieback into pieces and place in a food processor. Add the sugar and process to fine crumbs. Transfer to a medium bowl. Pour the butter over the mixture and toss until thoroughly coated and crumbly. Pour into the springform pan, and use your fingertips to press the crumbs evenly over the bottom. Refrigerate the crust.

To make the Cappuccino Cheesecake: In a small bowl, stir the espresso powder and vanilla into the sour cream; set aside. In the bowl of a stand mixer fitted with the paddle attachment, beat the cream cheese on the lowest speed just until smooth. Stop the mixer as needed to scrape down the sides of the bowl. Maintaining the same speed, add the sugar and beat until the mixture is completely smooth, stopping the mixer as needed to scrape down the sides of the bowl.

With the mixer on low speed, add the eggs, 3 to 4 tablespoons at a time, beating after each addition until incorporated and stopping the mixer to scrape down the sides of the bowl once or twice. Add the sour cream mixture and beat just until blended.

Pour a little more than half of the filling (4 cups/ 32 fl ounces/960 ml) onto the crumb crust in the springform pan. Transfer about 1 cup (8 fl ounces/240 ml) of the remaining batter to a small bowl and stir in the chocolate. Slowly pour the chocolate-studded filling over the filling in the pan, and spread as evenly as possible with a rubber spatula. Slowly pour the remaining batter on top, spreading it evenly and thinly over the chocolate layer to cover.

Bake the cheesecake until it still quivers slightly in the center when the pan is gently tapped, about 1 hour. Turn off the oven and leave the cheesecake in the oven for an additional 2 hours (the cheesecake will become firmer with no cracks). Transfer the pan to a wire rack and let cool to room temperature, about 2 hours. Cover the pan and refrigerate for several hours or up to overnight.

Remove the cheesecake from the refrigerator and sprinkle the cocoa powder and cinnamon randomly over the top. Slowly release the springform clasp and carefully remove the sides. If any portion of the cheesecake sticks to the sides, use a small metal spatula to separate it. You don't need to remove the cheesecake from the metal base.

To serve, cut the cold cheesecake into wedges with a sharp, thin-bladed knife, dipping the knife blade in hot water and wiping it dry with a towel before each cut. Or, use a long piece of dental floss to cut across the cake cleanly and easily.

Blackberry-Blueberry Chiffon Cream Pie

This majestic dessert evokes the summery pleasure of fresh berries and sweet cream. Whole blueberries and blackberries are gently folded into the filling to provide a refreshing burst of fruit flavor in every bite. The spicy gingersnap crust made with macadamia nuts is a crunchy counterpoint to the ethereal chiffon filling. Although this lofty dessert looks delicate, it's definitely sturdy enough to bring it to your next girls'-night-out get-together or to an alfresco dinner with a few friends on a warm summer evening. Gelatin is used judiciously in the filling to support the delicate, airy framework.

Note: Because this recipe uses uncooked eggs, it carries a risk of salmonella. Be sure to use clean, uncracked eggs. Unless you can find pasteurized eggs, I would not recommend this recipe for the elderly, the very young, the chronically ill, pregnant women, or others with a weakened immune system.   **YIELD: ONE 9-INCH PIE, 8 SERVINGS**

GINGERSNAP CRUMB CRUST

20 (5 OUNCES/140 GRAMS) STORE-BOUGHT GINGERSNAP COOKIES SUCH AS NABISCO BRAND

⅓ CUP (1½ OUNCES/40 GRAMS) SALTED OR UNSALTED MACADAMIA NUTS

1 TABLESPOON GRANULATED SUGAR

2 OUNCES (½ STICK/55 GRAMS) UNSALTED BUTTER, MELTED

BLACKBERRY-BLUEBERRY FILLING

1 CUP (8 FL OUNCES/240 ML) HEAVY CREAM

¾ CUP PLUS 1 TABLESPOON (5¾ OUNCES/165 GRAMS) GRANULATED SUGAR

⅔ CUP (4 OUNCES/115 GRAMS) BLACKBERRIES, PICKED OVER FOR STEMS, DIVIDED

⅔ CUP (4 OUNCES/115 GRAMS) BLUEBERRIES, PICKED OVER FOR STEMS, DIVIDED

2 TEASPOONS UNFLAVORED POWDERED GELATIN

3 TABLESPOONS WATER

3 LARGE EGGS, SEPARATED

½ CUP (4 FL OUNCES/120 ML) STRAINED FRESH ORANGE JUICE

1 TABLESPOON STRAINED FRESH LEMON JUICE

2 TEASPOONS FINELY GRATED LEMON ZEST

1 TEASPOON FINELY GRATED ORANGE ZEST

PINCH OF SALT

BERRY GARNISH

¼ CUP (1½ OUNCES/40 GRAMS) BLACKBERRIES, PICKED OVER FOR STEMS, AT ROOM TEMPERATURE

¼ CUP (1½ OUNCES/40 GRAMS) BLUEBERRIES, PICKED OVER FOR STEMS, AT ROOM TEMPERATURE

2 TABLESPOONS RED CURRANT JELLY

Before baking: Center a rack in the oven and preheat the oven to 350 degrees F. Lightly coat a 9-inch glass pie dish with nonstick spray or vegetable oil.

To make the crust: Break the gingersnaps into pieces and place them in a food processor. Add the macadamia nuts and sugar and process until fine crumbs form to yield 1¾ cups. Transfer to a medium bowl. Pour the butter over the mixture and toss until thoroughly coated and crumbly. Pour into the prepared pie dish, and use your fingertips to press the crumbs firmly and evenly over the bottom and up the sides of the dish.

Bake for 10 minutes only. The crust will be soft when lightly touched with a fingertip, but it will firm as it cools. Transfer to a wire rack and let cool completely.

To make the Blackberry-Blueberry Filling: Before you can assemble the filling, you must ready some of the components. Using a whisk or a handheld mixer, whip together the cream and 2 tablespoons of the sugar in a deep, medium bowl until soft peaks form. Cover and refrigerate. Place ⅓ cup (2 ounces/55 grams) each of the blackberries and blueberries in a small bowl; set aside. Place the remaining blackberries and blueberries in a small food processor or a blender and process until a smooth puree forms. Strain the puree through a fine-mesh sieve into a small bowl, pressing on the seeds with the back of a spoon or a rubber spatula. Discard the contents of the sieve, and set the puree aside. You should have about 6 tablespoons (3 fl ounces/75 ml). Half fill a large bowl with ice cubes and water to create an ice-water bath for cooling the filling; set aside. In a small bowl, sprinkle the gelatin over the 3 tablespoons water and set aside for at least 5 minutes to soften.

Place the egg whites in a small, deep bowl; set aside. Select a medium stainless-steel bowl that fits snugly and securely over a saucepan, and fill the pan one-fourth full of water. Place the egg yolks, scant ¼ cup (2 ounces/55 grams) of the remaining sugar, the orange and lemon juices and zests, and the salt in the bowl. Whisk to combine. Bring the water just to a gentle simmer, set the bowl over the saucepan, and continue to whisk until the mixture registers 170 degrees F on an instant-read thermometer. Remove from the heat and whisk the gelatin into the mixture until it has dissolved. Whisk in the fruit puree until thoroughly blended.

Set the bowl over the ice-water bath and stir the mixture frequently until it is slightly thickened and feels cooler than body temperature, 65 to 70 degrees F, when tested with your finger. This step will take roughly 10 to 12 minutes. Remove the bowl from the ice-water bath and set it aside at room temperature.

Proceed right away to whip the egg whites by hand with the whisk or the handheld mixer until they form soft peaks. Gradually add the remaining 3 tablespoons sugar and continue to whip until the whites are glossy and thick. Using a spatula, fold the reserved blackberries and blueberries into the egg yolk mixture. Without delay, fold in half of the egg whites, followed by half of the whipped cream until incorporated. Then fold in the remaining egg whites and whipped cream at the same time.

Gently pour the filling into the crumb crust, mounding it in the center. Refrigerate until the filling is set, about 3 hours. Then place plastic wrap directly on the surface of the filling, and keep the pie refrigerated for up to 30 minutes before serving. The pie can be prepared 1 day in advance.

To make the Berry Garnish: About 30 minutes before serving, place the berries in a large bowl. In a small, heavy saucepan, heat the jelly over low heat, stirring occasionally, until liquefied and no warmer than body temperature. Pour the jelly next to the berries in the bowl, gently slide a rubber spatula under the berries, and fold the fruit and jelly together. Repeat folding about three more times, or until the berries are lightly glazed by the jelly. Carefully scoop out the berries with a fork or spoon and arrange them over the top of the pie.

To serve, cut the pie into wedges with a sharp knife.

Minced-Fruit Strudel

Celebrate the bounty of autumn orchards any time of the year with this heartwarming fruit strudel. The fabulous filling, enriched with a cornucopia of dried and fresh fruits, is adapted from a recipe in *The Wine Lover's Dessert Cookbook*, written by fellow food buddies Mary Cech and Jennie Schacht. Not to be confused with its labor-intensive Austrian cousins, this dessert is really a strudel in name and shape only, relying on a baker-friendly cream cheese pastry dough that bakes up extra flaky. **YIELD: ONE 13-INCH-LONG STRUDEL, 8 SERVINGS**

½ RECIPE (11 OUNCES/310 GRAMS) FLAKY STRUDEL PASTRY (PAGE 364)

MINCED DRIED FRUIT FILLING

1½ CUPS (12 FL OUNCES/360 ML) FRESH ORANGE JUICE

¼ CUP (2 FL OUNCES/30 ML) WATER

3 TABLESPOONS GRANULATED SUGAR

2 TABLESPOONS ORANGE MARMALADE

8 DRIED FIGS (7½ OUNCES/215 GRAMS), CHOPPED SMALL TO YIELD ABOUT 1 CUP PLUS 2 TABLESPOONS

8 DRIED APRICOTS (3 OUNCES/85 GRAMS), CHOPPED SMALL TO YIELD ABOUT ½ CUP

⅓ CUP (2 OUNCES/55 GRAMS) DRIED CHERRIES, CHOPPED SMALL TO YIELD ABOUT ⅓ CUP

1 CUP (ABOUT 5 OUNCES/140 GRAMS) GOLDEN RAISINS, CHOPPED SMALL TO YIELD ABOUT 1 CUP

1 MEDIUM (8-OUNCE/225-GRAM) GOLDEN DELICIOUS APPLE, HALVED, CORED, AND CHOPPED SMALL TO YIELD ABOUT 1½ CUPS (7 OUNCES/200 GRAMS)

½ TEASPOON GROUND CINNAMON

3 OUNCES (85 GRAMS) ARTISANAL ITALIAN, FRENCH, OR SOURDOUGH BÂTARD OR BAGUETTE

2 OUNCES (½ STICK/55 GRAMS) SALTED BUTTER

1 TABLESPOON UNSALTED BUTTER, MELTED

1 TABLESPOON ALL-PURPOSE FLOUR

To prepare the pastry: On a lightly floured work surface, roll out the pastry into a 13 by 8-inch rectangle. Fold the dough into thirds like a business letter: working from a short end, lift one-third up over the center and then fold the top third down to cover. Rotate the dough 90 degrees, and repeat the rolling, this time into a 12 by 7-inch rectangle, and folding into thirds. Wrap in plastic and refrigerate until cold and firm, about 3 hours.

To make the Minced Dried Fruit Filling: In a medium saucepan, combine the orange juice, water, sugar, and marmalade over medium heat and bring to a boil. Add the dried figs, apricots, cherries, raisins, apple, and cinnamon and simmer gently, stirring occasionally, just until the apple pieces are tender, about 5 minutes. Remove from the heat and let cool to room temperature. You should have 1 quart (32 fl ounces/960 ml). You will need 1½ cups (12 fl ounces/360 ml) for this recipe. Freeze the remainder (pack it into 1-cup containers for convenience) for up to 1 month.

Before baking: Center a rack in the oven and preheat the oven to 375 degrees F. Line a rimmed baking sheet with parchment paper; set aside.

To assemble the strudel: Place the 1½ cups minced dried fruit filling in a sieve placed over a small bowl and let drain for about 15 minutes.

Pulse the bread in a food processor to produce coarse crumbs. In a 10-inch skillet, melt the salted butter over medium heat. Add the bread crumbs and toss just until golden. Remove from the heat and set aside to cool.

In a medium bowl, toss the drained fruit filling with the melted unsalted butter. Sprinkle the flour over the top and, using a rubber spatula, fold it in gently just until incorporated.

On a lightly floured work surface, roll out the pastry into a 13 by 8-inch rectangle. Spoon the filling lengthwise down the center of the pastry in a strip about 3 inches wide, leaving a 1-inch border uncovered on each short end. Sprinkle the butter bread crumbs over the filling. Fold each short end of the pastry over the filling, creating a 1-inch flap. Fold 1 uncovered long side over the filling, creating a flap about 2 1/2 inches wide. Then fold the other uncovered side over the filling, overlapping the first flap by about 3 inches. Press to seal. With both hands, gently lift the strudel and transfer it, seam side down, onto the prepared baking sheet. Using the tip of a paring knife, score the top of the strudel in a simple pattern of intersecting lines to form Xs. Cut 2 small holes in the top with the tip of the knife to allow steam to escape during baking.

Bake the strudel, rotating the baking sheet 180 degrees at the midpoint to ensure even baking, until golden, 35 to 40 minutes. (Some of the butter might melt from the pastry toward the end of baking, but it will remain within the rimmed pan. A small amount of butter leaking from the pastry doesn't affect the pastry.) Transfer the pan to a wire rack and let cool for about 15 minutes. Using a large metal spatula, carefully transfer the strudel to the rack and let cool almost completely before serving.

To serve, using a serrated knife, cut the strudel crosswise into 2- to 2 1/2-inch-wide slices. Serve warm or at room temperature. Lightly cover any leftover strudel with waxed paper and store at room temperature. Although the pastry is not as crisp the second day, it is still quite delicious.

Farmers' Market Fresh

BAKING HAS COME A LONG WAY in the last one hundred years. Recipes, techniques, and equipment have evolved to the point that anyone can turn out a luscious masterpiece. The availability of ingredients has changed, too.

A century ago, home baking was limited by the calendar and by where you lived. In fall you baked apple pies, in spring you made strawberry tarts, and summertime cobblers were peachy keen with that season's fruit. In one way, the newfound popularity of farmers' markets has taken us back to those days. Cooks and bakers look for fruits and vegetables that are ripe, fragrant, and full of flavor, but most of all they seek a connection to the people who work so hard to bring us great produce.

Fresh fruit is nature personified, and there is something about it that is a mood elevator for me. Maybe it's because there is so much tactile sensation working with fruit. By trimming, peeling, or—best of all—handpicking fresh fruit, I am inspired—not to gild the lily, but to unlock and develop the magnificent natural flavors.

Summer is prime time for fruit desserts. That's when I make the intriguing Golden Blueberry Cake—the berries end up on the bottom, not the top—or the luscious Double-Crust White Peach–Polenta Tart with Sweetened Crème Fraîche. In fall, I serve decadent Brown Butter Pear Tart or earthy Open-Faced Apple Galette with Quince Paste. Spring is when whimsical 24-Karat Cupcakes with Orange Cream Cheese Icing or Warm Mixed Cherry Clafouti shines as a seasonal showstopper.

At one time, I shied away from cooking fruit. It's already so colorful and flavorful, what could I do to improve on it? But what convinced me to set aside my reservations was when I realized that cooking intensifies the flavor. Now I know that I'm not interfering with pure flavors. Instead, I'm distilling their essence.

Top-of-the-Crop Blackberry-Ginger Pie

Fresh summer blackberries lend their vibrant color and signature sweet-tart flavor to this dessert, enlivened with just the right amount of spicy crystallized ginger. To showcase the stunning purple berries, use cookie cutters to form decorative pastry shapes for the top crust. Finish the dessert with a festive sprinkling of lavender flowers. **YIELD: ONE 9-INCH PIE, 8 SERVINGS**

½ RECIPE (TWO 10-OUNCE/280-GRAM DISKS) FOUR PIE CRUSTS AT ONE TIME (PAGE 357)

FILLING

4 TEASPOONS QUICK-COOKING (INSTANT) TAPIOCA

4 TEASPOONS WATER OR FRESH ORANGE JUICE

6 CUPS (ABOUT 1½ POUNDS/680 GRAMS) BLACKBERRIES, PICKED OVER FOR STEMS

¾ CUP PLUS 2 TABLESPOONS (6¼ OUNCES/175 GRAMS) GRANULATED SUGAR

3 TABLESPOONS CORNSTARCH

2 TEASPOONS FINELY MINCED CRYSTALLIZED GINGER

⅛ TEASPOON NUTMEG, PREFERABLY FRESHLY GRATED

⅛ TEASPOON SALT

2 TABLESPOONS UNSALTED BUTTER, MELTED AND COOLED

1 TABLESPOON FRESH LEMON JUICE

DECORATION

1 TABLESPOON GRANULATED SUGAR

¼ CUP (SCANT ¼ OUNCE/5 GRAMS) PESTICIDE-FREE DRIED LAVENDER FLOWERS (SEE SOURCES)

Before baking: Center a rack in the oven and preheat the oven to 425 degrees F. Have ready a 9-inch glass pie dish.

To line the pie dish with pastry: Following the directions on page 27 for rolling out pie pastry, roll out 1 pastry disk into an 11½-inch circle about ⅛ inch thick, loosely roll up the pastry around the rolling pin, and then unroll it, top side down, onto a baking sheet. Cover with a sheet of plastic wrap and refrigerate until it is time to decorate the top of the pie.

Roll out the remaining disk into an 11½-inch circle the same way. Following the directions on page 27 for lining a pie dish, transfer the pastry circle to the pie dish, flute the edges of the pastry, and freeze just to firm the dough, 10 to 20 minutes.

Following the directions for blind baking a pie crust on page 28, partially bake the pie crust for 25 to 30 minutes. Transfer to a wire rack and let cool completely before filling. Leave the oven on at 375 degrees F.

To make the filling: In a small bowl, scatter the tapioca over the water and set aside to soften for about 10 minutes. Place the blackberries in a large bowl. In a small bowl, whisk together the sugar, cornstarch, ginger, nutmeg, and salt. Sprinkle the sugar mixture over the berries and toss to coat the berries evenly. Then add the tapioca mixture and toss gently to coat evenly. Pour the butter and lemon juice over the berries and toss again just to blend evenly. Let the mixture stand for about 10 minutes to allow the tapioca time to absorb some of the berry juices. Using a rubber spatula, guide the berry filling from the bowl into the cooled pie crust.

Remove the circle of pastry from the refrigerator. Using a 3⅛-inch four-leaf cutter (or a 3⅛- to 3⅜-inch scalloped round cutter), cut out 7 shapes from the pastry. Using a metal spatula (to preserve the shape of the pastry as you move it), transfer 1 cutout to the top of the filling, placing it near the edge of the crust. Repeat with 5 more cutouts, spacing them ¼ to ½ inch apart to form a ring around the filling. Place the final cutout in the center. Lightly brush each pastry cutout with water, and then sprinkle with the sugar and lavender for decoration.

Bake the pie until the filling juices are bubbling and the pastry is golden brown, 20 to 25 minutes. Transfer to a wire rack to cool. Serve warm or at room temperature.

Warm Mixed Cherry Clafouti

Clafouti pronounced (kla-foo-TEE) is a homey French dessert that originated in the Limousin region of central France. It is essentially a sweet custard batter similar to a crepe batter (eggs, milk, and flour) poured over a layer of fresh fruit. Its texture is a cross between a cake and a pudding, and it naturally deflates just a bit as it cools. The amount of sugar depends on the sweetness of the fruit (in this case a variety of sweet cherries), so always taste the fruit first to determine how much to add. A *clafouti* takes only minutes to prepare, making it a good choice for spur-of-the-moment get-togethers. It also means that it can bake and cool while you are eating dinner, so you can enjoy a warm dessert when you finish. In the fall, substitute sliced prune plums or a seasonal mélange of plums and halved seedless grapes for the cherries.

YIELD: ONE 9-INCH ROUND DESSERT, 6 TO 8 SERVINGS

FOR THE PAN

1 TABLESPOON UNSALTED BUTTER, SOFTENED

2 TABLESPOONS POWDERED SUGAR

1 TABLESPOON GRANULATED SUGAR

BATTER

2 CUPS (8 TO 10 OUNCES/225 TO 280 GRAMS) MIXED BING AND RAINIER CHERRIES OR OTHER SWEET VARIETY, STEMMED, PITTED, AND LEFT WHOLE

1½ CUPS (12 FL OUNCES/360 ML) HALF-AND-HALF

4 LARGE EGGS

6 TABLESPOONS (1¾ OUNCES/50 GRAMS) ALL-PURPOSE FLOUR

2½ OUNCES (½ STICK PLUS 1 TABLESPOON/70 GRAMS) UNSALTED BUTTER, MELTED AND COOLED

¼ CUP (1¾ OUNCES/50 GRAMS) GRANULATED SUGAR

2 TABLESPOONS NATURAL OR BLANCHED SLICED ALMONDS

1 TABLESPOON HONEY

1 TABLESPOON KIRSCH (OPTIONAL)

2 TEASPOONS PURE VANILLA EXTRACT

⅛ TEASPOON SALT

2 TABLESPOONS POWDERED SUGAR

1 PINT PREMIUM ALMOND OR VANILLA ICE CREAM OR 1 CUP (8 OUNCES/225 GRAMS) CRÈME FRAÎCHE

Before baking: Center a rack in the oven and preheat the oven to 400 degrees F. To prepare the pan, generously rub the butter over the bottom and sides of a 9-inch glass pie dish or a 4-cup ceramic dish. Dust it with the powdered sugar and then the granulated sugar, tapping out the excess sugar.

To make the batter: Arrange the cherries over the bottom of the prepared pie dish. In a blender or food processor, combine the half-and-half, eggs, flour, butter, granulated sugar, almonds, honey, kirsch (if using), vanilla, and salt and process until a creamy, smooth batter forms. Slowly pour the batter evenly over the fruit.

Bake the *clafouti* until the custard is golden brown around the edges and puffy yet firm in the middle, 23 to 26 minutes. Transfer to a wire rack and, without delay (it deflates as it cools), dust the top with the powdered sugar. Serve warm or at room temperature accompanied with ice cream.

Golden Blueberry Cake

This is a great cake—great flavor and great for using up the egg yolks left over from making an angel food cake (page 208), financiers (page 252), a white cake (page 346), a meringue buttercream (page 329), or a Pavlova (page 265). During baking, the blueberries float to the bottom of the pan, creating an interesting effect: half of the cake with blueberries and the other half a plain yellow cake. **YIELD: ONE 10-INCH ROUND TUBE CAKE, 18 TO 20 SERVINGS (3 THIN SLICES PER SERVING)**

2½ CUPS PLUS 1 TABLESPOON (10½ OUNCES/300 GRAMS) CAKE FLOUR

2 TEASPOONS BAKING POWDER

½ TEASPOON SALT

¾ CUP (6 FL OUNCES/180 ML) WHOLE MILK

1 TEASPOON PURE VANILLA EXTRACT

½ TEASPOON PURE ALMOND EXTRACT

8 OUNCES (2 STICKS/225 GRAMS) UNSALTED BUTTER, AT ROOM TEMPERATURE

2 CUPS (14 OUNCES/400 GRAMS) GRANULATED SUGAR

8 LARGE (⅔ CUP/5½ FL OUNCES/165 ML) EGG YOLKS

1½ CUPS (ABOUT 8 OUNCES/225 GRAMS) BLUEBERRIES, PICKED OVER FOR STEMS

3 TABLESPOONS POWDERED SUGAR

Before baking: Center a rack in the oven and preheat the oven to 350 degrees F. Butter and flour a 10 by 4¼-inch tube pan with or without a removable bottom. Have all of the ingredients at room temperature.

Sift together the flour, baking powder, and salt onto a sheet of waxed paper; set aside. Pour the milk into a glass measuring cup, and add the vanilla and almond extracts; set aside. In the bowl of a stand mixer fitted with the paddle attachment, beat the butter on medium speed until creamy and smooth, 30 to 45 seconds. Stop the mixer and scrape down the sides of the bowl. On medium speed, add the sugar in a steady stream and continue to beat until the mixture is white and fluffy, 3 to 4 minutes. Stop the mixer as needed to scrape down the sides of the bowl.

With the mixer on medium speed, add the egg yolks, one at a time, beating after each addition until incorporated. On the lowest speed, add the flour mixture in three additions alternately with the milk mixture in two additions, beginning and ending with the flour mixture and mixing after each addition until incorporated. Stop the mixer occasionally to scrape down the sides of the bowl. Spoon one-third of the batter into the pan, spreading evenly with a rubber spatula. Using the spatula, fold the blueberries into the remaining batter. Then spoon the blueberry batter over the batter in the pan, again spreading evenly.

Bake the cake until it springs back when lightly touched in the center, a round wooden toothpick inserted in the center comes out free of cake, and the sides are beginning to come away from the pan, 60 to 65 minutes. Transfer to a wire rack and let cool in the pan for 10 minutes.

Tilt and rotate the pan while gently tapping it on a counter to release the cake sides. Invert a wire rack on top of the cake, invert the cake onto it, and carefully lift off the pan. Let the cake cool completely.

If serving the cake within 24 hours, wrap in plastic wrap and store it at room temperature. For longer storage, overwrap with aluminum foil, label with the contents and date, and freeze for up to 2 weeks. To thaw, remove the foil and leave at room temperature for 3 to 4 hours.

To serve, sprinkle the top of the cake lightly with powdered sugar and cut the cake into thin slices with a sharp knife.

Rhubarb-Cherry-Raspberry Crumb Pie

Every year around Father's Day, three of my favorite fruits—rhubarb, cherries, and raspberries—are in the market. But the window is short, so in celebration of the availability of these red fruits, I make this crumb pie. Adding cream to the fruit filling rounds out the tart flavors and aids in creating a delicious bubbly sauce when the pie is finished baking. In fact, I leave the cherries whole after pitting them so they trap the juicy liquid. I like to sprinkle the streusel topping in a ring around the perimeter of the filling, leaving the wide, colorful center open to be admired on its own.

Any combination of fresh fruits can be used to fill this 9-inch pie, as long as you begin with a total of 6½ to 7½ cups. (The fruit shrinks in volume during baking, so you need to start with a large amount and mound it in the pie dish.) You can also bake the pie in a deep-dish pie dish if you own one. But because it is deeper (2 inches) than a traditional 9-inch pie dish (1½ inches), you will need to increase the fruit to 1½ times the amount used here. If deep-dish glass pie dishes are scarce in the cookware stores where you live, look for them in antique shops and at yard or garage sales.   **YIELD: ONE 9-INCH PIE, 8 SERVINGS**

STREUSEL

¼ CUP (1¾ OUNCES/50 GRAMS) FIRMLY PACKED LIGHT
   BROWN SUGAR

¼ CUP (1¾ OUNCES/50 GRAMS) GRANULATED SUGAR

½ CUP (2¼ OUNCES/65 GRAMS) ALL-PURPOSE FLOUR

2 OUNCES (½ STICK/55 GRAMS) UNSALTED BUTTER, AT ROOM
   TEMPERATURE, CUT INTO 4 EQUAL PIECES

¼ TEASPOON SALT

1 RECIPE SINGLE-CRUST FLAKY PIE PASTRY (PAGE 354)

FRUIT FILLING

4 TEASPOONS QUICK-COOKING (INSTANT) TAPIOCA

4 TEASPOONS WATER OR FRESH ORANGE JUICE

1 CUP (7 OUNCES/200 GRAMS) GRANULATED SUGAR

3 TABLESPOONS CORNSTARCH

PINCH OF SALT

1 POUND (455 GRAMS) MEDIUM RHUBARB STALKS (6 OR 7),
   TRIMMED AND CUT INTO ½-INCH SLICES TO YIELD
   3½ CUPS (15 OUNCES/430 GRAMS)

2 CUPS (11 OUNCES/310 GRAMS) SWEET CHERRIES,
   PREFERABLY BING, STEMMED, PITTED, AND LEFT WHOLE

3 TABLESPOONS HEAVY CREAM

½ TEASPOON PURE ALMOND EXTRACT

2 CUPS (10 OUNCES/280 GRAMS) RED RASPBERRIES, PICKED
   OVER FOR STEMS

To make the streusel: In a small bowl, blend the sugars together with your fingertips, breaking up any lumps. Add the flour and mix to combine. Scatter the butter pieces over the sugar mixture. With your fingertips, blend in the butter until the mixture forms into small, irregular, crumbly clumps. If using right away; set aside. Or, transfer to an airtight container and refrigerate for up to 1 week or freeze for up to 1 month.

Before baking: Center a rack in the oven and preheat the oven to 425 degrees F. Have ready a 9-inch glass pie dish.

To line the pie dish: Following the directions on page 27, roll out the pastry into a 13-inch circle ⅛ to ³⁄₁₆ inch thick, transfer the pastry circle to the pie dish, flute the edges of the pastry, and refrigerate while preparing the filling.

To make the Fruit Filling: In a small bowl, scatter the tapioca over the water and set aside to soften for about 10 minutes. In a large bowl, whisk together the sugar, cornstarch, and salt. Add the rhubarb and cherries and toss to coat evenly with the sugar mixture. Add the cream and almond extract to the tapioca mixture, pour over the fruit, and toss just until the fruit is coated with the mixture. Let the mixture stand for about 10 minutes, gently tossing occasionally, to allow the thickeners (tapioca and cornstarch) to blend with the juices the sugar extracts from the fruit. (This process is known as sweating.) Sprinkle the raspberries on top and, using a rubber spatula, gently fold them into the mixture using only 3 or 4 strokes to avoid crushing them too much. Using the rubber spatula, guide the filling from the bowl into the pie crust.

Sprinkle the streusel in a 3-inch-wide border around the edge of the pie, leaving a 5-inch center portion of the filling uncovered.

Place the pan on a rimmed baking sheet (or 12-inch pizza pan) to catch any fruit juices that might overflow during baking. Bake for 10 minutes, then reduce the heat to 375 degrees F and continue to bake until the juices are bubbling and the crust is golden brown, 45 to 50 minutes longer. Transfer to a wire rack to cool. As the pie cools, the fruit juices will thicken, so the warmer the pie when served, the thinner the juices will be.

Serve the pie warm or at room temperature. For the best flavor, serve it the same day it is baked.

Double-Crust White Peach–Polenta Tart with Sweetened Crème Fraîche

There's nothing quite like ripe white (or yellow) peaches for eating out of hand, but heat them and their flavor intensifies. For this tart, you poach the peaches in white wine, sugar, cinnamon, and vanilla for an aromatic touch. The polenta in the pastry adds an unexpected sweet crunch, as does the raw sugar sprinkled on the top crust before baking. The pastry drapes the fruit as it bakes, capturing the peaches' beautiful curves.

Poach the fruit ahead so both the fruit and the pastry finish baking at same time. Poaching also releases some of the peaches' moisture, so that they don't exude as much juice during baking and make the pastry soggy. To intensify the taste of the peaches, they are cooled in the flavored poaching syrup. Basil, lemon balm, lemongrass, and mint are ideal choices in the summer, while sturdier flavorings, such as cinnamon, cloves, rosemary, aniseeds (not to be mistaken for fennel seeds), and star anise, are perfect selections in the fall (this recipe uses fall flavorings).

When freestone nectarines are in season, you can substitute them for the peaches. The skin of nectarines is thinner and more tender than peach skin, so there's no need to peel them.

YIELD: ONE 9½-INCH ROUND TART, 8 SERVINGS

FRUIT

6 MEDIUM (1¾ TO 2 POUNDS/800 TO 910 GRAMS) FIRM BUT RIPE WHITE OR YELLOW PEACHES

4 CUPS (1¾ POUNDS/800 GRAMS) GRANULATED SUGAR

2 CUPS (16 FL OUNCES/480 ML) WATER

2 CUPS (16 FL OUNCES/480 ML) WHITE WINE SUCH AS CHENIN BLANC OR SAUVIGNON BLANC OR WATER

1 CINNAMON STICK, 3 INCHES LONG

1 PIECE VANILLA BEAN, 3 INCHES LONG

5 BLACK PEPPERCORNS

3 WHOLE CLOVES

¾ TEASPOON ANISEEDS

CORNMEAL (POLENTA) PASTRY

2¼ CUPS (10¼ OUNCES/290 GRAMS) ALL-PURPOSE FLOUR

¾ CUP (5¼ OUNCES/150 GRAMS) GRANULATED SUGAR

⅔ CUP (3½ OUNCES/100 GRAMS) YELLOW CORNMEAL OR POLENTA

¾ TEASPOON SALT

8 OUNCES (2 STICKS/225 GRAMS) UNSALTED BUTTER, AT ROOM TEMPERATURE, CUT INTO ¼-INCH SLICES

3 LARGE (¼ CUP/2 FL OUNCES/60 ML) EGG YOLKS

RAW SUGAR, PEARL SUGAR, OR GRANULATED SUGAR FOR SPRINKLING

1 TABLESPOON GRANULATED SUGAR

1 CUP (8 OUNCES/225 GRAMS) CRÈME FRAÎCHE

To poach the fruit: To peel the peaches, score an X in the blossom end of each peach. Have ready a large bowl of ice water. Fill a medium saucepan two-thirds full of water and bring to a boil. Add 2 or 3 peaches and blanch for 1 minute. Using a sieve or a slotted spoon, scoop out the peaches and place them in the ice water. Using a paring knife, peel the peaches and then return them to the ice water for 1 minute. (This retards oxidation, which causes the flesh to darken.) Transfer to a large platter lined with paper toweling. Repeat with the remaining peaches. Cut all of the peaches in half lengthwise and pit them.

In a 2 1/2-quart saucepan, combine the sugar, water, wine, cinnamon stick, vanilla bean, peppercorns, cloves, and aniseeds and place over medium heat. Bring just to a boil, stirring to dissolve the sugar. Reduce the heat to medium-low to low and add the peaches. Place a couple of paper towels on top of the peaches to submerge the fruit completely in the syrup to keep it from discoloring. Cook at a slow simmer, turning the peaches occasionally so they cook evenly, for 7 to 20 minutes (the cooking time varies with the size, ripeness, and variety of the peaches). The fruit should just be tender when pierced with the point of a paring knife but still have some resistance.

Remove the pan from the heat and let the peaches cool in the syrup for 30 to 60 minutes. Using a slotted spoon, transfer the peaches to a storage container, and then add just enough of the syrup to cover the fruit. Cover and refrigerate until it is time to assemble the tart. Pour the remaining syrup through a fine-mesh sieve into a sturdy storage container, cover tightly, label with the contents and date, and freeze for another time. It will keep for up to 1 month.

Before baking: Center a rack in the oven and preheat the oven to 375 degrees F.

To make the Cornmeal (Polenta) Pastry: In the bowl of a stand mixer fitted with the paddle attachment, combine the flour, sugar, cornmeal, and salt and mix on low speed just until blended. Scatter the butter pieces over the flour mixture and mix on low speed until crumbly. Maintaining the same speed, add the egg yolks and mix just until the mixture comes together to form a dough.

Have ready a 9 1/2 by 1-inch round fluted tart pan with a removable bottom. Divide the dough in half (each half will weigh 14 1/2 to 15 ounces/415 to 445 grams) and shape each half into a flat disk. Wrap 1 disk in waxed paper and

set aside. On a lightly floured work surface, roll or pat the other disk into an 8-inch circle. Transfer the pastry circle to the tart pan and press the soft dough over the bottom and up the sides of the pan as evenly as possible.

To assemble the tart: Remove the peaches from the syrup and drain well on paper towels. Arrange the peach halves, cut sides down and close together, in the pastry-lined pan, covering the crust almost completely.

Place the remaining dough disk on a sheet of plastic wrap, and cover it with a sheet of waxed paper. Following the directions for rolling out tart pastry on page 29, roll out the pastry into an 11-inch circle about 3/16 inch thick. Peel off and discard the waxed paper from the pastry. Lift the plastic wrap with the pastry on it, and invert it, pastry side down, over the peaches. Gently peel away the sheet of plastic wrap and discard it. Press around the crust edges to seal. Cut off the excess dough to make the top crust flush with the tart pan sides. Brush the top crust lightly with water and sprinkle with the raw sugar.

Place the pan on a baking sheet (or 12-inch pizza pan) to catch any fruit juices that might overflow from the tart during baking. Bake the tart until the pastry is deep golden brown, 40 to 45 minutes. Transfer to a wire rack to cool for about 15 minutes. Then set the tart pan on a narrower elevated surface, such as a tin can, so the bottom of the pan is released as the metal rim slips down. Carefully transfer the tart still on its thin metal base onto a serving platter.

In a small bowl, stir the granulated sugar into the crème fraîche. Serve the tart warm or at room temperature. Accompany each serving with a dollop of the crème fraîche.

Open-Faced Apple Galette with Quince Paste

Picture thin apple slices neatly arranged on a buttery, crisp pastry with small pieces of intensely flavored rose-colored quince paste highlighting the fruit—attractive, homemade, and delicious. Quince paste, known in Spanish as *membrillo*, is made by cooking quinces with sugar and lemon juice to a thick, rosy paste. It is often paired with Spain's prized Manchego cheese, and is available in the cheese section of well-stocked food markets, in specialty cheese shops, and in Spanish groceries.   **YIELD: ONE 11-INCH GALETTE, 6 TO 8 SERVINGS**

PASTRY

1 CUP (4½ OUNCES/130 GRAMS) ALL-PURPOSE FLOUR

2 TABLESPOONS YELLOW CORNMEAL

1 TEASPOON GRANULATED SUGAR

¼ TEASPOON SALT

3½ OUNCES (¾ STICK PLUS 1 TABLESPOON/100 GRAMS) COLD UNSALTED BUTTER, CUT INTO ¼-INCH SLICES

¼ CUP (2 FL OUNCES/60 ML) ICE WATER

FILLING

3 SMALL (ABOUT 1 POUND/455 GRAMS) GOLDEN DELICIOUS APPLES, PEELED, HALVED, CORED, AND CUT CROSSWISE INTO ⅛-INCH-THICK SLICES TO YIELD 4 CUPS (14 OUNCES/400 GRAMS)

⅓ CUP (1½ OUNCES/40 GRAMS) WALNUTS, TOASTED (PAGES 15–16) AND COARSELY CHOPPED

3 TABLESPOONS GRANULATED SUGAR

2 TABLESPOONS UNSALTED BUTTER, MELTED AND COOLED

½ TEASPOON GROUND CINNAMON

¼ TEASPOON GROUND ALLSPICE

1 TABLESPOON GRANULATED SUGAR

2 OUNCES (55 GRAMS) QUINCE PASTE

To make the pastry: In a large bowl, stir together the flour, cornmeal, sugar, and salt. Scatter the butter pieces over the flour mixture. With a pastry blender, cut in the butter until the mixture has many pieces of butter ranging in size from cornmeal to rolled oats to small peas. Sprinkle the ice water, 1 tablespoon at a time, evenly over the flour mixture, using a fork to toss and distribute the moisture until the mixture is moist enough to stick together. Add additional cold water, 1 teaspoon at a time, if needed. With your hands, gather the moistened particles together, using the side of the bowl to shape them into a ball. Flatten the dough into a rough square shape, wrap in plastic wrap, and refrigerate for at least 2 hours or up to 1 day before rolling.

Before baking: Center a rack in the oven and preheat the oven to 400 degrees F. Line a large rimless baking sheet with parchment paper.

To assemble: If the dough is cold and firm from the refrigerator, let it stand at room temperature just until it is malleable enough to roll yet still cool to the touch, 15 to 30 minutes. On a lightly floured work surface, roll out the pastry into a 13 by 12-inch rectangle about ⅛ inch thick. Loosely roll up the pastry around the rolling pin, and then unroll it, top side down, onto the prepared baking sheet.

In a large bowl, toss the apple slices with the nuts, butter, sugar, cinnamon, and allspice. Arrange the apple mixture evenly on the pastry, leaving an uncovered border about 1½ to 2 inches wide on all sides. Fold the border over the filling, leaving a ¼-inch gap just inside the flap that is free of filling. (As the galette bakes, the fruit juices will bubble and push against the pastry flap. The gap allows for expansion and eases the pressure on the pastry, preventing the juices from leaking out during baking.)

Pleat the border evenly to form a kind of ruffle around the fruit filling, similar to a drawstring purse that is open in the center. Lightly brush the pleated border with water. Sprinkle the pastry border with the 1 tablespoon sugar.

Bake the galette until the pastry is golden brown and crisp and the apples are tender yet still moist, 40 to 50 minutes. Transfer to a wire rack and let cool on the pan for 10 minutes. Slip a wide offset spatula, a giant dough scraper, or a small rimless baking sheet under the galette and transfer it (without the parchment paper) to the rack to continue to cool, 30 to 45 minutes.

Cut the quince paste into about twenty 1 by ½ by ⅜-inch slices. Slip them randomly under several of the apple slices so they peek out and highlight the dessert. Transfer the galette to a serving plate or cutting board and serve warm or at room temperature. For the best taste and texture, serve the galette the same day it is baked.

If the galette is made early in the day, do not add the quince paste. Just before serving, reheat the galette in a preheated 325 degree F oven just until warm, 10 to 15 minutes. Then slip the quince slices randomly under the apple slices and serve.

Brown Butter Pear Tart

Pears are incredibly versatile, and their ability to marry seamlessly with a broad array of other flavors makes them a baker's dream. In this tart, a variation on a French classic, chopped chocolate lining the crust goes beautifully with the fruit, and a hint of anise in the brown butter filling adds a mysterious but welcome depth of flavor. **YIELD: ONE 11-INCH ROUND TART, 12 SERVINGS**

PASTRY

1¾ CUPS (8 OUNCES/225 GRAMS) ALL-PURPOSE FLOUR

⅓ CUP (2¼ OUNCES/65 GRAMS) GRANULATED SUGAR

¼ TEASPOON SALT

5 OUNCES (1¼ STICKS/140 GRAMS) COLD UNSALTED BUTTER, CUT INTO ¼-INCH SLICES

1 LARGE EGG

1 TEASPOON PURE VANILLA EXTRACT

FILLING

2 TO 3 OUNCES (55 TO 80 GRAMS) SEMISWEET CHOCOLATE, COARSELY CHOPPED

4 OUNCES (1 STICK/115 GRAMS) UNSALTED BUTTER

2 LARGE EGGS

⅔ CUP (4½ OUNCES/130 GRAMS) GRANULATED SUGAR

⅓ CUP (1½ OUNCES/40 GRAMS) ALL-PURPOSE FLOUR

½ TEASPOON PURE VANILLA EXTRACT

¾ TEASPOON ANISEEDS

4 MEDIUM (1¼ TO 1½ POUNDS/570 TO 680 GRAMS) FIRM YET RIPE BARTLETT PEARS

DECORATION

⅓ CUP (2½ FL OUNCES/75 ML) STRAINED APRICOT JAM, WARMED

To make the pastry: In a food processor, combine the flour, sugar, and salt and pulse 3 or 4 times to blend. Scatter the butter pieces over the flour mixture and pulse until the mixture is the consistency of cornmeal.

In a small bowl, whisk together the egg and vanilla. With the processor motor running, pour the egg mixture down the feed tube and process just until the ingredients start to form a ball.

Transfer the dough to a work surface. Beginning at the far end, and using the heel of your hand, push a small amount of the dough (about the size of an extra-large egg) away from you, smearing it on the work surface. Repeat with the remaining dough in small amounts. When you've worked all the dough in this manner, give it a couple more strokes to bring it together into a smooth, homogeneous unit. (This kneading technique, described on page 31, is known as *fraisage*.) Shape the dough into a flat disk. Set aside to rest for 15 minutes.

If not using the dough right away, wrap it in plastic wrap and refrigerate for up to 3 days. For longer storage, overwrap with aluminum foil, label with the contents and date, and freeze for up to 2 weeks. Thaw the dough in the refrigerator for at least 4 hours or up to overnight. Let it stand at room temperature just until it is malleable enough to roll yet still cool to the touch, 15 to 30 minutes.

Before baking: Center a rack in the oven and preheat the oven to 350 degrees F. Have ready an 11 by 1-inch round fluted tart pan with a removable bottom.

To line the pan with the pastry dough: On a lightly floured work surface, roll out the dough into a 13-inch circle about ⅛ inch thick. Following the directions on page 27, line the tart pan with the pastry circle. (The unbaked tart shell can be securely covered with plastic wrap and refrigerated for up to 3 days or frozen for up to 1 week.)

Partially bake the tart shell for 17 to 25 minutes as directed on page 29. Transfer the pan to a wire rack and let cool while you prepare the filling. Scatter the chocolate pieces over the tart dough so that they begin to melt. Increase the oven temperature to 375 degrees F.

To make the filling: Following the directions for making brown butter on page 19, melt the butter in a small, heavy saucepan over medium-low heat and heat just until it begins to turn a delicate brown, 5 to 7 minutes. Remove from the heat, pour into a small bowl, and set aside to cool for about 15 minutes.

In a medium bowl, whisk the eggs until blended. Whisk in the sugar, and then the flour, vanilla, and aniseeds. Gradually whisk in the cooled brown butter. Set aside while preparing the pears.

Peel the pears, cut them in half lengthwise, and core them. Cut each pear half crosswise into ⅛-inch-thick slices. With your fingertips, gently press down on the slices to fan them, keeping the original shape. Pour about three-fourths of the filling into the partially baked shell over the chocolate. With the aid of an offset spatula, transfer each sliced pear half to the pastry shell so that the wider portion rests close to the outer edge of the tart shell and the narrow portion points toward the center. Carefully pour the remaining filling around the pears (not over them). The tart will be filled almost to the top of the crust.

Although the filling will puff during baking without overflowing, place the tart on a rimmed baking sheet for security. Bake until the filling and the crust are golden, 50 to 60 minutes. As the tart bakes, the pears will release their juices, which will accumulate a bit on the top in the center of the tart. Note that the pastry around the edge of the tart will appear golden brown toward the end of baking; however, the pastry underneath the filling is just right. Transfer to a wire rack and let cool in the pan for about 15 minutes. To remove the tart from the pan, set the tart pan on a narrower elevated surface, such as a tin can, so the bottom of the pan is released as the metal rim slips down. Carefully transfer the tart still on its thin metal base onto a wire rack or serving platter.

Let the tart cool for another 15 minutes, and then brush the warm jam lightly over the surface of the tart. Serve warm or at room temperature, cut into wedges with a sharp knife.

Pastry-Topped Fig and Nectarine Cobbler

The classic cobbler takes on a fresh sophistication when it's crowned with a woven lattice pastry that showcases the colorful fruit below. Juicy nectarines and sweet, plump figs are a perfect match, providing an irresistible combination of flavors. I use granulated sugar and honey to sweeten the fruit: the honey adds an illusive flavor along with sweetness, while the sugar keeps everything in perfect harmony.   YIELD: ONE 9 BY 14-INCH COBBLER, 10 SERVINGS

FRUIT MIXTURE

ABOUT 15 (1 POUND/455 GRAMS) RIPE BLACK MISSION FIGS, STEMMED AND QUARTERED LENGTHWISE TO YIELD 3 CUPS

5 TO 6 MEDIUM (1¾ POUNDS/800 GRAMS) FIRM BUT RIPE NECTARINES, HALVED, PITTED, AND CUT INTO ½-INCH WEDGES TO YIELD 5 CUPS

½ TO ⅔ CUP (3½ TO 4½ OUNCES/100 TO 130 GRAMS) GRANULATED SUGAR, DEPENDING ON THE SWEETNESS OF THE FRUITS

3 TABLESPOONS ALL-PURPOSE FLOUR

2 TABLESPOONS HONEY

2 TABLESPOONS UNSALTED BUTTER, CUT INTO BITS

PASTRY

1¾ CUPS (8 OUNCES/225 GRAMS) ALL-PURPOSE FLOUR

1 TABLESPOON GRANULATED SUGAR

1 TABLESPOON BAKING POWDER

½ TEASPOON SALT

3 OUNCES (¾ STICK/85 GRAMS) COLD UNSALTED BUTTER, CUT INTO ¼-INCH SLICES

1 CUP (8 FL OUNCES/240 ML) HEAVY CREAM

1 TABLESPOON GRANULATED SUGAR

1 PINT PREMIUM VANILLA ICE CREAM

Before baking: Center a rack in the oven and preheat the oven to 425 degrees F. Generously butter a 14 by 9 by 2-inch oval gratin dish or a 13 by 9 by 2-inch glass or ceramic baking dish.

To make the fruit mixture: In a large bowl, gently toss together the figs, nectarines, sugar, flour, and honey. Arrange the fruit mixture in the prepared dish. Dot with the butter.

To make the pastry: Sift together the flour, sugar, baking powder, and salt into a large bowl. Scatter the butter pieces over the flour mixture. With a pastry blender, cut in the butter until the mixture is the consistency of coarse cornmeal. Gradually add the cream and, using a fork, stir it into the flour mixture just until it comes together as a dough.

On a lightly floured surface, flatten the dough and then roll it out until it is just slightly smaller than the diameter of the dish holding the fruit. Lift it with your hands or roll it onto the rolling pin and ease it onto the fruit. Brush the top of the pastry with any cream remaining in the carton. Sprinkle with the 1 tablespoon sugar. Trim the edges even with a knife, and cut several slits in the center to allow steam to escape.

Bake the cobbler until the pastry is golden and the fruit is bubbly at the edges, 20 to 25 minutes. Transfer to a wire rack to cool. Serve warm or at room temperature with a scoop of ice cream.

Flag-Raising Mixed-Berry Potpies

I like an assortment of soft fruits for these homespun pies, but most of the time I use fruit that I have on hand. Try all sorts of combinations, using similar quantities like a mélange of blueberries, blackberries, olallieberries, boysenberries, gooseberries, and raspberries; sliced peaches, apricots, mangoes, papaya, pineapple, and rhubarb; or apples, pears, plums, and pluots.

These potpies are the epitome of an American dessert and fit perfectly into a menu celebrating the Fourth of July. Assemble them hours ahead, set them on a baking sheet, cover with plastic wrap, and refrigerate. **YIELD: 6 SERVINGS**

1 RECIPE CREAM CHEESE PASTRY (PAGE 359)

1 TABLESPOON FINELY MINCED CRYSTALLIZED GINGER (OPTIONAL)

FRUIT

6 CUPS (ABOUT 1¾ POUNDS/800 GRAMS) MIXED BERRIES SUCH AS BLUEBERRIES, BLACKBERRIES, AND RED RASPBERRIES, PICKED OVER FOR STEMS

1 TO 1¼ CUPS (7 OUNCES/200 GRAMS TO 8¾ OUNCES/ 250 GRAMS) GRANULATED SUGAR, DEPENDING ON THE SWEETNESS OF THE BERRIES

3 TABLESPOONS CORNSTARCH

4 TEASPOONS QUICK-COOKING (INSTANT) TAPIOCA

1 TEASPOON GROUND CINNAMON

½ TEASPOON NUTMEG, PREFERABLY FRESHLY GRATED

⅛ TEASPOON SALT

2 TABLESPOONS HEAVY CREAM

2 TABLESPOONS UNSALTED BUTTER, CUT INTO 6 SLICES

GRANULATED SUGAR FOR SPRINKLING

Make the pastry as directed, adding the crystallized ginger, if desired, when you scatter the cheese cubes over the mixture and then pulsing just until the ingredients come together in a ball.

Divide the dough in half, shape each half into a 5-inch disk about ¾ inch thick (12½ ounces/355 grams), wrap in plastic wrap, and refrigerate until firm, about 4 hours.

Before baking: Center a rack in the oven and preheat the oven to 375 degrees F. Place six 1-cup ramekins or custard cups each about 4 inches in diameter on a large rimmed baking sheet.

To prepare the fruit: In a large bowl, gently toss together the berries, sugar, cornstarch, tapioca, cinnamon, nutmeg, and salt. Divide the fruit mixture evenly among the ramekins. Spoon 1 teaspoon of the cream over the fruit in each ramekin, and then top with a small pat of butter.

To top the potpies: On a lightly floured work surface, roll out 1 disk of the dough about ³⁄₁₆ inch thick. Using a 4½-inch round cookie or biscuit cutter (or other template), cut out circles. (You need circles that are just a bit larger than the diameter of your ramekins, so adjust the size as needed if your ramekins are a different diameter.) Set a pastry circle on top of each fruit-filled ramekin and, using your fingertips, gently press the pastry down into the ramekin around the edges. (The pastry doesn't need to be sealed to the edges. As the potpies bake, the pastry will appear to "melt" and "hug" the fruit.) Roll out the second dough disk and cut out circles to cover the remaining ramekins.

With a pastry brush, apply a light coating of water to the pastry on each ramekin, and then sprinkle some sugar over the top. Using a small paring knife, make a couple of slits in the center of each pastry to allow steam to escape.

Bake the potpies until the pastry is golden and the fruit is bubbly, 30 to 35 minutes. Transfer to a wire rack to cool. Serve warm or at room temperature (the fruit filling will thicken as it cools).

Sour Cream Custard Tart

When you are in the mood for something refreshing and creamy but not too rich or heavy, try this tangy tart that I bake in a square pan. In summer, arrange an assortment of fresh berries on top in a checkerboard pattern, and in the fall, scatter a handful of ruby pomegranate seeds over the top. The versatile sour cream filling complements both toppings equally well, so keep this recipe at the ready regardless of the season. You can also bake this tart in a rectangular or round tart pan: roll out the pastry into a 17 by 7-inch rectangle ³⁄₁₆ inch thick and line a 14 by 4 by 1-inch tart pan, or roll out the pastry into a 13-inch circle ³⁄₁₆ inch thick and line a 9¹⁄₂ by 1-inch tart pan.

YIELD: ONE 9-INCH SQUARE TART, 8 OR 9 SERVINGS

SHORTBREAD PASTRY

1 LARGE EGG YOLK

2 TEASPOONS WATER

1¼ CUPS (5½ OUNCES/155 GRAMS) ALL-PURPOSE FLOUR

¼ CUP (1¾ OUNCES/50 GRAMS) GRANULATED SUGAR

⅛ TEASPOON SALT

4 OUNCES (1 STICK/115 GRAMS) COLD UNSALTED BUTTER, CUT INTO 8 SLICES

SOUR CREAM FILLING

2 LARGE EGGS

1 CUP (8 OUNCES/225 GRAMS) SOUR CREAM

¼ CUP (2 OUNCES/55 GRAMS) CRÈME FRAÎCHE

½ TEASPOON PURE VANILLA EXTRACT

½ CUP (3½ OUNCES/100 GRAMS) GRANULATED SUGAR

1 TABLESPOON ALL-PURPOSE FLOUR

⅛ TEASPOON SALT

FRUIT TOPPING

80 (ABOUT 2 CUPS/10 OUNCES/280 GRAMS) RED RASPBERRIES, PICKED OVER FOR STEMS

80 (ABOUT 2 CUPS/10 OUNCES/280 GRAMS) BLACKBERRIES, PICKED OVER FOR STEMS

To make the Shortbread Pastry: In a small bowl, whisk together the egg yolk and water. In a food processor, combine the flour, sugar, and salt and pulse 3 or 4 times to blend. Scatter the butter slices over the flour mixture and pulse until the mixture has the consistency of cornmeal.

With the motor running, pour the egg yolk mixture down the feed tube and process just until tiny, moist balls form, 20 to 30 seconds. With your hands, scoop out the dough, place on a clean work surface, and gently press together until smooth and cohesive.

Shape the dough into a flat 4-inch square 1½ inches thick and use the pastry right away while it is malleable. If not using the dough right away, wrap in plastic wrap and refrigerate up to 3 days. For longer storage, overwrap with aluminum foil, label with the contents and date, and freeze for up to 1 month. Thaw the dough in the refrigerator for at least 4 hours or up to overnight. Let it stand at room temperature just until it is malleable enough for rolling, 15 to 30 minutes, before using.

Center a rack in the oven and preheat the oven to 350 degrees F. Have ready a 9 by 1½-inch square fluted tart pan with a removable bottom.

To line the pan with the pastry dough: Following the directions on page 27, roll out the pastry into a 10½-inch square about ³⁄₁₆ inch thick and line the tart pan. Chill the pastry-lined pan in the freezer for about 20 minutes or in the refrigerator for at least 30 minutes or up to 1 day.

Partially bake the tart shell for 17 to 25 minutes as directed on page 30. Transfer to a wire rack and let cool for at least 10 minutes before filling. The tart shell is fragile while warm but becomes crisp as it cools. Increase the oven temperature to 375 degrees F.

To make the Sour Cream Filling: In a deep, medium bowl, whisk the eggs until blended. Add the sour cream, crème fraîche, and vanilla and stir until blended. Mix in the sugar, flour, and salt, stirring until combined. Pour the filling into the cooled crust, spreading it evenly over the crust with a rubber spatula.

Bake the tart until the custard is soft but not liquid when lightly touched and doesn't quiver when you move the pan, about 20 minutes. Transfer to a wire rack and let cool completely. To remove the tart from the pan, set the tart pan on a narrower elevated surface, such as a tin can, so the bottom of the pan is released as the metal rim slips down. Carefully transfer the tart still on its thin metal base on a wire rack or serving platter.

Arrange the berries on top of the tart in a checkerboard fashion. Use 4 berries, closely spaced, for each square for a total of 160 berries, 80 berries of each kind. If not serving within 2 to 3 hours, refrigerate and serve chilled.

Rustic Sweet-Potato Crostata

Native to the Americas, sweet potatoes were one of Christopher Columbus's most delicious New World "discoveries." Here, I have used this New World ingredient to lend rich color, flavor, and texture to a classic Old World dessert. Sweet potatoes are available all year, but their true season kicks off in the autumn, which is my favorite time to purchase these naturally sweet tubers at my local farmers' market. Wonderful for harvest gatherings, this *crostata* lends itself to all sorts of variations. Instead of making a freeform tart, you can use the pastry to line a 12-inch pizza pan or 10-inch shallow tart pan or flan ring. Either way you form the *crostata*, you can skip making the cranberry marmalade and serve a wedge on a paper napkin for eating out of hand at an informal gathering. Or, you can make the marmalade for topping Mile-High Cheesecake (page 154) or Cheesecake Timbales (page 247, made without the Fruit Salad).   **YIELD: ONE 11-INCH *CROSTATA*, ABOUT 8 SERVINGS**

1 RECIPE SINGLE-CRUST CROSTATA PASTRY (PAGE 362)

SWEET POTATO FILLING

⅓ CUP (2¼ OUNCES/65 GRAMS) FIRMLY PACKED DARK
    BROWN SUGAR

1 TABLESPOON ALL-PURPOSE FLOUR

½ TEASPOON GROUND CINNAMON

¼ TEASPOON GROUND GINGER

⅛ TEASPOON GROUND ALLSPICE

⅛ TEASPOON GROUND BLACK PEPPER

PINCH OF SALT

1 CUP (8 OUNCES/225 GRAMS) SWEET POTATO PUREE
    (PAGE 371)

⅓ TO ⅔ CUP (2½ TO 5½ FL OUNCES/75 TO 165 ML)
    HALF-AND-HALF

1 LARGE EGG

CRANBERRY MARMALADE (OPTIONAL)

3 CUPS (ONE 12-OUNCE/340-GRAM PACKAGE) FRESH OR
    THAWED, FROZEN CRANBERRIES, PICKED OVER
    FOR STEMS

1 CUP (7 OUNCES/200 GRAMS) GRANULATED SUGAR

⅓ CUP (2½ FL OUNCES/75 ML) WATER

1 STRIP ORANGE PEEL, ABOUT 3 INCHES LONG AND
    ½ INCH WIDE

½ VANILLA BEAN, SPLIT LENGTHWISE

1 TO 2 TABLESPOONS GRAND MARNIER OR FRESH ORANGE
    JUICE, IF NEEDED

Before baking: Center a rack in the oven and preheat the oven to 375 degrees F. Line a large rimmed baking sheet with parchment paper.

Following the directions on page 31, roll out the pastry into a 12-inch circle about ³⁄₁₆ inch thick and shape into a *crostata* crust on the prepared baking sheet. Bake partially for 20 to 22 minutes. Remove the baking sheet to a wire rack and let the *crostata* crust cool for about 10 minutes while you prepare the filling.

To make the Sweet Potato Filling: In a medium bowl, whisk together the sugar, flour, cinnamon, ginger, allspice, pepper and salt. In a small bowl, stir together the sweet potato puree, ⅓ cup of the half-and-half, and the egg until blended. Stir the sweet potato mixture into the sugar mixture just until blended. If the filling is too thick to spread easily, add enough of the remaining half-and-half, 1 tablespoon at a time, to thin the filling until it can be spread but is not runny. Pour the filling into the partially baked pastry, spreading it evenly over the center portion with a rubber spatula. (The ¼-inch-thick filling will be almost level with the rim of the *crostata*.)

Bake the *crostata* until the pastry is golden and the filling is shiny on top, appears set, and feels firm when lightly pressed in the center, 18 to 22 minutes. Transfer to a wire rack and let cool on the pan completely before serving.

To make the Cranberry Marmalade: While the *crostata* is baking, in a heavy 1 1/2-quart saucepan, combine the cranberries, sugar, water, and orange peel. Place the pan over medium-low heat and cook, stirring occasionally, until the mixture registers 205 degrees F on a candy thermometer. Remove from the heat. Using a small paring knife, scrape the seeds from the vanilla bean into the pan, and stir them in with a silicone spatula. Pour the mixture onto a rimmed baking sheet, and spread out thinly to cool quickly. You want the consistency to be between that of chunky applesauce and a fruit conserve. If it is too thick, add the Grand Marnier as needed to thin. (Cranberries contain pectin, which will cause the mixture to continue to thicken after cooking.) You can make the marmalade in advance and store it in a tightly covered container in the refrigerator for up to 5 days.

To serve, cross 2 long, sturdy spatulas and slip under the *crostata*, or slip 1 large, wide metal spatula or a rimless baking sheet under the *crostata*, and transfer it to a serving plate. Cut into wedges with a sharp knife, and serve with a dollop of the thin, saucy marmalade, if desired, on the side.

Note: Sometimes I pipe a cream cheese spiral on the filling before the crostata *goes into the oven, creating a lacy pattern reminiscent of a paper doily. To make the spiral, in a small bowl, mix together 3 ounces (85 grams) cream cheese, at room temperature; 2 tablespoons granulated sugar; and 1 large egg yolk until well blended and smooth. Fashion a small cone out of parchment paper (page 26) and half fill it with the cream cheese mixture. Snip a small opening at the end of the paper cone to allow a thin flow. Or, spoon the mixture into a small disposable pastry bag fitted with a 1/8-inch plain open tip. Starting in the center of the* crostata, *and exerting light, even pressure, pipe the cheese mixture in a gradually expanding spiral over the filling. Then, draw the tip of a small paring knife, a narrow wooden skewer, or a round wooden toothpick back and forth across the lines of the spiral, pulling the cream cheese mixture slightly to create a marbling effect and wiping the knife tip clean between the strokes.*

Almost-Last-Minute Summer Fruit Crumble

Thanks to Mother Nature's bounty of summer fruits, this is one of the best recipes in my repertoire. If you have all of your ingredients on hand (and the streusel made ahead and stored in the refrigerator), you can put this dessert together easily at a moment's notice. I've called this recipe a crumble, which is its British moniker. In America, it is known as a crisp. By any name, it is absolutely scrumptious.   **YIELD: 8 TO 10 SERVINGS**

STREUSEL

1 ¼ CUPS (4 OUNCES/115 GRAMS) OLD-FASHIONED
  ROLLED OATS

1 CUP (4½ OUNCES/130 GRAMS) ALL-PURPOSE FLOUR

1 CUP FIRMLY PACKED (7 OUNCES/200 GRAMS) LIGHT
  BROWN SUGAR

5 OUNCES (1¼ STICKS/140 GRAMS) COLD
  UNSALTED BUTTER, CUT INTO ¼-INCH SLICES

1 TEASPOON BAKING POWDER

¾ TEASPOON GROUND CINNAMON

⅛ TEASPOON SALT

FRUIT MIXTURE (9 TO 10 CUPS/2 TO 2 ¼ POUNDS/ 900 GRAMS TO 1 KG TOTAL)

3 TO 4 CUPS (1 TO 1¼ POUNDS/455 TO 570 GRAMS) MIXED
  BERRIES SUCH AS BLUEBERRIES, BLACKBERRIES,
  BOYSENBERRIES, AND/OR RED RASPBERRIES, PICKED
  OVER FOR STEMS

1 CUP (ABOUT 6 OUNCES/170 GRAMS) BING, RAINIER,
  OR OTHER SWEET CHERRIES, STEMMED, PITTED,
  AND HALVED

3 TO 4 (4 OUNCES/115 GRAMS) RIPE BLACK MISSION FIGS,
  STEMMED AND QUARTERED LENGTHWISE

1 MEDIUM (5 OUNCES/140 GRAMS) FIRM BUT RIPE PEACH,
  PEELED, HALVED, PITTED, AND SLICED

1 EACH SMALL (4 TO 5 OUNCES/115 TO 140 GRAMS) FIRM BUT
  RIPE NECTARINE, PLUOT, APRICOT, AND PLUM, HALVED,
  PITTED, AND SLICED

2 TABLESPOONS FRESH LEMON JUICE

1 TEASPOON PURE VANILLA EXTRACT

¼ TEASPOON ALMOND EXTRACT

½ CUP PLUS 2 TABLESPOONS (4¼ OUNCES/120 GRAMS)
  GRANULATED SUGAR

1 TABLESPOON SNIPPED PESTICIDE-FREE FRESH LAVENDER,
  LEMON VERBENA, OR LEMON THYME (OPTIONAL)

3 TABLESPOONS ALL-PURPOSE FLOUR

WHIPPED CREAM SAUCE

2 CUPS (16 FL OUNCES/480 ML) COLD HEAVY CREAM

1 CUP (8 OUNCES/225 GRAMS) COLD CRÈME FRAÎCHE

1 TABLESPOON GRANULATED SUGAR

To make the streusel: In a large bowl, combine the oats, flour, sugar, butter, baking powder, cinnamon, and salt. Using your fingertips, mix the ingredients until a crumbly consistency forms that comes together when you press it between your fingers or squeeze it in your hand. If using right away, set aside. Or, cover the bowl and store at room temperature for 1 to 2 hours. For longer storage, spoon the streusel into a resealable plastic bag and refrigerate for up to 5 days.

Before baking: Center a rack in the oven and preheat the oven to 350 degrees F. Have ready a 13 by 9 by 2-inch oval gratin dish or glass or ceramic baking dish.

To prepare the fruit mixture: Combine all of the fruits in an oversized bowl (for ease in tossing the fruits). In a small bowl, stir together the lemon juice and the vanilla and almond extracts. Sprinkle the lemon juice mixture over the fruit. Next, sprinkle the sugar and lavender (if using) over the fruit, and then gently toss the fruit with a rubber spatula to coat evenly with the flavorings. Sprinkle the flour over the fruit, and again toss gently just until the flour is incorporated. Tilt the bowl and use the spatula to guide the fruits so they tumble into the gratin dish evenly. Scatter the streusel over the fruit to cover lightly (don't pack it down).

Bake the crumble until the fruit is soft, the juices are bubbling, and the topping is lightly browned, about 50 minutes. Transfer to a wire rack to cool.

To make the Whipped Cream Sauce: In a large bowl, whisk together the cream, crème fraîche, and sugar just until very softly whipped. Cover and refrigerate until serving.

Serve the crumble warm or at room temperature. Spoon a dollop of the sauce on top of or alongside each serving.

Stone-Fruit Cobbler with Cornmeal Biscuits

This rustic, feel-good dessert pays homage to the sunny flavors of summer. It is served the old-fashioned way—in bowls—so you can savor every delicious drop of juice. The delicate crunch of cornmeal biscuits provides a delectable counterpoint to the sweet succulence of the ripe fruit. A dollop of heavy cream or vanilla ice cream adds a luscious finishing touch. If you can't find freestone fruit, cut wedges around the pit. (Buy a bit more fruit than the recipe states, since the wedges won't release quite as easily.) **YIELD: ONE 9-INCH SQUARE COBBLER, 8 TO 12 SERVINGS**

FRUIT MIXTURE

5 OR 6 MEDIUM (ABOUT 1½ POUNDS/680 GRAMS) ASSORTED RIPE PURPLE AND RED PLUMS AND/OR PLUOTS, HALVED, PITTED, AND CUT INTO ½-INCH-THICK SLICES TO YIELD ABOUT 2 CUPS (1¼ POUNDS/570 GRAMS)

5 LARGE OR 7 MEDIUM (ABOUT 2½ POUNDS/1.1 KG) FIRM-RIPE, UNPEELED FREESTONE NECTARINES, HALVED, PITTED, AND CUT INTO ½-INCH-THICK SLICES TO YIELD 6 CUPS (2¼ POUNDS/ABOUT 1 KG)

2 TABLESPOONS FRESH LIME OR LEMON JUICE

1 TABLESPOON QUICK-COOKING (INSTANT) TAPIOCA

2 TEASPOONS FINELY GRATED LIME OR LEMON ZEST

1 TEASPOON PURE VANILLA EXTRACT

ABOUT ⅔ CUP (4½ OUNCES/130 GRAMS) GRANULATED SUGAR, DEPENDING ON THE SWEETNESS OF THE FRUITS

1 TABLESPOON CORNSTARCH

¼ TEASPOON GROUND ALLSPICE

PINCH OF SALT

BISCUIT DOUGH

1⅓ CUPS (6¼ OUNCES/175 GRAMS) ALL-PURPOSE FLOUR

¼ CUP (1½ OUNCES/40 GRAMS) YELLOW CORNMEAL

2 TEASPOONS BAKING POWDER

½ TEASPOON SALT

6 OUNCES (1½ STICKS/170 GRAMS) UNSALTED BUTTER, SOFTENED

3 TABLESPOONS GRANULATED SUGAR

1 LARGE EGG

⅓ CUP (2½ FL OUNCES/75 ML) WHOLE MILK

½ TEASPOON PURE VANILLA EXTRACT

2 TABLESPOONS WHOLE MILK

3 TABLESPOONS SANDING SUGAR

Before baking: Center a rack in the oven and preheat the oven to 375 degrees F. Butter a 9 by 2-inch square baking pan, preferably with straight sides.

To prepare the fruit mixture: Combine all of the fruits in an oversized bowl (for ease in tossing the fruits). Sprinkle the lime juice, tapioca, lime zest, and vanilla over the fruit and toss gently with a rubber spatula to coat evenly. Set aside for 15 minutes to allow the tapioca to soften.

Taste the fruit to check the sweetness for how much sugar to use. Then, in a small bowl, stir together the sugar, cornstarch, allspice, and salt. Sprinkle the sugar mixture over the fruit and toss gently to coat the fruit evenly. Tilt the bowl and use the rubber spatula to guide the fruits so they tumble into the prepared dish evenly.

To make the Biscuit Dough: Sift together the flour, cornmeal, baking powder, and salt onto a sheet of waxed paper; set aside. In a medium bowl, beat the butter and sugar with a handheld mixer on medium speed until creamy and smooth, about 30 seconds. Reduce the speed to medium-low, add the egg, and beat until incorporated.

On the lowest speed, add the flour mixture in two additions alternately with the milk in one addition, beginning and ending with the flour mixture and beating after each addition until incorporated. Add the vanilla during the final moments of mixing.

Using an ice cream scoop a scant 2 inches in diameter (#24) or a large spoon, drop about 1 1/2-tablespoon dollops of the dough over the fruit in 4 rows of 3 dollops each.

Lightly brush the tops of the dough with the milk and sprinkle with the sanding sugar. (As the cobbler bakes, the dollops of dough will spread to cover the fruit in an attractive pattern.)

Bake the cobbler until the crust is golden and the fruit juices are bubbling, 40 to 45 minutes. Transfer to a wire rack to cool. Serve warm or at room temperature.

Apricot-Almond-Berry Buckle

Beloved by American bakers since colonial times, a buckle belongs to the family of simple fruit-and-dough desserts that includes homespun relatives like slump, grunt, and pandowdy. The buckle can also be baked in a 9 by 2-inch square pan, with the same cooking time.

YIELD: ONE 9-INCH ROUND CAKE, 12 SERVINGS

CAKE

4 OUNCES (1 STICK/115 GRAMS) UNSALTED BUTTER, SOFTENED

2 TABLESPOONS SOUR CREAM

2 TABLESPOONS WHOLE MILK

1¼ CUPS (5 OUNCES/140 GRAMS) CAKE FLOUR

1 CUP (7 OUNCES/200 GRAMS) GRANULATED SUGAR

½ TEASPOON BAKING POWDER

¼ TEASPOON SALT

2 LARGE EGGS, LIGHTLY BEATEN

1 LARGE EGG YOLK (RESERVE THE WHITE FOR THE TOPPING)

1 TEASPOON PURE VANILLA EXTRACT

½ TEASPOON PURE ALMOND EXTRACT

FRUIT

5 TO 6 SMALL (10 OUNCES/280 GRAMS) FIRM BUT RIPE APRICOTS, HALVED, PITTED, AND HALVES QUARTERED LENGTHWISE TO YIELD ABOUT 1½ CUPS (9 OUNCES/255 GRAMS)

1 CUP (5 OUNCES/140 GRAMS) RED RASPBERRIES, PICKED OVER FOR STEMS

1 CUP (5 OUNCES/140 GRAMS) BOYSENBERRIES OR OTHER SEASONAL BERRIES, PICKED OVER FOR STEMS

ALMOND TOPPING

1 TO 2 TABLESPOONS EGG WHITE

1 TABLESPOON GRANULATED SUGAR

1 CUP (3½ OUNCES/100 GRAMS) NATURAL OR BLANCHED SLICED ALMONDS

Before baking: To soften the butter for the cake batter, remove it from the refrigerator about 2 hours ahead and place it in the bowl of a stand mixer. Center a rack in the oven and preheat the oven to 350 degrees F. Butter a 9-inch round springform pan with 2¾- or 3-inch sides, then flour it, tapping out the excess flour. Line the bottom with parchment paper. In a small bowl, stir together the sour cream and milk for the cake batter. Have all of the other ingredients at room temperature.

To make the cake: Sift together the flour, sugar, baking powder, and salt onto the butter in the mixer bowl. Add the sour cream mixture, eggs, egg yolk, and vanilla and almond extracts to the bowl. Attach the bowl to the mixer, fit it with the paddle attachment, and beat on low speed until creamy and smooth, 1 to 2 minutes, stopping the mixer occasionally to scrape down the sides of the bowl. Detach the paddle and bowl from the mixer, and tap the paddle against the side of the bowl to free the excess batter.

Using a rubber spatula, gently fold in the apricots and berries. Spoon the batter into the prepared pan and spread as evenly as possible with the spatula.

To make the Almond Topping: In a small bowl, use a fork to beat the egg white just to break it up; set aside. In a small bowl, sprinkle 1 tablespoon of the sugar over the nuts. Pour 1 tablespoon of the egg white on top of the nuts and toss with the fork to coat evenly. If needed, add more egg white to coat the almonds evenly. Scatter the almond mixture over the cake batter.

Bake the buckle just until it springs back when lightly touched in the center, a round wooden toothpick inserted in the center comes out free of cake, and the almond topping transforms into a shiny, crystalline golden crust, 55 to 60 minutes. Transfer to a wire rack and let cool in the pan for about 20 minutes.

Slowly release the springform clasp and carefully remove the pan sides. Invert a wire rack on top of the buckle, invert the buckle onto it, lift off the pan bottom, and slowly peel off the parchment liner and discard it. Invert a serving plate on top, invert the buckle so it is right side up, and remove the original rack. Serve warm or at room temperature.

24-Karat Cupcakes with Orange Cream Cheese Icing

King Midas would have loved these little cakes, which truly are worth their weight in gold. Although I will admit this recipe does call for more than twenty-four baby carrots, the combination of ingredients comes together to create the quintessential carrot cupcake. Topped with classic cream cheese frosting, the moist, tender cakes are enriched with walnuts, flaked coconut, and a delicate medley of spices. They are perfect as an afternoon snack—or get your day off to a decadent start by enjoying them for breakfast. The stubby carrots labeled baby carrots, packaged in plastic bags and sold in supermarket produce departments, are not immature roots but actually whittled down mature carrots.   **YIELD: 2 DOZEN CUPCAKES**

CUPCAKES

2 CUPS (11 OUNCES/310 GRAMS) PEELED BABY CARROTS

4 OUNCES (1 STICK/115 GRAMS) UNSALTED BUTTER, MELTED AND COOLED

¾ CUP (6 FL OUNCES/180 ML) CANOLA OIL

2 CUPS (9 OUNCES/255 GRAMS) ALL-PURPOSE FLOUR

1½ TEASPOONS BAKING POWDER

1½ TEASPOONS GROUND CINNAMON

1 TEASPOON BAKING SODA

½ TEASPOON SALT

½ TEASPOON NUTMEG, PREFERABLY FRESHLY GRATED

4 LARGE EGGS

1 CUP (7 OUNCES/200 GRAMS) GRANULATED SUGAR

½ CUP FIRMLY PACKED (3½ OUNCES/100 GRAMS) LIGHT BROWN SUGAR

1 TABLESPOON FRESH LEMON JUICE

1 TEASPOON PURE VANILLA EXTRACT

⅔ CUP (3 OUNCES/85 GRAMS) CHOPPED WALNUTS

½ CUP (4 OUNCES/115 GRAMS) SWEETENED FLAKED DRIED COCONUT

ORANGE CREAM CHEESE ICING

ONE 8-OUNCE (225-GRAM) PACKAGE CREAM CHEESE, SOFTENED

3 OUNCES (¾ STICK/85 GRAMS) UNSALTED BUTTER, SOFTENED

1 TEASPOON PURE VANILLA EXTRACT

1 CUP PLUS 3 TABLESPOONS (4¼ OUNCES/120 GRAMS) POWDERED SUGAR, SIFTED

1 TABLESPOON FINELY GRATED ORANGE ZEST

1 TEASPOON FINELY GRATED LEMON ZEST

ABOUT 1 TABLESPOON FRESH LEMON JUICE

Before baking: Center a rack in the oven and preheat the oven to 350 degrees F. Butter two 12-cup standard muffin pans. Or, lightly coat the cups with nonstick spray. Or, line the cups with fluted paper or foil liners. Have all of the ingredients at room temperature.

To make the cupcakes: In a food processor, pulse the carrots just until they are finely chopped to yield 2⅓ cups, lightly packed. Transfer the carrots to a small bowl and set aside. In another small bowl, stir together the butter and oil; set aside. Sift together the flour, baking powder, cinnamon, baking soda, salt, and nutmeg onto a sheet of waxed paper; set aside.

In the bowl of a stand mixer fitted with the paddle attachment or a handheld mixer, beat together the eggs and granulated and brown sugars on medium speed until light and fluffy, about 1½ minutes. Reduce the speed to low speed, add the butter-oil mixture, lemon juice, and vanilla and beat until well blended. With the mixer still on low speed, add the flour mixture in three additions, beating after each addition until incorporated and stopping the mixer to scrape down the sides of CONTINUED ▶

the bowl as needed. Detach the paddle and bowl from the mixer, and tap the paddle against the side of the bowl to free the excess batter. Using a rubber spatula, stir in the carrots, walnuts, and coconut until evenly distributed.

Using an ice cream scoop a scant 2 inches in diameter (#24) or a spoon, fill the prepared muffin cups three-fourths full. Bake the cupcakes until they are golden brown on top and feel firm yet spring back when gently touched, about 25 minutes. Transfer to wire racks and let cool in the pans for 10 minutes. Using the tines of a fork to aid in lifting, remove the cupcakes from the pans and let cool completely on wire racks.

To make the Orange Cream Cheese Icing: In the bowl of the stand mixer fitted with the paddle attachment, beat together the cream cheese, butter, and vanilla on medium-low speed until creamy and smooth, about 1 minute. Reduce the speed to low and gradually add the powdered sugar, continuing to beat until the mixture is smooth and has a spreading consistency. Detach the paddle and bowl from the mixer, and tap the paddle against the side of the bowl to free the excess frosting. Using a rubber spatula, stir in the orange and lemon zests. Add the lemon juice to taste.

With a flexible metal spatula, generously frost the top of each cooled cupcake, mounding the frosting in the center. Serve immediately, or arrange in a sturdy covered container or a cake box and store at room temperature for up to 2 days.

Singular Sensations

LONG BEFORE AND EVER SINCE I wrote my second book, *Sweet Miniatures*, I have been fascinated with diminutive desserts. Whether eaten out of hand or elegantly served on a plate, good flavors do come in small packages.

Exactly what those packages look like is open to many interpretations. Flaky Lemon-Marshmallow Turnovers and Year-Round Little Peach Pies are junior versions of their full-sized counterparts—lemon meringue and peach pies—and are perfect to pack in a picnic basket or snack on during the day.

Rich Coffee Cup Tiramisu or creamy Cheesecake Timbales draw hungry attention as they star at the end of a meal. For eaters who want just a bite or two of something sweet, the size fits. And Double-Cranberry Mini Cakes or Fruit Cocktail Trifles with Crème Anglaise will win as many raves for their handsome appearance as they will for their bright flavors.

Single servings also lend themselves to a knockout dessert buffet. Why not assemble a selection of tastes and textures: Brown Butter Bundtlettes speckled with a coffee glaze, nostalgic Milk Chocolate S'More Tartlets with Homemade Marshmallow Topping, and spice-laden Persimmon Bread Puddings. Such a lineup is also ideal for a cocktail party or an informal afternoon tea.

These desserts are treats you have the right not to share—they are all your own. Savor the moment.

Apple Cider Baby Chiffon Cakes

Enlivened with apple cider and a medley of autumnal spices, these small chiffon cakes capture the very essence of fresh apples. They're topped with an apple glaze, which is applied to the still-warm cake so that it spreads evenly and sets perfectly, cooling to a lustrous sheen. The garnish features cross sections of unpeeled, uncored apples, each revealing a natural star pattern at its center. Perfect for seasonal celebrations, the recipe for these little cakes is modeled after one created by three of the kindest, most generous people I know, longtime friends and bakers extraordinaire Gayle Ortiz and her partners, Joe Ortiz, Gayle's bread-baking genius husband, and Luisa Beers, of Gayle's Bakery in Capitola, California.

It's unusual to see a spongy chiffon cake recipe call for buttering and flouring the pan, but here the pan preparation provides the traction necessary for the batter to expand and grip the sides of the pan as the cake bakes. It also makes it possible to remove the cake from the pan while it is still slightly warm (not hot) from the oven. The cake is then easier to glaze because the residual warmth helps spread the glaze thinly and set up more quickly. **YIELD: 6 OR 8 MINIATURE TUBE CAKES**

CAKES

1 CUP PLUS 1 TABLESPOON (4¼ OUNCES/120 GRAMS) CAKE FLOUR

¾ CUP (5¼ OUNCES/150 GRAMS) GRANULATED SUGAR, DIVIDED

1 TEASPOON BAKING POWDER

½ TEASPOON FINE SEA SALT

½ TEASPOON GROUND CINNAMON

¼ TEASPOON GROUND GINGER

¼ TEASPOON GROUND CLOVES

2 OUNCES (½ STICK/55 GRAMS) UNSALTED BUTTER, MELTED AND COOLED

⅓ CUP (2½ FL OUNCES/75 ML) APPLE CIDER

3 LARGE EGGS, SEPARATED

½ TEASPOON PURE VANILLA EXTRACT

APPLE–CREAM CHEESE GLAZE

6 OUNCES (170 GRAMS) CREAM CHEESE, SOFTENED

⅔ CUP (2½ OUNCES/70 GRAMS) POWDERED SUGAR

2 TABLESPOONS WHOLE MILK

2 TABLESPOONS APPLE CIDER OR 1½ TEASPOONS EACH APPLE CIDER AND CALVADOS

DECORATION

FRESH APPLE CHIPS (OPPOSITE PAGE)

Before baking: Center a rack in the oven and preheat the oven to 350 degrees F (or 325 degrees F if the pans have a dark finish). Lightly coat eight ¾-cup or six 1-cup miniature tube pans with nonstick spray, then flour them, tapping out the excess. Or, butter and flour the pans. (You can also use a baking plaque with six 1-cup decorative-shaped molds or a muffin pan with oversized cups.) Set the prepared pans on a rimmed baking sheet.

To make the cakes: Sift together the flour, ½ cup plus 2 tablespoons (4½ ounces/130 grams) of the sugar, the baking powder, the salt, the cinnamon, the ginger, and the cloves into a large bowl. With a rubber spatula, make a well in the center of the flour mixture and set aside. In a tall, small bowl, combine the butter, apple cider, egg yolks, and vanilla and aerate with a whisk or a handheld mixer on medium-low speed, about 30 seconds. Stop the mixer occasionally and scrape down the sides of the bowl. Pour the egg yolk mixture into the well of the flour mixture and mix by hand or on low speed until smooth and homogeneous, about 20 seconds.

In the bowl of a stand mixer fitted with the whisk attachment, or a handheld mixer with clean beaters, whip the egg whites on medium speed until soft peaks form. Slowly add the remaining 2 tablespoons sugar and continue to whip on medium speed until moist, shiny stiff peaks form. Using the rubber spatula, gently stir one-third of the whipped whites into the batter to lighten it. Then gently fold in the remaining whites. Pour the batter into the prepared pans, filling them half to three-fourths full.

Bake the cakes until they spring back when lightly touched in the center, 15 to 20 minutes. Transfer to a wire rack and let cool in the pans for 15 to 30 minutes.

Tilt and rotate each pan while gently tapping it on a counter to release the cake sides and then invert the cake onto a wire rack. (If you have used a plaque or a muffin pan, tilt, rotate, and tap the pan the same way, invert a wire rack on top of the cakes; invert the cakes onto it, gently shaking the pan to release them; and carefully lift off the pan.) Turn the little cakes right side up on a baking sheet or large platter. The unfrosted cakes can be cooled completely and stored in a sturdy covered container at room temperature for up to 1 day. For longer storage, label with the contents and date and freeze for up to 2 weeks. Thaw at room temperature for about 2 hours.

To make the Apple–Cream Cheese Glaze: In a large bowl, vigorously mix together the cream cheese and sugar with a rubber spatula until smooth. Beat in the milk and apple cider until the mixture is creamy and smooth. If not thin enough for spreading consistency, add additional apple cider, 1 teaspoon at a time.

Brush the glaze over the cakes, allowing it to drip down the sides, if desired. Alternatively, using an offset spatula, spread the glaze over the tops of the cakes, allowing the excess to drip down the sides. Set the cakes aside until the glaze sets, about 2 hours. (You will have glaze left over for another use; cover and refrigerate for up to 2 days.)

When the glaze has set, stick an apple chip upright into the top of each baby cake, and serve.

Fresh Apple Chips

Thin lengthwise slices of unpeeled pears with core intact, or peeled, cored pineapple thinly sliced crosswise can be dried in the same manner as the apple chips.

YIELD: 20 TO 25 SLICES

1 CUP (8 FL OUNCES/240 ML) WATER
1 CUP (7 OUNCES/200 GRAMS) GRANULATED SUGAR
2 GOLDEN DELICIOUS OR GRANNY SMITH APPLES

In a heavy 1 1/2-quart saucepan, combine the water and sugar over low heat and heat, stirring, until the sugar dissolves. Raise the heat to medium-high, bring to a boil, and boil for 1 minute. Remove from the heat and let cool to room temperature.

Place a rack in the upper third and another rack in the lower third of the oven and preheat the oven to 140 degrees F. Line 1 large or 2 small rimmed baking sheets with silicone mats. Or, line with parchment paper and spray lightly with nonstick spray.

Using a mandoline or other slicer, cut off the bottoms of the unpeeled apples but do not core. Cut the apples crosswise into paper-thin slices (they should be about the thickness of a dime or even thinner). Place the slices in the syrup briefly (just a few seconds).

Drain the apple slices and arrange them in single layers, close together but not touching, on the baking sheet(s). Cover the slices with another silicone mat or with a sheet of parchment that has been coated with nonstick spray. If using the parchment, top with another baking sheet to keep the fruit slices flat. If you prefer fruit chips with ruffled edges, don't cover them while baking.

Bake the apple slices for about 35 minutes. Remove the top silicone mat, or the baking sheet and parchment, and return the slices to the oven to bake until they are dry and crisp, 1 to 1 1/2 hours. To test if the chips are ready, remove 1 slice to see if it becomes crispy as it cools. Remove the baking sheet(s) from the oven and transfer the chips to wire racks in a single layer. Let cool completely. As they cool, they will harden.

Store the slices in an airtight container at room temperature for up to 10 days.

Banana-Coconut Upside-Down Cupcakes

Upside-down cakes and tropical fruits have long been convivial companions. In this recipe, sliced bananas and shredded coconut are teamed with warm caramel to create a rich, gooey topping. Making these moist, tender little cakes couldn't be easier, and when you invert them onto a serving plate, you will see that they have actually decorated themselves. Festive yet unfussy, they're especially nice for brunch with family and friends. Or, enjoy them as a decadent afternoon snack, accompanied by a tall, cold glass of milk. **YIELD: 6 CUPCAKES**

CARAMEL TOPPING

1¼ CUPS (9 OUNCES/255 GRAMS) GRANULATED SUGAR

⅓ CUP PLUS 1 TABLESPOON (3 FL OUNCES/90 ML) WATER

3 TABLESPOONS UNSALTED BUTTER

⅛ TEASPOON FINE SEA SALT

2 MEDIUM BANANAS

⅔ CUP (2 OUNCES/55 GRAMS) UNSWEETENED MEDIUM-SHRED DRIED COCONUT

CUPCAKES

1½ CUPS PLUS 2 TABLESPOONS (6¾ OUNCES/190 GRAMS) CAKE FLOUR

½ TEASPOON BAKING POWDER

¼ TEASPOON BAKING SODA

¼ TEASPOON FINE SEA SALT

½ CUP (4 OUNCES/115 GRAMS) SOUR CREAM

¼ CUP (2 OUNCES/55 GRAMS) MASHED RIPE BANANA (ABOUT ½ MEDIUM)

1 TEASPOON PURE VANILLA EXTRACT

4½ OUNCES (1 STICK PLUS 1 TABLESPOON/130 GRAMS) UNSALTED BUTTER, AT ROOM TEMPERATURE

1⅓ CUPS (9¼ OUNCES/265 GRAMS) GRANULATED SUGAR

2 LARGE EGGS, LIGHTLY BEATEN

Before baking: Center a rack in the oven and preheat the oven to 350 degrees F. Using a 12-cup standard muffin pan, lightly coat every other cup with nonstick spray. Preparing alternate cups promotes even baking when not all of the cups are filled. Have all of the cupcake ingredients at room temperature.

To make the Caramel Topping: In a 1-quart, heavy saucepan, combine the sugar and water over medium-low heat and heat, stirring occasionally, until the sugar dissolves. Raise the heat to medium-high and cook, without stirring, until the mixture turns amber. Remove from the heat and stir in the butter (carefully, as it might bubble vigorously) and salt. Set aside to cool slightly, about 5 minutes. Spoon about 2 tablespoons of the hot caramel into each muffin cup. Cut the bananas into ³⁄₁₆-inch-thick slices; you need a total of 18 slices. Fit 3 slices in a circle, shingle fashion, on top of the caramel in each muffin cup. Sprinkle about 1 ½ tablespoons coconut over the banana slices in each cup.

To make the cupcakes: Sift together the flour, baking powder, baking soda, and salt onto a sheet of waxed paper; set aside. In a blender or small food processor, combine the sour cream, banana, and vanilla and process to a smooth liquid. You should have about ⅔ cup (5 ½ fl ounces/165 ml); set aside.

In the bowl of a stand mixer fitted with the paddle attachment, beat the butter on medium speed until creamy and smooth, about 30 seconds. Add the sugar and continue to beat until light and fluffy, 2 to 2 ½ minutes, stopping the mixer as needed to scrape down the sides of the bowl. Add the eggs, about 2 tablespoons at a time, beating after each addition until incorporated. On the lowest speed, add the banana mixture and mix until blended. Maintaining the same speed, gradually add the dry ingredients and mix just until incorporated, stopping the mixer occasionally to scrape down the sides of the bowl. Spoon an equal amount of the batter into each prepared cup, filling them about three-fourths full and spreading evenly.

Bake the cupcakes until their centers spring back when lightly touched, 23 to 25 minutes. Be careful not to over-bake. Transfer to a wire rack and let cool in the pan for about 5 minutes.

Tilt and rotate the pan while gently tapping it on a counter to release the sides of the cupcakes. Invert a wire rack on top of the cupcakes; invert the cupcakes onto it, gently shaking the pan to release them; and carefully lift off the pan. Turn the little cakes right side up on the rack and let cool completely.

Serve the cupcakes the same day they are baked. Or, freeze in a sturdy covered container for up to 2 weeks; thaw for about 1 hour at room temperature before serving.

Butterscotch-Pecan Mini Pies

Elevating the traditional pecan pie to a scrumptious new level, these diminutive desserts are distinguished by their intense butterscotch flavor. The chocolate cookie crust and crunchy toasted pecans perfectly complement the luscious filling. Making the pastry crust is simplicity itself: you just press it into the molds. For a showstopping treat, accompany each little pie with a scoop of premium vanilla or butter-pecan ice cream.   **YIELD: 15 MINIATURE PIES**

½ RECIPE CHOCOLATE TART PASTRY (PAGE 363)

FILLING

1 CUP (4 OUNCES/115 GRAMS) PECAN HALVES, TOASTED (PAGES 15–16)

½ CUP (6 OUNCES BY WEIGHT/170 GRAMS) DARK CORN SYRUP

¾ CUP FIRMLY PACKED (5¼ OUNCES/150 GRAMS) LIGHT BROWN SUGAR

3 OUNCES (¾ STICK/85 GRAMS) UNSALTED BUTTER, CUT INTO ¼-INCH SLICES

¼ CUP PLUS 2 TABLESPOONS (3 FL OUNCES/90 ML) HEAVY CREAM

¼ TEASPOON SALT

2 LARGE EGGS

2 TEASPOONS PURE VANILLA EXTRACT

Before baking: Center a rack in the oven and preheat the oven to 350 degrees F. Have ready one or two 12-cup plaques made up of 3-inch cups with 1-inch fluted, sloping sides (each cup holds 6 tablespoons). The dough is enough for 15 little pie shells, so if you own only 1 plaque, just repeat, forming 3 more pies after the first batch has baked and the pan has cooled.

To line the cups with the tart pastry: Freshly made dough can be shaped right away. If the dough is cold and firm from the refrigerator, let it stand at room temperature just until it is malleable yet still cool to the touch, 15 to 30 minutes. Pinch off 1 scant tablespoon of the dough, roll it into a ball between your palms, and drop it into a cup. Repeat until you have dropped a ball of dough into 15 cups. Space the balls evenly around the second plaque. This promotes even baking when not all of the cups are filled. Press the center of each dough ball with your index finger into the bottom and then up the sides of the cup, distributing the pastry evenly. The object is to use just enough dough to line the cups without creating a thick shell.

To make the filling: Coarsely chop the nuts on a cutting board, and spoon about 2 teaspoons of the nuts into the bottom of each pastry-lined cup. In a small saucepan, combine the corn syrup, sugar, butter, cream, and salt, in that order. Place over low heat and stir just until the butter is melted. Remove from the heat, stir the ingredients together until well blended, and set aside to cool. Stir in the eggs and vanilla until smooth.

Spoon about 1 tablespoon of the filling over the nuts in each cup. (It is difficult to measure the nuts and gooey filling exactly, and because I would rather that you have too much of each than too little, you will have some of both components left over.) They will keep covered and refrigerated for up to a day and can be used to make more mini pies—you will have used only half of the chocolate pastry recipe here—or something else.

Bake the pies until the edges of the crusts appear dull brown (not shiny) and dry and are slightly firm to the touch, 15 to 20 minutes. Transfer the plaques to wire racks and let cool until the pies can be touched, about 15 minutes.

To remove the pies from the plaques, slip the tip of a paring knife under the edge of each pastry shell to help lift the pie from its cup. Transfer the pies to the racks and let cool completely.

Serve at room temperature. To store, arranged the pies in an aluminum foil–lined sturdy, shallow box, cover, and keep at room temperature for up to 2 days.

Cheesecake Timbales

One of my favorite forms of culinary creativity is to give a classic dessert a fresh new personality. Here, miniature cheesecakes take on decidedly dramatic dimensions. Their statuesque shapes are a cinch to create, with timbale molds doing all the work for you. Of course, you can also bake the creamy little cakes in muffin pans or custard cups with equally delicious (and attractive) results.

YIELD: 10 SERVINGS

FOR THE MOLDS

2 TABLESPOONS UNSALTED BUTTER, SOFTENED, OR NONSTICK SPRAY

½ CUP (2 OUNCES/55 GRAMS) FINE GRAHAM CRACKER CRUMBS

FILLING

1¼ POUNDS (TWO 8-OUNCE/225-GRAM PACKAGES PLUS 2 OUNCES/55 GRAMS) CREAM CHEESE, AT ROOM TEMPERATURE

¾ CUP PLUS 1 TABLESPOON (5¾ OUNCES/165 GRAMS) GRANULATED SUGAR

2 LARGE EGGS

1 LARGE EGG YOLK

3 TABLESPOONS HEAVY CREAM

1 TEASPOON PURE VANILLA EXTRACT

FRUIT SALAD

1 CUP (5 OUNCES/140 GRAMS) STRAWBERRIES, HULLED

1 KIWIFRUIT, PEELED

1 SMALL RIPE MANGO, PEELED AND PITTED

1 SMALL, FIRM BUT RIPE NECTARINE, HALVED AND PITTED, OR 2 SPEARS PINEAPPLE, PREFERABLY GOLDEN VARIETY

10 SPRIGS FRESH MINT

Before baking: Center a rack in the oven and preheat the oven to 350 degrees F. Butter ten ½-cup round aluminum timbale molds, each 2⅛ inches in diameter and 2 inches deep. Or, coat the molds lightly with nonstick spray. Then coat the molds with the graham cracker crumbs, gently tapping out the excess crumbs. Have all of the remaining ingredients at room temperature.

To make the filling: In the bowl of a stand mixer fitted with the paddle attachment, beat the cream cheese on medium-low speed until smooth, stopping the mixer to scrape down the sides of the bowl as needed. Reduce the speed to low, add the sugar, and beat until blended. Then add the eggs and egg yolk, one at a time, mixing after each addition until incorporated. Add the cream and vanilla and continue to beat on low speed until the mixture has the consistency of heavy cream.

To ease pouring, transfer the mixture to a 4-cup measuring cup or pitcher. Pour the filling into the prepared molds, filling them almost to the top. Set the filled molds, not touching, in a shallow roasting pan about 2 inches deep, and pour hot water into the pan to come about two-thirds of the way up the sides of the molds.

Bake the cheesecakes until the tops are pale gold, about 35 minutes. Transfer to a wire rack and let cool in the molds for about 2 hours to allow time for the cakes to firm slightly.

Line a sturdy storage container with plastic wrap. To unmold the cheesecakes, gently tap the sides of each timbale mold on a counter to loosen the cake, invert the cake onto your palm, and then gently turn the cake right side up and set it in the container. Cover with a lid or aluminum foil and refrigerate for at least a few hours before serving or for up to 2 days.

To make the Fruit Salad: Finely dice the strawberries, kiwifruit, mango, and nectarine. In a large bowl, toss the fruits to combine.

To serve, center a chilled cheesecake on a plate, and spoon 2 to 3 tablespoons of the salad around each cake. Garnish each cake with a mint sprig.

Chocolate-Dipped Cheesecake-sicles

A whimsical treat for summer parties and barbecues, these are the coolest cheesecakes you have ever seen. Freezing gives the creamy cakes a rich, velvety texture all their own, while chocolate ganache adds a luxurious layer of decadence. For this riff on the classic Popsicle, bake the cheesecakes in muffin cups, then insert a wooden stick into each cake and pop them into the freezer. Once frozen, dip them in chocolate ganache and sprinkle them with macadamia nuts.

YIELD: 11 SERVINGS

1 RECIPE CHEESECAKE TIMBALES (PAGE 247), MADE WITHOUT THE FRUIT SALAD

CHOCOLATE GLAZE

2 CUPS (10 OUNCES/280 GRAMS) UNSALTED MACADAMIA NUTS, TOASTED (PAGES 15–16) AND FINELY CHOPPED

10 OUNCES (280 GRAMS) SEMISWEET CHOCOLATE, FINELY CHOPPED

1 CUP (8 FL OUNCES/240 ML) HEAVY CREAM

Before baking: Center a rack in the oven and preheat the oven to 350 degrees F. Lightly coat 11 cups of a 12-cup standard muffin pan (preferably nonstick) with nonstick spray. Then coat the molds with the graham cracker crumbs, gently tapping out the excess crumbs.

Prepare the cheesecake filling as directed. To ease pouring, transfer the mixture to a 4-cup measuring cup or pitcher. Pour the mixture into the prepared muffin cups, filling each cup to just below the rim. Set the muffin pan in a larger shallow pan, such as a 15½-by-10½-by-1-inch pan (jelly-roll pan), and pour in hot water to come about halfway up the sides of the muffin cups.

Bake the cheesecakes until they are ivory colored, appear dry, tiny cracks (not open crevices) are beginning to form in the tops, and they are slightly firm to the touch though still soft underneath, 35 to 40 minutes. Transfer the muffin pan to a wire rack and let stand until the cheesecakes are cool to the touch, about 30 minutes.

To unmold, tap the sides of the muffin pan on a counter to loosen the cheesecakes. Place a sheet of plastic wrap or waxed paper on top of the cakes and a cutting board

on top of the paper. Invert the pan onto the plastic wrap and cutting board. Lift off the pan and let the cheesecakes firm up slightly and cool completely, about 1 hour.

Line a deep storage container (deep enough to accommodate the stick that will be inserted in the cheesecakes) with plastic wrap, and transfer each cheesecake, right side up, to the container. Cover with a lid or aluminum foil and refrigerate for at least 2 hours or up to overnight to firm. Then insert a wooden Popsicle stick into each cheesecake, re-cover the container, and place in the freezer until frozen.

To coat the cheesecakes with the Chocolate Glaze: Have the same (but cleaned) muffin pan that the cheesecakes were baked in originally. Spoon a scant tablespoon of the chopped nuts in the bottom of each of 11 cups and set the pan aside.

To make the glaze, place the chocolate in a medium bowl. In a small saucepan, bring the cream just to a boil over medium-low heat. Pour the cream over the chocolate and let stand for 30 seconds. Whisk together until the chocolate melts and the mixture is smooth and shiny. Set aside just to cool slightly, about 5 minutes. Put the remaining nuts into a medium bowl.

Remove the cheesecakes from the freezer. Working with 1 cheesecake at a time, and holding it by its wooden stick, dip the cheesecake into the chocolate, immersing it to a depth of about 1 inch (about ¼ inch of the cheesecake should be chocolate free). Lift the cheesecake from the chocolate, check to make sure it is evenly coated with the glaze, and then allow any chocolate dripping from the base to fall back into the bowl. Turn the cheesecake upright very briefly to allow any excess chocolate to flow downward, coating the dipped area evenly. Then, without delay, dip the cheesecake, chocolate side down, into the nuts, applying by hand as many nuts as you wish to fill in any gaps. Gently press the nuts into the glaze. Set the cheesecake, chocolate side down (stick up), on top of the nuts in a muffin-pan cup (don't press it down into the cup; just rest it on the nuts for easy removal later). Repeat with the remaining cheesecakes.

Transfer the muffin pan to the refrigerator to set up the glaze, about 15 minutes. When the chocolate has firmed, carefully lift the cheesecakes by their sticks and return them, stick up, to the original plastic wrap–lined container. Cover and return to the freezer until serving. They will keep for up to 1 week.

Serve the cheesecake-sicles directly from the freezer. Or, if too firm, let them stand at room temperature for about 10 minutes before serving. Accompany each cold cheesecake-sicle with a large colorful napkin.

Coffee Cup Tiramisu

The inspiration for this divine classic dessert came from a business dinner in my home, catered by gifted and creative chef Ayelet Perry and her husband, Nir Perry, owners of Cassis Catering in Redwood City, California, and the Red Currant Restaurant in Menlo Park, California. They presented individual portions of tiramisu in square coffee cups, each topped with a crisp biscotti. My version, based on their clever coffee-cup presentation, calls for circles of vanilla sponge cake soaked in coffee syrup, layered with a fluffy mascarpone cheese filling, and finished with grated chocolate. Perfect for entertaining, the tiramisu actually benefits from being made 1 to 2 days ahead, freeing up your time before the party. **YIELD: 9 SERVINGS**

SPONGE SHEET CAKE

1 CUP PLUS 2 TABLESPOONS (4½ OUNCES/130 GRAMS)
    CAKE FLOUR

½ CUP (3½ OUNCES/100 GRAMS) GRANULATED SUGAR

6 LARGE (½ CUP/4 FL OUNCES/120 ML) EGG YOLKS

1 TEASPOON PURE VANILLA EXTRACT

4 LARGE (½ CUP/4 FL OUNCES/120 ML) EGG WHITES

COFFEE SYRUP

1 CUP (8 FL OUNCES/240 ML) BREWED ESPRESSO OR
    STRONG COFFEE

⅓ CUP (2¼ OUNCES/65 GRAMS) GRANULATED SUGAR

2 TABLESPOONS KAHLÚA OR OTHER COFFEE LIQUEUR

MASCARPONE FILLING

6 LARGE EGG YOLKS

⅔ CUP PLUS 2 TABLESPOONS (5½ OUNCES/155 GRAMS)
    GRANULATED SUGAR

½ CUP (4 FL OUNCES/120 ML) PLUS 1 TABLESPOON
    SWEET MARSALA

3 LARGE (⅓ CUP/2½ FL OUNCES/75 ML) EGG WHITES

TWO 8-OUNCE (225-GRAM) CONTAINERS MASCARPONE
    CHEESE, AT ROOM TEMPERATURE

1 TABLESPOON WHOLE MILK

5 OUNCES (140 GRAMS) BITTERSWEET CHOCOLATE, FINELY
    GRATED TO YIELD ABOUT ⅔ CUP

Before baking: Center a rack in the oven and preheat the oven to 350 degrees F. Line an 18 by 13 by 1-inch pan (half sheet pan) with aluminum foil, allowing the foil to extend about 4 inches beyond the 2 narrow sides and crimping the foil lightly along the edges of the pan. Lightly coat the foil with nonstick spray, then flour it, tapping out the excess flour. Or, butter and flour the foil.

To make the Sponge Sheet Cake: Sift together the flour and ¼ cup (1¾ ounces/50 grams) of the sugar onto a sheet of waxed paper; set aside. Place the remaining ¼ cup sugar in a small bowl; set aside.

In a medium bowl, using a handheld mixer, whip the egg yolks on high speed until they thicken, increase in volume, and appear pale yellow, 3 to 5 minutes. Add the vanilla during the final moments of whipping. To test if the yolks have thickened enough, lift the beater. If they fall back into the bowl in a ribbon that rests softly on the surface and remains there for 5 to 7 seconds, they are ready. But if the ribbon immediately dissolves into the surface, continue whipping until the yolks are the desired thickness. Detach the beaters and tap them against the side of the bowl to free the excess yolks.

In the bowl of a stand mixer fitted with the whisk attachment, whip the egg whites on medium-low speed until foamy. Increase the speed to medium and begin adding the reserved sugar, 1 teaspoon at a time, whipping until soft white peaks form, about 1 minute. Maintaining the same speed, gradually add the remaining sugar in a steady stream and continue to whip until glossy white, stiff but not dry peaks form, about 2 minutes.

Pour the yolks over the whites. Using a rubber spatula, fold the yolks and whites together using only a few strokes. Don't be too concerned if some of the yolks are still visible. Using a metal icing spatula, scoop up one-third of the flour mixture, sprinkle it over the surface, and fold it in with the spatula. Add the remaining flour mixture in two additions in the same way, folding just until incorporated. Using the spatula, scoop the batter from the bowl onto 5 or 6 different areas of the prepared pan. Then gently spread the batter to cover the pan in as even a layer as possible.

Bake the cake until it is barely colored (still remains pale yellow), its surface appears set, and it feels firm but still spongy when pressed gently with a finger in the center, 10 to 12 minutes. Transfer to a wire rack and let cool in the pan for 10 to 15 minutes.

To release the cake, loosen the foil from the two ends, invert a large wire rack on top of the pan, and invert the cake onto it. Lift off the pan, and carefully peel off the foil. Cover the cake with the bottom of the pan and invert the cake, right side up, onto the pan, and lift off the rack. Let the cake cool completely, 30 to 60 minutes.

Using a 2 $\frac{1}{2}$-inch round cutter, and cutting close together, cut out 22 circles of cake. (Only 18 are needed for this dessert; the extras are for insurance or snacking.) If assembling the dessert within 24 hours, cover the cake circles securely with aluminum foil or plastic wrap and store at room temperature. For longer storage, place the cake circles in a sturdy covered container, label with the contents and date, and freeze for up to 10 days. Thaw at room temperature for 45 minutes.

To make the Coffee Syrup: In a medium bowl, combine the coffee, sugar, and liqueur and stir until the sugar is dissolved; set aside.

To make the Mascarpone Filling: Fill a 4-quart saucepan two-thirds full of water and bring to a simmer. Half fill a large bowl with ice cubes and water to create an ice-water bath for cooling the filling. In a large heatproof bowl, whisk together the egg yolks and $\frac{2}{3}$ cup ($4\frac{1}{2}$ ounces/

130 grams) of the sugar. Whisk in $\frac{1}{2}$ cup of the Marsala, then rest the bowl over (not touching) the simmering water in the saucepan. Cook the mixture, whisking constantly, until it thickens and registers 160 degrees F on an instant-read thermometer, 3 to 5 minutes. Transfer the bowl to the ice-water bath and let stand, stirring occasionally, until cooled to room temperature, about 70 degrees F. Remove from the ice-water bath; set nearby.

Working with 2 cake circles at a time, dip them into the soaking syrup and place them in a single layer on a large platter. Set them aside (still on the platter) to allow the syrup to soak in while finishing the filling.

In a medium bowl, using a handheld mixer, whip the egg whites on medium-low speed until foamy. Increase the speed to medium and begin adding the remaining 2 tablespoons sugar, 1 teaspoon at a time, whipping until soft white peaks form, about 1 minute. Then, maintaining the same speed, begin adding the sugar in a steady stream and continue whipping until thick, stiff, glossy peaks form, 1 to 2 minutes. Set nearby.

In a large bowl, using a rubber spatula, briefly beat together the mascarpone cheese and milk until creamy, soft peaks form. Using the spatula, fold the cooled egg yolk mixture and the remaining 1 tablespoon Marsala into the mascarpone mixture. Then, fold the egg whites into the mascarpone mixture.

To assemble the tiramisu: Select 9 coffee cups or tumblers, each with a capacity of 1 cup, and set them on a large tray or rimmed baking sheet. Using an ice cream scoop a scant 2 inches in diameter (#24), deposit 2 $\frac{1}{2}$ to 3 tablespoons of the filling into the bottom of a coffee cup, and place a soaked cake round on top. Top with another 2 $\frac{1}{2}$ to 3 tablespoons of the filling, then another cake round, and finally, another 2 $\frac{1}{2}$ to 3 tablespoons filling. Fill the remaining 8 cups in the same way. Finish the top of each cup with a sprinkling of the grated chocolate.

Place a piece of plastic wrap over each cup to seal the dessert securely and refrigerate for at least 30 to 45 minutes or for up to 3 days. Let sit at room temperature for a few minutes to lessen the chill before serving.

Miniature Financier Teacups with Candied Kumquats

Guaranteed to lift your spirits, these French-inspired cakes are ideal whenever you crave a little something sweet. They are wonderfully adaptable, partnering equally well with everything from tea and coffee to wine, sherry, or port. These financiers are chewy, yet lighter and more delicate than traditional financiers, which are like tiny pound cakes. Enriched with browned butter, ground almonds, honey, and orange zest, you will never settle for eating just one. A Zyliss rotary grater is the ideal tool for grinding the nuts, quickly transforming them into a fine powder that blends smoothly into the batter. If you are lucky enough to find fresh red currants in the market near the end of June or early July, grab them for an easy, special summertime garnish. Rinse them carefully, drain them on a paper towel, and then place a few (even with stems) on top of each miniature financier.   **YIELD: 3 DOZEN MINIATURE CAKES (2 OR 3 PER SERVING)**

CANDIED KUMQUATS (OPTIONAL)

16 (6 OUNCES/170 GRAMS) KUMQUATS

1 CUP (8 FL OUNCES/240 ML) WATER

1 TABLESPOON LIGHT CORN SYRUP

1½ CUPS (10½ OUNCES/300 GRAMS) GRANULATED SUGAR

FINANCIERS

8 OUNCES (2 STICKS/225 GRAMS) UNSALTED BUTTER,
    PLUS 2 TABLESPOONS, MELTED, FOR PREPARING PANS

¼ CUP (1½ OUNCES/40 GRAMS) WHOLE NATURAL ALMONDS,
    FINELY GROUND TO YIELD ¾ CUP

2 CUPS (7 OUNCES/200 GRAMS) POWDERED SUGAR

½ CUP PLUS 2 TABLESPOONS (3 OUNCES/85 GRAMS)
    ALL-PURPOSE FLOUR

½ TEASPOON BAKING POWDER

¼ TEASPOON SALT

FINELY GRATED ZEST OF 1 ORANGE

¾ CUP (6 FL OUNCES/180 ML) EGG WHITES (5 TO 6 LARGE)

1 TABLESPOON HONEY

1 TEASPOON PURE VANILLA EXTRACT

½ TEASPOON PURE ALMOND EXTRACT

To make the Candied Kumquats: Using a small serrated knife, trim off the stem end from each kumquat and then cut crosswise into ¼-inch-thick slices. In a

medium, heavy saucepan, combine the water, corn syrup, and sugar over medium heat and heat until the sugar dissolves, stirring if needed. Raise the heat to medium-high and bring to a boil without stirring. Add the kumquat slices, reduce the heat to medium, and simmer until the fruit is tender and the sugar syrup is syrupy, 15 to 25 minutes. Transfer the kumquat slices and syrup to a heatproof bowl and set aside to cool to room temperature. To store, transfer to an airtight container and refrigerate for up to 1 month. You should have about ¾ cup (5 ounces/140 grams).

Advance preparation: First, following the directions for making brown butter on page 19, prepare the brown butter for the financiers' batter. In a heavy 1½-quart saucepan, melt the 8 ounces butter over medium-low heat and heat just until it begins to turn a delicate brown, about 8 minutes. Remove from the heat and pour into a small bowl. If you like, you can strain the butter through a fine-mesh sieve, but I prefer the golden specks in the batter. Set the butter aside to cool just until it is body temperature yet still melted. (To hasten the cooling, whisk the butter over an ice-water bath.) Meanwhile, prepare the pans for baking.

Before baking: Center a rack in the oven and preheat the oven to 350 degrees F. Brush three 12-cup miniature muffin pans with the melted butter, and put them in the refrigerator for about 15 minutes to solidify the butter. Or, lightly coat the pans with nonstick spray. Or, you can use any of the wide variety of shapes in a similar size available in nonstick flexible silicone molds and plaques (page 38). If using flexible silicone bakeware, arrange them next to one another on a perforated (or standard) baking sheet for even baking and for support when moving them in and out of the oven.

To make the Financiers: In a bowl, whisk together the nuts, sugar, flour, baking powder, salt, and orange zest; set aside. In another large bowl, whisk the egg whites just until foamy. Add the flour mixture and stir until combined. Gradually stir in the melted butter until thoroughly blended. Stir in the honey and the vanilla and almond extracts. Let the mixture rest at room temperature until just slightly thickened, about 30 minutes.

Using an ice cream scoop about 1 1/4 inches in diameter (#70) or a spoon, deposit the batter into the prepared muffin cups, filling them two-thirds full.

Bake the cakes until their tops are golden with lacy edges, appear set, and spring back when lightly pressed, 13 to 15 minutes. Transfer to wire racks and let cool in the pans for 5 to 10 minutes.

Gently tap each pan on a counter and then invert onto a wire rack. The cakes should release cleanly and quickly from the pans. Set them, lacy side down, on the racks and let cool completely.

To serve, turn the financiers lacy side up on individual plates or a platter. Using a slotted spoon, scoop the kumquats out of the syrup and drain briefly on paper toweling. Center a slice on each financier. Store the remaining kumquats in their syrup in the refrigerator for up to 1 month and use to garnish additional batches or another dessert.

Flaky Lemon-Marshmallow Turnovers

Just right for casual parties and buffets, these irresistible pastries are like miniature lemon meringue pies wrapped in a flaky phyllo crust. Inside each turnover, tangy citrus curd is paired with a fluffy marshmallow that melts into a soft, gooey accompaniment to the filling during baking. If you are using frozen phyllo dough, let it thaw overnight in the refrigerator. Then, for ease in handling, allow the phyllo, still in its packaging, to sit at room temperature for 2 hours before shaping. If the dough tears while you are folding the turnovers, don't worry. Just stick the pieces together with melted butter. After the turnovers bake, you won't notice the patchwork. **YIELD: 2 DOZEN TURNOVERS**

16 PHYLLO SHEETS, ABOUT 16 BY 12 INCHES, AT ROOM TEMPERATURE

8 OUNCES (2 STICKS/225 GRAMS) UNSALTED BUTTER, MELTED

1 RECIPE LEMON CURD (PAGE 370)

12 MINIATURE WHITE MARSHMALLOWS, CUT IN HALF

3 TABLESPOONS GRANULATED SUGAR

To assemble the turnovers: Line a rimmed baking sheet with a silicone mat or parchment paper. Unwrap the phyllo, unroll it, and then place the 16 stacked sheets on a work surface. Cut the sheets lengthwise into 4 equal strips each about 3 inches wide and 16 inches long. Cover the phyllo with waxed paper and a damp towel. You will have 64 strips. You need only 48 strips for this recipe, but because phyllo tears so easily, especially phyllo that has been frozen and thawed, I have included a cushion of extra strips here.

To form each turnover, stack 2 strips and then brush the top with melted butter. Spoon about 1 rounded teaspoon of the curd in the center at the base of the stacked strips, positioning it 1 inch from the end. (Don't use too much filling, or the turnovers will burst during baking.) Place a marshmallow in the center of the curd. Starting at the end near the curd, fold the right bottom corner over the filling to form a triangle (the bottom edge of the strip will be aligned with the left side of the strip). Now, fold the bottom of the triangle up so it is aligned with the left side of the strip. Fold again on the diagonal so the left edge is now aligned with the right edge. Continue folding back and forth, flag fashion, to the end of the strip, creating a multilayered triangle. Fold the corners tightly to prevent the filling from leaking out during baking. Set the pastry, seam side down, on the prepared baking sheet. Brush the folded package with the melted butter. Repeat to make 23 more pastries. (You won't need all of the curd.) Cover the pan with plastic wrap and chill for at least 30 minutes or up to a few hours before baking.

Before baking: Center a rack in the oven and preheat the oven to 350 degrees F.

Remove the plastic wrap, and sprinkle the turnovers lightly with the sugar. Bake the pastries until golden and crisp, 12 to 15 minutes. Transfer to a wire rack and let cool on the pan. Serve warm or at room temperature.

Double-Cranberry Mini Cakes

These versatile little cakes have a wholesome sort of decadence that makes them ideal for any time of day, from a brunch buffet to an afternoon pick-me-up to a casual dinnertime dessert. Enriched with a dollop of sour cream, the moist, tender butter cakes are studded with fresh and dried cranberries, toasted nuts, and crystallized ginger. They're finished with a simple powdered sugar glaze and a sprinkling of cranberries and bits of ginger that hint at the treasures inside. You can also bake the batter in six 1-cup Bundt pans. Butter the pans, lightly coat them with nonstick spray, then flour them, tapping out the excess flour. If the pans (or molds) have an intricate design or detail, prepare them as directed on page 24 to ensure the finished cakes release in one piece. Fill the pans two-thirds full and increase the baking time to 26 to 32 minutes.

YIELD: 2½ TO 3 DOZEN MINIATURE CAKES

CAKE

⅓ CUP (1¼ OUNCES/35 GRAMS) SMALL PECAN PIECES, TOASTED (PAGES 15–16)

⅓ CUP (1¼ OUNCES/35 GRAMS) FRESH CRANBERRIES, PICKED OVER FOR STEMS, CUT IN HALF OR, IF LARGE, COARSELY CHOPPED

⅓ CUP (1½ OUNCES/45 GRAMS) DRIED CRANBERRIES, COARSELY CHOPPED

3 PIECES CRYSTALLIZED GINGER, CUT INTO SMALL DICE TO YIELD 2 TABLESPOONS

1½ CUPS (6¾ OUNCES/195 GRAMS) ALL-PURPOSE FLOUR

¼ TEASPOON SALT

8 OUNCES (2 STICKS/225 GRAMS) UNSALTED BUTTER, AT ROOM TEMPERATURE

1 CUP PLUS 1 TABLESPOON (7½ OUNCES/210 GRAMS) GRANULATED SUGAR

4 LARGE EGGS

1 TABLESPOON SOUR CREAM

1 TEASPOON PURE VANILLA EXTRACT

¼ TEASPOON ORANGE OIL OR 1½ TEASPOONS FINELY GRATED ORANGE ZEST

BROWN BUTTER DRIZZLE

2 OUNCES (½ STICK/55 GRAMS) UNSALTED BUTTER

1¾ CUPS (7½ OUNCES/215 GRAMS) POWDERED SUGAR, SIFTED

3 TO 5 TABLESPOONS (2½ FL OUNCES/75 ML) WHOLE MILK

1 TEASPOON PURE VANILLA EXTRACT

DECORATION

¼ CUP (1¼ OUNCES/35 GRAMS) DRIED CRANBERRIES, COARSELY CHOPPED

2 TABLESPOONS VERY FINELY DICED CRYSTALLIZED GINGER

Before baking: Center a rack in the oven and preheat the oven to 350 degrees F. Butter three 12-cup miniature muffin pans, then flour them, tapping out the excess flour. Or, you can use any of the wide variety of shapes in a similar size available in nonstick flexible silicone molds and plaques (page 38). If using silicone bakeware, arrange them next to one another on a perforated (or standard) baking sheet for even baking and for support when moving them in and out of the oven. Have all of the ingredients at room temperature.

To make the cakes: In a bowl, mix together the nuts, fresh and dried cranberries, and ginger with your fingertips; set aside. Sift together the flour and salt onto a sheet of waxed paper; set aside.

In the bowl of a stand mixer fitted with the paddle attachment, beat the butter on medium speed until creamy and smooth, 30 to 45 seconds. Add the sugar and continue to beat until light and fluffy, about 6 minutes, stopping the mixer occasionally to scrape down the sides of the bowl. Add the eggs, one at a time, CONTINUED ▸

beating after each addition until incorporated. Then add the sour cream, vanilla, and orange oil and beat until blended.

On the lowest speed, gradually add the flour mixture and mix until incorporated, stopping the mixer occasionally to scrape down the sides of the bowl. Detach the paddle and bowl from the mixer, and tap the paddle against the side of the bowl to free the excess batter. Using a rubber spatula, gently fold in the cranberry mixture. Spoon the batter into the prepared muffin cups, filling them three-fourths full. You don't need to spread the batter evenly in each cup; it settles during baking. If you are not filling all of the cups in the third pan (the yield for the recipes varies between 2 1/2 and 3 dozen), space the cups you do fill evenly around the pan. Spacing the cups promotes even baking when not all of the cups are filled.

Bake the cakes until they spring back when lightly touched in the center and are beginning to come away from the sides of the pan, 14 to 16 minutes. Transfer to wire racks and let cool in the pans for 5 minutes.

Gently tap each pan on a counter and then invert onto a wire rack. Turn the cakes right side up on the racks and let cool completely.

To make the Brown Butter Drizzle: Following the directions for making brown butter on page 19, melt the butter in a small, heavy saucepan over medium-low heat and heat just until it begins to turn a delicate brown, 3 to 5 minutes. Remove from the heat, pour into a medium bowl, and stir in the sugar, 3 tablespoons of the milk, and the vanilla until the mixture is creamy and smooth. Add additional milk, 1 teaspoon at a time, until the glaze is liquid enough to drizzle over the cakes in a decorative way.

Slip a sheet of waxed paper under the racks to catch any drips, and drizzle the glaze over the cooled cakes from the tines of a fork. Decorate the tops with the cranberries and ginger. Set the cakes aside for at least 30 minutes to set up the glaze. Serve at room temperature.

Place the leftover cakes in sturdy covered containers, label with the contents and date, and freeze for up to 2 weeks. To thaw, remove the amount you need to a plate (return the container with the remaining cakes to the freezer), cover the cakes loosely with plastic wrap, and set aside at room temperature for 30 to 45 minutes.

Hand Galettes with Assorted Fruit

Handsome showcases for fresh seasonal fruit, these easy-to-assemble, rustic European-style tarts are small enough to be eaten out of hand; hence, their name. **YIELD: ABOUT 18 HAND GALETTES**

FILLING

ONE 8-OUNCE (225-GRAM) PACKAGE CREAM CHEESE, AT ROOM TEMPERATURE

1 CUP (3½ OUNCES/100 GRAMS) POWDERED SUGAR

1 LARGE EGG, LIGHTLY BEATEN

1 TABLESPOON APRICOT JAM

1 TEASPOON PURE VANILLA EXTRACT

¾ CUP (3 OUNCES/85 GRAMS) FINELY CHOPPED WALNUTS

½ RECIPE (TWO 10-OUNCE/280-GRAM DISKS) FOUR PIE CRUSTS AT ONE TIME (PAGE 357)

FRUIT

1 SMALL (4 OUNCES/115 GRAMS) FIRM BUT RIPE PEACH, PEELED, HALVED, PITTED, AND CUT LENGTHWISE INTO ½-INCH-THICK SLICES

1 CUP (5 OUNCES/140 GRAMS) RED RASPBERRIES, PICKED OVER FOR STEMS

1 MEDIUM BUNCH (4 OUNCES/115 GRAMS) SEEDLESS RED GRAPES, HALVED

To make the filling: In a deep, medium bowl, stir and mash the cream cheese with a rubber spatula until smooth. Add the sugar and mix until incorporated. Stir in the egg, jam, and vanilla until well blended. Stir in the walnuts. Cover the bowl with plastic wrap and refrigerate until needed. You should have about 1 ½ cups filling.

Before baking: Center a rack in the oven and preheat the oven to 400 degrees F. Line a large baking sheet with parchment paper.

To roll out the pastry: If the dough is cold and firm from the refrigerator, let it stand at room temperature just until it is malleable enough to roll yet still cool to the touch, 15 to 30 minutes. On a lightly floured work surface, roll out 1 dough disk into a 14-inch circle about ⅛ inch thick. Using a 4 ½-inch round cookie or biscuit cutter (or other template), cut out 7 circles close together. Reserve the dough scraps. Transfer the dough circles to

the prepared baking sheet, spacing them about 1 ½ inches apart. Repeat with the remaining dough disk, and add the circles to the baking sheet.

Combine the dough scraps from the 2 disks (about 6 ounces/170 grams) by stacking the leftover rolled portions (rather than mashing or kneading them together into a tight ball), and then gently shaping the dough into a round disk. Don't worry if the dough doesn't seem cohesive. As you roll it, it will come together. On a lightly floured work surface, roll out the dough into an 8-inch circle about ⅛ inch thick. Cut out 3 or 4 additional circles and place them on the baking sheet.

To form the hand galettes: Spoon about 1 tablespoon of the filling in the center of each dough circle. Using a small offset spatula, spread the filling thinly over the dough to within ¼ inch of the edge.

Cut each peach slice crosswise into 5 small pieces and place the pieces in a medium bowl. Add the raspberries and grape halves and toss to mix. Place 5 to 9 pieces (¼ to ⅓ cup/1 to 1 ½ ounces/30 to 40 grams) of fruit, depending on the size of the pieces, on top of the filling on each circle. With your fingertips, gently lift the edges of the dough circle and pleat them up over the fruit. Then, with your palm, cup the pastry to form a neat round package reminiscent of a money pouch, but don't pinch together the top edges to seal. The galettes will open during baking, which is part of their charm. Each one opens differently, creating its own "personality."

Bake the galettes until the pastry is golden and fruit is soft and appears juicy, 19 to 25 minutes. Transfer to a wire rack and let cool completely on the pan. Serve the galettes at room temperature. They are best eaten the same day they are baked.

Brown Butter Bundtlettes

Two of my favorite baking ingredients are sweet friendship and browned butter, both of which play a starring role in these bundtlettes. The browned butter cake recipe, given to me by talented pastry chef and friend Janet Rikala Dalton, is a cherished mainstay in my baking repertoire. One day, as I was preparing the cakes to give away as gifts, I added my powdered sugar glaze as a finishing touch. I mixed some finely ground coffee and the seeds from a vanilla bean into the glaze, and the result was the lustrous topping featured here, which adds its own special combination of flavor, texture, and sparkle. **YIELD: 8 SMALL CAKES, 8 OR 16 SERVINGS**

CAKES

8 OUNCES (2 STICKS/225 GRAMS) UNSALTED BUTTER

¾ CUP (6 FL OUNCES/180 ML) WELL-SHAKEN BUTTERMILK, AT ROOM TEMPERATURE

1 TEASPOON PURE VANILLA EXTRACT

2 CUPS (9¼ OUNCES/260 GRAMS) ALL-PURPOSE FLOUR

1 TEASPOON BAKING POWDER

¼ TEASPOON SALT

1½ CUPS (10½ OUNCES/300 GRAMS) GRANULATED SUGAR

2 LARGE EGGS, LIGHTLY BEATEN

GLAZE

¾ CUP (2½ OUNCES/70 GRAMS) POWDERED SUGAR

2 TABLESPOONS FINELY GROUND COFFEE

1 VANILLA BEAN, SPLIT LENGTHWISE

¼ CUP (2 FL OUNCES/60 ML) BOILING WATER

Advance preparation: First, following the directions for making brown butter on page 19, prepare the brown butter for the cake batter. In a heavy 1½-quart saucepan, melt the butter over medium-low heat and heat just until it begins to turn a delicate brown, about 8 minutes. Remove from the heat and pour into a small bowl. If you like, you can strain the butter through a fine-mesh sieve, but I prefer the golden specks in the batter. Set aside to cool completely. (To hasten the cooling, whisk the butter over an ice-water bath.) Cover and refrigerate until solid, at least 2 hours or for up to 1 week.

Before baking: Center a rack in the oven and preheat the oven to 350 degrees F (or 325 degrees F if the pans

have a dark finish). Butter eight 1-cup Bundt pans, lightly coat them with nonstick spray, then flour them, tapping out the excess flour. If the pans (or molds) have an intricate design or detail, prepare them as directed on page 24 to ensure the finished cakes release in one piece. (If you are using 2 plaques, each with six 1-cup molds to make the 8 cakes, space the 2 molds you prepare in the second plaque well apart. Spacing the molds promotes even baking when not all of the molds are filled.) Remove the brown butter from the refrigerator and allow it to warm at room temperature for about 20 minutes before proceeding to make the cake. In a small bowl, stir together the buttermilk and vanilla; set aside at room temperature. Have all of the other ingredients at room temperature.

To make the cakes: Sift together the flour, baking powder, and salt onto a sheet of waxed paper; set aside. In the bowl of a stand mixer fitted with the paddle attachment, beat the brown butter on medium speed until creamy and smooth, about 1 minute, stopping the mixer occasionally to scrape down the sides of the bowl. Maintaining the same speed, add the sugar in a steady stream and beat until the mixture is lighter in color and fluffy, 3 to 4 minutes, stopping the mixer as needed to scrape down the sides of the bowl.

On medium speed, add the eggs, 3 to 4 tablespoons at a time, beating after each addition until incorporated. On the lowest speed, add the flour mixture in three additions alternately with the buttermilk mixture in two additions, beginning and ending with the flour mixture and mixing after each addition until incorporated. Stop the mixer after each addition to scrape down the sides of the bowl. Detach the paddle and bowl from the mixer, and tap the paddle against the side of the bowl to free the excess batter.

Divide the batter evenly among the prepared pans (or prepared plaque cups), filling them two-thirds full and spreading the batter evenly with a rubber spatula.

Bake the cakes until a round wooden toothpick inserted in the center comes out free of cake and they are beginning to come away from the sides of the pans, 30 to 33 minutes. Transfer to a wire rack and let cool in the pans for 5 to 10 minutes. While the cakes are cooling, prepare the glaze.

To make the glaze: Place the powdered sugar in a small, deep bowl; set aside. Set a small fine-mesh sieve over a second small heatproof bowl and place the coffee in it. Using a small paring knife, scrape the seeds from the vanilla bean onto the sugar. Pour the boiling water over the ground coffee to make coffee. Then remove 2 teaspoons of the coffee grounds from the sieve and sprinkle them over the sugar. Remove the sieve and discard the remaining coffee grounds. Add 5 teaspoons of the coffee to the sugar mixture and mix together with a rubber spatula until smooth. Reserve the remaining coffee.

Tilt and rotate each pan while gently tapping it on a counter to release the cake sides. Invert a wire rack on top of the cake, invert the cake onto it, and carefully lift off the pan. (If using plaques, unmold the same way.) Arrange all of the cakes on a large rack, and slide a sheet of waxed paper under the rack to catch any drips from the glaze. With a pastry brush, apply a thin coating of the glaze all over the warm cakes. If the glaze is too thick, add additional coffee, 1/2 teaspoon at a time.

If serving the cakes the same day they are baked, set them aside at room temperature until needed. To store the cakes, transfer them to an aluminum foil–lined cake box or a sturdy covered container and keep at room temperature for up to 2 days.

Persimmon Bread Puddings

Persimmons were very much a part of my Indiana upbringing. Our family lived near a park where there were trees that produced tiny, fragrant persimmons. Each slightly bigger than a strawberry, these sweet local legends were intensely flavorful. Nowadays, I celebrate the autumn harvest with creamy little bread puddings featuring a spiced purée made from Hachiya persimmons. If you can't find persimmons, homemade or canned pumpkin puree makes a fine substitute.

The Hachiya persimmon season is brief. When my crop is abundant thanks to kind neighbors and friends who share, I puree the flesh, freeze 1-cup portions in individual resealable plastic bags, overwrap the bags with aluminum foil, and label with the contents and date. You can thaw the bags overnight in the refrigerator, or slip them into a bowl of very warm water for about 20 minutes.

YIELD: 6 SERVINGS

2 LARGE EGGS

3 LARGE (¼ CUP/2 FL OUNCES/60 ML) EGG YOLKS

1⅓ CUPS (10½ FL OUNCES/315 ML) WHOLE MILK

½ CUP (4 FL OUNCES/120 ML) PERSIMMON PUREE

6 TABLESPOONS FIRMLY PACKED (2¾ OUNCES/75 GRAMS) LIGHT BROWN SUGAR

1 TABLESPOON UNSULFURED MOLASSES

1 TEASPOON FINELY GRATED ORANGE ZEST

½ TEASPOON GROUND GINGER

½ TEASPOON GROUND CINNAMON

¼ TEASPOON GROUND CLOVES

¼ TEASPOON NUTMEG, PREFERABLY FRESHLY GRATED

¼ TEASPOON SALT

½ CUP PLUS 1 TABLESPOON (4½ FL OUNCES/135 ML) HEAVY CREAM

3 CUPS CRUST-FREE, CUBED (¾-INCH) DAY-OLD FRENCH OR ITALIAN BREAD

FOR GARNISH

½ CUP (4 FL OUNCES/120 ML) HEAVY CREAM

GROUND CINNAMON FOR SPRINKLING

Before baking: Center a rack in the oven and preheat the oven to 350 degrees F. Lightly butter six ¾-cup ramekins or custard cups.

In a large bowl, whisk together the eggs and egg yolks until blended; set nearby. In a medium saucepan, whisk together the milk, persimmon puree, sugar, molasses, orange zest, spices, and salt. Place over low heat and stir just until hot and the sugar is dissolved. Whisk half the hot milk mixture into the eggs, then whisk the combined mixtures back into the remaining milk mixture. Without delay, strain the custard through a fine-mesh sieve back into the large bowl. Stir in the cream.

Set the ramekins on a large baking sheet. Divide the bread cubes evenly among the ramekins. Pour the custard over the bread, dividing it evenly. Saturate the bread by gently pushing it down into the custard.

Bake the puddings on the baking sheet until a knife blade inserted in the center of a pudding comes out clean, about 25 minutes. Transfer to a wire rack to cool. The puddings will deflate as they cool.

Meanwhile, in a medium, deep bowl, whisk the cream until soft peaks form. Cover and refrigerate until serving.

Serve the puddings warm or at room temperature. Top each pudding with a dollop of the whipped cream, and dust the cream lightly with cinnamon.

Three Cheers for Tiny Pumpkin Pies

The three cheers you would hear at our house are coming from our three grandchildren: Joshua, Natalie, and Daniel. It's a family tradition to enjoy these little pies on Thanksgiving—and to prepare enough of them to share with the children's teachers and classmates. The pastry dough freezes beautifully, so it can be made well before the busy holiday season. When you are ready, just thaw the dough and press it into the muffin cups. (At this point, you can also cover the pastry-lined muffin pans with plastic wrap, and refrigerate them for up to 2 days before filling.) Then, while the oven is preheating, leave the cold pastry-lined pans at room temperature for 20 to 30 minutes. Prepare the filling (it's a snap) and bake, then sit back and enjoy the rave reviews from your own cheering section.   YIELD: 8 DOZEN MINIATURE PUMPKIN PIES

PASTRY

3 CUPS (13¾ OUNCES/390 GRAMS) ALL-PURPOSE FLOUR

½ TEASPOON SALT

12 OUNCES (3 STICKS/340 GRAMS) COLD UNSALTED BUTTER, CUT INTO ¼-INCH SLICES

9 OUNCES (ONE 8-OUNCE/225-GRAM PACKAGE PLUS 2 TABLESPOONS) COLD CREAM CHEESE, CUT INTO CHUNKS

PUMPKIN FILLING

3 CUPS (26 OUNCES/740 GRAMS) CANNED PUMPKIN PUREE

2 CUPS (14 OUNCES/400 GRAMS) GRANULATED SUGAR

1½ CUPS (12 OUNCES/340 GRAMS) SOUR CREAM

6 LARGE EGGS, LIGHTLY BEATEN

⅓ CUP (2½ FL OUNCES/75 ML) WHOLE MILK

1 TABLESPOON GROUND PUMPKIN PIE SPICE

FOR GARNISH

¾ CUP (6 FL OUNCES/180 ML) HEAVY CREAM

NUTMEG, PREFERABLY FRESHLY GRATED, FOR SPRINKLING

To make the pastry: In a food processor, combine the flour and salt and pulse 3 or 4 times to blend. With the motor running, gradually add the butter slices and cream cheese chunks through the feed tube and process just until the dough comes together in a ball. Divide the dough into thirds. If you are not using the dough right away, flatten each portion into a disk, wrap separately in plastic wrap, and refrigerate for up to 3 days. For longer storage, overwrap with aluminum foil, label with the contents and date, and freeze for up to 10 days. Thaw overnight in the refrigerator.

Before baking: Center a rack in the oven and preheat the oven to 375 degrees F. Have ready three 12-cup miniature muffin pans.

Place 1 dough portion on a work surface. Using an ice cream scoop about 1⅛ inches in diameter (#100) or a spoon, drop mounds of about 1½ teaspoons of the dough into 32 muffin cups. One by one, roll each piece of dough into a ball between your palms. This step aids in shaping the crusts more evenly. Dip your index finger into a small amount of flour and then press the center of each dough ball into the bottom and then up the sides of the cup, distributing it evenly.

To make the Pumpkin Filling: In a medium bowl, combine the pumpkin puree, sugar, sour cream, eggs, milk, and pumpkin pie spice and stir until well blended.

Fill each tart shell with a rounded teaspoon (be sure to use a measuring spoon, not a spoon from your flatware drawer) of the filling. Bake the pies for 15 minutes. Reduce the oven temperature to 350 degrees F and continue to bake just until the filling is puffy and feels firm when lightly touched and the pastry is light gold, 4 to 8 minutes longer. (Don't bake until the filling cracks or the pies will be overcooked.) Transfer to wire racks and let cool in the pans for 15 to 20 minutes.   CONTINUED ▶

Tilt each pan slightly and tap it gently on a counter to release the tiny pies. If necessary, carefully slip a small, flexible metal spatula between the pastry and the pan and trace around the perimeter of each pie to loosen the sides. Remove the pies and let cool completely on the racks. Repeat with the remaining dough and filling; you will need to bake 5 more panfuls to finish the dough and filling.

If you are not making a large batch, wrap the leftover dough in plastic wrap and overwrap with aluminum foil. Transfer the filling to a sturdy covered container. Label both packages with the contents and date and freeze for up to 10 days. Thaw in the refrigerator for several hours. Before using, remove from the refrigerator and allow the dough to warm until it is pliable and the filling to warm until it is close to room temperature, 30 to 40 minutes.

If serving the pies within 24 hours, transfer them to aluminum foil–lined cake boxes or sturdy covered containers and store at room temperature. For longer storage, freeze the pies in the sturdy containers for up to 2 weeks. Thaw at room temperature the day of serving. To freshen the pies, heat them in a preheated 300 degree F oven until warm, 8 to 10 minutes. Let cool before serving.

To garnish the pies: A half hour to an hour before serving, in a deep, medium bowl, whisk the cream until it is thick enough to spoon or pipe, then top each pie with a tiny dollop of whipped cream. Sprinkle the cream lightly with nutmeg.

Crème Fraîche Custard with Lacy Brûlée Wafers

This recipe, inspired by the classic crème brûlée, indulges dessert lovers with a surprise. Beneath the creamy custard there is a hidden layer of luscious prune puree, enlivened with aromatic oolong tea and a judicious dash of Armagnac. Crème fraîche gives the delicate custard a fresh, subtle tanginess that complements the complex sweetness of the puree. Thin, crisp, and fragrant with spices, the lacy cookie wafers, formed as wide or slightly wider than the diameter of the ramekins (I used ramekins 4 inches in diameter), are placed right on top, echoing crème brûlée's iconic caramelized topping.

The wafers recipe yields a large number of small wafers. Once you have made what you need for this recipe, you can use the remaining batter to make larger wafers for placing on top of old-fashioned tumblers ($3\frac{1}{2}$ inches high and 3 inches in diameter) or clear-glass, stemmed goblets filled with ice cream or a simple fruit dessert. **YIELD: 6 SERVINGS**

LACY BRÛLÉE WAFERS

2 OUNCES (½ STICK/55 GRAMS) UNSALTED BUTTER

¼ CUP (1¾ OUNCES/50 GRAMS) GRANULATED SUGAR

¼ CUP (3 OUNCES BY WEIGHT/85 GRAMS) DARK CORN SYRUP OR LYLE'S GOLDEN SYRUP

1 TABLESPOON FINELY GRATED ORANGE ZEST

¼ TEASPOON GROUND GINGER

¼ TEASPOON GROUND CINNAMON

⅛ TEASPOON GROUND CLOVES

½ CUP (2¼ OUNCES/65 GRAMS) ALL-PURPOSE FLOUR

½ TEASPOON PURE VANILLA EXTRACT

CRÈME FRAÎCHE CUSTARD

ABOUT ⅓ CUP (2½ OUNCES/70 GRAMS) DRIED PLUM-ARMAGNAC PUREE (PAGE 000)

½ CUP (4 OUNCES/115 GRAMS) CRÈME FRAÎCHE

1½ CUPS (12 FL OUNCES/360 ML) HEAVY CREAM

⅓ CUP (2¼ OUNCES/65 GRAMS) GRANULATED SUGAR

4 LARGE (⅓ CUP/2½ FL OUNCES/75 ML) EGG YOLKS

1½ TEASPOONS PURE VANILLA EXTRACT

ARMAGNAC FOR SERVING (OPTIONAL)

To make the Lacy Brûlée Wafers: Center a rack in the oven and preheat the oven to 350 degrees F. Have ready 2 baking sheets.

In a small saucepan, combine the butter, sugar, corn syrup, and orange zest, in that order, and bring to a boil over medium-low heat, stirring once or twice to combine the ingredients. Remove from the heat and stir in the ginger, cinnamon, cloves, and flour. Add the vanilla and stir until smooth.

To form each wafer, drop ½ teaspoon of the batter onto the baking sheet, spacing the wafers well apart since they spread considerably as they bake. (This is the amount that works to create a wafer that will cover a 3-inch-diameter ramekin; if your ramekins are a different size, adjust the amount as needed.) Don't bake more than 3 or 4 wafers at a time. They harden within seconds of being removed from the oven, and it is difficult to get more than that off the baking sheet quickly enough. You need only 6 wafers for this dessert, so once you have baked them, you can make larger wafers with the remaining batter if you like.

CONTINUED ►

Bake the wafers until golden brown, 4 to 5 minutes. Remove the baking sheet from the oven and let cool for 10 to 15 seconds. Then, with a metal spatula, lift 1 warm wafer at a time onto a wire rack to cool. Let the wafers cool completely. Repeat with the remaining batter. You should have about 5 dozen wafers 4¼ to 4½ inches in diameter. To store, stack the cooled wafers in an airtight container and keep at room temperature for up to 1 week. Leave the oven on if you will be baking the custards now.

To make the Crème Fraîche Custard: Reduce the oven temperature to 300 degrees F. Place six ½-cup 3-inch round ramekins or custard cups on a baking sheet.

Spoon about 2 teaspoons of the plum puree into each ramekin and use the back of the spoon to spread it evenly.

Place a fine-mesh sieve over a medium bowl. Put the crème fraîche, heavy cream, and sugar, in that order, in a heavy 1½-quart saucepan and heat over low heat, stirring occasionally, just until the sugar dissolves. Do not allow to boil. Remove from the heat. In a bowl, whisk together the egg yolks and vanilla until blended. Add the warm cream and stir with the whisk to combine. Pour the mixture

through the sieve (as the liquid flows through the sieve, it will catch any cooked egg yolk particles and deflate any bubbles that may have formed during stirring).

Divide the custard evenly among the ramekins and place the pan on a rack in the oven. Pour hot water into the pan to come almost halfway up the sides of the ramekins. Bake until the custard is just set (it doesn't quiver when a ramekin is lightly moved), 35 to 40 minutes. Be careful not to overbake. Using metal tongs, transfer the ramekins from the water bath to a wire rack. Allow the ramekins to cool until they can be touched, about 20 minutes.

Refrigerate the custards until well chilled (they firm as they cool), 1 to 2 hours, then serve directly from the refrigerator. Or, cover the chilled ramekins with plastic wrap and return them to the refrigerator for up to 2 days.

Just before eating, set a wafer on top of each ramekin. If desired, crack each wafer and pour about 1 teaspoon Armagnac on top.

A Dessert from Down Under with a Patriotic American Filling

This spirited dessert is based on one I enjoyed at the famed Balthazar Restaurant in New York. Its foundation is a Pavlova, a Down Under treat whose history evokes such lively debate among Australians and New Zealanders that I will not venture to describe its origins until the friendly controversy is resolved. Suffice it to say, a Pavlova is a meringue that is uniquely crisp on the outside and moist and tender on the inside. Here, Pavlovas are topped with a filling of whipped cream and berries that pays sweet tribute to America's patriotic red, white, and blue.

If you are short on time, you don't have to pipe the meringue. You can just spoon mounds onto the baking sheet, shape them into 3-inch rounds with a rubber spatula, and then use the back of a spoon to create a cuplike shape for holding the filling. The important ingredient in this recipe is the cream of tartar (or vinegar) because it influences the meringue's characteristic texture. Also, an easy way to free fresh red currants from the stem is to remove them gently a few at a time with the tines of a fork. **YIELD: 8 TO 10 SERVINGS**

DOWN UNDER PAVLOVA

1 ½ TEASPOONS PURE VANILLA EXTRACT

½ TEASPOON CREAM OF TARTAR OR 2 TEASPOONS WHITE WINE VINEGAR OR DISTILLED WHITE VINEGAR

1 ½ TABLESPOONS CORNSTARCH

1 ½ CUPS (10 ½ OUNCES/300 GRAMS) GRANULATED SUGAR

¾ CUP (6 FL OUNCES/180 ML) EGG WHITES (5 TO 6 LARGE)

PINCH OF SALT

PATRIOTIC AMERICAN FILLING

1 CUP (8 FL OUNCES/240 ML) HEAVY CREAM

2 TABLESPOONS GRANULATED SUGAR

2 TEASPOONS DARK RUM

1 TEASPOON PURE VANILLA EXTRACT

2 CUPS (10 OUNCES/280 GRAMS) RED RASPBERRIES, PICKED OVER FOR STEMS

2 CUPS (10 OUNCES/280 GRAMS) BLUEBERRIES, PICKED OVER FOR STEMS

1 CUP (4 OUNCES/115 GRAMS) FRESH RED CURRANTS, STEMMED (OPTIONAL)

Before baking: Center a rack in the oven and preheat the oven to 275 degrees F. Line a large baking sheet with parchment paper. Have ready a large pastry bag, either a clear-plastic disposable bag or a reusable bag (one from which you have already cut off the tip).

Pour the vanilla and vinegar (if using) into a small cup. In a small bowl, stir the cornstarch into the sugar. Set the cup and bowl aside.

In the bowl of a stand mixer fitted with the whisk attachment, whip together the egg whites, cream of tartar (if using), and salt on medium speed until soft peaks form when the whisk is lifted, about 2 minutes. Increase the speed to medium-high and slowly sprinkle in the sugar mixture. Then continue to beat until glossy, stiff peaks form when the whisk is lifted, 4 to 5 minutes. Add the vanilla during the final moments of whipping.

Without delay, spoon the meringue into the pastry bag, and instead of fitting the bag with a decorating tip, use scissors and a ruler to cut off a 2 ½-inch CONTINUED ▸

piece from its tip. Pipe the meringue into round mounds about 3 ½ inches in diameter on the baking sheet.

Bake the meringues until they are crisp, dry to the touch on the outside, and snow white, 50 to 60 minutes. The exterior should not be tan or cracked, and the interiors should have a marshmallow consistency. If the meringues begin to color or crack during baking, reduce the temperature to 250 degrees F. When the meringues are ready, transfer to a wire rack and let cool completely on the pan, at least 20 minutes.

Whether you are planning on serving the meringues an hour after baking or up to 3 days later, carefully lift them from the baking sheet, place them in a single layer in a sturdy airtight container, and leave them at room temperature. (If you do make the meringues in advance, be sure the container is airtight, as any humidity will soften them.)

To make the Patriotic American Filling: Using a whisk or a handheld mixer, whip together the cream, sugar, rum, and vanilla in a deep, medium bowl until soft peaks form. Cover and refrigerate. Just before serving, use a whisk just to bring the whipped cream together. In a bowl, combine the berries and currants (if using) and blend gently with a rubber spatula.

To assemble: Gently cut off the top one-fourth to one-third of each meringue with a sharp, thin-bladed knife. Set the bottoms on a serving platter or on individual plates. Fill each bottom with a spoonful of the whipped cream, and then spoon the fruit onto the whipped cream, leaving the edge of the shell uncovered. Place a meringue lid on top or lean it against the side. Serve the desserts right away before they become soggy. Pass any remaining cream and fruit at the table.

Fruit Cocktail Trifles with Crème Anglaise

Trifles look especially artistic when viewed through glass, which showcases the beauty of the colorful layers. Because these miniature versions are presented in individual tumblers or stemmed goblets, each dessert maintains its attractive appearance right down to the last luscious spoonful. Here, poppy seed cake (whose tiny black polka dots add visual intrigue) is layered with a mélange of strawberries, raspberries, cherries, mangoes, and red currants. You need only half of the cake to make the trifles; wrap the other half and reserve for another use, such as Frozen Fruit Rainbow Terrine (page 143), or keep it on hand for snacking. Variations are as boundless as your imagination: just use your favorite seasonal fruits.

For the best flavor and texture, chill the trifles for at least 3 hours before serving and eat them within 24 hours. **YIELD: 6 INDIVIDUAL TRIFLES**

FRUIT FILLING

4 CUPS (17½ OUNCES/500 GRAMS) MIXED FRESH FRUITS SUCH AS THINLY SLICED, HULLED STRAWBERRIES; RED RASPBERRIES, PICKED OVER FOR STEMS; FINELY DICED, PEELED RIPE MANGO; PITTED, QUARTERED CHERRIES; AND STEMMED FRESH RED CURRANTS, IN ANY COMBINATION

3 TO 4 TABLESPOONS GRANULATED SUGAR, DEPENDING ON THE SWEETNESS OF THE FRUITS

¼ CUP (2 FL OUNCES/60 ML) DRY WHITE WINE OR FRUIT JUICE (OPTIONAL)

½ (9 BY 6½ INCHES) SILVER CAKE WITH POPPY SEEDS (PAGE 346)

1 RECIPE CRÈME ANGLAISE (PAGE 369)

To prepare the fruit: Place all of the fruits in a large bowl and sprinkle them with the sugar. Using a rubber spatula, gently toss the fruits to coat them evenly with the sugar. Set aside for at least 1 hour to draw out the juices, tossing the fruit occasionally. If using, add the wine to the fruit and toss to coat evenly; set aside.

To assemble: Have ready 6 old-fashioned tumblers (3 ½ inches high and 3 inches in diameter) or clear-glass, stemmed goblets.

Using a 12-inch serrated knife, split the cake in half horizontally (page 25) to create 2 layers each 9 by 6 ½ inches and ¾ inch thick.

Place the two ¾-inch-thick layers, side by side, on a cutting board or a sheet of waxed paper. Using a 3-inch round cutter, cut out 6 circles from each layer, for a total of 12 circles. Place a cake circle in the bottom of each of the 6 tumblers, and spoon about 2 tablespoons of the fruit on top of each cake circle. Drizzle about 1 tablespoon of the juice that has accumulated in the fruit bowl over the fruit and cake. Top with another cake circle, spoon another 1 to 2 tablespoons of fruit on the cake, and drizzle with another tablespoon fruit juice. Spoon 2 tablespoons of the Crème Anglaise over the fruit. Cover each trifle with plastic wrap and refrigerate for at least 3 hours or up to overnight.

To serve, uncover each trifle and spoon another tablespoon or two of Crème Anglaise over the top, if desired.

Year-Round Little Peach Pies

I devised this recipe so that my honey could enjoy the summery flavors of his favorite homemade peach pie year-round—and so can you. The pies are modeled after little desserts I tasted at a bakery in New York. To re-create their charming home-baked appearance, I fit circles of one of my most-often-used pie doughs into muffin cups. For a filling that transcends the seasons, I've called for fresh peaches or readily available frozen sliced peaches (in convenient 1-pound/455-gram packages, each containing 3 cups). From my experience, the pies made with frozen peaches bake up every bit as juicy, colorful, and delicious as their fresh counterparts. You will be glad if you reroll the pastry scraps after you cut out the first circles, too. I couldn't tell the difference between crusts made from the original dough and the scraps, and by using the scraps, you can produce 4 additional pies, bringing the total to 16.   **YIELD: 16 LITTLE PIES**

1 RECIPE DOUBLE-CRUST FLAKY PIE PASTRY (PAGE 355)

STREUSEL

¾ CUP PLUS 1 TABLESPOON (3¾ OUNCES/105 GRAMS) ALL-PURPOSE FLOUR

½ CUP FIRMLY PACKED (3½ OUNCES/100 GRAMS) LIGHT BROWN SUGAR

¾ CUP (3 OUNCES/85 GRAMS) FINELY CHOPPED UNSALTED MACADAMIA NUTS

⅛ TEASPOON SALT

4 OUNCES (1 STICK/115 GRAMS) UNSALTED BUTTER, AT ROOM TEMPERATURE, CUT INTO 8 PIECES

FILLING

7 MEDIUM (2½ POUNDS/1.1 KG) RIPE PEACHES, PEELED, HALVED, PITTED, AND CUT LENGTHWISE INTO ½-INCH-THICK SLICES, TO YIELD ABOUT 6 CUPS (2 POUNDS/910 GRAMS), OR TWO 1-POUND (455-GRAM) PACKAGES FROZEN YELLOW PEACH SLICES, THAWED FOR 1 TO 1½ HOURS

½ CUP (3½ OUNCES/100 GRAMS) GRANULATED SUGAR

2 TABLESPOONS CORNSTARCH

1 TABLESPOON FINELY MINCED CRYSTALLIZED GINGER (OPTIONAL)

1 TABLESPOON FRESH LEMON JUICE

If the pastry is frozen, let it thaw in the refrigerator for about 4 hours or up to overnight. The dough should remain cold.

Before baking: Center a rack in the oven and preheat the oven to 400 degrees F. Have ready two 12-cup standard muffin pans.

Remove 1 of the dough packages from the refrigerator. Following the directions for rolling out pie pastry on page 28, roll out the dough into a 14-inch circle about ⅛ inch thick. Using a 4½-inch round cookie or biscuit cutter (or other template), cut out 6 circles close together. Reserve the dough scraps. Ease each pastry circle into a muffin cup, fitting it into the contours. Use your fingertips to pleat the dough around the edges and to push the pastry gently down into the cup. Since the dough circle is larger than the circumference of the cup, it is natural for the pastry to pleat. Set aside at room temperature.

Remove the second portion of dough from the refrigerator; allow it to sit for 10 minutes if it is very firm. Roll and cut the dough in the same way, and line 6 more cups. Stack the dough scraps from the 2 disks on top of one another (rather than mashing or kneading them together into a tight ball), and gently shape the dough into a disk. Don't worry if the dough doesn't seem cohesive. As you roll it, it will come together. On a lightly floured work surface, roll out the dough about ⅛ inch thick, cut out 4 additional circles, and line 4 more cups in the second muffin pan, spacing the cups evenly around the pan. Spacing the cups promotes even baking when not all of the cups are filled. At this point, you can cover the muffin pans securely with plastic wrap and refrigerate them for up to 2 days. Remove from the refrigerator 1 hour before assembling the little pies.

To make the streusel: Combine the flour, sugar, nuts, and salt, in that order, in a medium bowl and mix with your fingertips, breaking up any lumps. Scatter the butter pieces over the flour mixture, and mix with your fingertips until the mixture resembles coarse crumbs. If using right away, set aside. Or, refrigerate the streusel in an airtight container for up to 1 week or freeze for up to 1 month. Bring to room temperature before using.

To make the filling: Cut the peach slices in half crosswise to make bite-sized pieces and put them in a large bowl. In a small bowl, stir together the sugar and cornstarch. Stir in the ginger, if using. Sprinkle the lemon juice and then the sugar mixture over the peaches and toss to coat evenly.

Spoon the filling into the pastry-lined cups, filling them to the rim (a couple pieces of fruit might poke above the rim). Spoon 1 or 2 teaspoons of the juices from the bottom of the bowl over the filling. (Any leftover peach filling can be divided evenly among the peach-filled cups.) Sprinkle about 1 1/2 tablespoons of the streusel over the top of each little pie. Lightly press on the streusel to ensure it stays in place. Remove any streusel from the surface of the muffin pan so that it does not burn and stick in the oven.

Bake the pies until the filling bubbles lightly and the pastry edges are golden, 25 to 35 minutes. Transfer to a wire rack and let cool in the pan for about 15 minutes. Using a small, thin, flexible metal or plastic spatula, trace around the sides of each pie to ensure that it is not stuck to the pan (any overflow of the fruit juices also may cause them to stick). Leave the pies in the pan to cool for about 15 minutes longer (the pies are fragile when warm). Then, invert a rack or baking sheet on top of the pies and invert them onto the rack. Carefully turn the pies right side up on the rack.

Serve the pies warm or at room temperature. They are best eaten the same day they are baked. However, you can store them in an airtight container for up to 1 day. Or, for longer storage, place them in a sturdy covered container, label with the contents and date, and freeze for up to 2 weeks. Thaw completely at room temperature, then place on a parchment paper–lined baking sheet, heat in a preheated 325 degree F oven until warm, about 15 minutes, and serve warm.

Milk Chocolate S'More Tartlets with Homemade Marshmallow Topping

Inspired by the gooey campfire treats many of us enjoyed as kids, these playful tartlets are nostalgia personified. A crisp graham cracker crust is topped with rich, velvety milk chocolate ganache and a dollop of homemade marshmallow cream (the creamy marshmallow recipe was generously shared by pastry chef, consultant, and instructor Christine Law). If desired, run the tartlets under the broiler or use a kitchen torch to re-create that familiar fire-toasted flavor. Any way you serve them, your family, friends, or guests are guaranteed to want "s'more." **YIELD: 10 TARTLETS**

GRAHAM CRACKER TART DOUGH

1 ½ CUPS (7 ½ OUNCES/225 GRAMS) GRAHAM FLOUR

¾ CUP (3 ½ OUNCES/100 GRAMS) ALL-PURPOSE FLOUR

⅓ CUP FIRMLY PACKED (2 ¼ OUNCES/65 GRAMS) LIGHT BROWN SUGAR

½ TEASPOON FINE SEA SALT

⅛ TEASPOON BAKING SODA

3 OUNCES (¾ STICK/85 GRAMS) COLD UNSALTED BUTTER, CUT INTO 6 TO 8 PIECES

1 LARGE EGG

2 TABLESPOONS HONEY

1 TABLESPOON UNSULFURED MOLASSES

1 TABLESPOON WATER

MILK CHOCOLATE GANACHE

10 OUNCES (280 GRAMS) MILK CHOCOLATE, PREFERABLY EL REY OR GUITTARD, FINELY CHOPPED

¾ CUP (6 FL OUNCES/180 ML) HEAVY CREAM

MARSHMALLOW TOPPING

4 LARGE (½ CUP/4 FL OUNCES/120 ML) EGG WHITES, AT ROOM TEMPERATURE

¾ TEASPOON UNFLAVORED POWDERED GELATIN

PINCH OF SALT

¼ CUP (2 FL OUNCES/60 ML) WATER

¾ CUP (5 ¼ OUNCES/150 GRAMS) GRANULATED SUGAR

¼ CUP (3 OUNCES BY WEIGHT/85 GRAMS) LIGHT CORN SYRUP

To make the Graham Cracker Tart Dough: In a food processor, combine the flours, sugar, salt, and baking soda and pulse 3 or 4 times to blend. Scatter the butter pieces over the flour mixture and pulse using 1-second bursts until the butter disappears into the dough.

In a small bowl, whisk together the egg, honey, molasses, and water, in that order. With the motor running, pour the egg mixture down the feed tube and process just until the ingredients form a ball.

Transfer the dough to a work surface. Beginning at the far end, and using the heel of your hand, push a small amount of the dough (about the size of an extra-large egg) away from you, smearing it on the work surface. Repeat with the remaining dough in small amounts. When you've worked all the dough in this manner, give it a couple more strokes to bring it together into a smooth, homogeneous unit. (This kneading technique, described on page 31, is known as *fraisage*.)

Divide the dough in half. Roll out half of the dough between 2 sheets of waxed paper into an 11-inch circle about ⅛ inch thick. Repeat with the remaining dough. Leave the dough circles between the sheets of waxed paper and stack them on a baking sheet. Refrigerate until firm, at least 2 hours or up to 3 days. Or, wrap plastic wrap around the dough circles and the baking sheet, overwrap with aluminum foil, label with the contents and date, and freeze for up to 1 month.

Before baking: Center a rack in the oven and preheat the oven to 350 degrees F. On a very large baking sheet (or 2 smaller baking sheets), set 10 tartlet pans each 4 inches in diameter and ¾ inch deep.

Remove 1 dough circle at a time from the refrigerator. Peel off the top sheet of waxed paper, replace it loosely on top, and flip the entire package over onto the work surface. Peel off and discard the second sheet of waxed paper. Using a 4 1/2-inch round cookie or biscuit cutter (or other template), cut out 4 circles close together. Reserve the dough scraps. Set each dough circle on top of a tartlet pan. When the dough softens slightly, gently press the circles into the pans. Repeat with the other dough circle. Combine the dough scraps from the circles, press together into a disk, roll out between sheets of waxed paper, chill, cut out 2 more circles, and line the remaining 2 tartlet pans.

Prick the bottoms of the tartlet shells with the tines of a fork. Bake the shells on the baking sheet until golden, 9 to 12 minutes. Transfer to a wire rack and let cool completely on the baking sheet. Remove the cooled tartlet shells from their pans and set them on the baking sheet, spacing them 1 to 2 inches apart.

To make the Milk Chocolate Ganache: Place the chocolate in a medium bowl. In a small, heavy saucepan, bring the cream just to a boil over medium-low heat. Pour the cream over the chocolate and let stand for about 15 seconds. Whisk together until smooth and creamy. Set aside at room temperature just until the mixture cools a bit and begins to thicken.

To fill the tarts: Fashion a large cone out of parchment paper (page 26) and half fill it with the ganache. Snip a small opening at the end of the paper cone to allow a thin flow and pipe enough ganache into each shell to come one-third to halfway up the sides. Or, spoon the ganache into the shells. Store any leftover ganache in an airtight container in the refrigerator for up to 8 days, then reheat over a hot-water bath (100 degrees F) for another use. Set the ganache-filled pastry shells aside, and proceed to make the Marshmallow Topping.

To make the Marshmallow Topping: Have everything ready because once you start making the topping, you can't stop. In the bowl of a stand mixer fitted with the whisk attachment, place the egg whites. Sprinkle the gelatin and salt over the egg whites and let stand for at least 5 minutes to allow the gelatin to soften. Meanwhile, combine the water, sugar, and corn syrup in a heavy 2-quart saucepan over low heat and heat, stirring occasionally or swirling the pan to distribute the heat, until the sugar dissolves, about 5 minutes. Wash down the sides of the pan with a wet pastry brush as needed to prevent crystallization. Raise the heat to medium and cook, without stirring, until the syrup registers 240 degrees F on a candy thermometer.

When the sugar syrup is close to reaching 240 degrees F, begin whipping the egg whites on medium speed and continue whipping until they are opaque and fluffy. As soon as the sugar syrup reaches 240 degrees F, remove the pan from the heat, reduce the mixer speed to low, and slowly and carefully drizzle the hot syrup onto the egg whites. Try not to hit the whisk, which will throw bits of the hot syrup onto the sides of the bowl, where they will solidify. Stop the mixer occasionally to scrape down any sugar syrup on the sides of the bowl and incorporate it into the egg whites. When all of the sugar syrup has been added, raise the speed to medium and continue whipping until the egg whites are shiny, thick (not stiff), and a bit warm but not hot, 5 to 10 minutes.

Without delay, spoon a dollop of the marshmallow topping on the center of each tartlet. If desired, slip the tartlets under a preheated broiler to brown the marshmallow tops lightly or toast the tops with a kitchen torch.

Serve the tartlets at room temperature the same day they are assembled.

Say It with Cookies

EACH BAKER, like each artist, has a favorite medium to use as a creative outlet. Mine is the cookie. Cookies let me experiment with a whole palette of styles: crispy, crunchy, chewy, snappy, or melt-in-your-mouth tender.

And, because cookies are universally popular, they let me custom-bake something for the ones I love. My Dave likes the Neapolitan Bars and our grandchildren, Joshua, Natalie, and Daniel, like the Zebra Cookies and Susie's Raspberry Jam Squares.

One of my favorite ways to share cookies is through a cookie exchange. Friends and family bring their favorite cookies in airtight containers that double as a way to transport home their share of what everyone else has baked. Arrange everyone's offerings on platters or in colorful cloth- or tissue paper–lined boxes labeled with the name of the recipe and the baker. Then, use old-fashioned baker's math to split them: add up the number of cookies all of the bakers brought, divide that amount by the number of people participating, and the answer determines how many cookies each swapper may take.

I usually host an exchange at the holidays, but any special time is right: a bridal or baby shower, a school or church meeting, Valentine's Day, even a family reunion. Guests enjoy the energetic excitement and constant conversation at the event, and the varied collection of cookies they take home. Some excellent choices to offer are Chocolate-Vanilla Swirl Cookies, each one sporting a unique design; Nancy's Brown Butter Buttons, with their unmatched delicate texture; Heart-to-Heart-to-Heart Cookies, particularly for Valentine's Day; and Fruit-Nut Florentine Cookie Triangles, which are especially appealing in cooler weather.

Don't forget to use cookies for more than snacks or lunch-bag fillers. Rest Bonnie's Best-Selling Almond Tuiles on a scoop of ice cream like a jaunty hat for dessert, or use Hazelnut Shortbread Cookies to hold spoonfuls of jam or Nutella (hazelnut-chocolate spread).

Whatever you are trying to say, cookies will help you say it.

Bonnie's Best-Selling Almond Tuiles

This is the little black dress of cookie recipes. These thin, crisp, buttery cookies are flat versions of classic French tuiles. The recipe is from a former student who became a professional baker. Bonnie Yoshikawa presented her large, rectangular version of the cookies to me as a delicious gift, artfully stacked in a see-through container. You can shape yours any way you please, from oversized flat ovals or small rounds to whimsical rolled tubes with a fortune tucked inside. An attractive yet simple presentation is to center an oversized tuile on top of a scoop of favorite ice cream or sorbet.

To streamline baking, and make the best use of your time, try a baking relay system. It's ideal to work with 4 baking sheets, but if you have only 2 or 3 sheets, that's fine. Spread the dough on the prepared baking sheets, and set them aside so they are ready when it's time to bake. When 1 sheet comes out from the oven, immediately place another sheet of unbaked tuiles in the oven. Without delay, remove the baked tuiles to a wire rack to cool, and set the hot baking sheet aside to cool. It should be cool enough to handle in 7 to 9 minutes. Having 4 baking sheets is ideal because 1 sheet can be in the oven, you can be loading a second sheet, and 2 sheets can be cooling. **YIELD: 2 DOZEN COOKIES**

¾ CUP (5 ¼ OUNCES/150 GRAMS) GRANULATED SUGAR

¾ CUP (6 FL OUNCES/180 ML) EGG WHITES (ABOUT 5 LARGE)

1 ½ CUPS (5 ¼ OUNCES/150 GRAMS) SLICED NATURAL OR BLANCHED ALMONDS

3 ¼ OUNCES (¾ STICK PLUS 1 ½ TEASPOONS/90 GRAMS) UNSALTED BUTTER, MELTED AND COOLED TO TEPID

½ CUP PLUS 1 TABLESPOON (2 ½ OUNCES/70 GRAMS) CAKE FLOUR

Before baking: Center a rack in the oven and preheat the oven to 350 degrees F. Unwrap an end of a chilled stick of unsalted butter and rub it over 2 to 4 large non-stick baking sheets (see headnote) to apply a very thin film of fat, or coat very lightly with nonstick baking spray.

In a large bowl, blend together the sugar, egg whites, and almonds, in that order, with a rubber spatula. Stir in the butter, and then the flour until thoroughly combined. Loosely cover the bowl with plastic wrap and set aside at room temperature for 10 to 15 minutes. (Or, cover securely and refrigerate for up to 1 day to bake when it is convenient.)

Drop the batter by 1 tablespoonfuls onto a baking sheet, putting about 4 on the pan and spacing them about 2 ½ inches apart. Using an offset spatula, thinly spread each portion into an oversized oval or rectangle about 4 by 3 inches and the thickness of an almond slice (thinner than a playing card).

Bake the cookies until evenly golden (some of the nuts might remain ivory colored), 12 to 15 minutes. Transfer to a wire rack and let cool on the pan for only 15 seconds. Then, carefully slide a metal spatula, preferably offset, under the cookies, one at a time, and lift them onto the rack. Let cool completely. The cookies will crisp as they cool. Repeat the baking with the remaining batter and baking sheet(s).

Stack the cooled cookies in an airtight container and store at room temperature for up to 10 days. The tuiles are highly susceptible to any moisture in the air, so keep them in the container until serving to ensure their crispness.

Cacao Nib Meringue Kisses

When you first look at cacao nibs, you would never guess that these homely pellets embody the very soul of chocolate. They are roasted beans that have been hulled and crushed, and they have an intense chocolate flavor that perfectly balances the delicate sweetness of meringue. In these cookies, the crunchy nibs are also decorative, punctuating the meringue with handsome dark polka dots (pulse them in a small food processor to grind them finely). For a spicy, beautiful, and exotic variation, substitute pink peppercorns. (See Sources for where to order both cacao nibs and pink peppercorns.)

Once you have opened a package of cacao nibs, transfer them to an airtight container and store them in a cool, dry place for up to 1 month or in the freezer for up to 4 to 6 months. Before using them, heat them in a preheated 200 degree F oven for about 1 minute to bring out their flavor. This also melts any crystallized cocoa butter (a harmless grayish coating) that may have formed on them. **YIELD: ABOUT 3 DOZEN COOKIES**

2 LARGE EGG WHITES

¼ TEASPOON CREAM OF TARTAR

⅛ TEASPOON SALT

½ CUP (3½ OUNCES/100 GRAMS) GRANULATED SUGAR

1 TEASPOON PURE VANILLA EXTRACT

2 TABLESPOONS FINELY GROUND CACAO NIBS

Before baking: Center a rack in the oven and preheat the oven to 225 degrees F. Line a large baking sheet with parchment paper.

In the bowl of a stand mixer fitted with the whisk attachment, whip together the egg whites, cream of tartar, and salt on medium speed until soft peaks form, about 2 minutes. Maintaining the same speed, gradually add the sugar, about 1 tablespoon at a time, and continue to beat until glossy, white, stiff peaks form, 2 to 3 minutes. Add the vanilla during the final moments of whipping. Detach the whisk and bowl from the mixer, and tap the whisk against the side of the bowl to release the excess meringue. Using a rubber spatula, fold in the cacao nibs.

Spoon the meringue into a pastry bag fitted with a ½-inch plain open tip. Pipe a dab of the meringue under each corner of the parchment paper to secure the paper in place. Pipe kisses about 1 inch wide onto the prepared baking sheet, spacing them 1 inch apart. Alternatively, using an ice cream scoop about 1¼ inches in diameter (#70), drop about 1-tablespoon mounds onto the baking sheet, spacing them about 1 inch apart.

Bake the cookies until dry and crisp yet still white, about 1 hour. The timing will depend on the day's humidity. If necessary, reduce the oven heat to keep the meringues from coloring. Turn off the oven and let the meringues cool in the oven for 30 minutes. Transfer to a wire rack and let cool completely on the pan. Once cool, the cookies lift off the paper easily.

Stack the cooled cookies in an airtight container and store at room temperature for up to 1 week.

Chocolate Chip Cookie Logs

These slice-and-bake cookies are inspired by a vintage recipe on a bag of Fred's chocolate chips, a brand I discovered some two decades ago that is no longer available. They were exceptional semi-sweet chocolate chips, with a flat shape that I've re-created here with chocolate *pistoles*, flat wafers or disks each about ⅞ inch in diameter. The *pistoles* disperse randomly through the dough, so that slicing the logs into cookies creates an attractive mosaic, with little spokes of chocolate scattered here and there. Keep the logs on hand in the refrigerator, and enjoy freshly baked cookies at a moment's notice. For where to buy *pistoles*, see Sources.   **YIELD: ABOUT 4 DOZEN COOKIES**

1⅓ CUPS (6 ¼ OUNCES/175 GRAMS) ALL-PURPOSE FLOUR

½ TEASPOON BAKING SODA

¼ TEASPOON SALT

4 OUNCES (1 STICK/115 GRAMS) UNSALTED BUTTER, SOFTENED

½ CUP (3 ½ OUNCES/100 GRAMS) GRANULATED SUGAR

⅓ CUP FIRMLY PACKED (2 ¼ OUNCES/65 GRAMS) LIGHT BROWN SUGAR

1 LARGE EGG

2 TEASPOONS PURE VANILLA EXTRACT

½ CUP (3 OUNCES/85 GRAMS) 61% SEMISWEET PISTOLES SUCH AS GUITTARD BRAND

In a small bowl, whisk together the flour, baking soda, and salt just to blend. In the bowl of a stand mixer fitted with the paddle attachment, beat together the butter and sugars on medium-low speed just until the ingredients are well blended, yet the mixture appears sandy or grainy, 45 to 60 seconds. Do not overbeat. On low speed, add the egg and vanilla and beat just until blended, then stop the mixer and scrape down the sides of the bowl. On the lowest speed, gradually add the flour mixture and beat until incorporated. Detach the paddle and bowl from the mixer, and tap the paddle against the side of the bowl to free the excess dough. Using a rubber spatula, stir in the *pistoles*.

Divide the soft dough in half. On a clean work surface, pat one-half of the dough into a rough log about 5½ inches long. Repeat with the second half. Then, following the directions on page 32, compress each log so it is rounder,

more uniformly shaped, and about 7 inches long. Wrap the logs separately in the parchment paper used to compress them and refrigerate until cold and very firm, at least several hours or up to overnight. For longer storage, overwrap with aluminum foil, label with the contents and date, and freeze for up to 1 month. Thaw in the refrigerator for 8 hours or up to overnight.

Before baking: Center a rack in the oven and preheat the oven to 350 degrees F. Line 2 large baking sheets with parchment paper, so you can get a second pan ready while the first one is baking.

Using a sharp serrated knife and a sawing motion, cut the chilled dough logs into slices a scant ¼ inch thick. Place the slices on the prepared baking sheets, spacing them about 1½ inches apart.

Bake the cookies, 1 sheet at a time, until they are flat and light golden brown but still soft, 12 to 14 minutes. (They will crisp as they cool.) Transfer to a wire rack and let cool on the pan for about 3 minutes. Using a metal spatula, transfer the cookies to wire racks to cool completely.

Stack the cooled cookies in an airtight container and store at room temperature for up to 2 days or in the freezer for up to 1 month. Thaw in the container at room temperature.

Chocolate-Vanilla Swirl Cookies

The first word that came to mind when I saw these intricately swirled cookies was Rorschach: every one expresses something different, just like the famous inkblot test. The recipe is from my talented dear friend Nora Tong, owner of Nora's Patisserie in Daly City, California, about six miles south of San Francisco. She uses a special method of stretching and twisting the dough into two-tone logs, so that when the cookies are sliced, each is a unique work of art. For seasonal variations, customize the sugar coating on the outside of the logs, from red and green for Christmastime to spooky black and orange for Halloween. I always have one or two of these dough logs on hand in my refrigerator or freezer so I can slice and bake on demand.

This recipe exemplifies how weighing ingredients is more accurate than measuring by volume. For example, if you measure different brands of cocoa powder in a cup measure and then put them on a scale, you will discover they weigh differently. But if you use weight as your measuring method, you will always end up with the same amount of each ingredient and your cookies will always have the optimum amount of chocolate flavor. **YIELD: ABOUT 12 DOZEN COOKIES**

VANILLA DOUGH

2¾ CUPS (11 OUNCES/310 GRAMS) CAKE FLOUR

1 CUP PLUS 2 TABLESPOONS (4 OUNCES/115 GRAMS) POWDERED SUGAR

¼ TEASPOON SALT

8 OUNCES (2 STICKS/225 GRAMS) UNSALTED BUTTER, SOFTENED

1 TEASPOON PURE VANILLA EXTRACT

CHOCOLATE DOUGH

2¼ CUPS (9 OUNCES/255 GRAMS) CAKE FLOUR

1 CUP PLUS 2 TABLESPOONS (4 OUNCES/115 GRAMS) POWDERED SUGAR

½ CUP PLUS 1 TABLESPOON (2 OUNCES/55 GRAMS) UNSWEETENED NATURAL OR DUTCH-PROCESSED COCOA POWDER

¼ TEASPOON SALT

8 OUNCES (2 STICKS/225 GRAMS) UNSALTED BUTTER, SOFTENED

1 TEASPOON PURE VANILLA EXTRACT

2 CUPS (ABOUT 15 OUNCES/430 GRAMS) NONPAREIL SPRINKLES FOR DECORATION

To make the Vanilla Dough: In the bowl of a stand mixer fitted with the paddle attachment, combine the flour, sugar, and salt and mix on the lowest speed just to blend. Stop the mixer, place the butter on top of the flour mixture, and wrap a kitchen towel around the back and sides of the mixer bowl, or use a bowl shield to contain the mixture in the bowl, since even the lowest speed causes this amount of flour to fly out of the bowl. Resume mixing on the lowest speed and mix just until the mixture starts to appear lumpy. You should see small clusters that are just beginning to show signs of coming together. Stop the mixer, add the vanilla, and resume mixing on the lowest speed just until the mixture is thoroughly combined. Transfer the dough to a bowl, cover, and refrigerate for 15 minutes. Wash the bowl and paddle attachment and proceed to make the Chocolate Dough.

To make the Chocolate Dough: In the bowl of the stand mixer fitted with the paddle attachment, combine the flour, sugar, cocoa powder, and salt and mix on the lowest speed to blend. Stop the mixer, place the butter on top of the flour mixture, and wrap a kitchen towel around the back and sides of the mixer bowl, or use a bowl shield to contain the mixture in the bowl, since even the lowest speed causes this amount of flour to fly out of the bowl. Resume mixing on the lowest speed and mix just until the mixture starts to appear lumpy. You should see small clusters that are just beginning to show signs of coming together. Stop the mixer, add the vanilla, and resume mixing on the lowest speed just until the mixture is thoroughly combined. Transfer the dough to a bowl, cover, and refrigerate for 15 minutes.

To form into logs: Remove the Vanilla Dough from the refrigerator and divide it into thirds in the bowl, with each piece about 7 1/2 ounces (215 grams). Remove the Chocolate Dough from the refrigerator and divide it into thirds in the bowl, again with each piece about 7 1/2 ounces (215 grams). On a clean work surface, flatten each of the dough pieces with your fingertips into a 7 by 5-inch rectangle. Place a chocolate rectangle on top of a vanilla rectangle, and then tear the stack in half, to create 2 pieces each about 3 1/2 by 5 inches. (A dough scraper will be helpful in lifting the dough from the work surface.) Place one-half on top of the other half to create 4 layers. Pat the stack into a 9 by 4-inch rectangle. Using a dough scraper, cut the stack in half lengthwise to create two 9 by 2-inch pieces. Place 1 piece on top of the other to create a stack with 8 layers.

To marble the logs: Using both hands, twist the dough about three times and at the same time gently extend the dough package. Have each hand at a different point on the dough package as you manipulate it into a swirled pattern. (The exterior will look similar to a barber pole, only in black and white.) Set nearby on the work surface. Repeat the process with the remaining dough to form 2 more logs. Then, to make the logs easier to handle, cut each log in half crosswise. You will have 6 logs in all. Following the directions on page 32, compress each log so it is rounder, more uniformly shaped, and about 8 inches long and 1 1/4 inches in diameter.

Spread the nonpareil sprinkles in a large rectangular pan, such as a 9 by 13 by 2-inch pan (quarter sheet pan). One at a time, roll each dough log back and forth in the sprinkles to coat the outside of the log evenly. Set the coated logs on a baking sheet and refrigerate until firm enough to handle without disturbing the shape, about 1 hour. Then wrap in plastic wrap and return to the refrigerator until firm, 1 to 1 1/2 hours longer. For longer storage, overwrap with aluminum foil, label with the contents and date, and freeze for up to 1 month. Thaw in the refrigerator for several hours or up to overnight before baking.

Before baking: Center a rack in the oven and preheat the oven to 325 degrees F. Line 1 or to 2 large baking sheets (depending on how many cookies you want to bake) with parchment paper.

Using a sharp knife, cut 1 or more chilled logs into 1/4-inch-thick slices and arrange the slices on the prepared baking sheets, spacing them 1/2 inch apart.

Bake the cookies, 1 sheet at a time, just until they are no longer shiny on top and are lightly golden on the bottom, 10 to 12 minutes. Don't let them color on top. Using a metal spatula, transfer the cookies to wire racks and let cool completely.

Stack the cooled cookies in an airtight container and store at room temperature for up to 10 days.

Flavor Variations: To create a spicy cookie with a sweet kick, add 1/8 teaspoon chipotle chile powder (a smoky pepper) to the chocolate dough, mixing it with the dry ingredients. For a minty accent, substitute 1/2 teaspoon peppermint extract or a few drops of peppermint oil for the vanilla extract in the vanilla dough.

Zebra Cookies Variation

Waiting in line at a popular Colorado bakery, my imagination was captivated by striped cookie triangles nestled in a glass apothecary jar. For several days, I puzzled over how to re-create the intriguing geometric design—and the result is this recipe. The secret to shaping the cookies is to form the dough in square pans lined with heavy-duty aluminum foil. After you have layered the chilled squares of chocolate and vanilla dough, creating the cookies couldn't be easier. Just slice and bake.

YIELD: ABOUT 4 DOZEN COOKIES CONTINUED ▶

1 RECIPE CHOCOLATE DOUGH (PAGE 276)
1 RECIPE VANILLA DOUGH (PAGE 276)

Line a 6 by 2-inch square, straight-sided pan with aluminum foil, pressing it into the contours of the pan and allowing 3 to 4 inches to overhang 2 ends. (If possible use heavy-duty aluminum foil, which is less likely to tear than regular foil when lifting the chilled dough from the pan later.) Divide the Chocolate Dough into thirds, each about 7 1/2 ounces (215 grams). Then divide the Vanilla Dough into thirds, each about 7 1/2 ounces (215 grams).

Place 1 piece of dough between 2 sheets of waxed paper and roll it out into a rectangle about 6 by 3 inches. Repeat with the remaining 5 pieces of dough. Beginning with a vanilla rectangle, gently lift the dough from the waxed paper and layer it in the bottom of the prepared pan, pressing or rolling the layer evenly with a 2 1/2-inch to 4-inch pastry roller to fit the dimensions of the pan. Continue layering in this way, alternating the vanilla and chocolate doughs and ending with the chocolate dough. You should have 6 layers of dough about 2 inches high. Cover and refrigerate the dough until firm, about 4 hours or up to overnight.

Before baking: Center a rack in the oven and preheat the oven to 350 degrees F. Line a large baking sheet with parchment paper.

Using the foil flaps, lift the chilled dough from the pan. Peel off the foil and discard. With a sharp chef's knife, cut the dough into 3 strips, each 6 inches long by 2 inches wide and thick. Return 2 of the strips to the refrigerator to keep the dough cold while you cut the third one. Using the same knife, cut the third strip into 3/16-inch-thick squares. Cut each square in half on the diagonal, forming 2 triangles. Place the triangles on the prepared baking sheet, spacing them about 1/2 inch apart.

Bake the cookies just until they are no longer shiny on top and are pale gold on the bottom, 8 to 10 minutes. Using a metal spatula, transfer the cookies to a wire rack to cool completely. Repeat with the remaining strips, if desired.

Stack the cooled cookies in an airtight container and store at room temperature for up to 10 days.

Trufflewiches

Imagine an Oreo cookie taken to the pinnacle of luxurious decadence and you will have an idea of what these dramatic sandwich cookies are like. Twin circles of dark chocolate shortbread showcase a plump white-chocolate truffle center, enriched with lemon zest for a whisper of a tangy flavor. This recipe uses an easy, straightforward method for bringing the ingredients together that I refer to as reverse mixing (see page 31 for a detailed explanation). It is a foolproof way to make the dough without overaerating it, which ensures that the finished cookies won't fall apart when you bite into them. **YIELD: ABOUT 20 SANDWICH COOKIES**

DARK CHOCOLATE SHORTBREAD

1 ¾ CUPS (8 OUNCES/225 GRAMS) ALL-PURPOSE FLOUR

¾ CUP (5 ¼ OUNCES/150 GRAMS) GRANULATED SUGAR

½ CUP PLUS 1 TABLESPOON (2 OUNCES/55 GRAMS) UNSWEETENED DUTCH-PROCESSED COCOA POWDER

⅛ TEASPOON SALT

7 ½ OUNCES (1 ½ STICKS PLUS 3 TABLESPOONS/ 215 GRAMS) UNSALTED BUTTER, SOFTENED

1 LARGE EGG

1 TEASPOON PURE VANILLA EXTRACT

WHITE CHOCOLATE TRUFFLE FILLING

6 OUNCES (170 GRAMS) WHITE CHOCOLATE, FINELY CHOPPED

¼ CUP PLUS 2 TABLESPOONS (3 FL OUNCES/90 ML) HEAVY CREAM

1 TEASPOON FINELY GRATED LEMON ZEST

In the bowl of a stand mixer fitted with the paddle attachment, combine the flour, sugar, cocoa powder, and salt and beat on the lowest speed just to blend. Stop the mixer and place the butter on top of the flour mixture. Resume mixing on the lowest speed and mix just until the mixture starts to appear lumpy. You should see small clusters that are just beginning to show signs of coming together. Stop the mixer, add the egg and vanilla, and resume mixing on the lowest speed just until the mixture is thoroughly combined. Resume mixing on the lowest speed and mix just until the mixture starts to appear lumpy.

Divide the soft dough in half and shape each half into a disk. For easier handling, loosely wrap each disk in plastic wrap and freeze for 15 minutes or refrigerate for 30 minutes.

Place 1 dough portion between 2 sheets of waxed paper and roll out into a 10-inch circle about ¼ inch thick. Repeat with the remaining dough portion. Leaving the dough circles between the sheets of waxed paper, stack them on a baking sheet and refrigerate until firm, about 2 hours. Or, wrap plastic wrap around the dough circles and baking sheet and refrigerate for up to 3 days. For longer storage, overwrap with aluminum foil, label with the contents and date, and freeze for up to 1 month. To thaw, place the dough circles, still on the pan, in the refrigerator overnight.

Before baking: Center a rack in the oven and preheat the oven to 350 degrees F. Line 2 large baking sheets with parchment paper.

Remove 1 dough package from the refrigerator. Peel off the top sheet of waxed paper, replace it loosely on top, and flip the entire package over. Peel off and discard the second sheet of waxed paper. Using a 1 ½-inch round fluted cutter, cut out circles from the dough, cutting them as closely together as possible. Arrange the cutouts on a prepared baking sheet, spacing them about ½ inch apart. Reserve the scraps, if desired.

Bake the cookies until their surface is dull and their tops are close to firm when touched gently, about 10 minutes. Be careful not to overbake. Transfer the baking sheet to a wire rack and let the cookies cool on the pan for 5 minutes. Using a metal spatula, transfer the cookies to the rack to cool completely. The cookies CONTINUED ▶

will firm up as they cool. Repeat with the remaining dough circle and baking sheet. Then, if desired, reroll the scraps between 2 sheets of waxed paper, chill, cut out additional cookies, and bake as directed.

To make the White Chocolate Truffle Filling: Place the chocolate in a medium bowl. In a small, heavy saucepan, bring the cream with the lemon zest just to a boil over medium-low heat. Pour the hot cream over the chocolate and let stand for about 45 seconds. Whisk together until smooth and creamy. Cover with plastic wrap, pressing it directly onto the surface, and refrigerate just until the mixture is still creamy, yet firm enough to hold its shape, 35 to 45 minutes.

On a large tray or baking sheet, turn half of the cookies bottom side up. Using an ice cream scoop about 1⅛ inches in diameter (#100), scoop the truffle filling (about 1-inch balls) onto the cookies. Top with the remaining cookies, bottom side down. Press each sandwich cookie gently to secure the truffle between the 2 cookies, leaving a gap so the truffle is still round and visible. Refrigerate any leftover filling in a sturdy covered container for up to 1 week. To use as a filling or glaze, heat it over a bowl of hot water until it is the proper consistency.

To store the cookies: If filling later, stack unfilled cookies in an airtight container and store at room temperature for up to 10 days. Arrange sandwiched cookies in a single layer in a covered aluminum foil–lined cardboard box, such as a cake box, and store at room temperature for up to 2 days.

"Be My Valentine" Heartwiches

Guaranteed to win your valentine's heart, these luscious heart-shaped chocolate shortbread sandwiches with chocolate ganache centers are a delectable way to convey sweet sentiments. The top of each cookie is embellished with sparkling red sugar, which provides a colorful counterpoint to the dark chocolate. Present the cookies in a handsome box, accompanied by a message that lets your sweetheart know there is love in every bite.   **YIELD: 1½ TO 2 DOZEN SANDWICH COOKIES**

DOUGH

1½ CUPS (7 OUNCES/200 GRAMS) ALL-PURPOSE FLOUR

½ CUP (1¾ OUNCES/50 GRAMS) UNSWEETENED DUTCH-PROCESSED COCOA POWDER

⅛ TEASPOON SALT

PINCH OF GROUND CAYENNE PEPPER (OPTIONAL)

6 OUNCES (1½ STICKS/170 GRAMS) UNSALTED BUTTER, AT ROOM TEMPERATURE

⅔ CUP (4½ OUNCES/130 GRAMS) GRANULATED SUGAR

¼ CUP (¾ OUNCE/25 GRAMS) POWDERED SUGAR

RED DECORATING SUGAR FOR SPRINKLING

DARK CHOCOLATE TRUFFLE FILLING

6 OUNCES (170 GRAMS) SEMISWEET OR BITTERSWEET CHOCOLATE, FINELY CHOPPED

¼ CUP PLUS 2 TABLESPOONS (3 FL OUNCES/90 ML) HEAVY CREAM

To make the dough: In a medium bowl, briefly whisk together the flour, cocoa powder, salt, and cayenne (if using) to blend; set aside. In the bowl of a stand mixer fitted with the paddle attachment, beat the butter on medium-low speed until smooth, about 1 minute. Add the sugars and beat on low speed just until creamy and well blended, about 1 minute, stopping the mixer occasionally to scrape down the sides of the bowl. Stop the mixer and add the flour mixture. On the lowest speed, mix just until thoroughly combined, 45 to 60 seconds.

Divide the dough into thirds. Place 1 dough portion between 2 sheets of waxed paper and roll out into a 10-inch circle about ⅛ inch thick. Repeat with the remaining dough portions. Leaving the dough circles between the sheets of waxed paper, stack them on a baking sheet and refrigerate until firm, about 2 hours. Or, wrap plastic wrap around the dough circles and baking sheet and refrigerate for up to 3 days. For longer storage, overwrap with aluminum foil, label with the contents and date, and freeze for up to 10 days. To thaw, place the dough circles, still on the pan, in the refrigerator for at least 4 hours or up to overnight.

Before baking: Center a rack in the oven and preheat the oven to 325 degrees F. Line 2 large baking sheets with parchment paper.

Remove 1 dough package at a time from the refrigerator. Peel off the top sheet of waxed paper, replace it loosely on top, and flip the entire package over. Peel off and discard the second sheet of waxed paper. Using a 1½-inch heart-shaped cutter, cut out hearts from the dough, cutting them as closely together as possible. Arrange the cutouts on a prepared baking sheet, spacing them about ½ inch apart. Reserve the scraps, if desired. Sprinkle the tops of the cookies with the decorating sugar.

Bake the cookies until they appear set and their tops are close to firm when touched gently, 10 to 12 minutes. Cocoa burns easily so be careful not to overbake. (When the cookies have baked for almost 10 minutes, the aroma of chocolate will float through the air, which signals it's time to check if they have finished baking.) Transfer to a wire rack and let the cookies cool on the pan for 5 minutes (the cookies are very fragile when they emerge from the oven). Using a metal spatula, transfer the cookies to the rack to cool completely. The cookies will firm up as they cool. Repeat with the remaining dough circle and baking sheet. Then, if desired, reroll the scraps CONTINUED ▶

between 2 sheets of waxed paper, chill, cut out additional cookies, and bake as directed.

To make the Dark Chocolate Truffle Filling: Place the chocolate in a medium bowl. In a small, heavy saucepan, bring the cream just to a boil over medium-low heat. Pour the hot cream over the chocolate and let stand for about 45 seconds. Whisk together until smooth and creamy. Cover with plastic wrap, pressing it directly onto the surface, and refrigerate just until the mixture is still creamy yet firm enough to hold its shape, 35 to 45 minutes.

On a large tray or baking sheet, turn half of the cookies bottom side up. Using an ice cream scoop about 1⅛ inches in diameter (#100), scoop the truffle filling (about 1-inch balls) onto the cookies. Top with the remaining cookies,

sugared side up. Press each sandwich cookie gently to secure the truffle between the 2 cookies, leaving a gap so the truffle is still round and visible. Refrigerate any leftover filling in a sturdy covered container for up to 1 week. To use as a filling or glaze, heat it over a bowl of hot water until it is the proper consistency.

To store the cookies: If filling later, stack the unfilled cookies in an airtight container and store at room temperature for up to 10 days. Arrange sandwiched cookies in a single layer in a covered aluminum foil–lined cardboard box, such as a cake box, and store at room temperature for up to 2 days.

Fruit-Nut Florentine Cookie Triangles

As opulent as a Tuscan palazzo, these cookies resemble edible jewels. Cranberries glow like rubies, pistachios evoke pale green jade, and bits of candied orange peel mimic polished amber. Don't let their glamorous appearance fool you, though: these rich, chewy bar cookies are gratifyingly simple to make. Try them for holiday gatherings—or any time you need a lot of beautiful cookies.

YIELD: ABOUT 3 DOZEN COOKIES

PASTRY

2 CUPS (9 OUNCES/255 GRAMS) ALL-PURPOSE FLOUR

½ CUP (3½ OUNCES/100 GRAMS) GRANULATED SUGAR

¼ TEASPOON SALT

8 OUNCES (2 STICKS/225 GRAMS) COLD UNSALTED BUTTER, CUT INTO ¼-INCH SLICES

TOPPING

1 CUP (3½ OUNCES/100 GRAMS) NATURAL OR BLANCHED SLICED ALMONDS, TOASTED (PAGES 15–16)

⅓ CUP (1½ OUNCES/40 GRAMS) UNSALTED, SHELLED PISTACHIO NUTS

⅓ CUP (1¼ OUNCES/35 GRAMS) DRIED CRANBERRIES

¼ CUP (1¼ OUNCES/35 GRAMS) COARSELY CHOPPED CANDIED ORANGE PEEL

1 TABLESPOON FINELY CHOPPED CRYSTALLIZED GINGER

⅓ CUP (2½ FL OUNCES/75 ML) HEAVY CREAM

1 TABLESPOON MILD HONEY

1 TABLESPOON LIGHT CORN SYRUP

⅓ CUP (2¼ OUNCES/65 GRAMS) GRANULATED SUGAR

⅓ CUP FIRMLY PACKED (2¼ OUNCES/65 GRAMS) LIGHT BROWN SUGAR

3 OUNCES (¾ STICK/85 GRAMS) UNSALTED BUTTER

Before baking: Center a rack in the oven and preheat the oven to 350 degrees F. Have ready a 10½ by 15½ by 1-inch pan (jelly-roll pan).

To make the pastry: In a food processor, combine the flour, sugar, and salt and pulse 3 or 4 times to blend. Scatter the butter pieces over the flour mixture. Pulse until the mixture is the consistency of streusel. Scatter the dough over the bottom of the pan and, using your fingertips, press it evenly over the bottom to form the crust. (No need to press it up the sides of the pan.)

Bake the crust until set and pale gold on top, 16 to 18 minutes. Transfer to a wire rack and let cool in the pan while you prepare the topping. Leave the oven on.

To make the topping: In a small bowl, toss together the almonds, pistachios, cranberries, orange peel, and ginger to mix. Pour the cream, honey, corn syrup, and sugars, in that order, into a heavy 1½-quart saucepan. Stir to combine, and then add the butter. Place over medium-low heat and stir until the butter melts. Increase the heat to medium and cook, stirring constantly with a wooden spoon or a silicone spatula, until the mixture registers 235 degrees F on an instant-read thermometer and is straw colored, 8 to 10 minutes. Be sure to be diligent about stirring toward the end of cooking to prevent scorching. Remove from the heat and stir in the nut-fruit mixture.

Pour the thick, hot mixture onto the partially baked pastry, and spread thinly and evenly with the wooden spoon. Bake for 7 minutes, and then remove from the oven and spread the now more-liquid topping evenly over the pastry. Return to the oven and bake until golden on top, 13 to 14 minutes. The topping will bubble during baking, but the bubbles will form more slowly toward the end of the baking time. Transfer to a wire rack and let cool.

Using a sharp knife, cut the cooled cookie sheet crosswise into 2-inch-wide strips to yield seven 2 by 10-inch strips. Cut across each strip on the diagonal in alternate directions to yield 5 or 6 triangles per strip.

Stack the cookies between sheets of aluminum foil in an airtight container and store at room temperature for up to 1 week.

Simply Sweet Diamants

Simple never tasted so sweet—or so good. These cookies, based on a recipe by the inimitable French pastry chef Gaston Lenôtre, are special for me because they bring back childhood memories of a favorite box of cookies regularly sent to our family by my paternal grandfather. The box had a sturdy, bright red lid, and inside, two different cookies, one stacked on top of the other, were slipped into fluted, white paper cases. The cookie on top was always elaborately decorated, while the one on the bottom, though plain, was the best of the best in taste. It was a simple, delicious cookie that once again proved that appearances can be deceiving.   **YIELD: ABOUT 5 DOZEN COOKIES**

6 OUNCES (1½ STICKS/170 GRAMS) UNSALTED BUTTER, SOFT

½ CUP (3½ OUNCES/100 GRAMS) GRANULATED SUGAR

½ TEASPOON PURE VANILLA EXTRACT

1¾ CUPS (8 OUNCES/225 GRAMS) ALL-PURPOSE FLOUR

⅛ TEASPOON SALT

1 CUP (7¾ OUNCES/220 GRAMS) PEARL OR SANDING SUGAR

1 LARGE EGG WHITE, LIGHTLY BEATEN

In the bowl of a stand mixer fitted with the paddle attachment, beat together the butter, granulated sugar, and vanilla on the lowest speed until creamy and well blended, 1 to 2 minutes. Maintaining the same speed, add the flour and salt and mix just until combined.

Divide the dough into thirds. On a clean work surface, roll each piece into a log about 1¼ inches in diameter. Wrap the logs separately in plastic wrap and chill until firm, about 2 hours or up to 2 weeks. For longer storage, overwrap with aluminum foil, label with the contents and date, and freeze for up to 1 month. Thaw in the refrigerator for 8 hours or overnight.

Before baking: Center a rack in the oven and preheat the oven to 325 degrees F. Line 2 large baking sheets with parchment paper, so you can get a second pan ready while the first one is baking.

Remove the logs from the refrigerator. Spread the pearl sugar in a large rectangular pan, such as a 9 by 13 by 2-inch pan (quarter sheet pan). One at a time, brush each log with the egg white, and then roll in the pearl sugar to coat evenly. Press lightly so the sugar sticks to the dough. Using a sharp knife, cut 1 dough log into slices ½ inch thick. Place the slices on a prepared baking sheet, spacing them ½ inch apart.

Bake the cookies just until they are ivory colored on top and lightly golden on the bottom, about 12 minutes. Using a metal spatula, transfer the cookies to wire racks to cool completely. Repeat with the remaining logs.

Stack the cooled cookies in an airtight container and store at room temperature for up to 10 days.

Heart-to-Heart-to-Heart Cookies

This is truly a recipe from the heart, adapted from one that was generously shared with me by Susi Schuegraf, a passionate home baker who attended one of my baking classes in Seattle, Washington, many years ago. Perfect for giving to people you love and admire, each cookie features a trio of buttery walnut hearts in graduated sizes, joined by luscious layers of red currant jelly. If you are short on time, you can simply stack the three dough hearts on top of one another and then bake as directed. The pieces will attach automatically during baking. To form pyramids or stacks of cookies, you need to cut out an equal number of hearts (or whatever shape you desire) with three different-sized cutters of the same shape, such as a 2-inch, a 1½-inch, and a 1-inch cutter. And no matter what shape you choose, after trying just one of these cookies, you will discover for yourself how well they stack up. **YIELD: 2½ DOZEN STACKED COOKIES**

DOUGH

3 CUPS (13¾ OUNCES/390 GRAMS) ALL-PURPOSE FLOUR

1 CUP PLUS 1 TABLESPOON (4½ OUNCES/130 GRAMS) WALNUTS, FINELY GROUND TO YIELD 1½ CUPS PLUS 2 TABLESPOONS

¼ TEASPOON SALT

8¾ OUNCES (2 STICKS PLUS 1½ TABLESPOONS/250 GRAMS) UNSALTED BUTTER, AT ROOM TEMPERATURE

1 CUP (7 OUNCES/200 GRAMS) GRANULATED SUGAR

1 LARGE EGG

DECORATION

1 CUP (10 OUNCES/280 GRAMS) RED CURRANT JELLY

30 RED HOT CINNAMON CANDIES

Have ready 3 heart-shaped cutters in graduated sizes, such as 1¾ inches, 1 5/16 inches, and 1 1/16 inches. In a large bowl, whisk together the flour, ground nuts, and salt to blend; set aside.

In the bowl of a stand mixer fitted with the paddle attachment, beat the butter on medium-low speed until smooth, about 1 minute. Add the sugar, increase the speed to medium, and beat until well combined, smooth, and creamy, about 1 minute, stopping the mixer occasionally to scrape down the sides of the bowl. Add the egg, mixing just until it is incorporated. Stop the mixer and add all of the flour mixture at once. Resume mixing on the lowest speed and mix just until thoroughly combined, about 1 minute.

Divide the dough into thirds (each 11½ ounces/325 grams). Place 1 dough portion between 2 sheets of waxed paper and roll out into an 11-inch circle about ⅛ inch thick. Repeat with the remaining dough portions. Leaving the dough circles between the sheets of waxed paper, stack them on a baking sheet and refrigerate until firm, about 2 hours. Or, wrap plastic wrap around the dough circles and baking sheet and refrigerate for up to 3 days. For longer storage, overwrap with aluminum foil, label with the contents and date, and freeze for up to 1 month. To thaw, place the dough circles, still on the pan, in the refrigerator for at least several hours or up to overnight.

Before baking: Center a rack in the oven and preheat the oven to 300 degrees F. Line 2 large baking sheets with parchment paper.

Remove 1 dough package at a time from the refrigerator. Peel off the top sheet of waxed paper, replace it loosely on top, and flip the entire package over. Peel off and discard the second sheet of waxed paper. Using the 1¾-inch heart-shaped cutter, cut out 21 hearts from the dough. Arrange the cutouts on the baking sheet, spacing them ½ inch apart.

Bake the cookies, 1 sheet at a time, until they are pale gold, no longer appear raw or shiny, and CONTINUED ▶

feel slightly firm when gently touched, 13 to 15 minutes. Transfer to a wire rack and let the cookies cool on the pan for 5 minutes. Using a metal spatula, transfer the cookies to the rack to cool completely.

Remove a second dough package from the refrigerator, cut out 21 cookies with the 1 5/16-inch heart cutter and 21 cookies with the 1 1/16-inch heart cutter, bake for 10 to 14 minutes, and cool as directed. Closely monitor the baking of each cookie size so the cookies bake uniformly. If some cookies appear done before others, use a metal spatula to transfer them carefully to a wire rack, return the baking sheet to the oven, and resume baking the remaining cookies.

Then, remove the third dough package from the refrigerator and cut out 9 additional heart cookies of each size, 1 3/4 inches, 1 5/16 inches, and 1 1/16 inches. When you bake this final batch, you will need to remove the smallest cookies (they bake more quickly than the larger ones) after they bake 9 to 12 minutes, and then return the baking sheet to the oven to finish baking the larger cookies an additional minute or two.

To assemble and decorate the cookies: In a small saucepan, boil the currant jelly over medium-low heat for 2 minutes to evaporate some of its liquid. Let cool just until warm. Spoon a scant 1/8 teaspoon jelly in the center of all of the 1 3/4-inch cookies and the 1 5/16-inch cookies. Or, fashion a small cone out of parchment paper and use it to pipe the jelly (page 26). Center the medium-sized heart on top of the largest heart, pressing gently to connect the two. Next, center the smallest heart cookies on top of the medium-sized hearts, pressing gently so that all 3 cookies in each stack are attached.

Brush some jelly on the top of each stack, and immediately place a cinnamon candy in the center, pressing to adhere. Or, crush the candies slightly and sprinkle a tiny amount on each glazed cookie before the glaze dries.

To store the cookies: If decorating later, stack the undecorated cookies in an airtight container and store at room temperature for up to 10 days. Arrange the decorated cookies in a single layer in a covered aluminum foil–lined cardboard box, such as a cake box, and store at room temperature for up to 3 days.

Golden Gingersnap Stars

As festive as the holiday season itself, these glamorous cookie stars are embellished around the edges with real gold dust. The gingersnaps, notable for their exceptionally snappy spice flavor, are sturdy, keep well, and can be baked in a variety of sizes. **YIELD: 3 TO 4 DOZEN COOKIES**

DOUGH

1⅓ CUPS (6¼ OUNCES/175 GRAMS) ALL-PURPOSE FLOUR

¾ TEASPOON GROUND GINGER

½ TEASPOON BAKING SODA

½ TEASPOON GROUND CINNAMON

¼ TEASPOON GROUND CLOVES

⅛ TEASPOON GROUND ALLSPICE

⅛ TEASPOON GROUND BLACK PEPPER

⅛ TEASPOON SALT

3 OUNCES (¾ STICK/85 GRAMS) UNSALTED BUTTER, SOFTENED

½ CUP PLUS 1 TABLESPOON FIRMLY PACKED (SCANT 3¾ OUNCES/SCANT 105 GRAMS) LIGHT BROWN SUGAR

2 TABLESPOONS UNSULFURED MOLASSES

1 TABLESPOON COLD BREWED COFFEE

DECORATIONS (OPTIONAL)

SANDING OR GRANULATED SUGAR

EDIBLE GOLD DUST (SEE SOURCES)

PURE LEMON EXTRACT OR VODKA

To make the dough: Sift together the flour, ginger, baking soda, cinnamon, cloves, allspice, black pepper, and salt onto a sheet of waxed paper; set aside. In a large bowl, using a handheld mixer, beat together the butter and sugar on low speed just until the mixture is creamy and well blended, about 1 minute. Add the molasses and coffee and beat until blended. On the lowest speed, gradually add the flour mixture and mix just until a cohesive dough forms.

Divide the dough in half. Place 1 dough portion between 2 sheets of waxed paper and roll out into a 10-inch circle about ⅛ inch thick. Repeat with the remaining dough portion. Leaving the dough circles between the sheets of waxed paper, stack them on a baking sheet and refrigerate until firm, about 2 hours. Or, wrap plastic wrap around the dough circles and baking sheet and refrigerate

for up to 3 days. For longer storage, overwrap with aluminum foil, label with the contents and date, and freeze for up to 1 month. To thaw, place the dough circles, still on the pan, in the refrigerator for at least several hours or up to overnight.

Before baking: Center a rack in the oven and preheat the oven to 325 degrees F. Line 2 baking sheets with parchment paper, so you can get a second pan ready while the first one is baking.

Remove 1 dough package at a time from the refrigerator. Peel off the top sheet of waxed paper, replace it loosely on top, and flip the entire package over. Peel off and discard the second sheet of waxed paper. Using a 1½-inch star-shaped cutter, cut out stars from the dough, cutting them as closely together as possible. Arrange the cutouts on the baking sheet, spacing them ¼ to ½ inch apart. Reserve the scraps, if desired. Sprinkle the tops of the cookies with the sanding sugar, if desired.

Bake the cookies until they appear set and feel slightly firm to the touch, 7 to 10 minutes. The cookies will become crisp as they cool. Using a metal spatula, transfer to a wire rack to cool completely. Repeat with the remaining dough circle. Then, if desired, reroll the dough scraps between 2 sheets of waxed paper, chill, cut out additional cookies, and bake as directed.

To decorate with gold: In a small bowl, combine 1 tablespoon gold dust and a few drops of lemon extract and stir together to make a slurry, adding more gold dust or extract until the mixture is the consistency of paint. Then, using a small, clean sable paintbrush, paint along the edge of each cookie to emphasize its star shape.

Stack the cookies in an airtight container and store at room temperature for up to 10 days.

Hazelnut Shortbread Cookies

If you are looking for an ultrasimple way to create beautiful (and delicious) cookies, this is the recipe for you. Just right for bringing to a party or a cookie exchange, this Austrian-inspired shortbread is enriched with finely ground hazelnuts, which add their own sophisticated flavor and sweet, delicate aroma. You can bake the scalloped cookie rounds ahead of time, and then quickly decorate them at the last minute. Just before serving, finish the cookies by filling their indentations with a dollop of jewel-toned apricot or currant jelly.   YIELD: ABOUT 3 ½ DOZEN COOKIES

DOUGH

2 ½ CUPS (11 ½ OUNCES/325 GRAMS) ALL-PURPOSE FLOUR

½ CUP PLUS 1 TABLESPOON (3 OUNCES/85 GRAMS)
    HAZELNUTS, TOASTED AND SKINNED (PAGES 15–16)
    AND THEN FINELY GROUND TO YIELD 1 CUP

1 TEASPOON GROUND CINNAMON

¼ TEASPOON GROUND ALLSPICE

⅛ TEASPOON SALT

9 OUNCES (2 ¼ STICKS/255 GRAMS) UNSALTED BUTTER, AT
    ROOM TEMPERATURE

¾ CUP (5 ¼ OUNCES/150 GRAMS) GRANULATED SUGAR

DECORATION

POWDERED SUGAR FOR SPRINKLING

½ CUP (5 OUNCES/140 GRAMS) RED CURRANT JELLY

In a large bowl, whisk together the flour, ground hazelnuts, and cinnamon to blend; set aside. In the bowl of a stand mixer fitted with the paddle attachment, beat the butter on medium-low speed until smooth, about 1 minute. Add the sugar, increase the speed to medium, and beat until smooth and well blended, about 1 minute, stopping the mixer occasionally to scrape down the sides of the bowl. Stop the mixer, and add the flour mixture all at once. Resume mixing on low speed just until a cohesive dough forms, about 30 seconds.

Divide the dough in half. Place 1 dough portion between 2 sheets of waxed paper and roll out into a 10-inch circle about ⅛ inch thick. Repeat with the remaining dough portion. Leaving the dough circles between the sheets of waxed paper, stack them on a baking sheet and refrigerate until firm, about 2 hours. Or, wrap plastic wrap around the dough circles and baking sheet and refrigerate for up to 3 days. For longer storage, overwrap with aluminum foil, label with the contents and date, and freeze for up to 1 month. To thaw, place the dough circles, still on the pan, in the refrigerator for at least 4 hours or up to overnight.

Before baking: Center a rack in the oven and preheat the oven to 325 degrees F. Line 2 large baking sheets with parchment paper, so you can get a second pan ready while the first one is baking.

Remove 1 dough package at a time from the refrigerator. Peel off the top sheet of waxed paper, replace it loosely on top, and flip the entire package over. Peel off and discard the second sheet of waxed paper. Using a 1¾-inch scalloped round cutter, cut out circles from the dough, cutting them as closely together as possible. Arrange the cutouts on a prepared baking sheet, spacing them ½ inch apart. Using the tip of the handle on a wooden spoon, gently make a slight indentation in the center of each cookie. Reserve the scraps, if desired.

Bake the cookies, 1 sheet at a time, until they are beige, no longer appear raw or shiny, and feel slightly firm when gently touched, 15 to 17 minutes. Remove from the oven and if the indentations inflated slightly, gently poke them down. Using a metal spatula, transfer the cookies to the rack and let cool completely.

To decorate the cookies: Place the cookies on a large wire rack. Lightly sprinkle powdered sugar over the cookies (just a hint, not a complete coating of the surface).

In a small saucepan, boil the currant jelly over medium-low for 2 minutes to evaporate some of its liquid. Let cool just until warm. Spoon about $\frac{1}{8}$ teaspoon jelly into the indentation in each cookie. Or, fashion a small cone out of parchment paper and use it to pipe the jelly (page 26).

To store the cookies: If decorating later, stack the undecorated cookies in an airtight container and store at room temperature for up to 10 days. Arrange the decorated cookies in a single layer in a covered aluminum foil–lined cardboard box, such as a cake box, and store at room temperature for up to 3 days.

Nancy's Brown Butter Buttons

One of the most unusual cookies I've ever tasted, these homey delights were introduced to me by my good friend Nancy Kux, former owner of Nancy's Fancies in San Carlos, California, for over two decades. The heirloom recipe originated with Nancy's Swedish aunt, who called them Dream Cookies (and they truly are a dream come true). Showcasing the nutty flavor of browned butter, the cookies bake into puffy buttons with cracked tops. When you bite into them, they're indescribably rich and crumbly, melting luxuriously in your mouth. **YIELD: ABOUT 3½ DOZEN COOKIES**

8 OUNCES (2 STICKS/225 GRAMS) UNSALTED BUTTER

2 CUPS (9 OUNCES/255 GRAMS) ALL-PURPOSE FLOUR

½ TEASPOON BAKING SODA

1 TEASPOON PURE VANILLA EXTRACT

1 CUP (7 OUNCES/200 GRAMS) GRANULATED SUGAR

Before baking: Center a rack in the oven and preheat the oven to 350 degrees F. Line a large baking sheet with parchment paper.

Following the directions for making brown butter on page 000, melt the butter in a heavy 1½-quart saucepan over medium-low heat and heat just until it begins to turn a delicate brown, about 8 minutes. Remove from the heat and pour into a medium bowl. If you like, you can strain the butter through a fine-mesh sieve, but I prefer the golden specks in the batter. Set the butter aside to cool slightly, about 15 minutes. Meanwhile, sift together the flour and baking soda onto a piece of waxed paper; set aside.

Add the vanilla to the butter, and then stir in half of the sugar, blending well before adding the remaining sugar. Add the flour mixture in two additions, blending well after each addition. Set the mixture aside for 10 minutes to allow the flour to absorb the ingredients.

To shape each cookie, measure about 1½ teaspoons of the dough, or scoop up the dough with an ice cream scoop about 1¼ inches in diameter (#70). Work the crumbly dough between your palms to form cohesive balls, and place on the prepared baking sheet, spacing them about ½ inch apart.

Bake the cookies until they puff up, crack a bit on top, and are golden on the bottom, 15 to 18 minutes. Transfer the baking sheet to a wire rack and let the cookies cool on the pan for about 5 minutes. Using a metal spatula, transfer the cookies to a wire rack to cool completely.

Stack the cooled cookies in an airtight container and store at room temperature for up to 1 week or in the freezer for up to 1 month. Thaw at room temperature.

Neapolitan Bars

A sweet tribute to the colors of the Italian flag (and coincidentally, the Christmas season), these stunning bar cookies are a festive addition to any celebration. The rich shortbread pastry crust is topped with layers of ruby red raspberry jam and pale green almond frangipane filling and finished with a shiny dark chocolate glaze. When you cut the bars into squares, you instantly create dozens of perfect (and easily portable) petits fours, each offering a quartet of flavors in every bite. **YIELD: ABOUT 5 DOZEN 1½-INCH BARS**

PASTRY

2 CUPS (9 OUNCES/255 GRAMS) ALL-PURPOSE FLOUR

½ CUP (1¾ OUNCES/50 GRAMS) GRANULATED SUGAR

¼ TEASPOON SALT

6 OUNCES (1½ STICKS/170 GRAMS) COLD UNSALTED BUTTER, CUT INTO ½-INCH SLICES

2 LARGE EGG YOLKS

1 TEASPOON PURE VANILLA EXTRACT

FILLING

1 CUP PLUS 2½ TABLESPOONS PACKED (10 OUNCES/ 280 GRAMS) ALMOND PASTE, AT ROOM TEMPERATURE

⅔ CUP (4½ OUNCES/130 GRAMS) GRANULATED SUGAR

2 OUNCES (½ STICK/55 GRAMS) UNSALTED BUTTER, SOFTENED

4 LARGE EGGS

1 TEASPOON PURE VANILLA EXTRACT

4 OR 5 DROPS GREEN FOOD COLORING (OPTIONAL)

¾ CUP (7 OUNCES/200 GRAMS) SEEDLESS RED RASPBERRY JAM

SIMPLY CHOCOLATE GLAZE

1½ TABLESPOONS UNSALTED BUTTER

3 OUNCES (85 GRAMS) UNSWEETENED CHOCOLATE, FINELY CHOPPED

7 TABLESPOONS (3½ FL OUNCES/105 ML) WHOLE MILK

3 CUPS (10½ OUNCES/300 GRAMS) POWDERED SUGAR, SIFTED

⅛ TEASPOON SALT

1 TABLESPOON PURE VANILLA EXTRACT

Before baking: Center a rack in the oven and preheat the oven to 350 degrees F. Have ready a 15½ by 10½ by 1-inch pan (jelly-roll pan).

To make the pastry: In a food processor, combine the flour, sugar, and salt and pulse 3 or 4 times to blend. Scatter the butter pieces over the flour mixture. Pulse with 1-second bursts until the mixture has the consistency of cornmeal. In a small bowl, whisk together the egg yolks and vanilla. With the motor running, pour the egg mixture down the feed tube and process just until the ingredients form a ball.

Divide the dough into 8 equal pieces. Place 1 piece close to each corner of the pan. Place the remaining 4 dough pieces just off the pan's center. Using your fingertips, pat and spread the dough evenly over the bottom of the pan. To hasten spreading and to ensure the dough is evenly dispersed, place a sheet of plastic wrap on the surface of the dough, and use a 2½- to 4-inch pastry roller (or even a soda can) to help spread it evenly.

Bake the dough until it is cream colored and set (no longer shiny on top), about 15 minutes. Transfer to a wire rack and let cool completely in the pan. Leave the oven on.

To make the filling: In the bowl of a stand mixer fitted with the paddle attachment, beat the almond paste on low speed until it breaks up into fine crumbs, about 1 minute, depending on how soft it is. Add the sugar in a steady stream and beat until incorporated, about 1 minute. Maintaining the same speed, add the butter, 1 tablespoon at a time, and beat until incorporated, stopping the mixer occasionally to scrape down the sides of the bowl. Then add the eggs, one at a time, blending well after each addition. Detach the paddle and the bowl from CONTINUED ▶

the mixer and scrape off any batter clinging to the paddle. Using a rubber spatula, stir in the vanilla. Then stir in the food coloring, if using, until the filling is pale green. If the filling appears lumpy, push it though a medium-mesh sieve.

Stir the jam with a fork until smooth, and then spread it over the cooled pastry, preferably with an offset metal spatula. Gently spoon the filling over the jam-covered pastry, spreading it slowly and carefully to avoid mixing the jam into it.

Bake until the filling looks set on top and is just firm, not solid, to the touch (perhaps with just a few light brown spots here and there), 35 to 40 minutes. Transfer to a wire rack and let cool completely in the pan before topping with the glaze.

To make the Simply Chocolate Glaze: In a small, heavy saucepan, stir the butter, chocolate, and milk, in that order, over very low heat just until the butter and chocolate are melted and a soft, smooth mixture forms. Remove from the heat and stir in half of the powdered sugar and the salt and vanilla. Transfer the mixture to a medium bowl. Stir in the remaining sugar until the

mixture is smooth. If the glaze appears dull or too thick to spread, add additional warm milk, a teaspoon at a time. If it is too thin, add additional sifted powdered sugar, a tablespoon at a time.

Using a metal spatula, preferably offset, spread about three-fourths of the glaze evenly over the filling. Then apply more of the glaze if needed. (You will not need all of the glaze. Store the leftover glaze in a covered container in the refrigerator for up to 1 week, and use as a filling for sandwich cookies or as a glaze for cookies. Stir over hot water to soften to spreading consistency.) Set aside at room temperature for several hours to set the glaze, and up to 3 days at cool room temperature before cutting. (The bars stay fresh longer if you cut them as needed.)

Cut the pastry into squares (or rectangles) as needed. For small squares, cut lengthwise into seven 1 ½-inch-wide strips with a sharp knife. Then cut crosswise into eight 1 ½-inch-wide strips. For the best flavor and texture, serve them the same day they are cut. To store them before serving, arrange the bars in a single layer in a covered aluminum foil–lined cardboard box, such as a cake box, or a 2-inch-deep baking pan and cover the top of the pan with aluminum foil. Set aside at room temperature until serving.

Buttery Rosette Cookies

When making these blissfully buttery cookies, there's one simple secret to perfection: use a silicone mat, inverted so the textured side is facing up. If you pipe the dough onto an ungreased baking sheet, the cookies will stick as they cool and break when you try to remove them. Parchment paper will prevent sticking but the surface is too slippery and the dough won't adhere as you pipe. A silicone mat ensures flawless results. The consistency of the butter in this dough is important because the dough must be pliable enough to pipe easily. Allow enough time for the butter to sit at room temperature to soften.   **YIELD: ABOUT 3 DOZEN 2-INCH CIRCLE OR WREATH COOKIES**

1¼ CUPS PLUS 2 TABLESPOONS (6½ OUNCES/185 GRAMS) ALL-PURPOSE FLOUR

3 TABLESPOONS CORNSTARCH

½ TEASPOON FINE SEA SALT

6½ OUNCES (1½ STICKS PLUS 1 TABLESPOON/185 GRAMS) UNSALTED BUTTER, SOFTENED

½ CUP (1¾ OUNCES/50 GRAMS) POWDERED SUGAR

2 TEASPOONS PURE VANILLA EXTRACT

¼ CUP (2½ OUNCES/55 GRAMS) RASPBERRY JAM, WITH OR WITHOUT SEEDS

SANDING OR PEARL SUGAR FOR DECORATION (OPTIONAL)

Before baking: Center a rack in the oven and preheat the oven to 350 degrees F. Line a large baking sheet with a silicone mat, textured side up, or parchment paper.

Sift together the flour, cornstarch, and salt onto a sheet of waxed paper; set aside. In the bowl of a stand mixer fitted with the paddle attachment, beat together the butter and sugar on medium-low speed until light and creamy, 1½ to 2 minutes. Add the vanilla during the final moments of mixing. On the lowest speed, add the flour in three additions, beating after each addition until incorporated. Stop the mixer after each addition to scrape down the sides of the bowl. Detach the bowl from the mixer. Using a rubber spatula, stir the dough until it is smooth, well blended, and medium stiff (pliable enough to pipe). Be careful not to overmix.

If you have lined the pan with parchment paper, anchor it to the pan with a dab of dough under each corner. Spoon the dough into a large pastry bag fitted with a ³⁄₁₆-inch or ¼-inch star tip, filling it half full. Twist the top portion of the bag to pack the dough down firmly into the pastry tip to facilitate piping evenly. Holding the pastry bag perpendicular to the baking sheet and about ½ inch above it, press out a strip about 4½ inches long (each strip will be about 2¼ teaspoons dough). As you pipe, the strip will curve naturally, so twist the strip into a ring, directing the piped dough into the center of the ring to create a 2-inch-wide rosette. Repeat to form more rosettes, spacing them about 1 inch apart. Each time you finish piping a rosette, twist the pastry tip in the center of the spiral. This action stops the flow of dough and makes it easy to lift the dough away from the rosette. Using the end of a wooden spoon dipped in flour or a lightly moistened thumb, gently press a shallow indentation in the center of each cookie. Place a scant ⅛ to ¼ teaspoon jam in each indentation. Sprinkle the tops of the cookies with the sanding sugar, if using.

Bake the cookies until they are firm to the touch, pale gold on the bottom, and ivory on top, 12 to 13 minutes. Transfer to a wire rack and let the cookies cool on the pan for 3 minutes. Using a metal spatula, transfer the cookies to the rack to cool completely.

Stack the cooled cookies in an airtight container and store at room temperature for up to 2 days or in the freezer for up to 10 days. Thaw at room temperature.

Cookie-Dough Hamantaschen

The romantic story of Purim tells the tale of a queen named Esther, a villain named Haman, and a Persian king who spared the Jewish people for the love of Esther. Today, Jewish bakers traditionally celebrate the lighthearted holiday with these scrumptious cookie turnovers, formed in a triangular shape that replicates the wicked Haman's hat. This is one case in which you will be happy to eat your hats.   **YIELD: ABOUT 3 DOZEN COOKIES**

PRUNE PLUM–RAISIN–NUT FILLING

12 OUNCES (310 GRAMS) PITTED DRIED PRUNE PLUMS (2 CUPS LOOSELY PACKED)

½ CUP (2½ OUNCES/70 GRAMS) RAISINS

2 CUPS (16 FL OUNCES/480 ML) HOT WATER

2 TABLESPOONS FIRMLY PACKED LIGHT BROWN SUGAR

1 TABLESPOON HONEY

1 TEASPOON PURE VANILLA EXTRACT

½ TEASPOON GROUND CINNAMON

1 TABLESPOON FRESH LEMON JUICE

1 TEASPOON FINELY GRATED LEMON ZEST

½ CUP (2 OUNCES/55 GRAMS) CHOPPED TOASTED WALNUTS OR PECANS (PAGES 15–16)

COOKIE DOUGH

3 CUPS (13¾ OUNCES/390 GRAMS) ALL-PURPOSE FLOUR

2 TEASPOONS BAKING POWDER

½ TEASPOON SALT

4 OUNCES (1 STICK/115 GRAMS) UNSALTED BUTTER, AT ROOM TEMPERATURE

1 CUP (7 OUNCES/200 GRAMS) GRANULATED SUGAR

1 LARGE EGG

⅓ CUP (2½ FL OUNCES/75 ML) FRESH ORANGE JUICE

1 TEASPOON PURE VANILLA EXTRACT

To make the Prune Plum–Raisin–Nut Filling: Place the prune plums and raisins in a medium bowl. Pour the hot water over them and let soak until soft, about 10 minutes. Drain the fruit well, discarding the water, and place in a food processor. Add the sugar, honey, vanilla, cinnamon, and lemon juice and zest, in that order, and process until smooth. Spoon the mixture into a small bowl, and stir in the nuts. Set aside at room temperature and use the filling the same day. Or, if not using right away, refrigerate in a covered container for up to 2 weeks. You should have 1½ cups; you will have filling left over.

Before baking: Center a rack in the oven and preheat the oven to 350 degrees F. Line a large baking sheet with parchment paper.

To make the Cookie Dough: Sift together the flour, baking powder, and salt onto a sheet of waxed paper; set aside.

In the bowl of a stand mixer fitted with the paddle attachment, beat together the butter and sugar on medium speed until creamy and well blended, 1 to 2 minutes. Add the egg and continue beating just until smoothly incorporated. Reduce to speed to low and mix in the orange juice and vanilla. On the lowest speed, add the flour mixture, in three additions, mixing just until the dough forms a ball.

To form the cookies: Divide the dough in half and cover 1 portion with plastic wrap. On a lightly floured work surface, roll out the dough into a 13-inch circle about ⅛ inch thick. Using a 3-inch round cutter, cut out circles from the dough, cutting them as closely together as possible. Reserve the scraps. Place 1 teaspoon of the filling in the center of each circle. Moisten the edges of the dough with a little water. Bring the edges on 2 sides of the circle together over the filling, leaving about one-third of the circle open. Pinch 2 sides together, and then fold the open flap inward to meet the 2 edges and pinch all of the edges together firmly, forming a triangle. Arrange the cookies on the prepared baking sheet, spacing them about 1 inch apart. Repeat with the second half of the dough. Gather the scraps into a flat disk, reroll, and cut out and fill more circles, if desired.

Bake the cookies until golden brown on the bottom, about 15 minutes. Using a metal spatula, transfer the cookies to a wire rack and let cool completely.

Store the cookies in a single layer in an airtight container at room temperature for up to 2 days. Although they will be crisp initially, they will soften a bit after the first day. For longer storage, freeze in the container for up to 2 weeks. Thaw at room temperature for 2 hours.

Susie's Raspberry Jam Squares

Susie Block is an avid baker who supplied a popular local coffee shop with these soft bar cookies (and many other out-of-this-world treats) for years. Not being one to ask bakers to divulge professional secrets, I was reluctant to request the recipe until Susie and her husband were getting ready to move to the Midwest. She was delighted—and I am, too, because now I can share it with you. Combining a rich crust and striped cookie topping with a simple raspberry filling, the squares are classic companions for everything from hot coffee to ice-cold milk.   **YIELD: 2 DOZEN BARS**

8 OUNCES (2 STICKS/225 GRAMS) UNSALTED BUTTER, AT ROOM TEMPERATURE

1½ CUPS (10½ OUNCES/300 GRAMS) GRANULATED SUGAR

2 LARGE EGGS, LIGHTLY BEATEN

1 TEASPOON PURE VANILLA EXTRACT

3 CUPS (13¾ OUNCES/390 GRAMS) ALL-PURPOSE FLOUR

½ TEASPOON SALT

¾ CUP (3 OUNCES/85 GRAMS) CHOPPED WALNUTS OR MACADAMIA NUTS

1 CUP (10 OUNCES/280 GRAMS) RED RASPBERRY JAM WITH SEEDS

Before baking: Center a rack in the oven and preheat the oven to 350 degrees F. Press a sheet of aluminum foil to cover the outside bottom and sides of a 9 by 13 by 2-inch pan (quarter sheet pan). Lift off the foil, invert the pan, and gently press the form into the pan to fit the contours. Have all of the ingredients at room temperature.

In the bowl of a stand mixer fitted with the paddle attachment, beat together the butter and sugar on medium-low speed until creamy and well blended, 1 to 2 minutes. Stop the mixer occasionally to scrape down the sides of the bowl. Gradually add the eggs, mixing just until incorporated, stopping the mixer to scrape down the sides of the bowl as needed. Add the vanilla and beat just until smooth. On the lowest speed, gradually add the flour and salt and blend until a smooth dough forms, about 45 seconds. Detach the paddle and bowl from the mixer, and tap the paddle against the side of the bowl to free the excess dough.

Divide the soft dough into 2 portions, one about 2 cups (1¼ pounds/470 grams) and the other about 1½ cups (14 ounces/400 grams). Wrap the smaller portion in plastic wrap and refrigerate it to make it easier to handle when forming the dough into strips later. Divide the large portion into 6 pieces. Place 1 piece close to each corner of the prepared pan. Place the remaining 2 pieces just off the pan's center. Using floured fingertips, pat and spread the dough evenly over the bottom of the pan. To hasten spreading and to ensure the dough is evenly dispersed, place a sheet of plastic wrap on the surface of the dough, and use a 2½- to 4-inch pastry roller (or even a soda can) to help spread it evenly.

Sprinkle the nuts evenly over the dough, and gently press them into the dough slightly. Using an offset metal spatula, spread the raspberry jam evenly over the dough. Remove the smaller portion of dough from the refrigerator. You need to form 8 ropes of varying lengths with *similar* widths to create a striped pattern on top. Lightly flour your hands, and break off different amounts of the dough to roll and form the pattern. First, break off a scant ¼ cup (about 2⅛ ounces/60 grams) of the dough and roll it on a very lightly floured surface into a rope about 11 inches long. Then divide the remaining dough into 7 portions each 2½ to 3 tablespoons (1¼ to 1½ ounces/ 35 to 40 grams), and roll each of them into a rope 8 to 9 inches long.

Arrange the ropes on the jam layer, positioning them on the diagonal in one direction only and spacing them about ¾ inch apart, to create the striped pattern. Begin by placing the 11-inch rope diagonally in the center. Place all of the other ropes on either side of the center rope. Some ropes will be long enough and others will be too long. Trim each rope as needed to fit diagonally on top (it's easy to make adjustments, as the dough is quite pliable). Some ropes will be 8 to 8½ inches long, others will be 6 inches, and the ropes near the ends will be 2 to 2½ inches. If a space remains at the corners, roll some of the scraps or remaining dough into ropes 1 to 1½ inches long and place at each end. Be sure the jam and nuts are visible between the strips. (Keep in mind that the dough spreads somewhat during baking, and you want to be able to see the jam and nuts when you cut the squares after baking.) Pat the dough down lightly.

Bake until the dough is pale gold on top, the jam is set and not bubbling, and the underside of the dough is golden, 37 to 44 minutes. Transfer to a wire rack to cool partially, 30 to 40 minutes.

Place a cutting board or baking sheet on top of the pan, invert the pan onto it, and lift off the pan. Carefully peel off the foil and discard. Place another cutting board or baking sheet on top of the cookie plaque, invert the cookie plaque so it is right side up, and remove the original cutting board. Cut into 2-inch squares with a serrated knife, using a slow sawing motion (these are soft, not crisp, cookies). Let cool completely before serving or storing.

Stack the cookies, separating the layers with a sheet of waxed paper or aluminum foil, in a sturdy covered container at room temperature for up to 3 days or in the freezer for up to 2 weeks. Thaw in the container at room temperature for about 3 hours.

Espresso Shortbread-by-the-Dozen

Espresso takes its name from the Italian for "fast." In addition to describing the rich coffee flavor of these cookies, "espresso" also articulates their exceptional ease of preparation. One of the quickest, simplest ways I know to create a big batch of delicious cookies in a small amount of time, this "express" recipe relies on a bit of finely ground espresso to add sophisticated flavor. All you do is press the rich, buttery dough into a pan, bake, and cut into squares. For plain shortbread cookies, simply omit the espresso.   **YIELD: 1 DOZEN BARS**

2 CUPS (9 OUNCES/255 GRAMS) ALL-PURPOSE FLOUR

½ TEASPOON SALT

8 OUNCES (2 STICKS/225 GRAMS) UNSALTED BUTTER, AT
    ROOM TEMPERATURE

½ CUP PLUS 2 TABLESPOONS (4¼ OUNCES/120 GRAMS)
    GRANULATED SUGAR

2 TEASPOONS FINELY GROUND ESPRESSO-ROAST COFFEE

1 TO 2 TEASPOONS PURE VANILLA EXTRACT

12 SMALL ESPRESSO-ROAST COFFEE BEANS (OPTIONAL)

Before baking: Center a rack in the oven and preheat the oven to 300 degrees F. Line the bottom and 2 sides of an 8 x 2-inch square pan with parchment paper, leaving a 2- to 3-inch overhang on the sides.

Sift together the flour and salt onto a sheet of waxed paper; set aside. In the bowl of a stand mixer fitted with the paddle attachment, beat the butter on medium speed until creamy and smooth, about 30 seconds. With the mixer running, add the sugar and ground coffee all at once and beat until the mixture is light and fluffy, 5 to 6 minutes. Add the vanilla (use the larger amount if you like a stronger vanilla flavor) during the final moments of mixing. On the lowest speed, add the flour mixture in two additions and beat just until combined.

Divide the dough into 7 equal pieces. Place 1 piece close to each corner of the prepared pan. Place the remaining 3 dough pieces just off the pan's center. Using your

fingertips, pat and spread the dough evenly over the bottom of the pan. To hasten spreading and to ensure the dough is evenly dispersed, place a sheet of plastic wrap on the surface of the dough, and use a 2½- to 4-inch pastry roller (or even a soda can) to help spread it evenly. Prick the surface all over with the tines of a fork. Using a sharp knife, cut the dough into six 1¼-inch-wide strips, cutting all the way through the dough, then cut across these strips at the midpoint to form 4-inch-long rectangles. (After you cut the dough, a strip about ½ inch wide remains that will make a nice snack for the baker when the pan comes out of the oven.) Center a coffee bean on top of each cookie, if desired.

Bake the shortbread until pale gold yet not brown, 45 to 50 minutes. Transfer to a wire rack. Without delay, gently cut the warm shortbread along the marked lines with a small, sharp knife. (This prevents the squares from breaking once the shortbread has cooled.) When completely cool, using the ends of the parchment as handles, lift the shortbread out of the pan. If necessary, carefully break the shortbread into bars along the marked lines.

Stack the bars in an airtight container and store at room temperature for up to 2 weeks or in the freezer for up to 1 month. Thaw at room temperature for 2 to 3 hours.

Scalloped Butter Cookies
with Pistachio–Rose Water Glaze

A colorful contemporary painting at the San Francisco Museum of Modern Art inspired the geometric shapes of these sculptural cookies. The circular cookies feature cut-out square centers, creating a dramatic silhouette that looks beautiful on a serving platter. Adding yet another artistic dimension, the aromatic rose-water glaze is enlivened with bits of vibrant green pistachios and tangy orange zest. The unique combination of colors, flavors, and textures makes these tender butter cookies a memorable addition to your baking repertoire.

The rolled-out dough softens quickly, so after I cut out the cookies, I usually slip the cutouts back into the refrigerator for 10 to 15 minutes to firm up before I bake them.

YIELD: ABOUT 22 SANDWICH COOKIES

DOUGH

2 ¼ CUPS (10 ¼ OUNCES/290 GRAMS) ALL-PURPOSE FLOUR

¼ TEASPOON SALT

9 OUNCES (2 ¼ STICKS/255 GRAMS) UNSALTED BUTTER, ROOM TEMPERATURE

6 TABLESPOONS (2 ¾ OUNCES/75 GRAMS) GRANULATED SUGAR

1 TEASPOON PURE VANILLA EXTRACT

PISTACHIO–ROSE WATER GLAZE AND JELLY FILLING

2 TABLESPOONS UNSALTED, SHELLED PISTACHIO NUTS, FINELY GROUND TO YIELD A SCANT 3 TABLESPOONS

1 TEASPOON FINELY GRATED ORANGE ZEST

½ CUP (1 ¾ OUNCES/50 GRAMS) POWDERED SUGAR

4 TEASPOONS FRESH ORANGE OR LEMON JUICE OR WATER

¼ TEASPOON ROSE WATER, OR MORE TO TASTE

½ CUP (5 OUNCES/140 GRAMS) ROSE JELLY OR ORANGE MARMALADE

To make the dough: In a medium bowl, whisk together the flour and salt just to blend; set aside. In the bowl of a stand mixer fitted with the paddle attachment, beat the butter on medium-low speed until smooth, about 1 minute. Add the sugar and vanilla and beat just until combined, stopping the mixer to scrape down the sides of the bowl as needed. On the lowest speed, gradually add the flour mixture, mixing just until a cohesive dough forms.

Divide the dough in half. Place 1 dough portion between 2 sheets of waxed paper and roll out into an 11-inch circle about ³⁄₁₆ inch thick. Repeat with the remaining dough portion. Leaving the dough circles between the sheets of waxed paper, stack them on a baking sheet and refrigerate until firm, about 2 hours. Or, wrap plastic wrap around the dough circles and baking sheet and refrigerate for up to 3 days. For longer storage, overwrap with aluminum foil, label with the contents and date, and freeze for up to 1 month. To thaw, place the dough circles, still on the pan, in the refrigerator for at least 4 hours or up to overnight.

Before baking: Center a rack in the oven and preheat the oven to 325 degrees F. Line 2 large baking sheets with parchment paper, so you can get a second pan ready while the first one is baking.

Remove 1 dough package at a time from the refrigerator. Peel off the top sheet of waxed paper, replace it loosely on top, and flip the entire package over. Peel off and discard the second sheet of waxed paper. Using a 1 ¾-inch scalloped round cutter, cut out circles from the dough, cutting them as closely together as possible. If the dough softens, slide the soft dough with the cutouts (still on the waxed paper) onto a baking sheet, and CONTINUED ➤

place in the freezer or refrigerator until firm, about 10 minutes. Using a metal spatula, transfer the cutouts to the prepared baking sheet, spacing them about ½ inch apart. Reserve the scraps, if desired.

Bake the cookies until they are pale gold, no longer appear raw or shiny, and feel slightly firm when gently touched, 13 to 15 minutes. Transfer to a wire rack and let the cookies cool on the pan for 5 minutes. Using a metal spatula, transfer the cookies to the rack to cool completely.

Cut out 1¾-inch scalloped circles from the remaining dough circle. Then, using a ½-inch square cutter (such as the narrow end of a ⅝-inch plain open pastry tip), cut out a square (or you can cut circles if you prefer) from the center of each circle. Again, refrigerate or freeze the dough if it has softened, and then bake on the second prepared baking sheet as directed for the solid cookies, reducing the time to 12 to 14 minutes (the cookies with the holes bake faster than the solid cookies). Transfer to a wire rack and let cool on the pan for 5 minutes, then transfer the cookies to the rack to cool completely. Leave the oven on. Then, if desired, reroll the scraps between 2 sheets of waxed paper, chill, cut out additional cookies, and bake as directed.

Keep the oven rack in the same position and reduce the temperature to 140 degrees F. Line a clean baking sheet with parchment paper and transfer the cookies with holes to it; set aside.

To make the Pistachio–Rose Water Glaze: In a small bowl, stir together the pistachios, orange zest, sugar, orange juice, and rose water until smooth. With a pastry brush, spread a very thin layer of the glaze on each of the cookies with holes. Return the cookies to the oven until the glaze is set and dry and the tiny pistachio chips are still green, 2 to 4 minutes. Remove from the oven and set aside.

To assemble and decorate the cookies: In a small saucepan, boil the rose jelly over medium-low heat for 2 minutes to evaporate some of its liquid. Let cool just until warm. On a work surface, turn the solid cookies bottom side up. Spoon about ½ teaspoon jelly in the center of the bottom of a cookie. Center a glazed cutout circle on top of the jellied bottom, and press so the jelly fills the hole. Repeat with the remaining cookies.

To store the cookies: If decorating later, stack the undecorated cookies in an airtight container and store at room temperature for up to 10 days. Arrange the decorated cookies in a single layer in a covered aluminum foil–lined cardboard box, such as a cake box, and store at room temperature for up to 3 days.

Ultimate Coconut Macaroons

These coconut morsels are crispy on the outside and moist on the inside, and they always remind me of the famous coconut candy bar. The only difference is that the candy bar is enrobed in chocolate. But these cookies are so good that I doubt you will miss the chocolate. To make them suitable for Passover, omit the corn syrup. **YIELD: ABOUT 33 COOKIES**

3 CUPS (8 OUNCES/225 GRAMS) UNSWEETENED MEDIUM-
    SHRED DRIED COCONUT

1 CUP PLUS 2 TABLESPOONS (8 OUNCES/225 GRAMS)
    GRANULATED SUGAR

½ CUP (4 FL OUNCES/120 ML) EGG WHITES (3 TO 4 LARGE)

1 TABLESPOON UNSALTED BUTTER, SOFTENED

2 TEASPOONS WATER

2 TEASPOONS LIGHT CORN SYRUP

½ TEASPOON SALT

Before baking: Center a rack in the oven and preheat the oven to 375 degrees F. Line a large baking sheet with a silicone mat or parchment paper.

In a heavy 4-quart heavy saucepan, stir together the coconut, sugar, egg whites, butter, water, corn syrup, and salt. Place over low heat and cook, stirring constantly, until the mixture registers 120 degrees F on an instant-read or candy thermometer.

Spoon 1-tablespoon-sized mounds onto the prepared baking sheet, spacing them about 1 inch apart. Or, use an ice cream scoop about 1 ¼ inches in diameter (#70) to shape the mounds. Let the mounds dry at room temperature until the surface is no longer sticky, 5 to 10 minutes. Then, with your fingertips, shape the mounds into small pyramids, smoothing the rough edges (to avoid burning during baking).

Bake the cookies until they are browned on the top and bottom and feel firm to the touch, yet still somewhat soft inside, 10 to 12 minutes. Rotate the baking sheet 180 degrees halfway through baking to ensure the cookies brown evenly. Using a metal spatula, transfer the cookies to a wire rack and let cool completely.

Stack the cooled cookies in an airtight container and store at room temperature for up to 1 day or in the freezer for up to 3 weeks. Thaw at room temperature for 2 to 3 hours.

Mexican Wedding Cookies

As their name implies, these familiar melt-in-your-mouth cookies are traditionally associated with celebrations—and they certainly are something to celebrate. I've included them because they are perfect for gifting to guests as a memento of a wedding, a christening, or even a graduation. Baking big batches is a cinch with this dough if you use an ice cream scoop for forming the cookies. And the dough is amazingly adaptable. In fact, it is the chameleon of the cookie world. You can personalize it with your favorite nuts and flavorings, and you can fashion it into cutouts, slice-and-bake logs, crescents, or thumbprint cookies to fill with jelly. The only limit is your imagination.

YIELD: ABOUT 5 DOZEN COOKIES

2 CUPS (9 OUNCES/255 GRAMS) ALL-PURPOSE FLOUR

¼ TEASPOON SALT

⅔ CUP (2 ½ OUNCES/70 GRAMS) POWDERED SUGAR, DIVIDED, PLUS MORE FOR DECORATION

1 CUP (4 OUNCES/115 GRAMS) PECANS OR WALNUTS, TOASTED (PAGES 15–16) AND FROZEN

8 OUNCES (2 STICKS/225 GRAMS) UNSALTED BUTTER, SOFTENED

1 TEASPOON PURE VANILLA EXTRACT

Before baking: Center a rack in the oven and preheat the oven to 325 degrees F. Line 2 large baking sheets with parchment paper, so you can get a second pan ready while the first one is baking.

Sift together the flour and salt onto a sheet of waxed paper; set aside. Pour ⅓ cup (1 ¼ ounces/35 grams) of the sugar and the frozen pecans into a food processor. Process until the nuts are finely ground (some small nut pieces may remain—that's fine).

In the bowl of a stand mixer fitted with the paddle attachment, beat together the butter and the remaining ⅓ cup sugar until the mixture is light and fluffy. Add the vanilla during the final moments of mixing. On the lowest speed, add the nut mixture, and then add the flour mixture and mix until thoroughly combined.

Using an ice cream scoop about 1 ⅛ inches in diameter (#100), drop balls of dough onto the prepared baking sheets, spacing them 1 inch apart. Or, roll the dough

between your palms into 1- to 1 ½-inch balls. If you use the scoop, the release action puts a ripple imprint on top of each cookie. Leave the cookies as they are so they emerge from the oven with a charming, unique design.

Bake the cookies, 1 sheet at a time, until lightly golden on the bottom, 12 to 15 minutes. Transfer to a wire rack, leave the cookies on the pan, and immediately sift powdered sugar over the tops. Let the cookies cool completely on the pan.

Arrange the cooled cookies in a single layer in a sturdy container, dust the tops generously with more sugar, cover tightly, and store at room temperature for up to 10 days or in the freezer for up to 1 month. Thaw at room temperature for about 2 hours.

Four Variations on the Mexican Wedding Cookie Theme

Cutout Cookies

Divide the dough into thirds. Roll out each portion between 2 sheets of waxed paper into a 9-inch circle about ⅛ inch thick. Stack the 3 circles, still between the sheets of waxed paper, on a baking sheet, and refrigerate until firm, about 2 hours. Cut out shapes with cookie cutters and place them about ½ inch apart on parchment paper–lined baking sheets. Bake the cookies in the center of a preheated 325 degree F oven until lightly golden on the bottom, about 10 minutes. Transfer the cookies to a wire rack to cool. Dust with powdered sugar, or sandwich 2 cookies with a favorite filling.

Slice 'n' Bake

Divide the dough into thirds. Roll each portion into a log about 1 1/2 inches in diameter. Wrap in plastic wrap and refrigerate until firm, about 2 hours. Using a sharp knife, cut the logs into 1/4-inch-thick slices and place them about 1/2 inch apart on parchment-lined baking sheets. If desired, lightly and evenly sprinkle the tops with cinnamon sugar. Bake the cookies in the center of a preheated 325 degree F oven until lightly golden on the bottom, 12 to 15 minutes. Transfer the cookies to a wire rack to cool.

Austrian Crescents

Measure 2 level teaspoons of dough for each crescent. Shape the dough into a short rope about 1/2 inch in diameter, and form the rope into a crescent with slightly tapered ends. Place the crescents about 1/2 inch apart on parchment paper–lined baking sheets. Bake the cookies in the center of a 325 degree F oven until lightly golden on the bottom, 12 to 15 minutes. Dust with powdered sugar right out of the oven, then let cool completely on the pan. Dust again with powdered sugar before serving or when storing.

Thumbprints

With your palms, shape 1 to 2 teaspoons of the dough into balls and drop 1/2 inch apart on parchment paper–lined baking sheets. Using the end of a wooden spoon, gently make a shallow indentation in the center of each cookie. Bake the cookies in the center of a 325 degree F oven until lightly golden on the bottom, 13 to 15 minutes. Transfer the cookies to a wire rack to cool. When the cookies are completely cool, fill the indentations with a favorite chocolate ganache or fruit jam.

Gingery Crumb Wedges

I am a streusel fiend. Show me a recipe with streusel and I immediately want to make it. Evoking the magical flavor and texture of streusel, these ginger cookies bake up crunchy, buttery, and absolutely irresistible. After baking, you simply break the cookies into pieces like peanut brittle. Package them on a pretty paper plate for a casual gift, nibble them as a companion to coffee, or serve them as an accompaniment to everything from raw or poached fruit to ice cream or sorbet.

YIELD: 1 DOZEN COOKIES

¾ CUP PLUS 3 TABLESPOONS (4 ¼ OUNCES/120 GRAMS)
    ALL-PURPOSE FLOUR

¾ CUP (4 ½ OUNCES/130 GRAMS) FINE SEMOLINA

½ CUP (3 ½ OUNCES/100 GRAMS) GRANULATED SUGAR

1 ½ TEASPOONS BAKING POWDER

¼ TEASPOON SALT

2 TABLESPOONS FINELY CHOPPED CRYSTALLIZED GINGER

5 ½ OUNCES (1 STICK PLUS 3 TABLESPOONS/155 GRAMS)
    UNSALTED BUTTER, MELTED AND COOLED

1 ½ TEASPOONS PURE VANILLA EXTRACT

Before baking: Center a rack in the oven and preheat the oven to 350 degrees F. Have ready a 9-inch round springform pan (the height of the pan is not critical here).

Sift together the flour, semolina, sugar, baking powder, and salt into a large bowl. Stir in the ginger. Add the butter and vanilla and, using your fingertips, blend together to coat the dry ingredients with the butter. Squeeze some of the mixture in your hand so that it forms small clumps that look like large chunks of streusel, and then let the clumps fall from your hand over the bottom of the pan. Continue scattering clumps over the pan bottom as evenly as possible until all of the mixture is in the pan. Resist pressing on the crumbly mixture to pack it into the pan.

Bake until lightly golden, about 45 minutes. Transfer to a wire rack and let cool completely in the pan. Using a sharp knife, cut into 12 wedges.

Store the cooled cookies in an airtight container at room temperature for up to 1 week.

Red Letter Day Desserts

BAKING SOMETHING SCRUMPTIOUS signals to everyone today is special. Like an unwritten language, the appearance of a birthday cake with your favorite flavors or a slice of pie served to the guest of honor triggers a mental reaction that makes lips curl upward and taste buds salivate. If you want to signify a day of celebration, all you need to do is bake something grand, like Night and Day Torte or All-American Chocolate Cake with Divinity Frosting and Milk Chocolate Paint.

Of course, birthdays are the most obvious occasions for celebrating, but they are not alone. For a fitting end to a dinner that toasts a new job or promotion, serve Dulce de Tres Leches Fiesta Cake with a vibrant red fruit sauce on each plate. A more elegant occasion, like a New Year's Eve party, concludes with a slice of Flourless Chocolate Torte.

The most important celebrations in life—weddings, baby namings or christenings, milestone anniversaries, and celebrations of workplace or creative success—call for magnificent desserts to herald the happenings. Be forewarned: Dee-luscious Lemon Meringue Pie, with its creamy, dreamy topping just might steal the show. For an event celebrating the arrival of a baby, something sweet and delicate is in order, like Old-Fashioned Jelly Roll with a Twist, with the creative spin being its playful spiral of a fruity-jam filling.

Sit down now with your agenda, skim through this chapter, and mark some desserts to suit the festivities.

Coffee-Toffee Celebration Cake

Many years ago, San Franciscans had the pleasure of frequenting the legendary Blum's coffee shop, famous for its captivating confections and delectable desserts. Inspired by a wave of nostalgia, I've created a lofty layer cake whose signature flavors offer loving tribute to the bygone eatery's fabled coffee-toffee pie. I recommend coarsely chopping the hazelnuts in a nut mill (page 43).

YIELD: ONE 9-INCH, 2-LAYER ROUND CAKE, 10 SERVINGS

1 RECIPE FAVORITE BUTTERMILK CAKE (PAGE 344)

COFFEE-TOFFEE FILLING AND TOPPING

½ CUP (2 ½ OUNCES/70 GRAMS) HAZELNUTS, TOASTED AND SKINNED, THEN COARSELY CHOPPED TO YIELD ½ CUP PLUS 2 TABLESPOONS

1 CUP (2 OUNCES/55 GRAMS) SWEETENED FLAKED DRIED COCONUT, TOASTED (PAGE 53)

½ TEASPOON ESPRESSO COFFEE POWDER DISSOLVED IN ½ TEASPOON HOT WATER

3½ TABLESPOONS WATER

3 TABLESPOONS LIGHT CORN SYRUP

¾ CUP (5¼ OUNCES/150 GRAMS) GRANULATED SUGAR

1 TABLESPOON UNSALTED BUTTER

½ CUP (4 FL OUNCES/120 ML) HEAVY CREAM

PINCH OF SALT

To bake the Favorite Buttermilk Cake: Center a rack in the oven and preheat the oven to 350 degrees F. Butter two 9 by 2-inch round cake pans, then flour them, tapping out the excess flour. Or, lightly coat with nonstick spray and flour the pans. Line the bottoms with parchment paper.

Make the cake batter as directed and divide it between the prepared pans. Bake the cakes until they spring back when lightly touched in the center, a round wooden toothpick inserted in the center comes out free of cake, and the sides are just beginning to come away from the pans, 25 to 28 minutes. Transfer to wire racks and let cool in the pans for 5 to 10 minutes, then unmold and let cool completely as directed in the recipe.

To assemble the cake: Place 1 layer, bottom side down, on a sturdy cardboard round the same diameter as the cake. Bend over so your eyes are down to cake level to see if the cake is level on top. If it is not, gently press the area down. Set the other cake layer nearby and proceed to make the filling and topping.

To make the Coffee-Toffee Filling and Topping:
Place the hazelnuts and coconut in a large heatproof bowl; set it and the coffee mixture nearby.

In a heavy 1½-quart saucepan, combine the water, corn syrup, and sugar, place over low heat, and cook, stirring occasionally, just until the sugar is dissolved, about 5 minutes. Increase the heat to medium-high, bring the mixture to a boil, and boil, without stirring, until the mixture turns light amber, 4 to 5 minutes. Keep a pastry brush in a small glass of cold water nearby for washing down any sugar crystals that form along the sides of the pan. Remove from the heat, add the butter, cream, the reserved coffee mixture, and the salt, in that order, carefully stirring with a small wooden spoon or silicone spatula to blend. (Careful, the mixture is steamy and bubbles up.) If the caramel is not smooth, place it over very low heat and stir until it is. Set the caramel aside to cool for 10 minutes only.

Pour the hot caramel sauce over the nuts and coconut and fold with a silicone spatula to combine. Spoon half of the warm mixture on top of the cake and, using an offset spatula, spread it evenly over the top of the layer. Center the other cake layer, bottom side down, on top. Again, check if the cake is level and if not, press the area down gently. Without delay, spoon the remaining caramel mixture over the top and spread it to the edge of the cake.

Transfer the dessert to a cake stand or large cake plate. Serve at room temperature, cut into slices with a serrated knife.

Chocolate Roulade with Chocolate Diplomat Cream

Chocolate, doubled, is the short description of this dessert. If you have a passion for chocolate, this thin, tender cake rolled around a sumptuous creamy chocolate filling will definitely catapult you into rapturous bliss. For short, I've given it the name Slices of Chocolate Heaven. If you slip the assembled dessert into the refrigerator for a couple of hours, the filling will moisten the cake slightly, linking the duo together into one heavenly tasting roulade. YIELD: ONE 18-INCH ROLLED CAKE, 12 TO 16 SERVINGS

1 RECIPE CHOCOLATE GENOISE SHEET CAKE (PAGE 352)

CHOCOLATE DIPLOMAT CREAM

¾ CUP (6 FL OUNCES/180 ML) HALF-AND-HALF

½ CUP (3½ OUNCES/100 GRAMS) GRANULATED SUGAR

⅛ TEASPOON SALT

2 OUNCES BITTERSWEET CHOCOLATE, COARSELY CHOPPED

2 LARGE (2 TABLESPOONS PLUS 2 TEASPOONS) EGG YOLKS

1 TABLESPOON PLUS 2 TEASPOONS ALL-PURPOSE FLOUR

1 TEASPOON PURE VANILLA EXTRACT

1 TEASPOON DARK RUM

1 CUP (8 FL OUNCES/240 ML) HEAVY CREAM

¼ CUP (¾ OUNCES/25 GRAMS) POWDERED SUGAR (OPTIONAL)

Make the genoise sheet cake and let cool, tented with aluminum foil, as directed.

To make the Chocolate Diplomat Cream: Rest a fine-mesh sieve over a large bowl and set nearby for straining the pastry cream later. Pour the half-and-half into a heavy 1½-quart saucepan, add ¼ cup (1¾ ounces/50 grams) of the granulated sugar and the salt, and stir to combine. Add the chocolate pieces.

In a small bowl, whisk the egg yolks until blended, then whisk in the remaining ¼ cup sugar. Add the flour and whisk to combine; set aside. Bring the half-and-half mixture just to a boil over medium heat, stirring to aid the chocolate in melting. Remove from the heat and pour half of the hot half-and-half mixture into the yolk mixture while whisking constantly. Return the combined mixtures to the saucepan and whisk to combine. Return to medium heat and heat, stirring constantly, until the mixture just comes to a boil, 1 to 2 minutes. At this time it will thicken. Continue to stir and simmer until the mixture is smooth and thick, about 1 minute more. Remove from the heat and pour through the sieve into the bowl. (The large bowl provides enough room to fold in the whipped cream later.) Cover with plastic wrap, pressing it directly onto the surface to prevent a skin from forming. Poke a few slits in the plastic with the tip of a knife to allow steam to escape and set aside to cool for 15 to 20 minutes. (Once it has cooled, you can refrigerate it for up to 3 days.)

To assemble the dessert: Stir the vanilla and rum into the cooled pastry cream. Using a whisk or a handheld mixer, whip the heavy cream in a medium, deep bowl until soft peaks form. Using a rubber spatula, fold the whipped cream into the pastry cream just until combined. Refrigerate briefly while preparing the cake for rolling.

Discard the foil tent for the cake. Using a thin-bladed knife, gently release any portion of cake sticking to the long sides of the pan. One at a time, pull up on the foil overhangs to release the foil from the pan, and then transfer the cake on its foil liner to a work surface, with a long side facing you. Place another long sheet of aluminum foil on the work surface nearby. CONTINUED ➤

Remove the chocolate filling from the refrigerator. Using an offset spatula, spread the filling evenly over the cake, leaving a 1-inch border uncovered on the long side farthest from you. (Some of the filling will move to that end as you roll up the cake.) Begin rolling by flipping the edge of the cake nearest you over onto itself. Then, with the aid of the foil that extends beyond the short sides, roll up the cake lengthwise until you reach the far long side. As you work, wrap the foil around the roll to assist you in rounding the shape (otherwise the cake will stick to your hands). Place the roll in its foil across the bottom third of a 24-inch-long piece of parchment paper, and follow the directions on page 25 for compressing the cake into a uniform roll. Carefully lift the cake roll in the aluminum foil and set it, seam side down, onto the fresh sheet of foil on the work surface. Wrap the cake securely in the foil. Transfer the foil-wrapped roll to a baking sheet or shallow tray and refrigerate for at least 2 hours or up to 1 day.

To serve: Remove the cake from the refrigerator and peel off and discard the foil. Using a serrated knife and a sawing motion, cut off both ends of the roll on the diagonal for eye appeal, and add them to the pushed-out filling you reserved during compressing to provide 2 extra portions. Lightly dust the top of the cake roll with the powdered sugar, if using. Carefully lift the roll onto a serving plate with the aid of a long, wide spatula or a rimless baking sheet. Using the serrated knife, cut into 1-inch-thick slices. Cover any leftovers with plastic wrap and refrigerate for up to 2 days.

Dulce de Tres Leches Fiesta Cake with Red Fruit Sauce

In Latin American households, *tres leches* (three milks) cake is synonymous with celebration—and *dulce de leche* is synonymous with divine decadence. I've combined these two indulgences to create one fabulously festive dessert. The *dulce de leche* (caramelized sweetened condensed milk) is blended with whole milk and heavy cream, enlivened with a spirited splash of rum. A classic vanilla sponge cake, or genoise, has the perfect texture to soak up the rich, creamy custard sauce. To finish the dessert, drizzle some scarlet berry sauce around each slice and garnish with few fresh berries and a dollop of whipped cream.

Bake the cake at least 1 day ahead so that it dries out slightly to make it thirsty for the filling. This genoise may also for another dessert. It will remain moist, wrapped in plastic wrap, at room temperature for up to 2 days. For storage up to 10 days, overwrap with aluminum foil and freeze. Thaw unwrapped at room temperature for 2 to 3 hours.

Many of my students have questioned me about the difference between evaporated milk and sweetened condensed milk. Both products have had some of their water removed under vacuum. Evaporated milk, the more versatile of the two products, can be used in almost any recipe calling for milk. Sweetened condensed milk has added sugar, resulting in a thicker consistency. When it is combined with an acid ingredient like lemon juice or concentrated orange, pineapple, or apple juice, it thickens without heating. When it is heated with chocolate or cocoa, it thickens without crystallization, and no further cooking is required. Sweetened condensed milk can also be caramelized in the oven, on the stove top, or in the microwave. I prefer the oven method. Be sure to heed the warning on the label never to submerge a can of sweetened condensed milk in simmering or boiling water. The process is *very* unstable. **YIELD: ONE 8-INCH ROUND CAKE, 8 TO 12 SERVINGS**

YELLOW GENOISE

¾ CUP PLUS 2 TABLESPOONS (3 ½ OUNCES/100 GRAMS) CAKE FLOUR

½ CUP PLUS 1 TABLESPOON (4 OUNCES/115 GRAMS) GRANULATED SUGAR, DIVIDED

⅛ TEASPOON SALT

4 LARGE EGGS

1 TEASPOON PURE VANILLA EXTRACT

DULCE DE LECHE CREAM

ONE 14-OUNCE (400-GRAM) CAN SWEETENED CONDENSED MILK

DULCE DE LECHE FILLING

½ RECIPE (½ CUP/4 ¾ OUNCES/135 GRAMS) DULCE DE LECHE CREAM

¾ CUP PLUS 3 TABLESPOONS (7 ½ FL OUNCES/215 ML) HEAVY CREAM   CONTINUED ►

¾ CUP PLUS 2 TABLESPOONS (7 FL OUNCES/210 ML)
WHOLE MILK

⅛ TEASPOON SALT

2 TEASPOONS DARK RUM

SIMPLY BERRY SAUCE

1 CUP (5 OUNCES/140 GRAMS) STRAWBERRIES, HULLED AND
CUT IN HALF IF LARGE

½ CUP (2½ TO 3 OUNCES) RED RASPBERRIES, PICKED OVER
FOR STEMS

¼ CUP (2½ OUNCES/70 GRAMS) STRAWBERRY JAM

WHIPPED CREAM TOPPING

1 CUP (8 FL OUNCES/240 ML) HEAVY CREAM

1 TABLESPOON GRANULATED SUGAR

1 TEASPOON PURE VANILLA EXTRACT

1 TEASPOON DARK RUM (OPTIONAL)

Before baking: Center a rack in the oven and preheat the oven to 350 degrees F. Lightly coat only the sides of an 8 by 2-inch round cake pan with nonstick spray, then flour the sides, tapping out the excess flour. Line the bottom with parchment paper.

To make the Yellow Genoise: Sift together the flour, 1 tablespoon of the sugar, and salt onto a sheet of waxed paper; set aside. In the bowl of a stand mixer, whisk together by hand the eggs and the remaining ½ cup (3½ ounces/100 grams) sugar. Place the bowl in a shallow pan, such as a 10-inch skillet, and add water hot to the touch (120 to 130 degrees F) to the skillet to a depth of 1½ inches. To prevent the eggs from setting, whisk them continuously until the sugar has dissolved and the mixture is close to body temperature, about 100 degrees F on an instant-read thermometer or tested with a fingertip, 30 to 60 seconds.

Remove the bowl from the water bath, attach the bowl to the mixer, and fit the mixer with the whisk attachment. Whip on medium speed until the mixture has cooled, increased in volume (tripled or more), and appears light in texture and almost white, 3 to 4 minutes. To test if the mixture is ready, lift the whisk. The mixture should fall back into the bowl in a ribbon that rests softly on the surface and remains there for at least 15 to 20 seconds. If

it sinks into the batter right away, continue whipping for a few more minutes until it has the desired consistency. Add the vanilla during the final moments of whipping.

Detach the whisk and the bowl from the mixer, and tap the whisk against the side of the bowl to free the excess egg mixture. Using a long metal spatula, scoop up one-third of the flour mixture and scatter it over the egg mixture. Using a rubber spatula, gently fold in the flour mixture just until incorporated. Repeat with the remaining flour mixture in two additions, folding just until all of the flour has been absorbed. Gently pour the mixture into the prepared pan. With the rubber spatula, spread the batter from the center outward, creating a slightly raised ridge around the outside rim. (Since heat is conducted faster near the metal rim, mounding the batter around the edges ensures the cake will bake more evenly and will be more level.)

Bake the cake until the top springs back slightly when lightly touched, sounds spongy when tapped, and the sides are beginning to come away from the pan, 25 to 27 minutes. An aroma reminiscent of freshly scrambled eggs should pervade your kitchen when the cake is done. Transfer to a wire rack and let cool in the pan for 5 to 10 minutes.

Tilt and rotate the pan while gently tapping it on a counter to release the cake sides. Invert a rack on top of the cake, invert the cake onto it, and lift off the pan. Slowly peel off the parchment liner, turn it over so that the sticky side faces up, and reposition it on top of the cake. Invert another rack on top, invert the cake so it is right side up, and remove the original rack. Let cool completely. The cake may remain on the rack, unwrapped, at room temperature for up to 36 hours before assembling this dessert.

To make the Dulce de Leche Cream: Center a rack in the oven and preheat the oven to 425 degrees F. Open the can of condensed milk and pour the contents into a 9-inch pie dish. Cover the dish with aluminum foil and place the dish in a shallow roasting pan. Pour very hot (130 degrees F) water into the pan to come halfway up the sides of the pie dish. Bake the milk until it turns caramel brown and thick, 1 to 1 1/2 hours. Refill the roasting pan with hot water as needed during the baking to maintain the level.

Remove the pan from the oven and remove the pie dish from the water bath. Discard the foil and let the caramelized milk cool completely at room temperature. Use half of the caramelized cream right away, or cover the dish with plastic wrap and refrigerate for up to 4 days.

To assemble the cake: Transfer the cake to a shallow plate with a rim and proceed to make the Dulce de Leche Filling. In a small, heavy saucepan over low heat, stir together the Dulce de Leche Cream, 2 tablespoons of the heavy cream, 2 tablespoons of the milk, and the salt until smooth and warm. Remove from the heat and pour into a large bowl or medium pitcher. Stir in the remaining 3/4 cup plus 1 tablespoon (6 1/2 fl ounces/195 ml) cream, the remaining 3/4 cup (6 fl ounces/180 ml) milk, and the rum until well blended. Slowly pour the mixture over the cake so the cake absorbs the filling. Pause briefly, if necessary, to give the cake time to absorb what has been poured. Refrigerate the cake, loosely covered with plastic wrap, for several hours to allow the flavors to blend and the texture to set.

To make the Simply Berry Sauce: In a food processor, combine the berries and jam and process until pureed. Strain through a fine-mesh sieve placed over a small bowl to remove any seeds. Cover tightly and refrigerate until serving. You should have about 1 cup (8 fl ounces/240 ml).

To make the Whipped Cream Topping: Just before serving, combine the cream, sugar, vanilla, and rum (if using) in a deep, medium bowl. Using a whisk or a handheld mixer, whip until soft peaks form. Using an offset spatula, spread the whipped cream evenly over the top of the cake.

Using a sharp knife, cut the cake into slices. Drizzle some of the berry sauce decoratively over each plate, or pass the sauce at the table. Cover any leftover cake loosely with plastic wrap and refrigerate for up to 1 day.

Heirloom Banana Layer Cake with Prune Plum Filling and Seafoam Frosting

Sweet inspiration for this dessert came to me while getting a haircut at San Francisco's inimitable Joseph Cozza Salon. Over the years, Joseph's right-hand person (and dessert-maker extraordinaire), Diana Pelliccione, has become a special baking buddy. This luscious cake is based on an heirloom recipe that has been in Diana's family since the 1940s. Three layers of rich, moist banana cake are filled with a dried plum puree subtly flavored with oolong tea and a dash of Armagnac. Enrobed in an ethereal brown sugar meringue frosting, this lavish creation is tailor-made for unforgettable occasions. **YIELD: ONE 8-INCH, 6-LAYER ROUND CAKE, 12 SERVINGS**

BANANA CAKE

2 ½ CUPS (10 ¼ OUNCES/290 GRAMS) CAKE FLOUR

1 TEASPOON BAKING SODA

1 TEASPOON BAKING POWDER

½ TEASPOON SALT

1 CUP (9 OUNCES/255 GRAMS) MASHED RIPE BANANAS (2 MEDIUM OR 3 SMALL)

¾ CUP (6 FL OUNCES/180 ML) WELL-SHAKEN BUTTERMILK

6 OUNCES (1 ½ STICKS/170 GRAMS) UNSALTED BUTTER, AT ROOM TEMPERATURE

1 ½ CUPS (10 ½ OUNCES/300 GRAMS) GRANULATED SUGAR

2 LARGE EGGS, LIGHTLY BEATEN

½ CUP (2 OUNCES/55 GRAMS) CHOPPED TOASTED WALNUTS (PAGES 15–16)

1 RECIPE DRIED PLUM–ARMAGNAC PUREE (PAGE 373)

SEAFOAM FROSTING

2 LARGE EGG WHITES

⅓ CUP (2 ½ FL OUNCES/75 ML) WATER

1 ½ CUPS PACKED (10 ½ OUNCES/300 GRAMS) LIGHT BROWN SUGAR

PINCH OF SALT

1 TEASPOON PURE VANILLA EXTRACT

Before baking: Center a rack in the oven and preheat the oven to 350 degrees F. Butter three 8 by 2-inch round cake pans, then flour them, tapping out the excess flour.

Or, lightly coat the pans with nonstick spray and flour them. Line the bottoms with parchment paper. Have all of the ingredients at room temperature.

To make the Banana Cake: Sift together the flour, baking soda, baking powder, and salt onto a sheet of waxed paper; set aside. In a small bowl, mix together the bananas and buttermilk; set aside.

In the bowl of a stand mixer fitted with the paddle attachment, beat the butter on low speed until creamy, 30 to 45 seconds. On medium speed, add the sugar in a steady stream and beat until light and fluffy, 3 to 4 minutes. Add the eggs, 1 to 2 tablespoons at a time, beating after each addition until incorporated. Continue to beat, stopping the mixer once or twice to scrape down the sides of the bowl, until the mixture is fluffy, 1 to 2 minutes. On the lowest speed, add the flour mixture in three additions alternately with the banana mixture in two additions, beginning and ending with the flour mixture and mixing until smooth. Stop the mixer once or twice to scrape down the sides of the bowl.

Divide the batter evenly among the prepared pans. With a rubber spatula, spread the batter in each pan from the center outward, creating a slightly raised ridge around the outside rim. (Since heat is conducted faster near the metal rim, mounding the batter around the edges ensures the layers will bake more evenly and will be more level.) Distribute the nuts evenly over the batter in each pan.

Bake the cakes until they are pale gold on top, spring back when lightly touched in the center, a round wooden toothpick inserted in the center comes out free of cake, and the sides are beginning to come away from the pans, 24 to 27 minutes. Transfer to wire racks and let cool in the pans for 10 minutes.

Tilt and rotate a pan while gently tapping it on a counter to release the cake sides. Invert a rack on top of the cake, invert the cake onto it, and lift off the pan. Slowly peel off the parchment liner, turn it over so that the sticky side faces up, and reposition it on top of the cake. Invert another rack on top, invert the cake so it is right side up, and remove the original rack. Repeat with the remaining 2 layers. Let cool completely.

If you plan to assemble the dessert within 24 hours, wrap the cakes in plastic wrap and store at room temperature. For longer storage, overwrap with aluminum foil, label with the contents and date, and freeze for up to 2 weeks. Thaw at room temperature for 2 to 3 hours.

To assemble the cake: Using a 12-inch serrated knife, split each cake layer in half horizontally (page 25) to create 6 layers. Set 1 bottom layer, cut side up, on an 8-inch sturdy cardboard round. Using a metal icing spatula, spread $\frac{1}{4}$ cup (1 $\frac{3}{4}$ ounces/50 grams) of the dried plum puree evenly over the layer. Top with the second half of the layer, cut side down. Repeat with the remaining 2 split cake layers (they don't need to be on a cardboard round), filling each of them with $\frac{1}{4}$ cup of the puree, and place these 2 filled layers nearby. (You won't need all of the puree.) Proceed to make the frosting.

To make the Seafoam Frosting: Put the egg whites, water, sugar, and salt, in that order, in a large heatproof bowl that fits snugly over a heavy saucepan (or use a double boiler). Fill the saucepan about one-fourth full with water and bring the water to a bare simmer. Meanwhile, whisk the egg white mixture for about 30 seconds to blend the ingredients thoroughly. Place the bowl over (not touching) the simmering water. With a handheld mixer, beat the mixture on low speed until it thickens, glossy, soft peaks form, and it registers 165 degrees on an instant-read thermometer, 5 to 7 minutes. Remove from the heat, add the vanilla, and beat just to incorporate. Use the frosting right away.

Using a metal icing spatula, spread about $\frac{3}{4}$ cup of the frosting evenly over the surface of the filled layer cake on the cardboard. Center a second filled layer cake on top, and spread it with another $\frac{3}{4}$ cup of the frosting. Center the last filled layer cake on top, and then frost the sides and top of the cake with the remaining frosting. Transfer the cake to a serving platter.

For the best flavor and texture, serve the cake the same day it is made. Using a serrated knife, slice the cake, wiping the blade clean with a warm, moist cloth after each cut. Refrigerate any leftover cake, placing a piece of plastic wrap directly on the cut surface. The fluffy egg white frosting will still be soft but will be slightly sticky and not as attractive the next day.

Cupid's Strawberry Cake with Cream Cheese Buttercream

A celebration of sweet pleasures, this luxurious layer cake would delight Cupid himself. It's the perfect dessert for Valentine's Day, a Sweet 16 party, or to commemorate a sunny summer day when sparkling red strawberries are at their pinnacle of seasonal ripeness. Tender yellow butter cake is topped with currant jelly, a not-too-sweet cream cheese buttercream, and slices of juicy strawberries. **YIELD: ONE 9-INCH, 4-LAYER ROUND CAKE, 14 TO 16 SERVINGS**

1 RECIPE (TWO 9-INCH ROUND LAYERS) SIGNATURE YELLOW CAKE (PAGE 348)

CREAM CHEESE BUTTERCREAM

TWO 8-OUNCE (225-GRAM) PACKAGES COLD CREAM CHEESE

4 OUNCES (1 STICK/115 GRAMS) UNSALTED BUTTER, AT ROOM TEMPERATURE, CUT INTO ¼-INCH SLICES

4 LARGE (⅓ CUP/2½ FL OUNCES/75 ML) EGG YOLKS, AT ROOM TEMPERATURE

4 TABLESPOONS WATER

¾ TEASPOON UNFLAVORED POWDERED GELATIN

¾ CUP (5¼ OUNCES/150 GRAMS) GRANULATED SUGAR

⅓ CUP (1¼ OUNCES/35 GRAMS) POWDERED SUGAR, SIFTED

1 TEASPOON PURE VANILLA EXTRACT

1½ TEASPOONS FINELY GRATED LEMON ZEST

½ CUP (5 OUNCES/140 GRAMS) RED CURRANT JELLY

2 CUPS (10 OUNCES/280 GRAMS) STRAWBERRIES, HULLED AND CUT CROSSWISE INTO ⅛-INCH-THICK SLICES

Bake the cake layers as directed, and let cool completely on wire racks.

To make the Cream Cheese Buttercream: Have ready for easy access in the freezer about 15 ice cubes in a resealable plastic bag for cooling the buttercream quickly.

In the bowl of a stand mixer fitted with the paddle attachment, mix the cream cheese on the lowest speed just until spreading consistency. Scrape down the sides of the bowl as needed. Gradually add the butter, mixing just until smooth and homogeneous. Transfer the mixture to a medium bowl; set nearby.

Reattach the clean bowl with the whisk attachment to the mixer and whip the egg yolks on medium speed until light in color and fluffy, 2 to 4 minutes. Detach the whisk and the bowl from the mixer; set the whisk close by to use later. Pour 1 tablespoon of the water into a small microwave-safe glass. Sprinkle the gelatin over the water and set aside to soften for at least 5 minutes.

In a small, heavy saucepan, combine the remaining 3 tablespoons water and the sugar, place over low heat, swirling the pan occasionally to distribute the heat and dissolve the sugar. Continue to cook over low heat (don't boil) until the sugar completely dissolves, about 2 minutes. Keep a pastry brush in a small glass of cold water nearby for washing down any sugar crystals that form along the sides of the pan.

As soon as the sugar has dissolved, raise the heat to medium and boil, without stirring, until the mixture registers 238 degrees F (soft-ball stage) on a candy thermometer, about 4 minutes. Without delay, pour the syrup into the center of the whipped yolks and, using the mixer's whisk attachment, whisk vigorously by hand to combine.

Reattach the bowl and the whisk to the mixer and whip on medium speed until the egg yolk mixture thickens, increases in volume, lightens in color and texture, and cools to room temperature, about 4 minutes. As you begin to whip, hold the reserved plastic bag with ice cubes against the bottom of the bowl, or as close to the bottom of the bowl as possible, to speed the cooling. As soon as the mixture is cool (close to room temperature or slightly cooler to avoid it melting the cream cheese mixture when it is added), detach the whisk and replace it with the paddle attachment. Microwave the gelatin for 8 to 9 seconds only, to heat the mixture just enough to dissolve the gelatin. Stir or swirl the gelatin mixture and set aside briefly. On the lowest speed, slowly add the cream cheese mixture and blend after each addition until smooth. Add the gelatin mixture in the last moments of mixing. Detach the paddle and the bowl from the mixer and with a rubber spatula gently fold in the powdered sugar, vanilla, and lemon zest. Use the buttercream right away. (This buttercream, made with less butter than a classic buttercream, has a creamier, softer texture that is perfect for filling cake layers and frosting a cake. The small amount of gelatin provides just enough support to make the dessert easy to cut and serve. Leftover buttercream may be stored, covered, in the refrigerator for up to 2 days.)

To assemble the cake: Using a 12-inch serrated knife, split each layer in half horizontally (page 25) to create 4 layers, each about ¾ inch thick. Set the bottom layer of 1 cake, cut side up, on a sturdy cardboard round the same diameter as the cake. Using a metal icing spatula, spread ¼ cup (2½ ounces/70 grams) of the jelly evenly over the layer to the edge. Top with the second layer, cut side down.

Using an offset spatula, evenly spread about ¾ cup of the buttercream over the cake to the edge. Cover the buttercream to the edge with a single layer of strawberry slices, and then carefully spread (to keep the strawberries in place) about ⅓ cup of the buttercream over the strawberries. Center the bottom layer of the second cake layer, cut side up, on top. Spread the remaining ¼ cup jelly evenly over the cake. Top with the last cake layer, cut side down.

Spread the sides and top of the cake with buttercream. (You won't need all of the buttercream for this cake. Cover and refrigerate the remainder for another dessert. It will keep for up to 1 week. Remove from the refrigerator 20 to 30 minutes before using, to allow it to soften sufficiently to spread.) With a textured scraper, gently comb lines in the soft buttercream on the top and sides of the cake, forming a grid pattern. Arrange the remaining strawberry slices, overlapping them, around the top edge of the cake.

To serve, cut into slices with a serrated knife. Or, transfer the cake to a cake box or sturdy covered container and refrigerate for up to 2 days (the buttercream will firm up in the refrigerator yet remain creamy). For the best flavor and texture, let stand at room temperature for 30 minutes before serving.

Black Forest Cake

This stunning chocolate-and-cherry cake is my fond tribute to Schwarzwälder Kirschtorte, the famous epicurean dessert from Germany's Black Forest region. A kirsch-kissed chocolate cake is layered with sour cherries, cherry preserves, whipped cream, and a rich chocolate filling. The sour cherries are a classic ingredient for this dessert, enlivening it with their signature tanginess. Since fresh sour cherries—Montmorency and Morello are the most common varieties—have a short season and are simply unavailable in some areas, I look for jars of Morello cherries packed in light syrup. But sweet cherries such as Bing are good with this cake, too, so I have included directions for poaching fresh sweet or sour cherries (frozen cherries can be poached the same way). **YIELD: ONE 10-INCH, 3-LAYER ROUND CAKE, 14 TO 16 SERVINGS**

POACHED FRESH CHERRIES (OPTIONAL)

1 ½ CUPS (12 FL OUNCES/180 ML) WATER

½ CUP (3 ½ OUNCES/100 GRAMS) GRANULATED SUGAR

½ VANILLA BEAN

1 STRIP LEMON ZEST, 2 INCHES LONG

1 ⅓ CUPS (8 OUNCES/225 GRAMS) SWEET OR SOUR CHERRIES, STEMMED, PITTED, AND LEFT WHOLE

1 TABLESPOON FRESH LEMON JUICE

1 TEASPOON ROSE WATER

CHOCOLATE GENOISE

⅔ CUP (3 OUNCES/85 GRAMS) ALL-PURPOSE FLOUR

⅓ CUP (1 ¼ OUNCES/40 GRAMS) CAKE FLOUR

⅓ CUP (1 OUNCE/30 GRAMS) UNSWEETENED COCOA POWDER, PREFERABLY DUTCH PROCESSED

1 TABLESPOON PLUS ½ CUP (4 OUNCES/115 GRAMS) GRANULATED SUGAR

⅛ TEASPOON SALT

2 TABLESPOONS UNSALTED BUTTER

4 LARGE EGGS

1 TEASPOON PURE VANILLA EXTRACT

BLACK FOREST SYRUP

⅓ CUP (2 ½ FL OUNCES/75 ML) WATER

⅓ CUP (2 ¼ OUNCES/65 GRAMS) GRANULATED SUGAR

5 TABLESPOONS (2 ½ FL OUNCES/75 ML) KIRSCH OR FRAMBOISE, OR TO TASTE

½ TEASPOON ROSE WATER

FILLING, FROSTING, AND DECORATION

½ CUP (ABOUT 5 OUNCES/140 GRAMS) CHERRY PRESERVES, DIVIDED

8 TO 9 OUNCES (225 TO 255 GRAMS) SEMISWEET CHOCOLATE, DIVIDED

3 CUPS (24 FL OUNCES/720 ML) HEAVY CREAM

2 TABLESPOONS GRANULATED SUGAR

1 TABLESPOON KIRSCH OR FRAMBOISE

2 TEASPOONS PURE VANILLA EXTRACT

1 CUP (6 OUNCES/170 GRAMS) WELL-DRAINED JARRED PITTED SOUR CHERRIES IN LIGHT SYRUP OR POACHED FRESH CHERRIES

½ CUP (2 OUNCES/55 GRAMS) FRESH RED CURRANTS, STEMMED, IF IN SEASON

To poach fresh cherries: In a medium, heavy saucepan, combine the water, sugar, vanilla bean, and lemon zest. Bring just to a boil over medium-low heat, stirring to dissolve the sugar. Reduce the heat to low, add the cherries, return the syrup just to a simmer, and cook the cherries at a slow simmer, turning them occasionally in the syrup so that they poach evenly, until just tender, 7 to 10 minutes. They should offer some resistance when pierced with the tip of a paring knife. Be careful not to overcook to the point of mushiness. Remove from the heat, add the lemon juice and rose water, and let the cherries cool in the syrup for about 1 hour.

Using a slotted spoon, transfer the cherries to an airtight container. Discard the vanilla bean and lemon zest from the syrup, pour enough syrup over the cherries to cover, and cover and refrigerate for up to 4 days. If desired, boil down the remaining syrup until it is reduced by at least half. Let the syrup cool until just to room temperature, then pour into a sturdy container and refrigerate for up to 2 weeks to use over other fruits, over pancakes, to flavor lemonade, or for brushing on cake layers. When ready to use the cherries, line a sieve with paper towels and place over a bowl. Using a slotted spoon, transfer the cherries to the sieve and drain well.

Before baking: Center a rack in the oven and preheat the oven to 350 degrees F. Lightly coat only the sides of a 10 by 2-inch round cake pan with nonstick spray, then flour the sides, tapping out the excess flour. Line the bottom with parchment paper.

To make the Chocolate Genoise: Sift together the flours, cocoa powder, 1 tablespoon of the sugar, and the salt onto a sheet of waxed paper; set aside. In a small, heavy saucepan, melt the butter over low heat and pour into a small bowl (or melt in the microwave in a small bowl); set aside.

In the bowl of a stand mixer, whisk together by hand the eggs and the remaining ½ cup (3½ ounces/100 grams) sugar. Place the bowl in a shallow pan, such as a 10-inch skillet, and add water hot to the touch (120 to 130 degrees F) to the skillet to a depth of 1½ inches. To prevent the eggs from setting, whisk them continuously until the sugar has dissolved and the mixture is close to body temperature, about 100 degrees F on an instant-read thermometer or tested with a fingertip, 30 to 60 seconds.

Remove the bowl from the water bath, attach the bowl to the mixer, and fit the mixer with the whisk attachment. Whip on medium speed until the mixture has cooled and increased in volume (tripled or more), and appears light in texture and almost white, 5 to 6 minutes. To test if the mixture is ready, lift the whisk. The mixture should fall back into the bowl in a ribbon that rests softly on the surface and remains there for at least 15 to 20 seconds. If it sinks into the batter right away, continue whipping for

a few more minutes until it has the desired consistency. Add the vanilla during the final moments of whipping.

Detach the whisk and the bowl from the mixer, and tap the whisk against the side of the bowl to free the excess egg mixture. Using a long metal spatula, scoop up one-fourth of the flour mixture and scatter it over the egg mixture. Using a rubber spatula, gently fold in the flour mixture just until incorporated. Repeat with the remaining flour mixture in three additions, folding just until all of the flour has been absorbed. Gently pour about 1 cup (8 fl ounces/240 ml) of the batter into the reserved butter, and use the spatula to fold until combined. Return the butter mixture to the rest of the batter, and again fold to combine. Gently pour the mixture into the prepared pan. With the rubber spatula, spread the batter from the center outward, creating a slightly raised side around the outside rim. (Since heat is conducted faster near the metal rim, mounding the batter around the edges ensures the cake will bake more evenly and be more level.)

Bake the cake until the top springs back slightly when lightly touched, sounds spongy when tapped, and the sides are beginning to come away from the pan, 35 to 40 minutes. Transfer to a wire rack and let cool in the pan for 5 to 10 minutes.

Tilt and rotate the pan while gently tapping it on a counter to release the cake sides. Invert a rack on top of the cake, invert the cake onto it, and lift off the pan. Slowly peel off the parchment liner, turn it over so that the sticky side faces up, and reposition it on top of the cake. Invert another rack on top, invert the cake so it is right side up, and remove the original rack. Let cool completely.

If you plan to assemble the dessert within 24 hours, wrap the cake in plastic wrap and store at room temperature. For longer storage, overwrap with aluminum foil, label with the contents and date, and freeze for up to 2 weeks. Thaw at room temperature for at least 4 hours or up to overnight.

To make the Black Forest Syrup: In a small, heavy saucepan, combine the water and sugar, place over medium-low heat, and bring just to a CONTINUED ▶

simmer, stirring until the sugar is dissolved. Remove from the heat and let cool completely. Add the kirsch and rose water; set aside. (If you have reduced cherry syrup left over from poaching, you can substitute it for the kirsch and rose water.)

To assemble the cake: Using a 12-inch serrated knife, split the cake horizontally into 3 layers, each about $1/2$ inch thick (page 25). Set the bottom layer, cut side up, on a cardboard round the same diameter as the cake. Brush about $1/4$ cup (2 fl ounces/60 ml) of the syrup evenly over the layer to the edge. Using an offset spatula, evenly spread $1/4$ cup ($2 1/2$ ounces/70 grams) of the cherry preserves over the layer to the edge.

Finely chop 3 ounces (85 grams) of the chocolate. Half fill a bowl or a saucepan with hot water (120 degrees F). Put the chocolate in a bowl and place it over (but not touching) the hot water. Stir occasionally with a rubber spatula until melted and smooth. (Replace the water with more hot water if needed to melt the chocolate smoothly.) Transfer 1 tablespoon of the hot water from the lower bowl to the chocolate and stir until smooth with the spatula. Leave the mixture in the bowl over the water.

In the bowl of a stand mixer fitted with the whisk attachment, whip together the cream, sugar, kirsch, and vanilla on medium speed until very soft peaks form; set aside.

Remove the chocolate from the water bath. (It should be no warmer than body temperature. Dip a finger into it to be sure.) Add about $1 1/4$ cups of the whipped cream to the chocolate and whisk immediately to combine. (Keep the bowl holding the remaining whipped cream nearby.) Be careful not to overwhip the cream and chocolate, or the mixture will appear curdled. Without delay, spread the chocolate cream evenly over the cake layer with the offset spatula. Scatter the cherries and red currants randomly over the chocolate cream, and then press them gently into the cream.

Set the second cake layer on top, and repeat with the syrup and another $1/4$ cup of preserves. Spread about 1 cup of the whipped cream evenly over the layer. Top with the final layer of cake, cut side down. Frost the sides and top with the remaining whipped cream. (A cake-decorating turntable is helpful here, so if you have one, put the cake on its cardboard base on the turntable.) Refrigerate the cake for at least 2 hours or up to 1 day before serving to allow the flavors to meld.

To decorate with chocolate shavings: Holding a shallow metal tartlet pan (about 3 inches in diameter) in one hand, and working over a sturdy baking sheet, draw the edge of the pan down the surface of the remaining piece of chocolate (5 to 6 ounces/140 to 170 grams). Using a dough scraper, transfer the shavings to an airtight sturdy plastic container and freeze until needed. The chill keeps the chocolate dry, and the small fragments of chocolate are less likely to melt from the heat of your hand as you apply them to the cake.

To apply the shavings to the cake, place the container of shavings on a strip of aluminum foil or waxed paper. Hold the cake in one hand directly over the sheet of foil. Carefully tilt the cake slightly, and with the other hand, gently sprinkle or press the chocolate into the cream. Rotate the dessert until it is almost covered. Sprinkle the top to cover completely.

To ensure the cake is protected in the refrigerator, place it, still on its cardboard round, on the inverted lid of a plastic or metal container large enough to hold the cake. Now invert the container and place it over the cake. To avoid disaster and to remind yourself of this unique storage, mark "top" on the inverted container. Store it like this until serving.

For the best flavor and texture, remove the dessert from the refrigerator and allow it to stand at room temperature for about 30 minutes before serving. Set the cake on a serving platter, if desired. Cut into slices with a sharp knife.

Rhubarb and Pistachio Tart

Slender spokes of fresh rhubarb in the ground pistachio filling lend a vibrant tanginess while cleverly defining individual servings. If you can't find slim stalks, cut the 3-inch-long segments in half lengthwise.   **YIELD: ONE 13¾ BY 4¼-INCH TART, 11 SERVINGS**

1 RECIPE TENDER TART PASTRY (PAGE 361)

PISTACHIO FRANGIPANE FILLING

¾ CUP PLUS 1 TABLESPOON (4 OUNCES/115 GRAMS) SHELLED, UNSALTED PISTACHIO NUTS

4 OUNCES (1 STICK/115 GRAMS) UNSALTED BUTTER, AT ROOM TEMPERATURE

½ CUP (3½ OUNCES/100 GRAMS) GRANULATED SUGAR

2 LARGE EGGS

⅛ TEASPOON SALT

⅛ TEASPOON ALMOND EXTRACT

2 TABLESPOONS ALL-PURPOSE FLOUR

4 NARROW RHUBARB STALKS (9 TO 10 OUNCES/255 TO 280 GRAMS), TRIMMED AND CUT INTO 11 PIECES, EACH 3 INCHES LONG

Before baking: Center a rack in the oven and preheat the oven to 375 degrees F.

Have ready a 13¾ by 4¼ by 1-inch fluted tart pan with a removable bottom.

To line the pan with the pastry dough: Following the directions on page 29 for rolling out tart pastry, roll out the dough into a 16½ by 6½-inch rectangle about ⅛ inch thick, line the tart pan, and trim away the excess dough with the rolling pin. Place the pastry-lined pan in the freezer for 15 minutes or in the refrigerator for 30 minutes to firm and chill.

Prick the bottom of the pastry with the tines of a fork and partially bake as directed on page 30. Transfer to a wire rack and let cool for about 15 minutes before filling. Leave the oven on.

To make the Pistachio Frangipane Filling: Have all of the ingredients at room temperature. Grind the pistachios in a nut mill (page 43) until they have the consistency of cornmeal to yield 1 cup ground.

Place the butter in a deep 1½-quart bowl. Using a handheld mixer on low speed, beat the butter until smooth and soft, about 30 seconds. Add the sugar and beat until combined. Add the eggs, one at a time, beating after each addition just until incorporated. Add the salt and the almond extract and beat until combined. With a rubber spatula, stir in the flour and ground nuts. (Whipping air into the mixture is not necessary in this case. You just want to blend the ingredients together smoothly.)

Spoon the filling into the partially baked shell and spread it evenly with the rubber spatula. Press the 11 rhubarb pieces into the filling, one by one, in a row, parallel to the short ends of the tart and centered between the long sides, spacing them ½ to ¾ inch apart. (They should be shallow in the filling so the entire top of the rosy red sticks shows.)

Bake the tart until the rhubarb is tender when pierced with a skewer or round wooden toothpick and the filling is golden on top and feels somewhat firm, rather than soft, when lightly touched, 45 to 50 minutes. Transfer it to a wire rack and let cool completely in the pan.

Set the tart pan on a narrower elevated surface, such as a tin can, so the bottom of the pan is released as the metal rim slips down. Carefully slide the tart still on its thin metal base onto a serving platter. Serve at room temperature. Cut between the rhubarb sticks with a sharp knife to create the servings.

Black-Bottom Praline Chiffon Pie

Black-bottom pie has been a tradition in the American South for over a century. Today, this down-home dessert is a favorite all across the country. My version is dressed up with homemade hazelnut praline for glamorous occasions. Pralines are typically finely ground and used to enhance pastry creams or buttercreams. For this pie, half of the crunchy nut praline flavors the chiffon filling and the remaining praline is sprinkled on top for decoration. Time-pressed bakers can accommodate hectic schedules by preparing the elements of this split-level dessert over a few days. Rave reviews from an enthusiastic pie-loving audience will be worth every minute it took to create it.　**YIELD: ONE 9-INCH PIE, 12 SERVINGS**

HAZELNUT PRALINE

3 TABLESPOONS WATER

½ CUP PLUS 2 TABLESPOONS (4 ½ OUNCES/125 GRAMS) GRANULATED SUGAR

⅔ CUP (3 ½ OUNCES/100 GRAMS) HAZELNUTS, TOASTED AND SKINNED (PAGES 15–16)

1 RECIPE SINGLE-CRUST FLAKY PIE PASTRY (PAGE 354)

CHOCOLATE AND PRALINE CHIFFON FILLINGS

2 ½ OUNCES (70 GRAMS) BITTERSWEET OR SEMISWEET CHOCOLATE, COARSELY CHOPPED

⅔ CUP (4 ½ OUNCES/130 GRAMS) GRANULATED SUGAR

2 TABLESPOONS CORNSTARCH

⅛ TEASPOON SALT

4 LARGE (⅓ CUP/2 ½ FL OUNCES/75 ML) EGG YOLKS, LIGHTLY BEATEN

2 ½ CUPS (20 FL OUNCES/600 ML) PLUS 3 TABLESPOONS COLD WHOLE MILK

2 TEASPOONS UNFLAVORED POWDERED GELATIN

2 TABLESPOONS HAZELNUT LIQUEUR

1 TEASPOON PURE VANILLA EXTRACT

3 LARGE (⅓ CUP/2 ½ FL OUNCES/75 ML) EGG WHITES

½ CUP (4 FL OUNCES/120 ML) HEAVY CREAM, WHIPPED TO SOFT PEAKS

To make the Hazelnut Praline: Line a large rimmed baking sheet with aluminum foil or a silicone mat. In a small, heavy saucepan, combine the water and sugar, place over low heat, and heat, without stirring, until the sugar dissolves. Raise the heat to medium and cook, without stirring, just until the mixture turns amber, about 5 minutes. Add the hazelnuts and shake and swirl the pan until the nuts are coated evenly with the caramel. Pour the nut mixture onto the prepared baking sheet (it will spread on its own) and leave at room temperature to cool and harden, about 1 hour.

To break the hardened praline in half on the pan, position the blade of a chef's knife or cleaver on the praline and, with a mallet or rolling pin, apply enough force to the blade to break the praline into at least 2 large pieces. Then, break the large pieces into smaller pieces with your hands. The praline will keep in an airtight container at room temperature for up to 10 days.

Chop the praline just before you need it for the recipe. Place half of it in a heavy-duty resealable plastic bag and crush with a mallet or the end of a rolling pin until coarsely chopped. Or, place in a food processor and pulse with 1-second bursts until coarsely chopped. Place the pieces in a resealable plastic bag and set aside. Repeat with the second half of the praline, but crush or pulse this half until finely chopped. Place the pieces in a separate resealable plastic bag and set aside. If you are using a processor, be careful that you don't overprocess the praline. Doing this step by hand gives you more control.

Before baking: Center a rack in the oven and preheat the oven to 425 degrees F. Have ready a 9-inch pie dish.

To line the pie dish: Following the directions on page 27 for rolling out pie pastry, roll out the dough into a 13-inch circle ⅛ to 3/16 inch thick, transfer the pastry circle to the pie dish, and flute the edges of the pastry. Place the crust in the freezer for 20 minutes or in the refrigerator for at least 30 minutes to firm.

Following the directions for blind baking a pie crust on page 28, fully bake the pie crust. Transfer to a wire rack and let cool completely before filling.

To make the Chocolate and Praline Chiffon Fillings:
Have the bag of finely chopped praline nearby. Place the chocolate in a medium heatproof bowl and set aside.

In a heavy 2- to 2½-quart saucepan, whisk together ⅓ cup (2¼ ounces/65 grams) of the sugar, the cornstarch, and the salt. Whisk in the egg yolks until blended. Gradually add 2½ cups of the milk while whisking constantly. Place over medium-low heat and cook, whisking constantly, until the mixture thickens and an instant-read thermometer registers 160 to 170 degrees F, 6 to 8 minutes. It is natural to see wisps of steam rising from the pastry cream toward the end of cooking, but be careful it does not boil.

Without delay, remove the pan from the heat, measure out 2 cups (16 fl ounces/480 ml) of the pastry cream, and pour them over the chopped chocolate. Set the remaining pastry cream aside. Using a rubber spatula, stir the pastry cream and chocolate until the chocolate melts and the mixture is smooth and well blended. Set aside to cool slightly, about 15 minutes.

Meanwhile, half fill a large bowl with ice cubes and water to create an ice-water bath for cooling the filling later. In a small bowl, sprinkle the gelatin over the remaining 3 tablespoons milk and set aside to soften for at least 5 minutes. When the chocolate filling has cooled enough, pour it into the cooled pastry shell and refrigerate while preparing the praline chiffon layer.

Add the softened gelatin to the remaining hot pastry cream in the saucepan. Whisk over very low heat just until the gelatin dissolves and blends smoothly into the mixture, about 30 seconds. Do not allow it to boil. Pour the pastry cream into a large bowl and stir in the liqueur and vanilla. Set the bowl over the ice-water bath, and whisk occasionally to cool the cream and prevent any lumps from forming. When the filling is just slightly thickened and feels cooler than body temperature (65 to 70 degrees F), remove the bowl from the ice-water bath and set it aside at room temperature. This step takes 10 to 12 minutes. Proceed without delay to whip the egg whites.

Place the egg whites and 1 teaspoon of the remaining sugar in a medium bowl. Using a handheld mixer, whip the egg whites on medium speed until soft peaks form. Gradually add the remaining ⅓ cup sugar and continue to whip until fluffy, glossy white peaks form. Using a rubber spatula, fold about one-fourth of the whites into the soft gelatin mixture. Fold in the remaining whites just until incorporated. Then fold in the finely chopped praline. Using the spatula, gently guide the filling over the chocolate layer in the pie shell, mounding it in the center. Refrigerate until well chilled and set, 3 to 4 hours.

For the optimum flavor, serve the pie the same day it is made. Just before serving, spread the whipped cream over the top of the pie and sprinkle with the coarsely chopped praline. Serve the pie chilled.

Night and Day Torte

As memorable as the Cole Porter song that shares its name, this recipe was inspired by an enchanting black-and-white cake I glimpsed in the window of a Hong Kong bakery some twenty-five years ago. I was hurrying to an appointment and never got to taste the dessert, but I couldn't stop thinking about its fascinating design. I finally figured out how to replicate the magically alternating sections, and the result is this torte. Tender chocolate sponge cake is topped with velvety white and dark chocolate mousses, piped in strips to create a captivating optical effect that is repeated with each slice. Bakers, take note: making the torte is much simpler than figuring out how to do it.

When a sponge cake is large in size and tall, it needs to be cooled upside down, elevated above the work surface to preserve its delicate structure. However, the cake for this dessert is a thin layer and light as a feather, so it can be cooled upright without ruining its lovely texture. The cooled cake is just the right thickness and has enough structure to withstand being split in half to yield two moist, spongy layers.

When preparing the white and dark chocolate fillings, you add 1 tablespoon of water from each of the lower bowls used to melt the chocolates to the chocolates themselves. This tempers them, that is, brings them close to the temperature of the mixture into which you fold them, guaranteeing a smooth consistency. **YIELD: ONE 9-INCH, 2-LAYER SQUARE CAKE, 9 SERVINGS**

CHOCOLATE SPONGE CAKE

¼ CUP (1 OUNCE/30 GRAMS) CAKE FLOUR

¼ CUP PLUS 1 TABLESPOON (1 OUNCE/30 GRAMS) UNSWEETENED DUTCH-PROCESSED COCOA POWDER

½ CUP PLUS 1 TABLESPOON (3¾ OUNCES/105 GRAMS) GRANULATED SUGAR

4 LARGE EGGS

1 TEASPOON PURE VANILLA EXTRACT

½ TEASPOON CREAM OF TARTAR

⅛ TEASPOON SALT

VANILLA BEAN–RUM SYRUP

⅓ CUP (2¼ OUNCES/65 GRAMS) GRANULATED SUGAR

½ CUP (4 FL OUNCES/120 ML) WATER

½ VANILLA BEAN, SPLIT LENGTHWISE

1 TABLESPOON DARK RUM, OR TO TASTE

DARK AND WHITE CHOCOLATE MOUSSES

2 TEASPOONS COLD WATER

½ TEASPOON UNFLAVORED POWDERED GELATIN

3 OUNCES (85 GRAMS) WHITE CHOCOLATE, FINELY CHOPPED

3 OUNCES (85 GRAMS) SEMISWEET CHOCOLATE FINELY CHOPPED

1⅓ CUPS (10½ FL OUNCES/315 ML) HEAVY CREAM

Before baking: Center a rack in the oven and preheat the oven to 325 degrees F. Line the bottom of a 9 by 2-inch square pan with parchment paper. Have all of the cake ingredients at room temperature.

To make the Chocolate Sponge Cake: Sift together the flour, cocoa, and ¼ cup (1¾ ounces/50 grams) of the sugar onto a sheet of waxed paper; set aside. Place another ¼ cup of the sugar in a small bowl, and put the remaining

1 tablespoon sugar in another small bowl; set aside. Separate the eggs, placing the whites in the bowl of a stand mixer fitted with the whisk attachment, and the egg yolks in a deep 1½-quart bowl.

With a handheld mixer, whip the yolks on medium-high speed for 3 to 5 minutes. Add the vanilla and whip until incorporated. The mixture will have thickened, become pale yellow, and increased slightly in volume. To test if the mixture is ready, lift the beaters. The mixture should fall back into the bowl in a ribbon that rests softly on the surface and dissolves into the mixture very slowly. If it sinks into the batter right away, continue whipping for a few more minutes until it has the desired consistency.

Whip the whites on medium-low speed for 30 to 45 seconds to break them up. When small bubbles appear and the surface is frothy, stop the machine and sprinkle the cream of tartar and salt into the center. Resume whipping on medium speed and slowly sprinkle in the 1 tablespoon sugar. Continue to whip until the whites are glossy and stiff but not dry, about 4 minutes.

Detach the whisk and bowl from the mixer, and tap the whisk against the side of the bowl to free the excess whites. Pour the yolks onto the whites (notice that they float on the surface). Using just a few strokes, fold them together with a rubber spatula. Don't be concerned if streaks of the yolk mixture are visible.

Sprinkle the reserved ¼ cup sugar over the top and fold in to incorporate. Using a metal icing spatula, sprinkle about half of the flour mixture over the egg mixture, and fold it in with the spatula just until incorporated. Repeat with the remaining flour mixture. Use the rubber spatula to gently guide the batter into the prepared pan and to smooth the surface level.

Bake the cake until the top is set (dry rather than wet), it feels spongy and springs back when lightly touched with a finger, and a round wooden toothpick inserted in the center comes out clean, about 30 minutes. If you are in doubt about whether it is done, baking it for 5 more minutes won't harm it. The batter rises slowly during the first 15 minutes of baking. Toward the end of baking, it

will not rise very high. That's fine. As the cake cools, it will contract slightly. Transfer to a wire rack and let cool completely in the pan, about 1 hour.

Tilt and rotate the pan while gently tapping it on a counter to release the cake sides. If they don't release, slip a small metal spatula between the cake and the pan and run the spatula carefully along the entire perimeter of the pan. Invert a rack on top of the cake, invert the cake onto it, and lift off the pan. Slowly peel off the parchment liner, turn the paper over so that the sticky side faces up, and reposition it on top of the cake. Invert another rack on top, invert the cake so it is right side up, and remove the original rack. Let cool completely.

If you plan to assemble the dessert within 24 hours, wrap the cake in plastic wrap and store at room temperature. For longer storage, overwrap with aluminum foil, label with the contents and date, and freeze for up to 10 days. To thaw, remove the foil and set aside at room temperature in its packaging for 1 to 1½ hours.

To make the Vanilla Bean–Rum Syrup: In a small, heavy saucepan, combine the sugar, water, and vanilla bean over medium-low heat and heat, stirring, until the sugar dissolves. Raise the heat to medium and bring to a boil. Reduce the heat to low and simmer for 1 minute. Remove from the heat and remove the vanilla bean. Using a small paring knife, scrape the seeds from the vanilla bean into the syrup. Set aside to cool completely, then add the rum to taste.

To assemble the dessert: Using a 12-inch serrated knife, split the cake in half horizontally (page 25). Set the bottom layer, cut side up, on a cardboard square the same size as the cake. Set the other layer nearby. Brush about ¼ cup (2 fl ounces/60 ml) of the syrup over the layer.

To make the Dark and White Chocolate Mousse: Fit 2 pastry bags with ⁹⁄₁₆-inch plain open tips (a tad over ½ inch); set aside. Pour 1 teaspoon of the cold water each into 2 small, short microwave-safe glasses. Sprinkle ¼ teaspoon of the gelatin over each glass of water and set aside to soften for at least 5 minutes. CONTINUED ▶

Half fill a bowl with hot water (110 degrees F). Put the white chocolate in a 1-quart bowl and place it over (but not touching) the hot water. Half fill a second bowl with hot water (120 degrees F). Put the semisweet chocolate in a second 1-quart bowl and place it over (but not touching) the hot water. Stir the chocolates occasionally with rubber spatulas until melted and smooth. Meanwhile, microwave the gelatin for 8 to 9 seconds only, to heat the mixture just enough to dissolve the gelatin. Stir or swirl the gelatin mixtures and set aside briefly.

Transfer 1 tablespoon of water from each of the lower bowls to the white and dark chocolate and stir each with the rubber spatula until smooth. Allow the chocolates to remain over the water baths and proceed to whip the cream.

In the bowl of a stand mixer fitted with the whisk attachment, whip the cream on medium speed until soft peaks form on the surface, yet they have enough body to divide fairly easily later. (The cream remains somewhat liquid underneath; gently jiggle the bowl to detect how liquid it is.)

Remove the chocolates from their water baths. They should be at body temperature, no hotter or cooler. Pour 1 batch of gelatin into each bowl of melted chocolate and whisk briefly to blend. Add half of the whipped cream to one of the bowls and fold with a rubber spatula just until incorporated. The chocolate cream should be smooth. (Additional whisking after the mixtures are blended will stiffen their consistency. Too much additional manipulation will change the textures.) Spoon the mixture into one of the pastry bags and refrigerate it. Fold the remaining whipped cream into the other bowl of chocolate in the same way. Spoon the mixture into the other pastry bag. Use both chocolate creams right away.

Beginning at the corner on one end of the cake, pipe a stripe of the white chocolate mousse on the diagonal to the opposite corner on the cake. Pipe a stripe of the dark chocolate next to the white stripe. Then continue piping, alternating stripes of white and dark chocolate next to one another, to cover the surface of the cake. You will need to pipe about 16 strips to cover the cake. Top with the remaining cake layer, cut side down. Place the dessert in the refrigerator until the mousses firm, about 45 minutes. Cover the dessert with plastic wrap and return it to the refrigerator until about 30 minutes before serving.

To serve, transfer the cake to a serving plate. Using a sharp knife, cut 2 ½- to 3-inch squares of cake, wiping the blade clean with a damp towel after each cut. It's fun to see that piping the mousses on the diagonal creates a pattern that is repeated with each slice.

Deluxe Boston Cream Pie

Here's a delicious American tradition taken to the happy heights of decadence. Despite the name, it's not a pie at all, but two layers of rich buttermilk cake sandwiching an unctuous creamy custard filling. My version takes the idea of indulgence right over the top by covering the cake with whipped cream, then enrobing the entire dessert in a warm chocolate ganache. Cut the dessert and each slice reveals a visual symphony of luscious layers. There's no pressure to create this spectacular cake in one day. Prepare the cake and pastry cream a day or two in advance, then glaze the dessert with the chocolate in no time on the day you want to serve it.

YIELD: ONE 9½-INCH (AFTER FROSTING AND GLAZING), 2-LAYER ROUND CAKE, 12 SERVINGS

1 RECIPE FAVORITE BUTTERMILK CAKE (PAGE 344)

VANILLA DIPLOMAT CREAM FILLING

1 CUP (8 FL OUNCES/240 ML) WHOLE MILK

½ CUP (3½ OUNCES/100 GRAMS) GRANULATED SUGAR

1 VANILLA BEAN, SPLIT LENGTHWISE

3 LARGE (¼ CUP/2 FL OUNCES/60 ML) EGG YOLKS

3 TABLESPOONS ALL-PURPOSE FLOUR

2 TABLESPOONS UNSALTED BUTTER

⅔ CUP (5½ FL OUNCES/165 ML) HEAVY CREAM

1 TEASPOON PURE VANILLA EXTRACT

1 TEASPOON DARK RUM

WHIPPED CREAM FROSTING AND DARK CHOCOLATE GLAZE

2 CUPS (16 FL OUNCES/480 ML) HEAVY CREAM

10 OUNCES (280 GRAMS) SEMISWEET CHOCOLATE, FINELY CHOPPED

To make the Favorite Buttermilk Cake: Center a rack in the oven and preheat the oven to 350 degrees F. Butter a 9 by 2¾-inch round springform pan, then flour it, tapping out the excess flour. Or, lightly coat with nonstick spray and flour the pan. Line the bottom with parchment paper.

Make the cake batter as directed and pour into the prepared pan. Bake the cake until it springs back when lightly touched in the center, a wooden toothpick inserted in the center comes out free of cake, and the sides are beginning to come away from the pan, 30 to 35 minutes. Transfer to a wire rack and let cool in the pan for 5 to 10 minutes.

Slip a small metal spatula between the still-warm cake and the pan and run the spatula carefully along the entire perimeter of the pan. Release the springform clasp and remove the sides. Invert a rack on top of the cake, invert the cake onto it, and lift off the bottom of the pan. Slowly peel off the parchment liner, turn the paper over so that the sticky side faces up, and reposition it on top of the layer. Invert another rack on top, invert the cake so it is right side up, and remove the original rack. Let cool completely.

To make the Vanilla Diplomat Cream Filling: Rest a fine-mesh sieve over a 1-quart bowl and set nearby for straining the pastry cream later. Pour the milk and ¼ cup (1¾ ounces/50 grams) of the sugar into a 1½-quart saucepan. Using the tip of a small paring knife, scrape the seeds from the vanilla bean into the milk.

In a small bowl, whisk the egg yolks until blended, then whisk in the remaining ¼ cup sugar. Add the flour and whisk to combine; set aside. Bring the milk mixture just to a boil over medium heat. Remove from the heat and pour half of the milk mixture into the yolk mixture while whisking constantly. Return the combined mixture to the saucepan and whisk to combine. Return to medium heat and heat, stirring constantly, until the mixture just comes to a boil, 1 to 2 minutes. It will have thickened at this point. Continue to stir and simmer until it is smooth and thick, about 1 minute more. Remove from CONTINUED ▶

the heat, add the butter, and stir until the butter is melted and incorporated. Pour through the sieve into the bowl. Cover with plastic wrap, pressing it directly onto the surface to prevent a skin from forming. Poke a few slits in the plastic with the tip of a knife to allow steam to escape and set aside to cool for 15 to 20 minutes. (Once it has cooled, you can refrigerate it for up to 3 days.)

To assemble the dessert: In a medium, deep bowl, using a whisk or a handheld mixer, whip the heavy cream until soft peaks form. Refrigerate briefly while splitting the cake.

Using a 12-inch serrated knife, split the cake in half horizontally (page 25). Place the bottom layer, cut side up, on a sturdy cardboard round the same diameter as the cake. Spoon about ½ cup of the whipped cream into a pastry bag fitted with a ⁵⁄₁₆-inch plain open tip (a tad over ½ inch). Pipe a line of the whipped cream around the edge of the cake layer (page 26). Stir the vanilla and rum into the cold pastry cream until smooth. Then fold the remaining whipped cream into the pastry cream. Spoon the filling evenly over the cake layer on the cardboard round. Using an offset spatula, spread it evenly just to the line of whipped cream. Center the other cake layer, cut side down, on top.

To make the Whipped Cream Frosting and Dark Chocolate Glaze: In a medium, deep bowl, using a whisk or a handheld mixer, whip 1 cup (8 fl ounces/ 240 ml) of the cream until soft peaks form. Using a metal icing spatula, frost the top and sides of the cake with the whipped cream. Place the cake on a wire rack, and set the rack on a rimmed baking sheet or rimmed pizza pan that will fit in your freezer. Place it uncovered in the freezer for 40 minutes only (this is just enough time to chill the whipped cream frosting).

While the cake is in the freezer, prepare the chocolate glaze. Put the chocolate in a medium bowl. In a small, heavy saucepan, bring the remaining 1 cup cream just to a boil over medium-low heat. Pour the hot cream over the chocolate, let stand for about 20 seconds, and then whisk until smooth and shiny. Set aside to cool to body temperature.

Set the cake, still on its rack and baking sheet, on a work surface. Pour the chocolate glaze over the cake to cover the top and sides, using the metal icing spatula to assist in spreading the glaze over the top and down the sides. (Alternatively, set the cake directly on the baking sheet, and pour the glaze onto the center of the cake. Then, lift the cake on its cardboard base about 1 inch above the baking sheet and tilt it gently back and forth until the glaze covers the top and flows over the sides.) Refrigerate for at least 30 minutes before serving.

To serve, cut into slices with a serrated knife, dipping the blade in hot water and wiping it dry with a towel before each cut.

Caramel Chocolate Cream Pie

Remember those rich, gooey confections you used to fantasize about as a kid? Well, here's a dessert that is a sweet childhood dream come true. The creamy filling is actually a bittersweet chocolate pudding that is so rich and chocolaty it takes tremendous willpower to keep a tasting spoon out of the pan. It's layered on top of a buttery pastry crust lined with an outrageously creamy caramel. For a decidedly grown-up finishing touch, garnish the pie with brandy-spiked whipped cream, followed by a sprinkling of crunchy toffee bits. **YIELD: ONE 9-INCH PIE, 8 SERVINGS**

1 RECIPE SINGLE-CRUST FLAKY PIE PASTRY (PAGE 354)

CARAMEL
½ CUP (3 ½ OUNCES/100 GRAMS) GRANULATED SUGAR

2 TABLESPOONS UNSALTED BUTTER

⅓ CUP (2 ½ FL OUNCES/75 ML) HEAVY CREAM

CHOCOLATE PUDDING FILLING
3 CUPS (24 FL OUNCES/720 ML) WHOLE MILK, DIVIDED

⅓ CUP FIRMLY PACKED (2 ¼ OUNCES/65 GRAMS) LIGHT BROWN SUGAR

5 OUNCES (140 GRAMS) 60% BITTERSWEET CHOCOLATE, COARSELY CHOPPED

3 LARGE (¼ CUP/2 FL OUNCES/60 ML) EGG YOLKS

⅓ CUP (2 ¼ OUNCES/65 GRAMS) GRANULATED SUGAR

¼ CUP (1 OUNCE/30 GRAMS) CORNSTARCH

⅛ TEASPOON SALT

2 TABLESPOONS UNSALTED BUTTER

1 ½ TEASPOONS PURE VANILLA EXTRACT

TOPPING
¾ CUP (6 FL OUNCES/180 ML) HEAVY CREAM

1 TABLESPOON GRANULATED SUGAR

2 TEASPOONS COGNAC OR OTHER BRANDY

1 TEASPOON PURE VANILLA EXTRACT

½ CUP (2 ½ OUNCES/75 GRAMS) HEATH TOFFEE BITS

Before baking: Center a rack in the oven and preheat the oven to 425 degrees F. Have ready a 9-inch glass pie dish.

To line the pie dish: Following the directions on page 27 for rolling out pie pastry, roll out the dough into a 13-inch circle ⅛ to ³⁄₁₆ inch thick, transfer the pastry circle to the pie dish, and flute the edges of the pastry. Place the crust in the freezer for 20 minutes or in the refrigerator for at least 30 minutes to firm.

Following the directions for blind baking a pie crust on page 28, fully bake the pie crust as directed. Transfer to a wire rack and let cool completely before filling.

To make the caramel: Put the sugar in a heavy 1½-quart heavy saucepan and place over low heat. Let the heat touch the bottom of the saucepan for 3 to 4 minutes without stirring to give the bottom layer of sugar time to begin to melt. (Stirring at this point will cause the sugar to clump.) When a syrupy layer of melted sugar is visible, begin stirring occasionally with a small wooden spoon or silicone spatula until the sugar has dissolved. Increase the heat to medium-high and cook, without stirring, until the melted sugar turns amber, 5 to 7 minutes. Remove from the heat, add the butter, and then add the cream. (Be careful, the mixture bubbles madly.) Stir the ingredients with the spoon until they blend together smoothly. When the bubbling subsides, pour the caramel into a small heatproof bowl and set aside to cool, about 45 minutes. The caramel that remains in the saucepan is needed for the chocolate filling, so don't clean it.

To make the Chocolate Pudding Filling: Pour 1 cup (8 fl ounces/240 ml) of the milk, the brown sugar, and the chocolate into the caramel saucepan, and whisk over low heat until the sugar dissolves and the chocolate melts to produce a dark chocolate mixture, about 2 minutes. Add 1 cup of the remaining milk and whisk to combine. CONTINUED ▶

Place a fine-mesh sieve over a large bowl for straining the filling. In a medium bowl, whisk the egg yolks until blended and set aside. In a medium, heavy saucepan, whisk together the granulated sugar, cornstarch, and salt. Gradually whisk in the remaining 1 cup milk, then whisk in the egg yolks. Whisk in the chocolate mixture until well blended. Place the saucepan over medium heat and cook, stirring frequently with a silicone spatula until the mixture thickens, 6 to 8 minutes. Reduce the heat to low and simmer, stirring constantly, for 30 seconds longer to ensure the egg yolks are cooked. Remove from the heat and stir in the butter until melted. Pour through the sieve and set aside to cool for 5 minutes. Stir in the vanilla and cover with plastic wrap, pressing it directly onto the surface to prevent a skin from forming. Poke a few slits in the plastic with the tip of a knife to allow steam to escape and set aside to cool for 1 hour (it will not be completely cool).

Using a small offset spatula, spread the cooled caramel evenly over the crust. Remove the plastic wrap from the chocolate filling, pour the slightly warm filling over the caramel layer, and re-cover it with the plastic wrap, pressing it directly onto the surface. Refrigerate until chilled, 3 to 4 hours. It should be slightly firmer yet still creamy.

To make the topping: In a deep, medium bowl, combine the cream, sugar, Cognac, and vanilla. Using a whisk or a handheld mixer, whip together until soft peaks form.

Spoon the whipped cream into the center of the chilled pie, mounding it in a casual manner to allow the cream to spread naturally. Scatter the toffee pieces over the pie just before serving. Serve chilled, cut into wedges with a sharp knife.

Dee-luscious Lemon Meringue Pie

The expression "Life is short, eat dessert first!" could have been coined after eating a lemon meringue pie. This one features a silken, sweet-tart filling crowned with a lofty layer of meringue. To create a dramatically towering topping, I've called for an Italian meringue made with brown and granulated sugars, which also ensures the egg white mixture is safely cooked. For a contemporary (and fun) finishing touch, use a kitchen torch to brown the meringue, or be traditional and use your oven. This recipe was inspired by pastry chef Anne Baker's out-of-this-world lemon-lime meringue pie at Cindy Pawlcyn's renowned Mustards Grill in Yountville, California.   YIELD: ONE 9-INCH PIE, 8 SERVINGS

1 RECIPE SINGLE-CRUST FLAKY PIE PASTRY (PAGE 354)

LEMON FILLING

4 LARGE (⅓ CUP/2½ FL OUNCES/75 ML) EGG YOLKS

2 TABLESPOONS PLUS 1 CUP (8 OUNCES/225 GRAMS) GRANULATED SUGAR

3 TABLESPOONS CORNSTARCH

3 TABLESPOONS ALL-PURPOSE FLOUR

⅛ TEASPOON SALT

1½ CUPS (12 FL OUNCES/360 ML) COLD WATER

3 TABLESPOONS UNSALTED BUTTER, AT ROOM TEMPERATURE

⅓ CUP (2½ FL OUNCES/75 ML) STRAINED FRESH LEMON JUICE (1 TO 2 LEMONS)

1 TABLESPOON FINELY GRATED LEMON ZEST

ITALIAN MERINGUE

¾ CUP (6 FL OUNCES/180 ML) EGG WHITES (ABOUT 6 LARGE), AT ROOM TEMPERATURE

¼ TEASPOON CREAM OF TARTAR

¾ CUP (5¼ OUNCES/150 GRAMS) GRANULATED SUGAR

¾ CUP FIRMLY PACKED (5¼ OUNCES/150 GRAMS) BROWN SUGAR, PREFERABLY DARK

½ CUP (4 FL OUNCES/120 ML) WATER

Before baking: Center a rack in the oven and preheat the oven to 425 degrees F. Have ready a 9-inch glass pie dish.

To line the pie dish: Following the directions on page 27 for rolling out pie pastry, roll out the dough into a 13-inch circle ⅛ to ³⁄₁₆ inch thick, transfer the pastry circle to the pie dish, and flute the edges of the pastry. Place the crust in the freezer for 20 minutes or in the refrigerator for at least 30 minutes to firm.

Following the directions for blind baking a pie crust on page 28, fully bake the pie crust. Transfer to a wire rack and let cool completely before filling.

To make the Lemon Filling: In a small bowl, whisk together the egg yolks and 2 tablespoons of the sugar to combine and set aside. In a heavy, nonreactive 2-quart saucepan, combine the remaining 1 cup (7 ounces/ 200 grams) sugar, the cornstarch, the flour, and the salt. Gradually stir in the water to blend the ingredients thoroughly. Place over medium heat, bring the mixture just to a boil, and cook, stirring constantly with a silicone spatula, until smooth, clear, and thick, about 4 minutes. Reduce the heat to low and cook for 1 minute *only*, stirring often (but not vigorously) to prevent scorching (the mixture will get thicker).

Remove from the heat and gently stir a small amount of the hot mixture into the yolk mixture just to temper the yolks. Pour the combined mixtures into the saucepan and stir to blend (the mixture will thin a bit). Cook over low heat, stirring constantly to prevent scorching, just until the mixture thickens again and to cook the egg yolks, 1 minute *only*. Avoid overmixing. Remove from the heat and gently stir in the butter and the lemon juice and zest. Set aside at room temperature. Proceed to make the meringue.   CONTINUED ▸

To make the Italian Meringue: Have ready for easy access in the freezer about 15 ice cubes in a resealable plastic bag for cooling the meringue quickly. If you are using a kitchen torch to brown the meringue, set it nearby. If you are browning the meringue in the oven, preheat the oven to 375 degrees F and set aside a second 9-inch pie dish.

Place the egg whites and cream of tartar in the bowl of a stand mixer fitted with the whisk attachment. In a small, heavy saucepan, combine the sugars and water, place over low heat, and cook, stir occasionally, just until the sugars have dissolved. Keep a pastry brush in a small glass of cold water to wash down any sugar crystals that form along the sides of the pan. Increase the heat to medium, bring the mixture to a boil, and cook, without stirring, until the mixture registers 220 degrees F on a candy thermometer, 4 to 5 minutes.

As the syrup continues to boil, begin whipping the egg whites on medium-low speed until soft peaks form. Increase the speed to medium and continue whipping until thick, moist, glossy (not dry or granular) peaks form. Remove the sugar syrup from the heat when it registers 240 degrees F. (If the whites aren't thick and glossy yet, the syrup can wait briefly.)

With the mixer on its lowest speed, slowly pour the hot syrup into the meringue in a steady stream, aiming the syrup between the whisk and the bowl and taking care not to hit the whisk to avoid splattering the sides of the bowl. (No matter how careful you are, it's natural for some of the syrup to splatter. Try to incorporate as much of the hot syrup as possible.) As the hot syrup is poured onto the whipped whites, the mixture will expand immediately. When most of the sugar syrup has been added, increase the speed to medium-high and continue to whip until the mixture has thickened and forms glossy, stiff peaks with a marshmallow-like appearance. As you whip,

hold the reserved plastic bag with ice cubes against the bottom of the bowl, or as close to the bottom of the bowl as possible, for 2 to 3 minutes to speed the cooling.

Reduce the speed to low and continue to whip to set the structure of the meringue and to cool it to room temperature. (You will know when it is cooler because the outside of the metal bowl will no longer feel warm.)

With the aid of a rubber spatula, empty the lemon filling from the saucepan into the pie shell, spreading evenly with the spatula. Scoop large dollops of the thick meringue about 2 inches from the edges of the crust and onto 3 to 5 other areas on top of the filling. With a metal icing spatula, spread and coax the meringue over the filling just to cover the edges of the crust to seal in the filling and to prevent the meringue from shrinking away from the crust. Using the back of a spoon, decorate the meringue with deep, dramatic swirls.

Use the kitchen torch to brown the meringue. Or, set the pie dish in the set-aside extra pie pan and bake until the meringue is pale gold, 10 to 12 minutes. (The second pie dish helps insulate the filling from the oven's heat.) Remove the pie from the oven, lift it from the second pan, and place it on a wire rack to cool. Don't serve it until it has reached room temperature.

This pie is best eaten the same day it is baked. If you are serving it a few hours later in the day, refrigerate it and then remove it from the refrigerator about 30 minutes before serving so it is not too cold. To serve, cut into wedges with a sharp knife. If you have leftover pie, fashion a tent in aluminum foil to cover, being careful not to touch the meringue with the foil, and refrigerate for up to 2 days. To serve the cold pie, dip a sharp knife in cold water before cutting a wedge to ensure a clean cut through the meringue.

All-American Chocolate Cake with Divinity Frosting and Milk Chocolate Paint

Artistic inspiration for the dramatic decorating technique featured in this recipe comes from a late-nineteenth-century American layer cake described in *The Delectable Past*, by culinary historian Esther Aresty. My own creation features two layers of moist, tender full-flavored chocolate cake lavishly iced with a fluffy white divinity frosting. The frosting is covered with a thin film of creamy milk chocolate "paint" that covers the entire surface of the dessert. The handsome, sublime result is as delectable as the rich history that inspired it.   **YIELD: ONE 9-INCH, 2-LAYER ROUND CAKE, 10 TO 12 SERVINGS**

1 RECIPE DARK CHOCOLATE CAKE (PAGE 350), BAKED IN TWO 9 BY 2-INCH ROUND CAKE PANS

FLUFFY DIVINITY FROSTING

4 LARGE (½ CUP/4 FL OUNCES/120 ML) EGG WHITES

½ CUP (4 FL OUNCES/120 ML) WATER

¼ CUP (3 OUNCES BY WEIGHT/85 GRAMS BY WEIGHT) LIGHT CORN SYRUP

1½ CUPS (10½ OUNCES/300 GRAMS) GRANULATED SUGAR

¼ TEASPOON SALT

⅛ TEASPOON CREAM OF TARTAR

2 TEASPOONS PURE VANILLA EXTRACT

MILK CHOCOLATE PAINT

2 TABLESPOONS UNSALTED BUTTER

2 OUNCES (55 GRAMS) MILK CHOCOLATE, FINELY CHOPPED

Bake the 2 cake layers as directed, and let cool completely on wire racks.

To make the Fluffy Divinity Frosting: Have ready in your freezer for easy access 8 to 10 ice cubes in a resealable plastic bag for cooling the meringue later. Place the egg whites in the bowl of a stand mixer fitted with the whisk attachment.

In a deep 2-quart saucepan, combine the water, corn syrup, and sugar, place over low heat, and cook, stirring occasionally, until the sugar has dissolved and the mixture is clear, about 3 minutes. Keep a pastry brush in a small glass of cold water to wash down any sugar crystals that form along the sides of the pan. Increase the heat to medium-high, bring to a boil, and cook, without stirring, until the syrup registers 210 degrees F on a candy thermometer, 3 to 4 minutes. Be careful, as the mixture can overflow at this point (large bubbles will appear and the syrup will rise quickly in the pan). Reduce the heat slightly if the syrup does threaten to overflow. Eventually the syrup will stop climbing up the sides and just bubble lightly.

When the boiling syrup registers close to 225 degrees F, add the salt and cream of tartar to the egg whites and begin whipping the egg whites on medium-low speed until soft peaks form. Increase the speed to medium and continue whipping until thick, moist, glossy but not dry peaks form. Remove the sugar syrup from the heat as soon as it registers 240 degrees F. (If the whites aren't thick and glossy yet, the syrup can wait briefly.)

With the mixer on medium-low speed, slowly pour the hot syrup into the meringue in a steady stream, aiming the syrup between the whisk and the side of the bowl and taking care not to hit the whisk to   CONTINUED ▸

avoid splattering the sides of the bowl. (No matter how careful you are, it's natural for some of the syrup to splatter. Try to incorporate as much of the hot syrup as possible.) As the hot syrup is poured onto the whipped whites, the mixture will expand immediately. When all of the syrup has been added, without delay, increase the speed to medium and continue to whip until the mixture has thickened and formed glossy, stiff peaks with a marshmallow-like appearance, 2 to 3 minutes. As you begin to whip, hold the reserved plastic bag of ice cubes against the bottom of the bowl, or as close to the bottom of the bowl as possible, for 2 to 3 minutes to speed the cooling. When the meringue has cooled a bit (though it will still be quite warm) and stiff peaks have formed, reduce the speed to low, add the vanilla extract, and continue to whip to set the structure of the meringue and to cool it until it registers 93 to 96 degrees F on an instant-read thermometer. Don't overwhip the meringue. It becomes tricky to spread smoothly over the cake if it is too cool. Use right away.

To frost the cake: Place 1 of the cake layers on a sturdy cardboard round, or place it on a cake plate and slip about 3 strips of waxed paper under the cake to protect the plate. (A decorator's turntable is helpful when frosting the cake. If using the turntable, place the cake on its cardboard on the platform and frost as directed. After frosting the cake, transfer it on its cardboard base to a cake plate.) Using a long metal icing spatula, spread about ¾ cup of the frosting evenly over the layer all the way to the edges. Center the second layer on top. Apply large dollops of the frosting onto the sides and top of the cake by scooping it up with the metal spatula, and then spread it to cover completely. You can create a smooth finish or you can create deep swirls with the back of a spoon—the choice is yours. You don't have to be skimpy since there is plenty of frosting available, with a nice amount left over. Be sure to frost the entire cake before you finish spreading the frosting, as once the frosting cools, it sets up and is no longer spreadable. Use the leftover frosting to ice cupcakes or as a filling for sandwich cookies right away before it hardens.

To paint the cake: Let the cake stand at room temperature until the frosting is set and doesn't stick to your finger when lightly touched, 1 to 2 hours. In a small, heavy saucepan, combine the butter and chocolate and place over low heat just until melted. Remove from the heat and stir until creamy and smooth. Or, place in a microwave-safe bowl and melt in a microwave oven at 50 percent power (medium) for 30-second bursts, stirring after each burst. When most of the chocolate is melted, stir until creamy and smooth. Using a 1-inch-wide pastry brush, coat the entire surface of the frosting with the chocolate. Set the cake aside at room temperature for at least 30 minutes to give the chocolate time to set up before serving.

Transfer the cake to a plate or platter. To serve, cut into slices with a sharp knife, dipping the blade in hot water and wiping it dry with a towel before each cut.

Flourless Chocolate Torte

This is a family favorite that we have enjoyed repeatedly since the early 1970s. It's adapted from a recipe by the late, great Helen McCully, who was the food editor of *House Beautiful* and *McCall's* magazines for many years. Ground walnuts in the batter serve as an alternative to flour. For optimum flavor, I recommend making the cake a day ahead. You can decorate the top simply with a trio of toasted walnut halves. Or, you can fill three empty walnut shell halves with a few chopped walnuts, top each shell with a perfect walnut half, and then center the shells on top of the cake, pointing each shell outward in a different direction to create a simple, stunning décor. And for a very special occasion, decorate the top of the cake with tiny deposits of gold leaf.

YIELD: ONE 8-INCH ROUND CAKE, 12 SERVINGS

CAKE

4 OUNCES (1 STICK/115 GRAMS) UNSALTED BUTTER, CUT INTO ½-INCH SLICES

4 OUNCES (115 GRAMS) SEMISWEET CHOCOLATE, COARSELY CHOPPED

⅔ CUP (4½ OUNCES/130 GRAMS) GRANULATED SUGAR

FINELY GRATED ZEST OF 1 ORANGE

1 TABLESPOON GRAND MARNIER

3 LARGE EGGS

1½ CUPS (6 OUNCES/170 GRAMS) WALNUTS, FINELY GROUND TO YIELD 2 CUPS

GLAZE

3 OUNCES (¾ STICK/85 GRAMS) UNSALTED BUTTER, CUT INTO ¼-INCH SLICES

6 OUNCES (170 GRAMS) BITTERSWEET CHOCOLATE, FINELY CHOPPED

1 TABLESPOON HONEY

DECORATION

3 WALNUT HALVES, LIGHTLY TOASTED (PAGES 15–16)

EDIBLE GOLD LEAF (SEE SOURCES), OPTIONAL

Before baking: Center a rack in the oven and preheat the oven to 375 degrees F. Butter an 8 by 2-inch round cake pan, then flour it, tapping out the excess flour. Line the bottom with parchment paper.

To make the cake: In a small, heavy saucepan, melt the butter and chocolate over very low heat, stirring with a silicone spatula until smooth. (Or, combine in a medium microwave-safe bowl and melt in a microwave oven at 50 percent power for 30-second bursts, stirring after each burst, until melted, 1 to 1½ minutes.) Transfer the warm chocolate mixture to a large bowl. While it is still warm, add the sugar, orange zest, and liqueur and stir to mix. Let cool for 5 minutes. Stir in the eggs, one at a time, blending in thoroughly after each addition. Stir in the ground nuts. Pour the batter into the prepared pan.

Bake the cake until it feels soft but not liquid when gently pressed in the center, about 25 minutes. Do not overbake. The chocolate becomes firm as it cools. Transfer to a wire rack and let cool for 15 to 20 minutes.

Tilt and rotate the pan while gently tapping it on a counter to release the cake sides. Cover the cake with a sturdy cardboard round the same size as the cake, invert the cake onto it, and lift off the pan. Slowly peel off the parchment liner and discard it. Let the cake cool completely on the cardboard round.

If you plan to assemble the dessert within 2 days, wrap the cake in plastic wrap and store at room temperature. For longer storage, overwrap with aluminum foil, label with the contents and date, and freeze for up to 1 month. To thaw, remove the foil and set aside at room temperature in its packaging for 3 to 4 hours before applying the glaze. CONTINUED ▸

To make the glaze: Half fill a bowl with hot water (120 degrees F). Put the butter and chocolate in a 1-quart bowl and place it over (but not touching) the hot water. Stir occasionally with a rubber spatula until the mixture is smooth, shiny, and liquid. (Stir slowly so you don't produce bubbles in the glaze.) Remove the bowl from over the water, and gently stir in the honey. Use the glaze right away before it begins to set.

Place the cake on its cardboard round on a work surface. (A decorator's turntable can be helpful for this step.) Using a metal icing spatula, apply a thin coating of the glaze over the top and sides of the cake. This is a crumb coat—a bit like applying putty to hide any perfections—that will allow the remaining glaze to flow more smoothly over the cake, creating a shiny, attractive finish.

Place the cake still on its cardboard round on a wire rack over a rimmed baking sheet. Pour the glaze onto the center of the cake, and gently tilt it to help the glaze flow over the top and down the sides. Set cake on another rack or serving plate. When the glaze has set, place the 3 walnut halves on the top of the cake, placing them in the center in the shape of a triangle. If desired, using a small, clean sable paintbrush, apply tiny pieces of gold leaf or small dabs of gold leaf randomly on top of the cake.

Frangipane Ripple Chocolate Pound Cake

This unique Bundt cake is a work of confectionery art, each slice revealing ripples of dark chocolate pound cake and taupe-colored frangipane filling. Perfect party fare, it needs no additional embellishment (although a scoop of chocolate-almond ice cream wouldn't be out of place). Harried bakers will also appreciate the fact that this cake actually improves with age, so you don't need to feel guilty about baking it a day or two before you serve it.

I use Blue Diamond or American Almond (see Sources) canned almond paste. To keep the paste moist after you open the can, place a piece of plastic wrap directly on the surface, cover the can securely with a sheet of aluminum foil, and then replace the lid on top. It should be fine for a year in the refrigerator. **YIELD: ONE 10-INCH BUNDT CAKE, 20 SERVINGS (3 THIN SLICES PER SERVING)**

ALMOND PASTE FRANGIPANE

⅓ CUP (1¼ OUNCES/35 GRAMS) SLICED BLANCHED ALMONDS

½ CUP (4 OUNCES/115 GRAMS) ALMOND PASTE

¼ CUP (1¾ OUNCES/50 GRAMS) GRANULATED SUGAR

1 LARGE EGG

2 OUNCES (½ STICK/55 GRAMS) UNSALTED BUTTER, SOFTENED

CAKE

2 ⅓ CUPS (9¼ OUNCES/260 GRAMS) CAKE FLOUR

¾ CUP (2½ OUNCES/70 GRAMS) UNSWEETENED DUTCH-PROCESSED COCOA POWDER

2 TEASPOONS BAKING POWDER

¼ TEASPOON SALT

10 OUNCES (2½ STICKS/280 GRAMS) UNSALTED BUTTER, AT ROOM TEMPERATURE

2 CUPS (14 OUNCES/400 GRAMS) GRANULATED SUGAR

3 LARGE EGGS, LIGHTLY BEATEN

1 TEASPOON PURE VANILLA EXTRACT

1 CUP (8 FL OUNCES/240 ML) WHOLE MILK

To make the Almond Paste Frangipane: In a food processor, combine the almonds, almond paste, and sugar and process until the nuts are finely ground. Add the egg and butter and process until smoothly blended. Cover and refrigerate, and proceed to prepare the cake. (It will thicken just slightly in the refrigerator, which will make it easier to spread.)

Before baking: Center a rack in the oven and preheat the oven to 350 degrees F (or 325 degrees F if the pan has a dark finish). Butter a 10 by 3-inch Bundt pan, lightly coat it with nonstick spray, then flour it, tapping out the excess flour. If the pan has an intricate design or detail, prepare it as directed on page 24 to ensure the finished cake releases in one piece. Have all of the ingredients at room temperature.

To make the cake: Sift together the flour, cocoa powder, baking powder, and salt onto a sheet of waxed paper; set aside. In the bowl of a stand mixer fitted with the paddle attachment, beat the butter on medium speed until creamy and smooth, 30 to 45 seconds. Add the sugar in a steady stream and continue to beat until light in color and fluffy, 4 to 5 minutes, stopping the mixer occasionally to scrape down the sides of the bowl.

On medium speed, gradually add the eggs, 2 to 4 tablespoons at a time, beating after each addition until incorporated. Add the vanilla during the final moments of mixing. On the lowest speed, add the flour mixture in three additions alternately with the milk in two additions, beginning and ending with the flour mixture and mixing after each addition until incorporated. Stop the mixer to scrape down the sides of the bowl as needed. CONTINUED ➤

Remove the frangipane from the refrigerator. Spoon about 2 cups of the batter into the pan, and spread it evenly with a rubber spatula. Spoon half of the frangipane in dollops over the center of the batter. Using a small offset spatula, spread the frangipane evenly over the batter, avoiding the center tube and the sides of the pan (to achieve a neat, contained design). Spoon about 1 1/2 cups more of the batter evenly over the filling. Spoon the remaining frangipane over the batter, spreading evenly. Spoon the remaining batter over the top and spread evenly.

Bake the cake just until the top springs back when lightly touched in the center and the sides are beginning to come away from the pan, 60 to 67 minutes. Transfer to a wire rack and let cool in the pan for 15 to 20 minutes.

Tilt and rotate the pan while gently tapping it on a counter to release the cake sides. Invert a rack on top of the cake, invert the cake onto it, and lift off the pan. Let cool completely.

If serving the next day, wrap the cooled cake with plastic wrap and store at room temperature. To serve, cut into thin slices with a serrated knife.

Creamy Mint Napoleons

Buttery, flaky puff pastry and creamy, refreshing mint filling create an elegant dessert worthy of your most memorable occasions. Don't be intimidated by the length of the recipe. Much of it describes an efficient technique for crafting expertly shaped napoleon strips. Taught to me by pastry chef Pauline Lam, this clever technique, tailored to save time and frustration, entails using scissors to cut the chilled filling into rectangles that precisely fit the puff pastry strips, allowing you to stack as you go. **YIELD: 8 SERVINGS**

FRESH MINT PASTRY CREAM

2 CUPS (16 FL OUNCES/480 ML) WHOLE MILK

1 CUP (ABOUT 1 OUNCE/30 GRAMS) FRESH PEPPERMINT LEAVES, COARSELY CHOPPED

5 LARGE (6 TABLESPOONS/3 FL OUNCES/90 ML) EGG YOLKS

7 TABLESPOONS (3 OUNCES/85 GRAMS) GRANULATED SUGAR

3½ TABLESPOONS (SCANT 1 OUNCE/28 GRAMS) CORNSTARCH

½ RECIPE (1¼ POUNDS/570 GRAMS) WELL-CHILLED PDQ (PRETTY DARN QUICK) PUFF PASTRY (PAGE 367)

1 TABLESPOON UNSALTED BUTTER, MELTED

2 TEASPOONS GRANULATED SUGAR

POWDERED SUGAR FOR DECORATION

To make the Fresh Mint Pastry Cream: Select a rimmed baking sheet that will fit in your refrigerator or freezer and line it with plastic wrap; set aside. Place a fine-mesh sieve over a medium bowl; set aside. Pour the milk into a 1½-quart saucepan, add the mint, place over medium heat, and bring to a boil. Remove from the heat and allow the mixture to steep for 10 minutes. Pour the milk through the sieve, pressing against the mint with the back of a spoon to extract as much milk as possible, and then discard the mint. Rinse the sieve and saucepan, place the sieve over a small bowl, and set the pan and bowl aside. Measure the milk and add additional milk, if necessary, to make 2 cups (16 fl ounces/480 ml).

Place the yolks in the rinsed-out saucepan and whisk them to blend. Whisk in the sugar and cornstarch, then gradually whisk in the mint-infused milk until well

blended. Place over medium heat and bring to a gentle boil, stirring constantly with a silicone spatula for about 1 minute. Then switch to the whisk and beat the mixture while it cooks until it is smooth and thick and registers 180 degrees F on an instant-read thermometer, about 2 minutes. Pour the hot pastry cream onto the plastic wrap–lined baking sheet. Using the spatula, spread it into a strip about 12 by 7 inches by ¼ inch thick, squaring off the edges neatly with the spatula. Refrigerate, uncovered, until set and cool, about 30 minutes. If not using right away, place plastic wrap directly on the surface after it cools and refrigerate for up to 2 days.

Before baking: Center a rack in the oven and preheat the oven to 400 degrees F. Line a large rimmed baking sheet with parchment paper.

To bake the pastry: On a lightly floured surface, roll out the puff pastry into an 18 by 16-inch rectangle about ⅛ inch thick. To maintain the shape of the rectangle when transferring it to the prepared baking sheet, lay the rolling pin across the upper third of the dough. Lift the top edge and fold it toward you, draping it over the pin. The ends of the rolling pin will remain exposed. Roll the pin toward you, wrapping the remaining dough loosely around the pin. Transfer the dough to the baking sheet by lifting the rolling pin and suspending it 1 inch above the farthest edge of the prepared baking sheet. Flip over the last edge of dough rolled and unroll it toward you onto the baking sheet. (Unrolling the dough toward you, rather than away from you, is better because you can see the baking sheet and guide the dough precisely.) CONTINUED ▶

Trim 1 inch off of each long edge and 1½ inches off of each short edge to create a 16 by 13-inch rectangle. Prick the pastry all over with the tines of a fork. Refrigerate for 30 minutes. Brush the pastry with a thin coating of butter, and sprinkle the granulated sugar over the top. Again, prick the pastry all over with a fork. Bake until golden, 27 to 30 minutes. Transfer to a wire rack and let cool completely on the baking sheet.

To ready the pastry cream and pastry for assembling the napoleons: Place the baking sheet with the plastic-lined pastry cream in the freezer for 30 minutes before assembling the napoleons (not to freeze completely, just to get very cold and close to firm). Using the tip of a paring knife, make a few widely spaced dots lengthwise down the exact center of the pastry cream strip to use a guide for cutting. Following the dots and using kitchen scissors, cut through the plastic wrap and pastry cream to create two 3½ by 12-inch strips of pastry cream. Leave the strips on the plastic wrap on the baking sheet.

Using a ruler and a knife, cut the sheet of baked pastry lengthwise into three 4 by 12-inch strips. (Make a snack out of trimmings.) If large air pockets formed while baking, gently pat them down with your fingertips, leaving the large pastry flakes in the same spot as the bubbles were. (The pastry cream will cover these areas, and no one will ever know that broken pieces are there.) Turn the pastry strips so that 2 strips are flat sides up and 1 strip is flat side down.

To assemble the napoleons: Have the pastry strips and the pastry cream strips close by. Start with the pastry strip that is the flat side down. Using the plastic flaps of 1 of the pastry cream strips, place the strip parallel to the pastry strip. Then, still holding the plastic flaps, lift the cream strip and invert it onto the pastry strip. Gently peel off the plastic wrap and discard it. If a portion of the pastry cream splits, just spread over the break with a flexible metal spatula to cover the pastry strip evenly. (Note that the pastry cream is only 3½ inches wide, while the pastry is 4 inches, to compensate for the natural spread of the pastry cream once it is stacked.) Place a flat side up pastry strip on top of the first pastry cream strip, and then cover it with the second pastry cream strip, maneuvering it into the place the same way you did the first strip. Cover the stack with the third puff pastry strip, flat side up.

Cut the napoleon into eight 1½-inch-wide slices. For the first cut of each slice, use a very sharp paring knife, cutting through only the top layer of pastry, and then finish cutting with a long serrated knife. Push the slices together and upright again, if necessary. When all of the slices are cut, dust the tops with the powdered sugar and transfer the slices to a serving platter or individual plates. The napoleons are best served the same day they are prepared.

Old-Fashioned Jelly Roll with a Twist

When I was a child, a jelly roll was a familiar dessert at our house, showcasing the sun-warmed fruit flavors of our family's homemade preserves. As an adult, I elevated the simple to the sublime when I embellished the homespun recipe for a master class I was asked to teach at a conference of the International Association of Culinary Professionals. The classic jelly roll is sliced horizontally into two slender layers, which are then overlapped to form one long cake, which is rolled into a giant spiral that seems to go on forever. The colorful pinwheel effect is truly spectacular, and a short, sharp serrated knife makes it a cinch to create. A taste of vintage Americana, this festive dessert is perfect for birthdays, anniversaries, and other special occasions. **YIELD: ONE 10-INCH ROLLED CAKE, 12 SERVINGS**

CAKE

¾ CUP PLUS 2 TABLESPOONS (3 ½ OUNCES/100 GRAMS) CAKE FLOUR

¾ TEASPOON BAKING POWDER

¼ TEASPOON SALT

4 LARGE EGGS

1 CUP (7 OUNCES/200 GRAMS) GRANULATED SUGAR

1 TEASPOON PURE VANILLA EXTRACT

¼ CUP (2 FL OUNCES/60 ML) WATER

FILLING

1 ⅓ CUPS (12 OUNCES/340 GRAMS) SEEDLESS RASPBERRY JAM

1 TABLESPOON FINELY GRATED LEMON ZEST

DECORATION

POWDERED SUGAR OR 3 TABLESPOONS APRICOT JAM, 2 TEASPOONS FRESH LEMON JUICE, AND ½ CUP (2 ½ OUNCES/70 GRAMS) SHELLED, UNSALTED PISTACHIO NUTS, FINELY CHOPPED

Before baking: Center a rack in the oven and preheat the oven to 400 degrees F. Using a paper towel, lightly butter a small area in the center of a 15½ by 10½ by 1-inch pan (jelly-roll pan). Line the pan with aluminum foil, pressing the foil into the contours of the pan and leaving a 2-inch overhang at each short end (buttering the pan anchors the foil in place to make buttering the foil easier). Butter the foil, then flour it, tapping out the excess flour.

To make the cake: Sift together the flour, baking powder, and salt onto a sheet of waxed paper; set aside. Place the eggs in the bowl of a stand mixer and whisk lightly by hand just until blended. Add the sugar and whisk until combined.

Attach the bowl to the mixer and fit the mixer with the whisk attachment. Whip the eggs and sugar on medium speed until the mixture is light ivory in color and very fluffy, about 6 minutes. Add the vanilla during the final moments of whipping. Using a rubber spatula, gently fold in the flour mixer in three additions alternately with the water in two additions, beginning and ending with the flour and folding after each addition until incorporated. The batter will be fluffy yet thin. Gently pour the batter into the prepared pan and spread it evenly with an offset spatula.

Bake the cake until it is pale golden on top and springs back when lightly pressed in the center, 10 to 12 minutes. Transfer to a wire rack and let cool completely in the pan.

Using a thin-bladed knife, gently release any portion of cake sticking to the long sides of the pan. One at a time, pull up on the foil overhangs to release the foil from the pan, and then transfer the cake on its foil liner to a work surface. If necessary, trim any crisp edges. Using a small, sharp serrated knife (the blade should be about 5 inches long), cut a horizontal incision about 1 inch deep around the circumference of the cake. Then cut an inch or more deeper into the cake, moving the knife CONTINUED ▶

in a sawing motion, in and out, while simultaneously rotating the cake with the other hand, until you have again circumvented the entire cake. Continue to cut in this way, cutting deeper each time until you have split the thin cake in half horizontally into 2 very thin layers. If the layers are not perfectly even no one will know after the cake is rolled with the filling. Place a sheet of aluminum foil on the work surface next to one of the short ends of the cake. Gently and carefully flip 1 layer onto the foil on the work surface. Then position the second layer so that it overlaps a short end of the first layer by about ¼ inch to create a cake strip 30 inches long and 10 inches wide.

To make the filling and roll the cake: In a small bowl, stir the raspberry jam until smooth. Add the lemon zest and stir to combine. Using an offset spatula, spread the jam evenly and thinly over the cake's surface. Begin rolling by flipping a short edge of the cake over onto itself. Then, using your fingertips, roll up the cake until you reach the far end. As you roll, lift the foil to assist you in rolling the cake. When you finish rolling, wrap the foil around the cake and gently set the cake, seam side down, on a serving plate. Set aside at room temperature until 1 hour before serving.

To serve, remove and discard the foil from the cake roll, and trim both ends. Lightly dust the cake roll with powdered sugar. Or, in a small bowl, stir together the apricot jam and lemon juice, spread the mixture over the roll with a metal icing spatula, and sprinkle with the pistachio nuts. Using a serrated knife and a sawing motion, cut into ¾-inch slices and place the slices, cut side down, on dessert plates.

Wrap any leftover cake in plastic wrap and store at room temperature for up to 2 days.

For longer storage, omit the powdered sugar or jam and nuts garnish, wrap the cake roll in plastic wrap, overwrap with aluminum foil, and freeze for up to 2 weeks. To thaw, remove the foil and set aside at room temperature in its packaging for 2 to 3 hours. Apply the powdered sugar or the jam and nut garnish before serving.

NOTES

PART THREE

The Baker's Handbook
Basic Recipe Components

I LIKE TO THINK OF RECIPES as painting kits: they guide you through the process of creating masterworks. But instead of brilliant colors and a collection of brushes, they use rich flavors and a variety of tools to help you craft edible works of art.

Inside those paint boxes, the canvas, or foundation of each recipe, is key. The bold hues are exciting, to be sure, because each one adds a layer of depth to the finished artwork. But everything begins with the canvas. The cakes and pastries in this chapter are delectable on their own, before they are frosted, rolled, filled, or topped.

The recipes that appear on the following pages are integral to the assembled desserts in the rest of the book. They are reliable and adaptable by nature. And yet these recipes are more than mere canvases. You will also find them indispensable as you come up with your own combinations. Versatile cakes can hold just about any filling, adaptable tart shells can cradle sweet or savory mixtures, and multipurpose sauces and fillings can team with other components to form a completely original creation.

Take, for example, Croissant Pastry ASAP. To use the dough in a completely different manner than how it is used in this book, sprinkle it with cinnamon and sugar, cut it into strips, twist, and bake. Now you have something special to serve at breakfast. Or, use Cream Cheese Pastry to top a savory potpie or to wrap around a spicy meat filling for empañadas.

Embellishments like Lemon Curd and Crème Anglaise likewise find new applications as you work them into your repertoire. For example, spread the curd onto slices of toasted pound cake for an impromptu dessert or teatime snack, or spoon the custard sauce over a bowl of fresh fruit. Or, combine a pair of component recipes, such as Dried Plum–Armagnac Puree as a filling for turnovers made with All-Butter Flaky Pastry.

Stroll through any art museum and you will quickly realize that even though every painter starts with a canvas, each one decides just how much he or she wants to add to it. A splash of color can be just as effective as layer after layer—and even a blank canvas can make a memorable statement.

Favorite Buttermilk Cake

This terrific basic cake, perfect with many different fillings and frostings, marries well with a variety of flavors, such as chocolate, maple, citrus, all types of nuts, caramel, and more. It holds up beautifully as an integral part of Peanut Butter Crunch Cake, Squared (page 128) and Deluxe Boston Cream Pie (page 325), and promises to do the same in your dessert creations.

YIELD: ONE 8-INCH SQUARE CAKE

1 ¾ CUPS (7 OUNCES/200 GRAMS) CAKE FLOUR

½ TEASPOON BAKING POWDER

½ TEASPOON BAKING SODA

¼ TEASPOON SALT

⅔ CUP (5 ½ FL OUNCES/165 ML) WELL-SHAKEN BUTTERMILK

1 TEASPOON PURE VANILLA EXTRACT

5 ½ OUNCES (1 ⅓ STICKS/155 GRAMS) UNSALTED BUTTER, AT ROOM TEMPERATURE

1 ⅓ CUPS (9 ¼ OUNCES/260 GRAMS) GRANULATED SUGAR

3 LARGE EGGS, LIGHTLY BEATEN

Before baking: Center a rack in the oven and preheat to 350 degrees F. Lightly coat an 8 by 2-inch square pan with nonstick spray, then flour it, tapping out the excess flour. Or, butter and flour the pan. Line the bottom with parchment paper. Have all of the ingredients at room temperature.

Sift together the flour, baking powder, baking soda, and salt onto a sheet of waxed paper; set aside. In a small bowl, stir together the buttermilk and vanilla; set aside.

In the bowl of a stand mixer fitted with the paddle attachment, beat the butter on medium speed until it is lighter in color, clings to the sides of the bowl, and has a satiny appearance, 30 to 45 seconds. Increase the speed to medium-high and add the sugar in a steady stream, stopping the mixer occasionally to scrape down the sides of the bowl. Continue to beat on medium speed until the mixture is lighter in color and fluffy, 3 to 4 minutes.

With the mixer on medium speed, add the eggs, 1 to 2 tablespoons at a time, beating after each addition until incorporated. If at any time the batter appears watery or shiny (signs of curdling), increase the speed to medium-high and beat until the batter is smooth again. Then return to medium speed and resume adding the eggs, beating until smooth, stopping the mixer as needed to scrape down the sides of the bowl.

On the lowest speed, add the flour mixture in three additions alternately with the buttermilk mixture in two additions, beginning and ending with the flour mixture and mixing only until incorporated after each addition. Stop the mixer after each addition to scrape down the sides of the bowl.

Pour the batter into the prepared pan. With the rubber spatula, spread the batter from the center outward, creating a slightly raised ridge around the outside rim. (Since heat is conducted faster near the metal rim, mounding the batter around the edges ensures the cake will bake more evenly and will be more level.)

Bake the cake just until it is golden brown on top, springs back when lightly touched in the center, a round wooden toothpick inserted in the center comes out free of cake, and the sides are just beginning to come away from the pan, about 45 minutes. Transfer to a wire rack and let cool in the pan for 10 to 15 minutes.

Tilt and rotate the pan while gently tapping it on a counter to see if the cake sides release. If they don't release, slip a small metal spatula between the still-warm cake and the pan and run the spatula carefully along the entire perimeter of the pan. Invert a rack on top of the cake, invert the cake onto it, and carefully lift off the pan. Slowly peel off the parchment paper, turn it over so that the sticky side faces up, and reposition it on the top of the cake. Invert another rack on top, invert the cake so it is right side up, and remove the original rack. Let cool completely.

Use right away, or wrap in plastic wrap and store at room temperature for up to 1 day. For longer storage, overwrap with aluminum foil, label with the contents and date, and freeze for up to 2 weeks. To thaw, remove the foil and leave at room temperature for 2 to 3 hours.

Silver Cake with Poppy Seeds

As versatile as it is delicious, this is the ultimate white cake. You can use this delicate cake as an element to create other desserts, such as Frozen Fruit Rainbow Terrine (page 143) and Fruit Cocktail Trifles with Crème Anglaise (page 267), or you can enjoy it on its own, unfrosted or frosted (split into layers if you like) with a favorite frosting, with coffee or tea. The pristine white cake is polka-dotted with black poppy seeds, creating a festive appearance that particularly highlights the vibrant colors of fresh fruit. Enriching the cake with buttermilk gives it a light, tender texture and subtle tangy flavor. For an all-purpose white cake, omit the poppy seeds.   **YIELD: ONE 13 BY 9-INCH CAKE**

2¼ CUPS (8¾ OUNCES/250 GRAMS) CAKE FLOUR

2 TEASPOONS BAKING POWDER

½ TEASPOON BAKING SODA

¼ TEASPOON SALT

¼ CUP (2 FL OUNCES/60 ML) WHOLE MILK

½ VANILLA BEAN, SPLIT LENGTHWISE

½ CUP (4 FL OUNCES/120 ML) WELL-SHAKEN BUTTERMILK

¼ CUP (1 OUNCE/30 GRAMS) POPPY SEEDS

1 TABLESPOON FRESH LEMON JUICE

7 OUNCES (1¾ STICKS/200 GRAMS) UNSALTED BUTTER,
    AT ROOM TEMPERATURE

1½ CUPS (10½ OUNCES/300 GRAMS) GRANULATED SUGAR

4 LARGE (ABOUT ½ CUP/4 FL OUNCES/120 ML) EGG WHITES,
    LIGHTLY BEATEN

Before baking: Center a rack in the oven and preheat the oven to 350 degrees F. Lightly coat a 13 by 9 by 2-inch pan (quarter sheet pan) with nonstick spray, then flour it, tapping out the excess flour. Or, butter and flour the pan. Line the bottom with parchment paper. Have all of the ingredients at room temperature.

Sift together the flour, baking powder, baking soda, and salt onto a sheet of waxed paper; set aside. In a small saucepan, heat the milk with the vanilla bean just until lukewarm. Set aside to cool to room temperature, about 5 minutes. Remove the vanilla bean from the milk, scrape the seeds from the bean into the milk with a small paring knife, and discard the pod. Pour the vanilla-flavored milk into a small bowl, add the buttermilk, poppy seeds, and lemon juice, and stir to blend; set aside.

In the bowl of a stand mixer fitted with the paddle attachment, beat the butter on medium speed until it is lighter in color, clings to the sides of the bowl, and has a satiny appearance, 30 to 45 seconds. Add the sugar in a steady stream, then stop the mixer and scrape down the gritty, sandy mixture clinging to the sides of the bowl. Continue to beat on medium speed until the mixture is very light in color and fluffy, 3 to 4 minutes.

With the mixer on medium speed, add the egg whites, 1 to 2 tablespoons at a time, beating after each addition until incorporated before adding more. (This is especially important for egg whites because a large percentage of an egg white is water.) If at any time the batter appears watery or shiny (signs of curdling), stop the flow of egg whites, increase the speed to medium-high, and beat until the batter looks smooth again. Then return to medium speed and resume adding the egg whites. Continue to beat, stopping to scrape down the sides and bottom of the bowl at least once or twice, until all of the whites have been added and the mixture is fluffy.

On the lowest speed, add the flour mixture in three additions alternately with the buttermilk mixture in two additions, beginning and ending with the flour mixture and mixing after each addition until incorporated. Stop the mixer after each addition to scrape down the sides of the bowl.

Pour the batter into the prepared baking pan. With a rubber spatula, spread the batter from the center outward, creating a slightly raised ridge around the outside rim. (Since heat is conducted faster near the metal rim, mounding the batter around the edges ensures the cake will bake more evenly and will be more level.)

Bake the cake until it springs back slightly when lightly touched in the center, a round wooden toothpick inserted in the center comes out free of cake, and the sides are just beginning to come away from the pan, 38 to 42 minutes. Transfer to a wire rack and let cool in the pan for about 10 minutes.

Tilt and rotate the pan while gently tapping it on a counter to release the cake sides. If they don't release, slip a thin metal spatula between the still-warm cake and the pan

and run the spatula carefully along the entire perimeter of the pan. Invert a large wire rack on top of the cake, invert the cake onto it, and carefully lift off the pan. Slowly peel off the parchment paper, turn it over so that the sticky side faces up, and reposition it on the top of the cake. Invert another rack on top, invert the cake so it is right side up, and remove the original rack. Let cool completely.

Use right away or wrap in plastic wrap and store at room temperature for up to 1 day. For longer storage, overwrap with aluminum foil, label with the contents and date, and freeze for up to 2 weeks. To thaw, remove the foil and leave at room temperature for 2 to 3 hours.

Signature Yellow Cake

I always contemplate the "what if?" in baking. Research and experimentation keep me open to fresh material and make it possible to continue my quest of learning. A fine example of this approach occurred one day when I was adding whole eggs to a cake batter and also decided to add (rather than waste) three egg yolks left over from another recipe. The cake, which received rave reviews for its tender, fine-grained texture and moist, rich flavor, has since become a signature cake, a perfect component for many of my desserts.   **YIELD: TWO 9-INCH OR THREE 8-INCH CAKE LAYERS**

2½ CUPS PLUS 2 TABLESPOONS (10¾ OUNCES/305 GRAMS) CAKE FLOUR

2 TEASPOONS BAKING POWDER

½ TEASPOON SALT

8 OUNCES (2 STICKS/225 GRAMS) UNSALTED BUTTER, AT ROOM TEMPERATURE

2 CUPS (14 OUNCES/400 GRAMS) GRANULATED SUGAR

3 LARGE EGGS, LIGHTLY BEATEN

3 LARGE (¼ CUP/2 FL OUNCES/60 ML) EGG YOLKS

1 CUP (8 FL OUNCES/240 ML) WHOLE MILK

2 TEASPOONS PURE VANILLA EXTRACT

Before baking: Center a rack in the oven and preheat the oven to 350 degrees F. Lightly coat two 9 by 2-inch or three 8 by 2-inch round cake pans with nonstick spray, then flour them, tapping out the excess flour. Or, butter and flour the pans. Line the bottoms with parchment paper. Have all of the ingredients at room temperature.

Sift together the flour, baking powder, and salt onto a large sheet of waxed paper; set aside. In the bowl of a stand mixer fitted with the paddle attachment, beat the butter on medium speed until it is lighter in color, clings to the sides of the bowl, and is smooth and creamy, about 45 seconds. Add the sugar in a steady stream, and then stop the mixer to scrape down the sides of the bowl. Continue to beat on medium speed until the mixture is very light in color and texture, 4 to 5 minutes, stopping the mixer occasionally to scrape down the sides of the bowl.

With the mixer on medium speed, add the beaten whole eggs, 3 to 4 tablespoons at a time, beating after each addition until incorporated. Stop the mixer occasionally to scrape down the sides of the bowl. Then add the egg yolks, one at a time, again beating after each addition until incorporated. The entire process of adding and beating the eggs should take 3 to 4 minutes, at which point the mixture should appear fluffy and increased in volume.

On the lowest speed, add the flour mixture in four additions alternately with the milk in three additions, beginning and ending with the flour mixture and mixing well after each addition until incorporated. Stop the mixer often to scrape down the sides of the bowl, and add the vanilla during the last moments of mixing.

Spoon equal amounts of the batter into each pan. With a rubber spatula, spread the batter from the center outward, creating a slightly raised ridge around the outside rim. (Since heat is conducted faster near the metal rim, mounding the batter around the edges ensures the layers will bake more evenly and will be more level. Batters containing chemical leavenings—baking powder and baking soda—also have a tendency to bake higher in the middle, forming a slight dome, and the ridge compensates for that tendency.)

Bake the cakes until the tops spring back when lightly touched in the center and the edges are beginning to come away from the sides of the pans, 35 to 40 minutes. Transfer the pans to wire racks and let cool for about 10 minutes.

Tilt and rotate a pan while gently tapping it on a counter to release the cake sides. If they don't release, slip a thin metal spatula between the still-warm cake and the pan and run the spatula carefully along the entire perimeter of the pan. Invert a wire rack on top of the cake, invert the cake onto it, and carefully lift off the pan. Slowly peel off the parchment liner, turn it over so that the sticky side faces up, and reposition it on the top of the cake. Invert another rack on top, invert the cake so it is right side up, and remove the original rack. Repeat with the remaining layer(s). Let cool completely.

If serving the cake within 24 hours, wrap each layer in plastic wrap and store at room temperature. For longer storage, overwrap with aluminum foil, label with the contents and date, and freeze for up to 2 weeks. To thaw, remove the foil and leave at room temperature for 2 to 3 hours.

Dark Chocolate Cake

When Evie Lieb (page 184) and I met at a yard sale (predominantly cookbooks) many years ago, we discovered we had a lot in common, least of which was our mutual love of baking. Along the way we discovered that both of us had spotted a chocolate cake recipe in a magazine that we had adopted as one of our signature cakes for all types of occasions. Since it first came to our attention in the early 1970s, we have sung its praises to anyone who will listen. Here, I list it as a basic cake that stars in two great dessert recipes, Dark Chocolate Baby Cakes (page 136) and All-American Chocolate Cake with Divinity Frosting and Milk Chocolate Paint (page 331).

This recipe includes directions for baking in two different layer-cake pan sizes: 6 by 3-inch round pans, which are used for the Baby Cakes, and 9 by 2-inch round pans, which are used for All-American Chocolate Cake. But this cake is extremely popular, so here are two suggestions for making large cakes from this recipe. Bake the cake in a 9 by 13 by 2-inch pan (quarter sheet pan) for 40 minutes, let cool completely, frost, and cut into squares to serve. Or, double the recipe and bake the cake in an 18 by 13 by 1-inch pan (half sheet pan) for 35 minutes. Let the cake cool completely, then, following the directions for splitting a cake into layers on page 25, freeze the cake just until firm, cut it in half crosswise, and then split each half in half horizontally to yield 4 layers total. Use the layers to make two 2-layer, 13 by 9-inch cakes. Fill and frost as desired; each cake serves about 16.   **YIELD: TWO 6 BY 3-INCH ROUND CAKE LAYERS OR TWO 9 BY 2-INCH ROUND CAKE LAYERS**

3 OUNCES (85 GRAMS) UNSWEETENED CHOCOLATE, COARSELY CHOPPED

2 CUPS (8 OUNCES/225 GRAMS) CAKE FLOUR

1½ TEASPOONS BAKING SODA

½ TEASPOON SALT

1 CUP (8 OUNCES/225 GRAMS) SOUR CREAM

2 TEASPOONS PURE VANILLA EXTRACT

6 OUNCES (1½ STICKS/170 GRAMS) UNSALTED BUTTER, AT ROOM TEMPERATURE

2 CUPS FIRMLY PACKED (14 OUNCES/400 GRAMS) LIGHT BROWN SUGAR

3 LARGE EGGS, LIGHTLY BEATEN

1 CUP (8 FL OUNCES/240 ML) LUKEWARM COFFEE OR WATER

Before baking: Center a rack in the oven and preheat the oven to 350 degrees F. Lightly coat two 6 by 3-inch round cake pans or two 9 by 2-inch round cake pans with nonstick spray, then flour them, tapping out the excess flour. Or, butter and flour the pans. Line the bottoms with parchment paper. Have all of the ingredients at room temperature.

Half fill a bowl with hot water (120 degrees F). Put the chocolate in a bowl and place it over (but not touching) the hot water. Let the chocolate melt until creamy and smooth, stirring slowly occasionally. (Replace the water with more hot water, if needed, to melt the chocolate smoothly.) Remove from the water bath and set aside to cool to lukewarm.

Sift together the flour, baking soda, and salt onto a sheet of waxed paper; set aside. In a small bowl, stir together the sour cream and vanilla; set aside.

In the bowl of a stand mixer fitted with the paddle attachment, beat the butter on medium speed until it is lighter in color and creamy, clings to the sides of the bowl, and has a satiny appearance, about 45 seconds. Add the sugar in a steady stream, stopping the mixer occasionally to scrape down the sides of the bowl. Continue to beat on medium speed until the mixture is very light in color and fluffy, 3 to 4 minutes.

With the mixer on medium-low speed, add the eggs, 3 to 4 tablespoons at a time, beating after each addition until incorporated and stopping the mixer occasionally to scrape down the sides of the bowl. Continue to beat on medium-low speed until the mixture is well blended and lighter in color and texture, 3 to 4 minutes. Stop the mixer occasionally to scrape down the sides of the bowl.

On the lowest speed, add the flour mixture in three additions alternately with the sour cream in two additions, beginning and ending with the flour mixture and mixing after each addition until incorporated. Stop the mixer and scrape down the sides of the bowl after each addition. Detach the paddle and bowl from the mixer, and tap the paddle against the side of the bowl to release the excess batter. Slowly add the warm coffee, stirring with a rubber spatula until smooth. Spoon half of the batter into each prepared pan and spread evenly with the spatula.

Bake the cakes until the tops spring back when lightly pressed with a fingertip and a round wooden toothpick inserted in the center of each cake comes out free of cake, about 55 minutes for 6-inch round pans and 35 minutes for 9-inch round pans. Transfer to wire racks and let cool in the pans for 10 to 15 minutes.

Tilt and rotate a pan while gently tapping it on a counter to release the cake sides. If they don't release, slip a thin metal spatula between the still-warm cake and the pan and run the spatula carefully along the entire perimeter of the pan. Invert a wire rack on top of the cake, invert the cake onto it, and lift off the pan. Slowly peel off the parchment paper, turn it over so that the sticky side faces up, and reposition it on the top of the cake. Invert another rack on top, invert the cake so it is right side up, and remove the original rack. Repeat with the remaining cake. Let the cakes cool completely.

To store, wrap each cake layer in plastic wrap and store at room temperature for up to 2 days. For longer storage, overwrap with aluminum foil, label with the contents and date, and freeze for up to 1 month. Thaw at room temperature for about 2 hours before unwrapping, splitting into layers, and frosting,

Chocolate Genoise Sheet Cake

Buttering and flouring the aluminum foil that lines the pan for this cake helps spread the batter efficiently. If you used only a nonstick spray, the batter would float on top of the foil, making it difficult to spread it evenly. If you floured the spray, the flour would form an ultrathin layer during baking that cracks and flakes off and is unsightly when the cake is rolled.

To use this cake for other than a rolled cake, freeze it as directed, and then thaw only partially (it should still be firm). Cut the cake in half crosswise to yield two 13 by 9-inch layers and use the layers to make one 2-layer, 13 by 9-inch cake. Or, split each half in half horizontally to yield four 9 by 6½-inch layers total, and use the layers to make one 4-layer, 9 by 6½-inch cake. Fill and frost the cakes as desired; each cake serves 12 to 16. **YIELD: ONE 18 BY 13-INCH SHEET CAKE**

⅓ CUP (1½ OUNCES/40 GRAMS) CAKE FLOUR

⅓ CUP (1 OUNCE/30 GRAMS) UNSWEETENED DUTCH-PROCESSED COCOA POWDER

½ CUP PLUS 3 TABLESPOONS (4¾ OUNCES/135 GRAMS) GRANULATED SUGAR

⅛ TEASPOON SALT

4 LARGE EGGS

2 LARGE EGG YOLKS

1 TABLESPOON UNSALTED BUTTER, MELTED

1 TEASPOON PURE VANILLA EXTRACT

Before baking: Center a rack in the oven and preheat the oven to 400 degrees F. Moisten a paper or kitchen towel with water and rub the towel lightly only over the inside bottom of an 18 by 13 by 1-inch pan (half sheet pan). Line the pan with aluminum foil (use 2 sheets, one overlapping the other a bit, to cover the bottom and sides completely), pressing the foil into the contours of the pan and leaving at least a 2-inch overhang at each end (the water anchors the foil in place to make buttering it easier). Butter the foil, then flour it, tapping out the excess flour.

Sift together the flour, cocoa, 1 tablespoon of the sugar, and the salt onto a sheet of waxed paper; sift again and set aside.

Place the eggs, egg yolks, and the remaining ½ cup plus 2 tablespoons (4¼ ounces/120 grams) sugar in the bowl of a stand mixer. Holding the whisk attachment from the mixer in your hand, whisk the mixture to blend the ingredients. Attach the bowl to the mixer, and fit the mixer with the whisk attachment. Whip the egg mixture on medium speed until it is airy, pale, and tripled in volume, 4 to 5 minutes. When the whisk is lifted, the mixture should fall back into the bowl in a ribbon that rests softly on the surface and remains there for about 10 seconds. If the ribbon immediately dissolves into the mixture, continue whipping for 2 to 3 minutes longer. On the lowest speed, add the butter and vanilla in the final moments of whipping.

Detach the whisk and bowl from the mixer, and tap the whisk against the side of the bowl to free the excess batter. Sprinkle about one-third of the flour mixture over the batter and fold it in with a rubber spatula until incorporated. Fold in the remaining flour in two additions until no streaks of flour are visible. Gently pour the batter down the middle of the prepared pan. Using an offset spatula, spread the batter evenly.

Bake the cake until it appears set on top and springs back when lightly touched in the center, 11 to 13 minutes. If the cake doesn't test done, return it to the oven for another minute or two, watching it carefully.

Transfer the pan to a wire rack. Without delay, place 2 long sheets of foil, one at a time and slightly overlapping them, over the length of the cake. Manipulate the foil into a shallow tent (a tent holds in the moisture as the cake cools and prevents the foil from sticking to the top of the cake). Let the cake cool completely, 30 to 60 minutes.

Discard the foil tent. Using a thin-bladed knife, gently release any portion of cake sticking to the long sides of the pan. One at a time, pull up on the foil overhangs to release the foil from the pan, and transfer the cake on its foil liner to a work surface. Use as directed in individual recipes.

Or, to store, wrap the cake and sheet pan with plastic wrap, overwrap with aluminum foil, label and date with the contents, and freeze for up to 2 weeks. To thaw, unwrap and loosely cover with the plastic wrap, and then set aside at room temperature for about 1 hour.

Single-Crust Flaky Pie Pastry

This is a versatile, easy-to-handle all-purpose pastry, ideal for my Caramel Chocolate Cream Pie (page 327), Rhubarb-Cherry-Raspberry Crumb Pie (page 220), Dee-luscious Lemon Meringue Pie (page 329), and Black-Bottom Praline Chiffon Pie (page 320).   **YIELD: PASTRY FOR ONE 9-INCH SINGLE-CRUST PIE**

1 ¼ CUPS (5 ½ OUNCES/155 GRAMS) ALL-PURPOSE FLOUR

2 TEASPOONS GRANULATED SUGAR

¼ TEASPOON SALT

3 OUNCES (¾ STICK/85 GRAMS) COLD UNSALTED BUTTER, CUT INTO 6 SLICES

3 TABLESPOONS COLD SOLID VEGETABLE SHORTENING

3 TO 4 TABLESPOONS ICE WATER

In a large bowl, whisk together the flour, sugar, and salt. Scatter the butter pieces over the flour mixture. With a pastry blender, cut them in until they are no larger than peas. Add the shortening and cut it in until the particles vary in size from coarse crumbs to peas and are evenly distributed throughout the dough.

Sprinkle the ice water, 1 tablespoon at a time, over the flour mixture, tossing lightly with a fork, preferably a blending fork, after every addition, until the pastry is moist enough to hold together. Pinch a small portion of the dough between your fingers. If it won't hold together, add a little more water, 1 teaspoon at a time.

Transfer the dough to a lightly floured work surface, gently shape it into a ball, and flatten into a 5-inch disk about ½ inch thick (about 10 ½ ounces/300 grams). Wrap in plastic wrap and refrigerate until firm enough to roll, at least 2 hours or up to 2 days. For longer storage, overwrap with aluminum foil, label with the contents and date, and freeze for up to 1 month. Thaw in the refrigerator for about 4 hours or up to overnight. The dough should remain cold for rolling.

Use as directed in individual recipes. Or, to use for your own pies, follow the directions on page 27 for rolling out the pastry and lining a pie dish.

Double-Crust Flaky Pie Pastry

Like the Single-Crust Flaky Pie Pastry on page 354, this recipe calls for a little vegetable shortening to give the finished pastry a wonderful tenderness. I use it for my Double-Crust Butter-Pecan Apple Pie (page 62) and to make enough Year-Round Little Peach Pies (page 268) for a crowd. **YIELD: PASTRY FOR ONE 9-INCH DOUBLE-CRUST PIE**

2 ¼ CUPS (10 ¼ OUNCES/290 GRAMS) ALL-PURPOSE FLOUR

1 TABLESPOON GRANULATED SUGAR

½ TEASPOON SALT

5 OUNCES (1 ¼ STICKS/140 GRAMS) COLD UNSALTED BUTTER, CUT INTO ¼-INCH SLICES

⅓ CUP (2 ½ OUNCES/70 GRAMS) COLD SOLID VEGETABLE SHORTENING

6 TO 8 TABLESPOONS (3 TO 4 FL OUNCES/90 TO 120 ML) ICE WATER

In a large bowl, whisk together the flour, sugar, and salt. Scatter the butter pieces over the flour mixture. With a pastry blender, cut them in until they are no larger than peas. Add the shortening and cut it in until the particles vary in size from coarse crumbs to peas and are evenly distributed throughout the dough.

Sprinkle the ice water, 1 tablespoon at a time, over the flour mixture, tossing lightly with a fork, preferably a blending fork, after every addition, just until the pastry is moist enough to hold together. Pinch a small portion of the dough between your fingers. If it won't hold together, add a little more water, 1 teaspoon at a time.

Transfer the dough to a lightly floured work surface, divide it in half, and gently shape each half into a ball. Flatten each ball into a 5-inch disk about ½ inch thick (about 10½ ounces/300 grams each). Wrap each disk in plastic wrap and refrigerate until firm enough to roll, about 2 hours or up to 2 days. For longer storage, over-wrap with aluminum foil, label with the contents and date, and freeze for up to 1 month. Thaw in the refrigerator for about 4 hours or up to overnight. The dough should remain cold for rolling.

Use as directed in individual recipes. Or, to use for your own pies, follow the directions beginning on page 28 for rolling out the pastry for a double-crust pie.

All-Butter Flaky Pastry

To form this flaky pastry dough successfully, you must cut cold butter into the flour—either by hand with a pastry blender or in a food processor with the steel blade—until you have a variety of chunks that range in size from small lima beans to peas to lentils. The amount of water you will need to add to this dough is likely to change slightly from time to time, depending on such variables as humidity and the moisture content of your butter and sometimes even your flour. Rolling out and folding the dough twice and then refrigerating it for about 30 minutes helps to firm up the butter and relax the pastry, which ensures a flakier result. Use this pastry recipe the next time you make fruit turnovers or a rustic open-faced galette, rolling it out on a lightly floured work surface about ⅛ inch thick.   **YIELD: 1 POUND, 9 OUNCES (710 GRAMS) DOUGH, PASTRY FOR TWO 12-INCH GALETTES OR ONE 12-INCH DOUBLE-CRUST GALETTE**

2 ⅓ CUPS (10 ½ OUNCES/300 GRAMS) ALL-PURPOSE FLOUR

1 TEASPOON GRANULATED SUGAR

½ TEASPOON SALT

8 OUNCES (2 STICKS/225 GRAMS) COLD UNSALTED BUTTER, CUT INTO ¼-INCH SLICES

10 TO 12 TABLESPOONS (5 TO 6 FL OUNCES /150 TO 180 ML) ICE WATER

In a food processor, combine the flour, sugar, and salt and pulse 3 or 4 times to blend. Scatter the butter pieces over the flour mixture. Pulse with 1-second bursts until the mixture includes a variety of chunks the size of small lima beans, peas, and lentils (about 25 bursts). Transfer the mixture to a large bowl. Or, whisk the dry ingredients together in a large bowl, scatter the butter pieces over the top, and cut in the butter with a pastry blender.

Sprinkle the ice water, 1 tablespoon at a time, over the mixture, tossing gently with a fork, preferably a blending fork, after each addition. Aim each tablespoon of water at a section of the mixture that appears to need more moisture, and continue to add water and toss the mixture until the dough is evenly moist and masses roughly together. The butter pieces should still be visible and remain about the same size.

With your hands, scoop up the dough and transfer it to a lightly floured work surface. Gently pat and coax the

mass into a cohesive dough. (If the dough is sticking to your rolling surface, lift it with a dough scraper.) Gently flatten the dough with your hand (lightly flour the top if it is sticky) into a roughly 7 by 5 by 1 ½-inch rectangle. Lightly flour the work surface (and the top of the dough if necessary), and roll it out into a 16 by 8-inch rectangle about ½ inch thick. As you roll, lightly flour the dough and the work surface as needed; lift and move the dough to make sure it is gliding and expanding on the surface, not sticking to it; and never roll off the edges.

Fold the dough into thirds like a business letter: working from a short end, lift the bottom one-third of the rectangle up over the center and then fold the top third down to cover, forming an 8 by 5 ½-inch rectangle. Rotate the dough 90 degrees, lightly flour the work surface, and again roll the dough out into a 16 by 8-inch rectangle. Fold the dough again into thirds, wrap in plastic wrap, and refrigerate for at least 30 to 40 minutes to firm the butter and relax the pastry before using.

The dough can be refrigerated for up to 3 days. For longer storage, overwrap with aluminum foil, label with the contents and date, and freeze for up to 1 month. Thaw in the refrigerator for at least 8 and up to 24 hours and then use well chilled.

Four Pie Crusts at One Time

With just a few ingredients and a little effort, you can make your own pie crusts in less time than it takes to go out to purchase them. This is one of my all-time favorite pastry recipes because the dough is easy to mix, a dream to roll, and deliciously tender with any filling, sweet or savory. The egg enriches the crust and binds the ingredients together, while the vinegar relaxes the proteins to yield a superb, tender crust. Pie crusts keep well in the freezer, so it is to your advantage to roll out the dough and line pie dishes days in advance. Or, you can roll out the dough, freeze the circles, and then line the pie dishes just before you need them. Directions for both plan-ahead techniques are included in the method.

You are bound to end up with some dough scraps after lining the pans. Gather them up, roll them out about $1/8$ inch thick, and cut out shapes with cookie cutters or a knife. Sprinkle granulated sugar and ground cinnamon over the cutouts and bake in a preheated 350 degree F oven. These pastry cookies will not only create wonderful cookies for the children in the family, but they will also fill their memory banks for years to come. **YIELD: FOUR 10-OUNCE (280-GRAM) DOUGH DISKS, FOR FOUR 9-INCH SINGLE-CRUST PIES OR TWO 9-INCH DOUBLE-CRUST PIES**

4½ CUPS (1¼ POUNDS/570 GRAMS) ALL-PURPOSE FLOUR

1 TABLESPOON PLUS 2 TEASPOONS GRANULATED SUGAR

1½ TEASPOONS SALT

1 LARGE EGG

⅓ CUP (2½ FL OUNCES/75 ML) ICE WATER, PLUS 3 TO 4 TABLESPOONS

2 TEASPOONS VINEGAR, PREFERABLY CIDER

12 OUNCES (3 STICKS/340 GRAMS) COLD UNSALTED BUTTER

⅓ CUP (2 OUNCES/55 GRAMS) COLD SOLID VEGETABLE SHORTENING

Put the flour, sugar, and salt in the bowl of a stand mixer and whisk together by hand. In a small bowl, combine the egg, the ⅓ cup ice water, and the vinegar and beat together lightly with a fork; set aside in the refrigerator. Cut the butter into ¼-inch slices, and cut the shortening into 6 equal pieces. Scatter the butter and shortening pieces over the flour mixture.

With a rubber spatula, toss the flour mixture briefly to coat the butter and shortening with flour. Attach the bowl to the stand mixer, and fit the mixer with the paddle attachment. Wrap a kitchen towel around the back and sides of the mixer bowl, or use a bowl shield to contain the mixture in the bowl, since even the lowest speed causes this amount of flour to fly out of the bowl. Mix on the lowest speed just long enough to break up the butter and shortening pieces and to coat them lightly with the flour, about 30 seconds. The chunks will vary from the size of fava beans to lima beans to peas.

Without delay, resume mixing on the lowest speed while pouring the ice water–egg mixture on the flour in a steady stream—not too slowly or too quickly—taking 10 to 15 seconds. As soon as all of the liquid has been added, stop the mixer. Most of the butter chunks should look almost the way they did when you began mixing. The mixture will appear chunky, messy, and not cohesive. However, touch it and it will feel somewhat moist, but with some loose flour particles and somewhat chunky pieces in the bottom of the bowl. CONTINUED ➤

To bring this amount of dough together, you need to sprinkle on additional ice water, 1 tablespoon at a time, wherever the mixture still feels dry or crumbly. Using your fingertips or a fork (preferably a blending fork), scoop up a large portion of the dry flour particles from the bottom of the bowl and place them on the top. Sprinkle 1 tablespoon of the additional ice water over the mixture and toss briefly. Again, lift up a large portion of the mixture from the bottom of the bowl and place it on top. Sprinkle on another tablespoon of water and toss briefly. Scoop up another large portion of the particles from the bottom of the bowl and place them on top. Sprinkle another tablespoon of the ice water over the mixture and toss again. Scoop again but add more ice water only if needed. To test if the dough is ready to form or more ice water is needed, press a small amount in your hand. If it comes together without falling apart, it is ready. If not, sprinkle on another tablespoon of water and test again.

Tilt the bowl and gently scoop the mixture onto a work surface or a large rimmed baking sheet to contain the crumbly dough and make cleanup easy. Transfer any remaining crumbly bits onto the top and pat gently to form into a single very large mass of dough. Divide the dough into four 10-ounce (280-gram) portions, and form each portion into a disk 5 inches in diameter and ¾ inch thick. Wrap the disks individually in plastic wrap and refrigerate until firm enough to roll, 2 to 4 hours or up to 2 days. For longer storage, overwrap with aluminum foil, label with the contents and date, and freeze for up

to 1 month. Thaw in the refrigerator for several hours or overnight before using. Or, you can store the dough using one of the following techniques.

To line pie dishes ahead: Following the directions on page 27, roll out each dough disk into a 12-inch circle ⅛ to 3/16 inch thick, transfer to a 9-inch glass, aluminum, or foil pie pan; flute the edges of the pastry; and freeze just to firm the dough, 15 to 20 minutes. Then wrap the pastry-lined pie dish securely with plastic wrap, label with the contents and date, and freeze for up to 2 weeks.

To roll out dough circles ahead: Roll out each disk of dough as directed for lining pie pans, stack the circles, separated by sheets of waxed paper, on a baking sheet, and freeze just until firm, about 20 minutes. Wrap plastic wrap around the dough circles and the baking sheet, and then overwrap with aluminum foil, label with the contents and date, and freeze for up to 2 weeks. When needed, remove a circle of dough and set it aside at room temperature just until it is pliable, about 10 minutes. Transfer the dough to a glass, aluminum, or foil pie pan; fit it into the contours of the pan; and flute the edges of the pastry. Return to the freezer for about 15 minutes, and then proceed to make the pie as the recipe directs. Or, use a dough circle for a top crust as directed on page 28.

Bake the pie crusts directly from the freezer as needed, either filling them unbaked or blind baking them partially or fully (page 28) before filling.

Cream Cheese Pastry

This pastry is both foolproof and provides delicious results. It is the perfect dough to store in the freezer to make such desserts as Flag-Raising Mixed-Berry Potpies (page 229) on short notice. Or, use this pastry recipe for making strudels, tarts, or pies, rolling it out on a lightly floured work surface about 1/8 inch thick. To make sublime savory strudels, tarts, or pies with this pastry, omit the sugar and lemon zest. **YIELD: 1 POUND, 9 OUNCES (710 GRAMS) DOUGH**

2 1/4 CUPS (10 1/4 OUNCES/290 GRAMS) ALL-PURPOSE FLOUR

2 TABLESPOONS GRANULATED SUGAR

1 TEASPOON FINELY GRATED LEMON ZEST

1/4 TEASPOON SALT

8 OUNCES (2 STICKS/225 GRAMS) COLD UNSALTED BUTTER, CUT INTO 1/4-INCH SLICES

6 OUNCES (170 GRAMS) COLD CREAM CHEESE, CUT INTO SMALL CUBES

In a food processor, combine the flour, sugar, lemon zest, and salt and pulse 3 or 4 times to blend. Scatter the butter pieces over the flour mixture. Pulse until the mixture is the consistency of cornmeal. Scatter the cream cheese cubes over the mixture and pulse just until the ingredients come together in a ball.

On a clean work surface, divide the dough in half and shape each half into a 5-inch disk about 3/4 inch thick (12 1/2 ounces/355 grams), or divide as directed in individual recipes. Wrap each disk in plastic wrap and refrigerate until firm, about 4 hours, before using.

The dough can be refrigerated for up to 3 days. For longer storage, overwrap with aluminum foil, label with the contents and date, and freeze for up to 2 weeks. Thaw in the refrigerator for 4 hours or up to overnight and then use well chilled as directed in individual recipes.

Three Tart Shells at One Time

This dough can be pressed with the fingertips into pans, rather than rolled, but I find that rolling it out is faster and easier. The recipe is adapted from one I learned in a baking class taught by the talented Pascal Janvier, pastry chef and proprietor of the outstanding Fleur de Cocoa in Los Gatos, California.   YIELD: THREE 12½-OUNCE (355-GRAM) DOUGH DISKS, FOR THREE 9½-INCH TART SHELLS

4½ CUPS (1 POUND, 2 OUNCES/500 GRAMS) CAKE FLOUR

2 CUPS (7 OUNCES/200 GRAMS) POWDERED SUGAR

¼ TEASPOON SALT

11 OUNCES (2¾ STICKS/310 GRAMS) UNSALTED BUTTER, SOFTENED

1 LARGE EGG

1 LARGE EGG YOLK

1 TEASPOON PURE VANILLA EXTRACT

In the bowl of a stand mixer fitted with the paddle attachment, briefly mix together the flour, sugar, and salt on the lowest speed. Stop the mixer, cut the softened butter into about 6 pieces, scatter them over the flour mixture, and resume mixing on the lowest speed. Mix just until the mixture starts to appear lumpy. Stop the mixer and add the egg, egg yolk, and vanilla. Resume mixing on the lowest speed just until the mixture comes together.

Transfer the dough to a work surface. Beginning at the far end, and using the heel of your hand, push a small amount of the dough (about the size of an extra-large egg) away from you, smearing it on the work surface. Repeat with the remaining dough in small amounts. When you've worked all the dough in this manner, give it a couple more strokes to bring it together into a smooth, homogeneous unit. (This kneading technique, described on page 31, is known as *fraisage*.) Divide the dough into three 12 ½-ounce (355-gram) portions, and form each portion into a disk 6 inches in diameter.

At this point, following the directions on page 29, you can roll out each disk into a circle and line a 9 ½ by 1-inch round tart pan. Or, you can wrap the disks separately in plastic wrap and refrigerate for up to 3 days. For longer storage, overwrap with aluminum foil, label with the contents and date, and freeze for up to 1 month. Thaw in the refrigerator for several hours or overnight before using. When ready to use, remove a dough package from the refrigerator and set aside at room temperature until it is still firm yet pliable enough for rolling, 20 to 40 minutes, before using.

Tender Tart Pastry

This is an amazingly easy-to-prepare pastry, with a tender structure and buttery flavor that will elicit praise from anyone who tastes it. I use it for my Rhubarb and Pistachio Tart (page 319) and my Autumn Dried Fruit–Nut Tart (page 198), but it is sure to find more uses in your kitchen.

YIELD: PASTRY FOR ONE 9-INCH SQUARE OR 10¼-INCH ROUND TART SHELL

1 LARGE EGG YOLK

2 TEASPOONS WATER

1 TEASPOON PURE VANILLA EXTRACT

1¼ CUPS (5½ OUNCES/155 GRAMS) ALL-PURPOSE FLOUR

⅓ CUP (1¼ OUNCES/35 GRAMS) POWDERED SUGAR

⅛ TEASPOON SALT

4 OUNCES (1 STICK/115 GRAMS) COLD UNSALTED BUTTER,
    CUT INTO 8 SLICES

In a small bowl, whisk together the egg yolk, water, and vanilla; set aside. In a food processor, combine the flour, sugar, and salt and pulse 3 or 4 times to blend. Scatter the butter pieces over the flour mixture and pulse until the mixture is the consistency of cornmeal.

With the motor running, pour the egg yolk mixture down the feed tube and process just until small clumps form, about 10 seconds. With your hands, scoop out the dough, place on a floured work surface, and gently press together until smooth and cohesive. Shape the dough into a 5-inch disk and use as directed in individual recipes. Or, to use for your own tarts, follow the directions on page 29 for rolling out the pastry and lining a tart pan.

If not using the dough right away, wrap in plastic wrap and refrigerate for up to 3 days. For longer storage, over-wrap with aluminum foil, label with the contents and date, and freeze for up to 1 month. Thaw the dough in the refrigerator for at least 4 hours or up to overnight. Let it stand at room temperature just until it is malleable enough for rolling, 15 to 30 minutes, before using.

Single-Crust Crostata Pastry

Wonderfully pliable, this pastry dough is shaped directly on a baking sheet for my Pecan–Pine Nut Tassie Crostata (page 74) and Rustic Sweet-Potato Crostata (page 232). Use it as the base for your own *crostata* fillings. **YIELD: 12½ OUNCES (355 GRAMS) DOUGH, PASTRY FOR ONE 11-INCH CROSTATA**

1 LARGE EGG YOLK

2 TABLESPOONS WATER

½ TEASPOON PURE VANILLA EXTRACT

1½ CUPS (7 OUNCES/200 GRAMS) ALL-PURPOSE FLOUR

2 TABLESPOONS GRANULATED SUGAR

¼ TEASPOON SALT

3½ OUNCES (¾ STICK PLUS 1 TABLESPOON/100 GRAMS) COLD UNSALTED BUTTER, CUT INTO ½-INCH SLICES

In a small bowl, whisk together the egg yolk, water, and vanilla; set aside. In a food processor, combine the flour, sugar, and salt and pulse 3 or 4 times to blend. Scatter the butter pieces over the flour mixture. Pulse until the mixture has the consistency of coarse meal. Add the egg yolk mixture and pulse just until moist clusters begin to stick together without forming a ball.

Pinch a small portion of the dough between your fingers. If it won't hold together, pulse in additional water, 1 teaspoon at a time. Just when the mixture feels moist (not wet) and ready to come together, scrape the dough out onto a sheet of plastic wrap on your work surface. Gently pat the dough into a ball and then flatten it into a 6-inch disk. Enclose it in the plastic wrap and refrigerate for about 30 minutes or freeze for about 20 minutes, or until it is chilled (not firm) yet still pliable enough to roll, then use as directed in individual recipes. Or, to use for your own recipes, follow the directions on page 31 for rolling out and shaping the pastry for a *crostata*.

If not using the dough right away, refrigerate it in the plastic wrap for up to 2 days. For longer storage, overwrap with aluminum foil, label with the contents and date, and freeze for up to 1 month. Thaw in the refrigerator for several hours or up to overnight, and then leave at room temperature until it is malleable yet still cool to the touch, 15 to 30 minutes, before using.

Chocolate Tart Pastry

Similar to a cookie dough, this simple-to-prepare recipe is quite versatile in making a crisp yet tender tart shell for the Cheery Cherry Chocolate Tart (page 191) and crispy thin crusts for the Butterscotch-Pecan Mini Pies (page 246). For optimum chocolate flavor, use a quality cocoa powder. The aroma of chocolate perfuming the air and the crusts' dry and slightly firm edges are cues that the tart or tartlet shells are finished baking.   **YIELD: ONE 12½ OUNCE (355-GRAM) DOUGH DISK, FOR ONE 9½-INCH OR 10¼-INCH ROUND TART SHELL OR 15 BUTTERSCOTCH-PECAN MINI PIE SHELLS (PAGE 246)**

1 LARGE EGG WHITE

1 TEASPOON PURE VANILLA EXTRACT

1 CUP PLUS 2 TABLESPOONS (5 OUNCES/140 GRAMS) ALL-PURPOSE FLOUR

3 TABLESPOONS UNSWEETENED NATURAL OR DUTCH-PROCESSED COCOA POWDER

3 TABLESPOONS FIRMLY PACKED LIGHT BROWN SUGAR

3 TABLESPOONS GRANULATED SUGAR

⅛ TEASPOON SALT

3 OUNCES (¾ STICK/85 GRAMS) COLD UNSALTED BUTTER, CUT INTO ¼-INCH SLICES

In a small bowl, whisk together the egg white and vanilla; set aside. In a food processor, combine the flour, cocoa powder, sugars, and salt and pulse 3 or 4 times to blend. Scatter the butter pieces over the flour mixture. Pulse until the mixture is the consistency of cornmeal.

With the motor running, pour the egg white mixture down the feed tube and process just until the ingredients start to form a ball. Transfer the dough to a clean work surface. Using the heel of your hand, press the dough together until it is smooth and cohesive. Shape the dough into a disk.

If not using the dough right away, wrap it in plastic wrap and refrigerate for up to 3 days. For longer storage, overwrap with aluminum foil, label with the contents and date, and freeze for up to 2 weeks. Thaw the dough in the refrigerator for at least 4 hours or up to overnight. Let it stand at room temperature just until it is malleable enough to roll, 15 to 30 minutes.

Use as directed in individual recipes. Or, to use for your own tarts, follow the directions on page 29 for rolling out the pastry and lining a tart pan.

Flaky Strudel Pastry

I use this tender pastry for my Minced-Fruit Strudel (page 214) and Pumpkin Strudel (page 193), but it is also a good choice for turnovers and other individual pastries, both sweet and savory. (If using it for hors d'oeuvres or other savories, omit the sugar.)   **YIELD: 1 POUND, 6 OUNCES (625 GRAMS) DOUGH**

1 ¾ CUPS (8 OUNCES/225 GRAMS) ALL-PURPOSE FLOUR

2 TABLESPOONS GRANULATED SUGAR

¼ TEASPOON SALT

8 OUNCES (2 STICKS/225 GRAMS) COLD UNSALTED BUTTER, CUT INTO ¼-INCH SLICES

4 OUNCES (115 GRAMS) COLD CREAM CHEESE, CUT INTO 8 EQUAL CUBES

2 TABLESPOONS SOUR CREAM

In a food processor, combine the flour, sugar, and salt and pulse 3 or 4 times to blend. Scatter the butter pieces, cream cheese cubes, and sour cream over the flour mixture. Pulse with 1-second bursts until the mixture is the consistency of streusel. Transfer the mixture to a clean work surface and gather it into a dough.

Divide the dough in half (each about 11 ounces/310 grams), and form each half into a 6 by 4-inch rectangle. Wrap each rectangle in plastic wrap and refrigerate until firm, 2 to 3 hours or up to 3 days. For longer storage, overwrap with aluminum foil, label with the contents and date, and freeze for up to 1 month. Thaw in the refrigerator for at least 4 hours or up to overnight.

Before using, let the chilled pastry stand at room temperature for about 5 minutes. This allows the dough to warm just enough so it will roll out smoothly without cracking.

Croissant Pastry ASAP

The work needed to make this pastry dough *is* ASAP. It's the time between the steps that isn't. But your patience will be rewarded with pastry that is nearly as flaky as the classic version. Making croissant pastry is similar to making its cousin, puff pastry (page 367), which involves incorporating a "butter package" and rolling and folding the dough several times, with resting periods in between. The primary difference between the two is that croissant pastry calls for yeast. The result is a buttery-tasting flaky yeast pastry with a tender, sweet coffee-cake-like quality. It develops a nice puffy structure, though no dramatic lift, as it bakes, which makes it perfect for flaky buns (page 174), twisted sticks (page 175), and, yes, even croissants.   **YIELD: 2½ POUNDS (1.13 KG) DOUGH**

12 OUNCES (3 STICKS/340 GRAMS) COLD UNSALTED BUTTER

3¾ CUPS (1 POUND, 1 OUNCE/485 GRAMS) UNBLEACHED
    ALL-PURPOSE FLOUR

3 TABLESPOONS GRANULATED SUGAR

1 TABLESPOON (1 ENVELOPE PLUS ¾ TEASPOON)
    INSTANT YEAST

2 TEASPOONS SALT

¾ CUP (6 FL OUNCES/180 ML) WHOLE MILK

¼ CUP (2 FL OUNCES/60 ML) WATER

1 TABLESPOON CANOLA OIL

1 TEASPOON PURE VANILLA EXTRACT

Cut the butter into ½-inch-thick slices. Then cut each slice in half lengthwise to yield 12 to 16 oblong chunks per stick of butter. Since it takes time to cut this large amount of butter into pieces, once you have cut them, place them on a baking sheet and refrigerate for at least 10 minutes to retain their chill and firm up after handling.

In a medium bowl, combine ¾ cup (3¼ ounces/90 grams) of the flour, the sugar, the yeast, and the salt and whisk to blend. In a glass measuring cup, whisk together the milk, water, oil, and vanilla. Add the milk mixture to the flour mixture and stir just to blend; set nearby.

Place the remaining 3 cups (13¾ ounces/390 grams) flour in the bowl of a stand mixer. Scatter the butter pieces over the flour. With a rubber spatula, toss briefly to coat the butter pieces with the flour. Attach the bowl to the mixer, and fit the mixer with the paddle attachment.

Wrap a kitchen towel around the back and sides of the mixer bowl or use a bowl shield to contain the mixture in the bowl, since even the lowest speed causes this amount of flour to fly out of the bowl. Mix on the lowest speed just long enough for the flour to coat the butter lightly, about 15 seconds. The majority of the chunks should be from the size of lima beans to the size of unshelled almonds and should not be totally incorporated.

Without delay, resume the mixer's lowest speed while pouring the yeast mixture on the flour mixture in a steady stream, not too slowly or too quickly, taking 10 to 15 seconds. As soon as all of the liquid has been added, stop the mixer. Most of the butter chunks should look almost the way they did when you began mixing. The mixture should appear chunky, messy, and not cohesive. However, touch it and it will feel somewhat moist, but with some loose flour particles and somewhat chunky pieces in the bottom of the bowl.

Using your fingertips, scoop up a large portion of the dry flour particles from the bottom of the bowl, place them on top of the rough mass, and press them together in an attempt to form a dough. Don't be concerned if some dry particles remain.

Dust a work surface and your hands lightly with flour (1 to 1½ tablespoons). Transfer the rough mass to the work surface and press it into a cohesive 8-inch round mass. Place the dough in a large resealable plastic CONTINUED ▸

bag, or in a large bowl and cover it tightly with plastic wrap, and set it aside in a warm place (about 70 degrees F) until it is puffy and has grown 1 to 1 ½ inches higher, 1 to 2 hours. Refrigerate the dough, still in its bag or bowl, for at least 4 hours or up to overnight.

To layer the dough: Transfer the dough from the refrigerator (it will be fairly firm) to the work surface to begin the process of distributing the butter throughout the pastry to create the flaky layers. Lightly flour the surface and the top of the dough. Roll out the dough slowly, pressing on it firmly with the rolling pin and using even strokes, into a rectangle close to 16 by 8 inches and ½ inch thick. As you work, lightly dust the work surface and the top of the dough as needed with flour. With your fingertips, gently coax the dough to straighten the edges and square off the corners, and dab any areas of sticky butter with a little flour. Starting at a short end, fold the dough into thirds like a business letter: lift the bottom one-third of the rectangle up over the center and then fold the top third down to cover. This is called a single fold, or first "turn," and the dough won't be smooth.

Rotate the dough 90 degrees to the left so that the flap on top opens to the left like a book. Roll out the dough again on the lightly floured surface to a 16 by 8-inch rectangle. (If at any time the dough or the butter pieces in the dough start to soften, wrap the dough in plastic wrap or aluminum foil and freeze for 10 to 20 minutes to chill the butter and rest the dough. The butter pieces must remain layered throughout the dough to ensure flaky pastry.) Brush off any excess flour. With a short end facing you, again fold the rectangle into thirds like a business letter. You have just completed the second turn, and you will notice that the pastry has taken form. Wrap the pastry securely in plastic wrap, overwrap in aluminum foil, and refrigerate for at least 4 hours or preferably overnight. It will keep in the refrigerator for up to 2 days.

PDQ (Pretty Darn Quick) Puff Pastry

To ensure the best results, you must respect the proportions of the two flours used here. And because volume measures can vary among flour brands, weighing the flours is the most reliable way to do that. I have included approximate volume measures here, too, in case you lack a scale. This pastry is used to make Creamy Mint Napoleons (page 337) and Rhubarb, Apple, and Raspberry Jalousie (page 161), but it would work beautifully for nearly any recipe calling for puff pastry. **YIELD: 2 POUNDS, 7 OUNCES (1.11 KG) DOUGH**

1 POUND (4 STICKS/455 GRAMS) COLD UNSALTED BUTTER

12 OUNCES (340 GRAMS) UNBLEACHED ALL-PURPOSE FLOUR (2½ TO 2¾ CUPS)

4 OUNCES (115 GRAMS) CAKE FLOUR (SCANT 1 CUP)

¾ TEASPOON SALT

1 CUP (8 FL OUNCES/240 ML) ICE WATER

Cut the butter into ½-inch slices. Since it takes time to cut this large amount of butter into pieces, once you have cut them, place the pieces on a baking sheet and refrigerate for at least 10 minutes so they retain their chill and remain firm after handling.

Place the flours and salt in the bowl of a stand mixer; whisk by hand to blend. Scatter the butter pieces over the flour mixture. Have the ice water in a liquid measuring cup.

Attach the bowl to the mixer, and fit the mixer with the paddle attachment. Wrap a kitchen towel around the back and sides of the mixer bowl or use a bowl shield to contain the mixture in the bowl, since even the lowest speed causes this amount of flour to fly out of the bowl. Beat on the lowest speed just long enough for the flour to coat the butter lightly, about 10 seconds. The majority of the chunks should be the size of fava or lima beans. Without delay, resume the mixer's lowest speed while pouring the ice water on the flour in a steady stream, not too slowly or too quickly, taking 10 to 15 seconds. As soon as all of the water has been added, stop the mixer. Most of the butter chunks should look almost the way they did when you began mixing. The mixture will appear chunky,

messy, and not cohesive. However, touch it and it will feel somewhat moist, but with some loose flour particles in the bottom of the bowl.

Using your fingertips, scoop up a large portion of the dry flour particles from the bottom of the bowl, place them on top of the rough mass, and press them together in an attempt to form a dough. Don't be concerned if some dry particles remain.

Dust your hands and a work surface lightly with flour. Transfer the rough mass to the work surface. Pat it into an 8½ by 5½ by 1½-inch rectangle. Roll out the dough into a 16 by 10-inch rectangle, dusting lightly with flour if necessary. With your fingertips, gently coax the dough to straighten the edges and square off the corners, and dab any areas of sticky butter with a little flour. Starting at a short end, fold the dough into thirds like a business letter: working from a short end, lift the bottom one-third of the rectangle up over the center and then fold the top third down to cover. This is called a single fold, or first "turn," and the dough won't be smooth.

Rotate the dough 90 degrees to the left so that the flap on top opens to the left like a book. Roll out the dough again on the lightly floured surface to a 15 by 8-inch rectangle. Brush off any excess flour. With a short end facing you, repeat folding the rectangle into thirds like a business letter. Now the mixture is beginning to look like a dough, and you have just completed the second single fold, or second turn. CONTINUED ▶

Wrap the dough in aluminum foil and refrigerate for 20 minutes. You have completed two single folds in a short time, so a short resting time should be enough to chill and partially firm the dough. If at any time the dough resists rolling or the butter becomes too soft, you need to return the dough to the refrigerator to chill a bit longer.

Remove the dough from the refrigerator, and lightly dust the work surface and the dough with flour. Place the dough so that the last fold is at a right angle to you and the flap on top opens to the left like a book. Roll out the dough again on a lightly floured surface into a 16 by 8-inch rectangle. Brush off any excess flour. With a short end facing you, fold the short end closest to you up over the center of the rectangle and fold the other short end down over the center, again resembling a business letter. You have just completed the third single fold, or third turn, and you will notice the pastry is beginning to take form.

Position the dough again so that the last fold is at a right angle to you and the flap on top opens to the left like a book. Repeat the rolling and folding as directed previously. This is the fourth and final turn. Rewrap the dough in the foil and place it in the refrigerator to rest for at least 1 hour to chill it thoroughly before shaping it for use.

After the dough has rested, roll it into a more manageable shape, such as an 11 by 9-inch rectangle. Wrap in plastic wrap and refrigerate for up to 2 days. For longer storage, overwrap with aluminum foil, label with the contents and date, and freeze for up to 2 months. Thaw the dough in the refrigerator for about 24 hours before using.

Crème Anglaise

This classic sauce deserves to be high on your list of sauces you can't live without. Perhaps I'm partial to it because I was honestly raised on this "custard." My mother made it often in my early years to pour over Jell-O! And we never had an apple pie without a pitcher of this homemade sauce for dressing up each serving. **YIELD: ABOUT 1¼ CUPS**

1 CUP (8 FL OUNCES/240 ML) WHOLE MILK

¼ CUP (1¾ OUNCES/50 GRAMS) GRANULATED SUGAR, DIVIDED

3 LARGE (¼ CUP/2 FL OUNCES/60 ML) EGG YOLKS

1 TEASPOON PURE VANILLA EXTRACT

2 TEASPOONS GRAND MARNIER (OPTIONAL)

1 TEASPOON FINELY GRATED ORANGE ZEST (OPTIONAL)

Set a fine-mesh sieve on top of a 1-quart bowl and set aside for straining the custard after cooking. In a heavy 1½-quart saucepan, combine the milk and 2 tablespoons of the sugar; set aside. In a small bowl, whisk the egg yolks until blended, then whisk in the remaining 2 tablespoons sugar; set aside.

Place the saucepan over medium heat and bring the milk just to a boil. Remove from the heat and pour about half of the hot milk mixture into the egg yolk mixture while whisking constantly. Pour the combined mixtures back into the saucepan and whisk to combine. Return the pan to medium-low heat and cook, stirring constantly over the entire bottom of the pan with a wooden spoon, until an instant-read thermometer registers 165 to 170 degrees F, or until the custard is thick enough to coat the spoon and leave a clear path when your finger is drawn down its center, about 45 seconds. If you are not using a thermometer, look for steam, which signals that the mixture is approaching the correct temperature. Do not allow the mixture to boil or it will curdle.

Remove from the heat and quickly pour through the sieve. Set aside for 10 minutes, stirring occasionally. Stir in the vanilla and Grand Marnier and orange zest, if using, and then cover and refrigerate. The sauce thickens slightly as it cools. Serve within 2 to 3 days.

Lemon Curd

Use this smooth, tangy curd as a filling for cakes and tarts, or you can even spread it on scones warm from the oven. In this book, it is used in Frozen Lemon Glacier (page 140) and Flaky Lemon-Marshmallow Turnovers (page 254). **YIELD: 1½ CUPS (12 FL OUNCES/360 ML)**

2 LARGE EGGS

2 LARGE EGG YOLKS

½ CUP (3½ OUNCES/100 GRAMS) GRANULATED SUGAR

6 TABLESPOONS (3 FL OUNCES/90 ML) STRAINED FRESH LEMON JUICE

2 TEASPOONS FINELY GRATED LEMON ZEST

3 OUNCES (¾ STICK/85 GRAMS) COLD UNSALTED BUTTER, CUT INTO 6 PIECES

Set a fine-mesh sieve over a shallow 1½-quart bowl; set aside. Place the eggs and egg yolks in a heavy 1½-quart saucepan and whisk to combine. Add the sugar, lemon juice, and lemon zest, whisking to combine after each addition. Add the butter pieces, place the pan over medium heat, and cook, stirring constantly over the entire bottom of the pan with a silicone spatula, until the mixture begins to develop body and thicken, 2 to 3 minutes.

As the butter melts, it will become incorporated into the mixture. Watch the pan closely to make sure the mixture never boils. Boiling can cause it to curdle and the butter to separate from the curd. The curd is ready when an instant-read thermometer registers 160 degrees F. Without delay, remove from the heat and pour through the sieve, pushing it through with the spatula.

Cover with plastic wrap, pressing it directly onto the surface of the curd to keep the top from drying out. This also ensures the curd will be perfectly smooth and thick when cold. If it is left uncovered, it can form lumps. Poke 5 to 7 slits in the plastic with the tip of a knife to allow steam to escape, let cool, and then refrigerate for at least 3 hours or up to 10 days.

Sweet Potato Puree

Southern bakers are famous for their sweet potato pie, which looks and tastes a bit like pumpkin pie. I use the hearty tuber with equal success as the base for the spices-laced filling in my Rustic Sweet-Potato Crostata (page 232). **YIELD: ABOUT 1 CUP (8 OUNCES/225 GRAMS)**

1 LARGE (10 OUNCE/280 GRAMS) GARNET OR JEWEL SWEET
    POTATO (YAM)

Pierce the sweet potato a few times with the tip of a small paring knife. Place the sweet potato, uncovered, in the microwave on 100 percent power for 8 minutes. Check for doneness by piercing the potato with the tip of the paring knife. If the sweet potato is tender, set it aside until it is cool enough to handle. If not, return it to the microwave for 2 minutes more, or just until it tests tender.

With the paring knife, slit the skin down the center of the sweet potato, scoop the flesh into a small bowl, and discard the skin. Mash the flesh with a large fork or potato masher. Set aside to cool.

Measure 1 cup (8 ounces/225 grams) of the puree for the crostata. (Save any leftover puree to add to the broth of a favorite vegetable soup.) Use right away, or wrap in plastic wrap and refrigerate for up to 2 days. For longer storage, overwrap with aluminum foil, label with the contents and date, and freeze for up to 1 month. Thaw at room temperature for about 1 hour.

Red-Hot Poached Pears

A poached pear, a simple yet elegant dessert, becomes a dramatic addition to any number of desserts the moment you cut into it. The sweet, spicy poached pear is a beautiful red on the outside, yet maintains its pristine white interior. I am fond of partnering the poached fruit with one of my home-baked items, such as Red Velvet Cake Roll (page 85), Walnut Breton Cake (page 68), Double-Cranberry Mini Cakes (page 255), Heavenly Brownie-on-Shortbread Bars (page 64), or a medley of cookies.

You can use this same syrup, which is enough for poaching 1½ to 2 pounds (680 to 910 grams) of fruit, for poaching other fruits, too (for example, 3 to 4 medium apples weigh 1½ to 2 pounds, and 9 fresh figs weigh 1½ pounds.) When poaching any fruit, you want to cook it just enough to soften it. If you overcook it, it will be disappointingly mushy. Poached fruit can be refrigerated in its syrup for a few days. Freeze leftover syrup to poach another batch of fruit at another time. **YIELD: 6 SERVINGS**

6 FIRM BUT RIPE BOSC PEARS

½ LEMON

4 CUPS (32 FL OUNCES/960 ML) WATER

1½ CUPS (10½ OUNCES/300 GRAMS) GRANULATED SUGAR

⅓ CUP (ABOUT 1 OUNCE/30 GRAMS) RED HOT CINNAMON CANDIES

2 TABLESPOONS FRESH LEMON JUICE

½ VANILLA BEAN

1 STRIP LEMON PEEL, 4 INCHES LONG

1 CINNAMON STICK, 2½ INCHES LONG

⅔ CUP (5½ FL OUNCES/165 ML) HEAVY CREAM, LIGHTLY WHIPPED

Peel the pears, leaving the stems intact. Using a melon baller, scoop out the core from the bottom (blossom end) of each pear. To prevent discoloration, rub the pear surfaces with the cut side of the lemon half.

Select a large pot that will accommodate the pears in a single layer and add the water, sugar, candies, lemon juice, vanilla bean, lemon peel, and cinnamon stick to it. Place over medium heat and bring just to a boil, stirring to dissolve the sugar and candy. Add the pears, reduce the heat to low, and bring to a simmer. Cover the surface of the pears with a paper towel to keep the fruits immersed in the syrup. Cook the pears at a slow simmer, turning them occasionally in the syrup so that they cook evenly, 7 to 20 minutes (the cooking time depends on the size and degree of ripeness of the pears). The fruit should be just tender when pierced with the point of a paring knife but still have some resistance.

Remove from the heat and let the pears cool in the cooking syrup for about 1 hour (they will continue to cook). Using a slotted spoon, transfer the pears to a sturdy container with a tight-fitting cover. Remove the vanilla bean, lemon peel strip, and cinnamon stick from the syrup and discard them. Pour in enough syrup just to cover the pears, cover the container, and refrigerate until serving. The pears will keep for up to 4 days.

When ready to serve, gently lift the pears from the syrup with a slotted spoon to a dish. In a medium saucepan, boil the syrup until it is reduced by at least half, then remove from the heat and let cool until just warm or room temperature. Serve each pear with some of the syrup and a dallop of whipped cream.

Dried Plum–Armagnac Purée

I spread this sweet, dark puree between the layers of a banana cake (page 312) and use it to line the bottom of individual baked custards (page 263). It would also make a delicious filling for my Bohemian Kolaches (page 171).   **YIELD: ABOUT 1⅓ CUPS (ABOUT 9 OUNCES/255 GRAMS)**

2 OOLONG TEABAGS
2 CUPS (16 FL OUNCES/480 ML) WATER
30 PITTED (9 OUNCES/255 GRAMS) DRIED PRUNE PLUMS
2 TABLESPOONS ARMAGNAC OR OTHER BRANDY
¼ CUP (1¾ OUNCES/50 GRAMS) GRANULATED SUGAR

Place the tea bags in a teapot. Bring the water to a boil, add to the teapot, and let the tea steep for 5 minutes; discard the tea bags. Place the prune plums in a deep 1½-quart bowl, add the warm tea, and let soak for about 1 hour. Drain the prune plums, discarding the soaking liquid.

On a cutting board, coarsely chop the prunes with a cleaver or a 6- to 7-inch *santoku* knife (page 42) until you have a slightly sticky, smooth, thick puree. Transfer to a bowl and mix in the Armagnac and sugar. Use right away, or pack into a sturdy covered container and refrigerate for up to 3 days or freeze for up to 2 weeks. Thaw at room temperature.

PART FOUR

Sources

ONE OF THE MOST PLEASURABLE parts of baking is discovering new ingredients and equipment. The first places to shop for these items should always be your local kitchenware and specialty-foods stores. But since it's not possible for retail shops to stock every product available, I've made sure you'll have everything necessary to prepare my recipes by compiling this list of purveyors who will ship you what you need. To simplify your shopping, the information that accompanies some of the sources includes references to items used to prepare the recipes in this book.

Even when you're not seeking ingredients and equipment for a particular recipe, I predict you'll have fun window-shopping online. Whether you're getting ready to bake for a special occasion or equipping yourself to bake occasionally, I hope you'll enjoy using and exploring these wonderful resources as much as I do.

American Almond Products Company
103 Walworth Street
Brooklyn, NY 11205
800.825.6663
www.americanalmond.com

Home-baking ingredients, including nut pastes, marzipan, and flavored toppings and fillings (such as poppy seed).

American Egg Board
1460 Renaissance Drive
Park Ridge, IL 60068
847.296.7043
www.aeb.org

A wealth of information about eggs and egg products, including nutritional and safety guidelines.

Ateco
36 Sea Cliff Avenue
Glen Cove, NY 11542
800.645.7170
www.atecousa.com

All types of cake-decorating tools, such as pastry bags and tips, and other specialty baking accessories, plus extensive online instruction on decorating techniques.

Bakers Cash and Carry
367 West Paxton Avenue
Salt Lake City, UT 84101
801.487.3300
www.bakerscandc.com

Supplies for making and decorating cakes and several brands of chocolate in quantities for home bakers, some at competitive prices.

Beryl's Cake Decorating
and Pastry Supplies
P.O. Box 1584
North Springfield, VA 22151
800.488.2749
www.beryls.com

Extensive line of American, British, and French cake-decorating and pastry supplies. High-quality tools, huge assortment of cupcake liners and other paper goods, 22- and 24-karat gold leaf and gold dust, food colors, chocolate, Kosher products, pastry tampers, and many items you may have only dreamed of until now.

Blue Diamond Growers
1802 C Street
P.O. Box 1768
Sacramento, CA 95811
916.442.0771
www.bluediamond.com

Natural and flavored almonds in many forms, almond milk, and almond paste in a 7-pound can.

Bob's Red Mill Natural Foods
5209 SE International Way
Milwaukie, OR 97222
800.349.2173
www.bobsredmill.com

Over 400 products, including whole-grain flours, nut flours, a variety of sugars (maple), dried fruits, coconut in a choice of forms (including flour, flakes, shreds), rolled oats, grains, seeds, nuts, and spices. Many of Bob's items are also carried nationally in supermarkets and health-food, grocery, and specialty-foods stores.

Bridge Kitchenware
711 Third Avenue (enter on 45th)
New York, NY 10017
212.688.4220
www.bridgekitchenware.com

A broad array of imported professional-quality bakeware, tools, and pastry equipment.

Cachecreek Lavender Company
3430 Madrone Street
Rumsey, CA 95679
800.323.0063
www.cachecreeklavender.com

Culinary lavender grown in Northern California and sold as dried lavender flowers, lavender sugar, and lavender salt.

ChefTools
309 South Cloverdale Street C35
Seattle, WA 98108
866.716.2433
www.cheftools.com

Carries major appliance, bakeware, and utensil brands, as well as spices, seasonings, and edible decorations.

Chocolates El Rey
800.357.3999
www.chocolates-elrey.com

Family-owned Venezuelan company that sells quarter-sized disks, bars, blocks, and nibs. The chocolate selection includes white chocolate and milk and dark chocolate made exclusively from Venezuelan cacao.

Chocosphere
877.992.4626
www.chocosphere.com

An Internet-only chocolate shop with an enormous offering of products manufactured by thirty-eight chocolatiers from around the world.

Dagoba
1105 Benson Way
Ashland, OR 97520
800.393.6075
www.dagobachocolate.com

Organic chocolate bars, drops, syrup, and cocoa powder for bakers.

Duck Products
800.321.0253
www.duckproducts.com

Click on Non-Adhesive Shelf Liners to find material for keeping baked items in place during transport (page 24).

Focus Products Group
www.focuspg.com

Source for Chicago Metallic checkerboard cake kit (page 124). Click on the Where to Buy Chicago Metallic link in the Chicago Metallic section of this Web site for a list of stores and sites that carry the kit.

Fog City News
455 Market Street
San Francisco, CA 94105
415.543.7400
www.fogcitynews.com

A combination newsstand and chocolate shop that imports hundreds of premium chocolate bars from around the world. Detailed computer database enables the staff to discuss the flavor nuances of various chocolates with customers.

Ghirardelli Chocolate Company
1111 139th Avenue
San Leandro, CA 94578
888.402.6262
www.ghirardelli.com

Manufacturers of an extensive line of chocolate bars, chips, and cocoa products for baking. Retail sources are listed and some items are available online.

Giusto's
344 Littlefield Avenue
South San Francisco, CA 94080
866.972.6879
www.giustos.com

Family-owned mill producing quality organic flours of many types; also carries spices, oils, sea salts, and other ingredients for home bakers.

Green & Black's USA
389 Interpace Parkway
Parsippany, NJ 07054
877.299.1254
www.greenandblacks.com

U.S. head office of a U.K. manufacturer of organic chocolate and cocoa for baking, with retail sources listed on the Web site.

Guittard Chocolate Company
10 Guittard Road
Burlingame, CA 94010
800.468.2462
www.guittard.com

Family owned and operated since 1868; shop online for chocolate bars, chocolate wafers (pistoles), cocoa powder, and cocoa nibs.

Housewares & Beyond
401 West Route 59 (in Atrium Plaza)
Monsey, NY 10952
888.352.1238
www.housewaresandbeyond.com

Large collection of tools and bakeware and extensive line of paper party goods.

India Tree
1421 Elliott Avenue West
Seattle, WA 98119
800.369.4848
www.indiatree.com

Large selection of decorative sugars, food colorings, candied flowers, and sweet and savory seasonings.

J. B. Prince
36 East 31st Street
New York, NY 10016
800.473.0577
www.jbprince.com

Mind-boggling online catalog of fine chef's tools and equipment from around the world, including Pullman loaf pans and a big variety of Flexipan brand silicone molds for everything from muffins to savarins.

Kerekes Bakery and
Restaurant Equipment
6103 15th Avenue
Brooklyn, NY 11219
800.525.5556
www.bakedeco.com

*An enormous inventory of large and small bakery
and pastry-making equipment, tools, and supplies,
including silicone, disposable, and metal baking
pans and molds and storage containers.*

King Arthur Flour
135 Route 5 South (flagship store)
Norwich, VT 05055
800.827.6836
Baker's Hotline: 802.649.3717
www.kingarthurflour.com
www.bakerscatalog.com

*Visit the store or shop online for chocolate,
bakeware, ginger, gold leaf, yeast, rotary
nut mill (catalog #8666), giant spatula,
2½-inch silicone pastry roller, popover pans,
bake-and-take covered pans, scales, digital
timer, Everbake nonstick spray, and, of course,
a wide variety of flours.*

La Cuisine
323 Cameron Street
Alexandria, VA 22314
800.521.1176
www.lacuisineus.com

*A good selection of pastry tools and bakeware,
ceramics, Hammersong cutters, candied and dried
fruits, flavored sugars, couverture chocolates, and
European flavor essences (including pistachio).*

Market Hall Foods
5655 College Avenue
Oakland, CA 94618
888.952.4005
www.rockridgemarkethall.com

*A group of stores with a retail location and
online shopping, including candied flowers
and fruits, baking chocolate in pellets and
small drops, hard-to-find nut oils, and varietal
peppercorns. If you don't see what you want,
they will try to find it for you.*

Melissa's World Variety Produce
P.O. Box 21127
Los Angeles, CA 90021
800.588.0151
www.melissas.com

*Huge variety of organic and exotic fruits and
vegetables available through the Web site or at
retail stores listed there, along with a wealth of
information about selection, storage, nutritional
data, and preparation of each item.*

New York Cake Supplies
56 West 22nd Street
New York, NY 10010
800.942.2539, fax 212.675.7099
www.nycake.com

*Well-stocked store that meets the baking and
cake-decorating needs of the home and professional
baker, including Wilton merchandise, assorted
bakeware, food colorings, tools, chocolates, and
cutters. Order by phone or fax only.*

Parrish's Cake Decorating Supplies
225 West 146th Street
Gardena, CA 90248
800.736.8443
www.parrishsmagicline.com

*Major source of Magic Line baking pans in a
big array of sizes (from 4 inches in diameter),
shapes, and depths. All pans have straight sides,
and some have removable bottoms. Also, food
colorings (powders, pastes, and gels), pastry bags
and tips, cardboard rounds, spatulas, and other
professional tools. Call to request a catalog, then
order by mail or phone.*

Penzeys Ltd. Spice House
19300 West Janacek Court
Brookfield, WI 53008
800.741.7787
www.penzeys.com

*A vast inventory of top-quality spices, herbs, and
extracts, including exotic items and spice blends
available in quantities from 1 ounce and up. Web
site offers online catalog and list of retail locations
throughout the United States.*

The Perfect Purée of Napa Valley
2700 Napa Valley Corporate Drive, Suite L
Napa, CA 94558
800.556.3707
www.perfectpuree.com

*Purees in a multitude of common and exotic
fruit flavors shipped frozen. Also markets fruit
concentrates and citrus zests.*

Previn
2044 Rittenhouse Square
Philadelphia, PA 19103
888.285.9547, fax 215.985.0323
www.previninc.com

*Extensive line of professional pastry tools,
cake-decorating equipment, pans, molds, and
more. Order by phone or fax only.*

Scharffen Berger Chocolate Maker
914 Heinz Avenue
Berkeley, CA 94710
800.930.4528
www.scharffenberger.com

Chocolate bars, cocoa powder, and cocoa nibs.

Surfas Restaurant Supply
and Gourmet Food
8824 National Boulevard
Culver City, CA 90232
866.799.4770
www.surfasonline.com

*Pastry tools; chocolates for decorating and baking;
an extensive assortment of Magic Line and other
cake, springform, tube, sheet, and muffin pans;
paper products; disposable rigid aluminum foil
cups; and much more. The business card says it
all: "chef's paradise."*

Sur La Table
5701 Sixth Avenue South, Suite 486
Seattle, WA 98108
800.243.0852
www.surlatable.com

*A home baker can find everything from tools and
pans (oversized aluminum blending fork, Chicago
Metallic checkerboard cake kit) to tabletop
accessories. Order online or from print catalog or
shop at retail stores across the country.*

Sweet Celebrations
P.O. Box 39426
Edina, MN 55439
800.328.6722
www.sweetc.com

Formerly known as Maid of Scandinavia; hard-to-find Scandinavian molds and baking ingredients, all types of bakeware, dragées and other items for decorating, and cupcake liners in many sizes and patterns.

Trader Joe's
www.traderjoes.com

A national retail chain with an excellent, reasonably priced selection of nuts for baking (pistachio nuts, pine nuts, macadamia nuts, walnuts, hazelnuts, almonds, and pecans).

The Vanilla Company
P.O. Box 3206
Santa Cruz, CA 95063
800.757.7511
www.vanilla.com

A business with a strong social conscience. In addition to excellent organic vanilla extract (bottles in a variety of sizes) and vanilla beans from several sources around the world, you can purchase vanilla paste and vanilla salt.

The White Lily Foods Company
4740 Burbank Road
Memphis, TN 38118
800.595.1380
www.whitelily.com

Southern soft-wheat flour makes White Lily flour a preferred choice for certain cakes, biscuits, and cream puffs. Products mostly available in specialty-foods stores, with some products available for online ordering.

Williams-Sonoma
3250 Van Ness Avenue
San Francisco, CA 94109
P.O. Box 7456
San Francisco, CA 94120
877.812.6235
www.williams-sonoma.com

Known for their wide range of excellent-quality baking tools (spritz cookie press), baking equipment, bakeware (including straight-sided square pans and a line of nonstick pans), knives, specialty ingredients (Nielsen-Massey vanilla extract), and knowledgeable sales personnel. Retail stores are nationwide (Bak-klene nonstick spray is available only in the retail stores). Both printed and online catalog available.

Wilton Industries
2240 West 75th Street, 1B
Woodridge, IL 60517
800.794.5866
www.wilton.com

Decorating books, baking supplies, specialty shaped pans (licensed characters), pastry bags and tips, fun accessories, stencils, sets of cutters, candles, silicone molds, and a wide selection of invitations and party goods for celebratory occasions. All items available by mail, and some items sold in hobby stores across the United States.

Volume and Weight Measures

American, Imperial, and Metric Equivalents

Volume Equivalents   To measure liquids, American cooks typically use measuring spoons (teaspoons/tsp and tablespoons/T) and measuring cups. The latter include continuous markings for cups and fluid ounces (fl oz) printed vertically on the side. The imperial system used by British cooks uses the same fluid ounces.

AMERICAN	METRIC	IMPERIAL/AMERICAN
¼ tsp	1.25 ml	—
½ tsp	2.5 ml	—
1 tsp	5 ml	—
½ T (1 ½ tsp)	7.5 ml	—
1 T (3 tsp)	15 ml	—
2 T	30 ml	1 fl oz
2½ T	37.5 ml	1¼ fl oz
3 T	45 ml	1½ fl oz
3½ T	52.5 ml	1¾ fl oz
¼ cup (4 T)	60 ml	2 fl oz
⅓ cup (5 T)	75 ml	2½ fl oz
⅜ cup (6 T)	90 ml	3 fl oz
½ cup (8 T)	120 ml	4 fl oz
⅝ cup (10 T)	150 ml	5 fl oz
⅔ cup (11 T)	165 ml	5½ fl oz
¾ cup (12 T)	180 ml	6 fl oz
⅞ cup (14 T)	210 ml	7 fl oz
1 cup (16 T/US ½ pint)	240 ml	8 fl oz
1¼ cups	300 ml	10 fl oz (UK ½ pint)
1⅓ cups	315 ml	10½ fl oz
1⅜ cups	330 ml	11 fl oz
1½ cups	360 ml	12 fl oz
1⅝ cups	390 ml	13 fl oz
1⅔ cups	—	13½ fl oz
1¾ cups	420 ml	14 fl oz
2 cups (US 1 pint)	480 ml	16 fl oz
2½ cups	600 ml	20 fl oz (UK 1 pint)
4 cups (US 1 quart)	960 ml	32 fl oz

Weight Equivalents   Most scales are marked in ounces and grams, but if your scale weighs only ounces or grams, this conversion table will prove invaluable. The metric weights given here are not exact equivalents. For example, the true value of 1 ounce (oz) is 28.35 grams (g), but for the sake of simplification, the figure has been rounded to 30 grams. (To convert ounces to grams, multiply the number of ounces by 28.35.) Most scales available to home bakers register rounded equivalents to make measuring easier. This rounding will not affect your baking results because the balance of the ingredients will be consistent.

AMERICAN/IMPERIAL	METRIC
¼ oz	7 g
½ oz	15 g
¾ oz	20 g
1 oz	30 g
1¼ oz	35 g
1½ oz	40 g
1¾ oz	50 g
2 oz	55 g
2¼ oz	65 g
2½ oz	70 g
2¾ oz	75 g
3 oz	85 g
3¼ oz	90 g
3½ oz	100 g
3¾ oz	105 g
4 oz	115 g
4¼ oz	120 g
4½ oz	130 g
4¾ oz	135 g
5 oz	140 g
5¼ oz	150 g
5½ oz	155 g

CONTINUED ▶

Weight Equivalents continued

AMERICAN/IMPERIAL	METRIC
5¾ oz	160 g
6 oz	170 g
6¼ oz	175 g
6½ oz	185 g
7 oz	200 g
7¼ oz	210 g
7½ oz	215 g
8 oz	225 g
8¼ oz	230 g
8½ oz	240 g
8¾ oz	250 g
9 oz	255 g
9¼ oz	260 g
9½ oz	270 g
10 oz	280 g
10¼ oz	290 g
10½ oz	300 g
11 oz	310 g
11½ oz	325 g
12 oz	340 g
12¼ oz	350 g
12½ oz	355 g
13 oz	370 g
13½ oz	385 g
13¾ oz	390 g
14 oz	400 g
14½ oz	415 g
15 oz	430 g
15½ oz	445 g
16 oz (1 lb)	455 g

Weights for Some Common Ingredients

ALL-PURPOSE FLOUR, UNSIFTED (SPOON AND SWEEP)

	OUNCES	GRAMS
¼ cup	1	30
⅓ cup	1½	40
½ cup	2¼	65
1 cup	4½	130
2 cups	9	255

CAKE FLOUR, UNSIFTED (SPOON AND SWEEP)

	OUNCES	GRAMS
¼ cup	1	30
⅓ cup	1½	40
½ cup	2¼	60
1 cup	4	130
2 cups	8	225

GRANULATED SUGAR, UNSIFTED (SPOON AND SWEEP)

	OUNCES	GRAMS
¼ cup	1¾	50
⅓ cup	2¼	65
½ cup	3½	100
1 cup	7	200
2 cups	14	400

POWDERED SUGAR, UNSIFTED (SPOON AND SWEEP)

	OUNCES	GRAMS
¼ cup	¾	25
⅓ cup	1¼	35
½ cup	1¾	50
⅔ cup	2½	70
1 cup	3½	100
2 cups	7	200

UNSALTED BUTTER

	OUNCES	GRAMS
1 tablespoon	½	15
2 tablespoons	1	30
4 tablespoons	2	55
6 tablespoons	3	85
8 tablespoons	4	115 (1 stick)
12 tablespoons	6	170 (1½ sticks)
16 tablespoons	8 (½ lb)	225 (2 sticks)
32 tablespoons	16 (1 lb)	455 (4 sticks)

Dimensions and Capacity of Frequently Used Baking Pans

If you don't have the pan called for in a recipe, use this chart to substitute a pan of equivalent capacity.

LAYER CAKE PANS

6 by 3-inch round pan	6 cups
8 by 2-inch round pan	7 cups
9 by 2-inch round pan	8 cups
8 by 2-inch square pan	8 ½ cups
9 by 2-inch square pan	10 ½ cups
7 by 3-inch round pan	8 cups

BAKING SHEETS AND PANS

13 by 9 by 2-inch baking pan (quarter sheet pan)	12 cups
15 ½ by 10 ½ by 1-inch pan (jelly-roll pan)	9 ½ cups
18 by 13 by 1-inch pan (half sheet pan)	12 cups

TUBE AND BUNDT PANS

10 by 4¼-inch angel food cake pan	16 cups
10 by 3-inch Bundt pan	10 to 12 cups, depending on design
9 ½-inch ring mold	5 cups
10-inch ring mold	6 cups

SPRINGFORM PANS

9 by 3-inch pan	10 cups
10 by 2¾- to 3-inch pan	12 to 14 cups

LOAF PANS

14 by 3 by 3¼-inch mud pan	11 cups
13 by 4 by 4-inch Pullman loaf pan	13 cups
9 by 5 by 3-inch loaf pan	8 cups

Index by Recipe Categories

Index